P9-BZS-239

Women in Western European History, *First Supplement*

Women in Western European History, *First Supplement*

A Select Chronological, Geographical, and Topical Bibliography

Compiled and edited by
Linda Frey, Marsha Frey, and Joanne Schneider

GREENWOOD PRESS

New York • Westport, Connecticut • London

Library of Congress Cataloging-in-Publication Data

Frey, Linda.
Women in western European history. First supplement.

Includes index.
1. Women—Europe—History—Bibliography. I. Frey, Marsha. II. Schneider, Joanne. III. Title. IV. Title: Women in western European history. First supplement.
Z7961.F74 1982 Suppl. [HQ1587] 016.3054 86-22777
ISBN 0-313-25109-6 (lib. bdg. : alk. paper)

Library of Congress Catalog Card Number: 86-22777
ISBN: 0-313-25109-6

First published in 1986

Greenwood Press, Inc.
88 Post Road West, Westport, Connecticut 06881

Printed in the United States of America

The paper used in this book complies with the Permanent Paper Standard issued by the National Information Standards Organization [Z39.48-1984].

10 9 8 7 6 5 4 3 2 1

To our mothers, Dolores Frey and Anna Schneider,
and to our canine and feline cohorts.

CONTENTS

PREFACE

> "It is no small pity and should cause us no little shame . . .that we do not understand ourselves or know who we are."
>
> Theresa of Avila

The concern voiced by Theresa of Avila, a sixteenth century mystic, remains with us today. When we began this bibliographical project in 1978, we intended to provide a useful reference tool for anyone interested in women's experiences within the Western European historical framework. At that time, even compiling a simple reading list devoted to any facet of European women's history proved difficult. With the publication of volumes one and two of this bibliography, the task of locating research on women's history has been simplified for the teacher and student alike. The publication of this supplement to the earlier volumes highlights the gaps still present in certain areas of research. Certainly for those students of English, French, and German women's history, the wealth of material is overwhelming. Scholarship about Italian women has significantly progressed in the past ten years, as has that on women in the Low Countries, where social historians, closely related to their French counterparts, have done interesting work. Iberian women's history shows an interesting imbalance. While there is a fair amount written on and about women in Spanish literature and women writers themselves, the political, economic, and social sides of women's experiences have received uneven attention. It is still true that the sheer number of scholarly journals and anthologies makes current research a formidable task.

This bibliography, which covers the period from antiquity to the present, supplements and updates the earlier two volumes. The first, issued in 1982, covers antiquity to the French Revolution, and the second, issued in 1984, covers the nineteenth and twentieth centuries. This book includes works recently published, as well as those recently uncovered or discovered by us. We have also repeated a few entries (less than one hundred) from the earlier books. These entries are either significant new editions or translations, or works previously cited in the second volume which also covered topics dealt with in the first volume (for example, Mitterauer and Sieder, *The European Family: Patriarchy and Partnership from the Middle Ages to the Present,* 1982). We have basically followed the same format of the earlier two volumes and have organized the work according to traditional historical periodization, e.g. the Renaissance. The virtues of a recognizable organization overrode any difficulties inherent in such periodization. Citations covering more than two time periods are listed in the survey section. This work is further organized into geographical/political divisions and, within these, into broad and narrow topics, including individual figures of historical importance. Citations dealing with a particular period in general, rather than with a specific country, are entered within topical categories under a general division and precede the geographical ones. The detailed historical outline serves as a specific table of contents for the work and proceeds from the most general to the most specific. Cross-references are utilized where helpful. To facilitate use of the bibliography, subject, name, and author indexes are also included, with reference to the entry numbers of pertinent citations. We have further refined the subject index by also listing countries where relevant. For example, the entry Divorce lists citations covering the topic in general and then specific countries, e.g. Austria, Switzerland, and so on. Illustrative quotations introduce broad topical sections. Their authors are noted in the Guide to Quotations.

The following is a list of criteria used and procedures followed in compiling this volume.

- The entry must focus directly on the historical condition of women.
- It must deal with Western European countries.
- It must be published material.
- It must be accessible in the United States. In the case of a periodical, it must be available (full edition) in at least ten libraries nationwide. No rare editions or obscure periodicals are included.
- It may be a monograph or an article from a scholarly journal or anthology.
- The entry must be in English or one of the major Western European Languages.
- The latest and, if possible, the English edition is listed.
- An entry on an individual must focus on the life or historical setting of the figure. A purely literary or artistic analysis usually would not be included.
- This bibliography does not include primary sources such as memoirs or letters; nor does it include literary sources such as novels or poems.

- To avoid confusion, no abbreviations have been used.
- Women are listed under the country with which they are most commonly associated.

We have compiled this bibliography to help bring women's issues into the mainstream of historical research, to underscore the contribution of an evolving field. Since the inception of this project in 1978, the increasing incorporation of women's history and social history in general into traditional history marks the increasing sophistication and acceptance of this new field. Through the compilation of this and the earlier bibliographies, we have attempted to promote further research, to illuminate the role of women in Western European history, and to address the issue of "understanding ourselves." That issue, as articulated by Theresa of Avila in the sixteenth century and by others throughout history, still haunts us today.

ACKNOWLEDGMENTS

We would like to acknowledge the unfailing support of our immediate families, particularly Dolores Frey, who unhesitatingly and generously aided us. We must also extend a note of thanks to the librarians at Farrell Library, Kansas State University, especially Lucy Wilde; the John D. Rockefeller Library, Brown University; the Madeleine Clark Wallace Library, Wheaton College; and the Maureen and Mike Mansfield Library, University of Montana, especially Chris Mullin. The dedicated labors of generations of historians and the encouragement of colleagues and deans William Stamey, Howard E. Reinhardt, and Robert Kruh, have made this work possible as have, on a more practical level, our secretaries and typists: Julie McVay, Belinda Whaley, Nedra Sylvis, and Betty Bailey. Susan Matule deserves special mention for her meticulous attention to detail and limitless patience.

HISTORICAL OUTLINE AND TOPICAL GUIDE TO CITATIONS

GUIDE TO QUOTATIONS

Women in Western European History, *First Supplement*

I.
HISTORICAL SURVEYS

A. GENERAL

1. BIBLIOGRAPHIES

"But for the 'historian,' for whom the past is dead and irreproachable, the past is feminine. He loves it as mistress of whom he never tires and whom he never expects to talk sense."

Michael Oakeshott

00001. Cardinale, Susan, ed. Anthologies by and about Women, An Analytical Index. Westport, Ct.: Greenwood Press, 1982.

00002. Falk, Joyce Duncan. "The New Technology for Research in European Women's History: 'Online' Bibliographies." Signs 9 (Autumn 1983): 120-133.

00003. Fout, John C., ed. "An English-Language Bibliography on European and American Women's History." In German Women in the Nineteenth Century, pp. 368-423. New York: Holmes and Meier, 1984.

00004. Hufton, Olwen. "Survey Articles, Women in History, Early Modern Europe." Past and Present 101 (November 1983): 125-141.

00005. Olson, David H. and Markoff, Roxanne, eds. Inventory of Marriage and Family Literature 8 (1981). Beverly Hills, Ca.: Sage Publications, 1982.

00006. Rossum-Guyon, Francoise van. "Selection bibliographique." Revue des sciences humaines n.s. 168 (October-December 1977): 625-632.

00007. Rudenstein, Gail M; Kessler, Carol Farley; and Moore, Ann M. "Mothers and Daughters in Literature: A Preliminary Bibliography." In _The Lost Tradition Mothers and Daughters in Literature_, edited by Cathy N. Davidson and E.M. Broner, pp. 309-322. New York: Ungar, 1980.

00008. Scott, Joan. "Survey Articles, Women In History, The Modern Period." _Past and Present_ 101 (November 1983): 141-157.

00009. Sicherman, Barbara; Monter, E. William; Scott, Joan Wallach; and Sklar, Kathryn Kish. _Recent United States Scholarship on the History of Women._ Washington, D.C.: American Historical Association, 1980.

00010. Stineman, Esther and Loeb, Catherine. _Women's Studies: a Recommended Core Bibliography._ Littleton, Col.: Libraries Unlimited, 1979.

00011. Tormey, Judith. "Some Recent Words on Historical Attitudes Toward Women." _Journal of the History of Ideas_ 45 (October-December 1984): 619-623.

2. ENCYCLOPEDIAS AND DICTIONARIES

"The glory of women is, to make themselves but little talked of: . . . Women should only act, as one may say, behind the curtains; they cannot appear upon the stage until particular circumstances lead them there."

Charlotte Lennox
The Female Quixote

00012. Cooper, Jilly and Hartman, Tom. _Violets and Vinegar: Beyond Bartlett Quotations by and About Women._ New York: Stein and Day, 1982.

00013. James, Simon. _A Dictionary of Sexist Quotations._ New York: Barnes and Noble, 1984.

00014. Kay, Ernest, ed. _The World Who's Who of Women._ Cambridge: International Bibliographical Center, 1978.

00015. Partnow, Elaine, ed. _The Quotable Woman_, 2 vols. New York: Facts on File, 1982 and 1985.

00016. Sau, Victoria. _Un diccionario ideológico feminista._ Barcelona: Icaria, 1981.

00017. Weiser, Marjorie P.K. and Arbeiter, Jean S., eds. _Womanlist._ New York: Atheneum, 1981.

3. SURVEYS

"Providence, Designing from the beginning that the manner of life to be adopted by women should in many respects ultimately depend, not so much on their own deliberate choice, as on the determination, or at least on the interest and convenience, of the parent, of the husband, or of some near connection; has implanted in them a remarkable tendency to conform to the wishes and example of those for whom they feel a warmth of regard, and even of all those with whom they are in familiar habits of intercourse."

Thomas Gisborne
An Enquiry into the Duties of the Female Sex, 1797

00018. Alzon, Claude. _La femme potiche et la femme bonniche. Pouvoir bourgeois et pouvoir male._ Paris: F. Maspero, 1978.

00019. Ardener, Shirley. _Defining Females: the Nature of Women in Society._ New York: John Wiley and Sons, 1978.

00020. Bassein, Beth Ann. _Women and Death: Linkages in Western Thought and Literature._ Westport, Ct.: Greenwood Press, 1984.

00021. Bock, Gisela. "Historische Frauenforschung: Fragestellungen und Perspektiven." In _Frauen suchen ihre Geschichte, Historische Studien zum 19. und 20. Jahrhundert_, edited by Karin Hausen, pp. 22-60. Munich: Verlag C.H. Beck, 1983.

00022. Cambridge Women's Studies Group. _Women in Society. Interdisciplinary Essays._ London: Virago Press, 1981.

00023. Cervantes, Lucius F. "Woman's Changing Role in Society." _Thought_ 40 (Autumn 1965): 325-368.

00024. Crawford, Patricia, et al., eds. _Exploring Women's Past._ Boston: George Allen and Unwin, 1983.

00025. Davis, Natalie Zemon. "Women's History in Transition: The European Case." _Feminist Studies_ 3 (Spring-Summer 1976): 83-103.

00026. DuBois, Page. "'Tristes Topiques': Framing the Woman Question." _Massachusetts Review_ 21 (Summer 1980): 334-342.

00027. Dworkin, Andrea. _Women Hating._ New York: Dutton, 1974.

00028. Elshtain, Jean Bethke, ed. _The Family in Political Thought._ Amherst, Mass: University of Massachusetts Press, 1982.

00029. Elshtain, Jean Bethke. "Introduction: Toward a Theory of the Family and Politics." In *The Family in Political Thought*, edited by Jean Bethke Elshtain, pp. 7-30. Amherst, Mass.: University of Massachusetts Press, 1982.

00030. __________. "'Thank Heaven for Little Girls': The Dialectics of Development." In *The Family in Political Thought*, edited by Jean Bethke Elshtain, pp. 288-302. Amherst, Mass.: University of Massachusetts Press, 1982.

00031. Fernau, Joachim. *Und sie schamten sich nicht*. Munich: F.A. Herbig, 1974.

00032. Hassauer-Roos, Friederike J. "Das Weib und die Idee der Menschheit. Zur neueren Geschichte der Diskurse über die Frau." In *Frauen in der Geschichte* III, edited by Annette Kuhn and Jörn Rüsen, pp. 87-108. Düsseldorf: Schwann-Bagel Verlag, 1983.

00033. Hausen, Karin. "Einleitung." In *Frauen suchen ihre Geschichte, Historische Studien zum 19. und 20. Jahrhundert*, edited by Karin Hausen, pp. 7-20. Munich: Verlag C.H. Beck, 1983.

00034. Hausen, Karin, ed. *Frauen suchen ihre Geschichte: Historische Studien zum 19. und 20. Jahrhundert*. Munich: C.H. Beck, 1983.

00035. Janssen-Jurreit, Marielouise. *Sexism: The Male Monopoly on History and Thought*. New York: Farrar Straus and Giroux, 1982.

00036. Kelly, Joan. "The Social Relation of the Sexes: Methodological Implications of Women's History." In *Women, History and Theory: The Essays of Joan Kelly*, pp. 1-18. Chicago: University of Chicago Press, 1984.

00037. __________. *Women, History, and Theory, The Essays of Joan Kelly*. Chicago: University of Chicago Press, 1984.

00038. Kinnear, Mary. *Daughters of Time, Women in the Western Tradition*. Ann Arbor, Mich.: University of Michigan Press, 1982.

00039. Kuhn, Annette and Rüsen, Jörn, eds. *Frauen in der Geschichte III. Fachwissenschaftliche und fachdidaktische Beitrage zur Geschichte der Weiblichkeit vom fruhen Mittelalter bis zur Gegenwart mit geeigneten Materialien für den Unterricht*. Dusseldorf: Schwann, 1983.

00040. Leacock, Eleanor Burke. "Ideologies of Male Dominance as Divide and Rule Politics: An Anthropologist's View." In *Woman's Nature: Rationalizations of Inequality*, edited by Marian Lowe and Ruth Hubbard, pp. 111-121. New York: Pergamon Press, 1983.

00041. Leacock, Eleanor Burke. _Myths of Male Dominance: Collected Articles on Women Cross-Culturally_. New York: Monthly Review Press, 1980.

00042. Lowe, Marian and Hubbard, Ruth, eds. _Woman's Nature: Rationalizations of Inequality_. New York: Pergamon Press, 1983.

00043. McMillan, Margaret. "Woman in the Past and the Future." In _The Case for Women's Suffrage_, edited by Frederick John Shaw, pp. 106-121. London: T. Fisher Unwin, 1907.

00044. Millan, Betty. _Monstrous Regiment: Women Rulers in Men's Worlds_. Windsor Forest, Berks.: Kensal Press, 1982.

00045. Nichols, Thomas Low. _Woman in All Ages and All Nations_. New York: Fowler and Wells, 1854.

00046. Santucci, L. _Donne alla Mola_. Milan: Bietti, 1967.

00047. Scobie, Edward. "African Women in Early Europe." In _Black Women in Antiquity_, edited by Ivan Van Sertima, pp. 135-154. New Brunswick: Transaction Book, 1985.

00048. Showalter, Elaine, ed. _Women's Liberation and Literature_. New York: Harcourt, Brace, Jovanovich, 1971.

00049. Signorelli Martí, Rosa. _La Mujer en la historia_. Buenos Aires: La Pleyade, 1970.

00050. Smith, Joan. "Analysis of Gender: A Mystique." In _Woman's Nature: Rationalizations of Inequality_, edited by Marian Lowe and Ruth Hubbard, pp. 89-109. New York: Pergamon Press, 1983.

00051. Squire, Geoffrey, _Dress, Art and Society, 1560-1970_. London: Studio Vista, 1974.

00052. Stephenson, June. _Women's Roots: Status and Achievement in Western Civilization_. Napa, Ca.: Diemer Smith Publishing Co., 1981.

4. BIOGRAPHICAL SKETCHES

"Seek to be good, but aim not to be great,
A woman's noblest station is retreat,
Her fairest virtues fly from the public sight,
Domestic worth, that shuns too strong a light."
Lord Lyttelton

00053. Blashfield, Jean F. _Hellraisers, Heroines, and Holy Women, Women's Most Remarkable Contributions to History_. New York: St. Martin's, 1981.

00054. Fraser, Antonia, ed. Heroes and Heroines. New York: A and W Publishers, 1980.

00055. Gallo, Antonio. Donna sempre. Naples: A. Fiory, 1975.

00056. Latour, Anny. Uncrowned Queens. Translated by A.A. Dent. London: Dent, 1970.

00057. Love, Cornelia Spencer. Famous Women of Yesterday and Today. 1938. Reprint. Philadelphia, Pa.: R. West, 1977.

00058. Marlow, Joan. The Great Women. New York: A and W Publishing, 1979.

00059. Monaghan, Patricia. The Book of Goddesses and Heroines. New York: E. P. Dutton, 1981.

00060. Pasteur, Claude. Les Pionnières de l'histoire. Paris: Editions du Sud, 1963.

00061. Raven, Susan and Weir, Alison. Women of Achievement. Thirty-Five Centuries of History. New York: Harmony Books, 1981.

00062. Spender, Dale, ed. Feminist Theorists Three Centuries of Key Women Thinkers. New York: Pantheon Books, Random House, 1983.

00063. ____________. Women of Ideas and What Men Have Done to Them: From Aphra Behn to Adrienne Rich. London: Routledge, 1982.

00064. Uglow, Jennifer S., comp. and Hinton, Frances, eds. The International Dictionary of Women's Biography. New York: Continuum, 1985.

5. MATRIARCHY

> "The progress from the maternal to the paternal conception of man forms the most important turning point in the history of the relations between the sexes."
>
> J.J. Bachofen

00065. Aberle, David F. "Matrilineal Descent in Cross-Cultural Perspectives." In Matrilineal Kinship, edited by David M. Schneider and Kathleen Gough, pp. 655-730. Berkeley: University of California Press, 1962.

00066. Adler, Margot. "Meanings of Matriarchy." In The Politics of Women's Spirituality, edited by Charlene Spretnak, pp. 127-137. Garden City, N.Y.: Doubleday and Company, Inc., Anchor Press, 1982.

00067. Bamberger, Joan. "The Myth of Matriarchy: Why Men Rule in Primitive Society." In Woman, Culture and Society, edited by Michelle Rosaldo and Louise Lamphere, pp. 263-280. Stanford, Calif.: Stanford University Press, 1974.

00068. Fester, Richard, et al. Weib und Macht: 5 Millionen Jahre Urgeschichte der Frau. Frankfurt am Main: S. Fischer, 1979.

00069. Newton, Esther and Webster, Paula. "Matriarchy and Power." Quest 2 (Summer 1975): 67-72.

6. PATRIARCHY

> "So go to your quarters now and attend to your own works, the loom and the spindle, and see that the servants get on with theirs. The bow is the men's concern and mine above all, for I am master in this house."
>
> Telemachus to mother
> Odyssey

00070. Brown, Penelope. "Universals and Particulars in the Position of Women." In Women in Society, edited by the Cambridge Women's Studies Group, pp. 242-256. London: Virago Press, 1981.

00071. Coward, Rosalind. Patriarchal Precedents. London: Routledge and Kegan Paul, 1983.

00072. Flax, Jane. "Political Philosophy and the Patriarchal Unconscious: A Psychoanalytic Perspective on Epistemology and Metaphysics." In Discovering Reality, Feminist Perspectives on Epistemology, Metaphysics, Methodology, and Philosophy of Science, edited by Sandra Harding and Merrill B. Hintikka, pp. 245-281. Boston: D. Reidel Publishing Co., 1983.

00073. French, Marilyn. Beyond Power. On Women, Men and Morals. New York: Summit Books, 1985.

00074. Gross, Michael and Averill, Mary Beth. "Evolution and Patriarchal Myths of Scarcity and Competition." In Discovering Reality, Feminist Perspectives on Epistemology, Metaphysics, Methodology, and Philosophy of Science, edited by Sandra Harding and Merrill B. Hintikka, pp. 71-95. Boston: D. Reidel Publishing Co., 1983.

00075. Hubbard, Ruth. "Have Only Men Evolved?" In Discovering Reality, Feminist Perspectives on Epistemology, Metaphysics, Methodology, and Philosophy of Science, edited by Sandra Harding and Merrill B. Hintikka, pp. 45-69. Boston: D. Reidel Publishing Co., 1983.

00076. Iglitzin, Lynne B. "The Patriarchal Heritage." In Woman in the World: A Comparative Study, edited by Lynne B. Iglitzin and Ruth Ross, pp. 7-24. Santa Barbara, Ca.: Clio Books, 1976.

00077. Kuhn, Annette. "Structures of Patriarchy and Capital in the Family." In Feminism and Materialism: Women and Modes of Production, edited by Annette Kuhn and AnnMarie Wolpe, pp. 42-67. London: Routledge and Kegan Paul, 1978.

00078. Lieven, Elena. "Subjectivity, Materialism and Patriarchy." In Women in Society, edited by the Cambridge Women's Studies Group, pp. 257-275. London: Virago Press, 1981.

00079. McDonough, Roisin and Harrison, Rachel. "Patriarchy and Relations of Production." In Feminism and Materialism: Women and Modes of Production, edited by Annette Kuhn and AnnMarie Wolpe, pp. 11-41. London: Routledge and Kegan Paul, 1978.

7. POLITICAL

". . . the advent of modern industrial societies has so far failed to eradicate the age-old subordination of women and has often given rise to new forms of alienation and imbalance."

"Resolution on the Position of Women in the European Community"
European Parliament, 1981

a) Generic

00080. Bei, Neda. "Der politische Diskurs/der politische Diskurs der Frauen. Marginalien zur Szenographie der bürgerlichen Revolution." In Das ewige Klischee, zum Rollenbild und Selbstverständnis bei Mannern und Frauen, pp. 76-107. Vienna: Herman Böhlaus, 1981.

00081. Charzat, Gisèle. Femmes, violence, pouvoir. Paris: Jean-Claude Simoën, 1979.

00082. Elshtain, Jean Bethke. Public Man. Private Woman: Women in Social and Political Thought. Princeton, N.J.: Princeton University Press, 1981.

00083. McGuigan, Dorothy, ed. The Role of Women in Conflict and Peace: Papers. Ann Arbor: University of Michigan, 1977.

00084. Minoli, Lorenza. "Oltre le pareti dell'esculusione--Il caso dei salotti politico-letterari." In Esistere comme donne, pp. 63-72. Milan: Mazzotta, 1983.

00085. Stiehm, Judith Hicks. "The Man Question." In _Women's Views of the Political World of Men_, edited by Judith Hicks Stiehm, pp. 205-223. Dobbs Ferry, N.Y.: Transnational Publishers Inc., 1984.

00086. ____________. _Women's Views of the Political World of Men_. Dobbs Ferry, NY.: Transnational Publishers, Inc., 1984.

00087. Swerdlow, Amy and Lessinger, Hanna, eds. _Class, Race and Sex: The Dynamics of Control_. The Scholar and the Feminist Conference Series. Barnard College Women's Center, no. 2. Boston: G.K. Hall and Co., 1983.

b) Marxism and Socialism

00088. Agulhon, Maurice. "On Political Allegory: A Reply to Eric Hobsbawm." _History Workshop_ 8 (Autumn 1979): 167-173.

00089. Alexander, Sally; Davin, Anna; and Hostettler, Eve. "Labouring Women: A Reply to Eric Hobsbawm." _History Workshop_ 8 (Autumn 1979): 174-182.

00090. Hobsbawm, Eric. "Man and Woman in Socialist Iconography." _History Workshop_ 6 (Autumn 1978): 121-138.

00091. Macciocchi, Maria-Antonietta. "Quelques thèmes autour du Marxisme et du féminisme." In _Les femmes et leur maîtres_, pp. 387-441. Paris: C. Bourgeois, 1979.

00092. Mason, Tim. "The Domestication of Female Socialist Icons: A Note in Reply to Eric Hobsbawn." _History Workshop_ 7 (Spring 1979): 170-175.

00093. Mullaney, Marie Marmo. _Revolutionary Women: Gender and the Socialist Revolutionary Role_. New York: Praeger, 1983.

00094. ____________. "Women and the Theory of the 'Revolutionary Personality.' Comments, Criticisms, and Suggestions for Further Study." _Western Social Science Journal_ 21 (April 1984): 49-70.

00095. Norton, Theodore Mills. "Contemporary Critical Theory and the Family: Private World and Public Crisis." In _The Family in Political Thought_, edited by Jean Bethke Elshtain, pp. 254-268. Amherst, Mass.: University of Massachusetts Press, 1982.

00096. Riley, Denise. "Left Critiques of the Family." In _Women in Society_, edited by the Cambridge Women's Studies Group, pp. 75-91. London: Virago Press, 1981.

00097. Rushton, Peter. "Marxism, Domestic Labour and the Capitalist Economy: A Note on Recent Discussions." In The Sociology of the Family: New Directions for Britain, edited by Michael Harris, pp. 32-48. Totowa, N.J.: Rowman and Littlefield, 1979.

00098. Slaughter, Jane and Kern, Robert, eds. European Women on the Left: Socialism, Feminism, and the Problems Faced by Political Women, 1880 to the Present. Westport, Connecticut: Greenwood Press, 1981.

c) Legal

00099. Glendon, Mary Ann. "Power and Authority in the Family: New Legal Patterns as Reflections of Changing Ideologies." American Journal of Comparative Law 23 (Winter 1975): 1-33.

00100. Muller-Freienfels, Wolfram. "Unification of Family Law." American Journal of Comparative Law 16 (1968): 175-218.

00101. Rheinstein, Max. "Trends in Marriage and Divorce Law in Western Countries." Law and Contemporary Problems 18 (1953): 3-19.

00102. Sillano, Maria Teresa. "La sottomissione legalizzata--Le donne e i codici tra Settecento e Ottocento." In Esistere comme donna, pp. 73-78. Milan: Mazzotta, 1983.

Also refer to #149, 163.

d) Criminal

00103. Hobsbawm, Eric. Bandits. New York: Pantheon, 1981.

00104. Tahourdin, B. "Women and Violence Throughout History." International Journal of Offenders Therapy and Comparative Criminology 21 (1977): 234-236.

Also refer to #355.

e) Feminism

00105. Blair, Juliet. "Women's Self Concept and Belief: A Feminist Approach to Empowerment Symbolism." Women's Studies International Forum 8 (1985): 323-334.

00106. Brundson, Charlotte. "'It is well known that by nature women are inclined to be rather personal.'" In Women Take Issue: Aspects of Women's Subordination, pp. 18-34. London: Hutchinson, 1978.

00107. Chafetz, Janet Saltzman and Dworkin, Anthony Gary. Female Revolt. The Rise of Women's Movement in World and Historical Perspective. Totowa, N.J.: Rowman and Allanheld, 1986.

00108. Charvet, John. Feminism. London: J.M. Dent and Sons Ltd., 1982.

00109. Cutrufelli, Maria Rosa. L'invenzione della donna: miti e techniche di uno sfruttamenti. Milan: G. Mazzotto, 1975.

00110. Esistere come donna. Milan: Mazzotta, 1983.

00111. Frankforter, A. Daniel. "Was there a Woman's Movement in Western History?" International Journal of Women's Studies 5 (March-April 1982): 114-127.

00112. Hartsock, Nancy C.M. Money, Sex, and Power, Towards a Feminist Historical Materialism. New York: Longmans, 1983.

00113. Jaquette, Jane S. "Power as Ideology: A Feminist Ideology." In Women's Views of the Political World of Men, edited by Judith Hicks Stiehm, pp. 7-29. Dobbs Ferry, N.Y.: Transnational Publishers, Inc., 1984.

00114. Kelly, Joan. "Early Feminist Theory and the Querelle des Femmes, 1400-1789." In Women, History and Theory: The Essays of Joan Kelly, pp. 65-109. Chicago: The University of Chicago Press, 1984. Also in Signs 8 (Autumn 1982): 4-28.

Also refer to #121.

00115. Kuhn, Annette and Wolpe AnnMarie. "Feminism and Materialism." In Feminism and Materialism: Women and Modes of Production, edited by Annette Kuhn and AnnMarie Wolpe, pp. 1-10. London: Routledge and Kegan Paul, 1978.

00116. ______________________________, eds. Feminism and Materialism: Women and Modes of Production. London: Routledge and Kegan Paul, 1978.

00117. Marcil-Lacoste, Louise. "The Trivialization of the Notion of Equality." In Discovering Reality, Feminist Perspectives on Epistemology, Metaphysics, Methodology, and Philosophy of Science, edited by Sandra Harding and Merrill B. Hintikka, pp. 121-137. Boston: D. Reidel Publishing Co., 1983.

00118. Mitchell, Juliet. Women: The Longest Revolution. New York: Pantheon, 1984.

00119. Rosenberg, Rosalind. Beyond Separate Spheres: Intellectual Roots of Modern Feminism. New Haven, Conn.: Yale University Press, 1982.

00120. Sayers, Janet. Biological Politics: Feminist and Anti-Feminist Perspectives. London: Tavistock, 1982.

00121. Schibanoff, Susan. "Comment on Kelly's 'Early Feminist Theory and the Querelle des Femmes 1400-1789.'" Signs 9 (Winter 1983): 320-326.

00122. University of Birmingham, Centre for Contemporary Cultural Studies, Women's Studies Group. Women Take Issue: Aspects of Women's Subordination. London: Hutchinson, 1978.

00123. Whittick, Arnold. Woman into Citizen. Santa Barbara, Ca.: ABC-Clio, 1980.

Also refer to #62, 91, 98, 202, 217, 220, 227.

f) Military

00124. Hacker, Barten C. "Women and Military Institutions in Early Modern Europe: A Reconnaissance." Signs 6 (Summer 1981): 643-671.

00125. Huston, Nancy. "The Matrix of War: Mothers and Heroes." Poetics Today 6 (1985): 153-170.

8. ECONOMIC

"Eritha the priestess holds the lease of a communal plot from the village."

Linear B Tablets

00126. Aventurin, Elzea. "The Division of Labour and Sexual Inequality: the Role of Education." In Women Workers and Society International Perspectives, pp. 27-42. Geneva: International Labour Office, 1976.

00127. Beechey, Veronica. "Women and Production: A Critical Analysis of some Sociological Theories of Women's Work." In Feminism and Materialism: Women and Modes of Production, edited by Annette Kuhn and AnnMarie Wolpe, pp. 155-197. London: Routledge and Kegan Paul, 1978.

00128. Bennholdt-Thomsen, Veronika. "Subsistence Production and Extended Reproduction." In Of Marriage and the Market, edited by K. Young, J. Walkowitz, and R. McCullough, pp. 16-29. London: C.S.E. Books, 1981.

00129. Bland, Lucy, et al. "Relations of Production: Approaches Through Anthropology." In Women Take Issue: Aspects of Women's Subordination, pp. 155-175. London: Hutchinson, 1978.

00130. ________________. "Women 'Inside and Outside' the Relations of Production." In Women Take Issue: Aspects of Women's Subordination, pp. 35-78. London: Hutchinson, 1978.

00131. Bock, Gisela and Duden, Barbara. "Lavoro d'amore -- amore come lavoro." Casabella 45 (March 1981): 20-24.

00132. Bridenthal, Renate. "The Dialectics of Production and Reproduction in History." Radical America 10 (March-April 1976): 3-11.

00133. Charles-Roux, Edmonde. Les femmes et le travail du Moyen-Age à nos jours. Paris: Editions de la Courtille, 1975.

00134. Cohen, Marjorie. "Changing Perceptions of the Impact of the Industrial Revolution on Female Labor." International Journal of Women's Studies 7 (September-October 1984): 291-305.

00135. DePauw, Linda Grant. Seafaring Women. Boston: Houghton Mifflin, 1982.

00136. Harris, Olivia. "Households as Natural Units." In Of Marriage and the Market, edited by K. Young, J. Walkowitz, and R. McCullough, pp. 49-68. London: C.S.E. Books, 1981.

00137. Illich, Ivan. Gender. New York: Pantheon Books, 1983.

00138. Leibowitz, Lila. "Origins of the Sexual Division of Labor." In Woman's Nature: Rationalizations of Inequality, edited by Marian Lowe and Ruth Hubbard, pp. 123-147. New York: Pergamon, 1983.

00139. Lewenhak, Sheila. Women and Work. New York: St. Martin's, 1980.

00140. Lis, Catharina and Soly, Hugo. "Policing the Early Modern Proletariat, 1450-1850." In Proletarianization and Family History, edited by David Levine, pp. 163-228. New York: Academic Press, Inc., 1984.

00141. Mackintosh, Maureen. "The Sexual Division of Labour and the Subordination of Women." In Of Marriage and the Market, edited by K. Young, J. Walkowitz, and R. McCullough, pp. 1-15. London: C.S.E. Books, 1981.

00142. Madden, Janice T. "The Development of Economic Thought on the 'Woman Problem.'" Review of Radical Political Economics 4 (July 1972): 21-39.

00143. Stahl, Gisela. "Dalla casa all' appartamento: l'economizzazione della donna." Casabella 45 (March 1981): 10-15.

00144. Stolcke, Verena. "Women's Labours: The Naturalisation of Social Inequality and Women's Subordination." In Of Marriage and the Market, edited by K. Young, J. Walkowitz, and R. McCullough, pp. 30-48. London: C.S.E. Books, 1981.

00145. Young, K.; Walkowitz, J.; and McCullough, R. eds. Of Marriage and the Market. London: C.S.E. Books, 1981.

Also refer to #97, 112, 115, 116, 305, 336, 337.

9. RELIGION/MYTHOLOGY

"It is good for them [men] if they abide even as I. . . . But if they cannot contain, let them marry: for it is better to marry than to burn. . . ."
St. Paul

a) Generic

00146. Carmody, Denise Lardner. Women and World Religions. Nashville: Abingdon, 1979.

00147. Goldberg, Ben Zion. The Sacred Fire: The Story of Sex in Religion. New York: University Books, 1958.

00148. Hoch-Smith, Judith and Spring, Anita, eds. Women in Ritual and Symbolic Roles. New York: Plenum Press, 1978.

00149. Kidwai, Mushir Hosain. Woman Under Different Social and Religious Laws, Buddhism, Judaism, Christianity, Islam. Delhi: Seema Publications, 1978.

00150. Ochshorn, Judith. The Female Experience and the Nature of the Divine. Bloomington, Ind.: Indiana University Press, 1981.

00151. Preston, James J., ed. Mother Worship Themes and Variations. Chapel Hill, N.C.: University of North Carolina Press, 1982.

00152. Spretnak, Charlene, ed. The Politics of Women's Spirituality: Essays on the Rise of Spiritual Power with the Feminist Movement. New York: Anchor Press, 1982.

00153. Stone, Merlin. The Paradise Papers, The Suppression of Women's Rites. London: Virago, 1974.

Also refer to #53.

b) Goddesses

00154. Christ, Carol P. "Symbol of Goddess and God in Feminist Theology." In The Book of the Goddess, Past and Present. An Introduction to Her Religion, edited by Carl Olson, pp. 231-251. New York: Crossroad Publishing Co., 1983.

00155. ______________. "Why Women Need the Goddess: Phenomenological, Psychological and Political Reflections." In The Politics of Women's Spirituality, edited by Charlene Spretnak, pp. 71-86. Garden City, N.Y.: Doubleday Company, Inc., Anchor Press, 1982.

00156. Engelsman, Joan. _The Feminine Dimension of the Divine._ Philadelphia: Westminister Press, 1979.

00157. Olson, Carl. _The Book of the Goddess, Past and Present: An Introduction to Her Religion._ New York: Crossroad Publishing Co., 1983.

00158. Starhawk. "Witchcraft as Goddess Religion." In _The Politics of Women's Spirituality_, edited by Charlene Spretnak, pp. 49-56. Garden City, N.Y.: Doubleday and Company, Inc., Anchor Press, 1982.

00159. Stone, Merlin. _Ancient Mirrors of Womanhood, Our Goddesses and Heroine Heritage._ 2 vols. New York: New Sibylline, 1979.

Also refer to #59.

c) Women and Judaism

00160. Morrell, Samuel. "An Equal or a Ward: How Independent Is a Married Woman According to Rabbinic Law?" _Jewish Social Studies_ 44 (Summer-Fall 1982): 189-210.

00161. Neuberger, Julia. "Women in Judaism: The Fact and the Fiction." In _Women's Religious Experience_, edited by Pat Holden, pp. 132-142. Totowa, N.J.: Barnes and Noble Books, 1983.

00162. Umansky, Ellen M. "Women in Judaism: From the Reform Movement to Contemporary Jewish Religious Feminism" In _Women of Spirit_, edited by Rosemary Ruether and Eleanor McLaughlin, pp. 333-354. New York: Simon and Schuster, 1979.

00163. Webber, Jonathan. "Between Law and Custom: Women's Experience of Judaism." In _Women's Religious Experience_, edited by Pat Holden, pp. 143-162. Totowa, New Jersey: Barnes and Noble Books, 1983.

Also refer to #149.

d) Women and the Bible

00164. Bader, Clarisse. _La femme biblique._ Paris: Didier, 1878.

00165. Beissmann, Claus. "Gibt es eine christologische Begrundungen für eine Unterordnung der Frau im Neuen Testament?" In _Die Frau im Urchristentum_, edited by Gerhard Dautzenberg, et al., pp. 254-262. Freiburg: Herder, 1983.

00166. Blank, Josef. "Frauen in der Jesusuberlieferungen." In _Die Frau im Urchristentum_, edited by Gerhard Dautzenberg, et al., pp. 9-91. Freiburg: Herder, 1983.

00167. Brown, Raymond. "Roles of Women in the Fourth Gospel." *Theological Studies* 36 (1975): 688-699.

00168. Daughters of St. Paul. *Women of the Gospel*. Boston, Mass.: Daughters of St. Paul, 1975.

00169. Edwards, George R. *Gay/Lesbian Liberation: A Biblical Perspective*. New York: Pilgrim Press, 1984.

00170. Evdokimoff, Paul Nicolaeivitch. *La Femme et le salut du monde*. Paris: Casterman, 1958.

00171. Falk, Zeev. "Über die Ehe in den biblischen Prophetien." *Zeitschrift der Savigny Stiftung für Rechtsgeschichte (Romantische Abteilung)* 90 (1973): 36-44.

00172. Fischer, James A. *God Said: Let There Be Women: A Study of Biblical Women*. Staten Island, N.Y.: Alba House, 1979.

00173. Ford, J. Massyngberde. "Women Leaders in the New Testament." In *Women Priests, A Catholic Commentary on the Vatican Declaration*, edited by Leonard Swidler and Arlene Swidler, pp. 132-134. New York: Paulist Press, 1977.

00174. Geiger, Ruthild. "Die Stellung der geschiedenen Frau in der Umwelt des Neuen Testaments." In *Die Frau im Urchistentum*, edited by Gerhard Dautzenberg, et al., pp. 134-157. Freiburg: Herder, 1983.

00175. Gillialand, Dolores S. *Selected Women of the Scriptures of Stamina and Courage*. Spearfish, S.D.: Honor Books, 1978.

00176. Girard, René. "Scandal and the Dance: Salome in the Gospel of Mark." *New Literary History* 15 (Winter 1984): 311-324.

00177. Harris, Dixie L. *Twenty Stories of Bible Women*. Hicksville, N.Y.: Exposition Press, Inc., 1980.

00178. Harris, Kevin. *Sex, Ideology and Religion, The Representation of Women in the Bible*. Totowa, N.J.: Barnes and Noble, 1984.

00179. Hurley, James B. *Man and Woman in Biblical Perspective: A Study in Role Relationships and Authority*. Leicester: Inter-Varsity Press, 1981.

00180. Levy, Ludwig. "Sexual Symbolik in der biblischer Paradisgeschichte." *Imago* 5 (1917-1919): 8-26.

00181. Lohfink, Gerhard. "Weibliche Diakone im Neuen Testament." In *Die Frau im Urchristentum*, edited by Gerhard Dautzenberg, et al., pp. 320-338. Freiburg: Herder, 1983.

00182. Macartney, Clarence E. *Great Women of the Bible*. Grand Rapids, Mich.: Baker Book House, 1974.

00183. McKenzie, John L. "St. Paul's Attitude Toward Women." In Women Priests, A Catholic Commentary on the Vatican Declaration, edited by Leonard Swidler and Arlene Swidler, pp. 212-215. New York: Paulist Press, 1977.

00184. Martens, Thierry. La Promotion de la femme dans la Bible. Paris: Casterman, 1967.

00185. Merklein, Helmut. "'Es ist gut fur den Menschen, eine Frau nicht anzufassen.' Paulus und die Sexualitat nach 1 Kor 7." In Die Frau im Urchristentum, edited by Gerhard Dautzenberg, et al., pp. 225-253. Freiburg: Herder, 1983.

00186. Mollenkott, Virginia R. The Divine Feminine: The Biblical Imagery of God as Female. New York: Crossroad Publishing Co., 1981.

00187. Moltmann-Wendel, Elisabeth. The Women Around Jesus. New York: Crossroad, 1982.

00188. Müller, Karlheinz. "Die Haustafel des Kolosserbriefes und das antike Frauenthema. Eine kritische Ruckschau auf die alte Ergebnisse." In Die Frau im Urchristentum, edited by Gerhard Dautzenberg, et al., pp. 263-319. Freiburg: Herder, 1983.

00189. Murphy-O'Connor, J. "The Non-Pauline Character of I Corinthians 11:2-16?" Journal of Biblical Literature 95 (1976): 615-621.

00190. Nunnaly-Cox, Janice. Foremothers: Women of the Bible. Somers, Ct.: Seabury Press, 1981.

00191. Otwell, John H. And Sarah Laughed: The Status of Women in the Old Testament. Philadelphia: Westminster Press, 1977.

00192. Overby, Coleman. Bible Women. Austin, Tx.: Firm Foundation Publishing House, 1936.

00193. Phillips, John A. Eve, The History of an Idea. New York: Harper and Row, 1984.

00194. Phipps, William E. Was Jesus Married? New York: Harper, 1970.

00195. Pitt, Hubert. "Die Frauen und die Osterbotschaft. Synopse der Grabesgeschichten (Mk 16, 1-8; Mt 27, 62-28, 15; Lk 24, 1-12; Joh 20, 1-18)." In Die Frau im Urchristentum, edited by Gerhard Dautzenberg, et al., pp. 117-133. Freiburg: Herder, 1983.

00196. Roddy, Lee. Intimate Portraits of Women in the Bible. Chappaqua, N.Y.: Christian Harold Books, 1980.

00197. Roheim, Geza. "The Garden of Eden." Psychoanalytic Review 27 (January 1940): 1-26; 177-199.

00198. Ruether, Rosemary Radford. "The Subordination and Liberation of Women in Christian Theology: St. Paul and Sarah Grimke." Soundings 51 (1978): 168-181.

00199. Rusche, Helga. They Lived by Faith. Women in the Bible. Translated by Elizabeth Williams. Baltimore: Helicon, 1963.

00200. Schelkle, Karl H. The Spirit and the Bride: Woman in the Bible. Collegeville, Mn.: Liturgical Press, 1979.

00201. Schwarz, Paul. Die neue Eva. Goppingen: Kummerle, 1973.

00202. Stanton, Elizabeth Cady. The Original Feminist Attack on the Bible. New York: Arno. Press, 1974.

00203. Strom, Kay M. Special Women of the Bible. St. Louis, Mo.: Concordia Publishing House, 1980.

00204. Trible, Phyllis. "Depatriarchalizing the Bible." Journal of the American Academy of Religion 41 (1973): 30-47. Also in The Jewish Woman: New Perspectives, edited by Elizabeth Kolton, pp. 217-240. New York: Schocken, 1976.

00205. ______________. God and the Rhetoric of Sexuality. Philadelphia: Fortress Press, 1978.

00206. ______________. "Two Women in a Man's World: A Reading of the Book of Ruth." Soundings 59 (Fall 1976): 251-279.

00207. Zabriskie, Colleen. "A Psychological Analysis of Biblical Interpretations Pertaining to Women." Journal of Psychology and Theology 4 (August 1976): 304-312.

e) Christianity

(1) Non-specific

00208. Bottomley, F. Attitudes to the Body in Western Christendom. London: Lepus Books, 1979.

00209. Danniel, A. and Olivier, Brigitte. La Gloire de l'homme c'est la femme. Lyon: Chalet, 1965.

00210. Foote, John A. "Child Care in the Church." Catholic Historical Review n.s. 5 (April 1925): 56-74.

00211. Fuchs, Eric. Sexual Desire and Love: Origins and History of the Christian Ethic of Sexuality and Marriage. New York: Seabury Press, 1983.

00212. Maltz, Daniel N. "The Bride of Christ is Filled with His Spirit." In Women in Ritual and Symbolic Roles, edited by Judith Hock-Smith and Anita Spring, pp. 27-44. New York: Plenum Press, 1978.

00213. Orsy, Ladislas. "Faith, Sacrament, Contract, and Christian Marriage: Disputed Questions." Theological Studies 43 (September 1982): 379-398.

00214. Ruether, Rosemary Radford. Sexism and God-Talk: Toward a Feminist Theology. Boston: Beacon Press, 1983.

00215. Stevenson, Kenneth W. Nuptial Blessing: A Study of Christian Marriage Rites. London: Alcuin Club, 1982.

(2) Women

00216. Aubert, Jean-Marie. La Femme, antifeminisme et christianisme. Paris: Cerf/Desclee, 1975.

00217. Carmody, Denise Lardner, Feminism and Christianity: A Two-Way Reflection. Nashville, Tn.: Abingdon Press, 1982.

00218. Demarest, Victoria Booth, God, Woman, and Ministry. St. Petersburg, Fl.: Valkyrie Press, 1978.

00219. Fiorenza, Elisabeth Schussler. In Memory of Her: A Feminist Theological Reconstruction of Christian Origins. New York: Crossroad, 1984.

00220. Harkness, Georgia Elma. Women in Church and Society: A Historical and Theological Inquiry. Nashville: Abingdon Press, 1971.

00221. Lecarme, Philippe. L'Eglise et l'état contre la femme? Paris: Edition de l'Epi, 1968.

00222. Leflaive, Anne. La femme et l'église. Paris: France Empire, 1968.

00223. Rabuzzi, Kathryn Allen. The Sacred and the Feminine. Toward a Theology of Housework. New York: The Seabury Press, 1982.

00224. Ryrie, Charles Caldwell. The Place of Women in the Church. New York: Macmillan, 1958.

00225. Savramis, Demosthenes. The Satanizing of Women, Religion Versus Sexuality. Garden City, N.Y.: Doubleday and Co., 1974.

00226. Sit, Amy Wang. The Rib. Harrison, Ark.: New Leaf Press, 1977.

00227. Soelle, Dorothee. The Strength of the Weak: Toward a Christian Feminist Identity. Philadelphia, Pa.: Westminster Press, 1984.

f) Women as Priests

00228. Barnhouse, Ruth Tiffany; Fahey, Michael; Dram, Bridget; and Walker, Bailey. "The Ordination of Women to the Priesthood: An Annotated Bibliography." Anglican Theological Review Spec. Sup. 6 (June 1976): 81-106.

00229. Boucher, Madeleine I. "Women and the Apostolic Community." In Women Priests, A Catholic Commentary on the Vatican Declaration, edited by Leonard Swidler and Arlene Swidler, pp. 152-155. New York: Paulist Press, 1977.

00230. Cardman, Francine. "Non-Conclusive Arguments: Therefore, Non-Conclusion?" In Women Priests, A Catholic Commentary on the Vatican Declaration, edited by Leonard Swidler and Arlene Swidler, pp. 92-98. New York: Paulist Press, 1977.

00231. Carr, Anne. "Authentic Theology in Service of the Church." In Women Priests, A Catholic Commentary on the Vatican Declaration, edited by Leonard Swidler and Arlene Swidler, pp. 221-226. New York: Paulist Press, 1977.

00232. Casey, Juliana. "'Transitory Character' . . . Only in 'Disciplinary Cases of Minor Importance'?" In Women Priests, A Catholic Commentary on the Vatican Declaration, edited by Leonard Swidler and Arlene Swidler, pp. 202-204. New York: Paulist Press, 1977.

00233. Collins, Adela Yarbro. "The Ministry of Women in the Apostolic Generation." In Women Priests, A Catholic Commentary on the Vatican Declaration, edited by Leonard Swidler and Arlene Swidler, pp. 159-166. New York: Paulist Press, 1977.

00234. Fiorenza, Elisabeth Schüssler. "The Twelve." In Women Priests, A Catholic Commentary on the Vatican Declaration, edited by Leonard Swidler and Arlene Swidler, pp. 114-122. New York: Paulist Press, 1977.

00235. Ford, J. Massyngberde. "The 'Ordination' of Queens." In Women Priests, A Catholic Commentary on the Vatican Declaration, edited by Leonard Swidler and Arlene Swidler, pp. 303-306. New York: Paulist Press, 1977.

00236. ____________________. "'The Permanent Value of Jesus and the Apostles.'" In Women Priests, A Catholic Commentary on the Vatican Declaration, edited by Leonard Swidler and Arlene Swidler, pp. 183-190. New York: Paulist Press, 1977.

00237. Getty, Mary Ann. "God's Fellow Worker and Apostleship." In Women Priests, A Catholic Commentary on the Vatican Declaration, edited by Leonard Swidler and Arlene Swidler, pp. 176-182. New York: Paulist Press, 1977.

00238. Higgins, Jean M. "Fidelity in History." In _Women Priests, A Catholic Commentary on the Vatican Declaration_, edited by Leonard Swidler and Arlene Swidler, pp. 85-91. New York: Paulist Press, 1977.

00239. Hogan, Denise C. "Reflections on Discipleship." In _Women Priests, A Catholic Commentary on the Vatican Declaration_, edited by Leonard Swidler and Arlene Swidler, pp. 284-290. New York: Paulist Press, 1977.

00240. Hopko, Thomas, ed. _Women and the Priesthood_. Crestwood, N.Y.: St. Vladimir's Seminary Press, 1983.

00241. Jewett, Paul K. _The Ordination of Women: An Essay on the Office of Christian Ministry_. Grand Rapids, Mich.: Eerdmans Publishing Co., 1980.

00242. Karris, Robert J. "Women in the Pauline Assembly: To Prophesy, But Not To Speak?" In _Women Priests, A Catholic Commentary on the Vatican Declaration_, edited by Leonard Swidler and Arlene Swidler, pp. 205-208. New York: Paulist Press, 1977.

00243. Kilmartin, Edward J. "Bishop and Presbyter as Representatives of the Church and Christ." In _Women Priests, A Catholic Commentary on the Vatican Declaration_, edited by Leonard Swidler and Arlene Swidler, pp. 295-302. New York: Paulist Press, 1977.

00244. Perkins, Pheme. "Peter's Pentecost Sermon: A Limitation on Who May Minister . . . ?" In _Women Priests, A Catholic Commentary on the Vatican Declaration_, edited by Leonard Swidler and Arlene Swidler, pp. 156-158. New York: Paulist Press, 1977.

00245. Quitslund, Sonya A. "In the Image of Christ." In _Women Priests, A Catholic Commentary on the Vatican Declaration_, edited by Leonard Swidler and Arlene Swidler, pp. 260-270. New York: Paulist Press, 1977.

00246. Rausch, Thomas P. "Ordination and the Ministry Willed by Jesus." In _Women Priests, A Catholic Commentary on the Vatican Declaration_, edited by Leonard Swidler and Arlene Swidler, pp. 123-131. New York: Paulist Press, 1977.

00247. Ruether, Rosemary Radford. "Women Priests and Church Tradition." In _Women Priests, A Catholic Commentary on the Vatican Declaration_, edited by Leonard Swidler and Arlene Swidler, pp. 234-238. New York: Paulist Press, 1977.

00248. Schneiders, Sandra M. "Did Jesus Exclude Women from Priesthood?" In _Women Priests, A Catholic Commentary on the Vatican Declaration_, edited by Leonard Swidler and Arlene Swidler, pp. 227-233. New York: Paulist Press, 1977.

00249. Stuhlmueller, Carroll. "Bridegroom: A Biblical Symbol of Union, Not Separation." In Women Priests, A Catholic Commentary on the Vatican Declaration, edited by Leonard Swidler and Arlene Swidler, pp. 278-283. New York: Paulist Press, 1977.

00250. ____________________. "Leadership: Secular Gift Transformed by Revelation." In Women Priests, A Catholic Commentary on the Vatican Delaration, edited by Leonard Swidler and Arlene Swidler, pp. 307-309. New York: Paulist Press, 1977.

00251. Thompson, Thomas L. "The Divine Plan of Creation: 1 Cor 11:7 and Gen 2:18-24." In Women Priests, A Catholic Commentary on the Vatican Declaration, edited by Leonard Swidler and Arlene Swidler, pp. 209-211. New York: Paulist Press, 1977.

00252. Turner, Pauline and Cooke, Bernard. "Women Can Have a Natural Resemblance to Christ." In Women Priests, A Catholic Commentary on the Vatican Declaration, edited by Leonard Swidler and Arlene Swidler, pp. 258-259. New York: Paulist Press, 1977.

g) Mariology

00253. Kristeva, Julia. "Stabat Mater." Poetics Today 6 (1985): 133-152.

00254. McHugh, John. The Mother of Jesus in the New Testament. Garden City, N.Y.: Doubleday and Co., 1975.

00255. Mahoney, Robert. "Die Mutter Jesu im Neuen Testament." In Die Frau im Urchristentum, edited by Gerhard Dautzenberg, et al., pp. 92-116. Freiburg: Herder, 1983.

00256. Matter, E. Ann. "The Virgin Mary: A Goddess." In The Book of the Goddess, Past and Present: An Introduction to Her Religion, edited by Carl Olson, pp, 80-96. New York: Crossroad Publishing Co., 1983.

00257. Moss, Leonard W. and Cappannari, Stephen C. "The Black Madonna: An Example of Cultural Borrowing." Scientific Monthly 73 (1953): 319-324.

00258. ________________________________. "In Quest of the Black Virgin: She is Black Because She is Black." In Mother Worship Themes and Variations, edited by James J. Preston, pp. 54-74. Chapel Hill, N.C.: University of North Carolina Press, 1982.

00259. Oberman, Heiko A. "The Virgin Mary in Evangelical Perspective." Journal of Ecumenical Studies 1 (Spring 1964): 271-298.

00260. Patsch, Joseph. _Our Lady in the Gospels_. Westminster, Md.: Newman Press, 1958.

00261. Turner, Victor and Turner, Edith. "Postindustrial Marian Pilgrimage." In _Mother Worship Themes and Variations_, edited by James J. Preston, pp. 145-173. Chapel Hill, N.C.: University of North Carolina Press, 1982.

h) Canon Law

00262. Ariès, Philippe. "The Indissoluble Marriage." In _Western Sexuality_, edited by Philippe Ariès and André Bejin, pp. 140-157. New York: Blackwell, 1985.

00263. Evdokimoff, Paul Nicolaeivitch. _Sacrement de l'amour. Le mystère conjugal à la lumière de la tradition orthodoxe_. Paris: Theophanie de Brouwer, 1980.

00264. Mullenders, Joannes. _Le mariage présumé_. Rome: Gregorian University, 1971.

i) Witchcraft

00265. Ben-Yuda, N. "European Witch Craze of the 14th to 17th Centuries: A Sociologist's Perspective." _American Journal of Sociology_ 86 (July 1980): 1-31.

00266. Budapest, Z. "Witch is to Woman as Womb is to Birth." _Quest_ 2 (Summer 1975): 50-56.

00267. Cavendish, Richard. _The Black Arts_. London: Routledge and Kegan Paul, 1967.

00268. Certeau, Michel de. _L'abent de l'histoire_. Tours: Mame, 1973.

00269. Dahl, Jurgen. _Nachtfrauen und Galsterweiber; eine Naturgeschichte der Hexe_. Ebenhausen: Lengewiesche-Brandt, 1960.

00270. Easlea, Brian. _Witch Hunting, Magic and the New Philosophy: An Introduction to Debates of the Scientific Revolution, 1450-1750_. Sussex: Harvester Press, 1980.

00271. Ehrenreich, Barbara and English, Deidre. "Burn Witch Burn." _Women: A Journal of Liberation_ 3.2 (1972): 30-32.

00272. Garrett, Clarke. "Women and Witches: Patterns of Analysis." _Signs: Journal of Women in Culture and Society_ 3 (1977): 461-470.

00273. Graubard, Mark. _Witchcraft and the Nature of Man_. Lanham, Md.: University Press of America, 1985.

00274. Horsley, Richard A. "Further Reflections on Witchcraft and European Folk Religion." *History of Religions* 19 (1979): 71-95.

00275. Hoyt, Charles Alva. *Witchcraft*. Carbondale, Ill.: Southern Illinois University Press, 1981.

00276. Larner, Christina. *Witchcraft and Religion, The Politics of Popular Belief*. New York: Basil Blackwell, 1984.

00277. McFarland, Morgan. "Witchcraft: The Art of Remembering." *Quest* 1 (Spring 1975): 41-48.

00278. Mair, Lucy. "Witchcraft, Spirit Possession and Heresy." *Folklore* 91 (1980): 228-238.

00279. Matalene, Carolyn. "Women as Witches." *International Journal of Women's Studies* 1 (1978): 473-587.

00280. Summers, Montague. *The Discovery of Witches*. 1928. Reprint. New York: AMS Press, 1982.

10. SOCIAL

"Silence gives the proper grace to women."

Sophocles
Ajax

a) Generic

00281. Boslooper, Thomas. *The Image of Woman*. New York: Rose of Sharon Press, 1980.

00282. Braudel, Fernand. *The Structures of Everyday Life The Limits of the Possible*. New York: Harper and Row, 1982.

00283. Faderman, Lillian. *Surpassing the Love of Men: Romantic Friendship and Love Between Women, from the Renissance to the Present*. New York: Morrow, 1981.

00284. Greer, Germaine. *Sex and Destiny: The Politics of Human Fertility*. New York: Harper and Row, 1984.

00285. Harris, Barbara J. and McNamara, JoAnn K., eds. *Women and the Structure of Society*. Durham, N.C.: Duke University Press, 1984.

00286. Lampériѐre, Anna. *Le role social de la femme*. Paris: F. Alcan, 1898.

00287. Lantz, Herman R. "Romantic Love in Pre-Modern Period: A Social Commentary." *Journal of Social History* 15 (Spring 1982): 349-370.

00288. Spelman, Elizabeth V. "Woman as Body: Ancient and Contemporary Views." Feminist Studies 8 (Spring 1982): 109-131.

00289. Wahlen, Auguste. Moeurs, usages et costumes de tous les peuples du monde-Europe. Brussels: Librairie historique-artistique, 1844.

00290. Watkins, Susan Cotts. "Spinsters." Journal of Family History 9 (Winter 1984): 310-325.

Also refer to #137.

b) Folklore

00291. Benwell, Gwen and Waugh, Arthur. Sea Enchantress: The Tale of the Mermaid and Her Kin. London: Hutchinson, 1961.

00292. Blocker, Monica. "Frauenzauber-Zauberfrauen." Zeitschrift fur Schweizerische Kirchengeschichte 76 (1982): 1-39.

00293. Coffin, Tristram Potter. The Female Hero in Folklore and Legend. New York: Seabury Press, 1975.

00294. DeCaro, Francis A. Women and Folklore, A Bibliographic Survey. Westport, Ct.: Greenwood Press, 1983.

00295. Lemaire, Ria. "The Woman-Song Tradition in West-European Tradition." Folklore Women's Communication 25 (1981): 14-15.

00296. Lundell, Torborg. "Folktale Heroines and the Type and Motif Indexes." Folklore 94 (1983): 240-246.

00297. Meletinsky, Eleasar. "Die Ehe im Zaubermarchen." Acta Ethnographica Academiae Scientiarum Hungaricae 19 (1970): 281-292.

00298. Penzer, Norman. Poison Damsels and Other Essays in Folklore and Anthropology. London: J.C. Sawyer, 1952.

c) Demography

00299. Anderson, Michael. "Historical Demography after The Population History of England." Journal of Interdisciplinary History 15 (Spring 1985): 595-607.

00300. Bourgeois-Pichat, Jean. "Additions to the Study of 'The Factors of Non-controlled Fertility.'" In Natural Fertility, edited by Henri Leridon and Jane Menken, pp. 65-81. Liege: Ordina Editions, 1979.

00301. Festy, Patrick. La fécondité des pays occidentaux de 1870 à 1970. Paris: Presses Universitaires de France, 1979.

00302. Frinking, Gerard A.B. "L'incidence de la surmortalité masculine sur le cycle de la vie familiale." In <u>The Family Cycle in European Societies</u>, edited by Jean Cuisenier, pp. 277-283. Paris: Mouton, 1977.

00303. Grigg, David. <u>Population Growth and Agrarian Change: An Historical Perspective</u>. New York: Cambridge University Press, 1980.

00304. Henry, Louis. "Current Concepts and Empirical Results Concerning Natural Fertility." In <u>Natural Fertility</u>, edited by Henri Leridon and Jane Menken, pp. 15-28. Liege: Ordina Editions, 1979.

00305. Kupinsky, Stanley, ed. <u>The Fertility of Working Women: A Synthesis of International Research</u>. New York: Praeger, 1977.

00306. Marcy, Peter T. "Factors Affecting the Fecundity and Fertility of Historical Population: A Review." <u>Journal of Family History</u> 6 (Fall 1981): 309-326.

00307. Menken, Jane. "Introduction." In <u>Natural Fertility</u>, edited by Henri Leridon and Jane Menken, pp. 1-13. Liege: Ordina Editions, 1979.

00308. Mosley, W. Henry. "The Effects of Nutrition on Natural Fertility." In <u>Natural Fertility</u>, edited by Henri Leridon and Jane Menken, pp. 83-105. Liege: Ordina Editions, 1979.

00309. Ohadike, Patrick O. "Socio-Economic, Cultural and Behavioral Factors in Natural Fertility Variations." In <u>Natural Fertility</u>, edited by Henri Leridon and Jane Menken, pp. 285-313. Liege: Ordina Editions, 1979.

00310. Schofield, Roger S. "Through a Glass Darkly: <u>The Population History of England</u> as an Experiment in History." <u>Journal of Interdisciplinary History</u> 15 (Spring 1985): 571-593.

00311. ________________ and Wrigley, Edward Anthony. "Population and Economy: From the Traditional to the Modern World." <u>Journal of Interdisciplinary History</u> 15 (Spring 1985): 561-569.

00312. Smith, James E. "How First Marriage and Remarriage Markets Mediate the Effects of Declining Mortality on Fertility." In <u>Marriage and Remarriage in the Populations of the Past</u>, edited by Jacques Dupâquier, et al., pp. 229-243. New York: Academic Press, 1981.

00313. Tilly, Charles. "Demographic Origins of the European Proletariat." In <u>Proletarianization and Family History</u>, edited by David Levine, pp. 1-85. New York: Academic Press, Inc. 1984.

00314. Trussell, James. "Natural Fertility: Measurement and Use in Fertility Models." In _Natural Fertility_, edited by Henri Leridon and Jane Menken, pp. 29-64. Liege: Ordina Editions, 1979.

00315. Watkins, Susan Cotts and Van de Walle, Etienne. "Nutrition, Mortality and Population Size: Malthus' Court of Last Resort." _Journal of Interdisciplinary History_ 14 (Autumn 1983): 205-226.

Also refer to #344.

d) Family

(1) Bibliographies

00316. Flandrin, Jean-Louis. "Histoire de la famille et histoire des mentalites." _Canadian Historical Association Historical Papers_ 1983: 136-149.

00317. Jordanova, L.J. "The History of the Family." In _Women in Society_, edited by the Cambridge Women's Studies Group, pp. 41-54. London: Virago Press, 1981.

00318. Lasch, Christopher. "The Family in History." _New York Review of Books_ (13 November 1975): 33-38.

00319. Morgan, David H.J. "New Directions in Family Research and Theory." In _The Sociology of the Family: New Directions for Britain_, edited by Michael Harris, pp. 3-18. Totowa, N.J.: Rowman and Littlefield, 1979.

00320. Plakans, Andrejas. _Kinship in the Past, An Anthropology of European Family Life 1500-1900_. Oxford: Basil Blackwell, 1985.

00321. Stone, Lawrence. "Family History in the 1980's." _Journal of Interdisciplinary History_ 12 (Summer 1981): 51-87.

00322. Treaton, J.R. "Marriage and the Family. 1. History and Sociology of the Family - - Recent Books." _Revue francaise de sociologie_ 17 (July-September 1976): 677-680.

(2) Non-specific

00323. Anderson, Michael. "The Relevance of Family History." In _The Sociology of the Family: New Directions for Britain_, edited by Michael Harris, pp. 49-73. Totowa, N.J.: Rowman and Littlefield, 1979.

00324. Behrman, S.J., et al., eds. _Fertility and Family Planning: A World View_. Ann Arbor: University of Michigan Press, 1969.

00325. Cuisenier, Jean, ed. The Family Life Cycle in European Societies. The Hague: Mouton, 1977.

00326. ______________. "Type d'organisation familiale et cycle: changement ou mutation dans les societes europeennes." In The Family Life Cycle in European Societies, edited by Jean Cuisenier, pp. 483-494. Paris: Mouton, 1977.

00327. Devereux, George. "The Family: Historical Function, Dysfunction, Lack of Function and Schizophrenia." Journal of Psychohistory 8 (Fall 1980): 183-193.

00328. Garigue, Philippe. Famille et humanisme. Montreal: Lemeac, 1973.

00329. Goode, William J. "Family Cycle and Theory Construction." In The Family Cycle in European Societies, edited by Jean Cuisenier, pp. 59-74. Paris: Mouton, 1977.

00330. ______________. World Revolution and Family Patterns. New York: Free Press, 1963.

00331. Goody, Jack. The Development of the Family and Marriage in Europe. New York: Cambridge University Press, 1983.

00332. Harris, Christopher C. The Family in Industrial Society. Boston: George Allen and Unwin, 1983.

00333. Hill, Reuben. "Social Theory and Family Development." In The Family Cycle in European Societies, edited by Jean Cuisenier, pp. 9-38. Paris: Mouton, 1977.

00334. Kelly, Joan. "Family and Society." In Women, History and Theory: The Essays of Joan Kelly, pp. 110-155. Chicago: The University of Chicago Press, 1984.

00335. Laslett, Peter. "Le cycle familial et le processur de socialisation: caracteristiques du schema occident considere dans le temps." In The Family Life Cycle in European Societies, edited by Jean Cuisenier, pp. 318-338. Paris: Mouton, 1977.

00336. ______________. "Family and Household as Work Group and Kin Group: Areas of Traditional Europe Compared." In Family Forms in Historic Europe, edited by Richard Wall, Jean Robin, and Peter Laslett, pp. 513-563. New York: Cambridge University Press, 1983.

00337. Medick, Hans. "The Proto-Industrial Family Economy: The Structural Function of Household and Family During the Transition from Peasant Society to Industrial Capitalism." Social History (October 1976): 291-316. Also in Sozialgeschichte der Familie in der Neuzeit Europas, edited by Werner Conze, pp. 254-282. Stuttgart: Ernstklett Verlag, 1976.

00338. Mitterauer, Michael and Sieder, Reinhard. The European Family: Patriarchy and Partnership from the Middle Ages to the Present. Chicago: University Press, 1982.

00339. Mount, Ferdinand. The Subversive Family. Winchester, Mass.: Allen and Unwin, 1983.

00340. Rodgers, Roy H. "The Family Life Cycle Concept: Past, Present, and Future." In The Family Cycle in European Societies, edited by Jean Cuisenier, pp. 39-57. Paris: Mouton, 1977.

00341. Rosof, Patricia J.F. and Zeisel, William, eds. Family History. New York: Institute for Research in History, 1985.

00342. Thadani, Veena-N. "The Logic of Sentiment: The Family and Social Change." Population and Development Review 4 (1978): 457-499.

00343. Tilly, Louise A. "Demographic History Faces the Family: Europe Since 1500. In Family History edited by Patricia J.F. Rosof and William Zeisel, pp. 45-68. New York: Institute for Research in History, 1985.

00344. ______________ and Cohen, Miriam. "Does the Family Have a History? A Review of Theory and Practice in Family History." Social Science History 6 (Spring 1982): 131-179.

00345. Todd, Emmanuel. La troisième planete: Structures familiales et systemes idéologiques. Paris: du Seuil, 1983.

00346. Wall, Richard. "Introduction." In Family Forms in Historic Europe, edited by Richard Wall, Jean Robin, and Peter Laslett, pp. 1-63. New York: Cambridge University Press, 1983.

00347. ____________; Robin, Jean; and Laslett, Peter, eds. Family Forms in Historic Europe. New York: Cambridge University Press, 1983.

Also refer to #95, 96, 99, 100, 302.

(3) Motherhood

00348. Badinter, Elizabeth. The Myth of Motherhood. London: Souvenir Press, 1981.

00349. Callaway, Helen. "'The Most Essentially Female Function of All': Giving Birth." In Defining Females: The Nature of Women in Society, edited by Shirley Ardener, pp. 163-185. New York: John Wiley and Sons, 1978.

00350. Ross, Mary Ellen and Ross, Cheryl Lynn. "Mothers, Infants, and the Psychoanalytic Study of Ritual." Signs 9 (Autumn 1983): 26-39.

00351. Wilson, Stephen. "The Myth of Motherhood A Myth: the Historical View of European Child-Rearing." Social History 9 (May 1984): 181-198.

Also refer to #451.

(4) Childhood

00352. Ende, Aurel. "Children in History: A Personal Review of the Past Decade's Published Research." Journal of Psychohistory 11 (Summer 1983): 65-88.

00353. Fildes, Valerie. A Social History of Infant Feeding. Edinburgh: University Press, 1986.

00354. Mecke, Richard Alan. "Childhood and the Historian." Journal of Family History 9 (Winter 1984): 415-424.

00355. Rush, Florence. The Best Kept Secret: Sexual Abuse of Children. New York: McGraw Hill, 1981.

00356. Sommerville, C. John. The Rise and Fall of Childhood. Beverly Hills, Ca.: Sage Publications, 1982.

00357. Suransky, Valerie Polakow. The Erosion of Childhood. Chicago: University of Chicago Press, 1982.

00358. Zglinicki, Friedrich von. Geburt. Eine Kulturgeschichte in Bildern. Braunschweig: Westermann, 1983.

Also refer to #210, 385, 634.

e) Marriage

00359. Ariès, Philippe. "Love in Married Life." In Western Sexuality, edited by Philippe Ariès and André Béjin, pp. 130-139. New York: Blackwell, 1979.

00360. Aspects de la vie populaire en Europe, amour et mariage. Liege: Musee de la Vie Wallonne, 1975.

00361. Braddock, Joseph. The Bridal Bed. New York: John Day, Co., 1961.

00362. Dupâquier, Jacques; Helin, Etienne; Laslett, Peter; Livi-Bacci, Massimo; and Sogner, Solvi, eds. Marriage and Remarriage in Populations of the Past. New York: Academic Press, 1981.

00363. Fox, Robin. Kinship and Marriage; An Anthropological Perspective. New York: Cambridge University Press, 1983.

00364. Hutchinson, H.N. Marriage Customs in Many Lands. London: Seeley and Co., 1897.

00365. Kaplan, Marion A., ed. The Marriage Bargain: Women and Dowries in European History. New York: Harrington Park, 1985.

00366. Kohler, Josef. On the Prehistory of Marriage. Chicago: University of Chicago Press, 1975.

00367. Lerner, Laurence David. Love and Marriage in its Social Context. New York: St. Martin's, 1979.

00368. Métral, Marie-Odile. Le mariage: les hesitations de l'Occident. Paris: Aubier-Montaigne, 1977.

00369. Rose, H.A. "The Development of Bride-Price and of Dowry." Folklore 36 (1925): 189-193.

00370. Scott, George Ryley. Curious Customs of Sex and Marriage. London: Torchstream, 1953.

00371. Segalen, Martine. "Mentalité populaire et remariage en Europe occidentale." In Marriage and Remarriage in Populations of the Past, edited by Jacques Dupaquier, et al., pp. 67-77. New York: Academic Press, 1981.

00372. Watkins, Susan Cotts. "Regional Patterns of Nuptuality in Europe 1870-1960." Population Studies 35 (July 1981): 199-216.

00373. Wood, Edward J. The Wedding Day in all Ages and Countries. New York: Harper and Bros., 1869.

Also refer to #101, 173, 211, 213, 215, 261-264, 297, 312, 322, 331.

f) Sex Life and Morals

(1) Non-Specific

00374. Andreas-Salomé, Lou. "Der Mensch als Weib." Neue Deutsche Rundschau 10 (1899): 225-243.

00375. Archer, John. Sex and Gender. New York: Penguin, 1984.

00376. Ariès, Philippe. "Thoughts on the History of Homosexuality." In Western Sexuality, edited by Philippe Ariès and André Béjin, pp. 62-75. New York: Blackwell, 1985.

00377. Ariès, Philippe and Béjin, André, eds. Western Sexuality Practice and Precept in Past and Present Times. New York: Blackwell, 1985.

00378. Benjamin, Jessica. "Master and Slave: The Fantasy of Erotic Domination." In Powers of Desire: The Politics of Sexuality, edited by Ann Snitow, Christine Stansell and Sharon Thompson, pp. 280-299. New York: Pergamon Press, 1983.

00379. Caplan, Jane. "Sexuality and Homosexuality." In Women in Society, edited by the Cambridge Women's Studies Group, pp. 149-167. London: Virago Press, 1981.

00380. Coveney, Lal et al., eds. The Sexuality Papers. London: Hutchinson, 1984.

00381. Coveney, Lal; Jackson, Margaret; Jeffreys, Sheila; Kay, Leslie; and Mahony, Pat. "Introduction." In The Sexuality Papers, edited by Lal Coveney et al., pp. 9-21. London: Hutchinson, 1984.

00382. Dinnerstein, Dorothy. The Mermaid and the Minotaur: Sexual Arrangements and Human Malaise. New York: Harper and Row, 1977.

00383. Ellis, Havelock. Man and Woman A Study of Secondary and Tertiary Sexual Characters. Boston: Houghton Mifflin Co., 1929.

00384. ______________. Sex in Relation to Society. New York: Random House, 1936.

00385. Fishmann, Sterling. "The History of Childhood Sexuality." Journal of Contemporary History 17 (April 1982): 269-283.

00386. Freedman, Estelle B. et al., ed. The Lesbian Issue, Essays from Signs. Chicago: University of Chicago Press, 1985.

00387. Goldstein, Melvin. "Some Tolerant Attitudes toward Female Homosexuality throughout History." Journal of Psychohistory 9 (Spring 1982): 437-460.

00388. Goodland, Roger. A Bibliography of Sex Rites and Customs. London: G. Routledge and Sons, 1931.

00389. Hutt, Corinne. Males and Females. Hamondsworth: Penguin Books, 1972.

00390. Klaich, Dolores. Femme et femme. Paris: Editions des femmes, 1979.

00391. Molino, Jean. "Le mythe de l'androgyne." In Aimer en France 1760-1860, edited by Paul Vialleneix and Jean Ehrard, 2: 401-411. 2 vols. Clermont-Ferrand: Association des Publications de la Faculte des Lettres et Sciences Humaines de Clermont-Ferrand, 1980.

00392. Moorhead, John. "Adam and Eve and the Discovery of Sex." Parergon n.s. 1 (1983) 1-9.

00393. Mosse, George L. Nationalism and Sexuality: Respectability and Abnormal Sexuality in Modern Europe. New York: Howard Fertig, 1985.

00394. Rose, H.A. "Customary Restraints on Celibacy." Folklore 30 (1919): 63-70.

00395. Ross, Ellen and Rapp, Rayna. "Sex and Society: A Research Note from Social History and Anthropology." In Powers of Desire: The Politics of Sexuality, edited by Ann Snitow, Christine Stansell, and Sharon Thompson, pp. 51-73. New York: Pergamon Press, 1983.

00396. Shoham, S. Giora. Sex as Bait: Eve, Casanova, and Don Juan. New York: University of Queensland Press, 1983.

00397. Singer, Irving. The Nature of Love. Chicago: University of Chicago Press, 1984.

00398. Snitow, Ann; Stansell, Christine; and Thompson, Sharon, eds. Powers of Desire: The Politics of Sexuality. New York: Monthly Review Press, 1983.

00399. Warren, Mary Anne. Gendercide, The Implications of Sex Selection. Totowa, N.J.: Rowman and Allanheld, 1985.

00400. Whitbeck, Caroline. "Love, Knowledge and Transformation." Women's Studies International Forum 7 (1984): 393-405.

Also refer to #147, 169, 180, 359, 454.

(2) Prostitutes

00401. Bullough, Vern L. "Problems and Methods for Research in Prostitution and the Behavioral Sciences." Journal of the History of the Behavioral Science 1 (July 1965): 244-251.

00402. Jagger, Alison M. "Prostitution." In The Philosophy of Sex, edited by Alan Soble, pp. 348-368. Totowa, N.J.: Rowman and Littlefield, 1980.

g) Fashion/Manners

00403. Barwick, Sandra. A Century of Style. London: Allen and Unwin, 1984.

00404. Bigelow, Marybelle S. *Fashion in History: Western Dress, Prehistoric to Present*. Minneapolis, Minn.: Burgess Publishing Co., 1979.

00405. Blätter für Kostümkunde. *Historische und Volks-Trachten*. Berlin: Lipperheide, 1876-1878.

00406. Bradshaw, Angela. *World Costumes*. London: Black, 1959.

00407. Bruhn, W. and Tilke, M. *A Pictorial History of Costume: A Survey of Costume . . . Including National Costume in Europe and Non-European Countries*. London: Zwemmer, 1955.

00408. Chalmers, Helena. *Clothes, On and Off the Stage; A History of Dress from the Earliest Times to the Present Day*. 1928. Reprint. Detroit, Mich.: Gale Research Co., 1976.

00409. Corson, Richard. *Fashions in Hair: The First 5,000 Years*. London: Peter Owen, 1980.

00410. ______________. *Fashions in Make-Up from Ancient to Modern Times*. New York: Universe Books, 1972.

00411. Curtin, Michael. "A Question of Manners: Status and Gender in Etiquette and Courtesy." *Journal of Modern History* 57 (September 1985): 395-423.

00412. Elias, Norbert. *The History of Manners*. New York: Pantheon Books, 1978.

00413. ________________. *Dress and Undress: A History of Women's Underwear*. New York: Drama Book Specialists, 1978.

00414. Ewing, Elizabeth. *Underwear: A History*. New York: Theatre Arts Books, 1972.

00415. Fox, Lilla M. *Folk Costumes of Southern Europe*. London: Chatto, Boyd and Oliver, 1972.

00416. Frei, Rose Marie. *Geschichte des Kostums*. Wadenswil: Statz, 1977.

00417. Gilbert, John. *National Costumes of the World*. London: Hamlyn, 1972.

00418. Hansen, Henny Harald. *Costume Cavalcade*. 1956. Reprint. London: Methuen, 1968.

00419. Hollander, Ann. *Seeing Through Clothes*. New York: Aron, 1980.

00420. Kemper, Rachel H. *Costume*. New York: Newsweek Books, 1977.

00421. Kohler, Carl. *A History of Costume*. Philadelphia: D. McKay Co., 1928.

00422. Kunzle, David. *Fashion and Fetishism, A Social History of the Corset, Tight-Lacing and Other Forms of Body Sculpture in the West*. Totowa, N.J.: Barnes and Noble, 1981.

00423. Laver, James. *Costume in the Theatre*. London: Harrap, 1964.

00424. Lipperheide, Franz Joseph, Freiherr von. *Katalog der Freiherrlich von Lipperheide'schen Kostumbibliothek. Reprint.* 1896-1905. New York: Saifer, 1965.

00425. Lurie, Alison. *The Language of Clothes*. New York: Random House, 1981.

00426. Mann, Kathleen. *Peasant Costume in Europe*. London: Black, 1950.

00427. Marly, Diana de. *Costume on the Stage, 1600-1940*. Totowa, N.J.: Barnes and Noble, 1982.

00428. Nienholdt, Eva and Wagner, Gretel. *Katalog der Lipperheideschen Kostümbibliothek*. 2 vols. New York: Hacker, 1967.

00429. Nunn, Joan. *Fashion and Costume*. New York: Schocken Books, 1984.

00430. Racinet, A. *Le costume historique. Types principaux du vetement . . . dans tous les temps et chez tous les peuples*. 6 vols. Paris: Firman-Didot, 1888.

00431. Snowden, James. *European Folk Dress*. London: Costume Society, 1973.

00432. ____________. *The Folk Dress of Europe*. New York: Mayflower, 1979.

00433. Victoria and Albert Museum. *A List of Works on Costume in the National Art Library*. London: Eyre and Spottiswoode, 1881.

00434. Wilcox, R. Turner. *Folk and Festival Costume of the World*. New York: Scribner, 1965.

00435. Yarwood, Doreen. *European Costume: 4000 Years of Fashion*. London: Batsford, 1975.

Also refer to #51, 289.

h) Health/Medical

(1) Birth Control

00436. Heinsohn, Gunnar and Steiger, Otto. "The Elimination of Birth Control and the Witch Trials of Modern Times." *International Journal of Women's Studies* 5 (May-June 1983): 193-214.

(2) Women in Medicine

00437. Glendinning, Chellis. "The Healing Powers of Women." In _The Politics of Women's Spirituality_, edited by Charlene Spretnak, pp. 280-293. Garden City, N.Y.: Doubleday and Company, Inc., Anchor Press, 1982.

00438. Levin, Beatrice S. _Women and Medicine_. Metuchen, N.J.: Scarecrow Press, 1980.

00439. Nutting, Mary Adelaide and Dock, Lavinia L. _A History of Nursing Systems from the Earliest Times to the Foundation of the First English and American Training Schools for Nurses_. Buffalo, N.Y.: Heritage Press, 1974.

(3) Women and Health

00440. Gruppi, Nicoletta. "L'esistenza mutilata." In _Esistere comme donna_, pp. 17-26. Milan: Mazzotta, 1983.

00441. Knibiehler, Yvonne and Fouquet, Catherine. _La Femme et les medecins_. Paris: Hachette, 1983.

(4) Psychology

00442. Burniston, Steve, et al. "Psychoanalysis and the Cultural Acquisition of Sexuality and Subjectivity." In _Women Take Issue: Aspects of Women's Subordination_, pp. 109-132. London: Hutchinson, 1978.

00443. Cixous, Hélène and Clement, Catherine. _La Jeune nee_. Paris: Union générale d'éditions, 1975.

00444. Holmstrom, Nancy. "Do Women have a Distinct Nature?" _Philosophical Forum_ 14 (Fall 1982): 25-42.

00445. Rawlinson, Mary C. "Psychiatric Discourse and the Feminine Voice." _Journal of Medicine and Philosophy_ 7 (May 1982): 153-177.

00446. Stevens, Gwendolyn. _The Women of Psychology_. Cambridge, Mass.: Schenkman Publishing, 1982.

11. CULTURAL

". . . in Antiquity and among simpler peoples the woman sings and dances and is no less a woman. Gracefulness is her domain and even her duty."

Renoir

a) Education

00447. Kersey, Shirley Nelson, ed. _Classics in the Education of Girls and Women_. Metuchen, N.J.: Scarecrow Press, 1981.

00448. Parker, Franklin and Parker, Betty June, eds. _Women's Education--A World View, Annotated Bibliography of Books and Reports_. Westport, Ct.: Greenwood Press, 1981.

Also refer to #126.

b) Literature

(1) Non-specific

(a) Women in Literature

00449. Atkins, John. _The Erotic Impulse in Literature_. London: Calder and Boyars, 1970.

00450. Daghistany, Ann. "The Picara Nature." _Women's Studies_ 5 (1977): 51-60.

00451. Davidson, Cathy N. and Broner, E.M., eds. _The Lost Tradition: Mothers and Daughters in Literature_. New York: Ungar, 1980.

00452. Donovan, Josephine. "The Silence is Broken." In _Women and Language in Literature and Society_, edited by Sally McConnel-Ginet, pp. 205-218. New York: Praeger, 1980.

00453. Jacobus, Mary. "Is There a Woman in this Text?" _New Literary History_ 14 (Autumn 1982): 117-141.

00454. Kronhausen, Phyliss. _Erotic Fantasies: A Study of the Sexual Imagination_. New York: Bell Publishing Co., 1970.

00455. Larcher, Louis Julian. _La femme jugée par les grands écrivains des deux sexes_. 1854. Reprint. New Haven: Research Publications, 1975.

00456. Lewis, Linda K. "Women in Literature: A Select Bibliography." _Bulletin of Bibliography_ 35 (1978): 116-122, 131.

00457. May, Keith M. _Characters of Women in Narrative Literature_. New York: St. Martin's Press, 1981.

00458. Miller, Nancy K. "Rereading as a Woman: The Body in Practice." Poetics Today 6 (1985): 291-299.

00459. Myers, Carol Fairbanks. Women in Literature: Criticism of the Seventies. Metuchen, N.J.: Scarecrow Press, 1976.

(b) Women Authors

00460. Bradbrook, Muriel Clara. The Collected Papers of Muriel Bradbrook. Totowa, N.J.: Barnes and Noble, 1982.

00461. Delany, Sheila. Writing Woman: Woman Writers and Women in Literature, Medieval to Modern. New York: Schocken, 1983.

00462. Jacobus, Mary, ed. Women Writing and Writing About Women. New York: Barnes and Noble, 1979.

00463. Kristeva, Julia. "Féminité et écriture. En response a deux questions sur Polylogue." Revue des sciences humaines n.s. 168 (October-December 1977): 495-501.

00464. Russ, Joanna. How to Suppress Women's Writing. Austin, Tx.: University of Texas Press, 1984.

00465. Schwartz, Narda Lacey. Articles on Women Writers 1960-1975: A Bibliography. Oxford: Clio Press, 1977.

00466. Sukenick, Lynn. "On Women and Fiction." In The Authority of Experience, edited by Arlyn Diamond and Lee R. Edwards, pp. 28-44. Amherst: University of Massachusetts Press, 1977.

00467. Todd, Janet, ed. Gender and Literary Voice. New York: Holmes and Meier, 1980.

00468. Wiesmayr, Elisabeth. "Weiblicher Lebens- und Schreibzusammenhang: Fragmentarische Uberlegungen zum Thema Frauen und Kreativität." In Das ewige Klischee, zum Rollenbild und Selbstverstandnis bei Mannern und Frauen, pp. 206-219. Vienna: Hermann Böhlaus, 1981.

Also refer to #452.

(c) Feminist Criticism

00469. Barnes, Annette. "Female Criticism: A Prologue." In The Authority of Experience, edited by Arlyn Diamond and Lee R. Edwards, pp. 1-15. Amherst: University of Massachusetts Press, 1977.

00470. Gilbert, Sandra M. and Gubar, Susan. "Sexual Linguistics, Gender, Language and Sexuality." New Literary History 16 (September 1985): 515-543.

00471. Jehlen, Myra. "Archimedes and the Paradox of Feminist Criticism." Signs 6 (Summer 1981): 575-601.

00472. Landy, Marcia. "The Silent Woman: Towards A Feminist Critique." In The Authority of Experience, edited by Arlyn Diamond and Lee R. Edwards, pp. 16-27. Amherst: University of Massachusetts Press, 1977.

(2) Philology

00473. Allen, Suzanne. "Plus-outre." Revue des sciences humaines n.s. 168 (October-December 1977): 503-515.

00474. Beardsley, Elizabeth Lane. "Referential Genderization." In Women and Philosophy: Toward A Theory of Liberation, edited by Carol C. Gould and Marx W. Wartofsky, pp. 285-293. New York: G.P. Putnam's, 1976.

00475. Hintikka, Merrill B. and Hintikka, Jaakko. "How Can Language Be Sexist?" In Discovering Reality, Feminist Perspectives on Epistemology, Metaphysics, Methodology, and Philosophy of Science, edited by Sandra Harding and Merrill B. Hintikka, pp. 139-148. Boston: D. Reidel Publishing Co., 1983.

00476. McConnel-Ginet, Sally, et al., eds. Women and Language in Literature and Society. New York: Praeger, 1980.

00477. Tyler, Mary. "Das Sprachverhalten des Mannes." In Das ewige Klischee, zum Rollenbild und Selbstverständnis bei Mannern und Frauen, pp. 220-231. Vienna: Herman Böhlaus, 1981.

(3) Philosophy

00478. Bell, Linda A., ed. Visions of Women. Clifton, N.J.: Humana Press, 1983.

00479. Femininity, "Masculinity" and "Androgyny": A Modern Philosophical Discussion. Totowa, N.J.: Rowman and Littlefield, 1982.

00480. Harding, Sandra. "Why Has the Sex/Gender System Become Visible Only Now?" In Discovering Reality, Feminist Perspectives on Epistemology, Metaphysics, Methodology, and Philosophy of Science, edited by Sandra Harding and Merrill B. Hintikka, pp. 311-324. Boston: D. Reidel Publishing Co., 1983.

00481. ____________ and Hintikka, Merrill B., eds. Discovering Reality, Feminist Perspectives on Epistemology, Metaphysics, Methodology, and Philosophy of Science. Boston: D. Reidel Publishing Co., 1983.

00482. Hartsock, Nancy C.M. "The Feminist Standpoint: Developing the Ground for a Specifically Feminist Historical Materialism." In _Discovering Reality, Feminist Perspectives on Epistemology, Metaphysics, Methodology, and Philosophy of Science_, edited by Sandra Harding and Merrill B. Hintikka, pp. 283-310. Boston: D. Reidel Publishing Co., 1983.

00483. Keller, Evelyn Fox and Grontkowski, Christine R. "The Mind's Eye." In _Discovering Reality, Feminist Perspectives on Epistemology, Metaphysics, Methodology, and Philosophy of Science_, edited by Sandra Harding and Merrill B. Hintikka, pp. 207-224. Boston: D. Reidel Publishing Co., 1983.

00484. Moulton, Janice. "A Paradigm of Philosophy: The Aversary Method." In _Discovering Reality, Feminist Perspectives on Epistemology, Metaphysics, Methodology, and Philosophy of Science_, edited by Sandra Harding and Merrill B. Hintikka, pp. 149-164. Boston: D. Reidel Publishing Co., 1983.

00485. Saxonhouse, Arlene. _Women in the History of Political Thought: Ancient Greece to Machiavelli_. Westport, Ct.: Greenwood Press, 1985.

(4) Drama

00486. Schwanitz, Dietrich. "Die Zeit ist aus den Fugen, aber das Leben geht weiter: 'Hamlet' oder 'Die Witwe von Ephesus.'" _Germanisch-Romanische Monatsschrift_ n.s. 31 (1981): 265-282.

(5) Prose

00487. Armstrong, Judith. _The Novel of Adultery_. New York: Barnes and Noble, 1976.

00488. Baruch, Elaine Hoffman. "The Feminine _Bildungsroman_: Education Through Marriage." _Massachusetts Review_ 22 (Summer 1981): 335-357.

c) Art

(1) Women in Art

00489. Broude, Norma and Garrard, Mary D. _Feminism and Art History: Questioning the Litany_. New York: Harper and Row, 1982.

00490. ________________. "Feminism in Art History." In _Feminism and Art History: Questioning the Litany_, pp. 1-18. New York: Harper and Row, 1982.

00491. Deonna, Waldemar. "La femme et la grenouille." _Gazette des Beaux Arts_ 94 no. 2 (November 1952): 229-240.

00492. La donna ideale nella grade pittura. Milan: Rizzoli Editori, 1965.

00493. Kahr, Madlyn Millner. "Delilah." In Feminism and Art History: Questioning the Litany, edited by Norma Broude and Mary D. Garrard, pp. 118-145. New York: Harper and Row, 1982. Also in Art Bulletin 54 (1972): 282-299.

00494. Nabakowski, Bislind. Frauen in der Kunst. Cambridge, Mass.: Suhrkamp Insel Publishers Boston Inc., 1980.

00495. Nikolenko, Lena. "The Beauties' Galleries." Gazette des Beaux Arts 108 no. 1 (January 1966): 19-23.

00496. Parker, Rozsika and Pollock, Griselda. Old Mistresses: Women, Art and Ideology. New York: Pantheon, 1982.

00497. Reid, Jane Davidson. "The True Judith." Art Journal 28 (Summer 1969): 376-387.

00498. Taslitzky, Boris. "A propos et hors de propos de 'La femme inspiratrice des arts plastiques.'" Europe 427-428 (November-December 1964): 159-165.

00499. Tufts, Eleanor. "Beyond Gardner, Gombrich, and Janson: Towards a Total History of Art." Arts 55 (April 1981): 150-154.

Also refer to #88-90, 92.

(2) Women Artists

(a) Non-specific

00500. Anscombe, Isabelle. A Woman's Touch, Women in Design from 1860 to the Present Day. New York: Viking, 1984.

(b) Musicians

00501. Borroff, Edith. "Women Composers: Reminiscence and History." College Music Symposium 15 (Fall 1975): 26-33.

00502. Bruyr, Jose. "La femme, la musique et les musiciennes." Europe 427-428 (November-December 1964): 171-176.

00503. Cohen, Aaron I. International Encyclopedia of Women Composers. New York: Bowker, 1981.

00504. Loesser, Arthur. Men, Women and Pianos: A Social History. New York: Simon and Schuster, 1954.

00505. Meggett, Joan M. Keyboard Music by Women Composers. Westport, Ct.: Greenwood Press, 1982.

00506. Neuls-Bates, Carol, ed. Women in Music. New York: Harper and Row, 1982.

00507. Pool, J.G. Women in Music History: A Research Guide. Published by author, 1981.

00508. Weissweiler, Eva. Kompositinnen aus 500 Jahren:eine Kultur und Wirkungsgeschichte in Biographie und Werkbeispielen. Frankurt am Main: Fischer Taschenbuch Verlag, 1981.

00509. Zelenka, K. Komponierende Frauen: ihr Leben, ihre Werke. Cologne: Ellenburg, 1980.

(c) Painters

00510. Brodsky, Judith K. "Some Notes on Women Printmakers." Art Journal 35 (Summer 1976): 374-377.

00511. Codell, Julie. "Women's Art and Art History." Giltedge n.s. 2 (1981): 90-94.

00512. Ellet, Elizabeth Fries Lummis. Women Artists in All Ages and Countries. New York: Harper Bros., 1859.

00513. Gabhart, Ann and Broun, Elizabeth. "Old Mistresses, Women Artists of the Past." The Walters Art Gallery Bulletin 24 (April 1972): 1-8.

00514. Krull, Edith. Kunst von Frauen: das Berufsbild der bildenden Kunstlerinnen in vier Jahrhunderten. Frankfurt am Main: Weidlich, 1984.

00515. Slatkin, Wendy. Women Artists in History: From Antiquity to the 20th Century. Englewood Cliffs, N.J.: Prentice Hall, 1985.

00516. Women Artists, 1600-1980: Selections from Five College Collections: March 12 through April 21, 1980. Amherst, Mass.: The Mead Art Museum, [1980].

d) Science and Technology

00517. Bush, C.G. "Women and the Assessment of Technology: To Think, to Be; to Unthink, to Free." In Machina ex Dea: Perspectives on Technology, edited by Joan Rothschild, pp. 151-170. New York: Pergamon Press, 1983.

00518. Davis, Herman S. "Women Astronomers (400 A.D.-1750)." Popular Astronomy 6 (May 1898): 129-138.

00519. Fee, Elizabeth. "Women's Nature and Scientific Objectivity." In Woman's Nature: Rationalizations of Inequality, edited by Marian Lowe and Ruth Hubbard, pp. 9-27. New York: Pergamon Press, 1983.

00520. Gearhart, Sally. "Aim to Technology: A Modest Proposal." In Machina ex Dea: Perspectives on Technology, edited by Joan Rothschild, pp. 171-182. New York: Pergamon Press, 1983.

00521. Hanmer, Jalna. "Reproductive Technology: The Future for Women." In Machina ex Dea: Perspectives on Technology, edited by Joan Rothschild, pp. 183-197. New York: Pergamon Press, 1983.

00522. Keller, Evelyn Fox. "Gender and Science." In Discovering Reality, Feminist Perspectives on Epistemology, Metaphysics, Methodology, and Philosophy of Science, edited by Sandra Harding and Merrill B. Hintikka, pp. 187-205. Boston: D. Reidel Publishing Co., 1983.

00523. King, Ymestra. "Toward an Ecological Feminism and a Feminist Ecology." In Machina ex Dea: Perspectives on Technology, edited by Joan Rothschild, pp. 119-129. New York: Pergamon Press, 1983.

00524. Merchant, Carolyn. "Isis' Consciousness Raised." Isis 73 (September 1982): 398-409.

00525. ________________. "Mining the Earth's Women." In Machina ex Dea: Perspectives on Technology, edited by Joan Rothschild, pp. 99-117. New York: Pergamon Press, 1983.

00526. Rappaport, Karen D. "Women Mathematicians: A Bibiliography." Women's Studies Newsletter 6 (Fall 1978): 15-17.

00527. Rothschild, Joan, ed. Machina ex Dea: Perspectives on Technology. New York: Pergamon Press, 1983.

00528. Stanley, Autumn. "Women Hold Up Two-Thirds of the Sky: Notes for a Revised History of Technology." In Machina ex Dea: Perspectives on Technology, edited by Joan Rothschild, pp. 5-22. New York: Pergamon Press, 1983.

B. BRITAIN

1. SURVEYS

> Women's "inferiority and infirmities are absolutely incurable."
>
> Hume

00529. Biographical Dictionary of British Women. London: Europe, 1984.

00530. Brunt, Rosalind and Rowan, Caroline, eds. Feminism, Culture and Politics. London: Wishart, 1982.

00531. Carpenter, Edward. Woman and Her Place in a Free Society. Manchester: Labour Press Society, 1894.

00532. Crawford, Patricia. "From the Woman's View: Pre-industrial England, 1500-1750." In Exploring Women's Past, pp. 49-85. Boston: George Allen and Unwin, 1983.

00533. Harper, Charles G. Revolted Women--Past, Present and to Come. London: Elkin Mathews, 1894.

00534. Lewis, Jane, ed. Women's Welfare: Women's Rights. London: Croom Helm, 1983.

00535. Marshall, Rosalind Kay. Virgin and Viragos: a History of Women in Scotland from 1080 to 1980. Chicago: Academy 1983.

00536. Prior, Mary, ed. Women in English Society 1500-1800. New York: Methuen, 1985.

2. POLITICAL

> " . . . it is impossible ever to govern subjects rightly, without knowing as well what they really are as what they only seem, which the Men can never be supposed to do, while they labor to force Women to live in constant masquerade."
>
> Sophia
> Woman Not Inferior to Man, 1739

a) Generic

00537. McIntosh, Mary. "The State and the Oppression of Women." In Feminism and Materialism: Women and Modes of Production, edited by Annette Kuhn and AnnMarie Wolpe, pp. 254-289. London: Routledge and Kegan Paul, 1978.

00538. Park, John. "Housing and the Family--Policy Issues." In Family Matters Perspectives on the Family and Social Policy, edited by Alfred White Franklin, pp. 57-62. New York: Pergamon Press, 1983.

b) Legal

00539. Glendon, Mary Ann. "Legal Concepts of Marriage and the Family." In Loving, Parenting and Dying, edited by Vivian C. Fox and Martin H. Quitt, pp. 95-109. New York: Psychohistory Press, Publishers, 1980.

00540. Groves, Dulcie. "Member and Survivors: Women and Retirement-Pensions Legislation." In Women's Welfare, Women's Rights, edited by Jane Lewis, pp. 38-63. London: Croom Helm, 1983.

00541. Rayden, William. The Practice and Law of Divorce, edited by Joseph Jackson, R.B. Rowe, and Margaret Booth. London: Butterworths, 1967.

00542. Sachs, Albert Louis and Wilson, Joan Hoff. Sexism and the Law: A Study of Male Beliefs and Judicial Bias in Britain and the United States. New York: Free Press, 1979.

00543. Spring, Eileen. "Law and the Theory of the Affective Family." Albion 16 (Spring 1984): 1-20.

Also refer to #576, 590, 635, 636.

c) Feminism

00544. Allen, Sandra, et al. Conditions of Illusion, Papers from the Women's Movement. Leeds: Feminist Books, 1974.

00545. Banks, Olive. Faces of Feminism: A Study of Feminism as a Social Movement. New York: St. Martin's, 1982.

00546. Bouchier, David. The Feminist Challenge: The Movement for Women's Liberation in Britain and the United States. New York: Schocken Books, 1984.

00547. Coote, Anna. Sweet Freedom: The Struggle for Women's Liberation. Oxford: Blackwells, 1982.

00548. Ferguson, Moira, ed. First Feminists, British Women Writers, 1578-1799. Bloomington, Ind.: Indiana University Press, 1985.

00549. Jessel, Penelope. The Ascent of Women. London: Liberal Publication Department, 1975.

00550. London Feminist Group. The Sexual Dynamics of History: Men's Power, Women's Resistance. London: Pluto Press, 1983.

00551. Newsome, Stella. Women's Freedom League, 1907-1957. London: n.p., n.d.

00552. Rooke, Patrick J. Women's Rights. London: Wayland, [1972].

00553. Rose, Catherine. The Female Experience. The Story of the Woman Movement in Ireland. Galway, Ireland: Arlen House, 1975.

Also refer to #530.

d) Suffrage

00554. Liddington, Jill. One Hand Tied Behind Us: The Rise of the Women's Suffrage Movement. London: Virago, 1978.

00555. Mason, Bertha. The Story of the Women's Suffrage Movement. London: Sheratt & Hughes, 1912.

00556. Strauss, Sylvia. "Traitors to the Cause": The Men's Campaign for Women's Rights. Westport, Ct.: Greenwood Press, 1982.

Also refer to #551, 552.

e) Political Roles

00557. McLeod, Kirsty. The Wives of Downing Street. London: Collins, 1976.

00558. Somerset, Anne. Ladies in Waiting: From the Tudors to the Present Day. New York: Alfred A. Knopf, 1984.

3. ECONOMIC

"One Higginson, a journeyman carpenter in the Borough having last week sold his wife to a brother workman in a fit of conjugal indifference at the alehouse . . . "

Annual Register, 1766

a) Generic

(1) Bibliographies

00559. Caskey, S.A. and Connolly, S.J. "Select Bibliography of Writings on Irish Economic and Social History Published in 1976." Irish Economic and Social History 4 (1977): 79-83.

00560. Caskey, S.A. and McCracken, D.P. "Select Bibliography of Writings on Irish Economic and Social History Published in 1977." Irish Economic and Social History 5 (1978): 78-83.

00561. ________________. "Select Bibliography of Writings on Irish Economic and Social History Published in 1978." Irish Economic and Social History 6 (1979): 81-90.

00562. Connolly, S.J. and Geary, T.P. "Select Bibliography of Writings on Irish Economic and Social History Published in 1973." Irish Economic and Social History 1 (1974): 67-70.

00563. ________________. "Select Bibliography of Writings on Irish Economic and Social History Published in 1974." Irish Economic and Social History 2 (1975): 66-71.

00564. Connolly, S.J. and Greenlees, S.R. "Select Bibliography of Writings on Irish Economic and Social History Published in 1975." Irish Economic and Social History 3 (1976): 83-87.

00565. Gillespie, Raymond and Kirkham, Graeme. "Select Bibliography of Writings on Irish Economic and Social History Published in 1979." Irish Economic and Social History 7 (1980): 99-105.

00566. Gillespie, Raymond and Kirkham, Graeme. "Select Bibliography of Writings on Irish Economic and Social History Published in 1980." Irish Economic and Social History 8 (1981): 113-124.

00567. Keating, Carla and Kirkham, Graeme. "Select Bibliography of Writings on Irish Economic and Social History Published in 1981." Irish Economic and Social History 9 (1982): 80-93.

00568. ________________. "Select Bibliography of Writings on Irish Economic and Social History Published in 1982." Irish Economic and Social History 10 (1983): 100-114.

00569. ________________. "Select Bibliography of Writings on Irish Economic and Social History Published in 1983." Irish Economic and Social History 11 (1984): 127-141.

(2) Non-specific

00570. Hughes, Therle. English Domestic Needlework: 1660-1860. London: Abbey Fine Arts Ltd., n.d.

00571. Middleton, Chris. "Patriarchal Exploitation and the Rise of English Capitalism." In Gender, Class and Work, edited by Eva Gamarnikow, et al., pp. 11-27. London: Heinemann, 1983.

00572. Prior, Mary. "Women and the Urban Economy: Oxford 1500-1800." In Women in English Society 1500-1800, pp. 93-117. New York: Methuen, 1985.

00573. Tebbutt, Melanie. Making Ends Meet: Pawnbroking and Working-Class Credit. New York: St. Martins's Press, 1983.

00574. Young, James D. Women and Popular Struggles, A History of Scottish and English Working-Class Women, 1500-1984. Atlantic Highlands, N.J.: Humanities Press, 1985.

Also refer to #540, 608, 613, 615, 637, 641.

b) Woman's Employment

00575. Boston, Sarah. Women Workers and the Trade Union Movement. London: Davis-Poynter, 1980.

00576. Bruegel, Irene. "Women's Employment, Legislation and the Labour-Market." In Women's Welfare, Women's Rights, edited by Jane Lewis, pp. 130-169. London: Croom Helm, 1983.

00577. Cuthbert, Norman H. The Lace Makers Society: a Study of Trade Unionism in the British Lace Industry, 1760-1960. Nottingham: Amalgamated Society of Operative Lace Makers and Auxiliary Workers, 1960.

00578. Davidson, Caroline. A Woman's Work is Never Done: A History of Housework in the British Isles, 1650-1950. London: Chatto: 1982.

00579. Duffin, Lorna, ed. Women and Work in Pre-Industrial Britain. London: Croom Helm, 1985.

00580. Hollis, Patricia. "Working Women." History 62 (1977): 439-445.

00581. Hunt, Felicity. "The London Trade in the Printing and Binding of Books: An Experience in Exclusion, Dilution and Deskilling for Women Workers." Women's Studies International Forum 6 (1983): 517-524.

00582. Kussmaul, Ann. Servants in Husbandry in Early Modern England. Cambridge: University Press, 1981.

00583. Middleton, Chris. "Women's Labour and the Transition to Pre-Industrial Capitalism." In Women and Work in Pre-Industrial Britain, edited by Lorna Duffin, pp. 181-206. London: Croom Helm, 1985.

00584. Ormsbee, Thomas Hamilton. "The Women Silversmiths of England." American Collector 6 (May 1938): 8-9.

00585. Prior, Mary. Fisher Row: Fishermen, Bargemen, and Canal Boatmen in Oxford, 1500-1900. New York: Oxford University Press, 1982.

00586. Roberts, Michael. "Sickles and Scythes: Women's Work and Men's Work at Harvest Time." History Workshop 7 (Spring 1979): 3-28.

00587. Stewart, Margaret and Hunter, L. The Needle is Threaded: The History of an Industry. Southampton: Heinemann, 1964.

4. RELIGION

> "Never til she is valued and educated as man's equal will unions be perfect and their consequences blissful."
>
> Catherine Booth

a) Generic

00588. Johnson, Dale A. Women in English Religion, 1700-1925. Lewiston, N.Y.: Edwin Mellen Press, 1983.

b) Mariology

00589. Fuller, Reginald. "The Role of Mary in Anglicanism." *Worship* 51 (May 1977): 214-224.

c) Canon Law

00590. Ingram, Martin. "Spousals Litigation in the English Ecclesiastical Courts c. 1350-c. 1640." In *Marriage and Society Studies in the Social History of Marriage*, edited by R.B. Outhwaite, pp. 35-57. New York: St. Martin's Press, 1981.

d) Witchcraft

00591. Adams, W.H. Davenport. *Witch, Warlock, and Magician, Historical Sketches of Magic and Witchcraft in England and Scotland*. London: Chatto and Windus, 1889.

00592. Anderson, Alan and Gordon, Raymond. "Witchcraft and the Status of Women--the Case of England." *British Journal of Sociology* 29 (June 1978): 171-184.

00593. Bruford, Alan. "Scottish Gaelic Witch Stories: A Provisional Type-List." *Scottish Studies* 11 (1967): 13-47.

00594. Forster, J. Margaret. "Folklore of County Monaghan, Ireland. Twenty Years Later." *California Folklore Quarterly* 2 (1943): 309-314.

00595. Larner, Christina. *Enemies of God, The Witch-Hunt in Scotland*. Baltimore: Johns Hopkins University Press, 1981.

00596. ________________. "Witch Beliefs and Witch-Hunting in England and Scotland." *History Today* 31 (February 1981): 32-36.

00597. Linton, Elizabeth Lynn. *Witch Stories*. London: Chatto and Windus, 1861.

00598. Maple, Eric. "Witchcraft and Magic in the Rochford Hundred." *Folk-Lore* 76 (1965): 213-224.

5. SOCIAL

"Make not too dangerous wit a vain pretence
But wisely rest content with modest sense;
For wit like wine intoxicates the brain,
Too strong for feeble women to sustain."
Lord Lyttelton

a) Generic

00599. Ambrose, Peter J. The Quiet Revolution: Social Change in a Sussex Village, 1871-1971. London: Chatto and Windus, 1974.

00600. Chamberlain, Mary. Fenwomen: A Portrait of Women in an English Village. 1975. Reprint. Boston: Routledge and Kegan Paul, 1984.

00601. Lewis, Jane. Women in England 1870-1950. Sexual Divisions and Social Change. Bloomington, Ind.: Indiana University Press, 1985.

00602. Wall, Richard. "Women Alone in English Society." Annales de demographie historique (1981): 303-317.

Also refer to #559-569.

b) Demography

00603. Gaunt, David; Levine, David; and Moodie, Elspeth. "The Population History of England 1541-1871: A Review Symposium." Social History 8 (May 1983): 139-168.

00604. Hair, P.E.H. "Bridal Pregnancy in Rural England." In Loving, Parenting and Dying, edited by Vivian C. Fox and Martin H. Quitt, pp. 193-200. New York: Psychohistory Press, Publishers, 1980.

00605. Lee, Ronald. "Population Homeostasis and English Demographic History." Journal of Interdisciplinary History 15 (Spring 1985): 635-660.

00606. Levine, David. "Production, Reproduction, and the Proletarian Family in England, 1500-1851." In Proletarianization and Family History, edited by David Levine, pp. 87-127. New York: Academic Press, Inc., 1984.

00607. ____________. "Proto-Industrialization and Demographic Upheaval." In Essays on the Family and Historical Change, edited by Leslie Page Moch and Gary D. Stark, pp. 9-34. College Station: Texas A&M University Press, 1983.

00608. Lindert, Peter H. "English Population, Wages and Prices: 1541-1913." Journal of Interdisciplinary History 15 (Spring 1985): 609-634.

00609. McLaren, Dorothy. "Marital Fertility and Lactation 1570-1720." In Women in English Society 1500-1800, edited by Mary Prior, pp. 22-53. New York: Methuen, 1985.

00610. Mitchell, B.R. "Population and Vital Statistics 8, Population of the Principal Towns of the United Kingdom, 1801-1951." Abstracts of British Historical Statistics 1962: 24-27.

00611. Morgan, Valerie. "A Case Study of Population Change over Two Centuries: Blaris, Lisburn 1661-1848." Irish Economic and Social History 3 (1976): 5-16.

00612. Morrow, Richard B. "Family Limitation in Pre-Industrial England: A Reappraisal." Economic History Review 2nd ser. 31 (1978): 419-428.

00613. Olney, Martha L. "Fertility and the Standard of Living in Early Modern England: In Consideration of Wrigley and Schofield." Journal of Economic History 43 (March 1983): 71-77.

00614. Pearce, David and Farid, Samir. "Illegitimate Births: Changing Patterns." Population Trends 9 (Autumn 1977): 20-23.

00615. Wall, Richard. "The Household: Demographic and Economic Change in England, 1650-1970." In Family Forms in Historic Europe, edited by Richard Wall, Jean Robin, and Peter Laslett, pp. 493-512. New York: Cambridge University Press, 1983.

00616. ____________. "Inferring Differential Neglect of Females from Mortality Data." Annales de demographie historique (1981): 119-140.

00617. Weir, David R. "Rather Never Than Late: Celibacy and Age at Marriage in English Cohort Fertility 1541-1871." Journal of Family History 9 (Winter 1984): 340-355.

00618. Wilson, C. "Natural Fertility in Pre-Industrial England, 1600-1799. Population Studies 38 (July 1984): 225-240.

00619. Wrigley, Edward Anthony, "Family Reconstitution." In An Introduction to English Historical Demography, edited by Peter Laslett, D.E.C. Eversley, and W.A. Armstrong, pp. 96-159. New York: Basic Books, 1966.

c) Family

(1) Non-specific

00620. Clawson, Mary Ann. "Early Modern Fraternalism and the Patriarchal Family." Feminist Studies 6 (Summer 1980): 368-391.

00621. Crowther, M.A. "Family Responsibility and State Responsibility in Britain before the Welfare State." *Historical Journal* 25 (1982): 131-145.

00622. Delphy, Christine. "Sharing the Same Table: Consumption and the Family." In *The Sociology of the Family: New Directions for Britain*, edited by Michael Harris, pp. 214-231. Totowa, N.J.: Rowman and Littlefield, 1979.

00623. Fox, Vivian C. and Quitt, Martin H., eds. *Loving, Parenting and Dying: The Family Cycle in England and America Past and Present*. New York: Psychohistory Press, 1980.

00624. ______________________________. "Uniformities and Variations in the English and American Family Cycle: Then and Now." In *Loving, Parenting and Dying*, pp. 4-90. New York: Psychohistory Press, Publishers, 1980.

00625. Harris, Michael, ed. *The Sociology of the Family: New Directions for Britain*. Totowa, N.J.: Rowman and Littlefield, 1979.

00626. Laslett, Peter. "Parental Deprivation in the Past." In *Loving, Parenting and Dying*, edited by Vivian C. Fox and Martin H. Quitt, pp. 446-456. New York: Psychohistory Press, Publishers, 1980.

00627. Levine, David, ed. *Proletarianization and Family History*. New York: Academic Press, 1984.

00628. __________, et al. *Essays on the Family and Historical Change*. College Station, Tx.: Texas A&M University Press, 1983.

00629. Medick, Hans and Sabean, David Warren, eds. *Interest and Emotion, Essays on the Study of Family and Kinship*. New York: Cambridge University Press, 1985.

00630. ______________________________. "Interest and Emotion in Family and Kinship Studies: A Critique of Social History and Anthropology." In *Interest and Emotion, Essays on the Study of Family and Kinship*, pp. 9-27. New York: Cambridge University Press, 1985.

00631. Shanley, Mary Lyndon. "The History of the Family in Early Modern England." *Signs* 4 (Summer 1979): 740-750.

00632. Stone, Lawrence. "Patriarchalism and the English Family." In *Loving, Parenting and Dying*, edited by Vivian C. Fox and Martin H. Quitt, pp. 379-385. New York: Psychohistory Press, Publishers, 1980.

Also refer to #538, 539, 543, 606, 612, 619.

(2) Motherhood

00633. Mathieu, Nicole-Claude. "Biological Paternity, Social Maternity: On Abortion and Infanticide as Unrecognized Indicators of the Cultural Character for Maternity." In The Sociology of the Family: New Directions for Britain, edited by Michael Harris, pp. 232-240. Totowa, N.J.: Rowman and Littlefield, 1979.

(3) Childhood

00634. Pollock, Linda A. Forgotten Children: Parent-Child Relations from 1500-1900. New York: Cambridge University Press, 1983.

Also refer to #633, 680.

(4) Battered Wives

00635. Eisenberg, Sue E. and Micklow, Patricia L. "The Assaulted Wife: 'Catch 22' Revisited." Women's Rights Law Reported 3 (1977): 138-161.

00636. Gibson, Ian. The English Vice: Beating, Sex and Shame in Victorian England and After. London: Duckworth, 1978.

d) Marriage

00637. Breen, Richard. "Dowry Payments and the Irish Case." Comparative Studies in Society and History 26 (April 1984): 280-296.

00638. Cressy, David. "The Seasonality of Marriage in Old and New England." Journal of Interdisciplinary History 16 (Summer 1985): 1-21.

00639. Gillis, John R. For Better, For Worse: British Marriages, 1600 to the Present. New York: Oxford University Press, 1986.

00640. ____________. "Peasant, Plebeian, and Proletarian Marriage in Britain, 1600-1900." In Proletarianization and Family History, edited by David Levine, pp. 129-162. New York: Academic Press, Inc., 1984.

00641. Griffith, J. "Economy, Family and Remarriage, Theory of Remarriage and Application to Pre-Industrial England." Journal of Family Issues 1 (1980): 479-496.

00642. Kussmaul, Ann. "Time and Space, Hoofs and Grain: The Seasonality of Marriage in England." Journal of Interdisciplinary History 15 (Spring 1985): 755-779.

00643. Levine, David. "'For their own Reasons': Individual Marriage Decisions and Family Life." Journal of Family History 7 (Fall 1982): 255-264.

00644. Macfarlane, Alan. Marriage and Love in England, Modes of Reproduction 1300-1840. New York: Basil Blackwell, 1986.

00645. Menefee, Samuel Pyeatt. Wives for Sale: An Ethnographic Study of British Popular Divorce. New York: St. Martin's, 1981.

00646. Outhwaite, R.B., ed. Marriage and Society Studies in the Social History of Marriage. New York: St. Martin's, 1981.

00647. Schofield, Rogers. "English Marriage Patterns Revisited." Journal of Family History 10 (Spring 1985): 2-20.

00648. Smith, Richard M. "Some Reflections on the Evidence for the Origins of the 'European Marriage Pattern' in England." In The Sociology of the Family: New Directions for Britain, edited by Michael Harris, pp. 74-112. Totowa, N.J.: Rowman and Littlefield, 1979.

00649. Smout, T.C. "Scottish Marriage, Regular and Irregular 1500-1940." In Marriage and Society Studies in the Social History of Marriage, edited by R.B. Outhwaite, pp. 204-236. New York: St. Martin's Press, 1981.

00650. Todd, Barbara J. "The Remarrying Widow: A Stereotype Reconsidered." In Women in English Society 1500-1800, edited by Mary Prior, pp. 54-92. New York: Methuen, 1985.

Also refer to #539, 541, 590, 604, 609, 617.

e) Fashion/Manners

00651. Arnold, Janet. Patterns of Fashion: Englishwoman's Dresses and Their Construction. London: Macmillan, 1972.

00652. Baines, Barbara B. Fashion Revivals from the Elizabethan Age to the Present Day. London: B.T. Batsford, 1981.

00653. Bradfield, Nancy M. Historical Costumes of England from the Sixteenth to the Twentieth Century. New York: Barnes and Noble, 1971.

00654. Courtois, Georgine de. Woman's Headdress and Hairstyles in England from AD 600 to the Present Day. London: B.T. Batsford, 1973.

00655. Dunbar, John Telfer. The Costume of Scotland. London: B.T. Batsford, 1981.

00656. Ewing, Elizabeth. Women in Uniform through the Centuries. Totowa N.J.: Rowman and Littlefield, 1975.

00657. Gibbs-Smith, Charles H. Costume. An Index to the More Important Material in the Victoria and Albert Museum Library. London: Victoria and Albert Museum Library, 1936.

00658. Landsdowne, Avril. Occupational Costume and Working Clothes, 1776-1976. Aylesbury: Shire Publications, 1977.

00659. Stevenson, Sara and Bennett, Helen. Van Dyck in Check Trousers: Fancy Dress in Art and Life, 1700-1900. Edinburgh: Scottish National Portrait Gallery and The National Museum of Antiquities of Scotland, 1978.

00660. Walkley, C. The Way to Wear 'em: Punch on Fashion. Atlantic Highlands, N.J.: Humanities Press, 1985.

00661. Yarwood, Doreen. English Costume from the Second Century B.C. to 1972. London: Batsford, 1972.

f) Health/Medical

(1) Birth Control

00662. Francome, Colin. Abortion Freedom: A Worldwide Movement. Boston: George Allen and Unwin, 1984.

00663. Greenwood, Karen and King, Lucy. "Contraception and Abortion." In Women in Society, edited by the Cambridge Women's Studies Group, pp. 168-184. London: Virago Press, 1981.

00664. Peel, John. "The Manufacture and Retailing of Contraceptives in England." Population Studies 17 (November 1963): 113-125.

Also refer to #633.

(2) Women in Medicine

00665. Chamberlain, Mary. Old Wive's Tales: Their History, Remedies, and Spells. London: Virago, 1981.

00666. Haldane, Elizabeth. The British Nurse in Peace and War. London: J. Murray, 1923.

00667. Wyman, A.L. "The Surgeoness: The Female Practitioner of Surgery 1400-1800." Medical History 28 (January 1984): 22-41.

(3) Women and Health

00668. Dow, Derek. The Rotten Row: The History of the Glasgow Royal Maternity Hospital 1834-1984. Carnforth, Lincs.: Parthenon, 1984.

00669. Oakley, Ann. The Captured Womb. A History of the Medical Care of Pregnant Women. New York: Basil Blackwell, 1984.

00670. Showalter, Elaine. The Female Malady: Women, Madness and English Culture, 1830-1980. New York: Pantheon, 1986.

g) Recreation

00671. Fletcher, Sheila. Women First: The Female Tradition in English Physical Education, 1880-1980. London: Athlone Press, 1984.

6. CULTURAL

"Almost all girls of quality are educated as if they were to be great ladies, which is often as little to be expected as an immoderate heat of the sun in northern Scotland. You should teach yours to confine their desires to probabilities, to be useful as possible to themselves, and to think privacy (as it is) the happiest state of life."

Lady Mary Wortley Montague
"The Education of Children--
Letter to Countess of Bute"
19 February 1749

a) Education

00672. Cressy, David. "Levels of Illiteracy in England, 1530-1730." Historical Journal 20 (1977): 1-23.

00673. Findlay, Joseph John. Children of England: A Contribution to Social History and to Education. London: Methuen, 1923.

00674. O'Day, Rosemary. Education and Society 1500-1800: The Social Foundations of Education in Early Modern Britain. London: Longmans, 1982.

00675. Okely, Judith. "Privileged, Schooled and Finished: Boarding Education for Girls." In Defining Females: The Nature of Women in Society, edited by Shirley Ardener, pp. 109-139. New York: John Wiley and Sons, 1978.

00676. Scrimgeour, R.M. ed. The North London Collegiate School, 1850-1950: A Hundred Years of Girls' Education. London: Oxford University Press, 1950.

b) Literature

(1) Non-specific

(a) Women in Literature

00677. Belaval, Yvon. "The Author and Love." Yale French Studies 11 (1953): 5-11.

00678. Cadogan, Mary and Craig, Patricia. You're a Brick, Angela! A New Look at Girls' Fiction from 1839-1975. London: Gollancz, 1976.

00679. Hull, Suzanne W. Chaste, Silent and Obedient: English books for Women, 1475-1640. San Marino: Huntington Library, 1982.

00680. Pattison, Robert. The Child Figure in English Literature. Athens: University of Georgia Press, 1978.

00681. Pearson, Carol and Pope, Katherine. The Female Hero in American and British Literature. New York: R.R. Bowker, 1981.

00682. Stephane, Nelly. "La femme et la litterature en Angleterre." Europe 427-428 (November-December 1964): 130-137.

(b) Women Authors

00683. Cotton, Nancy. Women Playwrights in England, c. 1363-1750. Lewisburg: Bucknell University Press, 1980.

00684. Figes, Eva. Sex and Subterfuge: Women Writers to 1830. London: Macmillan, 1982.

00685. Jelinek, Estelle C., ed. Women's Autobiography Essays in Criticism. Bloomington, Ind.: Indiana University Press, 1980.

00686. Perry, Ruth. "Introduction." In Mothering the Mind, Twelve Studies of Writers and Their Silent Partners, edited by Ruth Perry and Martine Watson Brownley, pp. 3-24. New York: Holmes and Meier, 1984.

00687. __________ and Brownley, Martine W., eds. Mothering the Mind: Twelve Studies of Writers and Their Silent Partners. New York: Holmes and Meier, 1984.

00688. Winston, Elizabeth. "The Autobiographer and Her Readers: From Apology to Affirmation." In Women's Autobiography, Essays in Criticism, edited by Estelle C. Jelinek, pp. 93-111. Bloomington, Ind.: Indiana University Press, 1980.

Also refer to #548.

(2) Prose

00689. Cockshut, Anthony Oliver John. Man and Woman: A Study of Love and the Novel 1740-1940. New York: Oxford University Press, 1978.

00690. Dancyger, Irene. A World of Women: An Illustrated History of Women's Magazines, 1700-1970. Dublin: Gill, 1978.

00691. Taylor, Anne Robinson. Male Novelists and Their Female Voices: Literary Masquerades. Troy, N.Y.: Whitston Publishing Co., 1981.

00692. Todd, Janet, ed. Men by Women. Women and Literature, vol. 2. New York: Holmes and Meier, 1982.

00693. Zeman, Anthea. Presumptuous Girls: Women and their World in the Serious Novel. London: Weidenfeld and Nicholson, 1977.

c) Intellectuals

00694. Smith, Bonnie. "The Contribution of Women to Modern Historiography in Great Britain, France and the United States, 1750-1940." American Historical Review 89 (June 1984): 709-732.

d) Art

00695. Findlater, Richard. The Player Queens. London: Weidenfeld and Nicholson, 1976.

00696. Herrmann, Frank. The English as Collecters. New York: Norton, 1972.

e) Science

00697. Kidwell, Peggy Aldrich. "Women Astronomers in Britain, 1780-1930." Isis 75 (September 1984): 534-545.

C. FRANCE

1. SURVEYS

"One has the right to judge women on appearances . . . ."
Diderot

00698. Benoît, Nicole; Morin, Edgar; and Paillard, Bernard. La femme majeure. Paris: Du Seuil, 1973.

00699. Darmon, Pierre. Mythologie de la femme dans l'Ancienne France. Paris: Seuil, 1983.

00700. Gillet, Marcel. "Pas d'histoire, les femmes du Nord?" Revue du Nord 58 (July-September 1981): 559-568.

00701. Havel, Jean Eugene Martial. La condition de la femme. Paris: A. Colin, 1961.

00702. Kaim, Julius Rudolph. Pariserinnen. Munich: List Verlag, 1965.

00703. Ravis-Giordani, Georges. "La femme corse dans la villageoise traditionnelle: status et rôles." In Femmes corses et femmes méditerranéennes, pp. 6-19. Provence: Centre d'Etudes Corses de l'université de Provence, 1976.

00704. Sarde, Michele. Regard sur les françaises Xe siècle-XXe siècle. Paris: Stock, 1983.

00705. Thieme, Hugo Paul. Women of Modern France. Vol. 7 of Women in All Ages and in All Countries. Philadelphia: Rittenhouse Press, 1907.

00706. Weitz, Margaret C. Femmes: Recent Writings on French Women. Boston: Hall, 1985.

2. POLITICAL

> "Without the female electorate--but I don't regret it--I would have beaten General de Gaulle in 1965 and . . . Giscard d'Estaing in 1974."
>
> Mitterand

a) Criminal

00707. Gelfand, Elessa. Imagination in Confinement, Women's Writings from French Prisons. Ithaca, N.Y.: Cornell University Press, 1983.

Also refer to #752, 757, 795.

b) Marxism/Socialism

00708. Sowerwine, Charles. Sisters or Citizens? Women and Socialism in France Since 1876. Cambridge: University Press, 1982.

c) Feminism

00709. Angenot, Marc. Les Champions des femmes. Examen du discours sur la supériorité des femmes, 1400-1800. Montreal: Presses de l'Université du Québec, 1978.

00710. Ascoli, Georges. "Bibliographie pour servir à l'histoire des idées féministes depuis le milieu du XVIe jusqu'à la fin du XIIIe siècle." Revue de synthese historique 13 (August 1906): 99-106.

00711. Lever, Maurice. "L'antiféminisme du Moyen Age à la Revolution." Histoire 54 (1983): 38-51.

00712. Offen, Karen M. "'First Wave' Feminism in France: New Work and Resources." Women's Studies International Forum 5 (1982): 685-689.

00713. Rabaut, Jean. Histoire des feminismes français. Paris: Stock, 1978.

00714. Zylberg-Hocquard, Marie Helene. Femmes et feminisme dans le mouvement ouvrier français. Paris: Editions ouvrieres, 1981.

d) Political Roles

00715. Brooks, Geraldine. Dames and Daughters of the French Court. 1904. Reprint. Freeport, N.Y.: Books for Libraries Press, 1968.

3. ECONOMIC

> "In all cases when women can do the job as well and as fast as men, they are preferred. This stems from the first economic law. . . that the force displaced should be exactly to the result obtained."
>
> Jules Simon

00716. Barbier, Jean-Marie. Le quotidien et son economie. Essai sur les origines historiques et sociales de l'economie familiale. Paris: CNRS, 1981.

00717. Fairchilds, Cissie C. Domestic Enemies: Servants and Their Masters in Old Regime France. Baltimore, Md.: Johns Hopkins University Press, 1984.

00718. Gutton, Jean-Pierre. Domestiques et serviteurs dans la France de l'ancien regime. Paris: Aubier Montaigne, 1981.

00719. Parent-Lardeur, Françoise. Les demoiselles de magasin. Paris: Editions Ouvrieres, 1970.

00720. Perrot, Marguerite. Le mode de vie des familles bourgeoises. Paris: Presses de la Fondation nationale des sciences politiques, 1982.

00721. Shaffer, John W. Family and Farm, Agrarian Change and Household, Organization in the Loire Valley, 1500-1900. Albany N.Y.: State University of New York Press, 1982.

Also refer to #714.

4. RELIGION

[Eve like Adam was a] "preeminent speciman of Divine wisdom, justice and goodness."

Calvin

00722. Braun, Pierre. "La sorcellerie dans les lettres de remission du Trésor des Chartes." In Actes du 102e Congres national des Sociétés savantes, Limoges, 1977. Section de Philologie et d'histoire jusqu'à 1610, 2: Etudes sur la sensibilité, pp. 257-278. Paris: Bibliothèque National, 1979.

00723. Casta, Francois J. "L'eglise corse et la femme." In Femmes corses et femmes mediterraneennes, pp. 286-309. Provence: Centre d'Etudes Corses de l'Universite de Provence, 1976.

00724. Farret-Saada, Jeanne. Deadly Words. Witchcraft in the Bocage. Cambridge: University Press, 1980.

00725. Garrisson-Estebe, Janine. L'Homme protestant. Paris: Hachette, 1980.
[See especially ch. VII, "La Femme protestante."]

00726. LeBrun, Francois, ed. Histoire des catholiques en France. Toulouse: Privat, 1980.

00727. Perouas, Louis. "Les religieuses dans le pays creusois du XVIIIe au XXe siecle." Cahiers d'histoire 24 no. 2 (1979): 17-43.

00728. Weaver, F. Ellen. "Women and Religion in Early Modern France: A Bibliographical Essay on the State of the Question." Catholic Historical Review 67 (1981): 50-59.

5. SOCIAL

"How essential it is that a woman annex herself to a man of sense! You are for the most part only what we wish you to be."

Diderot

a) Generic

(1) Non-specific

00729. Aldrich, Robert. "Customs and Traditions." In Economy and Society in Burgundy Since 1850, pp. 177-208. New York: St. Martin's, 1984.

00730. Assier-Andrieu, Louis. Coutume et rapports sociaux. Etude anthropologique des communautes paysannes du Capcir. Paris: Ed. du C.N.R.S., 1981.

00731. Dupeux, Georges. French Society 1789-1970. New York: Barnes and Noble, 1976.

00732. Jeanton, Gabriel. Le Mâconnais traditionaliste et populaire, vol. 1: Le peuple; le costume; l'habitation. Macon: Protat, 1920.

00733. Levy, Charles and Louis, Henry. "Ducs et Pairs sous l'ancien regime." Population 15 (October-December 1960): 807-830.

00734. Morazé, Charles. La France bourgeoise (XVIIIe-XXe siecles). Paris: Colin, 1946.

00735. Pouyez, C. "Démographie, structures foncières et société: evolution d'un village d'Artois du VIe au XIXe siècle." Canadian Historical Association Historical Papers 1973: 269-300.

(2) Women

00736. Auzias, Jean-Marie. "Ni Vierge ni martyre: tentative de description anthropologique de la femme vivaraise." In Femmes corses et femmes meditéranéennes, pp. 80-97. Provence: Centre d'Etudes Corses de l'Universite de Provence, 1976.

00737. Roubin, Lucienne. "Espace masculin, espace féminin en communauté provençale." Annales: économies, sociétés, civilisations 25 (March-April 1970): 537-560.

b) Demography

00738. Bideau, Alain. "A Demographic and Social Analysis of Widowhood and Remarriage: The Example of the Castellany of Thoissey-in-Dombes, 1670-1840." Journal of Family History 5 (1980): 28-43.

00739. Calot, Gerard. "The Demographic Situation in France. Population Trends 25 (Autumn 1981): 15-20.

00740. Fauve-Chamoux, Antoinette. "Les structures familiales au royaume des familles souches: Esparros." Annales: économies, sociétés, civilisations 39 (May 1984): 513-528.

00741. Gouhier, Pierre. Port-en-Bessin, 1597-1792. Etude d'histoire démographique. Caen: Annales de Normandie, 1962.

00742. Henry, Louis. "Fecondité des mariages dans le quart Sud-Est de la France de 1670 à 1829." Population 33 (July-October 1978): 835-884.

00743. Odgen, Philip E. and Huss, Marie-Monique. "Demography and Pronatalism in France in the Nineteenth and Twentieth Centuries." *Journal of the History of Geography* 8 (1982): 283-298.

00744. Pomponi, Francis. "La femme corse: approche monographique et démographique du problème." In *Femmes corses et femmes meditérranéennes*, pp. 323-357. Provence: Centre d'Etudes Corses de l'Universite de Provence, 1976.

00745. Ronsin, François. *La grève des ventres: propagande néo-malthusienne et baisse de la natalité française XIXe-XXe siècles*. Paris: Aubier Montaigne, 1980.

00746. Tilly, Charles. "Population and Pedagogy in France." *History of Education Quarterly* 13 (Summer 1973): 113-128.

00747. Tugault, Yves. *Fecondite et urbanisation*. Paris: Presses Universitaires de France, 1975.

Also refer to #735.

c) Family

(1) Non-specific

00748. Dupâquier, Jacques. "Naming--Practices, Godparenthood, and Kinship in the Vexin, 1540-1900." *Journal of Family History* 4 (1980): 135-155.

00749. Gutton, Jean-Pierre. *La sociabilité villageoise dans l'ancienne France: Solidarités et voisinages du XVIe au XVIIIe siècle*. Paris: Hachette, 1979.

00750. Vovelle, Michel. "Y a-t-il un modèle de la famille méridionale?" *Provence historique* 25 (July-September 1975): 487-507.

Also refer to #620, 716, 720, 721, 740.

(2) Motherhood

00751. Knibiehler, Yvonne and Fouquet, Catherine. *L'histoire des mères du Moyen-Age à nos jours*. Paris: Montalba, 1980.

(3) Childhood

00752. Ancel, Marc and Molines, Henri, eds. *La Protection judiciare de l'enfant en fonction de l'évolution du droit et des institutions judiciares*. Paris: A. Pedone, 1980.

00753. Demars-Sion, Veronique. "Illégitimité et abandon d'enfant: la position des provinces du Nord (XVIe-XVIIIe)." Revue du Nord (July 1983): 481-506.

00754. Gelis, Jacques; Laget, Mirreille; and Morel, Marie-France. Entrer dans la vie: naissances et enfances dans la France traditionnelle. Paris: Editions Gallimard, 1978.

00755. Grimmer, Claude. La Femme et la bâtard. Amours illégitimes et secrètes de l'ancienne France. Paris: Presses de la Renaissance, 1983.

00756. Meyer, Philippe. The Child and the State: The Intervention of the State in Family Life. New York: Cambridge University Press, 1983.

Also refer to #772.

d) Marriage

00757. Darmon, Pierre. Damning the Innocent: A History of the Persecution of the Impotent in Pre-Revolutionary France. Translated by Paul Keegan. New York: Viking, 1986.

00758 Segalen, Martine. Nuptialité et alliance: le choix du conjoint dans une commune de l'Eure. Paris: G.-P. Maisonneuve et Larose, 1971.

Also refer to #646, 738, 742.

e) Fashion/Manners

00759. Agron, Suzanne. Le Costume féminin. Paris: J. Lanore, 1976.

00760. Aubert, Octave Louis. Les costumes bretons, leur histoire--leur evolution. St. Brieuc: Aubert, 1936.

00761. Bernoville, Gaetan. Le Pays des Basques, types et coutumes. Dessins originaux de Inigo Bernoville. Paris: Horizons de France, 1930.

00762. Bigot, Maurice. Les coiffes bretonnes; cent modeles differents. St. Brieuc: Aubert, 1928.

00763. Bily-Brossard, Jeanne. Coiffes et costumes feminins du Poitou. Niort: Soulisse-Martin, 1952.

00764. Charles-Roux, Jules. Souvenirs de passé: le costume en Provence. 2 vols. Paris: Lemerre, 1907.

00765. Choleau, Jean. Costumes et chants populaires de Haute Bretagne. Vitre: Unvaniez-Arvor, 1953.

00766. Creston, R-Y. Les costumes des populations bretonnes. (Travaux du Laboratoire d'anthropologie generale.) Rennes: Les Nouvelles de Bretagne, 1953-1959.

00767. Darjou, Alfred. Costumes de la Bretagne. Paris: Plon, n.d.

00768. Dartiguenave, Alfred. Costumes des Pyrenees dessines d'après nature. Pau: A. Bassy, n.d.

00769. Delaye, Edmond. Les anciens costumes des Alpes du Dauphiné. Lyon: Grange et Giraud, 1922.

00770. Delpierre, Madeleine. La Mode et ses métiers du XVIIIe siècle à nos jours. Paris: Musée de la Mode et du Costume, 1981.

00771. ______ and Falluel, Fabienne. Chapeaux 1750-1960. Paris: Musee de la Mode et du Costume, 1980.

00772. ______. Modes enfantines, 1750-1950: [exposition], juin-novembre 1979. Paris: Musee de la Mode et du Costume, 1979.

00773. ______. Secrets d'elegance (1750-1950). Paris: Musee de la Mode et du Costume, 1978.

00774. Flandreysy, Jeanne de. La femme provençale. Marseille: Detaille, 1922.

00775. Gallois, Emile. Provinces françaises. Costumes decoratifs. Paris: Editions Art et architecture, 1936.

00776. Gauthier, Joseph. L'art populaire français: costumes paysans. Paris: Massin, 1930.

00777. Gelle, P. and Arnaud, C. Vues et costumes pittoresques du département des Deux-Sèvres. Niort: Morisset, 1844.

00778. Harding, J.D. The Costumes of the French Pyrenees Drawn on Stone ... From Original Sketches by J. Johnson. London: James Carpenter and Son, 1832.

00779. Helias, Pierre. Costumes de Bretagne. Chateaulin: Jos Le Doare, 1969.

00780. Jeanton, Gabriel. Costumes bressans et mâconnais. Macon: Renaudier, 1937.

00781. Keim, Aline. Les costumes du pays de France. Paris: Nilsson, 1929.

00782. Lalaisse, Hippolyte. Costumes et coiffes de Bretagne: cent phototypies d'après les compositions de Hippolyte Lalaisse. Paris: Laurens, 1932.

00783. Le Bondidier, L. Les vieux costumes pyrénéens. Pau: Garet-Haristoy, [1917].

00784. Lepage-Medvey, E. French Costumes. Paris: Hyperion, 1939.

00785. Maurice, C. Costumes pittoresques. Paris: E. Morier, [1859].

00786. Murphy, Michelle. Two Centuries of French Fashion. Brooklyn: Brooklyn Museum, 1949.

00787. Musée Cosmopolite. Costume français. Paris, 1850-63.

00788. La Normandie illustrée; sites et costumes de la Seine-Inférieure, de l'Eure, du Calvados, de l'Orne et de la Manche. Nantes: Charpentier, 1852-55.

00789. Pingret, Edouard. Costumes des Pyrén(n)ées. Paris: Gihaut, [1840].

00790. Robert, Jean. Le costume traditionnel dans les Pyrenees françaises. Lourdes: Musée pyrénéen, 1969.

00791. Royere, Henry; Gardillanne, Gratiane de; and Moffat, Elizabeth Whitney. Les costumes regionnaux de la France. 5 vols. Paris: Ed. du Pegase, 1929.

00792. Sainsard, A. and Pierre, F. Costumes folkloriques; provinces francaises. Paris: Fleurus, 1972.

f) Health/Medical

00793. McLaren Angus. Sexuality and Social Order: The Debate Over the Fertility of Women and Workers in France, 1770-1920. New York: Holmes and Meier, 1983.

00794. Petaux, Jean. Le Maine-et-Loire face à l'avortement: l'évolution des mentalités en Anjou. Cholet: Editions du Choletais, 1979.

00795. Soutoul, Jean Henri. Conséquences d'une loi: Après 600 jours d'avortements l'égaux. Paris: Table Ronde, 1977.

Also refer to #751.

6. CULTURAL

"There have been very learned women as there have been women lawyers, but there have never been women inventors."

Voltaire

a) Education

(1) Non-specific

00796. Chartier, Roger; Compere, Marie Madeleine; and Julia, Dominique. L'education en France du XVIe au XVIIIe siècle. Paris: Société d'édition d'enseignement supérieur, 1976.

00797. Hodgson, Gerald. Studies in French Education from Rabelais to Rousseau. Gloucester, Mass.: Peter Smith, 1964.

00798. Marquet, Pierre Bernard. L'Enseignement ne sut a rien. Paris: E.S.S., 1978.

00799. Zimmerman, Axel. Baccalaureat: Abitur und Sekundarschule in Frankreich. Rheinstatten: Schindele, 1976.

Also refer to #716, 746.

(2) Women

00800. Clark, Linda L. Schooling the Daughters of Marianne: Textbooks and the Socialization of Girls in Modern French Primary Schools. Albany, N.Y.: State University of New York Press, 1984.

00801. Perrel, Jean. "L'enseignement feminin sous l'Ancien regime: Les écoles populaires en Auvergne, Bourbonnais et Velay." Cahiers d'histoire 23 (1978): 193-210.

b) Literature

00802. Fabre, Daniel. "L'Image de la femme dans le discours juvenile en Languedoc." In Femmes corses et femmes mediterranéennes, pp. 48-79. Provence: Centre d'Etudes Corses de l'Universite de Provence, 1976.

00803. Furet, François and Ozouf, Jacques. Lire et écrire: l'alphabétisation des français de Calvin à Jules Ferry. Paris: Minuit, 1977.

00804. Giacomo-Marcellini, Mathee. "Reflets de la condition de la femme corse dans le langage de la communauté rurale a sotta." In Femmes corses et femmes meditérranéennes, pp. 160-173. Provence: Centre d'Etudes Corses de l'Université de Provence, 1976.

00805. Hermann, Claudine. Les voleuses de langue. Paris: Éditions des femmes, 1976.

00806. Kern, Edith. "Author or Authoress?" Yale French Studies 27 (1961): 3-11.

00807. Milhaud, Marianne. "La femme au miroir du roman-feuilliton." Europe 427-428 (November-December 1964): 108-117.

00808. Yaguello, Marina. Les mots et les femmes. Paris: Payot, 1979.

Also refer to #677, 694.

c) Art

00809. Dowley, F.H. "French Portraits of Ladies as Minerva." Gazette des beaux-arts 6th ser. 45 (May 1955): 261-286, 323-330.

00810. La Femme artiste: d'Elisabeth Vigée-Lebrun à Rosa Bonheur. Mont-de-Marsan: Impr. Lacoste, 1982.

00811. George, Waldemar. "Les femmes mesure de l'art français." L'art et les artistes n.s. 35 (February 1938): 145-175; n.s. 36 (May 1938): 253-262.

00812. Paris. Grand Palais. La femme peintre et sculpteur du XVIIe siècle au XXe siècle. 1975.

00813. Sadoul, Charles and Las Cases, Philippe de. L'art rustique en France: Lorraine. Paris: Albin-Michael, n.d.

D. THE GERMANIES

1. BIBLIOGRAPHIES

> "A new Eve--she already senses that the taste of that seductive fruit of knowledge will exclude her for ever from the paradise of hee innocence and all the blessed happiness of blindness."
>
> Gabriele Reuter

00814. "Emanzipation durch Emanzipations Literatur? Bücher zur Frauenfrage aus den Jahren 1971 und 1972." Buch und Bibliothek 25 (January 1973): 36-44.

2. SURVEYS

"When will activity of one's own choosing ever cease to be the royal prerogative of the men."
Theodor Gottlieb von Hippel

00815. Becker-Cantarino, Barbara, ed. _Die Frau von der Reformation zur Romantik: Die Situation der Frau vor dem Hintergrund der Literatur und Sozialgeschichte._ Bonn: Bouvier Verlag Herbert Grundmann, 1980.

00816. Goodman, Kay and Sanders, Ruth N. eds. _Women and German Studies: An Interdisciplinary and Comparative Approach._ Oxford, Oh.: Miami University, 1977.

00817. Kohler-Irrgang, Ruth. _Die Sendung der Frau in der deutschen Geschichte._ Leipzig: Hase und Koehler, 1940.

00818. Netting, Robert M. "Eine lange Ahnenreihe. Die Fortdauer von Patrilinien uber mehr als drei Jahrhunderte in einem schweizerischen Bergdorf." _Schweizerische Zeitschrift für Geschichte_ 29 (1979): 194-215.

3. POLITICAL

" . . . A woman's demand for emancipation and her qualifications for it are in direct proportion to the amount of maleness in her."
Otto Weininger
Sex and Character

a) Generic

00819. Dertinger, Antje. _Weiber und Gendarm. Vom Kampf staatsgefährdender Frauenspersonen um ihr Recht auf politische Arbeit._ Cologne: Bund-Verlag, 1981.

b) Marxism and Socialism

00820. Forschungsgemeinschaft Geschichte des Kampfes der Arbeiterklasse um die Befreiung der Frau an der Padagogischen Hochschule Clara Zetkin Leipzig. _Die Frau und die Gesellschaft._ Leipzig: Verlag für die Frau, 1974.

c) Legal

00821. Huebner, Rudolf. _A History of Germanic Private Law._ 1918. Reprint. South Hackensack, N.J.: Rothman Reprints, 1968. [See especially Book IV, Family Law.]

d) Feminism

00822. Freier, Anna-E. "Dem Reich der Freiheit sollst Du Kinder gebären." Der Antifeminismus der proletarischen Frauenbewegung im Spiegel der "Gleichheit," 1891-1971. Frankfurt am Main: Haag und Herchen Verlag, 1981.

00823. Greven-Aschoff, Barbara. "Sozialer Wandel und Frauenbewegung." Geschichte und Gesellschaft 7 (1981): 328-346.

00824. Kawan, Hildegard and Weber, Barbara. "Reflections on a Theme: The German Woman's Movement, Then and Now." In The Women's Liberation Movement, edited by Jan Bradshaw, pp. 421-433. New York: Pergamon Press, 1982.

00825. Koepcke, Cordula. Frauenbewegung zwischen den Jahren 1800 und 2000. Heroldsberg bei Nürnberg: Glock und Lutz, 1979.

00826. Schenk, Herrad. Die feministische Herausforderung: 150 Jahre Frauenbewegung in Deutschland. Munich: Beck, 1980.

00827. Woodtli, Susanna. Gleichberechtigung: Der Kampf um die politischen Rechte der Frau in der Schweiz. Frauenfeld: Huber, 1975.

Also refer to #820.

4. ECONOMIC

> "Even though both sexes are equal, still it is not absolutely necessary that both are destined for the same occupations. The man is destined for an active life and the woman for for a domestic one."
>
> Marianne Ehrmann

00828. Barchewitz, Jutta. Von der Wirtschaftstatigkeit der Frau in der vorgeschichtlichen Zeit bis zur Entfaltung der Stadtwirtschaft. Breslau: Priebatsch, 1937.

00829. Braunwarth, Henry. Die Spanne zwischen Männer- und Frauenlöhnen. Cologne-Deutz: Bund Verlag G.m.b.h., 1955.

00830. Gaunt, David. "The Property and Kin Relationships of Retired Farmers in Northern and Central Europe." In Family Forms in Historic Europe, edited by Richard Wall, Jean Robin and Peter Laslett, pp. 249-279. New York: Cambridge University Press, 1983.

00831. Handl, Johann. "Education Chances and Occupational Opportunities of Women: A Sociohistorical Analysis." Journal of Social History 17 (Spring 1984): 463-487.

00832. Quartaert, Jean H. "The Shaping of Women's Work in Manufacturing: Guilds, Households and the State in Central Europe, 1648-1870." American Historical Review 90 (December 1985): 1122-1148.

5. RELIGION

"Even though poetic experience may seem difficult for female frailty, yet always relying on heavenly grace and not on my own power, I have tried to compose. . . "

Hrotsvit of Gandersheim

00833. Lechner, Gregor Martin. "Die Madonna als Hauszeichen." Alte Stadt 10 no. 4 (1983): 348-360.

00834. Monter, E. William. "Women in Calvinist Geneva (1550-1800). Signs 6 (Winter 1980): 189-209.

00835. Schrader, Franz. "Die katholisch gebliebenen Zisterzienserinnenklöster in den Bistümern Magdeburg und Halberstadt und ihre Beziehung zum Ordensverband." Zeitschrift der Savigny Stiftung für Rechtsgeschichte. (Kanonistische Abteilung) 60 (1974): 168-212.

6. SOCIAL

". . . the woman (as daughter) must now see her parents pass away with natural emotion and yet with ethical resignation, for it is only at the cost of this condition that she can come to that individual existence of which she is capable."

Hegel
The Phenomenology of the Mind

a) Generic

00836. Bodmer-Gessner, Verena. Die Bündnerinnen. Zurich: Verlag Berichthaus, 1973.

00837. Duller, Eduard. Das deutsche Volk in seinen Mandanten, Sitten, Gebräuchen, Heften und Trachten. Leipzig: Wigand, 1847.

00838. Kramer, Karl-Sigismund. Volksleben in Fürstentum Ansbach und seinen Nachbargebieten (1500-1800). Würzburg: Kommissions Verlag F. Schöningh, 1961. [See especially "Haus und Familie," pp. 191-236.]

b) Demography

00839. Imhof, Arthur E. "La mortalité infantile differentielle en Allemagne du 18e au 20e siècle. Resultats de recherches. Certitudes et hypotheses." _Population et famille_ 50-51 (1980): 137-178.

00840. ______________. "Remarriage in Rural Populations and in Urban Middle and Upper Strata in Germany from the Sixteenth to the Twentieth Century." In _Marriage and Remarriage in Populations of the Past_, edited by Jacques Dupaquier, et al., pp. 335-346. New York: Academic Press, 1981.

00841. Knodel, John. "The Influence of Child Mortality in a Natural Fertility Setting: An Analysis of German Villages." In _Natural Fertility_, edited by Henri Leridon and Jane Menken, pp. 273-284. Liege: Ordina Editions, 1979.

c) Family

(1) Non-specific

00842. Becker, Horst. _Die Familie_. Leipzig: Moritz Schafer, 1938.

00843. Beuys, Barbara. _Familienleben in Deutschland. Neue Bilder aus der deutschen Vergangenheit_. Reinbeck bei Hamburg: Rowohlt, 1980.

00844. Schmidtbauer, P. "The Changing Household: Austrian Household Structure from the Seventeenth to the Early Twentieth Century." In _Family Forms in Historic Europe_, edited by Richard Wall, Jean Robin, and Peter Laslett, pp. 347-378. New York: Cambridge University Press, 1983.

Also refer to #821, 830.

(2) Childhood

00845. Boesch, Hans. _Kinderleben in der deutschen Vergangenheit_. 1924. Reprint. Cologne: Diederichs, 1979.

00846. Ende, Aurel. "Zur Geschichte der Stillfeindlichkeit in Deutschland 1850-1978." _Kindheit_ 1 (September 1979): 203-214.

00847. Kreis, Rudolf. "The History of Childhood Through German Literature: A Psychogenic Model." _Journal of Psychohistory_ 9 (Winter 1982): 311-319.

00848. ____________. _Die verborgene Geschichte des Kindes in der deutschen Literatur. Deutschunterricht als Psychohistorie_. Stuttgart: J.B. Metzler, 1980.

00849. Theopold, Wilhelm. _Das Kind in der Votivmalerei_. Munich: Karl Thiemig, 1981.

00850. ______________. _Votivmalerei und Medizin_. Munich: Verlag Karl Thiemig, 1981.

Also refer to #839, 841.

d) Marriage

00851. Mitterauer, Michael. "Marriage without Co-Residence: A Special Type of Historic Family Forms in Rural Carinthia." _Journal of Family History_ 6 (Summer 1981): 177-181.

00852. Pedlow, Gregory W. "Marriage, Family Size and Inheritance Among Hessian Nobles, 1650-1900." _Journal of Family History_ 7 (Winter 1982): 333-352.

00853. Sozan, Michael. "Mate Selection Through History in a European Ethnic Community." _East European Quarterly_ 17 (Summer 1983): 229-250.

Also refer to #840, 925.

e) Fashion/Manners

00854. Adelmann, Paula. _Das Mieder in der Volkstracht des Oberrheins_. Heidelberg: C. Winter, 1939.

00855. Alexander, William. _Picturesque Representations of the Dress and Manners of the Austrians, Illustrated in Fifty Coloured Engravings with Descriptions_. London: M'lean, [1813].

00856. Arx-Lüthy, Frieda von. _Die Solothurner Trachten_. Solothurn: 1950.

00857. Au, Hans von der. _Odenwalder Tracht_. Darmstadt: Leske, 1952.

00858. Bader, Joseph. _Badische Volkssitten und Trachten_. Karlsruhe: Kunstverlag, 1843-44.

00859. Baur-Heinhold, Margarete. _Deutsche Trachten_. Konigstein: Langewiesche, 1958.

00860. Becker, Karl August. _Die Volkstrachten der Pfalz_. Kaiserslautern: Verlag der Pfälzischen Gesellschaft zur Förderung der Wissenschaften, 1952.

00861. Behnisch, Franz Joachim. _Die Tracht Nurnbergs und seines Umlandes vom 16. bis zur Mitte des 19. Jahrhunderts_. Nuremberg: Spindler, 1963.

00862. Bohnenblust, Roger. *Costumes fribourgeois*. Fribourg: La Liberté, 1971.

00863. Brand, L. *Zeichnungen nach dem gemeinen Volke besonders der Kaufruf in Wien*. 1775. Reprint. Vienna: Burgverlag 1924.

00864. Brockmann-Jerosch, H. *Schweizer Volksleben, Sitten, Brauchen, Wohnstatten*. Zurich: H.B-J, 1929.

00865. Deibel, Hans. *Die Volkstrachten des Schlitzerlandes*. Marburg: Elwert, 1967.

00866. Ewig, Ursula. *Die Frauentracht des Breidenbacher Grundes*. Marburg: Elwert, 1964.

00867. Fochler, Rudolf. *Costumes in Austria*. Munich: Welsermuhl, 1980.

00868. Fox, Nikolaus. *Saarlandische Volkskunde*. Bonn: F. Klopp, 1927.

00869. Friebertshauser, Hans. *Die Frauentrachten des alten Amtes Blankenstein*. Marburg: Elwert, 1966.

00870. Gaul, Franz. *Österreichisch-ungarische National-Trachten*. Vienna: Lechner, 1881-1888.

00871. Gerbing, Luise. *Die Thüringer Trachten in Wort und Bild*. Berlin: Stubenrauch, 1936.

00872. Gesellschaft fur den Volkskundeatlas in Österreich, *Österreichischer Volksundeatlas*. Vienna: Austrian Academy of Science, 1959-1971.

00873. Gierl, Irmgard. *Miesbacher Trachtenbuch. Die Bauern Tracht zwischen Isar und Inn*. Weissenhorn: Konrad, 1971.

00874. ————. *Pfaffenwinkler Trachtenbuch. Kulturlandschaft und Tracht in Weilheim, Murnau und Werdenfels*. Weissenhorn: Konrad, 1971.

00875. Gleichauf, Rudolf. *Badische Landestrachten im Auftrage des Grossherzog Badischen Handelsministeriums*. Stuttgart: Muller, 1862.

00876. Heierli, Julie. *Die Volkstrachten der Mittel- und Westschweiz. Luzen, Zug, Aargau, Solothurn, Basel, Waadt, Neuenberg und Geuf*. Erlenbach-Zurich: Rentsch, 1932.

00877. ————. *Die Volkstrachten der Ostschweiz, Thurgau, St. Gallen, Glarus, Appenzell*. Erlenbach-Zurich: Rentsch, 1922-1932.

00878. ————. *Die Volkstrachten von Bern, Freiburg und Wallis*. Erlenbach-Zurich: Rentsch, 1928.

00879. Heierli, Julie. Die Volkstrachten von Zurich, Schaffhausen, Graubunden und Tessin. Erlenbach-Zurich: Rentsch, 1930.

00880. Helm, Rudolf. Deutsche Volkstrachten aus der Sammlung des Germanischen Museums in Nurnberg. Munich: Lehmann, 1932.

00881. __________. Hessische Bauerntrachten. Marburg: Elwert, 1949.

00882. Henssen, Dorothee. Die Frauentracht des alten Amtes Biedenkopf. Marburg: Elwert, 1963.

00883. Hottenroth, Friedrich. Deutsche Volkstrachten-städtliche und ländliche vom XVI. Jahrhundert bis zum Anfange des XIX. Jahrhunderts. 3 vols. Frankfurt: Keller, 1898-1902.

00884. Ilg, Karl. Landes- und Volkskunde, Geschichte, Wirtschaft und Kunst Vorarlbergs. 4 vols. Innsbruck: Wagner, 1961-1968.

00885. Justi, Ferdinand. Hessische Trachtenbuch. Marburg: Elwert, 1905.

00886. Kaisig, Frieda. Schönwald. 32 Trachtenbilder aus einem deutschen Dorf in Oberschliesen. Hamburg: Knackstedt, 1920.

00887. Kretschmer, Albert. Deutsche Volkstrachten. Leipzig: Bach, 1887-1890.

00888. Laugel, Anselme. Trachten und Sitten in Elsass. Strasbourg: Fischbach, 1902.

00889. Laur, Ernst; Vial, Marie; and Schluep-Gruber, Martha. Kleiden und Wohnen in Bauernhaus. Bern: Buchverlag Verbandsdruckerei AG, 1951.

00890. Laur, Ernst and Wirth, Kurt. Schweitzer Trachten. Zurich: Silva, 1954.

00891. Leopoldi, Hans Heinrich. Mecklenburgische Volkstrachten, I: Bauerntrachten. Leipzig: Hofmeister, 1957.

00892. Lepage-Medvey, E. National Costumes. Paris: Hyperion, 1939.

00893. Lipp, Franz. Volkstracht. Zur Geschichte und landschaftlicher Gliederung der österreichischen Volkstracht. In Österreichische Volkskunde für Jederman, edited by Adolf Mais. Vienna, 1952.

00894. Lory, Gabriel and Moritz, F.W. Costumes suisses. . . dessins d'après nature. Neuchâtel: Wolrath, 1824.

00895. Lucking, W. and Nedo, Paul. Die Lausitz. Sorbische Trachten. Berlin: Akademie, 1956.

00896. Mathis, Burkard and Angehrn, Siegward. Um Kleid und Tracht. Einsiedeln, 1954.

00897. Meschgang, Jan. *Sorbische Volkstrachten II: Die Tracht der katholischen Sorben.* Bautzen: Domowina, 1957.

00898. Moleville, M. Bertrand de. *The Costume of the Hereditary States of the House of Austria, Displayed in Fifty Coloured Engravings.* London: Miller, 1804.

00899. Nedo, Paul. *Sorbische Volkstrachten.* Bautzen: Domowina, 1954.

00900. Nowak-Neumann, Martin. *Sorbische Volkstrachten IV: Die Tracht der niederlausitzer Sorben.* Bautzen: Domowina, 1965.

00901. ____________________ and Nedo, Paul. *Sorbische Volkstrachten I: Die Tracht der Sorben um Schleife.* Bautzen: Domowina, 1954.

00902. *Die oberösterreichische Landestracht fur Frauen.* Linz: O.o. Heimatverein, 1935.

00903. Perkonig, Josef Friedrich and Scherer, Hedi. *Brauch und Tracht in Österreich.* Innsbruck: Tyrolia, 1937.

00904. Pettigrew, Dora W. *Peasant Costume of the Black Forest.* London: Black, 1937.

00905. Rattelmüller, Paul Ernst. *Dirndl, Janker, Lederhosen: Künstler entdecken die oberbayerischen Trachten.* Munich: Grafer und Unzer, 1970.

00906. Rehm, Maria. *Österreichs Trachtenbüchlein.* London: Thorsons, 1956.

00907. Reinhardt, Albert. *Schwarzwälder Trachten.* Karlsruhe: Badenia, 1968.

00908. Retzlaff, Hans. *Deutsche Bauerntrachten.* Berlin: Atlantis, 1934.

00909. Ringler, Josef and Karasek, Gretel. *Tiroler Trachten.* Innsbruck: Tyrolia, 1961.

00910. Schadler, Karl. *Die Lederhose in Bayern und Tirol.* Innsbruck: Wagner, 1962.

00911. Schmidt, Leopold. *Volkstracht in Niederosterreich.* Linz: Trauner, 1969.

00912. Schneider, Erich. *Sorbische Volkstrachten III: Die Tracht der Sorben um Hoyerswerda [Wojerec].* Bautzen: Domowina, 1959.

00913. *Steirische Trachten.* Graz: Steirisches Volksbildungswerk, 1959.

00914. Stockar, Jurg. Zurich Mode durch die Jahrhunderte. Zurich: Orell Fussli Verlag, 1974.

00915. Stracke, Johannes C. Tracht und Schmuck Altfrieslands nach der Darstellung im Hausbuch des Hauptlings Unico Manninga. Zurich: Verlag Ostfriesische Landschaft, 1967.

00916. Weitnauer, Alfred. Tracht und Gewand im Schwabenland. Beschreibung der letzten bodenstandigen Trachten im Gebiet des Regierungsbezirks Schwaben. Kempten: Verlag fur Heimatpflege, 1957.

00917. Wille, Louis. Die Trachten des Harzlandes. Braunlage: Bonewitz, 1967.

00918. Witzig, Louise. Les costumes suisses. Berne: Hallwag, 1954.

00919. Wrede, Adam Joseph. Eifeler Volkskunde. 1914. Reprint. Bonn: Rohrscheid, 1960.

00920. Wyss, P. Trachten des Kantons Bern. Langna: Emmenthalerblatt, 1944.

00921. Zell, F. Bauern-Trachten aus dem bayerischen Hochland. Munich, 1903.

f) Health/Medical

00922. Hubbard, Ruth. "Prenatal Diagnosis and Eugenic Ideology." Women's Studies International Forum 8 (1985): 567-576.

00923. Sagmeister, Raimund. Fristenlösung-Wie kam es dazu? Salzburg: Anton Pustet, 1981.

Also refer to #850.

7. CULTURAL

"The destiny of nations lies far more in the hands of women--the mothers, than in the possessors of power. . . ."

Friedrich Froebel

a) Literature

00924. Burkhard, Marianne, ed. Gestaltet und Gestaltind Frauen in der deutschen Literatur. Amsterdamer Beiträge zur neuren Germanistik, no. 10. Amsterdam: Rodopi, 1980.

00925. Debus, Friedhelm. "Die deutschen Bezeichnungen für die Heiratsverwandtschaft." In Deutsche Wortforschung in europäischen Bezügen, edited by Ludwig Erich Schmitt, 1: 1-116. Giessen: Wilhelm Schmitz Verlag, 1958.

00926. Endres, Elisabeth. "Über das Schicksal der schreibenden Frauen." In Neue Literatur der Frauen edited by Heinz Puknus, pp. 7-19. Munich: C.H. Beck, 1980.

00927. Horsley, Ritta Jo. "Women and German Literature: A Bibliography." Female Studies 9 (1975): 202-211.

00928. Puschel, Ursula. Mit allen Sinnen: Frauen in der Literatur. Leipzig: Mitteldeutscher Verlag, 1980.

b) Art

00929. Keisch, Claude and März, Roland. Deutsche bildende Künstlerinnen von der Goethezeit bis zur Gegenwart. Berlin: National-Galerie, [1976?].

Also refer to #849, 850.

E. IBERIA

1. SURVEYS

"Give me lions or tigers to guard,
give me crocodiles, but do not
give me a beautiful young girl."

Lope de Vega

00930. Bennassar, Bartolomé. The Spanish Character Attitudes and Mentalities from the Sixteenth to the Nineteenth Century. Translated by Benjamin Keen. Los Angeles: University of California Press, 1979.
[See especially Ch. 7 "All the Forms of Love."]

00931. Campo de Alange, Maria de los Reyes Laffitte de Salamanca, Condesa del. La Mujer en España: cien anos de su historia, 1860-1960. Madrid: Aquilar, 1963.

00932. Mujer y sociedad en España, 1700-1975. Madrid: Ministerio de Cultura Estudios Sobre la Mujer, 1982.

00933. Ossorio y Gallardo, Angel. Mujeres. Barcelona: Ediciones Grijalbo, 1977.

00934. Pescatello, Ann M. "Latina Liberation: Tradition, Ideology, and Social Change in Iberian and Latin American Cultures." In Liberating Women's History, edited by Berenice A. Carroll, pp. 161-178. Urbana: University of Illinois Press, 1976.

2. POLITICAL

"I am perhaps the only writer in Spain who has never obtained from any government some compensation. . . . My sex has been an eternal obstacle. . . . With wounded vanity I had to accept their reasons as valid, although they are based merely on my lack of a beard."

Avellaneda

a) Generic

00935. Entrena Klett, Carlos Maria. Matrimonio, separacion y divorcio: (en la legislacion actual y en la historia). Pamplona: Aranzadi, 1982.

00936. Thiercelin, Raquel. "Les femmes espagnoles et la politique." In Femmes et politique autour de la Méditerranée, edited by Christiane Souriau, pp. 11-24. Paris: L'Harmattan, 1980.

b) Feminism

00937. Capmany, Maria Aurélia and Alcalde, Carmen. El feminismo ibérica. Barcelona: Libros Tau, 1970.

00938. Pilar Onate, María del. El feminismo en la literatura española. Madrid: Espasa-Calpe, 1938.

3. SOCIAL

"I was living with my daughter in the village when he came into my house, became my friend, began to take liberties with my daughter, violated her . . . and she bore his child and he left the settlement. But what is worse, he took a quantity of goods, money, wool and other things from my house."

A father

a) Family

00939. García Cárcel, Ricardo; Vincent, Bernard; and Casey, James. "La familia en España." Historia 16 (1981): 47-73.

b) Sex Roles and Morals

00940. Gilmore, David D. "Sexual Ideology in Andalusian Oral Literature: A Comparative View of a Mediterranean Complex." Ethnology 22 (July 1983): 241-252.

c) Fashion/Manners

00941. Aguilera, E.M. Los trajes populares de España. Barcelona: Omega, 1948.

00942. Anderson, Ruth M. Spanish Costume: Extramadura. New York: Hispanic Society, 1951.

00943. Carreras y Candi, F. Folklore y costumbres de espana. 2 vols. Barcelona: A. Martin, 1943-1946.

00944. Delineations of the Most Remarkable Costumes of the Different Provinces of Spain. London: Stokes, 1822.

00945. Gallois, Émile. Le costume en Espagne et au Portugal. Paris: Laurens, 1954.

00946. ______________. Costumes espagnols. Paris: Laurens, 1939.

00947. Garcia Boiza, Antonio. El traje regional Salmantino. Madrid: Espasa-Calpe, 1940.

00948. Gomez Tabanera, José Manuel. Trajes populares y costumbres tradicionales. Madrid: Tesoro, 1950.

00949. Hispanic Society of America. Extramadura costume: women's festival dress at Montehermoso, Caceres. New York: Hispanic Society, [1931].

4. CULTURAL

"The men, not satisfied after having reserved for themselves positions, honors, compensations for their work, in other words everything that could excise the studiousness and dedication of women, have also deprived the members of our sex of the satisfaction of having an enlightened mind."

Josefa Amar y Borbon

a) Literature

(1) Bibliographies

00950. Billick, David J. "Women in Hispanic Literature: A Checklist of Doctoral Dissertations and Master's Theses, 1905-1975." Women's Studies Abstracts 6 (Summer 1977): 1-11.

(2) Non-specific

(a) Women in Literature

00951. Miller, Beth, ed. Women in Hispanic Literature, Icons and Fallen Idols. Berkeley, Ca.: University of California Press, 1983.

Also refer to #938, 940.

(b) Women Authors

00952. Fox-Lockert, Lucia. Women Novelists in Spain and Spanish America. Metuchen, N.J.: The Scarecrow Press, 1979.

(3) Drama

00953. Bearse, Grace M. "Evolution of the Comendador's Daughter in Three Centuries of Spanish Drama." Hispanofilia 69 (May 1980): 17-26.

00954. Bravo Villasante, Carmen. La mujer vestida de hombre en el teatro español. Madrid: Revista de occidente, 1955.

F. ITALY

1. SURVEYS

"This immutable, inviolable, and fundamental truth: Matrimony was not instituted or re-established by men, but God, the Author of Nature. . ."

Piux IX

00955. Bargellini, Piero. La donna italiana del tempo antico. Florence: CYA, 1948.

00956. Palumbo, Pier Fausto. "La donna italiana nella storia e nella vita." Emporium 93 (April 1941): 152-162.

00957. Trollope, Thomas Adolphus. A Decade of Italian Women, 2 vols. London: Chapman & Hall, 1859.

2. POLITICAL

"The Laws have less confidence in a woman."

Bardus

00958. Alloatti, Franca and Mingardo, Mirella. "<<L'Italia Femminile>>--Il fiorire della stampa delle donne tra Ottocento e Novecento." In Esistere come donna, pp. 153-158. Milan: Mazzotta, 1983.

00959. Calapso, Jole. Donne ribelli: un secolo di lotte femminili in Sicilia. Palermo: S.F. Flaccovio, 1980.

00960. L'Emancipazione femminile in Italia: un secolo di discussioni 1861-1961. Florence: Nuova Italia, 1963.

00961. Librando, Vito. "Italian Law." In The Reform of Family Law in Europe: The Equality of the Spouses, Divorce, Illegitimate Children, edited by A.G. Chloros, pp. 151-182. Boston: Kluwer, 1978.

00962. Patane, Olga. "La femme italienne et la politique." In Femmes et politique autour de la Méditerranée, edited by Christiane Souriau, pp. 57-69. Paris: L'Harmattan, 1980.

3. RELIGION

"Wherever the gospel is preached in the whole world, what she has done will be told in memory of her."
Mark 14:9

00963. Fornari, Virginia. "Sante italiane." In La donna italiana descritta da scrittici, pp. 63-74. Florence: G. Civelli, 1890.

00964. Rosa, Gabriele de. Vescovi, populo e magia nel Sud: Ricerche di storia socio-reliogiosa dal XVII al XIX secolo. Naples: Guida, 1971.

00965. Tentori, Tullio. "An Italian Religious Feast. The Fujenti Rites of the Madonna dell'Arco, Naples." In Mother Worship Themes and Variations, edited by James J. Preston, pp. 95-122. Chapel Hill, N.C.: University of North Carolina Press, 1982. Also in Cultures 3 (1976): 117-140.

4. SOCIAL

"For all human tasks . . . are a common obligation and are common for men and women, and none is necessarily appointed for either one exclusively, but some pursuits are more suited to the nature of one, some to the other, and for this reason some are called men's work and some women's. But whatever things have reference to virtue, these one would properly say are equally appropriate to the nature of both. . . ."
C. Muscnius Rufus
"Should Daughters Receive the Same Education as Sons?"

a) Generic

00966. Bruno, Emilio, ed. La donna nella beneficenza in Italia. Turin: Botta, 1910-1913.

Also refer to #959, 961.

b) Folklore

00967. Canziani, Estella. "Piedmontese Proverbs in Dis-praise of Women." Folk-Lore 24 (1913): 91-96.

00968. Pietropaoli, Lydia Q. "Folklore from the Heart of Italy." New York Folklore Quarterly 19 (1963): 163-182, 282-295.

c) Demography

00969. Livi Bacci, Massimo. *A History of Italian Fertility During the Last Centuries*. Princeton, N.J.: Princeton University Press, 1977.

00970. Pina, Marco Della. "Le crisi di mortalità en un territorio a crescente specializzazione economica: Carrara 1600-1830." *Società et Storia* 3 (1978): 465-480.

00971. Sannino, Anna Lisa. "Illegittimi ed esposti nella societa Lucana dal XVII al XIX secolo." In *Studi di storia sociale e religiosa. Scritti in onore di Gabriele de Rosa*, pp. 1473-1494. Naples: Editrici Ferraro, 1980.

00972. Schiaffino, Andrea. "Il declino della fecondità in ambiente urbano: Reggio Emilia fra otto e novecento." *Instituto di Statistica-Quaderno* 3 (1979): 7-275.

00973. ________________. "Un modello interpretative delle strutture demografiche del regno di Napole nell XVIII e XIX secolo: intervento di un demographo." *Società e storia* 5 (1979): 521-560.

d) Family

00974. Lelli, Marcello; Merler, Alberto; and Petto, Cesare. "Hypothèse pour la comprehension du rapport entre famille et industrialisation la Sardaigne." In *Femmes corses et femmes meditérranéennes*, pp. 396-411. Provence: Centre d'Etudes Corses de l'Université de Provence, 1976.

Also refer to #961, 971.

e) Marriage

00975. Buonanno, Milly. *Le Funzioni sociali del matrimonio: modelli e regole della scelta del coniuge dal XIV al XX secolo*. Milan: Edizioni de Comunità, 1980.

00976. Merzario, Raul. *Il paese stretto. Strategie matrimoniale nella diocesi di Corro, secoli XVI-XVIII*. Turin: Einaudi, 1981.

Also refer to #961.

f) Sex Life and Morals

00977. Barzaghi, Antonio. *Donne o cortegiane? la prostituzione a Venezia documenti di costume dal XVI al XVIII secolo*. Verona: Bertani editore, 1980.

g) Fashion/Manners

00978. Calderini, Emma. Il costume populare in Italia. Milan: Sperling and Kupfer, 1946.

00979. Carta Raspi, Raimondo. Costumi sardi. Cagliari: [1930].

00980. D'Orlandi, L. and Perusini, G. Il costume populare Carnico. Udine: Doretti, 1966.

00981. Görlich, Giovanni Gualtiero, ed. Costumi populari italiani. 3 vols. Milan: Gorlich, 1951-1958.

00982. Levi Pisetzky, Rosita. Storia de costume in Italia. 5 vols. Milan: Instituto editoriale italiano, 1964-1969.

00983. Miceli, Biagio. Arte e costume in Sicilia. Ragusa: E.N.A.D., 1968.

00984. Perusini, G. Il costume populare Udinese. Udine: Doretti, 1966.

5. CULTURAL

"The emancipation of women must be one of the central problems of the renewal of the Italian state and society."

Togliatti

00985. Morand, Bernadette. "La femme dans le roman et le théâtre italiens." Europe 427-428 (November-December 1964): 123-130.

Also refer to #850.

G. THE LOW COUNTRIES

1. SOCIAL

"When their [Flemish women] husbands come home tired. . . they [the wives] turn them out of doors to seek distractions at a tavern. . . and the wives run around and gossip, to the neglect of their households."

Juan Luis Vives

a) Demography

00986. Vries, Jan de. "The Population and Economy of the Preindustrial Netherlands." Journal of Interdisciplinary History 15 (Spring 1985): 661-682.

b) Fashion/Manners

00987. Gardilanne, Gratiane de and Moffat, Elizabeth Whitney. National Costumes of Holland London: G.G. Harrap and Co., 1932.

00988. Groen, A. Dutch Costume. Delft: Elmar, 1977.

00989. Madou, J.B. and Eedhout, J.J. Collection des provinces de la Belgique. Brussels: Burggraaf, 1835.

00990. Valeton, Elsa M. Dutch Costumes. Amsterdam: De Driehoek, 1959.

00991. Vries, R.W.P. de. Dutch National Costumes. Amsterdam: Meulenhoff, [1930].

2. CULTURAL

"Do you think there's anything our husbands
labor for and not for our ends?
Are we shut out of counsailes, privacies,
And onely lymitted our household business?
No, certain, Lady, we partakes with all,
Or our good men pertake no rest."

Dutch women to an English woman
Fletcher's Tragedy of Sir John van Olden Barnavelt

00992. Lampaert, I. Le nu dans l'art moderne belge: 26 juin-23 aout 1981, Galerie CGER. Brussels: R. Coolen, 1981.

II. ANTIQUITY

A. GENERAL

1. BIBLIOGRAPHY

"It would have been better for men to have gotten their children in some either way, and women need not have existed. Then life would have been good."
Jason in *Medea*, Euripides

00993. Dickison, Sheila K. "Women in Antiquity: A Review Article." *Helios* n.s. 4 (Fall 1976): 59-69.

00994. Pomeroy, Sarah B. with Kraemer, Ross S. and Kampen, Natalie Boymel. "Selected Bibliography on Women in Classical Antiquity." In *Women in the Ancient World, The Arethusa Papers*, edited by John Peradotto and J. P. Sullivan, pp. 315-372. Albany, N.Y.: State University of New York, 1984.

2. SURVEYS

"But Hector, you are father and noble mother to me and brother as well, and you are my tender husband."
Andromache

00995. Bernhöft, Franz. *Frauenleben in der Vorzeit.* Wismar: n.p. 1893.

00996. Bingham, Marjorie Wall and Gross, Susan Hill. *Women in Ancient Greece and Rome.* St. Louis Park, Minn.: Glenhurst Pub., 1983.

00997. Blazquez, Niceto. "La mujer en el socialismo antiquo." Arbor 93 (January 1976): 79-90.

00998. Cameron, Averil and Kuhrt, Amelie, eds. Images of Women in Antiquity. Detroit, Mich.: Wayne State University Press, 1984.

00999. Foley, Helene P., ed. Reflections of Women in Antiquity. New York: Gordon and Breach Science Publishers, 1981.

01000. Klimberg H. Von Frauen des Altertums. Münster: Aschendorf, 1949.

01001. Lefkowitz, Mary R. Heroines and Hysterics. New York: St. Martin's, 1981.

01002. ________________. "Influential Women." In Images of Women in Antiquity, edited by Averil Cameron and Amelie Kuhrt, pp. 49-64. Detroit: Wayne State University Press, 1983.

01003. ________________ and Fant, Maureen B., eds. Women's Life in Greece and Rome. Baltimore, Md.: Johns Hopkins University Press, 1982.

01004. Seltman, Charles Theodore. Women in Antiquity. 1956. Reprint. Westport, Ct.: Hyperion Press Inc., 1981.

01005. Specht, Edith. "Streiflichter zur Situation der Frau in antiken Kulturen." In Das ewige Klischee, zum Rollenbild und Selbstverstandnis bei Mannern und Frauen, pp. 11-19. Vienna: Hermann Böhlaus, 1981.

01006. Wilkinson, L.P. "Classical Approaches." Encounter 50 (May 1978): 223-251.

3. POLITICAL

"God, who created man from clay, and formed woman from one of his ribs, joined her to him as one of his members, that she, being aware of her origin might learn from this to preserve her kindness and affection uncontaminatd from her husband."

New Constitutions of the Emperor Leo

a) Generic

01007. Andreasen, Niels-Erik. "The Role of the Queen-Mother in Israelite Society." Catholic Biblical Quarterly 45 (1983): 179-194.

b) Legal

01008. Arbois de Jubainville, Henri. Etudes sur le droit celtique. Paris: Thorin et fils, 1895.

01009. Gardascia, Guillaume. "Egalité et inegalité des sexes en matière d'atteinte aux moeurs dans le Proche-Orient ancien." Welt Orients 11 (1980): 7-16.

01010. MacDonald, Elizabeth Mary. The Position of Women as Reflected in Semitic Codes of Law. Toronto: Univ. of Toronto Oriental Studies, Univ. of Toronto Press, 1931.

Also refer to #1012.

c) Feminism

01011. Wilkinson, L.P. "Women's Liberation." In Classical Attitudes to Modern Issues, pp. 47-78. London: William Kimber, 1979.

4. RELIGION/MYTHOLOGY

"Sextilia, a vestal, found guilty of incest, and buried alive."

Livy

a) Generic

01012. Brown, John Pairman. "The Role of Women and the Treaty in the Ancient World." Biblische Zeitschrift 25 (1981): 1-28.

01013. Grottanelli, Cristiana. "The King's Grace and the Helpless Woman: A Comparative Study of the Stories of Ruth, Charila, Sita." History of Religions 22 (August 1982): 1-24.

01014. Mortley, Raoul. Womanhood: The Feminine in Ancient Hellenism, Gnosticism, Christianity, and Islam. Sydney, Australia: Delacrois, 1981.

01015. Perlman, Alice and Perlman, Polly. "Women's Power in the Ancient World." Women's Caucus-Religious Studies 3 (Summer 1975): 4-6.

b) Goddesses

01016. Barstow, Anne Llewellyn. "The Prehistoric Goddess." In The Book of the Goddess, Past and Present: An Introduction to Her Religion, edited by Carl Olson, pp. 7-15. New York: Crossroad Publishing Co., 1983.

01017. Berger, Pamela. The Goddess Obscured Transformation of the Grain Protectress from Goddess to Saint. Boston: Beacon Press, 1985.

01018. Debrida, Bella. "Drawing from Mythology in Women's Quest for Selfhood." In The Politics of Women's Spirituality, edited by Charlene Spretnak, pp. 138-151. Garden City, N.Y.: Doubleday and Company, Inc., Anchor Press, 1982.

01019. Drinker, Sophie. "The Origins of Music: Women's Goddess Worship." In The Politics of Women's Spirituality, edited by Charlene Spretnak, pp. 39-48. Garden City, N.Y.: Doubleday and Company, Inc., Anchor Press, 1982.

01020. Dunand, Francoise. Le culte d'Isis dans le bassin oriental de la Mediterranee. EPRO 26. Leiden: Brill, 1973.

01021. Gimbutas, Marija. The Goddesses and Gods of Old Europe. Berkeley, Ca.: University of California Press, 1982.

01022. ______________. "Women and Culture in Goddess-Oriented Old Europe." In The Politics of Women's Spirituality, edited by Charlene Spretnak, pp. 22-31. Garden City, N.Y.: Doubleday and Company, Inc., Anchor Press, 1982.

01023. Rich, Adrienne. "Prepatriarchal Female/Goddess Image." In The Politics of Women's Spirituality, edited by Charlene Spretnak, pp. 32-38. Garden City, N.Y.: Doubleday and Company, Inc., Anchor Press, 1982.

01024. Solie, Pierre. La Femme essentielle. Mythanalyse de la grand mère et de ses fils amants. Paris: Seghers, 1980.

01025. Solmsen, Friedrich. Isis Among the Greeks and the Romans. Cambridge, Mass.: Harvard, 1979.

01026. Stone, Merlin. "The Great Goddess: Who Was She?" In The Politics of Women's Spirituality, edited by Charlene Spretnak, pp. 7-21. Garden City, N.Y.: Doubleday and Company, Inc., Anchor Press, 1982.

01027. ____________. "The Three Faces of Goddess Spirituality." In The Politics of Women's Spirituality, edited by Charlene Spretnak, pp. 64-70. Garden City, N.Y.: Doubleday and Company, Inc., Anchor Press, 1982.

01028. Suhr, Elmer G. The Spinning Aphrodite: The Evolution of the Goddess from Earliest Pre-Hellenic Symbolism Through Late Classical Times. New York: Helios, 1969.

01029. Swidler, Leonard. "Goddess Worship and Women Priests." In Women Priests, A Catholic Commentary on the Vatican Declaration, edited by Leonard Swidler and Arlene Swidler, pp. 167-175. New York: Paulist Press, 1977.

c) Jews

01030. Archer, Léonie J. "The Role of Jewish Women in the Religion, Ritual and Cult of Graeco-Roman Palestine." In Images of Women in Antiquity, edited by Averil Cameron and Amélie Kuhrt, pp. 273-287. Detroit: Wayne State University Press, 1983.

01031. Brooten, Bernadette J. Women Leaders in the Ancient Synagogue: Inscriptional Evidence and Background Issues. Chicago, Ill.: Scholars Press, 1982.

d) Gnostics

01032. Buckley, Jorunn Jacobsen, "Two Female Gnostic Interpreters." History of Religions 19 (February 1980): 259-269.

5. SOCIAL

> "For nothing is stronger and better than this:
> when a man and a wife live together in their home,
> their thoughts of one accord . . ."
>
> The Odyssey

a) Generic

01033. Badian, E. "The Lives of Ancient Women." New York Review of Books (30 October 1975): 28-31.

01034. Philarète, Charles. L'Antiquité. Paris: Charpentier, 1876.

01035. Vardiman, E.E. Die Frau in der Antike. Sittengeschichte der Frau im Altertum. Vienna: Econ, 1982.

b) Demography

01036. Wilkinson, L.P. "Population and Family Planning." In Classical Attitudes to Modern Issues, pp. 15-43. London: William Kimber, 1979.

c)Family

(1) Non-specific

01037. Arbois de Jubainville, Henri. La famille celtique. Paris: E. Bouillon, 1905.

01038. Eyben, Emiel. "Family Planning in Greece-Roman Antiquity." Ancient Society 11-12 (1980-1981): 5-82.

01039. Guichard, Pierre. "De l'Antiquité au Moyen Age: Famille large et famille entroite." Cahiers d'histoire 24 no. 4 (1979): 45-60.

01040. Pembroke, Simon G. "The Early Human Family: Some Views 1770-1870." In Classical Influences on Western Thought A.D. 1650-1870, edited by R.R. Bolgar, pp. 275-291. Cambridge: University Press, 1979.

(2) Infanticide

01041. Boswell, John Eastburn. "*Expositio* and *Oblatio*: The Abandonment of Children and the Ancient and Medieval Family." *American Historical Review* 89 (February 1984) 10-33.

d) Marriage

01042. Engels, Donald. "The Problem of Female Infanticide in the Greco-Roman Woman." *Classical Philology* 75 (April 1980): 112-120.

01043. Doucet-Bon, Lise Vincent. *Le mariage dans les civilisations anciennes*. Paris: Albin Michel, 1975.

01044. Lefkowitz, Mary R. "Wives and Husbands." *Greece and Rome* 2nd ser. 30 (April 1983): 31-47.

01045. Pearson, Karl. "Kindred Group--Marriage-- I. Mother Age Civilization." In *Chances of Death and Other Studies in Evolution*, 2: 92-111. New York: E. Arnold, 1897.

e) Sex Life and Morals

01046. Atkins, John A. *The Classical Experience of the Sexual Impulse*. London: Calder and Boyars, 1973.

01047. Ford, Clellan S. "Some Primitive Societies." In *Sex Roles in Changing Society*, edited by Georgene H. Seward and Robert C. Williamson, pp. 25-44. New York: Random House, 1970.

01048. Johns, Catherine. *Sex or Symbol: Erotic Images of Greece and Rome*. London: Colonade, 1982.

01049. Klein, Theodore M. "Ariadne, the *Qadesha*, the *Hagne*, *Une femme de Bonne Volonte*." *Helios* n.s. 8(Autumn 1981): 55-62.

01050. Verstraete, Beert C. "Homosexuality in Ancient Greek and Roman Civilization: A Critical Bibiliography." *Journal of Homosexuality* 3 (Autumn 1977): 79-90.

Also refer to #1158.

f) Fashion

01051. Hope, Thomas. *Costumes of the Ancients*. London: Chatto and Windus, 1875.

01052. Houston, Mary Galway. *Ancient Greek, Roman and Byzantine Costume and Decoration*. 2nd. ed. London: A.C. Black, 1963.

6. CULTURAL

"A man would be considered a coward who was only as brave as a brave woman."
Aristotle

a) Literature

01053. Greenberg, Caren. "Reading Reading: Echo's Abduction in Language." In Women and Language in Literature and Society, edited by Sally McConnel-Ginet, pp. 300-309. New York: Praeger, 1980.

01054. Menage, Gilles. The History of Women Philosophers. Translated by Beatrice H. Zedler. Lanham, Md.: University Press of America, 1984.

01055. Ochshorn, Judith. "Mothers and Daughters in Ancient Near Eastern Literature." In The Lost Tradition Mothers and Daughters in Literature, edited by Cathy N. Davidson and E.M. Broner, pp. 5-14. New York: Ungar, 1980.

b) Art

01056. Delporte, H. L'image de la femme dans l'art prehistorique. Paris: Picard, 1979.

01057. Marshack, A. "European Ice Age Art and Symbol. Archeology 31 (May 1978): 52-55.

01058. Schlossman, Betty L. and York, Hildreth. "Women in Ancient Art." Art Journal 35 (Summer 1976): 345-351.

01059. Schmidt-Chevalier, M. "Were the Cave Painting in South-West France Made by Women?" International Journal of Contemporary Visual Artists 14 (Autumn 1981): 382-383.

Also refer to #1018.

B. GREECE

1. SURVEYS

"Let us too face the fight which favoreth none. For we, we women be not creatures cast in diverse mold from men."
Quintus Smyrnaeus about Trojan women

a) Generic

01060. Andrewes, Antony. Greek Society. London: Hutchinson, 1967.

01061. Arthur, Marylin B. "Early Greece: The Origins of the Western Attitude Toward Women." In _Women in the Ancient World, The Arethusa Papers_, edited by John Peradotto and J. P. Sullivan, pp. 7-58. Albany, N.Y.: State University of New York Press, 1984. Also in _Arethusa_ 6 (Spring 1973): 7-58.

01062. Ide, Arthur Frederick. _Woman in Ancient Greece_. Mesquite, Tex.: Ide House, 1980.

01063. ____________________. _Women in Greek Civilization before 100 B.C._ Mesquite, Tex.: Ide House, 1983.

01064. Just, Roger. Conceptions of Women in Classical Athens." _Anthropological Society of Oxford Journal_ 6 (1975): 153-170.

01065. Mosse, Claude. _La femme dans la Grèce antique_. Paris: Albin Michel, 1983.

01066. ____________. "La femme dans la société homérique." _Klio_ 63 (1981): 149-157.

01067. Pomeroy, Sarah B. _Women in Hellenistic Egypt: From Alexander to Cleopatra_. New York: Schocken Books, 1984.

b) Amazons

01068. Chesler, Phyllis. "The Amazon Legacy." In _The Politics of Women's Spirituality_, edited by Charlene Spretnak, pp. 97-113. Garden City, N.Y.: Doubleday and Company, Inc., Anchor Press, 1982.

01069. DuBois, Page. _Centaurs and Amazons, Women and the Pre-History of the Great Chain of Being_. Ann Arbor, Mich.: University of Michigan Press, 1982.

01070. Kleinbaum, Abby Wettan. _The War Against the Amazons_. New York: McGraw Hill, 1983.

01071. Leonhard, Walther. _Hettiter und Amazonen, die griechische Tradition über die "Chatti" und ein Versuch zu ihrer historischen Verwertung_. Leipzig: B. G. Teubner, 1911.

01072. Samuel, Pierre. _Amazones, guerrières et gaillardes_. Grenoble: Presses Universitaires de Grenoble, 1975.

01073. Tiffany, Sharon W. and Adams, Kathleen J. _The Wild Woman: An Inquiry to the Anthropology of an Idea_. Cambridge, Mass.: Schenkman Pub. Co., 1985.

01074. Tyrrell, William Blake. _Amazons, a Study in Athenian Mythmaking_. Baltimore: Johns Hopkins University Press, 1984.

01075. Weber, M. "Die Amazonen von Ephesos." Jahrbuch des Deutschen Archaologischen Instituts 91 (1976): 28-96.

Also refer to #1081.

2. POLITICAL

"It is proper for women who are wise
to let men act for them in everything."
Euripides

a) Generic

01076. Bremmer, J. "Gejon's Wife and the Carthaginian Ambassadors." Mnemosyne 33 (1980): 366-368.

01077. Cohen, G. M. "The Marriage of Lysimachus and Nicea." Historia Zeitschrift fur Alte Geschichte 22 (1973): 354-356.

01078. Cromey, Robert D. "Perikles' Wife: Chronological Considerations." Greek, Roman, and Byzantine Studies 23 (Autumn 1982): 203-212.

01079. Hartsock, Nancy C.M. "Prologue to a Feminist Critique of War and Politics." In Women's Views of the Political World of Men, edited by Judith Hicks Stiehm, pp. 121-150. Dobbs Ferry, N.Y.: Transnational Publishers Inc., 1984.

01080. Keuls, Eva. The Reign of the Phallus: Sexual Politics in Ancient Athens. New York: Harper and Row, 1984.

10181. Merck, Mandy. "The City's Achievements: The Patriotic Amazonmachy and Ancient in Athens." In Tearing the Veil, Essays on Feminity, edited by Susan Lipshitz, pp. 93-115. London: Routledge and Kegan Paul, 1978.

01082. Schaps, David M. "The Women of Greece in Wartime." Classical Philology 77 (July 1982): 193-213.

b) Legal

01083. Jones, J. Walter. The Law and Legal Theory of the Greeks. Oxford: Clarendon Press, 1956.

01084. Loraux, Nicole. Les infants d'Athéna. Idees athéniennes sur la citoyenneté et la division des sexes. Paris: François Maspero, 1981.

01085. MacDowell, Douglas M. The Law in Classical Athens. London: Thames and Hudson, 1978.

01086. Miller, Molly Broadbent. "Classical Athenian Family Law." In Studies in Greek Genealogy, pp. 113-239. Leyden: E. J. Brill, 1968.

01087. Modrzejewski, Joseph. "La Structure juridique du mariage grec." In Scritti in Onore di Orsolina Montevecchi, pp. 231-268. Bologna: Clueb, 1981.

01088. ______________. "Zum hellenistischen Eheguterrecht im griechischen und romischen Agypten." Zeitschrift der Savigny Stiftung für Rechtsgeschichte (Romanistische Abteilung) 87 (1970): 50-84.

01089. Sealey, Raphael. "The Athenian Courts for Homicide." Classical Philology 78 (October 1983): 275-297. [See especially III. "The Insecure Wife."]

01090. Vidal-Naquet, Pierre. "Esclavage et gynecocratie dans la tradition, le mythe, l'utopie." In Recherches sur les structures sociales dans l'antiquité classique, edited by C. Nicolet, pp. 63-80. Paris: Editions du centre national de la recherche scientifique, 1970.

Also refer to #1202, 1204.

c) Political Roles

01091. Homeyer, Helene. Die spartanische Helene und der Trojanische Krieg. Wiesbaden: Steiner, 1977.

01092. Newman-Gordon, Pauline. Helene de Sparte: la fortune du mythe en France. Paris: Pebresse, 1968.

01093. West, Martin Lichfield. Immortal Helen. London: Bedford College, 1975.

Also refer to #1194, 1196-1198, 1200, 1201, 1230.

3. ECONOMIC

"The disorder of women not only of itself gives an air of indecorum to the state, but tends to foster avarice."
Aristotle

01094. Billigmeier, Jon-Christian and Turner, Judy A. "The Socio-economic Roles of Women in Mycenaean Greece: A Brief Survey from Evidence of the Linear B Tablets." In Reflections of Women in Antiquity, edited by Helene P. Foley, pp. 1-18. New York: Gordon and Breach Science Publishers, 1981. Also in Women's Studies 8 (1981): 21-46.

01095. Fitton Brown, A. D. "The Contribution of Women to Ancient Greek Agriculture." Liverpool Classical Monthly 9 no. 5 (1984): 71-74.

01096. Uchitel, Alexander. "Women at Work. Pylos and Knossos, Lagash and Ur." _Historia Zeitschrift für Alte Geschichte_ 33 (1984): 257-282.

01097. Van Bremen, Riet. "Women and Wealth." In _Images of Women in Antiquity_, edited by Averil Cameron and Amelie Kuhrt, pp. 223-242. Detroit: Wayne State University Press, 1983.

4. RELIGION/MYTHOLOGY

> "No, my child, not for you are the works of warfare. Rather
> concern yourself only with the lovely secrets of marriage,
> while all this (warfare) shall be left to Athene and sudden Ares"
>
> _Iliad_ Zeus to Aphrodite
> Book V. 428-430.

a) Generic

01098. Brown, Christopher. "Dionysus and the Women of Elis: _PMG_ 871." _Greek, Roman and Byzantine Studies_ 23 (Winter 1982): 305-314.

01099. Calame, Claude. _Les Choeurs de jeunes filles en Grece archaique. I Morphologie, II Alcman._ Rome: Edizioni dell Ateneo & Bizzarri, 1977.

01100. Cantarella, Eva. "Dangling Virgins: Myth Ritual and the Place of Women in Ancient Greece." _Poetics Today_ 6 (1985): 91-101.

01101. Castner, Catherine J. "Epicurean Hetairai as Dedicants to Healing Deities?" _Greek, Roman and Byzantine Studies_ 23 (Spring 1982): 51-57.

01102. Cole, Susan Guettel. "New Evidence for the Mysteries of Dionysos." _Greek, Roman, and Byzantine Studies_ 21 (1980): 223-238.

01103. Farber, Ada. "Segmentation of the Mother: Women in Greek Myth." _Psychoanalytic Review_ 62 (Spring 1976): 29-47.

01104. Henrichs, Albert. "Greek Maenadism from Olpmpias to Messaline." _Harvard Studies in Classical Philology_ 82 (1978): 121-160.

01105. Johansen, J. P. "The Thesmophoria as a Women's Festival." _Temenos_ 11 (1975): 78-87.

01106. Kerenyi, Karoly. _Eleusis: Archetypal Image of Mother and Daughter_. New York: Pantheon, 1967.

01107. Kerenyi, Karoly and Jung, Carl. Essays on the Science of Mythology: The Myth of the Divine Child and the Mysteries of Eleusis. New York: Pantheon, 1949.

01108. Kraemer, R.S. "Ecstasy and Possession: The Attraction of Women to the Cult of Dionysius." Harvard Theological Review 72 (January-April 1979): 55-80.

01109. Lefkowitz, Mary R. "Women in Greek Myth." The American Scholar 54 (Spring 1985): 207-219.

01110. Padel, Ruth. "Women: Model for Possession by Greek Daemons." In Images of Women in Antiquity, edited by Averil Cameron and Amelie Kuhrt, pp. 3-19. Detroit: Wayne State University Press, 1983.

01111. Rousselle, Robert. "Comparative Psychohistory: Snake Handling in Hellenistic Greece and the American South." Journal of Psychohistory 11 (Spring 1984): 477-489.

01112. Skov, G.E. "The Priestess of Demeter and Kore and Her Role in the Initiation of Women at the Festival of the Heloa at Eleusis." Temenos 11 (1975): 136-147.

01113. Steiner, George. Antigones: How the Antigone Legend Has Endured in Western Literature, Art and Thought. New York: Oxford, 1984.

01114. Walcot, P. "Greek Attitudes Toward Women: The Mythological Evidence." Greece and Rome 36 (1984): 37-47.

b) Goddesses

01115. Berg, William. "Pandora: Pathology of a Creation Myth." Fabula 17 (1976): 1-25.

01116. Bergman, Jan. Ich Bin Isis. Studien zum memphitischen Hintergrund der griechischen Isisaretalogien. Uppsala: Almquist & Wiskell, 1968.

01117. Detienne, M. "Athena and the Mastery of the Horse." History of Religions 11 (November 1971): 161-184.

01118. Downing, Christine. "Ariadne, Mistress of the Labyrinth." In Facing the Gods, edited by James Hillman, pp. 135-149. Irving, Tex.: Spring, 1980.

01119. __________. "The Mother Goddess Among the Greeks." In The Book of the Goddess, Past and Present: An Introduction to Her Religion, edited by Carl Olson, pp. 49-59. New York: Crossroad Publishing Co., 1983.

01120. Friedrich, P. The Meaning of Aphrodite. Chicago: University of Chicago Press, 1979.

01121. Hörig, Monika. Dea Syria: Studien zur religiosen Tradition der Fruchtbarkeitsgottin in Vorderasien. Neukirchen: Neukirchener Verlag, 1979.

01122. Kerényi, Károly. Athene: Virgin and Mother in Greek Religion. Irving, Tex.: Spring Publications, 1979.

01123. ______________. Goddesses of Sun and Moon: Circe/Aphrodite/Medea/Niobe. Irving, Tex.: Spring Publications, 1979.

01124. ______________. Zeus and Hera: Archetypal Image of Father, Husband and Wife. Princeton: Princeton University Press, 1975.

01125. King, Helen. "Bound to Bleed: Artemis and Greek Women." In Images of Women in Antiquity, edited by Averil Cameron and Amelie Kuhrt, pp. 109-127. Detroit: Wayne State University Press, 1983.

01126. LeCorsu, France. Isis mythe et mystères. Paris: Belles lettres, 1977.

01127. Levin, Saul. "The Perfumed Goddess." Bucknell Review 24 (Spring 1978): 49-59.

01128. Lincoln, B. "Rape of Persephone: A Greek Scenario of Women's Initiation." Harvard Theological Review 72 (July-October 1979): 223-235.

01129. Mellor, Ronald. Thea Rome: The Worship of the Goddess Roma in the Greek World. Gottingen: Vandenhoeck und Ruprecht, 1975.

01130. Spretnak, Charlene. Lost Goddesses of Early Greece: A Collection of Pre-Hellenic Myths. Boston: Beacon Press, 1981.

01131. Zeitlin, Froma A. "Cultic Models of the Female: Rites of Dionysus and Demeter." Arethusa 15 (Spring-Fall 1982): 129-157.

01132. Zuntz, Gunther. Persephone: Three Essays on Religion in Magna Graecia. Oxford: Clarendon, 1971.

Also refer to #1016, 1024, 1068, 1090, 1109, 1112, 1114, 1207.

5. SOCIAL

"Of all things which are living. . . we women are the most unfortunate. . . it is required for us to buy a husband and take for our bodies a master; for not to take one is even worse."

Medea
Euripides

a) Generic

01133. Marcovich, M. "How to Flatter Women: P. Oxy, 2891." Classical Philology 70 (April 1975): 123-124.

01134. Schaps, David M. "The Woman Least Mentioned: Etiquette and Women's Names." Classical Quarterly 27 (1977): 323-330.

01135. Shelley, Percy Bysshe. "A Discourse on the Manners of the Ancient Greeks Relative to the Subject of Love." In Shelley's Prose, edited by David Lee Clark, pp. 216-223. Albuquerque: University of New Mexico Press, 1954.

01136. Walker, Susan. "Women and Housing in Classical Greece: the Archaeological Evidence." In Images of Women in Antiquity, edited by Averil Cameron and Amelie Kuhrt, pp. 81-91. Detroit: Wayne State University Press, 1983.

Also refer to #1094.

b) Family

01137. Billigmeier, Jon-Christian. "Studies on the Family in the Aegean Bronze Age and in Homer." In Family History, edited by Patricia J.F. Rosof and William Zeisel, pp. 9-18. New York: Institute for Research in History, 1985.

01138. Bourriot, F. "La famille et le milieu social de Cleon." Historia Zeitschrift fur Alte Geschichte 31 (1982): 404-453.

01139. French, Valerie. "Sons and Mothers." Helios n.s. 4 (Fall 1976): 54-56.

01140. Gomme, Arnold W. The Population of Athens in the Fifth and Fourth Centuries B.C. Oxford: B. Blackwell, 1933.

[See especially "The Size of Athenian Families and the Exposure of Children, pp. 75-83.]

01141. Humphreys, Sally C. The Family, Women and Death: Comparative Studies. London: Routledge and Kegan Paul, 1983.

01142. Lacey, W.K. The Family in Classical Greece. Reprint. 1968. Ithaca: Cornell University Press, 1984.

01143. Pomeroy, Sarah B. "The Family in Classical and Hellenistic Greece." In _Family History_, edited by Patricia J.F. Rosof and William Zeisel, pp. 19-26. New York: Institute for Research in History, 1985.

01144. ______________. "Infanticide in Hellenistic Greece." In _Images of Women in Antiquity_, edited by Averil Cameron and Amelie Kuhrt, pp. 207-222. Detroit: Wayne State University Press, 1983.

01145. Ungaretti, J.R. "Pederasty, Heroism, and the Family in Classical Greece." _Journal of Homosexuality_ 3 (1978): 291-300.

Also refer to #1042, 1086, 1106, 1119, 1122, 1174, 1187, 1191, 1204.

c) Marriage

01146. Cartwright, P. "Spartan Wives: Liberation or Licence." _Classical Quarterly_ n.s. 31 (1981): 84-105.

01147. Lenz, Carl Gotthold. _Geschichte der Weiber im heroischen Zeitalter_. 1790. Reprint. Selb: Notos, 1976.

01148. Lewis, Naphtali. "Dryton's Wives: Two or Three?" _Chronique d'Egypte_ 57 (1982): 317-321.

Also refer to #1043, 1044, 1087, 1088, 1090, 1124, 1174.

d) Sex Life and Morals

01149. Cole, Susan Guettel. "Greek Sanctions Against Sexual Assault." _Classical Philology_ 79 (1984): 97-113.

01150. Dover, K.J. "Classical Greek Attitudes to Sexual Behaviour." In _Women in the Ancient World, the Arethusa Papers_, edited by John Peradotto and J.P. Sullivan, pp. 143-157. Albany, N.Y.: State University of New York Press, 1984. Also in _Arethusa_ 6 (Spring 1973): 59-73.

01151. Sealey, Raphael. "On Lawful Concubinage in Athens." _Classical Antiquity_ 3 no. 1 (1984): 111-133.

Also refer to #1048, 1050, 1195.

e) Fashion/Manners

01152. Bieber, Margarete. _Entwicklungsgeschichte der griechischen Tracht_. Berlin: Mann, 1967.

01153. Heuzey, Jacques. "Le Costume féminin en Grèce à l'époque archaïque." Gazette des Beaux Arts 80 no. 1 (March 1938): 127-148.

Also refer to #1134, 1135.

f) Recreation

01154. Spears, Betty. "A Perspective of the History of Women's Sport in Ancient Greece." Journal of Sport History 11 (1984): 32-47.

g) Health/Medical

01155. Freund, Richard. "The Ethics of Abortion in Hellenistic Judaism." Helios 10 (1983): 125-137.

01156. Lloyd, G.E.R. Science, Folklore and Ideology. New York: Cambridge University Press, 1983.

[See especially part II, "The Female Sex: Medical Treatment and Biological Theories in the Fifth and Fourth Centuries B.C."]

Also refer to #1052, 1203.

6. CULTURAL

"A woman is necessarily an evil."
Menander

a) Education

01157. Cole, Susan Guettel. "Could Greek Women Read and Write?" In Reflections of Women in Antiquity, edited by Helene P. Foley, pp. 219-245. New York: Gordon and Breach Science Publishers, 1981. Also in Women's Studies 8 (1981): 129-155.

Also refer to #1173, 1405.

b) Literature

(1) Non-specific

01158. Bal, Mieke. "Sexuality, Semiosis and Binarism: A Narratological Comment on Bergren and Arthur." Arethusa 16 (Spring-Fall 1983): 117-135.
Also refer to #1159, 1205.

01159. Bergren, Ann L.T. "Language and the Female in Early Greek Thought." Arethusa 16 (Spring-Fall 1983): 69-95.

01160. Vernant, Jean-Pierre. "From Oedipus to Periander: Lameness, Tyranny, Incest in Legend and History." Arethusa 15 (Spring-Fall 1982): 19-38.

01161. Wlosok, Antonie. "Amor and Cupid." Harvard Studies in Classical Philology 79 (1975): 165-179.

(2) Philosophy

(a) Aristotle

01162. Campesi, Silvia and Gastaldi, Silvia. La Donna e i filosofi: archeologia di un'immagine culturale/testi di Platone, Aristotele, Presocratici. Bologna: Zanichelli, 1977.

01163. Clark, Stephen R. "Arsitotle's Woman." History of Political Thought 3 (1982): 177-191.

01164. Elshtain, Jean Bethke. "Aristotle, the Public-Private Split and the Case of the Suffragists." In The Family in Political Thought, pp. 51-65. Amherst, Mass.: University of Massachusetts Press, 1982.

01165. Lange, Lydia. "Woman is Not a Rational Animal: On Aristotle's Biology of Reproduction." In Discovering Reality, Feminist Perspectives on Epistemology, Metaphysics, Methodology, and Philosophy of Science, edited by Sandra Harding and Merrill B. Hintikka, pp. 1-15. Boston: D. Reidel Publishing Co., 1983.

01166. Markowski, Mieczyslaw. "Die Kommentare zum Liber de sex principiis in den mittelalterlichen Handschriften der Staatsbibliothek München." In Mélanges offerts à René Crozet, 2: 1275-1282. Poitiers: Société d'Etudes Médiévales, 1966 2: 1275-1282.

01167. Modrak, Deborah K. "Philosophy and Women in Antiquity." Rice University Studies 64 (Winter 1978): 1-11.

01168. Spelman, Elizabeth V. "Aristotle and the Politicization of the Soul." In Discovering Reality, Feminist Perspectives on Epistemology, Metaphysics, Methodology, and Philosophy of Science, edited by Sandra Harding and Merrill B. Hintikka, pp. 17-30. Boston: D. Reidel Publishing Co., 1983.

01169. Thom, Paul. "Stiff Cheese for Women." Philosophical Forum 8 (Fall 1976): 94-107.

b) Plato

01170. Canto, Monique. "The Politics of Women's Bodies: Reflections in Plato." Poetics Today 6 (1985): 275-289.

01171. Dickason, Anne. "Anatomy and Destiny: The Role of Biology in Plato's Views of Women." In Women and Philosophy: Toward a Theory of Liberation, edited by Carol C. Gould and Marx W. Wartofsky, pp. 45-53. New York: Putnam, 1976. Also in Philosophical Forum 5 (Fall-Winter 1973-1974): 45-53.

01172. DuBois, Page. "Phallocentrism and its Subversion in Plato's Phaedrus." Arethusa 18 (Spring 1985): 91-103.

01173. Lange, Lydia. "The Function of Equal Education in Plato's Republic and Laws." In The Sexism of Social and Political Theory: Woman and Reproduction from Plato to Nietzsche, edited by M.G. Clark and Lydia Lange, pp. 3-15. Toronto: University Press, 1979.

01174. Okin, Susan Moller. "Philosopher Queens and Private Wives: Plato on Women and the Family." In The Family in Political Thought, edited by Jean Bethke Elshtain, pp. 31-50. Amherst, Mass.: University of Massachusetts Press, 1982. Also in Philosophy and Public Affairs 6 (Summer 1977): 345-369.

01175. Osborne, Martha Lee. "Plato's Unchanging View of Woman: A Denial that Anatomy Spells Destiny." Philosophical Forum 6 (Summer 1975): 447-452.

01176. Smith, Janet Farrell. "Plato, Irony and Equality." Women's Studies International Forum 6 (1983): 597-607.

01177. Wender, Dorothea. "Plato: Misogynist, Paedophile, and Feminist." In Women in the Ancient World, The Arethusa Papers, edited by John Peradotto and J.P. Sullivan, pp. 213-228. Albany, N.Y.: State University of New York Press, 1984. Also in Arethusa 6 (Spring 1973): 75-90.

Also refer to #81, 1162, 1167.

(3) Drama

(a) General

01178. Case, Sue-Ellen. "Classic Drag: The Greek Creation of Female Parts." Theatre Journal 37 (October 1985): 317-327.

01179. Foley, Helene P. "The Conception of Women in Athenian Drama." In Reflections of Women in Antiquity, edited by Helene P. Foley, pp. 127-168. New York: Gordon and Breach Science Publishers, 1981.

01180. Henderson, Jeffrey. The Maculate Muse, Obscene Language in Attic Comedy. New Haven, Ct.: Yale University Press, 1975.

01181. Shaw, M. "Female Intruder: Women in Fifth Century Drama." Classical Philology 70 (October 1975): 255-266.

01182. Washington, Ida H. and Tobol, Carol E.W. "Kriemhild and Clytemnestra--Sisters in Crime or Independent Women?" In The Lost Tradition Mothers and Daughters in Literature, edited by Cathy N. Davidson and E.M. Bromer, pp. 15-21. New York: Ungar, 1980.

(b) Individuals

[1] Aeschylus

01183. Podlecki, Anthony J. "Aeschylus' Women." Helios n.s. 10 (Spring 1983): 23-47.

01184. Zeitlin, Froma I. "The Dynamics of Misogyny: Myth and Mythmaking in the Oresteia." In Women in the Ancient World, The Arethusa Papers, edited by John Peradotto and J.P. Sullivan, pp. 159-194. Albany, N.Y.: State University of New York Press, 1984. Also in Arethusa 11 (Spring and Fall 1978): 149-184.

01185. ________________. "Myth and Society: Women in Aeschylean Drama." Helios n.s. 5 (Spring 1977): 43-45.

[2] Aristophanes

01186. Henderson, Jeffrey. "Lysistrade: The Play and its Themes." Yale Classical Studies 26 (1980): 153-218.

01187. Saxonhouse, Arlene W. "Men, Women, War and Politics: Family and Polis in Aristophanes and Euripides." Political Theory 8 (1980): 65-81.

01188. Zeitlin, Froma I. "Travesties of Gender and Genre in Aristophanes' Thesmophoriazousae." In Reflections of Women in Antiquity, edited by Helene P. Foley, pp. 169-217. New York: Gordon and Breach Science Publishers, 1981. Also in Critical Inquiry 8 (Winter 1981): 301-327.

[3] Euripides

01189. Burnett, Anne. "Trojan Women and the Ganymede Ode." Yale Classical Studies 25 (1977): 291-316.

01190. Corelis, Jon. "Artemis and the Symbolism of the Hippolytos." Helios n.s. 4 (Fall 1976): 52-54.

01191. Easterling, P.E. "The Infanticide in Euripides' Medea." Yale Classical Studies 25 (1977): 177-192.

01192. Halporn, James. "The Skeptical Electra." Harvard Studies in Classical Philology 87 (1983): 101-118.

01193. Knox, B.M.W. "The Medea of Euripides." Yale Classical Studies 25 (1977): 192-226.

01194. Pippin, Anne Newton. "Euripides' Helen: A Comedy of Ideas." Classical Philology 55 (July 1960): 151-163.

01195. Segal, Charles. "The Menace of Dionysius: Sex Roles and Reversals in Euripides' Bacchae." In Women in the Ancient World, The Arethusa Papers, edited by John Peradotto and J.P. Sullivan, pp. 195-212. Albany, N.Y.: State University of New York Press, 1984. Also in Arethusa 11 (Spring and Fall 1978): 185-202 and Helios n.s. 5 (Spring 1977): 45-46.

01196. _____________. "The Two Worlds of Euripides' Helen." Transactions of the American Philological Association 102 (1971): 553-614.

01197. Sinkewicz, Thomas J. "Euripides Trojan Women: An Interpretation." Helios n.s. 6 (Spring 1978): 81-95.

01198. Solmsen, Friedrich. "Onoma and Progma in Euripides' Helen." Classical Review 48 (1934): 119-121.

01199. Vellacott, Philip. Ironic Drama, A Study of Euripides' Method and Meaning. Cambridge: Cambridge University Press, 1975.

01200. Wolff, Christian. "On Euripides' Helen." Harvard Studies in Classical Philology 77 (1973): 61-84.

01201. Zuntz, Gunther. "On Euripides' Helen: Theology and Irony." In Euripide, sept exposes et discussions, Entretiens sur l'antiquite classique, 6: 201-227. Geneva: n.p. 1960.

Also refer to #1187.

[4] Menander

01202. Macdowell, Douglas M. "Love Versus the Law: An Essay on Menander's Aspis." Greece and Rome 29 (April 1982): 42-52.

[5] Sophocles

01203. Holt, Philip. "Disease, Desire and Deianeira: A Note on the Symbolism of the Trachiniai." Helios n.s. 8 (Autumn 1981): 63-73.

(4) Poetry

(a) Individuals

[1] Hesiod

01204. Arthur, Marilyn B. "Cultural Strategies in Hesiod's Theogony: Law, Family, Society." Arethusa 15 (Spring-Fall 1982): 63-82.

01205. ________________. "The Dream of a World without Women: Poetics and the Circles of Order in the Theogony Prooemium." Arethusa 16 (Spring-Fall 1983): 97-116.

01206. Marquardt, Patricia A. "Hesiod's Ambiguous View of Woman." Classical Philology 77 (October 1982): 283-291.

01207. Olstein, Katharine. "Pandora, Dike and the History of Work in Hesiod's Works and Days." Helios n.s. 5 (Spring 1977): 37-39.

01208. Sussman, Linda Small. "Workers and Drones: Labor, Idleness and Gender Definition in Hesiod's Beehive." In Women in the Ancient World, The Arethusa Papers, edited by John Peradotto and J.P. Sullivan, pp. 79-93. Albany, N.Y.: State University of New York Press, 1984. Also in Helios n.s. 5 (Spring 1977): 39-41.

[2] Homer

01209. Arthur, Marylin B. "The Divided World of Iliad VI." In Reflections of Women in Antiquity, edited by Helene P. Foley, pp. 19-44. New York: Gordon and Breach Science Publishers, 1981. Also in Women's Studies 8 (1981): 21-46.

01210. Beye, Charles Rowan. "Male and Female in the Homeric Poems." Rasmus 3 (1974): 87-101.

01211. Bickerman, E.J. "Love Story in the Homeric Hymn to Aphrodite." Athenaeum 54 (1976): 229-254.

01212. Delebecque, Edovard. Construction de l'Odysée. Paris: Belles Lettres, 1980.

[See especially ch. 8 "Homère et les femmes," pp. 129-135.]

01213. Foley, Helene P. "'Reverse Similes' and Sex Roles in the Odyssey." In Women in the Ancient World, The Arethusa Papers, edited by John Peradotto and J.P. Sullivan, pp. 59-78. Albany, N.Y.: State University of New York Press, 1984. Also in Arethusa 11 (Spring and Fall 1978): 7-26.

01214. King, Katherine Cullen. "Achilles Amator." Viator 16 (1985): 21-64.

01215. Schadewalt, Wolfgang. Von Homers Welt und Werk. Leipzig: Koehler & Amelang, 1944.

01216. Scheinberg, Susan. "The Bee Maidens of the Homeric Hymn to Hermes." Harvard Studies in Classical Philology 83 (1979): 1-28.

01217. Wickert-Micknat, G. Die Frau. Gottingen: Vandenhoeck und Ruprecht, 1982.

[3] Others

01218. Cameron, Alan. "Asclepiades' Girl Friends." In Reflections of Women in Antiquity, edited by Helene P. Foley, pp. 275-302. New York: Gordon and Breach Science Publishers, 1981.

01219. Carson, Anne. "Wedding at Noon in Pindar's Ninth Pythian." Greek, Roman and Byzantine Studies 23 (Summer 1982): 121-128.

01220. Cohen, Shayne J.D. "The Beauty of Flora and the Beauty of Sarai." Helios n.s. 8 (Autumn 1981): 41-53.

01221. Foley, Helene P. "Sex and State in Ancient Greece." Diacritics 5 (Winter 1975): 31-36.

01222. Gans, Eric. "The Birth of the Lyric Self: From Feminine to Masculine." Helios n.s. 8 (Spring 1981): 33-47.

01223. Griffin, Allen N.F. "Unrequited Love: Polyphemus and Galatea in Ovid's Metamorphoses." Greece and Rome 2nd ser. 30 (October 1983): 190-197.

01224. Griffiths, Frederick T. "Home before Lunch: The Emancipated Woman in Theocritus." In Reflections of Women in Antiquity, edited by Helene P. Foley, pp. 247-273. New York: Gordon and Breach Science Publishers, 1981.

01225. Ziegler, Konrat. "Kallimachos und die Frauen." Die Antike 13 (1937): 20-42.

Also refer to #1053, 1315.

(b) Women Poets

[1] Erinna

01226. Arthur, Marylin B. "The Tortoise and the Mirror: Erinna PSI 1090." Classical World 74 (1980): 53-65.

01227. Levin, Donald Norman. "Quaestiones Erinneanae." Harvard Classical Studies in Classical Philology 66 (1962): 193-204.

01228. Pomeroy, Sarah B. "Supplementary Notes on Erinna." Zeitschift Papyrologie und Epigraphik 32 (1978): 17-22.

Also refer to #1240.

[2] Sappho

01229. Devereux, George. "The Nature of Sappho's Seizure in Fr. 31 LP as Evidence of her Inversion." Classical Quarterly n.s. 20 (1970): 17-31.

01230. DuBois, Page. "Sappho and Helen." In Women in the Ancient World, The Arethusa Papers, edited by John Peradotto and J.P. Sullivan, pp. 95-105. Albany, N.Y.: State University of New York Press, 1984. Also in Arethusa 11 (Spring and Fall 1978): 89-99.

01231. Lanata, Giuliana. "Sul linguaggio amoroso di Saffo." Quaderni Urbanita di Cultura Classica 2 (1966): 63-79.

01232. Manieri, Fiavio. "Saffo: appunti di metodologia generale per un approccio psichiatrico." Quaderni Urbinati di Cultura Classica 14 (1972): 46-64.

01233. Merkelbach, Reinhold. "Sappho und ihr Kreis." Philologus 101 (1957): 1-29.

01234. Schadewaldt, Wolfgang. Sappho: Welt und Dichtung: Dasein in der Liebe. Potsdam: E. Stichnote, 1950.

01235. Sellman, Jane. "Sappho." Women: A Journal of Liberation 3.2 (1972): 24-25.

01236. Stigers, Eva Stehle. "Retreat from the Male: Catullus 62 and Sappho's Erotic Flowers." Ramus 6 (1977): 83-102.

01237. __________________. "Sappho's Private World." In Reflections of Women in Antiquity, edited by Helene P. Foley, pp. 45-61. New York: Gordon and Breach Science Publishers, 1981. Also in Women's Studies 8 (1981): 47-63.

01238. Winkler, Jack. "Gardens of Nymphs: Public and Private in Sappho's Lyrics." In Reflections of Women in Antiquity, edited by Helene P. Foley, pp. 63-89. New York: Gordon and Breach Science Publishers, 1981. Also in Women's Studies 8 (1981): 65-91.

[3] Others

01239. Segal, Charles P. "Pebbles in Golden Urns: The Date and Style of Corinna." Eranos 73 (1975): 1-8.

01240. Wiggers, Nancy. "Sexual Stereotypes in the Writings of Four Greek Women." Helios n.s. 4 (Fall 1976): 50-52.

(5) Other Works

(a) Herodotus

01241. Dewald, Carolyn. "Women and Culture in Herodotus' Histories." In Reflections of Women in Antiquity, edited by Helene P. Foley, pp. 91-125. New York: Gordon and Breach Science Publishers, 1981. Also in Women's Studies 8 (1981): 93-127.

01242. Roselline, Michele and Said, Suzanne. "Usages des femmes et autres nomoi chez les 'sauvages' d'Herodote: essai de lecture structurale." Annali della Scuoloa Normale Superiore di Pisa 8 (1978): 949-1005.

(b) Plutarch

01243. Bremmer, J. "Plutarch and the Naming of Greek Women." American Journal of Philology 102 (Winter 1981): 425-426.

01244. Goessler, Lisette. Plutarchs Gedanken über die Ehe. Zurich: Buchdrückerei Berichthaus, 1962.

01245. Le Corsu, France. Plutarque et les femmes dans les vies paralleles. Paris: Les Belles Lettres, 1981.

01246. Plutarch. Selected Essays: On Love, the Family, and the Good Life. New York: Mentor Books, 1957.

Also refer to #1013.

(c) Thucydides

01247. Harvey, David. "Women in Thucydides." Arethusa 18 (Spring 1985): 67-90.

(d) Xenophon

01248. Oost, S.I. "Xenophon's Attitude Toward Women." Classical World 71 (1977): 225-236.

c) Art and Artifacts

(1) Women in Art

01249. Blümel, C. "Attisches Frauenköpfchen." Deutsches Archaologisches Institut Jahrbuch 51 (1936): 154-157.

01250. Cameron, Alan. "Notes on Erotic Art of Rufinus." Greek, Roman and Byzantine Studies 22 (Summer 1981): 179-186.

01251. Coates, Irene. "The Taming of the Bull." Architectural Design 45 (August 1975): 461-462.

01252. Edenbaum, R.I. "Panthea: Lucian and Ideal Beauty." Journal of Aesthetics 25 (Fall 1966): 65-70.

01253. Havelock, Christine Mitchell. "Mourners on Greek Vases: Remarks on the Social History of Women." In Feminism and Art History: Questioning the Litany, edited by Norma Broude and Mary D. Garrard, pp. 44-61. New York: Harper and Row, 1982.

01254. Kunze-Götte, Erika. Frauengemachbilder in der Vasenmalerei des fünften Jahrhunderts. Munich: Uni-Druk, 1957.

01255. McNally, Sheila. "The Maenad in Early Greek Art." In Women in the Ancient World, The Arethusa Papers, edited by John Peradotto and J.P. Sullivan, pp. 107-141. Albany, N.Y.: State University of New York Press, 1984. Also in Arethusa 11 (Spring and Fall 1978): 101-135.

01256. Richter, Gisela Marie Augusta. Korai: Archaic Greek Maidens. London: Phaidon, 1968.

01257. Scully, Vincent. "The Great Goddess and the Palace Architecture of Crete." In Feminism and Art History: Questioning the Litany, edited by Norma Broude and Mary D. Garrard, pp. 32-43. New York: Harper and Row, 1982.

01258. Williams, Dyfri. "Women on Athenian Vases: Problems of Interpretation." In Images of Women in Antiquity, edited by Averil Cameron and Amelie Kuhrt, pp. 92-106. Detroit: Wayne State University Press, 1983.

(2) Women Artists

01259. Kampen, Natalie Boymeel. "Hellenistic Artists: Female." Archeologie Classica 27 (1975): 9-17.

C. ROME

1. SURVEYS

> "Our ancestors did not want women to conduct any--not even private--business without a guardian; they wanted them to be under the authority of parents, brothers, or husbands; we (God help us!) even now let them snatch at the government and meddle in the Forum and our assemblies."
>
> Cato the Elder quoted in Livy

01260. Clark, Gillian. "Roman Women." Greece and Rome 2nd ser. 28 (October 1981): 193-212.

01261. Ferrero, Guglielmo. The Nastiest Women in Ancient Rome. Albuquerque, N.M.: Gloucester Art, 1979.

01262. Herrin, Judith. "In Search of Byzantine Women: Three Avenues of Approach." In _Images of Women in Antiquity_, edited by Averil Cameron and Amélie Kuhrt, pp. 167-189. Detroit: Wayne State University Press, 1983.

01263. Ide, Arthur Frederick. _Woman in Ancient Rome_. Mesquite, Tex.: Ide House, 1981.

01264. Pelletier, Andre. _La Femme dans la société gallo-romaine_. Paris: Picard, 1984.

01265. Pomeroy, Sarah B. "Women in Roman Egypt. A Preliminary Study Based on Papyri." In _Reflections of Women in Antiquity_, edited by Helene P. Foley, pp. 303-322. New York: Gordon and Breach Science Publishers, 1981.

01266. Warren, Larissa Bonfante. "The Women of Etruria." In _Women in the Ancient World, The Arethusa Papers_, edited by John Peradotto and J.P. Sullivan, pp. 229-239. Albany, N.Y.: State University of New York Press, 1984. Also in _Arethusa_ 6 (Spring 1973): 91-101.

2. MATRIARCHY

"Let us improve the status of women and reject the patriarchal notion of the degradation of nature."

Sherry Ortner

01267. Weisweiler, Josef. "Die Stellung der Frau bei den Kelten und das Problem des keltisches Mutterrechts." _Zeitschrift fur celtische Philologie_ 21 (1940): 205-279.

3. POLITICAL

"When a freed woman is living in concubinage with her patron, she can leave him without his consent, and unite with another man either in matrimony or in concubinage."

Ulpianus

a) Generic

01268. Dixon, Suzanne. "A Family Business: Women's Role in Patronage and Politics at Rome 80-44 B.C." _Classica et Mediaevalia_ 34 (1983): 91-112.

01269. MacMullen, Ramsay. "Woman in Public in the Roman Empire." _Historia Zeitschrift fur Alte Geschichte_ 29 (1980): 208-218.

01270. Raepsaet-Charlier, Marie-Therese. "Epouses et familles de magistrats dans les provinces romaines aux deux premiers siecles de l'empire." _Historia Zeitschrift fur Alte Geschichte_ 31 (1982): 56-69.

b) Legal

01271. Castillo, Arcadio del. La emancipacion de la mujer romana en el siglo I D. C. Granada: Universidad, Secretariado de Publicaciones y Departamento de Historia Antigua, 1976.

01272. Jolowicz, H.F. "Marriage." In The Roman Law Reader, edited by F. H. Lawson, pp. 49-53. Dobbs Ferry, N.Y.: Oceana Publications, 1969.

01273. Marshall, Anthony J. "The Case of Valeria: An Inheritance-Dispute in Roman Asia." Classical Quarterly 25 (1975): 82-87.

01274. Nelli, Simonetta. Lo scioglimento del matrimonio nella storia del diritto italiano. Milan: A. Giuffre, 1976.

01275. Odier, Pierre Gabriel. Droit romain. Empêchements au mariage. Paris: Librairie Nouvelle de Droit et de jurisprudence, 1890.

01276. Schafik, Allam. "Eheschliessung und Scheidung in Altagypten." Altertum 29 (1983): 117-123.

01277. Sirks, A.J.B. "A Favour to Rich Freed Women (libertinae) in 51 A.D. on Sue. Cl. and the Lex Papia." Revue internationale des droite de l'antiquité 27 (1980): 283-294.

01278. Treggiari, Susan. "Consent to Roman Marriage: Some Aspects of Law and Reality." Classical Views 1 (1982): 34-44.

01279. Ward, John O. "Women, Witchcraft, and Social Patterning in the Later Roman Lawcodes." Prudentia 13 (1981): 99-118.

01280. Zannini, Pierluigi. Studi sulla tutela mulierum. Turin: G. Giappichelli, 1976.

c) Feminism

01281. Sirago, V.A. Femminismo a Roma nel Primo Impero. Catanzaro: Rubbettino Editore, 1983.

d) Political Roles

(1) Cleopatra

01282. Benoist-Mechin, Jacques Gabriel Paul Michel. Cleopatre. Lausanne: Clairefontaine, 1973.

01283. Cowherd, Carrie. "Cleopatra: Portrait of a Queen and Mistress." Augustan Age 3 (1983-1984): 13-25.

01284. Griffin, Jasper. "Propertius and Antony." Journal of Roman Studies 67 (1977): 12-26.

01285. Pablon, Stanley J. "Julius Caesar: The Political Uses of Sex." Medical Aspects of Human Sexuality 5 (October 1971): 84-107.

(2) Galla Placidia

01286. Burckhardt, Felix. "Galla Placidia." Schweizerische Rundschau 25 (1925-1926): 409-419; 481-489.

01287. Caffin, Philippe. Galla Placidia. Paris: Perrin, 1977.

01288. Storoni Mazzolani, Lidia. Galla Placidia. Milan: BUR, 1981.

(3) Others

01289. Braund, D.C. "Berenice in Rome." Historia Zeitschrift fur Alte Geschichte 33 (1984): 120-123.

01290. Cameron, Alan. "The Empress and the Pact: Paganism and Politics at the Court of Theodosius II." Yale Classical Studies 27 (1982): 217-290.

01291. Carp, Teresa. "Two Matrons of the Late Republic." In Reflections of Women in Antiquity, edited by Helene P. Foley, pp. 343-354. New York: Gordon and Breach Science Publishers, 1981. Also in Women's Studies 8(1981): 189-200.

01292. Castritius, Helmut. "Zu den Frauen der Flavier." Historia Zeitschrift fur Alte Geschichte 18 (1969): 492-502.

01293. Daube, David. "The Marriage of Justinian and Theodora Legal and Theological Reflections." Catholic University Law Review 16 (1966-1967): 380-399.

01294. Fisher, Elizabeth A. "Theodora and Antonina in the Historia Arcana: History and/or Fiction?" In Women in the Ancient World, The Arethusa Papers, edited by John Peradotto and J.P. Sullivan, pp. 287-313. Albany, N.Y.: State University of New York, 1984. Also in Arethusa 11 (Spring and Fall 1978): 253-279.

01295. Flory, Marleen Boudreau. "Sic exempla parantur: Livia's Shrine to Concordia and the Porticus Liviae." Historia Zeitschrift fur Alte Geschichte 33 (1984): 309-330.

01296. Giacosa, Giorgio. Portraits of the Women of the Caesars. Translated by R. Ross Holloway. Monclair, New Jersey: Allanheld and Schram, 1977.

01297. Halley, Shelly P. "The Five Wives of Pompey the Great." Greece and Rome 32 (April 1985): 49-60.

01298. Holum, Kenneth G. Theodosian Empresses: Women and Imperial Dominion in Late Antiquity. Berkeley, Ca.: University of California Press, 1982.

01299. Humphrey, John. "The Three Daughters of Agrippina Maior." American Journal of Ancient History 4 (1979): 125-143.

01300. Linderski, Jerzy. "The Mother of Livia Augusta and the Aufidii Lurcones of the Republic." Historia Zeitschrift fur Alte Geschichte 33 (1974): 462-480.

01301. McDermott, William C. "Plotina Augusta and Nicomachus of Gervasia." Historia Zeitschrift fur Alte Geschichte 26 (1977): 192-203.

01302. Mazzei, Francesco. Messalina, Milan: Rusconi, 1983.

01303. Merriman, Joseph Francis. "The Empress Helena and the Aqua Augustea." Archeologia Classica 29 (1977): 436-446.

01304. Nicols, John. "Antonia and Sejanus." Historia Zeitschrift fur Alte Geschichte 24 (1975): 48-58.

01305. Rapke, Terence T. "Julia and C. Proculeius: A Note on Suetonius Augustus 63.2." Liverpool Classical Monthly 9 (1984): 21-22.

01306. Skinner, Marilyn B. "Clodia Metelli." Transactions of the American Philological Association 113 (1983): 273-287.

01307. Syme, Ronald. "Princesses and Others in Tacitus." Greece and Rome 28 (April 1981): 40-52.

01308. Wiseman, T.P. "The Wife and Children of Romulus." Classical Quarterly 33 (1983): 445-452.

4. ECONOMIC

> "Women are not only frail and easily tired, relax control, and they become ferocious, ambitious schemers, circulating among the soldiers, ordering company-commanders about."
>
> Aulus Caecina Severus

01309. Hobson, Deborah. "Women as Property Owners in Roman Egypt." Transactions of the American Philological Association 113 (1983): 311-321.

01310. Kampen, N. Image and Status: Roman Working Women in Ostia. Berlin: Mann, 1981.

01311. Treggiari, Susan. "Jobs in the Household of Livia." Papers. British School of Rome 43 (1975): 48-77.

01312. Treggiari, Susan. "Questions on Women Domestics in the Roman West." Schiavitù, manomissione e classi dipendenti nel mondo antico (Università degli studi di Padova pubblicazioni dell'istituto di storia antica) 13 (1979): 185-201.

5. RELIGION/MYTHOLOGY

"It is good for a man not to touch a woman..."
St. Paul

a) Goddesses

01313. Bryce, T.R. "The Arrival of the Goddess Leto in Lycia." Historia Zeitschrift für Alte Geschichte 32 (1983): 1-13.

01314. Dunand, Françoise. "Le statut des hiereiai en Égypte romaine." In Hommages à Maarten J. Vermaseren, edited by M. B. de Boer and T. A. Edridge, 1: 352-374. Leiden: Brill 1978.

01315. Porte, Danielle. "Claudia Quinta et le probleme de la lavatio de Cybele en 204 av. J.C." Klio 66 (1984): 93-103.

01316. Salzman, M. Renee. "Magna Mater: Great Mother of the Roman Empire." In The Book of the Goddess, Past and Present: An Introduction to Her Religion, edited by Carl Olson, pp. 60-67. New York: Crossroad Publishing Co., 1983.

Also refer to #1016, 1024.

b) Vestal Virgins

01317. Carettoni, Gianfilippo. "La domus virginum Vestalium e la domus publica del periodo repubblicano." Rendiconti della Pontificia Accademia di Archeologia 51-52 (1979-1980): 325-355.

c) Jews

01318. Davies, Eryl. "Inheritance Rights and the Hebrew Levirate Marriage." Vetus Testament 31 (1981): 138-144, 257-268.

Also refer to #1031.

d) Early Christianity

(1) Non-specific

01319. Bal, Mieke. "Sexuality, Sin and Sorrow: The Emergence of the Female Character (A Reading of Genesis 1-3)." Poetics Today 6 (1985): 21-42.

01320. Boucher, Madeleine, et al. "Women and Priestly Ministry: The New Testament Evidence." Catholic Biblical Quarterly 41 (1979): 608-613.

01321. Brooten, Bernadette. "Junia . . . Outstanding Among the Apostles (Romans 16:7)." In Women Priests, A Catholic Commentary on the Vatican Declaration, edited by Leonard Swidler and Arlene Swidler, pp. 141-144. New York: Paulist Press, 1977.

01322. Bullough, Vern L. "Introduction: The Christian Inheritance." In Sexual Practices and the Medieval Church, edited by Vern L. Bullough and James Brundage, pp. 1-12. Buffalo, N.Y.: Prometheus Books, 1982.

01323. Cameron, Averil. "'Neither Male nor Female.'" Greece and Rome 2nd ser. 27 (April 1980): 60-68.

01324. Crouzel, Henri. "Divorce et remariage dans l'Eglise primitive." Nouvelle revue théologique 98 (December 1976): 891-917.

01325. D'Angelo, Mary Rose. "Women and the Earliest Church: Reflecting on the Problematique of Christ and Culture." In Women Priests, A Catholic Commentary on the Vatican Declaration, edited by Leonard Swidler and Arlene Swidler, pp. 191-201. New York: Paulist Press, 1977.

01326. Fiorenza, Elizabeth Schussler. "The Apostleship of Women in Early Christianity." In Women Priests, A Catholic Commentary on the Vatican Declaration, edited by Leonard Swidler and Arlene Swidler, pp. 135-140. New York: Paulist Press, 1977.

01327. ______________. "The Study of Women in Early Christianity: Some Methodological Considerations." In Critical History and Biblical Faith: New Testament Perspectives, edited by J. T. Ryan, pp. 30-58. Villanova: College Theology Society, 1979.

01328. ______________. "Women Apostles: The Testament of Scripture." In Women and Catholic Priesthood, edited by AM. Gardiner, pp. 94-102. New York: Paulist Press, 1976.

01329. ______________. "Word, Spirit and Power: Women in Early Christian Communities." In Women of Spirit, edited by Rosemary Ruether and Eleanor McLaughlin, 29-70. New York: Simon and Schuster, 1979.

01330. Foucault, Michel. "The Battle for Chastity." In Western Sexuality, edited by Philippe Aries and Andre Bejin, pp. 14-25. New York: Blackwell, 1985.

01331. Griffe, Elie. "Le Concile d'Elvire devant le remariage des femmes." Bulletin de la littérature ecclesiastique 75 (July-September 1974): 210-214.

01332. Gryson, Roger. The Ministry of Women in the Early Church. Collegeville, Minn.: Liturgical Press, 1976.

01333. Hirst, Desirée. "The Catholic Concept of the Feminine." Bucknell Review 24 (Spring 1978): 60-71.

01334. Ide, Arthur Frederick. Woman in Early Christianity and Christian Society. Mesquite Tex.: Ide House, 1980.

01335. ____________________. Woman in the Apostolic Age. Mesquite, Tex.: Ide House, 1981.

01336. ____________________ and Ide, Charles A. Woman in the Age of Christian Martyrs. Mesquite, Tex.: Ide House, 1980.

01337. Koch, Hugo. Virgines Christi, die Gelübde der gottgeweihten Jungfrauen in den ersten drei Jahrhunderten. Leipzig: J.C. Hinrichs, 1907.

01338. Kötting, Bernhard. Der Zolibat in der alten Kirche. Munster: Verlag Aschendorff, 1968.

01339. Kraemer, R. "The Conversion of Women to Ascetic Forms of Christianity." Signs 6 (1980): 298-307.

01340. Labriolle, P. de. "Le mariage spirituel dans l'antiquité chrétienne." Revue historique 137 (1921): 204-225.

01341. McNamara, Jo Ann. "Muffled Voices: The Lives of Consecrated Women in the Fourth Century." In Medieval Religious Women, vol. 1, Distant Echoes, edited by John A. Nichols and Lilliam Thomas. 11-29. Kalamazoo, Mich.: Cistereian Publications, 1984.

01342. ________________. A New Song: Celibate Christian Women in the First Three Centuries. New York: Institute for Research in History, 1983.

01343. Munier, Charles. "Divorce, remariage et penitence dans l'église primitive." Revue des sciences religieuses 52 (April 1978): 97-117.

01344. Ruether, Rosemary. "Mothers of the Church: Ascetic Women in the Late Patristic Age." In Women of Spirit, edited by Rosemary Ruether and Eleanor McLaughlin, pp. 71-98. New York: Simon and Schuster, 1979.

01345. ________________. "Patristic Spirituality and the Experience of Women in the Early Church." In Western Spirituality: Historical Roots, Ecumenical Routes, edited by Matthew Fox, pp. 164-192. Santa Fe, N.M.: Bear and Co., Inc., 1981.

01346. Weiser, Alfons, SAL. "Die Rolle der Frau in der urchristlichen Mission." In Die Frau im Urchristentum, edited by Gerhard Dautzenberg, et al., pp. 158-181. Freiburg: Herder, 1983.

01347. Wilson-Kastner, Patricia, et al., A Lost Tradition: Women Writers of the Early Church. Lanham, Md.: University Press of America, 1981.

Also refer to #1274, 1396, 1403.

(2) St. Paul

01348. Achelis, Hans. Virgines subintroductae. Leipzig: J.C. Hinrichs, 1902.

01349. Ariès, Philippe. "St. Paul and the Flesh." In Western Sexuality, edited by Philippe Ariès and André Béjin, pp. 36-39. New York: Blackwell, 1985.

01350. Fiorenza, Elizabeth Schussler. "Women in the Pre-Pauline and Pauline Churches." Union Seminary Quarterly Review 33 (1978): 153-166.

01351. Hurley, James B. "Did Paul Require Veils or the Silence of Women? A Consideration of I Corinthians 11:2-16 and I Corinthians 14:33b-36." Westminster Theological Journal 35 (1973): 190-220.

01352. Pagels, Elaine. "Paul and Women: A Response to Recent Discussion." Journal of the American Academy of Religion 42 (September 1974): 538-549.

01353. Scroggs, Robin. "Paul and the Eschatological Woman: Revisited." Journal of the American Academy of Religion 42 (September 1974): 532-537.

01354. Walker, William O., Jr. "1 Corinthians 11: 2-16 and Paul's Views Regarding Women." Journal of Biblical Literature 94 (March 1975): 94-110.

Refer also to #184, 190, 198, 242.

(3) Fathers of the Church

(a) General

01355. Crouzel, Henri. "Le remariage après separation pour adultère selon les Peres latins." Bulletin de la littérature ecclesiastique 75 (July-September 1974): 189-204.

01356. Koch, Hugo. Virgo Eva-Virgo Maria: Neue Untersuchungen über die Lehre von der Jungfrauschaft und der Ehe Mariens in der ältesten Kirche. Berlin: W. de Gruyter, 1937.

01357. Osiek, Carolyn. "The Church Fathers and the Ministry of Women." In Women Priests, A Catholic Commentary on the Vatican Declaration, edited by Leonard Swidler and Arlene Swidler, pp. 75-80. New York: Paulist Press, 1977.

(b) Individuals

[1] St. Augustine

01358. Børresen, Kari Elisabeth. Subordination and Equivalence: The Nature and Role of Women in Augustine and Thomas Aquinas. Washington, D.C.: University Press of American, 1981.

01359. Hultgren, Gunnar. Le Commandment d'amour chez Augustine. Interprètation philosophique et théologique d'après les éscrits de la periode. Paris: Vrin, 1939.

[2] St. Tertullian

01360. Crouzel, Henri. "Deux textes de Tertullien concernant la procedure et les rites du mariage chretien." Bulletin de littérature ecclesiastique. 74(January-March 1973): 3-13.

Also refer to #1356.

(4) Saints/Religious Women

01361. Brester, Paul G. "The Legend of St. Marcella, Virgin Martyr." Western Folklore 16 (1957): 179-183.

01362. Cross, J.E. "Euphemia and the Ambrosian Missal." Notes and Queries n.s. 30 (February 1983): 18-22.

01363. Gavigan, John J. "The Mother of St. Augustine." American Ecclesiastical Review 119 (October 1948): 254-280.

01364. Gerontius. The Life of Melania the Younger. Translated by Elizabeth Clark. New York: Edwin Mellen Press, 1984.

01365. Luckett, Richard. "St. Cecilia and Music." Proceedings of the Royal Music Association 99 (1972-1973): 15-30.

01366. McNamara, JoAnn. "Cornelia's Daughters: Paula and Eustochium." Women's Studies 11 (1984): 9-27.

01367. Marchi, Luigi de. Sant 'Agnese, vergine e martire. Alba: Pia società san Paolo, 1941.

01368. Tervarent, Guy de. "Contribution to the Iconography of Saint Catherine." Gazette des Beaux Arts 85 no. 1 (May 1943): 308-310.

01369. Vogt, Josef. "Helena Augusta, the Cross and the Jews. Some Enquiries about the Mother of Constantine the Great." Classical Folia 31 (1977): 135-151. Also in Saeculum 27 (1976): 211-222.

6. SOCIAL

"He who loves his wife too passionately destroys the marriage."

St. Jerome

a) Generic

01370. Balsdon, D. "Der Alltag der Frau im alten Rom." Antike Welt 10 (1979): 40-56.

01371. Herzig, H. E. "Frauen in Ostia. Ein Beitrag zur Sozialgeschichte der Hafenstadt Roms." Historia Zeitschrift fur Alte Geschichte 32 (1983): 77-92.

01372. MacMullen, Ramsay. Roman Social Relations, 50 B.C. to A. D. 284. New Haven: Yale University Press, 1981.

01373. Porter, J. R. "The Daughters of Lot." Folklore 89 (1978): 127-141.

01374. Treble, Henry Arthur and King, K.M. Everyday Life in Rome in the Time of Caesar and Cicero. Oxford: Clarendon Press, 1930.

b) Demography

01375. Salmon, Pierre. Population de depopulation dans l'Empire romain. Brussels: Latomus, 1974.

Also refer to #1395.

c) Family

01376. Africa, Thomas. "The Mask of an Assassin: A Psychohistorical Study of M. Junius Brutus." Journal of Interdisciplinary History 8 (1978): 599-626.

01377. Franciosi, Gennaro. Clan gentilizio e strutture monogamiche: contributo alla storia della famiglia romana. Naples: Jovene, 1978.

01378. Hallett, Judith P. Fathers and Daughters in Roman Society: Women and the Elite Family. Princeton, N.J.: University Press, 1984.

01379. Kepartová, Jana. "Kinder in Pompeji. Eine epigraphische Untersuchung." Klio 66, no. 1 (1984): 192-209.

01380. Lacombe, Paul. La famille dans la société romaine. Paris: Lecrosnier et Babé, 1889.

01381. Phillips, Jane E. "Roman Mothers and the Lives of Their Adult Daughters." Helios n.s. 6 (Spring 1978): 69-80.

01382. Plescia, Joseph. "Patria Potestas and the Roman Revolution." In The Conflict of Generations in Ancient Greece and Rome, edited by Stephan Bertman, pp. 143-169. Amsterdam: Gruner, 1976.

01383. Wallace, Kristine Gilmartin. "Kinship Terms in Tacitus." Helios n.s. 5 (Fall 1977): 56-59.

Also refer to #1042.

d) Marriage

01384. Blockely, R. C. "Roman Barbarian Marriages in the Late Empire." Florilegium 4 (1982): 63-79.

01385. Bonfante, Larissa. "Etruscan Couples and the Aristocratic Society." In Reflections of Women in Antiquity, edited by Helene P. Foley, pp. 323-342. New York: Gordon and Breach Science Publishers, 1981. Also in Women's Studies 8 (1981): 157-187.

01386. Bush, Archie C. and McHugh, Joseph J. "Patterns of Roman Marriage." Ethnology 14 (January 1975): 25-45.

01387. Nisbet, R.G.M. "Felicitas at Surrentum (Statius, Silvae, II.2)." Journal of roman Studies 68 (1978): 1-11.

01388. Richlin, Amy. "Approaches to the Sources on Adultery at Rome." In Reflections of Women in Antiquity, edited by Helene P. Foley, pp. 379-404. New York: Gordon and Breach Science Publishers, 1981. Also in Women's Studies 8 (1981): 225-250.

01389. Rokbach, August. Untersuchungen über die römische Ehe. Stuttgart: Carl Mäcken, 1853.

01390. Treggiari, Susan. "Contubernales in CIL 6." Phoenix 35 (Spring 1981): 42-69.

Also refer to #1043, 1044, 1089, 1270, 1272, 1274-1276, 1278, 1318, 1324, 1331, 1343, 1355, 1360, 1403, 1411.

e) Sex Life and Morals

01391. Adams, J. N. The Latin Sexual Vocabulary. London: Duckworth, 1982.

01392. MacMullen, Ramsay. "Roman Attitudes to Greek Love." Historia Zeitschrift für Alte Geschichte 31 (1982): 484-502.

01393. Treggiari, Susan. "Concubinae." Papers of the British School at Rome 49 (1981): 59-81.

Also refer to #1048, 1050, 1322, 1413, 1423.

f) Fashion/Manners

01394. Sichel, Marion. Costume Reference 1. Roman Britain and the Middle Ages. Boston: Plays Inc., 1977.

g) Health/Medical

01395. Frier, Bruce. "Roman Life Expectancy: Ulpian's Evidence." Harvard Studies in Classical Philology 86 (1982): 213-251.

01396. Gorman, Michael J. Abortion and the Early Church: Christian, Jewish and Pagan Attitudes in the Greco-Roman World. Downers Grove, IL: Intervarsity Press, c1982.

01397. McDaniel, Walton Brooks. "The Medical and Magical Significance in Ancient Medicine of Things Connected with Reproduction and Its Organs." Journal of the History of Medicine 3 (Autumn 1948): 525-546.

Also refer to #1052.

h) Burial Customs

01398. Flory, Marleen Boudreau. "Where Women Precede Men: Factors Influencing the Order of Names in Roman Epitaphs." Classical Journal 79, no. 3 (1984): 216-224.

01399. Gabelmann, Hanns. Die Werkstattgruppen der oberitalischen Sarkophage. Bonn: Rheinland-Verlag 1973.

01400. Kleiner, D. E. E. Roman Group Portraiture. The Funerary Reliefs of the Late Republic and Early Empire. New York: Garland Publishing, 1978.

01401. Mansulli, Guido Achille. Le stele romano del territorio ravennate e del Basso Po. Ravenna: A. Longo, 1967.

01402. Shaw, Brent D. "Latin Funery Epigraphy and Family Life in the Later Roman Empire." Historia Zeitschrift fur Alte Geschichte 34 (1984): 457-497.

01403. Testini, Pasquale. "Aspetti di vita matrimonia--le in intiche iscrizione funerarie cristiane." Lateranum 42 (1976): 150-164.

01404. Zanker, P. "Grabreliefs romischer Freigelassner." Jahrbuch Deutschen Archeologischen Instituts 90 (1975): 267-315.

7. CULTURAL

"The golden hair that Galla wears
Is hers; who would have thought it?
She swears 'tis hers, and true she swears,
For I know where she bought it."
Martial

a) Generic

01405. Gilleland, M. E. "Female Speech in Greek and Latin." American Journal of Philology 101 (Summer 1980): 180-183.

01406. Pascal, H. Education et culture de la femme romaine a la fin de la Republique. Abbeville: Imprimerie F. Paillart, 1916.

Also refer to #1365.

b) Literature

(1) Non-Specific

01407. Hallett, Judith P. "Rapacious and Licentious Soldiery: Perusinae Glandes and Augustus' Beseiged Mentula." Helios n.s. 4 (Fall 1976): 57-58.

(2) Drama

01408. Johnston, Patricia A. "Poenulus I, 2 and Roman Women." Transactions and Proceedings of the American Philological Association 110 (1980): 143-159.

01409. Schuhmann, Elisabeth. "Zur sozialen Stellung der Frau in den Komodien des Plautus." Altertum 24 (1978): 97-105.

(3) Poetry

(a) Women in Poetry

01410. Luck, Georg. "The Woman's Role in Latin Love Poetry." In Perspectives of Roman Poetry, edited by G. Karl Galinsky, pp. 15-31. Austin: University of Texas Press, 1974.

(b) Poets

[1] Catullus

01411. Badian, E. "The Case of the Door's Marriage (Catullus 67.6)." Harvard Studies in Classical Philology 84 (1980): 81-89.

Also refer to #1236.

[2] Martial

01412. Watson, L. C. "Three Women in Martial." Classical Quarterly 33 (1983): 258-264.

[3] Ovid

01413. Curran, Leo C. "Rape and Rape Victims in the Metamorphoses." In Women in the Ancient World, The Arethusa Papers, edited by John Peradotto and J. P. Sullivan, pp. 263-286. Albany, N.Y.: State University of New York, 1984. Also in Arethusa 11 (Spring-Fall 1978): 213-241.

01414. Fantham, Elaine. "Sexual Comedy in Ovid's Fasti: Sources and Motivation." Harvard Studies in Classical Philology 87 (1983): 185-216.

01415. Picklesimer, Maria Luisa. "Proserpina: La image de la heroina jouen en las "Metamorfosis" de Ovidio." Arbor 94 (July-August 1976): 37-46.

Also refer to #1053, 1223, 1315.

[4] Virgil

01416. Fantham, Elaine. "Virgil's Dido and Seneca's Tragic Heroines." Greece and Rome 22 (April 1975): 1-10.

01417. Perkell, Christine G. "On Creusa, Dido and the Quality of Victory in Virgil's Aeneid." In Reflections of Women in Antiquity, edited by Helene P. Foley, pp. 355-377. New York: Gordon and Breach Science Publishers, 1981. Also in Women's Studies 8 (1981): 201-223.

(c) Woman Poet

01418. Santirocco, Matthew S. "Sulpicia Reconsidered." Classical Journal 74 (1979): 229-239.

(4) Elegy

01419. Allen, Archibald W. "Elegy and the Classical Attitude Toward Love: Propertius I:1." Yale Classical Studies 11 (1950): 255-277.

01420. Hallett, Judith P. "The Role of Women in Roman Elegy: Counter-Culture Feminism." In Women in the Ancient World, The Arethusa Papers, edited by John Peradotto and J. P. Sullivan, pp. 241-262. Albany, N.Y.: State University of New York, 1984. Also in Arethusa 6 (1973): 103-124 and 7 (1974): 211-219.

01421. King, Joy K. "Sophistication versus Chastity in Propertius' Latin Love Elegy." Helios n.s. 4 (Fall 1976): 69-76.

01422. Lilja, Sara. The Roman Elegist's Attitude to Women. 1965. Reprint. New York: Garland Publishers, 1978.

(5) Prose

01423. Bird, H.W. "Aurelius Victor on Women and Sexual Morality." Classical Journal 77 (October-November 1982): 44-48.

01424. Philippides, S. N. "Narrative Strategies and Ideology in Livy's 'Rape of Lucretia.'" Helios 10 (1983): 113-119.

01425. Richlin, Amy. "Invective Against Women in Roman Satire." Arethusa 17 (Spring 1984): 67-80.

Also refer to #1307.

c) Art and Artifacts

01426. Alföldi-Rosenbaum, Elisabeth. "Portrait Bust of a Young Lady of the Time of Justinian." Metropolitan Museum Journal 1 (1968): 19-40.

01427. Briguet, M. F. "Petite tête féminine étrusque." La Revue du Louvre et des musées de France 24 (1974): 247-252.

01428. Brilliant, Richard. Gesture and Rank in Roman Art: The Use of Gestures to Denote Status in Roman Sculpture and Coinage. New Haven: The Academy, 1963.

01429. Fuchs, S. "Neue Frauenbildnesse der frühen Kaiserzeit." Antike 14 (1938): 255-280.

01430. Goethert-Polaschek, Karin. Studien zur Ikonographie der Antonia Minor. Rome: L'erma di Bretschneider, 1973.

01431. Hafner, G. "Frauen-und Mädchenbilder aus Terrakotta im Museo gregoriano etrusco." Deutsches Archeologisches Institut Mitteilungen Romische Abte. 72 (1965): 41-61.

01432. Horst, M. "Portrait einer Romerin aus tiberischer Zeit." Münchner Jahrbuch der bildenden Kunst 24 (1973): 7-20.

01433. Kampen, Natalie Boymel. "Social Status and Gender in Roman Art: The Case of the Saleswoman." In Feminism and Art History: Questioning the Litany, edited by Norma Broude and Mary D. Garrard, pp. 62-77. New York: Harper and Row, 1982.

01434. L'Orange, H. P. "Zum frührömischen Frauenporträt." Deutsches Archaologisches Institut Mitteilungen Römische Abteilung 44 (1929): 167-179.

01435. Schauenburg, Konrad. "Frauen im Fenster." Deutsches Archaologisches Institut Mitteilungen Römische Abteilung 79 (1972): 1-15, 80 (1973): 271-273.

01436. Schmidt, Erika E. Römische Frauenstatuen. n.p., 1967.

Also refert o #1385, 1399-1401.

d) Science

01437. Penella, Robert J. "When Was Hypatia Born?" Historia Zeitschrift für Alte Geschichte 33 (1984): 126-128.

III. MIDDLE AGES

A. GENERAL

1. SURVEYS

"This woman had such great and lofty character that she never once condescended to unite with a man but remained a virgin her entire life."
Christine de Pisan

01438. Arcari, P.M. "La donn." In *Idee sulla donna nel medioevo: fonti e aspetti guiridici, antropologici, religiosi, sociali e litterari della condizione femminile*, edited by Mari Consiglia De Matteis, pp. 67-118. Bologne: Pàtron, 1981.

01439. Brunner, Karl and Daim, Falko. *Ritter, Knabben, Edelfrauen. Ideologie und Realitat du Rittertums im Mittelalter.* Vienna: Bohlau, 1981.

01440. De Matteis, Mari Consiglia, ed. *Idee sulla donna nel medioevo: fonti e aspetti guiridici, antropologici, religiosi, sociali e litterari della condizione femminile.* Bologne: Patron, 1981.

01441. Ennen, Edith. *Frauen im Mittelalter.* Munich: C. H. Beck, 1984.

01442. *La Femme dans les civilisations des Xe-XIIIe siècles: actes du colloque tenu à Poitiers les 23-25 septembre 1976* Poitiers: Université de Poitiers, Centre d'études supérieures de civilisation médiévale, 1977.

01443. Hoher, Friederike. "Hexe, Maria und Hausmutter--Zur Geschichte der Weiblichkeit im Spatmittelalter." In *Frauen in der Geschichte III*, edited by Annette Kuhn and Jorn Rusen, pp. 13-62. Düsseldorf: Schwann-Bagel Verlag, 1983.

01444. Ide, Arthur Frederick. Woman in the European Middle Ages. Mesquite, Tex.: Ide House, 1981.

01445. Ker, Margaret. "Brides of Christ and Poor Mortals: Women in Medieval Society." In Exploring Women's Past, edited by Patricia Crawford, et al., pp. 7-47. Boston: George Allen and Unwin, 1983.

01446. Pereira, Michele, ed. Ne Eva ne Maria. Condizione femminile e immagine della donna nel medioevo. Bologne: Zanichelli, 1983.

01447. Power, E. "Le idee medievali sulla donna." In Idee sulla donna nel medioevo: fonti e aspetti guiridici, antropologici, religiosi, sociali e litterari della condizione femminile, edited by Mari Consiglia De Matteis, pp. 47-66. Bologne: Patron, 1981.

01448. Shahar, Shulamith. The Fourth Estate: A History of Women in the Middle Ages. New York: Methuen, 1984.

Also refer to #2138.

2. POLITICAL

"[Woman is not] among those persons who cannot obligate themselves because she regularly celebrates all contracts in her name."

Rolandino Passaggieri

01449. Bellomo, Manlio. "La condizione giuridica della donna nel medioevo." In Ne Eva ne Maria. Condizione femminile e immagine della donna nel medioevo, edited by Michele Pereira pp. 55-63. Bologne: Zanichelli, 1983.

01450. Bloss, C. A. Heroines of the Crusades. London: Auburn and Rochester, 1853.

01451. Demougeot, Emilienne. "Le conubium dans les lois barbares du XIe siècle." Recueil de mémoires et travaux publié par la Société d'histoire du droit et des institutions des anciens pays du droit écrit 12 (1983): 69-82.

01452. Stafford, Pauline. Queen, Concubines, and Dowagers: The King's Wife in the Early Middle Ages. Athens, Ga.: University of Georgia Press, 1983.

Also refer to #1493.

3. ECONOMIC

"If anyone buys a maiden, she is to be bought
with a [bride] payment, if there is no fraud."
Aethelberht, 77

01453. Casey, K. "Donne, lavoro e potere." In _Ne Eva ne Maria. Condizione femminile e immagine della donna nel medioevo_, edited by Michele Pereira, pp. 46-55. Bologne: Zanichelli, 1983.

01454. Herlihy, David. _Medieval Households_. Cambridge, Mass.: Harvard University Press, 1985.

01455. Howell, Martha C. _Women's Work: The Structure of Market Production and Patriarchy in Late Medieval Cities of Northern Europe_. Chicago, Ill.: University of Chicago Press, 1986.

01456. Lehmann, A. "Il lavoro dell donne nel medioevo." In _Ne Eva ne Maria. Condizione femminile e immagine della donna nel medioevo_, edited by Michele Pereira, pp. 37-46. Bologne: Zanichelli, 1983.

01457. Verdon, J. "Le fonti per una storia della donna in Occidente nei secoli X-XIII." In _Idee sulla donna nel medioevo: fonti e aspetti guiridici, antropologici, religiosi, sociali e litterari della condizione femminile_, edited by Mari Consiglia De Matteis, pp. 119-176. Bologne: Patron, 1981.

Also refer to #1515.

4. RELIGION

"The world being dead to [the nuns],
they were dead to the world, and becoming unseen
by all, after their vocation laid over their eyes
and faces a thick veil, like a shroud."
Peter the Venerable

a) Generic

01458. Atkinson, Clarissa W. "Precious Balsam and Fragile Glass: The Ideology of Virginity in the Later Middle Ages." _Journal of Family History_ 8 (Summer 1983): 131-143.

01459. Barstow, Anne Llewellyn. _Married Priests and the Reforming Papacy: The Eleventh-Century Debates_. New York: Edwin Mellen Press, 1982.

01460. Bartoli, Marie Claude. "La femme a Bonifacio à la fin du moyen âge." In _Femmes corses et femmes méditeranéennes_, pp. 310-322. Provence: Centre d'Études Corses de l'Université de Provence, 1976. Also in _Études Corses_ 4 (1975): 310-322.

01461. Bolton, B.M. "Le donne nella vita religiosa." In _Ne Eva ne Maria. Condizione femminile e immagine della donna nel medioevo_, edited by Michele Pereira, pp. 71-82. Bologne: Zanichelli, 1983.

01462. Børresen, Kari Elisabeth. "L'ordine della creazione." In _Idee sulla donna nel medioevo: fonti e aspetti guiridici, antropologici, religiosi, sociali e litterari della condizione femminile_, edited by Mari Consiglia De Matteis, pp. 177-257. Bologne: Patron, 1981.

01463. Bynum, Caroine Walker. _Jesus as Mother, Studies in the Spirituality of the High Middle Ages_. Berkeley, Ca.: University of California Press, 1982.

01464. D'Alverny, M.T. "Come vedono la donna i teologi ed i filosofi." In _Idee sulla donna nel medioevo: fonti e aspetti guiridici, antropologici, religiosi, sociali e litterari della condizione femminile_, edited by Mari Consiglia De Matteis, pp. 259-303. Bologne: Patron, 1981.

01465. ____________. "Le opinioni dei teologi e dei filosofi sulla donna." In _Ne Eva ne Maria. Condizione femminile e immagine della donna nel medioevo_, edited by Michele Pereira, pp. 122-134. Bologne: Zanichelli, 1983.

01466. D'Avray, David L. and Tausche, M. "Marriage Sermons in ad status Collections of the Central Middle Ages." _Archives d'histoire doctrinale et littéraire du Moyen Âge_ 47 (1980): 71-119.

01467. Dedek, John F. "Premarital Sex: The Theological Argument from Peter Lombard to Durand." _Theological Studies_ 41 (December 1980): 643-667.

01468. Kiesling, Christopher. "Aquinas on Persons' Representation in Sacraments." In _Women Priests, a Catholic Commentary on the Vatican Declaration_, edited by Leonard Swidler and Arlene Swidler, pp. 253-257. New York: Paulist Press, 1977.

01469. Kottje, Raymond. "Ehe und Eheverstandnis in den vorgratianischen Bussbüchern." In _Love and Marriage in the Twelfth Century_, edited by Willy Van Hoecke and Andries Welkenhuysen, pp. 18-40. Louvain: Leuven University Press, 1981.

01470. Leclercq, Jean. "L'amour et le mariage vue par les clercs et des religieux, specialement au XIIe siècle." In _Love and Marriage in the Twelfth Century_, edited by Willy Van Hoecke and Andries Welkenhuysen, pp. 102-115. Louvain: Leuven University Press, 1981.

01471. ____________. _Monks on Marriage: A Twelfth Century View_. New York: Seabury Press, 1981.

01472. McLaughlin, Eleanor. "Les femmes et l'hérésie médiévale Un problème dans l'histoire de la spritualité." Concilium 111 (1976): 73-90.

01473. __________. "La presenza delle donne nei Movimenti ereticali." In Ne Eva ne Maria. Condizione femminile e immagine della donna nel medioevo, edited by Michele Pereira, pp. 82-92. Bologne: Zanichelli, 1983.

01474. __________. "Women, Power and the Pursuit of Holiness in Medieval Christianity." In Women of Spirit, edited by Rosemary Ruether and Eleanor McLaughlin, pp. 99-130. New York: Simon and Schuster, 1979.

01475. Matter, E. Ann. "Innocent III and the Keys to the Kingdom of Heaven." In Women Priests, A Catholic Commentary on the Vatican Declaration, edited by Leonard Swidler and Arlene Swidler, pp. 145-151. New York: Paulist Press, 1977.

01476. Mölk, Ulrich. "Saint Alexis et son épouse dans la legende latine et la première chanson française." In Love and Marriage in the Twelfth Century, edited by Willy Van Hoecke and Andries Welkenhuysen, pp. 162-170. Louvain: Leuven University Press, 1981.

01477. Nichols, John A. and Shank, Lillian Thomas, eds. Medieval Religious Women. Vol. I, Distant Echoes. Kalamazoo, Michigan: Cistercian Publications, 1984.

01478. Schulenburg, Jane Tibbetts. "The Heroics of Virginity Brides of Christ and Sacrificial Mutilation." In Women in the Middle Ages and the Renaissance, edited by Mary Beth Rose, pp. 29-72. Syracuse, N.Y.: Syracuse University Press, 1986.

01479. Tavard, George H. "The Scholastic Doctrine." In Women Priests, A Catholic Commentary on the Vatican Declaration, edited by Leonard Swidler and Arlene Swidler, pp. 99-106. New York: Paulist Press, 1977.

Also refer to #1322, 1333, 1358, 1543, 1549-1553, 1600, 1603.

b) Saints/Religious Women

01480. Bynum, Caroline Walker. "Women Mystics and Eucharistic Devotion in the Thirteenth Century." Women's Studies 11 (1984): 179-214.

01481. Grange, Isabelle. "Metamorphoses chrétiennes des femmes-cygnes. Du folklore à l'hagiographie." Ethnologie francaise 13 (1983): 139-150.

01482. Rouche, Michel. "La femme au moyen âge, histoire ou hagiographie?" Revue du Nord 63 (July-September 1981): 581-584.

01483. Tavormina, M. Theresa. "Of Maidenhood and Maternity: Liturgical Hagiography and the Medieval Idea of Virginity." American Benedictine Review 31 (1980): 384-399.

Also refer to #1367, 1477, 1589.

c) Monastic Life

01484. Leclercq, Jean. "La femme dans le théologie monastique au moyen âge." Communio 7 (1982): 64-70.

01485. Schulenberg, Jane Tibbetts, "Strict Active Enclosure and Its Effects on the Female Monastic Experience (ca. 500-1100)." In Medieval Religious Women, vol. 1, Distant Echoes, edited by John A. Nichols and Lillian Thomas: 51-86. Kalamazoo, Michigan: Cistercian Publications, 1984.

Also refer to #1468, 1536, 1541.

d) Canon Law

01486. Brooke, Christopher, N. L. "Aspects of Marriage Law in the Eleventh and Twelfth Centuries." In Proceedings of the Fifth International Congress of Medieval Canon Law, edited by Stephan Kuttner and Kenneth Pennington, pp. 333-344. Citta del Vaticano: Biblioteca Apostolica Vaticana, 1980.

01487. Brundage, James A. "Adultery and Fornication: A Study in Legal Theology." In Sexual Practices and the Medieval Church, edited by Vern L. Bullough and James Brundage, pp. 129-134. Buffalo, N.Y.: Prometheus Books, 1982.

01488. ________________. "Carnal Delight: Canonistic Theories of Sexuality." In Proceedings of the Fifth International Congress of Medieval Canon Law, edited by Stephan Kuttner and Kenneth Pennington, pp. 361-385. Citta del Vaticano: Biblioteca Apostolica Vaticana, 1980.

01489. ________________. "Concubinage and Marriage in Medieval Canon Law." In Sexual Practices and the Medieval Church, edited by Vern L. Bullough and James A. Brundage, pp. 118-128. Buffalo, N.Y.: Prometheus Books, 1982. Also in Journal of Medieval History 1 (April 1975): 1-17.

01490. ________________. "Let Me Count the Ways: Canonists and Theologians Contemplate Coital Positions." Journal of Medieval History 10 (June 1984): 81-93.

01491. Brundage, James A. "Prostitution in the Medieval Canon Law." In Sexual Practices and the Medieval Church, edited by Vern L. Bullough and James Brundage, pp. 149-160. Buffalo, N.Y.: Prometheus Books, 1982. Also in Signs 1 (Summer 1976): 825-845 and 2 (Summer 1977): 922-924.

01492. ________. "Rape and Seduction in the Medieval Canon Law." In Sexual Practices and the Medieval Church, edited by Vern L. Bullough and James Brundage, pp. 141-148. Buffalo, N.Y.: Prometheus Books, 1982.

01493. ________. "Sex and Canon Law: A Statistical Analysis of Samples of Canon and Civil Law." In Sexual Practices and the Medieval Church, edited by Vern L. Bullough and James A. Brundage, pp. 89-101. Buffalo, N.Y.: Prometheus Books, 1982.

01494. Donahue, Charles Jr. "The Canon Law on the Formation of Marriage and Social Practice in the Later Middle Ages." Journal of Family History 8 (Summer 1983): 144-158.

01495. Duggan, Charles. "Equity and Compassion in Papal Marriage Decretals to England." In Love and Marriage in the Twelfth Century, edited by Willy Van Hoecke and Andries Welkenhuysen, pp. 59-87. Louvain: Leuven University Press, 1981.

01496. Flandrin, Jean-Louis. "Sex in Married Life in the Early Middle Ages: The Church's Teaching and Behavioural Reality." In Western Sexuality, edited by Philippe Aries and Andre Bejin, pp. 114-129. New York: Blackwell, 1985.

01497. Gaudemet, Jean. "La formation de la théorie canonique du mariage." Revue du droit canonique 32 (1982): 101-108.

01498. ________. "Recherche sur les origines historiques de la faculté de rompre le mariage non consommé." In Proceedings of the Fifth International Congress of Medieval Canon Law, edited by Stephan Kuttner and Kenneth Pennington, pp. 309-331. Citta del Vaticano: Biblioteca Apostolica Vaticana, 1980.

01499. Gold, Penny Schine. "The Marriage of Mary and Joseph in the Twelfth-Century Ideology of Marriage." In Sexual Practices and the Medieval Church, edited by Vern L. Bullough and James Brundage, pp. 102-117. Buffalo, N.Y.: Prometheus Books, 1982.

01500. Lefebvre-Teillard, Anne. "Regle et realité dans le droit matrimonial à la fin du Moyen Age." Revue de droit canonique 30 (1980): 41-54.

01501. ________. "Regle et realité: les nullités de mariage à la fin du Moyen-Age." Revue de droit canonique 32 (1982): 145-155.

01502. Metz, R. "La donna nelle fonti del diritto canonico medioevale." In Ne Eva ne Maria. Condizione femminile e immagine della donna nel medioevo, edited by Michele Pereira, pp. 63-71. Bologne: Zanichelli, 1983.

01503. Payer, Pierre, J. Sex and the Penitentials: The Development of a Sexual Code 550-1150. London: University of Toronto Press, 1984.

01504. Tejéro Tejero, Eloy. "Matrimonio y sacramento en la escolástica incipiente." Revue de droit canonique 29 (1979): 138-144.

01505. Vogel, C. "Le rôle du liturge dans la formation du lien conjugal." Revue de droit canonique 30 (1980): 7-27.

01506. Weigand, Rudolf. "Liebe und Ehe bei den Dekretisten des 12. Jahrhunderts." In Love and Marriage in the Twelfth Century, edited by Willy Van Hoecke and Andries Welkenhuysen, pp. 41-58. Louvain: Leuven University Press, 1981.

Also refer to #1548.

e) Heresy

01507. Devlin, Dennis. "Feminine Lay Piety in the High Middle Ages: The Beguines." In Medieval Religious Women, vol. 1, Distant Echoes, edited by John A. Nichols and Lillian Thomas: 183-196. Kalamazoo, Michigan: Cistercian Publications, 1984.

01508. Greven, J. Die Anfänge der Beginen. Ein Beitrag zur Geschichte der Volksfrömmigkeit und der Ordenswesens in Hochmittelalter. Münster: Aschendorff, 1912.

f) Witchcraft

01509. Bullough, Vern L. "Postscript: Heresy, Witchcraft, and Sexuality." In Sexual Practices and the Medieval Church, edited by Vern L. Bullough and James Brundage, pp. 206-217. Buffalo, N.Y.: Prometheus Books, 1982.

01510. Pearson, Karl. "Woman as Witch--Evidences of Mother-Right in the Customs of Medieval Witchcraft." In Chances of Death and Other Studies in Evolution, 2: 1-50. New York: E. Arnold, 1897.

5. SOCIAL

> "The reticence and shame with which the modern world has frequently surrounded the everyday functions of birth, death, and love-making were feelings unknown in the medieval breast since there was no possible way in which they could be shunted aside and veiled from the gaze of others. Indeed, it would be difficult to think of any other age in which the facts of life came closer to being no more than just that."
>
> Charles T. Wood
> The Quest for Eternity

a) Generic

01511. Berschin, Walter. "'Richter', Ritter, Frauen. . . Die Laienstande nach Bonizo." In Love and Marriage in the Twelfth Century, edited by Willy Van Hoecke and Andries Welkenhuysen, pp. 116-129. Louvain: Leuven University Press, 1981.

01512. Chapelot, Jean and Fossier, Robert. The Village and House in the Middle Ages. Berkeley, Ca.: University of California Press, 1986.

01513. Chydenius, Johan. Love and the Medieval Tradition. Helsinki: Helsingfors, 1977.

01514. Colafemmina, Cesare. "Donne, ebrei e cristiana." Quaderni medievali 8 (1980): 117-125.

01515. Duby, Georges. "Les femmes et le revolution féodale." Pensée 61 (1984): 185-194.

01516. Gossmann, Elisabeth. "Anthropologie und soziale Stellung der Frau nach Summen und Sentenzenkommentaren des 13. Jahrhunderts." In Soziale Ordnungen im Selbstverstandnis des Mittelalters, edited by Albert Zimmerman and Gudrun Vuillemin-Diem, 1: 281-297. New York: Walter de Gruyter, 1979.

01517. Haucourt, Genevieve d'. Life in the Middle Ages. Translated by Veronica Hull and Christopher Feman. New York: Walker and Co., 1963.

01518. Jaeger, C. Stephen. The Origins of Courtliness: Civilizing Trends and the Formation of Courtly Ideals, 929-1210. Philadelphia, Pa.: University of Pennsylvania Press, 1985.

01519. Schulz, Knut. "Die Stellung der Gesellen in der spätmittelalterlichen Stadt." In Haus und Familie in der spätmitteralterlichen Stadt, edited by Alfed Haverkamp, pp. 304-326. Cologne: Böhlau, 1984.

b) Family

(1) Non-specific

01520. Guerreau-Jalabert, Anita. "Sur les structures de parenté dans l'Europe médiévale." *Annales: économies, sociétés, civilisations* 36 (November-December 1981): 1028-1049.

01521. Haverkamp, Alfred, ed. *Haus und Familie in der spätmitteralterlichen Stadt*. Cologne: Bohlau, 1984.

01522. Herlihy, David. "Donne, Terre e famiglia nell'Europa medievale." In *Ne Eva ne Maria. Condizione femminile e immagine della donna nel medioevo*, edited by Michele Pereira, pp. 23-37. Bologne: Zanichelli, 1983.

01523. _____________. "The Making of the Medieval Family: Symmetry, Structure and Sentiment." *Journal of Family History* 8 (Summer 1983): 116-130.

01524. Higounet-Nadal, Arlette. "Haus und Familie in Perigueux im ausgehenden Mittelalter. Eine Fallstudie." In *Haus und Familie in der spätmitteralterlichen Stadt*, edited by Alfred Haverkamp, pp. 244-256. Cologne: Bohlau, 1984.

01525. Mitterauer, Michael. "Familie und Arbeitsorganisation in stadtischen Gesellschaften des spaten Mittelalters und der fruhen Neuzeit." In *Haus und Familie in der spatmitteralterlichen Stadt*, edited by Alfred Haverkamp, pp. 1-36. Cologne: Bohlau, 1984.

01526. Wiegand, Rudolf. "Ehe- und Familienrecht in der mittelalterlichen Stadt." In *Haus und Familie in der spätmitteralterlichen Stadt*, edited by Alfred Haverkamp, 161-194. Cologne: Bohlau, 1984.

01527. Wemple, Suzanne F. "The Medieval Family: European and North American Research Directions." In *Family History*, edited by Patricia J.F. Rosof and William Zeisel, pp. 27-44. New York: Institute for Research in History, 1985.

(2) Childhood

01528. Arnold, Klaus. *Kind und Gesellschaft in Mittelalter und Renaissance: Beiträge und Texte zur Geschichte der Kindheit*. Paderborn: Ferdinand Schoningh, 1980.

01529. Bonney, Francoise. "Enfance divine et enfance humaine." In *L'enfant au moyen âge*, pp. 7-24. Aix-en-Provence: Université, 1980.

01530. *L'enfant au moyen age*. Aix-en-Provence: Universite, 1980.

01531. Goodich, Michael. "Bartholomaeus Anglicus on Child-Rearing." *History of Childhood Quarterly* 3 (Summer 1975): 75-84.

01532. Goodich, Michael. "Encyclopaedic Literature: Child-Rearing in the Middle Ages." History of Education 12 (1983): 69-85.

01533. Kroll, Jerome. "The Concept of Childhood in the Middle Ages." Journal of the History of the Behavioral Sciences 13 (October 1977): 384-393.

01534. Nitschke, August. "Die Stellung des Kindes in der Familie im Spätmittelalter und der Renaissance." In Haus und Familie in der spätmitteralterlichen Stadt, edited by Alfred Haverkamp, pp. 215-243. Cologne: Bohlau, 1984.

01535. Poirion, Daniel. "Edyppus ou l'énigme du roman médiéval." In L'enfant au moyen âge, pp. 285-298. Aix-en-Provence: Université, 1980.

01536. Shahar, Shulamith. "Infants, Infant Care, and Attitudes toward Infancy in the Medieval Lives of Saints." Journal of Psychohistory 10 (Winter 1983): 281-309.

01537. Sigal, Pierre-Andre. "Le vocabulaire de l'enfance et de l'adolescence dans les recueils de miracles latins des XIIe et XIIIe siècles." In L'enfant au moyen âge, pp. 141-160. Aix-en-Provence: Université, 1980.

Also refer to #1041.

c) Marriage

01538. Aries, Philippe. "Indissoluble Marriage." Proceedings of the Ninth Annual Meeting of the Western Society for French History, pp. 1-14. Lawrence, Ks.: University of Kansas Press, 1982.

01539. Brooke, Christopher N. L. "Marriage and Society in the Central Middle Ages." In Marriage and Society Studies in the Social History of Marriage, edited by R. B. Outhwaite, pp. 17-34. New York: St. Martin's Press, 1981.

01540. Ertzdorff, Xenja von and Wynn, Marianne, eds. Liebe-Ehe-Ehebruch in der Literatur des Mittelalters. Giessen: Wilhlem Schnitz, 1984.

01541. Glasser, Marc. "Marriage in Medieval Hagiography." Studies in Medieval and Renaissance History n.s. 4(1981): 1-34.

01542. Hughes, Diane Owen. "From Brideprice to Dowry in Meditterranean Europe." In The Marriage Bargain: Women and Dowries in European History, edited by Marion A. Kaplan, pp. 13-58. New York: Harrington Park, 1985.

01543. McNamara, Jo Ann. "Chaste Marriage and Clerical Celibacy." In _Sexual Practices and the Medieval Church_, edited by Vern L. Bullough and James A. Brundage, pp. 22-23. Buffalo, N.Y.: Prometheus Books, 1982.

01544. Payer, Pierre J. "Early Medieval Regulations Concerning Marital Sexual Relations." _Journal of Medieval History_ 6 (1980): 353-376.

01545. Schnur, Harry C. "Judische Ehe und Familie im Mittelalter." In _Love and Marriage in the Twelfth Century_, edited by Willy Van Hoecke and Andries Welkenhuysen, pp. 88-101. Louvain: Leuven University Press, 1981.

01546. Van Hoecke, Willy and Welkenhuysen, Andries, eds. _Love and Marriage in the Twelfth Century_. Louvain: Leuven University Press, 1981.

Also refer to #1451, 1459, 1466, 1469-1471, 1486, 1489, 1494-1501, 1504-1506, 1526, 1580, 1581.

d) Sex Life and Morals

(1) Non-specific

01547. Atkins, John A. _Sex in Literature: The Medieval Experience_. London: Calder and Boyars, 1979.

01548. Brundage, James A. "Prostitution, Miscegenation and Sexual Purity in the First Crusade." In _Crusade and Settlement_, edited by Peter W. Edbury, pp. 57-65. Cardiff, Wales: University College, 1985.

01549. Bullough, Vern L. "Formation of Medieval Ideals: Christian Theory and Christian Practice." In _Sexual Practices and the Medieval Church_, edited by Vern L. Bullough and James A. Brundage, pp. 14-21. Buffalo, N.Y.: Prometheus Books, 1982.

01550. _______________. "Sex Education in Medieval Christianity." _The Journal of Sex Research_ 13 (August 1977): 185-196.

01551. _______________. "The Sin Against Nature and Homosexuality." In _Sexual Practices and the Medieval Church_, edited by Vern L. Bullough and James A. Brundage, pp. 55-71. Buffalo, N.Y.: Prometheus Books, 1982.

01552. _______________. "Transvestism in the Middle Ages." In _Sexual Practices and the Medieval Church_, edited by Vern L. Bullough and James A. Brundage, pp. 43-54. Buffalo, N.Y.: Prometheus Books, 1982. Also in _American Journal of Sociology_ 79 (May 1974): 1381-1394.

01553. Bullough, Vern L. and Brundage, James, eds. Sexual Practices and the Medieval Church. Buffalo, N.Y.: Prometheus Books, 1982.

01554. Derouet-Bessen, Marie-Claude. "'Inter duos scopulos.' Hypothèses sur la place de la sexualité dans les modeles de la représentation du monde au XIe siècle." Annales: économies, sociétés, civilisations 36 (September-October 1981): 922-945.

01555. Lemay, Helen Rodnite. "Human Sexuality in Twelfth- through Fifteenth-Century Scientific Writing." In Sexual Practices and the Medieval Church, by Vern L. Bullough and James Brundage, pp. 187-205. Buffalo, N.Y.: Prometheus Books, 1982.

Also refer to #1322, 1458, 1467, 1488, 1490-1493, 1503, 1509, 1544, 1576-1577, 1588.

(2) Prostitutes

01556. Bullough, Vern L. "The Prostitute in the Early Middle Ages." In Sexual Practices and the Medieval Church, edited by Vern L. Bullough and James A. Brundage, pp. 34-42. Buffalo, N.Y.: Prometheus Books, 1982.

01557. ________________. "Prostitution in the Later Middle Ages." In Sexual Practices and the Medieval Church, edited by Vern L. Bullough and James Brundage, pp. 176-186. Buffalo, N.Y.: Prometheus Books, 1982.

01558. Lewinsohn, Richard. "Medieval Prostitution." In For Court, Manor and Church, edited by Donna R. Barnes, pp. 169-172. Minneapolis: Burgess, 1971.

01559. Pilosu, Mario. "L'atteggiamento della chiesa medievale verso la prostituzione continuità e novità nei secoli XII e XIII." Studi storico-religiosi 6 (1982): 143-162.

Also refer to #1548.

e) Fashion

01560. Newton, Stella Mary. Fashion in the Age of the Black Prince: A Study of the Years 1340-1365. Totowa, N.J.: Rowman and Littlefield, 1980.

01561. Scott, Margaret. The History of Dress: Late Gothic Europe, 1400-1500. Atlantic Highlands, N.J.: Humanities Press, 1981.

Also refer to #1394.

f) Health/Medical

01562. Bell, Rudolph M. *Holy Anorexia*. Chicago, Ill.: University of Chicago Press, 1986.

01563. Biller, P.P.A. "Birth-Control in the West in the Thirteenth and Early Fourteenth Centuries." *Past and Present* 94 (February 1982): 3-26.

01564. Brundage, James A. "The Problem of Impotence." In *Sexual Practices and the Medieval Church*, edited by Vern L. Bullough and James Brundage, pp. 135-140. Buffalo, N.Y.: Prometheus Books, 1982.

01565. Bullough, Vern L. "La medicina medievale e l'inferiorità femminile." In *Ne Eva ne Maria. Condizione femminile e immagine della donna nel medioevo*, edited by Michele Pereira, pp. 135-145. Bologne: Zanichelli, 1983.

01566. ___________ and Campbell, C. "Female Longevity and Diet in the Middle Ages." *Speculum* 55 (April 1980): 317-325.

01567. Rowland, Beryl, and Jennings, Margaret. "Medieval Multiple Birth." *Neuphilologische Mitteilungen*, 81 (1980): 169-173.

01568. Salvat, Michel. "L'accouchement dans la littérature scientifique médiévale." In *L'enfant au moyen âge*, pp. 87-106. Aix-en-Provence: Université, 1980.

01569. Talbot, C.H. "Dame Trot and Her Progeny." *Essays and Studies* n.s. 25 (1972): 1-14.

01570. Thomasset, Claude. "Quelques principles de l'embryologie médiévale (de Salerne à la fin du XIIIe siècle)." In *L'enfant au moyen âge*, pp. 107-121. Aix-en-Provence: Université, 1980.

01571. Wood, C.T. "Medieval Doctors' Dilemma: Sin, Salvation and the Menstrual Cycle in Medieval Thought." *Speculum* 56 (October 1981): 710-727.

6. CULTURAL

> "Now consider my daughter since thus it is, that you who are a weak feminine creature must take pains, whatever good fortune you may have, to conduct yourself graciously in perfect humility, especially toward your lord and husband."
>
> Anne of France

a) Generic

01572. Bell, Susan Groag. "Medieval Women Book Owners: Arbiters of Lay Piety and Ambassadresses of Culture." *Signs* 7 (Summer 1982): 742-768.

01573. Dinzelbacher, Peter. "Über die Entdeckung der Liebe im Hochmittelalter." Saeculum 32 (1981): 185-208.

01574. Lejeune, R. "Le donne e l'origine della letteratura in volgare." In Ne Eva ne Maria. Condizione femminile e immagine della donna nel medioevo, edited by Michele Pereira, pp. 111-112. Bologne: Zanichelli, 1983.

01575. Power, E. "L'educazione della donne." In Ne Eva ne Maria. Condizione femminile e immagine della donna nel medioevo, edited by Michele Pereira, pp. 101-110. Bologne: Zanichelli, 1983.

Also refer to #1550.

b) Literature

(1) Non-specific

(a) Women in Literature

01576. Bec, Pierre. "L'accès au lieu érotique: motifs et exorde dans la lyrique popularisante du moyen âge à nos jours." In Love and Marriage in the Twelfth Century, edited by Willy Van Hoecke and Andries Welkenhuysen, pp. 250-299. Louvain: Leuven University Press, 1981.

01577. Berger, Sidney L. "Sex in the Literature of the Middle Ages: The Fabliaux." In Sexual Practices and the Medieval Church, edited by Vern L. Bullough and James Brundage, pp. 162-175. Buffalo, N.Y.: Prometheus Books, 1982.

01578. Bornstein, Diane. The Lady in the Tower: Medieval Courtesy Literature for Women. New York: Archon Books, 1983.

01579. Brewer, Derek S. "Ideal of Feminine Beauty in Medieval Literature." Modern Language Review 50 (1955): 257-269.

01580. Dasllapiazza, Michael. "Spätmittelalterliche Ehediadaktik." In Liebe-Ehe- Ehebruch in der Literatur des Mittelalters, edited by Xenja von Ertzdorff and Marianne Wynn, pp. 161-172. Giessen: Wilhelm Schnitz, 1984.

01581. Ertzdorff, Xenja von. "Liebe- Ehe- Ehebruch und der Untergang des Artus-Reichs im 'Prosa-Lancelot." In Liebe-Ehe-Ehebruch in der Literatur des Mittelalters, edited by Xenja von Ertzdorff and Marianne Wynn, pp. 99-110. Giessen: Schnitz, 1984.

01582. John, Robert. "The Lady as Symbolical Figure in Medieval Literature." Perspectives in Literary Symbolism: Yearbook of Comparative Criticism 1 (1968): 170-180.

01583. Muller, Irmgard. "Liebestranke, Liebeszauber und Schlafmittel in der mittelalterlichen Literatur." In Liebe-Ehe-Ehebruch in der Literatur des Mittelalters, edited by Xenja von Ertzdorff and Marianne Wynn, pp. 71-87. Giessen: Wilhelm Schnitz, 1984.

01584. Payen, Jean-Charles. "Images littéraires de la femme médiévale." In La Condition féminine, Centre d'études et de recherches marxistes, pp. 221-234. Paris: Editions sociales, 1978.

01585. Rabine, Leslie W. "The Establishment of Patriarchy in Tristan and Isolde." Women's Studies 7 no. 3 (1980): 19-38.

01586. Schmidt, Paul Gerhard. "Amor als Ärgernis." In Liebe-Ehe-Ehebruch in der Literatur des Mittelalters, edited by Xenja von Ertzdorff and Marianne Wynn, pp. 16-24. Giessen: Wilhelm Schnitz, 1984.

01587. ____________. "Hercules indutus vestibus Ioles." In From Wolfram and Petrarch to Goethe and Grass: Studies in Literature in Honour of Leonard Forster, edited by D.H. Green, L.P. Johnson and Dieter Wuttker, pp. 103-107. Baden-Baden: Verlag Valentin Koerner, 1982.

01588. Thomasset, Claude. "La représentation de la sexualité et de la generation dans la pensée scientifique médiévale." In Love and Marriage in the Twelfth Century, edited by Willy Van Hoecke and Andries Welkenhuysen, pp. 1-17. Louvain: Leuven University Press, 1981.

Also refer to #1540, 1547.

(b) Women Authors

01589. Schibanoff, Susan. "Early Women Writers: In-Scribing, or, Reading the Fine Print." Women's Studies International Forum 6 (1983): 475-489.

01590. Wilson, Katharine M., ed. Medieval Women Writers. Athens, Ga.: University of Georgia Press, 1984.

(2) Poetry

01591. Plummer, John F. "Introduction." In Vox Feminae: Studies in Medieval Woman's Songs, pp. 5-17. Kalamazoo, Mich.: Western Michigan University, 1981.

01592. ____________, ed. Vox Feminae: Studies in Medieval Woman's Songs. Kalamazoo, Mich.: Western Michigan University, 1981.

01593. Regan, Mariann Sanders. Love Words, The Self and Text in Medieval and Renaissance Poetry. Ithaca, New York: Cornell University Press, 1982.

01594. Schotter, Anne Howland. "Woman's Song in Medieval Latin." In Vox Feminae: Studies in Medieval Woman's Songs, edited by John F. Plummer, pp. 19-33. Kalamazoo, Mich.: Western Michigan University, 1981.

(3) Troubadours

01595. Köhler, Erich. "Les troubadours et la jalousie." In Mélanges de langue et de littérature du Moyen Age et de la Renaissance offerts à Jean Frappier. Geneva: Droz, 1970.

01596. Paden, William. "The Troubadour's Lady: Her Marital Status and Social Rank" Studies in Philology 72 (1975): 28-50.

c) Chivalry

(1) Courtly Love

01597. Ertzdorff, Xenja von. "Tristan und Lanzelot. Zur Problematik der Liebe in den höfischen Romanen des 12. und fruhen 13. Jahrhunderts." Germanisch-Romanische Monatsschrift n.s. 33 (1983): 21-52.

01598. Marchello-Nizia, Christiane. "Amour courtois, société masculine et figures de pouvoir." Annales: économies, sociétés, civilisations 36 (November-December 1981): 969-982.

01599. Nelli, R. "Amore cortese ed eresia catara nella vita delle donne." In Ne Eva ne Maria. Condizione femminile e immagine della donna nel medioevo, edited by Michele Pereira, pp. 92-101, Bologne: Zanichelli, 1983.

01600. Russell, Jeffrey B. "Courtly Love as Religious Dissent." Catholic Historical Review 51 (April 1965): 31-44.

d) Art

(1) Women in Art

01601. Kitzinger, Ernst. "A Virgin's Face: Antiquarianism in 12th Century Art." Art Bulletin 62 (March 1980): 6-19.

01602. Kraus, Henry. "Eve and Mary: Conflicting Images of Medieval Woman." In Feminism and Art History: Questioning the Litany, edited by Norma Broude and Mary D. Garrard, pp. 78-99. New York: Harper and Row, 1982. Also in The Living Theatre of Medieval Art, ch. 3. Bloomington: University of Indiana Press, 1967.

01603. Seidl, Linda. "Salome and the Canons." Women's Studies 11 (1984): 29-66.

(2) Women Artists

01604. Davidson, Clifford. "Women and the Medieval Stage." Women's Studies 11 (1984): 99-113.

B. BRITISH ISLES

1. SURVEYS

"Lies, tears, and spinning are the things God gives by nature to a woman while she lives."
Chaucer

01605. Davies, Wendy. "Celtic Women in the Early Middle Ages." In Images of Women in Antiquity, edited by Averil Cameron and Amelie Kuhrt, pp. 145-166. Detroit: Wayne State University Press, 1983.

01606. Fell, Christine; Clark, Cecily; and Williams, Elizabeth. Women in Anglo-Saxon England and the Impact of 1066. Bloomington, Indiana: Indiana University Press, 1985.

01607. Lucas, Angela M. Women in the Middle Ages: Religion, Marriage and Letters. New York: St. Martin's Press, 1983.

01608. Templeton, Darlene. Women in Medieval England. Mesquite, Tex.: Ide House, 1980.

01609. ________________. Woman in Yorkist England. Mesquite, Tex.: Ide House, 1981?

2. MATRILINY

"Mother right is not confined to any particular people, but marks a cultural stage."
J.J. Bachofen

01610. Millery, Molly. "Matriliny by Treaty: The Pictish Foundation-Legend." In Ireland in Early Medieval Europe edited by Dorothy Whitelock, et al., pp. 133-161. Cambridge: University Press, 1982.

3. POLITICAL

"For since legally a woman is completely in the power of her husband, it is not surprising that her dower and all of her property are clearly deemed to be at his disposal."

Glanvill

a) Legal

01611. Bennett, Judith M. "Spouses, Siblings and Surnames: Reconstructing Families from Medieval Court Rolls" Journal of British Studies 23 (Fall 1983): 26-46.

01612. Binchy, Daniel A. "The Legal Capacity of Women in Regard to Contracts." In Studies in Early Irish Law, edited by Daniel A. Binchy, pp. 207-234. Dublin: Royal Irish Academy, 1936.

01613. _______________, ed. Studies in Early Irish Law. Dublin: Royal Irish Academy, 1936.

01614. Charles-Edwards, T.M. "Nau kynywedi teithiauc." In The Welsh Law of Women, edited by Dafydd Jenkins and Morfydd E. Owen, pp. 23-39. Cardiff: University Press, 1980.

01615. Dillon, Myles. "The Relationship of Mother and Son, of Father and Daughter, and the Law of Inheritance with Regard to Women." In Studies in Early Irish Law, edited by Daniel A. Binchy, pp. 129-179. Dublin: Royal Irish Academy, 1936.

01616. Donahue, Charles, Jr. "What Causes Fundamental Legal Ideas? Marital Property in England and France in the Thirteenth Century." Michagan Law Review 78 (November 1979): 59-88.

01617. Engdahl, David E. "English Marriage Conflicts Law before the Time of Bracton." American Journal of Comparative Law 15 (1966-1967): 109-135.

01618. Klinck, Anne Lingard. "Anglo-Saxon Women and the Law." Journal of Medieval History 7 (1982): 107-121.

01619. Knoch, August. "Die Ehescheidung im alten irischen Recht." In Studies in Early Irish Law, edited by Daniel A. Binchy, pp. 235-268. Dublin: Royal Irish Academy, 1936.

01620. Milson, S.F.C. "Inheritance by Women in the Twelfth and Early Thirteenth Centuries." In On the Laws and Customs of England, edited by Morris S. Arnold, et al., pp. 60-89. Chapel Hill, N.C.: University of North Carolina Press, 1981.

01621. Mulchrone, Kathleen. "The Rights and Duties of Women with Regard to the Education of their Children." In Studies in Early Irish Law, edited by Daniel A. Binchy, pp. 187-206. Dublin: Royal Irish Academy, 1936.

01622. Palmer, Robert C. "Contests of Marriage in Medieval England: Evidence for the Kings' Court circa 1300." Speculum 59 (January 1984): 42-67.

01623. Post, J.B. "Sir Thomas West and the Statute of Rapes, 1382." Bulletin of the Institute of Historical Research 53 (1980): 24-30.

01624. Power, Nancy C. "Classes of Women Described in the Senchas Mar." In Studies in Early Irish Law, edited by Daniel A. Binchy, pp. 81-108. Dublin: Royal Irish Academy, 1936.

01625. Ryan, John. "The Cain Adomain." In Studies in Early Irish Law, edited by Daniel A. Binchy, pp. 269-276. Dublin: Royal Irish Academy, 1936.

01626. Sheringham, J.G.T. "Bullocks with horns as long as their ears." Bulletin of the Board of Celtic Studies 29 (1982): 691-708.

01627. Thurneysen, Rudolf. "Heirat." In Studies in Early Irish Law, edited by Daniel A. Binchy, pp. 109-128. Dublin: Royal Irish Academy, 1936.

01628. Walters, D.B. "The European Legal Context of the Welsh Law of Matrimonial Property." In The Welsh Law of Women, edited by Dafydd Jenkins and Morfydd E. Owen, pp. 115-131. Cardiff: University Press, 1980.

01629. Waugh, Scott L. "Marriage, Class and Royal Lordship in England under Henry III." Viator 16 (1985): 181-207.

Also refer to #1646, 1680, 1681.

b) Criminal

01630. Carter, John Marshall. Rape in Medieval England: An Historical and Sociological Study. Lanham, Md.: University Press of America, 1985.

01631. ____________________. "Rape in Medieval English Society: The Evidence of Yorkshire, Wiltshire and London, 1218-1276." Comitatus 13 (1982): 33-63.

01632. ____________________. "The Status of Rape in Thirteenth Century England: 1218-1275." International Journal of Women's Studies 7 (May-June 1984): 248-259.

01633. Garay, Kathleen E. "Women and Crime in Later Medieval England: An Examination of the Evidence of the Courts of Gaol Delivery, 1388 to 1409." Florilegium 1 (1979): 87-109.

Also refer to #1623.

c) Political Roles

01634. Chandler, Victoria. "Ada de Warenne, Queen Mother of Scotland (c. 1123-1178)." Scottish Historical Review 60 (October 1981): 119-139.

01635. Crawford, Anne. "The King's Burden?- The Consequences of Royal Marriage in Fifteenth-Century England." In Patronage, the Crown and the Provinces in Later Medieval England, pp. 33-56. Atlantic Highlands, N.J.: Humanities Press, 1981.

01636. Menache, Sophia. "Isabelle of France, Queen of England - A Reconsideration." Journal of Medieval History 10 (June 1984): 107-124.

01637. Nitzsche, Jane Chance. "The Anglo-Saxon Woman as Hero: The Chaste Queen and the Masculine Woman Saint." Allegorica 5 (Winter 1980): 139-148.

01638. Parsons, John Carmi. "The Year of Eleanor of Castile's Birth and Her Children by Edward I." Medieval Studies 46 (1984): 245-265.

01639. Reid, Norman. "Margaret 'Maid of Norway' and Scottish Queenship." Reading Medieval Studies 8 (1982): 75-96.

01640. Searle, Eleanor. "Women and the Legitimization of Succession at the Norman Conquest." In Proceedings of the Battle Conference on Anglo-Norman Studies, edited by R. Allen Brown, pp. 159-170 and 226-229. Woodbridge: Boydell Press, 1981.

01641. Waara, Elizabeth R. "Wardships, Marriages, and the King's Men during the Reign of Henry III." Michigan Academician 13 (1980): 227-236.

01642. Wimsatt, James I. "The Blessed Virgin and the Two Coronations of Griselda." Mediaevalia 6 (1980): 187-207.

01643. Zital-Mareille, Joseph. La vie ardente d'Eleanor d'Aquitaine. Paris: E. Flammarion, 1931.

4. ECONOMIC

"If this is a manor where there is no dairy, it is always good to have a woman there at much less cost than a man."
Medieval English treatise on husbandry

01644. Hilton, Rodney H. "Women Traders in Medieval England." Women's Studies 11 (1984): 139-155.

01645. Hutton, Diane. "Women in Fourteenth Century Shrewsbury." In *Women and Work in Pre-Industrial Britain*, edited by Lorna Duffin, pp. 83-99. London: Croom Helm, 1985.

01646. Jenkins, Dafydd. "Property Interests in the Classical Welsh Law of Women." In *The Welsh Law of Women*, edited by Dafydd Jenkins and Morfydd E. Owen, pp. 69-92. Cardiff: University Press, 1980.

01647. Lacey, Kay E. "Women and Work in Fourteenth and Fifteenth Century London." In *Women and Work in Pre-Industrial Britain*, edited by Lorna Duffin, pp. 24-82. London: Croom Helm, 1985.

01648. Middleton, Chris. "Peasants, Patriarchy and the Feudal Mode of Production in England: A Marxist Appraisal. I. Property and Patriarchal Relations within the Peasantry." *Sociological Review* n.s. 29 (February 1981): 105-135.

01649. ________________. "Peasants, Patriarchy and the Feudal Mode of Production in England. II. Feudal Lords and the Subordination of Peasant Women." *Sociological Review* n.s. 29 (February 1981): 137-154.

5. RELIGION

". . . that the high might of the Trinity is our Father, and the deep wisdom of the Trinity is our Mother, and the great love of the Trinity is our Lord. The Second Person which is our Mother substantially, the same dear worthy person is now become our Mother sensual; for we double of God's making; that is to say substantial and sensual."

Julian of Norwich
XVI Revelations of Divine Love

a) Generic

01650. Aston, Margaret. "Lollard Women Priests?" *Journal of Ecclesiastical History* 31 (1980): 441-461.

01651. Bell, L. Michael. "'Hel Our Queen': An Old Norse Analogue to an Old English Female Hell." *Harvard Theological Review* 76 (April 1983): 263-268.

01652. Tudor, Victoria. "The Misogyny of Saint Cuthbert." *Archaeologia Aeliana* 5 (1984): 157-167.

b) Goddesses

01653. Cathasaigh, Donal O. "The Cult of Brigid: A Study of Pagan-Christian Syncretism in Ireland." In *Mother Worship Themes and Variations*, edited by James J. Preston, pp. 75-94. Chapel Hill, N.C.: University of North Carolina Press, 1982. Also in *Mankind Quarterly* 19 (June 1979): 311-328.

c) Saints/Religious Women

(1) Julian of Norwich

01654. Bancroft, Anne. The Luminous Vision: Six Medieval Mystics and Their Teachings. London: Allen and Unwin, 1982.

01655. Barker, Paula S. Datsko. "The Motherhood of God in Julian of Norwich's Theology." Downside Review 100 (October 1982): 290-304.

01656. Bradford, C.M. "Julian of Norwich and Margery Kempe." Theology Today 35 (July 1978): 153-158.

01657. Jones, Catherine. The English Mystic: Julian of Norwich." In Medieval Women Writers, edited by Katharine M. Wilson, pp. 269-296. Athens, Ga.: University of Georgia Press, 1984.

01658. McIlwain, James T. "The 'bodelye syeknes' of Julian of Norwich." Journal of Medieval History 10 (September 1984): 167-180.

01659. Pelphrey, Brant. Love was His Meaning: The Theology and Mysticism of Julian of Norwich. Salzburg: Institut fur Anglistik und Amerikanistik, 1982.

01660. Vinje, Patricia Mary. An Understanding of Love according to the Anchoress Julian of Norwich. Salzburg: Institut fur Anglistik und Amerikanistik, 1983.

01661. Watkins, Renee Neu. "Two Women Visionaries and Death. Catherine of Siena and Julian of Norwich." Numen 30 (December 1983): 174-198.

Also refer to #1665.

(2) Margery Kempe

01662. Atkinson, Clarissa. Mystic and Pilgrim. The Book and World of Margery Kempe. Ithaca, NY: Cornell University Press, 1983.

01663. Provost, William. "The English Religious Enthusiast: Margery Kempe." In Medieval Women Writers, edited by Katharine M. Wilson, pp. 297-319. Athens, Ga.: University of Georgia Press, 1984.

01664. Thornton, Martin. Margery Kempe. London: S.P.C.K., 1960.

01665. Watkin, Edward Ingram. On Julian of Norwich, and in Defense of Margery Kempe. Exeter: University of Exeter, 1979.

Also refer to #1656, 2118.

(3) Others

01666. Lowry, M.J.C. "Caxton, St. Winifred, and the Lady Margaret Beaufort." Library 6th ser. 5 (June 1983): 101-117.

01667. Rollason, D.W. The Mildreth Legend A Study in Early Medieval Hagiography in England. Atlantic Highlands, N.J.: Humanities Press, 1982.

Also refer to #1637, 1672, 1674.

d) Mariology

01668. Heffernan, Thomas J. "The Virgin as an Aid to Salvation in Some Fifteenth-Century English and Latin Verses." Medium Aevum 52 (1983): 229-238.

e) Monastic Life

01669. Elkins, Sharon K. "The Emergence of a Gilbertine Identity." In Medieval Religious Women, vol. 1, Distant Echoes, edited by John A. Nichols and Lillian Thomas, pp. 169-182. Kalamazoo, Mich.: Cistercian Publications, 1984.

01670. Graves, Coburn V. "Stixwould in the Market Place." In Medieval Religious Women, vol. 1, Distant Echoes, edited by John A. Nichols and Lillian Thomas, pp. 213-234. Kalamazoo, Mich.: Cistercian Publications, 1984.

01671. Meyer, Marc Anthony. "Patronage of the West Saxon Royal Nunneries in Late Anglo-Saxon England." Revue Benedictine 91 (1981): 332-358.

01672. Millinger, Susan. "Humility and Power: Anglo-Saxon Nuns in Anglo-Norman Hagiography." In Medieval Religious Women, vol. 1, Distant Echoes, edited by John A. Nichols and Lillian Thomas, pp. 115-129. Kalamazoo, Mich.: Cistercian Publications, 1984.

01673. Nichols, John A. "Medieval Cistercian Nunneries and English Bishops." In Medieval Religious Women, vol. 1, Distant Echoes, edited by John A. Nichols and Lillian Thomas, pp. 237-249. Kalamazoo, Mich.: Cistercian Publications, 1984.

01674. Talbot, Charles. "Christina of Markyate: a Monastic Narrative of the Twelfth Century." Essays and Studies n.s. 15 (1962): 13-26.

01675. Thompson, Sally. "Why English Nunneries Had No History: A Study of the Problems of the English Nunneries Founded after the Conquest." In Medieval Religious Women, vol. 1, Distant Echoes, edited by John A. Nichols and Lillian Thomas, pp. 131-149. Kalamazoo, Mich.: Cistercian Publications, 1984.

01676. Warren, Ann K. "The Nun as Anchoress: England, 1100-1500." In Medieval Religious Women, vol. 1, Distant Echoes, edited by John A. Nichols and Lillian Thomas, pp. 197-212. Kalamazoo, Mich.: Cistercian Publications, 1984.

f) Witchcraft

01677. Neary, Anne. "The Origins and Character of the Kilkenny Witchcraft Case of 1324." Proceedings of the Royal Irish Academy section c, 83 (1983): 333-350.

6. SOCIAL

> "Man does not just aim at generating offspring for the multiplication of the species, like a beast; he aims at living a good and peaceful life with his wife."
>
> John Baconthorpe

a) Generic

01678. Colker, Marvin L. "The Lure of Women, Hunting, Chess and Tennis: A Vision." Speculum 59 (January 1984): 103-105.

01679. Hamlin, Ann and Foley, Clair. "A Women's Graveyard at Carrickmore, County Tyrone and the Separate Burial of Women." Ulster Journal of Archeology ser.3 46 (1984): 41-46.

01680. McAll, Christopher. "The Normal Paradigms of a Woman's Life in the Irish and Welsh Texts." In The Welsh Law of Women, edited by Dafydd Jenkins and Morfydd E. Owen, pp. 7-22. Cardiff: University Press, 1980.

01681. Owen, Marfydd E. "Shame and Reparation: Woman's Place in the Kin." In The Welsh Law of Women, edited by Dafydd Jenkins and Morfydd E. Owen, pp. 40-68. Cardiff: University Press, 1980.

01682. Ross, Barbara. "Vipers and Gardens of Balsam: St. Thomas and the Virtues of Purity and Prudence." In St. Thomas Cantilupe, Bishop of Hereford: Essays in His Honor, pp. 73-81. Hereford: Friends of Hereford Cathedral, 1982.

01683. Tilly, Louise A. "Kin and neighbours in a Thirteenth Century Suffolk Community." Journal of Family History 4 (1979): 137-152.

b) Demography

01684. Hallam, H.E. "Age at First Marriage and Age at Death in the Lincolnshire Fenland, 1251-1478." Population Studies 39 (March 1985): 55-70.

01685. Hatcher, John. "Mortality in the Fifteenth Century: Some New Evidence." Economic History Review 2nd series 39 (February 1986): 19-38.

c) Family

(1) Non-specific

01686. Bennett, Judith M. "The Tie That Binds: Peasant Marriages and Families in Late Medieval England." Journal of Interdisciplinary History 15 (Summer 1984): 111-129.

01687. Hanawalt, Barbara A. The Ties That Bind, Peasant Families in Medieval England. New York: Oxford University Press, 1986.

01688. Lanahan, W.F. "What's in a Name? Family Surnames and Social Upheaval in Medieval England." Social Studies 65 (1974): 218-222.

Also refer to #1611, 1615.

(2) Childhood

01689. Attreed, Lorraine C. "From Pearl Maiden to Tower Princes: Towards a New History of Medieval Childhood." Journal of Medieval History 9 (March 1983): 43-58.

Also refer to #1621, 1714.

d) Marriage

01690. Bennett, Judith M. "Medieval Peasant Marriage: An Examination of Marriage License Fines in the Liber Gersumarum." In Pathways to Medieval Peasants, edited by J.A. Raftis, pp. 193-246. Toronto: Pontifical Institute of Medieval Studies, 1981.

01691. Brand, Paul A. and Hyams, Paul R. "Seigneurial Control of Women's Marriage." Past and Present 99 (1983): 123-133.

Also refer to #1694, 1698.

01692. Davies, R.R. "The Status of Women and the Practice of Marriage in Late-Medieval Wales." The Welsh Law of Women, edited by Dafydd Jenkins and Morfydd E. Owen, pp. 93-114. Cardiff: University Press, 1980.

01693. DeAragon, RaGena C. "In Pursuit of Aristocratic Women: A Key to Success in Norman England." Albion 14 (Winter 1982): 258-267.

01694. Faith, Rosamund. "Seigneurial Control of Women's Marriage." Past and Present 99 (1983): 133-148.

Also refer to #1691, 1698.

01695. Hill, Rosalind. "Marriage in Seventh Century England." In Saints, Scholars and Heroes, edited by Margot H. King and Wesley M. Stevens, 2:67-75. Collegeville, Minn.: Hill Monastic Manuscript Library, 1979.

01696. Rosenthal, Joel T. "Aristocratic Marriage and the English Peerage, 1350-1500: Social Institution and Personal Bond." Journal of Medieval History 10 (September 1984): 181-194.

01697. Ross, Margaret Clunies. "Concubinage in Anglo-Saxon England." Past and Present 108 (August 1985): 3-34.

01698. Searle, Eleanor. "A Rejoinder." Past and Present 99 (1983): 148-160.

01699. Sellar, W.D.H. "Marriage, Divorce and Concubinage in Gaelic Scotland." Transactions of the Gaelic Society of Inverness 51 (1978-1980): 464-493.

Also refer to #1616, 1617, 1619, 1622, 1626-1629, 1641, 1684, 1685, 1709, 1717, 1720, 1729, 1738, 1749, 1756, 1762-1765.

e) Sex Life and Morals

01700. Post, J.B. "A Fifteenth-Century Customary of the Southwark Stews." Journal of the Society of Archivists 5 (1977): 418-428.

Also refer to #1623, 1630-1632, 1748.

f) Health/Medical

01701. Manchester, K. "Secondary Cancer in an Anglo-Saxon Female." Journal of Archaeological Science 10 (1983): 475-82.

7. CULTURAL

"But God forbid that you should say or take me for a teacher for I do not intend that nor ever did so, for I am a woman, ignorant, weak, and frail."

Julian of Norwich

a) Education

01702. Leibell, Jane Frances. _Anglo-Saxon Education of Women from Hilda to Hildegarde_. Washington D.C.: n.p. 1922.

01703. Orme, Nicholas. _English Schools in the Middle Ages_. New York: Barnes and Noble, 1973. [See especially pp. 52-55.]

Also refer to #1621.

b) Literature

(1) Non-specific

(a) Women in Literature

01704. Damico, Helen. "The Valkyrie Reflex in Old English Literature." _Allegorica_ 5 (Winter 1980): 149-167.

01705. Harris, Adelaide E. _Heroine of the Middle English Romances_. 1928. Reprint. Folcroft Penn.: Folcroft Library Editions, 1973.

01706. Morrison, Stephen. "The Figure of 'Christus Sponsus' in Old English Prose." In _Liebe-Ehe-Ehebruch in der Literatur des Mittelalters_, edited by Xenja von Ertzdorff and Marianne Wynn, pp. 5-15. Giessen: Wilhelm Schnitz, 1984.

01707. Schmitz, Gotz. _Die Frauenklage: Studien zur elegischen Verserzahlung in der englischen Literatur des Spatmittelalters und der Renaissance_. Tubingen: Max Niemeyer, 1984.

01708. Schrader, Richard J. _God's Handiwork: Images of Women in Early Germanic Literature_. Westport, Ct.: Greenwood Press, 1983.

01709. Wood, Juliette. "The Calumnated Wife in Medieval Welsh Literature." _Cambridge Medieval Celtic Studies_ 10 (Winter 1985): 25-38.

(2) Poetry

(a) Chaucer

01710. Aers, David. "Criseyde: Woman in Medieval Society." *Chaucer Review* 13 (1979): 177-200.

01711. Amsler, Mark E. "Mad Lovers and Other Hooked Fish: Chaucer's *Complaint of Mars*." *Allegorica* 4 (Summer-Winter 1979): 301-314.

01712. Arn, M.J. "Three Ovidian Women in Chaucer's Troilus: Medea, Helen, Oenone." *Chaucer Review* 15 (Summer 1980): 1-10.

01713. Azelrod, Steven. "The Wife of Bath and the Clerk." *Annuale Mediaevale* 15 (1974): 109-124.

01714. Baron, F. Xavier. "Children and Violence in Chaucer's *Canterbury Tales*." *Journal of Psychohistory* 7 (Summer 1979): 77-103.

01715. Bassil, Veronica. "The Faces of Griselda: Chaucer, Prior and Richardson: A Discussion of Four Portrayals of Female Virtue including *The Not-Brown Mayd*." *Texas Studies in Language and Literature* 26 (1984): 157-182.

01716. Beichner, Paul E. "Confrontation, Contempt of Court, and Chaucer's Cecilia." *Chaucer Review* 8 (Winter 1974): 198-204.

01717. Benson, Donald R. "The Marriage 'encomium' in the *Merchant's Tale*: A Chaucerian Crux." *Chaucer Review* 14 (1979): 48-60.

01718. Bergner, Heinz. "Der gelöste Konflikt. Zu Chaucers 'Franklin's Tale.'" In *Liebe-Ehe-Ehebruch in der Literatur des Mittelalters*, edited by Xenja von Ertzdroff and Marianne Wynn, pp. 140-147. Giessen: Wilhelm Schnitz, 1984.

01719. Bolton, W.F. "The Wife of Bath: Narrator as Victim." In *Gender and Literary Voice*, Women and Literature, vol. 1, edited by Janet Todd, pp. 54-65. New York: Holmes and Meier, 1980.

01720. Boren, James. "Alysoun of Bath and the Vulgate 'perfect wife.'" *Neuphilologische Mitteilungen* 76 (1975): 247-256.

01721. Brewer, Derek S. "Honour in Chaucer." *Essays and Studies* n.s. 26 (1973): 1-19.

01722. Brown, Eric D. "Transformation and the Wife of Bath's Tale: A Jungian Discussion." *Chaucer Review* 10 (Spring 1976): 303-315.

01723. Burnley, J.D. "Criseyde's Heart and the Weakness of Women: An Essay in Lexical Interpretation." _Studia Neophilologica_ 54 (1982): 25-38.

01724. Clark, Susan L. and Wasserman, Julian N. "Constance as Romance and Folk Heroine in Chaucer's Man of Law's Tale." _Rice University Studies_ 64 (Winter 1978): 13-24.

01725. Clasby, E. "Chaucer's Constance: Womanly Virtue and the Heroic Life." _Chaucer Review_ 13 (Winter 1979): 221-233.

01726. Delany, Sheila. "'Mulier est hominis confusio': Chaucer's Anti-Popular _Nun's Priest Tale_." _Mosaic_ 17 (Winter 1984): 1-8.

01727. ______________. "Sexual Economics, Chaucer's Wife of Bath, and _The Book of Margery Kempe_." In _Writing Woman_, pp. 76-92. New York: Schocken Books, 1983.

01728. ______________. "Slaying Python: Marriage and Misogyny in a Chaucerian Text." In _Writing Woman_, pp. 47-75. New York: Schocken Books, 1983.

01729. ______________. "Womanliness in _The Man of Law's Tale_." In _Writing Woman_, pp. 36-46. New York: Schocken Books, 1983. Also in _Chaucer Review_ 9 (1974): 63-72.

01730. Delasanta, Rodney. "_Quoniam_ and the Wife of Bath." _Papers on Language and Literature_ 8 (Spring 1972): 202-206.

01731. Diamond, Aryln. "Chaucer's Women and Women's Chaucer." In _The Authority of Experience_, edited by Arlyn Diamond and Lee R. Edwards, pp. 60-83. Amherst: University of Massachusetts Press, 1977.

01732. Edwards, Robert. "_The Book of the Duchess_ and the Beginnings of Chaucer's Narrative." _New Literary History_ 13 (Winter 1982): 189-204.

01733. Fries, Maureen. "'Slydynge of Corage': Chaucer's Criseyde as Feminist and Victim." In _The Authority of Experience_, edited by Arlyn Diamond and Lee R. Edwards, pp. 45-59. Amherst: University of Massachusetts, 1977.

01734. Gallacher, Patrick J. "Dame, Dice and the Nobility of Pleasure." _Viator_ 13 (1982): 275-293.

01735. Gallagher, Joseph E. "Criseyde's Dream of the Eagle: Love and War in _Troilus and Criseyde_." _Modern Language Quarterly_ 36 (June 1975): 115-132.

01736. Galway, Margaret. "Philippa Pan, Philippa Chaucer." _Modern Language Review_ 55 (October 1960): 481-487.

01737. Glasser, Marc. "'He Nedes Moste Hire Wedde: "The Forced Marriage in the 'Wife of Bath's Tale' and Its Middle English Analogues." Neuphilologische Mitteilungen 85 (1984): 239-241.

01738. Hansen, Elaine Tuttle. "Irony and the Antifeminist Narrator in Chaucer's Legend of Good Women." Journal of English and Germanic Philology 82 (1983): 11-31.

01739. Jacobs, Kathryn. "The Marriage Contract of the Franklin's Tale. The Remaking of Society." Chaucer Review 20 (1985): 132-143.

01740. Kerhan, Anne. "The Archwife and the Eunuch." English Literary History 41 (Spring 1974): 1-25.

01741. Leicester, H. Marshall, Jr. "Of a Fire in the Dark: Public and Private Feminism in the Wife of Bath's Tale." Women's Studies 11 (1984): 157-178.

01742. Luecke, Janemarie. "Three Faces of Cecilia: Chaucer's Second Nun's Tale." American Benedictine Review 33 (December 1982): 335-348.

01743. Lunz, Elisabeth. "Chaucer's Prudence as the Ideal of the Virtuous Woman." Essays in Literature 4 (Spring 1977): 3-10.

01744. Miller, Robert P. "Constancy Humanized: Trivet's Constance and the Man of Law's Custance." Costerus 4 (1975): 49-71.

01745. Oberembt, Kenneth J. "Chaucer's Anti-Misogynist Wife of Bath." Chaucer Review 10 (Spring 1976): 287-302.

01746. Patterson, Lee. "'For the Wyves love of Bathe': Feminine Rhetoric and Poetic Resolution in the Roman de la Rose and the Canterbury Tales." Speculum 58 (July 1983): 656-695.

01747. Reiss, Edmund. "Chaucer's Deerne Love and the Medieval View of Secrecy in Love." In Chaucerian Problems and Perspectives. Essays Presented to Paul E. Beichner, C.S.C., edited by Edward Vasta and Zacharias P. Thundy, pp. 164-179. Notre Dame, Ind.: University of Notre Dame Press, 1979.

01748. Renoir, Alain. "The Inept Lover and the Reluctant Mistress: Remarks on Sexual Inefficiency in Medieval Literature." In Chaucerian Problems and Perspectives. Essays Presented to Paul E. Beichner, C.S.C., edited by Edward Vasta and Zacharias P. Thundy, pp. 180-206. Notre Dame, Ind.: University of Notre Dame Press, 1979.

01749. Rudat, Wolfgang E.H. "Gentilesse and the Marriage Debate in the Franklin's Tale: Chaucer's Squires and the Question of Nobility." Neophilologus 68 (July 1984): 451-470.

01750. Sands, D.B. "Non-comic, Non-tragic Wife: Chaucer's Dame Alys as Sociopath." Chaucer Review 12 (Winter 1978): 171-182.

01751. Spisak, James. "Anti-feminism Bridled: Two Rhetorical Contexts." Neuphilologische Mitteilungen 81 (1980): 150-160.

01752. Weissman, Hope Phyllis. "Antifeminism and Chaucer's Characterization of Women." In Geoffrey Chaucer, edited by George D. Economous, pp. 93-110. New York: McGraw-Hill, 1975.

01753. Witte, Stephen. "Muscipula Diaboli and Chaucer's Portrait of the Prioress." Papers on Language and Literature 13 (Summer 1977): 227-237.

(b) Others

01754. Abraham, Lenore MacGaffey. "Cynewulf's Juliana. A Case at Law." Allegorica 3 (Summer 1978): 172-189.

01755. Eadie, John. "Sir Gawain and the Ladies of Ill-Repute." Annuale Mediaevale 20 (1981): 52-66.

01756. Edwards, A.S.G. "Marriage, Harping and Kingship: The Unity of Sir Orfeo." American Benedictine Review 32 (1981): 282-291.

01757. Fries, Maureen. "Medieval Concepts of the Female and Their Satire in the Poetry of William Dunbar." Fifteenth-Century Studies 7 (1983): 55-77.

01758. ______________. "The 'Other' Voice: Woman's Songs Its Satire and Its Transcendence in Late Medieval British Literature." In Vox Feminae: Studies in Medieval Woman's Songs, edited by John F. Plummer, pp. 155-178. Kalamazoo, Mich.: Western Michigan University, 1981.

01759. Lehmann, Ruth P.M. "Woman's Songs in Irish, 800-1500." In Vox Feminae: Studies in Medieval Woman's Songs, edited by John F. Plummer, pp. 111-134. Kalamazoo, MI: Western Michigan University, 1981.

01760. McCarthy, Shaun. "'Syne maryit I a marchand' - Dunbar's Mariit Women and Their Audience." Studies in Scottish Literature 19 (1983): 138-156.

01761. Plummer, John F. "The Woman's Song in Middle English and Its European Backgrounds." In Vox Feminae: Studies in Medieval Woman's Songs, edited by John F. Plummer, pp. 135-154. Kalamazoo, Mich.: Western Michigan University, 1981.

01762. Sichert, Margit. "Liebe in den Mittelenglischen Pastourellen." In Liebe-Ehe-Ehebruch in der Literatur des Mittelalters, edited by Xenja von Ertzdorff and Marianne Wynn, pp. 125-139. Giessen: Wilhelm Schnitz, 1984.

01763. Tavormina, M. Theresa. "'Bothe two ben gode': Marriage and Virginity in Piers Plowman c. 18. 68-100." Journal of English and Germanic Philology 81 (1982): 320-330.

01764. ____________________. "Kindly Similitude: Langland's Matrimonial Trinity." Modern Philology 80 (1982): 117-128.

(3) Prose

01765. Blangez, Gerard. "Dissuasio Valerii ou la dissuasion de mariage de Gautier Map." In Melanges d'etudes anciennes offerts a Maurice Lebel, edited by Jean-Benoit Caron, et al., pp. 385-394. Quebec: Les Editions du Sphinx, 1980.

01766. Bornstein, Diane. "Anti-feminism in Thomas Hoccleve's Translation of Christine de Pizan's Epistre au Dieu d'Amours." English Language Notes 19 (1981): 7-14.

01767. Guynonvarc'h, Christian-J. "La mort de Muirchertach, fils d'Erc. Texte irlandais du tres Haut Moyen Age: La femme, le saint et le roi." Annales: economies, societes, civilisations 38 (September-October 1983): 985-1015.

01768. Olsen, Alexandra Hennessey. "Inversion and Political Purpose in the Old English Judith." English Studies 63 (1982): 216-219.

01769. Randolph, Mary Claire. "Female Satirists of Ancient Ireland." Southern Folklore Quarterly 6 (June 1942): 75-87.

c) Chivalry

(1) Courtly Love

01770. Bennett, Michael Q. "Courtly Literature and North West England in the Late Middle Ages." In Court and Poet, edited by Glyn S. Burgess, et al., pp. 69-78. Liverpool: Francis Cairns, 1981.

01771. Senior, Michael. "The Phaedra Complex Amour Courtois in Malory's 'Mort d'Arthur.'" Folklore 82 (Spring 1971): 36-59.

d) Art

(1) Women in Art

01772. Smith, Jeffrey Chipps. "The Tomb of Anne of Burgundy, Duchess of Bedford. In _Musée du Louvre_." _Gesta_ 23 (1984): 39-50.

C. FRANCE

1. SURVEYS

> "Every good quality is obscured in the girl or woman whose virginity falters. . . riches, beauty, and all other virtues are lost and as nothing in a woman so stained."
>
> Le Menagier de Paris

01773. Duby, Georges. "Notes brèves sur le fait féminin au XIIe siècle." In _Le Fait féminin_, edited by Evelyne Sullerot, pp. 421-424. Paris: Fayard, 1978.

01774. Pernoud, Régine. _La femme au temps des cathédrales_. Paris: Stock, 1980.

2. POLITICAL

> "Women are not as cruel as the men who rule the world. They do not kill, disinherit others, draw up false agreements or cause harm to the kingdom."
>
> Christine de Pisan

a) Legal

01775. Angers, Denise. "La femme en Basse-Normandie: droit et realité." _Revue de l'Université d'Ottawa_ 52 (1982): 210-219.

01776 Coulet, Noel. "Une curiosité notariale: Le testament congonctif d'un couple aixois en 1476." _Recueil de mémoires et travaux publié par la Société d'histoire du droit et des institutions des anciens pays du droit écrit_ 12 (1983): 59-63.

01777. Gaudemet, Jean. "Indissolubilité et consommation du mariage. L'apport d'Hincmar de Reims." _Revue de droit canonique_ 30 (1980): 28-40.

01778. Gouron, André. "Un échec des glossateurs: l'egalité des rapports matrimonaux et la pratique meridionale." Recueil de mémoires et travaux publié par la Société d'histoire du droit et des institutions des anciens pays du droit écrit 12 (1983): 93-105.

01779. Hajdu, Robert. "The Position of Noblewomen in the Pays des Coutomes, 1100-1300." Journal of Family History 5 (Summer 1980): 122-144.

01780. Malaussena, Paul-Louis La vie en Provence orientale aux XIVe et XVe siecles. Paris: Librarie generale de droit et de jurisprudence, 1969.

01781. Porteau-Bitker, A. "Criminalité et delinquance féminines dans le droit penal des XIIIe et XIVe siècles." Revue historique de droit française et étranger 58 (1980): 13-56.

01782. Turlan, Juliette M. and Timbal, Pierre C. "Justice laique et lien matrimonial en France au Moyen Age." Revue de droit canonique 30 (1980): 347-363.

Also refer to #1616, 1817.

b) Political Roles

(1) Joan of Arc

01783. Bancal, Jean. Jeanne d'Arc, princesse royale. Paris: Robert Lafont, 1971.

01784. Bernard, Jose. Joana d'Arc, a donzela d'Orleans. Petrópolis: Editora Vozes, 1961.

01785. Colson, Jean. Domremy; ou La vallée inspirée. Paris: Editions S.O.S., 1973.

01786. David-Darnac, Maurice. Le Dossier de Jehanne. Paris: J.J. Pauvert, 1968.

01787. ____________________. Histoire veridique et merveilleuse de la Pucelle d'Orléans. Paris: La Table ronde, 1969.

01788. Gies, Frances. Joan of Arc: The Legend and the Reality. New York: Harper and Row, 1981.

01789. Guillemin, Henri. Jeanne dite Jeanne d'Arc. Paris: Gallimard, 1977.

01790. Hanna, Martha. "Iconology and Ideology: Images of Jean of Arc in the Idiom of the Action française, 1908-1931." French Historical Studies 14 (Fall 1985): 215-239.

01791. Liocourt, Ferdinand de. La mission de Jeanne d'Arc. Paris: Nouvelles Editions latines, 1974.

01792. Raknem, Ingvald. Joan of Arc in History, Legend, and Literature. Oslo: Universitetsforlaget, 1971.

01793. Ready, Dolores. Joan, the Good Soldier: Joan of Arc. Minneapolis: Winston Press, 1977.

01794. Ribera-Perville, Claude. "Jeanne d'Arc au pays des images." Histoire 15 (1979): 58-67.

01795. Sackville-West, Victoria. Saint Joan of Arc: Burned as a Heretic, May 30, 1430: Canonized as a Saint, May 16, 1920. 1973. Reprint. Boston: G.K. Hall, 1984.

01796. Searle, William. The Saint and the Skeptics. Joan of Arc in the Works of Mark Twain, Anatole France and Bernard Shaw. Detroit, Mich.: Wayne State University Press, 1976.

01797. Walker, Kathrine Sorley. Joan of Arc. London: Jackdaw, 1965.

01798. Warner, Marina. Joan of Arc: The Image of Female Heroism. New York: Vintage Books, 1982.

01799. Weintraub, Stanley. Saint Joan: Fifty Years After. Baton Rouge, La.: Louisiana State University Press, 1973.

Also refer to #1824.

(2) Isabella of Bavaria

01800. Grandeau, Yann. "Isabeau de Bavière ou l'amour conjugal." In Actes du 102e Congres national des Sociétés savantes, Limoges 1977. Section de philologie et d'histoire jusqu'à 1610, 2: Études sur la sensibilité, pp. 117-148. Paris: Bibliothèque national, 1979.

01801. Markale, Jean. Isabeau de Bavière. Paris: Payot, 1982.

01802. Saller, Martin. Königin Isabeau. Munich: Nymphenburger, 1979.

01803. Verdon, Jean. Isabeau de Bavière. Paris: Tallandier, 1981.

(3) Agnès Sorel

01804. Kemp-Welch, Alice. "Agnes Sorel." In Nineteenth Century and After 58 (September 1905): 416-426.

01805. Philippe, Robert. Agnès Sorel. Paris: Hachette, 1983.

01806. Pollitzer, Marcel. La règne du favorite Agnès Sorel. Avignon: Aubanel, 1933.

01807. Schlumberger, E. "Agnès Sorel et sa legende: un exposition à Loches, France." In Connaissance des Arts 219 (May 1970): 90-97.

(4) Others

01808. Boutaric, Edgard. "Marguerite de Provence, son caractère, son rôle politique." Revue des questions historiques 3 (October 1867): 417-458.

01809. Bruguière, Marie-Bernadette. "Le mariage de Philippe Auguste et d'Isambour de Danemark: aspects canoniques et politiques." In Mélanges offerts à Jean Dauvillier, pp. 135-156. Toulouse: Centre d'histoire juridique meridionale, 1979.

01810. Caix de Saint-Aymour, Amédee Vicomte de. Anne de Russie, reine de France et Comtesse de Valois au XIe siècle. 2nd. ed. Paris: Champion, 1896.

01811. Elliott, Alison Goddard. "The Emperor's Daughter": An Old Catalan Account of Charlemagne's Mother." Romance Philology 34 (May 1981): 398-416.

01812. Hyam, Jane. "Ermentrude and Richildis." In Charles the Bald: Court and Kingdom, edited by Margaret Gibson, Janet Nelson and David Ganz, pp. 153-168. Oxford: British Archaeological Reports, 1981.

01813. Vallée-Karcher, Aline. "Jeanne de Bourgogne, épouse de Philippe VI de Valois: une reine Maudite?" Bibliothèque Ecole Chartres 138 (January- June 1980): 94-96.

01814. Yannick, Hillion. "La Bretagne et la rivalité Capétiens-Plantagenets. Un exemple: la duchesse Constance (1186-1202)." Annales de Bretagne et des Pays de l'Ouest 92 (1985): 111-144.

3. RELIGION

"Whoever has received knowledge and eloquence and speech from God should not be silent or conceal it, but demonstrate it willingly."

Marie de France

a) Generic

01815. Berier, François. "L'humaniste, le prêtre et l'enfant mort: le sermon 'De Sanctis Innocentibus' de Nicolas de Clamanges." In L'enfant au moyen âge, pp. 123-140. Aix-en Provence: Université, 1980.

01816. Brennan, Brian. "'Episcopae': Bishops Wives Viewed in Sixth Century Gaul." Church History 54 (September 1985): 311-323.

01817. Turlan, Juliette M. "Instigante diablo." In *Mélanges offerts à Jean Dauvillier*, pp. 803-808. Toulouse: Centre d'histoire juridique méridionale, 1979.

b) Saints/Religious Women

01818. Bambeck, Manfred. "'Element' und 'virginitet' in der altfranzosischen Eulaliasiquenz." *Archiv für das Studium der neueren Sprachen und Literaturen* 220 (1983): 88-109.

01819. Barnett, F.J. "Some Notes to the *Sequence of St. Eulalia*." In *Studies in Medieval French Presented to Alfred Ewert*, pp. 1-25. Oxford: Oxford University Press, 1961.

01820. Brzoska, Emil. *Barbaraverehrung und Bergbau mit Berucksichtigung des oberschlesischen Industriegebiets*. Dulmen: Laumann-Verlag, 1982.

01821. Caprio, Betsy. *The Woman Sealed in the Tower--Being A View of Feminine Spirituality as Revealed by the Legend of Saint Barbara*. New York: Paulist Press, 1982.

01822. Constable, Giles. "Troyes, Constantinople, and the Relics of St. Helen in the Thirteenth Century." In *Mélanges offerts à René Crozet* 2: 1035-1042. Poitiers: Société d'Etudes Médiévales, 1966.

01823. Dubois, Jacques. *Sainte Geneviève de Paris*. Paris: Beauchesne, 1982.

01824. Vauchez, André. "Jeanne d'Arc et le prophetisme féminin des XIVe et XV siècles." In *Jeanne d'Arc: Une époque, un rayonnement*, pp. 159-168. Paris: CNRS, 1982.

Also refer to #1783-1799.

c) Mariology

01825. Lefrancois-Pillion, Louise. "Les statues de la Vierge dans la sculptière français au XIVe siècle." *Gazette des Beaux Arts* 77 no. 2 (July-December 1935): 129-149; 204-227.

01826. Rickard, Marcia R. "The Iconography of the Virgin Portal at Amiens." *Gesta* 22 (1983): 147-157.

Also refer to #1847.

d) Monastic Life/Religious Orders

(1) Non-specific

01827. Blair, Peter Hunter. *The World of Bede*. New York: St. Martin's Press, 1971.

01828. Boulard, Marie-Odile. "Les chanoinesses de Remiremont, du XIVe siècle au début du XVIIe siècle." In Remiremont, l'abbaye et la ville, edited by Michel Parisse, pp. 61-69. Nancy: Université, 1980.

01829. Connor, Elizabeth. "Ten Centuries of Growth: The Cistercian Abbey of Soleilmont." In Medieval Religious Women, vol. 1, Distant Echoes, edited by John A. Nichols and Lillian Thomas: 251-267. Kalamazoo, Mich.: Cistercian Publications, 1984.

01830. Gold, Penny Schine. "Male/Female Cooperation: The Example of Fontevrault." In Medieval Religious Women, vol. 1, Distant Echoes, edited by John A. Nichols and Lillian Thomas: 151-168. Kalamazoo, Mich.: Cistercian Publications, 1984.

01831. Guillaume, Jean-Marie. "Les abbayes de femmes en pays franc, des origines à la fin du VIIe siècle." In Remiremont, l'abbaye et la ville, edited by Michel Parisse, pp. 39-46. Nancy: Université, 1980.

01832. Leclercq, Jean. "Does St. Bernard Have a Special Message for Nuns?" In Medieval Religious Women, vol. 1, Distant Echoes, edited by John A. Nichols and Lillian Thomas: 269-278. Kalamazoo, Mich.: Cistercian Publications, 1984.

01833. Müssigbrod, Axel. "Frauenkonversionen in Moissac." Historisches Jahrbuch 104 (1984): 113-129.

01834. Skinner, Mary. "Benedictine Life for Women in Central France, 850-1100: A Feminist Revival." In Medieval Religious Women, vol. 1, Distant Echoes, edited by John A. Nichols and Lillian Thomas: 87-113. Kalamazoo, MI: Cistercian Publications, 1984.

(2) Héloïse

01835. Benton, John F. "Fraud, Fiction and Borrowing in the Correspondence of Abelard and Héloïse." In Pierre Abelard-Pierre le Vénérable, Proceedings of the International Symposium of the Centre National de la Recherche Scientifique (July 2-9, 1972) 546: 469-511. Paris: Editions du centre national de la recherche scientifique, 1975.

01836. Charrier, Charlotte. Héloïse: Dans l'histoire et dans la legende. Paris: Libraire Ancienne Honoré Champion, 1933.

01837. McLaughlin, Mary Martin. "Peter Abelard and the Dignity of Women: Twelfth Century 'Feminism' in Theory and Practice." In Pierre Abelard-Pierre le Vénérable, Proceedings of the International Symposium of the Centre National de la Recherche Scientifique (July 2-9, 1972) 546: 287-333. Paris: Editions du centre national de la recherche scientifique, 1975.

01838. Monfrin, Jacques. "Le problème de l'authenticité de la correspondance d'Abelard et Héloïse." In Pierre Abelard-Pierre le Vénérable, Proceedings of the International Symposium of the Centre National de la Recherche Scientifique (July 2-9, 1972) 546: 409-424. Paris: Editions du centre national de la recherche scientifique, 1975.

01839. Moos, Peter von. "Le silence d'Héloïse et les idéologies modernes." In Pierre Abelard-Pierre le Vénérable, Proceedings of the International Symposium of the Centre National de la Recherche Scientifique (July 2-9, 1972) 546: 425-468. Paris: Editions du centre national de la recherche scientifique, 1975.

01840. Radice, Betty. "The French Scholar-Lover: Héloïse." In Medieval Women Writers, edited by Katharine M. Wilson, pp. 90-108. Athens, Ga.: University of Georgia Press, 1984.

01841. Zerbi, Piero. "Abelardo ed Eloisa: il problema di un amore e di una corrispondenza." In Love and Marriage in the Twelfth Century, edited by Willy Van Hoecke and Andries Welkenhuysen, pp. 130-161. Louvain: Leuven University Press, 1981.

e) Witchcraft

01842. Forbes, Thomas Rogers. "Perrette the Midwife: A Fifteenth Century Witchcraft Case." Bulletin of the History of Medicine 36 (March-April 1962): 124-129.

4. SOCIAL

"When your husband wishes to embrace you, suffer his advances obediently as the monk obeys his abbot."

Robert of Blois

a) Generic

01843. Bloch, Marc. French Rural History. Translated by Janet Sondheimer. Berkeley, CA: University of California Press, 1966.

01844. Commeaux, Charles. La vie quotidienne en Bourgogne au temps des ducs valois (1364-1477). Paris: Hachette, 1979.

01845. Deregnaucourt, Jean-Pierre. "L'inventaire après décès d'Ysabel Malet, bourgeoise douaisienne, en 1359. Document pour servir à l'histoire de la vie quotidienne de la bourgeoisie médiévale." Revue du Nord 64 (July-December 1982): 707-729.

01846. Derville, Alain. "Le nombre d'habitants des villes de l'Artois et de la Flandre Wallonne (1300-1450)." Revue du Nord 65 (April-June 1983): 277-299.

01847. Gold, Penny Schine. The Lady and the Virgin: Image, Attitude, and Experience in Twelfth-Century France. Chicago: University of Chicago Press, 1985.

01848. Kerherve, Jean. "Un accouchement dramatique à la fin du Moyen Âge." Annales de Bretagne 89 (1982): 391-396.

01849. Lorcin, Marie-Thérèse. Vivre et mourir en Lyonnais. Paris: Editions du CNRS, 1981.

01850. Scully, Terence. "'Douce dame d'honour': Late Fourteenth Century Qualifications of the Lady." Medioevo romanzo 7 (1980): 37-47.

b) Family

(1) Non-specific

01851. Bessmerny, J. "Les structures de la famille paysanne dans les villages de la France au IXe siècle." Le Moyen Âge 90 (1984): 165-193.

01852. Bouchard, Constance B. "The Structure of a Twelfth-Century French Family: The Lords of Seignelay." Viator 10 (1979): 39-56.

01853. Hajdu, Robert. "Family and Feudal Ties in Poitou, 1100-1300." Journal of Interdisciplinary History 8 (Summer 1977): 117-140.

01854. Hennebicque, Regine. "Structures familiales et politiques au neuvième siècle: un groupe familial de l'aristocratie française." Revue histoire 538 (April-June 1981): 289-333.

(2) Childhood

01855. Ashby, Genette. "Une analyse stylistique des formules épiques contenant 'enfant' ou l'un de ses synonymes." In L'enfant au moyen âge, pp. 219-231. Aix-en-Provence: Université, 1980.

01856. Autrand, Françoise. "Naissance illégitime et service de l'Etat: les enfants naturels dans le milieu de robe parisien, XIVe-XVe siècle." Revue histoire 542 (April-June 1982): 289-303.

01857. Caluwe, Jacques de. "L'enfant dans Daurel et Beton." In L'enfant au moyen âge, pp. 315-334. Aix-en-Provence: Université, 1980.

01858. Combarieu, Micheline de. "Enfance et démesure dans l'epopée médiévale française." In L'enfant au moyen âge, pp. 405-456. Aix-en-Provence: Université, 1980.

01859. Deschaux, Robert. "Eloy d'Amerval et l'éducation des enfants." In L'enfant au moyen âge, pp. 375-388. Aix-en-Provence: Université, 1980.

01860. Michaud-Frejaville, Françoise. "Les enfants au travail, contrats d'apprentissage en Orléanais (1380-1450)." In L'enfant au moyen âge, pp. 61-71. Aix-en-Provence: Université, 1980.

Also refer to #1815, 1870, 1873, 1874, 1876, 1877, 1919, 1925, 1928, 1933, 1936.

c) Marriage

01861. Bouchard, Constance B. "Consanguinity and noble Marriages in the Tenth and Eleventh Centuries." Speculum 56 (1981): 268-287.

01862. Critchlow, F.L. "On the Forms of Betrothal and Wedding Ceremonies in the Old French romans d'aventure." Modern Philology 2 (April-1905): 497-537.

01863. David, Marcel. "Le mariage dans la société féodale." Annales: économies, sociétés, civilisations 36 (November-December 1981): 1050-1055.

01864. Duby, George. The Knight, the Lady and the Priest. The Making of Modern Marriage in Medieval France. Translated by Barbara Bray. New York: Pantheon Books, Random House, 1983.

01865. __________. "The Matron and the Mismarried Woman: Perception of Marriage in Northern France Circa 1100." In Social Relations and Ideas, edited by T.H. Aston et al., pp. 89-108. Cambridge: University Press, 1983.

Also refer to #1616, 1776-1778, 1782, 1817, 1872, 1875, 1892, 1893, 1930, 1932.

d) Sex Life and Morals

(1) Prostitutes

01866. Otis, Leah. Prostitution in Medieval Society, History of an Urban Institution in Languedoc. Chicago: University of Chicago Press, 1985.

Also refer to #1882, 1934.

e) Burial Customs

01867. Pegeot, Pierre and Fajal, Bruno. "Le tombeau d'Alice de Vaudémont à Clairlieu." Annales de l'Est n.s. 36 (1984): 111-122.

5. CULTURAL

"I desired to keep you whom I loved beyond measure for myself alone."

Abelard of Héloïse

a) Literature

(1) Non-specific

01868. Accarie, Maurice. "Féminisme et antiféminisme dans le Jeu'Adam." Le Moyen Age 87 (1981): 207-226.

01869. Bec, Pierre. "Trobairitz occitanes et chansons de femme francaises." Perspective médiévales 5 (1979): 59-76.

01870. Berkvam, Doris Declais. Enfance et maternité dans la littérature française des XIIe et XIIIe siècles. Paris: Honoré Champión, 1981.

01871. Blakesless, Merritt R. "Eros and Thanatos: The Erotic Element in the Macabre Tradition in Continental Art and Literature of the Fifteenth Century." Fifteenth Century Studies 3 (1980): 1-20.

01872. Caluwé, Jacques de. "L'amour et le mariage, moteurs seconds, dans la littérature epique francaise et occitane du XIIe siècle." In Love and Marriage in the Twelfth Century, edited by Willy Van Hoecke and Andries Welkenhuysen, pp. 171-182. Louvain: Leuven University Press, 1981.

01873. Demarolle, Pierre. "Image de l'enfant et conceptions sociales dans deux oeuvres littéraires du XVe siècle." In L'enfant au moyen âge, pp. 359-374. Aix-en-Provence: Université, 1980.

01874. Payen, Jean-Charles. "L'enfance occultée; note sur un problème de typologie littéraire au Moyen-Age." In L'enfant au moyen âge, pp. 177-200. Aix-en-Provence: Université, 1980.

01875. ________________. "La 'mise en roman' du mariage dans la littérature francaise des XIIe et XIIIe siècles: de l'évolution idéologique à la typologie des genres." In Love and Marriage in the Twelfth Century, edited by Willy Van Hoecke and Andries Welkenhuysen, pp. 219-235. Louvain: Leuven University Press, 1981.

01876. Plouzeau, May. "Vingt regards sur l'enfançonnet, ou fragments du corps puéril dans l'ancienne littérature française." In L'enfant au moyen âge, pp. 201-218. Aix-en-Provence: Université, 1980.

01877. Vitale-Brovarone, Alessandro. "Le modele du developpement psychologique de l'enfant chez Fulgence le Mythographe." In L'enfant au moyen âge, pp. 161-176. Aix-en-Provence: Universite, 1980.

Also refer to #1855, 1859, 1862.

(2) Poetry

(a) Women in Poetry

[1] Non-specific

01878. Donaire Fernández, María Luisa. La mujer en la epica francesa. Oviedo: Univers. 1982.

01879. Fenster, Thelma S. "Joei Mêleé de Tristouse: The Maiden with the Cut-off Hand in Epic Adaptation." Neophilologus 65 (July 1981): 345-357.

01880. Johnson, Lesley. "Women on Top: Antifeminism in the Fabliaux." Modern Language Review 78 (1983): 298-307.

01881. Lorcin, Marie-Thérèse. "La feu apprivoise. L'homme, la femme et le feu dans les fabliaux." Revue historique 268 (1982): 3-15.

01882. ______________. "La prostituée des fabliaux est-elle intégrée ou exclus?" In Exclus et systèmes d'exclusion dans la littérature et la civilisation médiévales, pp. 105-118. Paris: C.U.E.R.M.A., 1978.

01883. Roffman, Marian H. "As the Poet Saw Her: Images of Woman in the Pastorals and the Fabliaux." Proceedings of the Annual Meeting of the Western Society for French History 8 (1980): 33-41.

01884. Romeo, Luigi. "A Sociolinguistic View of Medieval Romance Erotic Poetry." Forum italicum 7-8 (December 1973-March 1974): 81-101.

01885. Weinberger, Stephen. "Women: Property and Poetry in Eleventh Century Provence." Proceedings of the Annual Meeting of the Western Society for French History 8 (1980): 24-32.

01886. White, Sarah Melhado. "Sexual Language and Human Conflict in Old French Fabliaux." Comparative Studies in Society and History 24 (April 1982): 185-210.

[2] Chrétien de Troyes

01887. Frappier, Jean. Chrétien de Troyes: The Man and His Work. Athens, Ohio: Ohio University Press, 1982.

01888. Han, Françoise. "Enide et Yseult." Europe 427-428. (November-December 1964): 14-24.

01889. Mussetter, Sally. "The Education of Chrétien's Enide." Romanic Review 73 (1982): 147-166.

01890. Nelson, Deborah. "Enide: amie or femme?" Romance Notes 21 (Spring 1981): 358-363.

01891. Noble, Peter S. Love and Marriage in Chrétien de Troyes. Cardiff: University of Wales Press, 1982.

01892. Topsfield, Leslie T. "Fin' Amours in Marcabru, Bernart de Ventadorn and the Lancelot of Chrétien de Troyes." In Love and Marriage in the Twelfth Century, edited by Willy Van Hoecke and Andries Welkenhuysen, pp. 236-249. Louvain: Leuven University Press, 1981.

01893. Williamson, Joan B. "Suicide and Adultery in the 'Chevalier de la Charrette.'" In Mélanges de littérature du Moyen Age au XXe siécle offerts à Mademoiselle Jeanne Lods, pp. 571-587. Paris: Ecole normale Supérieure de Jeunes Filles, 1978.

[Others]

01894. Guidot, Bernard. "Figures féminines et chanson de geste: l'exemple de Guilbert d'Andrenas." In Mélanges de philologie et de littératures romanes offerts à Jeanne Wathelet-Willem, edited by Jacques De Caluwe and Henri Sepulchre, pp. 189-206. Liège: Cahiers de L'A.R.U.Lg., 1978.

01895. Harrison, Ann Tukey. "Aude and Bramimunde: Their Importance in the Chanson de Roland." French Review 54 (1981): 672-679.

01896. Kay, Sarah. "Love in a Mirror: An Aspect of the Imagery of Bernart de Ventadorn." Medium Aevum 52 (1983): 272-285.

01897. Ruiz Doménec, J.E. Amor y moral matrimonial: El testimonio de Guilhem de Peiteu. Bellaterra: Universidad Autonoma de Barcelona, 1983.

01898. Winn, Mary Beth. "Poems by 'the Lady' in La Chasse et le depart d'Amours (1509)." In Vox Feminae: Studies in Medieval Woman's Songs, edited by John F. Plummer, pp. 179-198. Kalamazco, Mich.: Western Michigan University, 1981.

Also refer to #1892.

(b) Women Poets

[1] Christine de Pisan

01899. Altman, Leslie. "Christine de Pisan: First Professional Women of Letters." In *Female Scholars*, edited by J.R. Brink, pp. 7-23. St. Albans, Vt.: Eden Press, 1980.

01900. Bornstein, Diane. "The Ideal of the Lady of the Manor as Reflected in Christine de Pizan's *Livre des trois vertus*." In *Ideals for Women in the Works of Christine de Pizan*, edited by Diane Bornstein, pp. 117-128. Detroit, Mich.: Corsortium for Medieval and Early Modern Studies, 1981.

01901. ______________, ed. *Ideals for Women in the Works of Christine de Pizan*. Detroit Mich.: Consortium for Medieval and Early Modern Studies, 1981.

01902. ______________. "Self-Consciousness and Self Concepts in the Work of Christine de Pizan." In *Ideals for Women in the Works of Christine de Pizan*, edited by Diane Bornstein, pp. 11-28. Detroit, Mich.: Consortium for Medieval and Early Modern Studies, 1981.

01903. Delany, Sheila. "A City, A Room: The Scene of Writing in Christine de Pisan and Virginia Woolf." In *Writing Woman*, pp. 181-197. New York: Schocken Books, 1983.

01904. Durley, Maureen Slattery. "The Crowned Dame, Dame Opinion, and Dame Philosophy: the Female Characteristics of Three Ideals in Christine de Pizan's *L'Avision Christine*." In *Ideals for Women in the Works of Christine de Pizan*, edited by Diane Bornstein, pp. 29-50. Detroit, Mich.: Consortium for Medieval and Early Modern Studies, 1981.

01905. Erhard, A. Blum. "Christine de Pisan. Un pioniere del lavoro intellettuale femminile." In *Idee sulla donna nel medioevo: fonti e aspetti guiridici, antropologici, religiosi, sociali e litterari della condizione femminile*, edited by Mari Consiglia De Matteis, pp. 305-313. Bologne: Pàtron, 1981.

01906. Finkel, Helen Ruth. "The Portrait of Woman in the Works of Christine de Pisan." *Les Bonnes Feuilles* 3 (Fall 1974): 138-151.

01907. Hindman, Sandra L. "With Ink and Mortar: Christine de Pizan's *Cité des dames* (an art essay)." *Feminist Studies* 10 (Fall 1984): 457-484.

01908. Kelly, F. Douglas. "Reflections on the Role of Christine de Pisan as a Feminist Writer." *Sub-Stances* 2 (1972): 63-71.

01909. Kennedy, Angus J. *Christine de Pizan: A Bibliographical Guide*. London: Grant and Cutler, 1984.

01910. Pernoud, Regine. Christine de Pisan. Paris: Calmann-Lévy, 1982.

01911. Pisan, Christine de. The Book of the City of Ladies. Translated by Earl Jeffrey Richards. New York: Persea Books, 1982.

01912. Price, Paola Malpezzi. "Masculine and Feminine Personae in the Love Poetry of Christine de Pisan." In Gender and Literary Voice, Women and Literature, vol. 1, edited by Janet Todd, pp. 37-53. New York: Holmes and Meier, 1980.

01913. Reno, Christine. "Virginity as an Ideal in Christine de Pizan's Cité des dames." In Ideals for Women in the Works of Christine de Pizan, edited by Diane Bornstein, pp. 69-90. Detroit, Mich.: Consortium for Medieval and Early Modern Studies, 1981.

01914. Willard, Charity Cannon. Christine de Pizan: Her Life and her Works. New York: Persea Books, 1984.

01915. ____________________. "Christine de Pizan and the Order of the Rose." In Ideals for Women in the Works of Christine de Pizan, edited by Diane Bornstein, pp. 51-67. Detroit, Mich.: Consortium for Medieval and Early Modern Studies, 1981.

01916. ____________________. "Christine de Pizan's Livre des trois vertus: Feminine Ideal or Practical Advice?" In Ideals for Women in the Works of Christine de Pizan, edited by Diane Bornstein, pp. 91-116. Detroit, Mich.: Consortium for Medieval and Early Modern Studies, 1981.

01917. ____________________. "The Franco-Italian Professional Writer: Christine de Pizan." In Medieval Women Writers edited by Katharine M. Wilson, pp. 333-363. Athens, GA: University of Georgia Press, 1984.

01918. Yenal, Edith. Christine de Pisan: A Bibliography of Writings By and About Her. Metuchen, N.J.: Scarecrow Press, 1982.

Also refer to #1766, 2127.

[2] Marie de France

01919. Ferrante, Joan M. "The French Courtly Poet: Marie de France." In Medieval Women Writers, edited by Katharine M. Wilson, pp. 64-89. Athens, Ga.: University of Georgia Press, 1984.

01920. Huchet, Jean-Charles. "Nom de femme et écriture féminine au Moyen Age. Les lais de Marie de France." Poétique 48 (1981): 407-430.

01921. Poe, Elizabeth Wilson. "Love in the Afternoon: Courtly Play in the 'Lai de Lanval.'" Neuphilologische Mitteilungen 84 (1983): 301-310.

01922. Wathelet-Willem, Jeanne. "L'enfant dans les Lois de Marie de France." In L'enfant au moyen âge, pp. 299-313. Aix-en-Provence: Université, 1980.

01923. Woods, William S. "Femininity in the Lais of Marie de France." Studies in Philology 47 (January 1950): 1-19.

(3) Prose

01924. Akehurst, F. Ronald P. "Abashed and impotent: Conon de Bethune's 'si voirement con . . . (R. 303).'" Romanic Review 74 (1983): 260-270.

01925. Buschinger, Danielle. "L'enfant dans les romans de Tristan en France et en Allemagne." In L'enfant au moyen âge, pp. 253-268. Aix-en-Provence: Université, 1980.

01926. Cabaniss, Allen. "France's First Woman of Letters." In Judith Augusta, A Daughter-in-Law of Charlemagne and Other Essays, pp. 51-64. New York: Vantage Press, 1974.

01927. Delany, Sheila. "Flore et Jehane: The Bourgeois Woman in Medieval Life and Letters." In Writing Woman, pp. 22-35. New York: Schocken Books, 1983. Also in Science and Society 45 (Fall 1981): 274-287.

01928. Larmat, Jean. "L'enfant dans L'Escoufle de Jean Renart." In L'enfant au moyen âge, pp. 269-283. Aix-en-Provence: Université, 1980.

01929. Planche, Alice. "Culture et contre-culture dans l'Epinette amoureuse de Jean Froissart: les écoles et les jeux." In L'enfant au moyen âge, pp. 389-403. Aix-en-Provence: Université, 1980.

01930. Shirt, David J. "Cliges: A Twelfth-Century Matrimonial Case-Book." Forum for Modern Language Studies 18 (1982): 75-89.

01931. Villon, François de. Le Fort expugnable de l'honneur du sexe féminin. 1555. Reprint. New York: Johnson Reprint Corp., 1970.

01932. Wolfzettel, Friedrich. "Thermatisierungen der Ehe in der französischen 'Novellistik' des 13. Jahrhunderts." In Liebe-Ehe-Ehebruch in der Literatur des Mittelalters, edited by Xenja von Ertzdorff and Marianne Wynn, pp. 41-55. Giessen: Wilhlem Schnitz, 1984.

(4) Troubadours, Trouvères

01933. Colliot, Régine. "Enfants et enfrance dans Raoul de Cambrai." In L'enfant au moyen âge, pp. 233-252. Aix-en-Provence: Université, 1980.

01934. Harvey, Ruth. "The Harlot and the Chimera in the Song of the Troubadour Marcabru." Reading Medieval Studies 10 (1984): 39-78.

01935. Rouillan-Castex, Sylvette. "L'amour et la société féodale." Revue historique 552 (October-December 1984): 295-329.

01936. Tavera, Antoine. "'Non ai de sen per en efan', les troubadours et le refus de la cohérence." In L'enfant au moyen âge, pp. 335-357. Aix-en-Provence: Université, 1980.

b) Chivalry

(1) Courtly Love

(a) Andreas Capellanus

01937. Andreas Capellanus. On Love. Edited by P.G. Walsh. London: Duckworth, 1982.

01938. Paepe, Abbé Norbert de. "Amor und verus amor bei Andreas Capellanus. Versuch einer Lösung des reprobatio-Problems." In Mélanges offerts à René Crozet 2: pp. 921-927. Poitiers: Société d'Etudes Médiévales, 1966.

01939. Schmolke-Hasselmann, Beate. "Accipiter et Chirotheca. Die Artusepisode des Andreas Capellanus -- eine Liebes -- allegorie?" Germanisch-Romanische Monatsschrift n.s. 32 (1982): 387-417.

Also refer to #2085.

(b) Jean de Meun

01940. Le Débat sur le Roman de la Rose. Paris: Champion, 1977.

01941. Quilligan, Maureen. "Words and Sex: The Language of Allegory of De planctu naturae, the Roman de la Rose and Book II of The Faerie Queen." Allegorica 2 (Spring 1977): 195-216.

Also refer to #1746.

c) Art

01942. Dronke, Peter. "The Provençal Trobairitz: Castelloza." In Medieval Women Writers, edited by Katherine M. Wilson, pp. 131-152. Athens, Ga.: University of Georgia Press, 1984.

01943. Sherman, Claire Richter. "Taking a Second Look: Observations on the Iconography of a French Queen, Jeanne de Bourbon (1338-1378)." In Feminism and Art History: Questioning the Litany, edited by Norma Broude and Mary D. Garrard, pp. 100-117. New York: Harper and Row, 1982.

Also refer to 1807, 1825, 1826, 1833.

D. THE GERMANIES

1. SURVEYS

"Arise . . . and stand upon your feet . . .
Play the man and let your heart take courage."
angel to Elizabeth von Schönau

01944. Ennen, Edith. "Die Frau in der mittelalterlichen Stadtgesellschaft Mitteleuropas." Hansische Geschichtsbibliothek 98 (1980): 1-22.

01945. Heimann, Heinz-Dieter. "Küche, Kinder, Kirche in der Überwindung der Krise des Spätmittelalters." In Haus und Familie in der spätmitteralterlichen Stadt, edited by Alfred Haverkamp, pp. 338-357. Cologne: Böhlau, 1984.

01946. Ketsch, Peter. "Aspekte der rechtlichen und politisch-gesellschaftlichen Situation von Frauen im frühen Mittelalter (500-1150)." In Frauen in der Geschichte II, edited by Annette Kuhn and Jörn Rüsen pp. 11-71. Düsseldorf: Schwann, 1982.

01947. Tellenbach, Gerd. Studien und Vorarbeiten zur Geschichte des Grossfrankischen und Fruhdeutschen Adels. Freibourg-en-Breisgau: E. Albert, 1957.

2. POLITICAL

"Since she was bedridden and unable to bear a child,
she was by the advice of his [Charlemagne's] devout
clergy, put on one side as if already dead."
Said of Charlemagne's wife
Monk of Sankt Gallen

01948. Dienst, Heide. "Dominus vir. Von Herzogin-Markgräfin Agnes und anderen Frauen des Hochmittelalters." In Das ewige Klischee, zum Rollenbild und Selbstverständnis bei Mannern und Frauen, pp. 20-44. Vienna: Hermann Böhlaus, 1981.

01949. Hlawitschka, Eduard. "Zur Bleitafelinschrift aus dem Grab der Kaiserin Gisela." Historisches Jahrbuch 97-98 (1977-1978): 439-445.

01950. Jenks, Stuard. "Frauensiegel in den Würzburger Urkunde des 14. Jahrhunderts." Zeitschrift für bayerische Landesgeschichte 45 (1982): 541-553.

01951. Struve, Tilman. "Zwei Briefe der Kaiserin Agnes." Historisches Jahrbuch 104 (1984): 411-424.

3. ECONOMIC

"Lo we give you first ten boys and an equal number of girls, ten horses and an equal number of mules. . . "
Leges Visigothorum

01952. Kroemer, Barbara. "Von Kauffrauen, Beamtinnen, Ärztinnen -- erwerbstätige Frauen in deutschen mittelalterlichen Städten." In Frauen in der Geschichte II, edited by Annette Kuhn and Jörn Rüsen, pp. 73-96. Düsseldorf: Schwann, 1982.

01953. Pia, Sister Maria. "The Industrial Position of Women in the Middle Ages." Catholic Historical Review n.s. 4 (January 1925): 556-560.

01954. Wensky, Margaret. "Die Stellung der Frau in Familie, Haushalt und Wirtschaftsbetrieb im spatmittelalterlich-fruhneuzeitlichen Köln." In Haus und Familie in der spatmittelalterlichen Stadt, edited by Alfred Haverkamp, pp. 289-303. Cologne: Böhlau, 1984.

01955. ______________. "Women's Guilds in Cologne in the Later Middle Ages." Journal of European Economic History 11 (Winter 1982): 631-650.

Also refer to #1992.

4. RELIGION/MYTHOLOGY

a) Mythology

"Now to the scandal of men, women are prophesying."
Hildegard of Bingen

01956. List, Edgar A. "Is Frau Holda the Virgin Mary?" German Quarterly 29 (March 1956): 80-84.

b) Saints/Religious Women

(1) Elizabeth of Hungary

01957. Adriani, Barbara. Quattro Personaggi in cerea di regista. Turin: Paravia, 1975.

01958. Ancelet-Hustache, Jeanne. Gold Tried by Fire: St. Elizabeth of Hungary. Translated by Paul J. Oligny and Sister Venard O'Donnell. Chicago: Franciscan Herald Press, 1963.

01959. Cabrera, Ypiña de Corsi, Matilde. Santa Isabel de Hungría. Mexico: Impreso en Editografica Guadalajara, 1983.

01960. Hoppe, Günther. Elisabeth, Landgräfin von Thüringen. Eisenach: Wartburg-Stiftung, 1981.

01961. Lang, Justin. Elisabeth von Thüringen. Zurich: Benziger, 1983.

(2) Hildegard of Bingen

01962. Gmelch, Joseph. Die Kompositionen der heiligen Hildegard. Dusseldorf: L. Schwann, 1913.

01963. Kraft, Kent. "The German Visionary: Hildegard of Bingen." In Medieval Women Writers, edited by Katharine M. Wilson, pp. 109-130. Athens, Ga.: University of Georgia Press, 1984.

01964. Krauss, Wilhelmine. "Die Musik der heiligen Hildegard von Bingen." Gregoriusblatt 61 (n.d.) 17-22.

01965. Newman, Barbara. "Hildegard of Bingen: Visions and Validation." Church History 54 (June 1985): 163-175.

01966. Scholz, Bernhard W. "Hildegard von Bingen on the Nature of Woman." American Benedictine Review 31 (1980): 361-383.

(3) Others

01967. Bombach, Berthold von. Das Leben der heiligen Luitgard von Wittichen (1291-1348). Stein am Rhein: Christiana Verlag, 1978.

01968. Howard, John. "The German Mystic: Mechthild of Magdeburg." In Medieval Women Writers, edited by Katharine M. Wilson, pp. 153-185. Athens, Ga.: University of Georgia Press, 1984.

01969. Köster, Kurt. "Elisabeth von Schönau." Archiv für Mittelrhein 3 (1951): 243-315.

01970. Lewis, Gertrud Jaron. "Christus als Frau. Eine Vision Elisabeths von Schönau." Jahrbuch für Internationale Germanistik 15 no. 1 (1983): 70-80.

Also refer to #1998-2003.

c) Religious Orders

01971. Blessin, Elmar. "Frauenklöster nach der Regeln des Hl. Benedikt in Baden-Wurttenberg (735-981)." Zeitschrift für Württembergische Landesgeschichte 41 (1982): 233-249.

01972. Dopsch, Heinz. "Die Petersfrauen." In Die älteste Kloster im Sprachraum: St. Peter in Salzburg, pp. 85-90. Salzburg: Amt der Salzburger Landesregierung-Kulturabteilung, 1982.

01973. Parisse, Michel. "Les Chanoinesses dans l'Empire germanique (IXe-XIe siècles). Francia 6 (1979): 107-126.

d) Mariology

01974. Stafski, Heinz. "Die Statuette einer Maria in Erwartung aus dem Dominikanerinnenkloster Kreuz in Regensburg." Zeitschrift des deutschen Vereins für Kunstwissenschaft 27 (1973): 55-62.

Also refer to #2031.

e) Monastic Life

01975. Kuchenbuch, Ludolf. Bäuerliche Gesellschaft und Klosterherrschaft im 9. Jahrhundert. Studien zur Sozialstruktur der Familie der Abtei Prüm. Wiesbaden: Franz Steiner Verlag, 1978.

f) Witchcraft

01976. Camerlynck, Eliane. "Féminité et sorcellerie chez les théoriciens de la démonologie à la fin du Moyen Age: étude du Malleus Maleficarum." Renaissance and Reformation n.s. 7 (1983): 13-25.

5. SOCIAL

"Nor can they [a married couple] be disjoined so that only one part of the body, either that which is in the man or that which is the woman observes continence while the other is polluted."

Hincmar

a) Generic

01977. Bahlow, Hans. "Metronymika. Frauennamen des Mittelalters als Familiennamen." Zeitschrift für deutsches Altertum und deutsche Literatur 108 (1979): 448-466.

01978. Dimt, Gunter. "Haus and Wohnung zwischen Mittelalter und Neuzeit am Beispiel Oberösterreichs." In Haus und Familie in der spätmitteraltlerlichen Stadt, edited by Alfred Haverkamp, pp. 66-98. Cologne: Böhlau, 1984.

01979. Dirlmeier, Ulf. "Zum Problem von Versorgung und Verbrauch privater Haushalte im Spätmittelalter." In Haus und Familie in der spätmitteraltlerlichen Stadt, edited by Alfred Haverkamp, pp. 257-288. Cologne: Böhlau, 1984.

01980. Kuhn-Refus, Maren. "Die soziale Zusammensetzung der Konvente in den oberschwabischen Frauenzisterzen." Zeitschrift für Württembergische Landesgeschichte 41 (1982): 7-31.

01981. Kuhnel, Harry. "Das Alltagsleben im Hause der spätmittelalterlichen Stadt." In Haus und Familie in der spätmitteraltlerlichen Stadt, edited by Alfred Haverkamp, pp. 37-65. Cologne: Böhlau, 1984.

01982. Lorenzen-Schmidt, Klaus-Joachim. "Zur Stellung der Frauen in der frühneuzeitlichen Stadtgesellschaft Schleswigs und Holsteins." Archiv für Kulturgeschichte 61 (1979): 317-339.

01983. Schwob, Ute Monika. "'Herrinnen' in Tiroler Quellen. Zur rechtlichen und sozialen Stellung der adeligen Frau im Mittelalter." In Literatur und bildende Kunst im Tiroler Mittelalter pp. 157-182. Innsbruck: Selbstverlag, 1982.

01984. Todd, Malcolm. Everyday Life of the Barbarians; Goths, Franks and Vandals. New York: G.P. Putnam's Sons, 1972.

b) Demography

01985. Dubuis, Pierre. "Démographie et peuplement dans le diocèse de Sion au Moyen Age." Schweizerische Zeitschrift für Geschichte 29 (1979): 144-158.

c) Family

01986. Cuvillier, Jean-Pierre. "L'enfant dans la tradition féodale germanique." In L'enfant au moyen âge, pp. 43-59. Aix-en-Provence: Université, 1980.

01987. Hammer, Carl I. "Family and Familia in Early-Medieval Bavaria." In Family Forms in Historic Europe, edited by Richard Wall, Jean Robin, and Peter Laslett, pp. 217-248. New York: Cambridge University Press, 1983.

01988. Köbler, Gerhard. "Das Familienrecht in der spätmittelalterlichen Stadt." In Haus und Familie in der spätmitteralterlichen Stadt, edited by Alfred Haverkamp, pp. 136-160. Cologne: Böhlau, 1984.

01989. Maschke, Erich. Die Familie in der deutschen Stadt des später Mittelalters. Heidelberg: Carl Winter Universitäts Verlag, 1980.

01990. Nonn, Ulrich. "Erminethrud - - eine vornehme Dame um 700." Historisches Jahrbuch 102 (1982): 135-143.

01991. Schmidt-Wiegand, Ruth. "Ehe und Familie in der lehrhaften Dichtung des 14. und 15. Jahrhunderts." In Haus und Familie in der spätmitteralterlichen Stadt, edited by Alfred Haverkamp, pp. 195-214. Cologne: Böhlau, 1984.

01992. Sprandel, Rolf. "Der handwerkliche Familienbetrieb des Spätmittelalters und seine Probleme." In Haus und Familie in der spätmitteralterlichen Stadt, edited by Alfred Haverkamp, pp. 327-337. Cologne: Böhlau, 1984.

01993. Uitz, E. "Zu einigen Aspekten der gesellschaftlichen Stellung der Frau in mittelalterlicher Stadt." Jahrbuch für Geschichte des Feudalismus 5 (1981): 57-88.

01994. ______. "Zur Darstellung der Städtbürgerin, ihre Rolle in Ehe, Familie, und Öffentlichkeit in der Chronistik und in des Rechtsquellen der spätmittelalterlichen deutschen Stadt." Jahrbuch für Geschichte des Feudalismus 7 (1983): 130-136.

Also refer to #1954, 1995.

d) Marriage

01995. Klassen, John M. "Marriage and Family in Medieval Bohemia." East European Quarterly 19 (Fall 1985): 257-274.

Also refer to #1991, 1993, 1994, 2005-2007, 2011, 2014-2015, 2025, 2026.

e) Fashion

01996. Lindskog-Wallenburg, Gudrun. *Bezeichnungen für Frauenkleidungstucke und Kleiderschmuck*. Berlin: n.p., 1977.

f) Health/Medical

01997. Calagan, Jennifer Lynn. "The Conjoined Twins Born Near Worms, 1495." *Journal of the History of Medicine and Allied Sciences* 38 (October 1983): 450-451.

Also refer to #1952.

6. CULTURAL

"It grieves me more to the heart that I,
a sinful woman must so write."
Mechthild of Magdeburg

a) Literature

(1) Drama

(a) Hrotsvitha of Gandersheim

01998. Butler, Mary Marguerite. "Hrotsvitha of Gandersheim: The Playable Dramas of a Women Playwright of the Tenth Century." In *New Research on Women at the University of Michigan*, edited by Dorothy G. McGuigan, pp. 213-215. Ann Arbor, Mich.: University of Michigan, Center for Continuing Education of Women, 1974.

01999. Köpke, Ernst Rudolf. *Die alteste deutsche Dichterin*. Berlin: E.S. Mittler and Sohn, 1869.

02000. Schwarz, Alexander. "Die Liebeserklärung: ein Sprechakt in der deutschen Literatur des XII. Jahrhunderts." In *Love and Marriage in the Twelfth Century*, edited by Willy Van Hoecke and Andries Welkenhuysen, pp. 183-196. Louvain: Leuven University Press, 1981.

02001. Wilson, Katharine M. "Ego Clamor Validus-- Hrotsvit and Her Poetic Program." *Germanic Notes* 14 (1983): 17-18.

02002. ________________. "Hrotsvit and the Sounds of Harmony and Discord." *Germanic Notes* 14 (1983): 54-56.

02003. ________________. "The Saxon Canoness: Hrotsvit of Gandersheim." In *Medieval Women Writers*, edited by Katharine M. Wilson, pp. 30-63. Athens, Ga.: University of Georgia Press, 1984.

(b) Others

02004. Senne, Linda P. "The Dramatic Figure in Das Spiel von den zehn Jungfrauen." Germanic Review 51 (May 1976): 161-171.

(2) Poetry

(a) Women in Poetry

02005. Boon, Pieter. "Die Ehe des 'Armen Heinrich': Eine Mesalliance?" Neophilologus 66 (January 1982): 92-101.

02006. Ertzdorff, Xenja von. "Ehe und höfische Liebe im Tristan Gottfrieds von Strassburg." In Love and Marriage in the Twelfth Century, edited by Willy Van Hoecke and Andries Welkenhuysen, pp. 197-218. Louvain: Leuven University Press, 1981.

02007. ________________. "Liebe, Ehe, Ehebruch und Tod in Gottfrieds 'Tristan'." In Liebe-Ehe-Ehebruch in der Literatur des Mittelalters, edited by Xenja von Ertzdorff and Marianne Wynn, pp. 88-98. Giessen: Wilhelm Schnitz, 1984.

02008. Heinen, Hubert. "The Woman's Songs of Hartmann von Aue." In Vox Feminae: Studies in Medieval Woman's Songs, edited by John F. Plummer, pp. 95-110. Kalamazoo, Mich.: Western Michigan University, 1981.

02009. Jillings, Lewis G. "The Ideal of Queenship in Hartmann's Erec." In The Legend of Arthur in the Middle Ages (Arthurian Studies) 7: 113-128. Cambridge: D.S. Brewer, 1983.

02010. Lewis, Gertrud Jaron. "Das vil edel wip. Die Haltung zeitgenossischer Kritiker zur Frauengestalt der mittelhochdeutschen Epik." In Die Frau als Heldin und Autortin, edited by Wolfgang Paulsen, pp. 66-81. Munich: Francke Verlag, 1979.

02011. Lomnitzer, Helmut. "Geliebte und Ehefrau im Deutschen Lied des Mittelalters." In Liebe-Ehe-Ehebruch in der Literatur des Mittelalters, edited by Xenja von Ertzdorff and Marianne Wynn, pp. 111-124. Giessen: Wilhelm Schnitz, 1984.

02012. McDonald, William C. "Flight from Love: The Falcon in Late-Medieval German Love Poetry." Fifteenth-Century Studies 6 (1983): 149-170.

02013. Mowatt, D.G. "Tristan's Mothers and Iwein's Daughters." German Life and Letters 23 (1969-1970): 18-31.

02014. Schnell, Rüdiger. "Gottfrieds Tristan und die Institution der Ehe." Zeitschrift für deutsche Philologie 101 (1982): 334-369.

02015. Thelen, Lynn. "The Internal Source and Function of King Gunther's Bridal Quest." Monatshefte 76 (Summer 1984): 143-155.

02016. Wailes, Stephen. "The Romance of Kudrun." Speculum 58 (April 1983): 347-367.

02017. Walshe, M. O'C. "Frauenlob. Profile of a Late Medieval Poet." German Life and Letters 5 (January 1952): 121-125.

02018. Wilson, H.B. "Ordo and the Portrayal of the Maid in Der arme Heinrich." Germanic Review 44 (March 1969): 83-94.

02019. Wynn, Marianne. "Nicht-Tristanische Liebe in Gottfrieds 'Tristan'. Liebesleidenschaft in Gottfrieds Elterngeschichte." In Liebe-Ehe-Ehebruch in der Literatur des Mittelalters, edited by Xenja von Ertzdorff and Marianne Wynn, pp. 56-70. Giessen: Wilhelm Schnitz, 1984.

(3) Prose

02020. Ehrismann, Otfrid. "Der tivel brahte mich ze dir--Vom Eheleben in Erzahlungen des Strickers." In Liebe-Ehe-Ehebruch in der Literatur des Mittelalters, edited by Xenja von Ertzdorff and Marianne Wynn, pp. 25-40. Giessen: Wilhelm Schnitz, 1984.

02021. Marchand, James. "The Frankish Mother: Dhuoda." In Medieval Women Writers, edited by Katharine M. Wilson, pp. 1-29. Athens, Ga.: University of Georgia Press, 1984.

Also refer to #1182, 1708, 1925.

(4) Minnesingers

02022. Harvey, Ruth. "Minnesang and the 'Sweet Lyric.'" German Life and Letters 17 (1963-1964): 14-26.

02023. Jackson, William E. Reinmar's Women: A Study of the Woman's Song ("Frauenlied" and "Frauenstrophe" of Reimar der Alte. Amsterdam: John Benjamins, 1981.

02024. ________________. "The Woman's Song in Medieval German Poetry." In Vox Feminae: Studies in Medieval Woman's Songs, edited by John F. Plummer, pp. 47-94. Kalamazoo, Mich.: Western Michigan University, 1981.

02025. Karnein, Alfred. "Liebe, Ehe und Ehebruch im minnedidaktischen Schrifttum." In Liebe-Ehe-Ehebruch in der Literatur des Mittelalters, edited by Xenja von Ertzdorff and Marianne Wynn, pp. 148-160. Giessen: Wilhelm Schnitz, 1984.

02026. Mertens, Volker. "Dienstminne, Tageliederotik und Eheliebe in den Liedern Wolframs von Eschenbach." Euphorion 77 (1983): 233-246.

02027. Milnes, Humphrey. "Ulrich von Lichtenstein and the Minnesang." German Life and Letters 17 (1963-1964): 27-41.

02028. Morral, E.J. "Heinrich von Morungen's Conception of Love." German Life and Letters 13 (1959-1960): 81-87.

02029. Wisbey, Roy. "Fortune and Love, Reason and the Senses: Traditional Motifs in Walther's Song 'Ich freudehelfelöser man (L54, 37ff).'" Oxford German Studies 13 (1982): 115-142.

b) Chivalry

(1) Courtly Love

02030. Blumstein, Andree Kahn. Misogyny and Idealization in the Courtly Romance. Studien zur Germanistik, Anglistik und Komparatistik, no. 41. Bonn: Boumer Verlag, Herbert Grundmann, 1977.

c) Art

02031. Petzsch, Christoph. "Weltliches in Marianischen Lied." Germanish-Romanische Monatsschrift n.s. 27 (1977): 369-375.

Also refer to #1962-1966, 1974.

E. IBERIA

1. SURVEYS

> "Eve means 'life' or 'disaster' or 'woe'--
> life because she was the origin of being
> born; disaster or woe because through
> transgression she became the cause of
> dying."
>
> Isidore of Seville

02032. Dillard, Heath. Daughters of the Reconquest: Women in Castilian Town Society 1100-1300. New York: Cambridge Press, 1985.

02033. Vinyoles I Vidal, Teresa-Maria. Les barcelonines a les darreries de l'Edat Mitjana, 1370-1410. Barcelona: Fundació Salvador Vives Casajuana, 1976.

2. POLITICAL

"When a father finds his daughter committing adultery with a man in his own house, or in that of his son-in-law, he has a right to kill her and the man."
Las Siete Partidas

a) Legal

02034. Carlé, María del Carmen. "Apuntes sobre el matrimonio en la Edad Media Española." Cuadernos de historia de España 63-64 (1980): 115-177.

02035. Claramunt, Salvador. "La mujer en el fuero de Cuenca." In Estudio en memoria del professor D. Salvador de Moxó, 1: 297-313. Madrid: Univers. Comp., 1982.

02036. De Arvizu, Fernando. "La femme dans le Code d'Euric." Revue historique de droit français et étranger 62 (1984): 391-405.

Also refer to #2087.

b) Political Roles

02037. Brundage, James A. "Matrimonial Politics in Thirteenth-Century Aragon: Moncada v. Urgel." Journal of Ecclesiastical History 31 (1980): 271-282.

02038. Figanière, Frederico Francisco de la. Memorias das Rainhas de Portugal: D. Theresa - Santa Isabel. Lisbon: Typographia Universal, 1859.

02039. Jenssen, Einar. "Cristina, la Princesa de Covarrubias. Relaciones Hispano-Noruegas en el Siglo XIII." Historia 16, no. 9 (March 1984): 41-48.

02040. LoRe, Anthony George. La leyenda de dona Maria Coronel. Valencia: Albatros Ediciones/Hispanofila, 1980.

02041. Oliveira, Fernando de. Três ensaios sobre figuras medievais. Lisbon: Scarpa, 1970.

02042. Reilly, Bernard F. The Kingdom of Léon-Castilla under Queen Urraca: 1109-1126. Princeton, N.J.: Princeton University Press, 1982.

02043. Ruiz Domenec, J.E. "Estragias matrimoniales y sistemas de Alianza entre Castilla y Cataluna en el siglo XII." Hispania 40 (May-August 1980): 271-284.

3. RELIGION

"I lack in service, lack in love,
Yet never cease in my desire."
Philipa of Avis and Lancaster
"To Holy Jesus"

a) Generic

02044. Arranz, Ana. "El Demonio Femonino. Mujer, Iglesia y Religiosidad en el Bajo Medievo Hispanico." Historia 16, no. 8 (November 1983): 59-68.

02045. Bertran I. Roigé, Prim. "Donacions de la Comtesa Dolca d'Urgell als Ordres Religiosos (1184-1210)." Analecta sacra tarraconensia 49-50 (1976-1977): 41-56.

02046. Marín Padelea, Encarnación. "Relacion judeoconversa durante la segunda mitad del siglo XV en Aragon: Matrimonio." Sefarad 42 (1984): 243-298.

b) Saints/Religious Women

02047. Calvo Moralijo, Gaspar. "Santa Maria de la Cruz." Antonianum 50 (July-December 1975): 561-576.

02048. La Borderie, Arthur de. Saint Lunaire (Leonor), son histoire, son eglise, ses monuments. Rennes: Plinon, 1881.

02049. Spero, Nancy. "Ende." Women's Studies 6 (1978): 3-11.

Also refer to #1827.

4. SOCIAL

"A Husband who finds a vile man in his house or in any other place in the act of intercourse with his wife, can kill him without being liable to any penalty. . ."
Las Siete Partidas

a) Generic

02050. Da Silva, José Gentil. "Le Moyen Age et les modernes: à propos des femmes et du mariage dans le sud-ouest européen." Annales de la Faculté des Lettres et Sciences humaines de Nice 39 (1983): 472-488.

02051. Dillard, Heath. "Medieval Women in Castilian Town Communities." Women's Studies 11 (1984): 115-138.

02052. Lewis, A.R. The Development of Southern French and Catalan Society, 718-1050. Austin, Tex.: University of Texas Press, 1965.

02053. Mitre, Emilio. La España medieval. Sociedades, Estadoes, Culturas. Madrid: Ediciones ISTMO, 1979.

02054. Powers, J.F. "Frontier Municipal Baths and Social Interaction in Thirteenth-Century Spain." American Historical Review 84 (June 1979): 649-667.

02055. Salisbury, Joyce E. "Fruitful in Singleness" Journal of Medieval History 8 (1982): 97-106.

02056. Vinyoles I Vidal, Teresa Maria. "Ajudes a donzelles pobres a maridar." In La pobreza y la assistencia los pobres en la Cataluña medieval, edited by Manuel Riu, pp. 295-362. Barcelona C.S.I.C., 1980.

Also refer to #2034, 2037, 2043, 2046, 2059, 2076, 2087.

b) Family

02057. Ashley, Kathleen. "Voice and Audience: The Emotional Worlds of the cantigas de amigo." In Vox Feminae: Studies in Medieval Woman's Songs, edited by John F. Plummer, pp. 35-46. Kalamazoo, Mich.: Western Michigan University, 1981.

02058. Sablonier, Roger. "The Aragonese Royal Family Around 1300." In Interest and Emotion, Essays on the Study of Family and Kinship, edited by Hans Medick and David Warren Sabean, pp. 210-239. New York: Cambridge University Press, 1985.

c) Sex Roles

02059. Ratcliffe, Marjorie. "Adulteresses, Mistresses and Prostitutes: Extra Marital Relationships in Medieval Castile." Hispania 67 (September 1984): 346-350.

d) Fashion

02060. Hamarneh, Sami. "The First Known Independent Treatise on Cosmetology in Spain." Bulletin of the History of Medicine 39 (July-August 1965): 309-325.

5. CULTURAL

"Men can do best, and women know it well.
Preeminence in all and each is yours;
Yet grant some small acknowledgment of ours."
Teresa de Cartagena
Admiraçión

a) Literature

(1) Non-specific

(a) Women in Literature

02061. Aizenberg, Edna. "_Una judía may fermosa_: The Jewess as Sex Object in Medieval Spanish Literature and Lore." _La Coronica_ 12 (1984): 187-194.

02062. Gerli, E. Michael. "La 'Religion de Amor' y el antifeminismo en las letras castellanas del sigol XV." _Hispanic Review_ 49 (1981): 65-86.

02063. Goldberg, Harriet. "Sexual Humor in Misogynist Medieval Exempla." In _Women in Hispanic Literature, Icons and Fallen Idols_, edited by Beth Miller, pp. 67-83. Berkeley, Ca.: University of California Press, 1983.

02064. ________________. "Two Parallel Medieval Commonplaces: Antifeminism and Antisemitism in the Hispanic Literary Tradition." In _Aspects of Jewish Culture in the Middle Ages_, edited by Paul E. Szarmach, pp. 85-119. Albany, N.Y.: SUNY Press, 1979.

02065. Irizarry, Estelle. "Echoes of the Amazon Myth in Medieval Spanish Literature." In _Women in Hispanic Literature, Icons and Fallen Idols_, edited by Beth Miller, pp. 53-66. Berkeley, Ca.: University of California Press, 1983.

02066. Ornstein, Jacob. "La misoginía y el profeminismo en la literatura castellana." _Revista de filología española_ 3 (1941): 219-232.

02067. Pelaez, Manuel J. "La mujer en la obra de Francisco Ximenes: un ejemplo de literatura antifeminista en la baja edad media." _Collectanea Franciscana_ 53 (1983): 41-49.

02068. Podol, Peter L. "The Stylized Portrait of Women in Spanish Literature." _Hispanofilia_ 71 (January 1981): 1-21.

02069. Rubio Alvarez, Fernando. "Desfavorable concepto moral de la mujer en algunas obras de origen oriental." _Ciudad de Dios_ 177 (1964): 267-287.

(b) Women Writers

02070. Deyermond, Alan. "Spain's First Women Writers." In _Women in Hispanic Literature, Icons and Fallen Idols_, edited by Beth Miller, pp. 27-52. Berkeley, Ca.: University of California Press, 1983.

(2) Poetry

(a) Women in Poetry

[1] Non-specific

02071. Battesti, Jeanne. "Du mythe de la femme sauvage à la bergère courtoise: la femme dans la poésie medievale espagnole." In _Femmes corses et femmes méditerranéennes_, pp. 209-240. Provence: Centre d'Etudes Corses de l'Université de Provence, 1976.

02072. Cortina, Lynn Rice. "The Aesthetics of Morality: Two Portraits of Mary of Egypt in the _Vida de Santa Maria Egipciaca_." _Hispanic Journal_ 2 (Fall 1980): 41-45.

02073. Deyermond, Alan. "Medieval Spanish Epic Cycles: Observation on their Formation and Development." _Kentucky Romance Quarterly_ 23 (1976): 281-303.

02074. Pinto, Mario di. _Due contrasti d'amore nella Spagna medievale_. [Razon de amor e Eleyna y Maria.] Pisa: Libreria Golliardica Editrice, 1959.

02075. Smith, Colin and Walker, Roger M. "Did the Infantes de Carrion intend to kill the Cid's Daughters?" _Bulletin of Hispanic Studies_ 56 (January 1979): 1-10.

02076. Weil, Jurgen W. "Girls from Morocco and Spain: Selected Poems from an 'adab' collection of poetry." _Archiv orientalni_ 52 (1984): 36-41.

[2] Juan Ruiz

02077. Álvarez, Nicolás Emilio. "'Loco Amor.' Goliardismo, Amor Cortes y 'Buen amor': El desenlace amoroso del episodio de Dona Garoca en el _Libro de Buen Amor_." _Journal of Hispanic Philology_ 7 (Winter 1983): 107-119.

02078. Bergstrom, Stanford. "A Structural Constant in the _Libro de buen amor_: Variations on the Duality of Love." _Journal of Hispanic Philology_ 3 (Autumn 1978): 37-48.

02079. de Ferraresi, Alicia C. _De amor y poesía en la España medieval: prólogo a Juan Ruiz_. Mexico: El Colegio de Mexico, 1976.

02080. Gimeno, Rosalie. "Women in the _Book of Good Love_." In _Women in Hispanic Literature, Icons and Fallen Idols_, edited by Beth Miller, pp. 84-96. Berkeley, Ca.: University of California Press, 1983.

02081. Knorst, Judith Irene. "The Element of Temptation in _Libro de buen amor_." _Hispania_ 64 (March 1981): 53-59.

02082. Laurence, Kemlin M. "The Battle between Don Carnal and Dona Cuaresma in the Light of Medieval Tradition." In _'Libro de buen amor' Studies_, edited by G.B. Gybbon-Monypenny, pp. 159-176. London: Tamesis Books Ltd., 1970.

02083. Lemartinel, Jean. "La belle selon Juan Ruiz." _Cresol_ 1 (1983): 1-16.

02084. Walker, Roger M. "Con miedo de la muerte la miel non es sabrosa: Love, Sin and Death in the _Libro de buen amor_." In _'Libro de buen amor' Studies_, edited by G.B. Gybbon-Monypenny, pp. 231-252. London: Tamesis Books Ltd., 1970.

02085. Wise, David O. "Reflections on Andreas Capellanus's _De Reprobatio amoris_ in Juan Ruiz, Alfonso Martinez and Fernando de Rojas." _Hispania_ 63 (September 1980): 506-513.

[3] Others

02086. Gerli, E. Michael. "La tipologia biblica y la introduccion a los _Milagros de Neustra Senora_." _Bulletin of Hispanic Studies_ 62 (January 1985): 7-14.

02087. Pavlovic, Milija N. and Walker, Roger M. "Money, Marriage and the Law in the _Poema de Mio Cid_." _Medium Aevum_ 51 (1982): 197-212.

02088. Scarborough, Connie L. "The Virgin as Midwife: Verbalization and Visualization in Alfonso X's _Cantigas de Santa Maria_." _Michigan Academician_ 15 (1982): 137-144.

(b) Poets

02089. Snow, Joseph. "The Spanish Love Poet: Florencia Pinar." In _Medieval Women Writers_, edited by Katharine M. Wilson, pp. 320-332. Athens, Ga.: University of Georgia Press, 1984.

(3) Prose

02090. Boggs, Ralph S. "La mujer mandona de Shakespeare y de Juan Manuel." _Hispania_ 10 (December 1927): 419-422.

02091. Gascon-Vera, Elena. "La ambiguedad en el concepto del amor y de la mujer en la prosa castellana del siglo XV." Boletin de la Real academia Española 59 (1979): 119-155.

02092. Sala-Molins, Louis. La Philosophie de l'amour chez Raymond Lulle. Paris: Mouton, 1974.

02093. Waley, Pamela. "Càrcel de amor and Grisel y Mirabella: A Question of Priority." Bulletin of Hispanic Studies 50 (1973): 340-356.

(4) Legends

02094. Bluestine, Carolyn. "The Power of Blood in the 'Siete infantes de Lara.'" Hispanic Review 50 (Spring 1982): 201-217.

02095. Burt, John R. "The Bloody Cucumber and Related Matters in the 'Siete Infantes de Lara.'" Hispanic Review 50 (Summer 1982): 345-352.

(5) Ballads

02096. Odd, Frank L. "Women of Romancero: A Voice of Reconciliation." Hispania 66 (September 1983): 360-368.

F. ITALY

1. BIBLIOGRAPHY

"A Woman and a minor on account of their incapacity and weakness cannot renounce [rights] unless they are vouched for."

Bardus

02097. Bartoli, Marco. "Donna e società nel tardo medioeve. Guida bibliografica." Cultura e scuola 19 (1980): 81-88.

2. POLITICAL

"If anyone shall be proved to have slept with a Muslim woman with her consent, let him be castrated and let her nose be cut off."

Council of Nablus

a) Legal

02098. Barni, Gian Luigi. "Un contratto di concubinato in Corsica nel XIII secolo." Revista di storia del Diritto Italiano 22 (1949): 131-155.

02099. Bellomo, Manlio. "Die Familie und ihre rechtliche Struktur in den italienischen Stadtkommunen des Mittelalters." In Haus und Familie in der spätmitteralterlichen Stadt, edited by Alfred Haverkamp, pp. 99-135. Cologne: Bohlau, 1984.

02100. Izbicki, Thomas M. "'Ista questio est antiqus': two consilia on Widow's Rights." Bulletin of Medieval Canon Law. n.s. 8 (1978): 47-50.

02101. Kirshner, Julius and Pluss, Jacques. "Two Fourteenth-Century Opinions on Dowries, Paraphernalia and Non-dotal Goods." Bulletin of Medieval Canon Law n.s. 9 (1979): 65-77.

02102. Kuehn, Thomas. "Cum consensu mundualdi: Legal Guardianship of Women in Quattrocento Florence." Viator 13 (1982): 309-333.

02103. ____________. Emancipation in Late Medieval Florence. New Brunswick, N.J.: Rutgers University Press, 1981.

02104. Leicht, P.S. "Il matrimonio del "captivus ab hostibus" in una lattera del pontifice Leone Magno." Rivista di storia del diritto Italiano 22 (1949): 181-185.

02105. Leisching, Peter. Beiträge zur Geschichte des mittelalterlichen Eherechts. Innsbruck: P. Leisching, 1978.

3. ECONOMIC

> ". . . sisters beware of all pride, vain ambition, envy, greed, and of taking part in the cares and busy ways of the world."
>
> Clare of Assisi
> Rule and Testament, 1253

02106. Brown, Judith and Goodman, Jordan. "Women and Industry in Florence." Journal of Economic History 40 (1980): 73-80.

02107. Kirshner, Julius and Molho, Anthony. "Il monte delle doti a Firenze dalla sua fondazione nel 1425 alla meta del sedicesimo secolo. Abbozzo di una ricerca." Ricerche storiche 10 (1980): 21-47.

02108. Riemer, Eleanor S. "Women, Dowries, and Capital Investment in Thirteenth-Century Siena." In The Marriage Bargain: Women and Dowries in European History, edited by Marion A. Kaplan, pp. 59-80. New York: Harrington Park, 1985.

Also refer to #2101.

4. RELIGION

"God has taken our wives from us and now Satan has give us sisters."

St. Francis of Assisi opposing additional nunneries

a) Generic

02109. Benvenuti Papi, Anna. "Penitenza e santità femminile in ambiente cateriniano e bernardiniano." In Atti del simposio internationale cateriniano-bernardiniano, edited by Domenico Maffei and Paolo Nardi, pp. 359-371. Siena: Accademia Senese degli Intronati, 1982.

02110. Hamilton, Bernard. "The House of Theophlact and the Promotion of Religious Life among Women in Tenth Century Rome." Studia Monastica 12 (1970): 195-217.

02111. Manson, Michel. "Quelques remarques sur le 'puer Ascanius' do Codex Vaticanus 3225, pictura 16." In L'enfant au moyen âge, pp. 25-41. Aix-en-Provence: Université, 1980.

02112. Policelli, Eugene F. "Medieval Women: Preacher's Point of View." International Journal of Women's Studies 1 (May-June 1978): 281-296.

b) Saints/Religious Women

(1) Clare of Assisi

02113. Brogliato, Bortolo. Assisi, incontro vivo con frate Francesco e sorella Chiara. Vicenza: L.I.E.F., 1976.

02114. Daniel-Rops, Henry. Claire sans la clarte. Paris: Fayard, 1962.

02115. Dhont, René Charles. Claire parmi ses soeurs. Paris: Apostolat des editions, 1973.

02116. Marina, Vittoria. Chiara d'Assisi. Padua: Messaggero, 1975.

(2) Others

02117. Berrigan, Joseph. "The Tuscan Visionary: Saint Catherine of Siena." In Medieval Women Writers, edited by Katherine M. Wilson, pp. 252-268. Athens, Ga.: University of Georgia Press, 1984.

02118. Brentano, Robert. "Catherine of Siena, Margery Kempe, and 'a caterva virginum.'" In Atti del simposio internazionale cateriniano-bernardiniano, edited by Domenico Maffei and Paolo Nardi, pp. 45-55. Siena: Accademia Senses degli Intronati, 1982.

(c) Monastic Life

02119. Abrahamse, Dorothy de F. "Byzantine Asceticism and Women's Monasteries in Early Medieval Italy." In Medieval Religious Women, vol. 1, Distant Echoes, edited by John A. Nichols and Lillian Thomas: 31-49. Kalamazoo, Mich.: Cistercian Publications, 1984.

02120. Mongelli, Giovanni. "Le abbadesse mitrate di San Benedetto di Conversano." Archivi 2nd ser. 26 (1959): 342-401.

5. SOCIAL

". . . have no fear of poverty, toil, tribulation, reviling, and the world's scorn, but rather. . . hold them as delectable things."

Clare of Assisi
Rule and Testament, 1253

(a) Family

02121. Herlihy, David and Klapisch-Zuber, Christiane. The Tuscans and Their Families: A Study of the Florentine Catasto of 1427. New Haven: Yale University Press, 1984.

02122. Sambin, Paolo. "La Familia di un vescovo italiano del' 300." Rivista di storia della Chiesa in Italia 4 (1950): 237-247.

Also refer to #2099, 2103, 2111.

b) Marriage

02123. Brooke, Christopher N.L. "Aspetti del matrimonio e della famiglia nel mondo di Santa Caterina e di San Bernardino." In Atti del simposio internazionale cateriniano-bernardiniano, edited by Domenic Maffei and Paolo Nardi, pp. 877-889. Siena: Accademic Senese degli Intronati, 1982.

02124. Garufi, Carlo Alberto. Ricerche sugli usi nuziale nel Medio Evo in Sicilia. Bologna: A. Forni, 1978.

02125. Klapisch-Zuber, Christiane. "Le complexe de Griselda. Dot et dons de mariage au Quattrocento." In Mélanges de l'Ecole Française de Rome. Moyen Age- Temps modernes 94 (1982): 7-43.

Also refer to #2100, 2104, 2105.

6. CULTURAL

"Amalsuntha proved to be endowed with wisdom and regard for justice in the highest degree, displaying to a great extent the masculine temper."

Procopius

02126. Colonna, Enza. "Figuri femminile in Liutprando da Cremona." _Quaderni medievali_ 14 (1982): 29-60.

02127. Dulac, Liliane. "Inspiration mystique et savoir politique: les conseils aux veuves chez Francesco da Barberino et chez Christine de Pizan." In _Mélanges à la mémoire de Franco Simone: France et Italie dans la culture européenne. I: Moyen Age et Renaissance_ 113-141. Geneva: Editions Slatkine, 1980.

02128. Klapisch-Zuber, Christine. "L'attribution d'un prénom à l'enfant en Toscane à la fin du Moyen-Age." In _L'enfant au moyen âge_, pp. 73-85. Aix-en-Provence: Universite, 1980.

02129. Lemay, Helen Rodnite. "William of Saliceto on Human Sexuality." _Viator_ 12 (1981): 165-181.

G. THE LOW COUNTRIES

1. RELIGION

"There was a defect in the formation of the first woman since she was formed from a bent rib, that is, a rib from the breast, which is bent as it were in a contrary direction to a man."

Malleus Maleficarum

02130. D'Haenens, Albert. "Femmes excédentaires et vocation religieuse dans l'ancien diocèse de Liège lors de l'essor urbain (fin du XIIe-début du XIIIe siècle). Le cas d'Ide de Nivelles (1200-1231)." In _Hommages à la Wallonie_, edited by Herve Hasquin, pp. 217-235. Brussells: Université libre de Bruxelles, 1981.

02131. Schmitt, Jean-Claude. _Mort d'une heresie: l'Eglise et les clercs face aux beguines et aux beghards du Rhin superieur du XIVe au XVe siècle_. New York: Mouton, 1978.

02132. Vanderauwera, Ria. "The Brabant Mystic: Hadewijch." In _Medieval Women Writers_, edited by Katharine M. Wilson, pp. 186-203. Athens, Ga.: University of Georgia Press, 1984.

2. SOCIAL

"A man and woman taken in adultery were stripped before the whole army. After their hands had been tied behind their backs, they were forced to walk around the whole army, while being roughly beaten with sticks by the executioners. . ."

Guibert of Nogent about the crusaders

(a) Demography

02133. Prevenier, Walter. "La démographie des villes du Comté de Flandre aux XIVe et XVe siècles. Etat de la question. Essai d'interpretation." Revue du Nord 65 (April-June 1983): 255-275.

Also refer to #1846.

(b) Family

02134. Nicholas, David. The Domestic Life of a Medieval City, Women, Children and the Family in Fourteenth-Century Ghent. Lincoln, Neb.: University of Nebraska Press, 1985.

3. CULTURAL

"Love appears every day for one who offers love, that wisdom is enough."

Hadewijch
"Poem on the Seven Names of Love"

(a) Art

02135. Schneebalg-Perelman, Sophie. "'La Dame à la licorne.' A été tissée à Bruxelles." Gazette des Beaux Arts 109 no. 2 (November 1967): 253-278.

IV. RENAISSANCE/REFORMATION

A. GENERAL

1. SURVEYS/BIBLIOGRAPHIES

"The hostilities . . . were so fierce that neither the two sovereigns could compromise . . . to talk of reconciliation . . . how easy for the ladies . . . to make the advances in such an undertaking."

Margaret of Austria - peacemaking in 1529

02136. Irwin, Joyce. "Society and the Sexes." In Reformation Europe: A Guide to Research, edited by S.E. Ozment, pp. 343-359, St. Louis: Center for Reformation Research, 1982.

02137. Kelly, Joan. "Did Women Have a Renaissance?" In Women, History and Theory: The Essays of Joan Kelly, pp. 19-50, Chicago: The University of Chicago Press, 1984.

02138. Rose, Mary Beth, ed. Women in the Middle Ages and the Renaissance. Syracuse, N.Y.: Syracuse University Press, 1986.

Also refer to #1443, 2560.

2. ECONOMIC

"I imagined that I alone was queen, but here I see hundreds whose attire vies with my own."

Joanna of Navarre, on her arrival in Flanders

02139. Bornstein, Diane. "Women at Work in the Fifteenth Century." Fifteenth-Century Studies 6 (1983):33-40.

02140. Hauser, Henri. Le travail industriel des femmes aux xve siècles. Paris: Girard et Brière, 1897.

3. RELIGION

"I allowed myself to be persuaded by an aunt of mine . . . to enter into witchcraft; after her death I did nothing for about a year, and then I began to go out in this way, that is she called men . . . then I greased myself with the ointment I had brought with me . . . and was transformed into a cat, left the body at home, descended the stair, and went out by the door."

Polissena of San Macario

a) Saints/Religious Women

02141. Liebowitz, Ruth P. "Virgins in the Service of Christ: The Dispute over an Active Apostolate for Women during the Counter-Reformation." In Women of Spirit, edited by Rosemary Ruether and Eleanor McLaughlin, pp. 131-152. New York: Simon and Schuster, 1979.

b) Witchcraft

02142. Horsley, Richard A. "Further Reflections on Witchcraft and European Folk Religion." History of Religions, 19(August 1979:71-95).

02143. Klaits, Joseph. Servants of Satan, The Age of the Witch Hunts. Bloomington, Ind.: Indiana University Press, 1985.

02144. Larner, Christine. "The Crime of Witchcraft in Europe. In Crime and the Law, the Social History of Crime in Western Europe since 1500, edited by V.A. Gatrell et al., pp. 49-75. London: Europa Publications, 1980.

02145. Schoeneman, Thomas J. "The Role of Mental Illness in the European Witch Hunts of the Sixteenth and Seventeenth Centuries: An Assessment." Journal of the History of the Behavioral Sciences 13 (October 1977):337-351.

Also refer to #2154.

4. SOCIAL

"There is nothing that doeth so commend, advance, set forth, adorn, deck, trim and garnish a maid as silence."

English tract

a) Generic

02146. Chamberlin, E.R. Everyday Life in Renaissance Times. New York: Putnam, 1966.

02147. Hale, J.R. _Renaissance Europe, Individual and Society_. New York: Harper and Row, 1971.
[See especially "Family and Personal Relationships" pp. 124-173.]

Also refer to #2145.

b) Family

02148. Ozment, Steven E. _When Fathers Ruled: Family Life in Reformation Europe_. Cambridge, Mass.: Harvard University Press, 1983.

Also refer to #1528.

c) Marriage

02149. Margolin, J.C. "Charivari et mariage ridicule au temps de la Renaissance." In _Les Fêtes de la Renaissance_, edited by J. Jacquot and E. Konigson, 3:579-601. Paris: Editions du Centre National de la recherche scientifique, 1975.

d) Fashion/Manners

02150. Amman, Jost. _Die Frauenzimmer Die Frauen Europas und ihre Trachten_. 1586. Reprint. Dortmund: Harengerg, 1980.

5. CULTURAL

"Eve because she had helped to seduce her husband hath inflicted on her, an especial bane. In sorrow shalt thou bring forth thy children, thy desires shall be subject to thy husband and he shall rule over thee."
Lawes Resolution of Womens' Rights

a) Generic

02151. Schlumbohm, Christa. "Die Glorifizierung der Barockfürstin als 'Femme forte.'" In _Europäische Hofkultu im 16. und 17. Jahrhundert I_, Wolfenbutteler Arbeiten zur Barockforschung, vol. 9, edited by August Buck, Georg Kauffmann, Blake Lee Spahr and Conrad Wiedemann, pp. 113-122. Hamburg: Dr. Ernest Hauswedell und. Co., 1981.

b) Literature

02152. Meijer, Marianne S. "Thomas More, Lodovico Domenichi et 'L'Honneur du Sexe Féminin.'" _Moreana_ 38 (June 1973):37-42.

02153. Still, Roger. Love and Death in Renaissance Tragedy. Baton Rouge: Louisiana State University Press, 1976.

Also refer to #1593.

c) Art

02154. Hoak, Dale. "Witch-Hunting and Women in the Art of the Renaissance." History Today 31 (February 1981):22-26.

02155. Lunenfeld, Marvin E. "Royal Image: Symbol and Paradigm in Portraits of early Modern Female Sovereigns and Regents." Gazette des Beaux Arts, 6th ser. 97, (April 1981):157-162.

B. BRITISH ISLES

1. SURVEYS

"A spaniel, a woman, and a walnut tree. The more they are beaten, the better they be."

Elizabethan chant

02156. Andre, Caroline S. "Some selected aspects of the role of women in sixteenth century England." International Journal of Women's Studies 4 (January-February 1981):76-88.

02157. Emerson, Kathy Lynn. Wives and Daughters: The Women of Sixteenth-Century England. Troy, New York: Whitson Pub. Co., 1985.

02158. James, Mervyn. Family, Lineage, and Civil Society: A Study of Society, Politics, and Mentality in the Durham Region, 1500-1640. Oxford: Clarendon, Press, 1974.

02159. Warnicke, Retha M. Women of the English Renaissance and Reformation. Westport, Ct.: Greenwood Press, 1983.

02160. Woodbridge, Linda. Women and the English Renaissance. Chicago: University of Illinois Press, 1984.

02161. Youings, Joyce. Sixteenth Century England. London: Allen Lane, Penguin Books, 1984. [See especially Ch. 15, "Marriage and Household," pp. 361-384 and Ch. 6, "Inflation of Population and Prices," pp. 130-154.]

2. POLITICAL

"How great soever may be the bounties I have received, the joy that I felt in being loved by a King whom I adore, and to whom I would with pleasure make a sacrifice of my heart, if fortune had rendered it worthy of being offered to him ..."

Anne Boleyn

a) Political Roles

(1) Individuals

(a) Elizabeth I

02162. Clifford, Esther. "Marriage of True Minds." Sixteenth Century Journal 15 (Spring 1984): 37-46

02163. Erickson, Carolly. The First Elizabeth. New York: Summit Press, 1983.

02164. Haugaard, William P. "Elizabeth Tudor's Book of Devotions: A Neglected Clue to the Queen's Life and Character." Sixteenth Century Journal 12 (Summer 1981): 79-106.

02165. Jones, Norman L. "Elizabeth, Edification and the Later Prayer Book of 1560." Church History 53 (June 1984):174-186.

02166. King, John N. "The Godly Woman in Elizabeth's Iconography." Renaissance Quarterly 38 (Spring 1985): 41-85.

02167. Woolf, D.R. "Two Elizabeths? James I and the Late Queen's Famous Memory." Canadian Journal of History 20 (August 1985): 167-191.

Also refer to #2184, 2197, 2277, 2306.

(b) Lady Jane Grey

02168. Ashdown, Dulcie. "Lady Jane Grey." British History Illustrated 3 (December 1976-January 1977):37-45.

02169. Fronville, Marguerite. Jane Grey, reine de 9 jours. Geneva: Perret-Gentil, 1975.

02170. Levin, Carole. "Lady Jane Grey: Protestant Queen and Martyr." In Silent but for the Word. Tudor Women as Patrons, Translators, and Writers of Religious Works, edited by Margaret P. Hannay, pp. 92-106. Kent, Ohio: Kent State University Press, 1985.

02171. Meroff, Deborah. *Coronation of Glory*. Grand Rapids, Michigan. Zondervan Publishing House, 1979.

(c) Henry VIII and his Wives

02172. Dowling, Maria. "Anne Boleyn and Reform." *Journal of Ecclesiastical History* 35 (January 1984): 30-46.

02173. ________. "Humanist Support for Katherine of Aragon." *Bulletin of the Institute for Historical Research* 57 (May 1984): 46-55.

02174. Flügel, J.C. "The Character and Married Life of Henry VIII." In *Psychoanalysis and History*, edited by Bruce Mazlish, pp. 124-149. Englewood, N.J.: Prentice-Hall, 1963.

02175. Harwood, Alice. "Virtuous Lady Queen Catherine Parr." *Fortnightly* 170 (September 1948): 187-192.

02176. King, John N. "Patronage and Piety: The Influence of Catherine Parr." In *Silent but for the Word. Tudor Women as Patrons, Translators, and Writers of Religious Works*, edited by Margaret P. Hannay, pp. 43-60. Kent, Ohio: Kent State University Press, 1985.

02177. Paget, H. "The Youth of Anne Boleyn." *Bulletin of the Institute of Historical Research* 54 (1981):162-170.

02178. Vena, Gaetano. *Boleyn, Sidney, Coleridge, Wilde, Eliot*. Cosenza: Pellegrini, 1975.

02179. Warnicke, Retha M. "The Fall of Anne Boleyn: A Reassessment." *Historical Journal* 70 (February 1985):1-15.

(d) Mary I

02180. Erickson, Carolly. "Bloody Mary: 'images of burning flesh and grim-eyed vengeance.'" *In Britain* 34 (April 1979): 30-33.

02181. Lewis, Brenda Ralph. "A most unhappy queen." *British History Illustrated* 3 (February-March 1977): 37-45.

02182. Tittler, Robert. *The Reign of Mary I*. New York: Longman, 1983.

(e) Mary, Queen of Scots

02183. Donaldson, Gordon. *Mary Queen of Scots*. London: English Universities Press, 1974.

02184. Plowden, Alison. Elizabeth Tudor and Mary Stewart: Two Queens in One Isle. Totowa, N.J.: Barnes and Noble, 1984.

(f) Arabella Stuart

02185. Cooper, E. Life and Letters of Lady Arabella Stuart. London: Hurst and Blackett, 1866.

02186. Seymour, William. "Arabella Stuart and William Seymour." History Today 22 (August 1972): 583-589.

02187. Smith, Emily Tennyson. Arabella Stuart. London: R. Bentley and Son, 1889.

(2) Others

02188. Buchanan, Patricia Nill. Margaret Tudor, New York: Columbia University Press, 1986.

02189. Gairdner, James. "The Death of Amy Robsart." English Historical Review 1 (1886): 235-259.

02190. Rowse, A.L. "Bess of Hardwick." In Eminent Elizabethans, pp. 1-40. Athens, Ga: University of Georgia Press, 1983.

02191. Simon, Linda. Of Virtue Rare: Margaret Beaufort, Matriarch of the House of Tudor. Boston: Houghton Mifflin, 1982.

02192. Stevenson, J., ed. The Life of Jane Dormer, Duchess of Feria. London: Burns and Oates, 1887.

Also refer to #1666

b) Gynecocratic Controversy

02193. Jordan, Constance. "Feminism and the Humanists: The Case of Sir Thomas Elyot's Defence of Good Women." Renaissance Quarterly 36 (Summer 1983): 181-201.

3. ECONOMIC

"There are in this town diverse young women and maidens who keep themselves out of service and work for themselves in diverse men's houses contrary to the statute."
Leet Records

02194. Roberts, Michael. "'Words they are Women, and Deeds they are Men'" "Images of Work and Gender in Early Modern England." In _Women and Work in Pre-Industrial Britain_, edited by Lorna Duffin, pp. 122-180. London: Croom Helm, 1985.

02195. Wright, Sue. "'Churmaids, Huswyfes and Hucksters': The Employment of Women in Tudor and Stuart Salisbury." In _Women and Work in Pre-Industrial Britain_, edited by Lorna Duffin, pp. 100-121. London: Croom Helm, 1985.

4. RELIGION

"Women are of two sorts; some of them are wiser, better learned, discreeter, and more constant than a number of men; but another and worse sort of them are fond, foolish, wanton, flibbergibs, tattlers, triflers . . ."
Bishop John Aylmer, from a sermon given before Queen Elizabeth I

a) Generic

02196. Greaves, Richard L. "The Role of Women in Early English Nonconformity." _Church History_ 52 (September 1983): 299-311.

02197. Levin, Carole. "John Foxe and the Responsibilities of Queenship." In _Women in the Middle Ages and the Renaissance Literary and Historical Perspectives_, edited by Mary Beth Rose, pp. 113-133. Syracuse, N.Y.: Syracuse University Press, 1986.

02198. Prior, Mary. "Reviled and Crucified Marriages: The Position of Tudor Bishops' Wives." In _Women in English Society, 1500-1800_, pp. 118-148. New York: Methuen, 1985.

02199. Rowlands, Marie B. "Recusant Women 1560-1640." In _Women in English Society 1500-1800_, edited by Mary Prior, pp. 149-180. New York: Methuen, 1985.

02200. Thompsett, Fredrica Harris. "Women Inclined to Holiness: Our Reformation Ancestry." _Historical Magazine of the Protestant Episcopalian Church_ 51 (December 1982):337-345.

Also refer to #2218.

b) Saints/Religious Women

(1) Women

(a) Individuals

[1] Margaret Clitherow

02201. Claridge, Mary. "Blessed Margareth Clitherow and the York plays (1572)." The Month n.s. 31 (June 1964): 347-354.

02202. Dessain, Mary Joanna. St. Margaret Clitherow. Slough, England: St. Paul, 1971.

02203. Longley, Katherine M. "The 'Trial' of Margaret Clitherow." Ampleforth Journal (Autumn 1970): 335-364.

(b) Others

02204. Beilin, Elaine V. "Anne Askew's Self-Portrait in the Examinations." In Silent but for the Word. Tudor Women as Patrons, Translators, and Writers of Religious Works, edited by Margaret P. Hannay, pp. 77-91. Kent, Ohio: Kent State University Press, 1985.

02205. Bornstein, Diane. "The Style of the Countess of Pembroke's Translation of Philippe de Mornay's Discours de la vie et de la mort." In Silent but for the Word. Tudor Women as Patrons, Translators, and Writers of Religious Works, edited by Margaret P. Hannay, pp. 126-134. Kent, Ohio: Kent State University Press, 1985.

02206. Derrick, Michael. "Critical and Historical Notes on Blessed Margaret of Salisbury." Month 177 (May-June 1941): 270-275.

02207. Fischer, Sandra K. "Elizabeth Cary and Tyranny, Domestic and Religious." In Silent but for the Word. Tudor Women as Patrons, Translators, and Writers of Religious Works, edited by Margaret P. Hannay, pp. 225-237. Kent, Ohio: Kent State University Press, 1985.

02208. Fisken, Beth Wynne. "Mary Sidney's Psalmes: Education and Wisdom. In Silent but for the Word. Tudor Women as Patrons, Translators, and Writers of Religious Works, edited by Margaret P. Hannay, pp. 166-183. Kent, Ohio: Kent State University Press, 1985.

02209. Hannay, Margaret P. "Doo What Men May Sing:" Mary Sidney and the Tradition of Admonitory Dedication. In Silent but for the Word. Tudor Women as Patrons, Translators, and Writers of Religious Works, edited by Margaret P. Hannay, pp. 149-165. Kent, Ohio: Kent State University Press, 1985.

02210. Lamb, Mary Ellen. "The Countess of Pembroke and the Art of Dying," In Women in the Middle Ages and the Renaissance Literary and Historical Perspectives, edited by Mary Beth Rose, pp. 207-226. Syracuse, N.Y.: Syracuse University Press, 1986.

02211. Lewalski, Barbara K. "Of God and Good Women: The Poems of Aemilia Lanyer." In Silent but for the Word. Tudor Women as Patrons, Translators, and Writers of Religious Works, edited by Margaret P. Hannay, pp. 203-224. Kent, Ohio: Kent State University Press, 1985.

02212. Verbrugge, Rita. "Margaret More Roper's Personal Expression in the Devout Treatise Upon the Pater Noster." In Silent but for the Word. Tudor Women as Patrons, Translators, and Writers of Religious Works, edited by Margaret P. Hannay, pp. 30-42. Kent, Ohio: Kent State University Press, 1985.

Also refer to #2248.

c) Canon Law

02213. Thurston, Herbert. "The Canon Law of the Divorce." English Historical Review 19 (October 1904): 632-645.

d) Puritans

02214. Hill, Christopher. "The Spiritualization of the Household." In Society and Puritanism in Pre-Revolutionary England, pp. 443-481. New York: Schocken Books, 1967.

Also refer to #2235, 2237.

e) Witchcraft

02215. Estes, Leland. "The Medical Origins of the European Witch Craze: A Hypothesis." Journal of Social History 17 (Winter 1983): 271-284.

02216. Pollock, Adrian. "Social and Economic Characteristics of Witchcraft: Accusations in Sixteenth and Seventeenth Century Kent." Archaeologica Cantiana 95 (1979): 37-48.

02217. Rushton, Peter. "Women, Witchcraft, and Slander in Early Modern England: Cases from the Church Courts of Durham, 1560-1675." Northern History 18 (1982): 116-132.

Also refer to #2203.

5. SOCIAL

"If you let your wife stand on your toe tonight, she'll stand on your face tomorrow."
Sir Thomas More *Epigrams*, No. 140 (1520)

a) Generic

(1) Non-specific

02218. Greaves, Richard L. *Society and Religion in Elizabethan England*. Minneapolis: University of Minnesota Press, 1981.

02219. Sanderson, Margaret H.B. *Scottish Rural Society in the Sixteenth Century*. Atlantic Highlands, N.J.: Humanities Press, 1982.

02220. Willan, T.S. "House and Home." In *Elizabethan Manchester*, pp. 106-123. Manchester: Printed for the Chetham Society, 1980.

Also refer to #2214.

(2) Women

02221. Fussell, George Edwin. "Countrywomen in old England." *Agricultural History* 50 (January 1976): 175-178.

b) Demography

02222. Cowgill, Ursula M. "Life and Death in the Sixteenth Century City of York." *Population Studies* 21 (July 1967): 53-62.

c) Family

(1) Non-specific

02223. Pearson, Lu Emily. "Changes Wrought by Death." In *Loving, Parenting and Dying*, edited by Vivian C. Fox and Martin H. Quitt, pp. 407-421. New York: Psychohistory Press, Publishers, 1980.

02224. Rosenthal, Joel T. "Aristocratic Widows in Fifteenth-Century England." In *Women and the Structure of Society*, edited by Barbara J. Harris and JoAnn K. McNamara, pp. 36-47. Durham, N.C.: Duke University Press, 1984.

02225. Travitsky, Betty S. "The New Mother of the English Renaissance: Her Writings on Motherhood." In *The Lost Tradition Mothers and Daughters in Literature*, edited by Cathy N. Davidson and E.M. Broner, pp. 33-43. New York: Ungar, 1980.

02226. Wrightson, Keith. "Household and Kinship in Sixteenth-century England." History Workshop 12 (Autumn 1981): 151-158.

Also refer to #2257, 2258, 2287.

(2) Childhood

02227. Byman, Seymour. "Child Raising and Melancholia in Tudor England." Journal of Psychohistory 5 (Spring 1978): 67-92.

02228. Carlton, Charles H. "The Administration of London's Court of Orphans." In Loving, Parenting and Dying, edited by Vivian C. Fox and Martin H. Quitt, pp. 456-466. New York: Psychohistory Press, Publishers, 1980.

02229. Hoffer, Peter C. and Hull, N.E.H. Murdering Mothers: Infanticide in England and New England, 1558-1603. New York: New York University Press, 1981.

02230. McCracken, Grant. "The Exchange of Children in Tudor England: An Anthropological Phenomenon in Historical Context." Journal of Family History 8 (Winter 1983): 303-313.

02231. McLaren, Dorothy. "Nature's Contraceptive: Wet-nursing and prolonged lactation: the case of Shesham, Buckinghamshire, 1578-1601." Medical History 23 (October 1979): 426-446.

02232. Stone, Lawrence. "Corporal Punishment, 1500-1600." In Loving, Parenting and Dying, edited by Vivian C. Fox and Martin H. Quitt, pp. 289-297. New York: Psychohistory Press, Publishers, 1980.

02233. Wooden, W.W. "The Topos of Childhood in Marian England." Journal of Medieval and Renaissance Studies 12 (1982): 179-194.

d) Marriage

02234. Davies, Kathleen M. "Continuity and Change in Literary Advice on Marriage." In Marriage and Society: Studies in the Social History of Marriage, edited by R.B. Outhwaite, pp. 58-80. New York: St. Martin's Press, 1981.

02235. __________. "The sacred condition of Equality -- How original were Puritan doctrines of marriage?" Social History 5 (May 1977): 563-580.

02236. Harris, Barbara J. "Marriage Sixteenth-Century Style: Elizabeth Stafford and the Third Duke of Norfolk." Journal of Social History 15 (Spring 1982): 371-382.

02237. Leites, Edmund. "The Duty to Desire: Love, Friendship and Sexuality in Some Puritan Theories of Marriage." _Journal of Social History_ 15 (Spring 1982): 383-408.

02238. Pearson, Lu Emily. "Founding and Maintaining an English Home." In _Loving, Parenting and Dying_, edited by Vivian C. Fox and Martin H. Quitt, pp. 163-177. New York: Psychohistory Press, Publishers, 1980.

02239. Stone, Lawrence. "The Stability of Marriage." In _Loving, Parenting and Dying_, edited by Vivian C. Fox and Martin H. Quitt, pp. 177-182. New York: Psychohistory Press, Publishers, 1980.

Also refer to #2198, 2207, 2213, 2261, 2263, 2266, 2270, 2273, 2290.

e) Sex Life and Morals

02240. Bashar, Nazife. "Rape in England between 1550 and 1700." In _The Sexual Dynamics of History_, edited by the London Feminist History Group, pp. 28-42. London: Pluto Press, 1983.

f) Fashion/Manners

02241. Sichel, Marion. _Costume Reference 2. Tudors and Elizabethans_. Boston: Plays Inc., 1977.

g) Health/Medical

02242. Aveling, James H. _The Chamberlens and the Midwifery Forceps_. London: J. and A. Churchill, 1882.

02243. Dewhurst, John. "The Alleged Miscarriages of Catherine of Aragon and Anne Boleyn." _Medical History_ 28 (January 1984): 49-56.

02244. Eccles, Audrey. _Obstetrics and Gynecology in Tudor and Stuart England_. Kent, Ohio: Kent State University Press, 1982.

02245. Guy, John R. "The Episcopal Licensing of Physicians, Surgeons and Midwives." _Bulletin of the History of Medicine_ 56 (Winter 1982): 528-542.

02246. Strong, L.D. and McCawley, E.L. "A Verification of a Hitherto Unknown Prescription of the Sixteenth Century. _Bulletin of the History of Medicine_ 21 (November-December 1947): 898-904.

Also refer to #2215.

6. CULTURAL

"Will my daughter prove a good musician? I think she'll sooner prove a soldier."
Shakespeare

a) Education

02247. Lamb, Mary Ellen. "The Cooke Sisters: Attitudes toward Learned Women in the Renaissance." In _Silent but for the Word. Tudor Women as Patrons, Translators, and Writers of Religious Works_, edited by Margaret P. Hannay, pp. 107-125. Kent, Ohio: Kent State University Press, 1985.

b) Patrons

02248. Hannay, Margaret P., ed. _Silent but for the Word. Tudor Women as Patrons, Translators, and Writers of Religious Works_. Kent, Ohio: Kent State University Press, 1985.

02249. Lamb, Mary Ellen. "The Countess of Pembroke's Patronage." _English Literary Renaissance_ 12 (Spring 1982): 162-179.

02250. ________________. "The Myth of the Countess of Pembroke." _Yearbook of English Studies_ 11 (1981):194-202.

02251. Quitslund, Jon A. "Spenser and the Patronesses of the _Fowre Hymnes_: Ornaments of all True Love and Beautie." In _Silent but for the Word. Tudor Women as Patrons, Translators, and Writers of Religious Works_, edited by Margaret P. Hannay, pp. 184-202. Kent, Ohio: Kent State University Press, 1985.

02252. Underwood, Malcolm G. "The Lady Margaret and her Cambridge Connections." _Sixteenth Century Journal_ 13 (Spring 1982):67-81.

02253. Warnicke, Retha M. "Margaret, Countess of Richmond. A Noblewoman of Independent Wealth and Status." _Fifteenth Century Studies_ 9 (1984):215-248.

c) Literature

(1) Non-specific

02254. Waller, Gary F. "Struggling into Discourse: The Emergence of Renaissance Women Writing." In _Silent but for the Word. Tudor Women as Patrons, Translators, and Writers of Religious Works_, edited by Margaret P. Hannay, pp. 238-256. Kent, Ohio: Kent State University Press, 1985.

02255. Woodbridge, Linda. _Women and the English Renaissance: Literature and the Nature of Womankind, 1540-1620._ Chicago: University of Illinois, 1984.

Also refer to #1708, 1941, 2160, 2204, 2205, 2207-2212, 2234.

(2) Drama

(a) Women

02256. Keyishian, Harry. "Griselda on the Elizabethan Stage: The Patient Grissie of Chettle, Dekker, and Haughton." _Studies in English Literature_ 16 (1976):253-261.

02257. McLuskie, Kate. "'Tis but a Woman's Jar': Family and Kinship in Elizabethan Domestic Drama." _Literature and History_ 9 (Autumn 1983):228-239.

02258. Wilson, Edward M. "Family Honour in the Plays of Shakespeare's Predecessors and Contemporaries." _Essays and Studies_ n.s. 6 (1953):19-40.

Also refer to #2201.

(b) Shakespeare

02259. Andresen-Thom, Martha. "Shrew-taming and Other Rituals of Aggression: Baiting and Bonding on the Stage and in the Wild." _Women's Studies_ 9 1982):121-143.

02260. Bamber, Linda. _Comic Women, Tragic Men: A Study of Gender and Genre in Shakespeare._ Stanford: University Press, 1982.

02261. Boose, Lynda E. "The Father and the Bride in Shakespeare." _PMLA_ 97 (May 1982):325-347.

02262. Charney, Maurice and Charney, Hanna. "The language of madwomen in Shakespeare and his fellow dramatists." _Signs_ 3 (Winter 1977): 451-460.

02263. Dash, Irene G. _Wooing, Wedding, and Power: Women in Shakespeare's Plays._ New York: Columbia University Press, 1981.

02264. Erickson, Peter B. "The Failure of Relationship between Men and Women in _Love's Labor's Lost_." _Women's Studies_ 9 (1981):65-81.

02265. Estrin, Barbara L. "'Behind a Dream': Cleopatra and Sonnett 129." _Women's Studies_ 9 (1982):177-188.

02266. Fineman, Joel. "Fratricide and Cuckoldry: Shakespeare's Doubles." Psychoanalytic Review 64 (Fall 1977):409-453.

02267. Garner, Shirley Nelson. "A Midsummer Night's Dream: 'Jack shall have Jill;/Nought shall go ill.'" Women's Studies 9 (1981):47-63.

02268. Gohlke, Madelon. "'All that is spoke is marred': Language and Consciousness in Othello." Women's Studies 9 (1982):157-176.

02269. Greene, Gayle. "Feminist and Marxist Criticism: An Argument for Alliances." Women's Studies 9 (1981):29-45.

02270. Hill, W. Speed. "Marriage as Destiny: An Essay on All's Well that Ends Well." English Literary Renaissance 5 (Autumn 1975): 344-359.

02271. Jacobs, R. "Sex and money: a note on Hamlet I. iii. Shakespeare Quarterly 31 (Spring 1980):88-90.

02272. Jameson, Anna B. Shakespeare's Heroines. 1913. Reprint. Folcroft, Pa.: Folcroft Library Editions, 1977.

02273. Kahn, Coppélia. "The Taming of the Shrew: Shakespeare's Mirror of Marriage." In The Authority of Experience, edited by Arlyn Diamond and Lee R. Edwards, pp. 84-100. Amherst: University of Massachusetts Press, 1977.

02274. Klein, Joan Larsen. "'Angels and Ministers of Grace': Hamlet IV v-vii." Allegorica 1 (Fall 1976):156-176.

02275. Leverenz, David. "The Women in Hamlet: An Interpersonal View." Signs 4 (Winter 1978):291-308.

02276. Mackenzie, Agnes Mure. The Women in Shakespeare's Plays: A Critical Study from the Dramatic and Psychological Points of View and in Relation to the Development of Shakespeare's Art. 1924. Reprint. Philadelphia: R. West, 1978.

02277. Marcus, Leah S. "Shakespeare's Comic Heroines, Elizabeth I and the Political Uses of Androgyny." In Women in the Middle Ages and the Renaissance Literary and Historical Perspectives, edited by Mary Beth Rose, pp. 135-153. Syracuse, N.Y.: Syracuse University Press, 1986.

02278. Mowat, Barbara A. "Images of Woman in Shakespeare's Plays." Southern Humanities Review 11 (1977):145-157.

02279. Neely, Carol Thomas. "Feminist Modes of Shakespearean Criticism: Compensatory, Justificatory, Transformational." Women's Studies 9 (1981):3-15.

02280. Novy, Marianne. "Demythologizing Shakespeare." Women's Studies 9 (1981):17-27.

02281. Novy, Marianne. _Love's Argument: Gender Relations in Shakespeare_. Chapel Hill, North Carolina: University of North Carolina Press, 1984.

02282. Okerlund, Arlene N. "In Defense of Cressida: Character as Metaphor." _Women's Studies_ 7 no. 3 (1980):1-17.

02283. Parten, Anne. "Re-establishing Sexual Order: The Ring Episode in _The Merchant of Venice_." _Women's Studies_ 9 (1982):145-155.

02284. Proudfoot, Richard. "'Love's Labours Lost' Sweet Understanding and the Five Worthies." _Essays and Studies_ n.s. 37 (1984):16-30.

02285. Rackin, Phyllis. "Anti-Historians: Women's Roles in Shakespeare's Histories." _Theatre Journal_ 37 (October 1985):329-344.

02286. Richmond, Velma. "Shakespeare's Women." _Midwest Quarterly_ 19 (Summer 1978): 330-342.

02287. Schotz, Myra Glazer. "The Great Unwritten Story: Mothers and Daughters in Shakespeare." In _The Lost Tradition Mothers and Daughters in Literature_, edited by Cathy N. Davidson and E.M. Broner, pp. 44-54. New York: Ungar, 1980.

02288. Sprengnether, Madelon. "Annihilating Intimacy in _Coriolanus_." In _Women in the Middle Ages and the Renaissance Literary and Historical Perspectives_, edited by Mary Beth Rose, pp. 89-111. Syracuse, N.Y.: Syracuse University Press, 1986.

02289. Sundelson, David. "Misogyny and Rule in _Measure for Measure_." _Women's Studies_ 9 (1981):83-91.

02290. Wheeler, Richard P. "Marriage and Manhood in _All's Well that Ends Well_." _Bucknell Review_ 21 (Spring 1973):103-124.

02291. Williamson, Marilyn L. "Doubling, Woman's Anger and Genre." _Women's Studies_ 9 (1982):107-119.

02292. Wilt, Judith. "Comment on David Leverenz's 'The Women in _Hamlet_.'" _Women's Studies_ 9 (1981):93-97.

02293. Ziegler, Georgianna. "A Supplement to the Lenz-Greene-Neely Bibliography on 'Women and Men in Shakespeare' based on the Collections of the Furness Shakespeare Library." _Women's Studies_ 9 (1982):203-213.

Also refer to #2090, 2640.

(c) Others

02294. Johnson, Marilyn Laurine. "Images of Women in the Works of Thomas Heywood. Salzburg, Austria: Institut für Englische Sprache und Literatur, 1974.

(3) Poetry

02295. Barnstone, Alike. "Women and the Garden: Andrew Marvell, Emilia Lanier, and Emily Dickinson." In Men by Women, Women and Literature, edited by Janet Todd, 2:147-167. New York: Holmes and Meier, 1982.

02296. DuBois, Page Ann. "'The Devil's Gateway': Women's Bodies and Earthly Paradise." Women's Studies 7 no. 3 (1980): 43-58.

02297. Kau, Joseph. "Delia's Gentle Lover and the Eternizing Conceit in Elizabethan Sonnets." Anglia 92 (1974): 334-348.

02298. Long, Percy W. "The Story of Spenser's Sonnets: Spenser and Lady Carey." Modern Language Review 3 (1908): 257-267.

02299. Schmitz, Götz. "Cresseid's Trial A Revision. Fame and Defamation in Henryson's 'Testament of Cresseid.'" Essays and Studies n.s. 32 (1979): 44-56.

Also refer to #2211, 2518.

C. FRANCE

1. POLITICAL

"Her forehead was haughty, her eyes hard, and her nose domineering. Her mouth, tightlipped and drawn in seemed made not to be kissed but to keep a secret."
said about
Diane de Poitiers

a) Political Roles

(1) Women

02300. Ryley, M. Beresford. Queens of the Renaissance. 1905. Reprint. Williamstown, Ma.: Corner House, 1982.

(2) Individuals

(a) Catherine de Medici

02301. Garrison-Estèbe, Janine. "Catherine de Medici:un grand roi." Histoire 22 (1980): 26-35.

02302. Trollope, Thomas Adolphus. The Girlhood of Catherine de Medici. London: Chapman and Hall, 1856.

(b) Margaret of Navarre

02303. Blaisdell, Charmarie Jenkins. "Marguerite de Navarre and Her Circle." In Female Scholars, edited by J.R. Brink, pp. 36-53. St. Albans, Vt.: Eden Press, 1980.

02304. Losse, Deborah N. "Distortion as a Means of Reassessments: Marguerite de Navarre's Heptameron and the 'Querelle des Femmes!" Journal of the Rocky Mountain Medieval and Renaissance Association 3 (1982): 57-84.

02305. Mariejol, Jean H. La Vie de Marguerite de Valois, reine de Navarre et de France. Paris: Libraire Hachette, 1928.

02306. Prescott, Anne Lake. "The Pearl of the Valois and Elizabeth I: Marguerite de Navarre's Miroir and Tudor England." In Silent but for the Word. Tudor Women as Patrons, Translators, and Writers of Religious Works, edited by Margaret P. Hannay, pp. 61-76. Kent, Ohio: Kent State University Press, 1985.

02307. Saulnier, V.L. "Marguerite de Navarre aux temps de Briconnet." Bibliothèque d'humanisme et renaissance 40 (1978):193-237.

02308. Wildenstein, Georges. "L'inventaire après décès de Marguerite de Navarre, reine de France, 1615." Gazette des Beaux Arts 100 no. 1 (March 1958):149-156.

02309. Winandy, André. "Piety and Humanistic Symbolism in the Works of Marguerite d'Angoulême, Queen of Navarre." Yale French Studies 47 (1972):145-169.

Also refer to #2300.

(3) Others

02310. Chombard de Lauwe, Marc. Anne de Beaujeu ou la passion du pouvoir. Paris: Tallandier, 1980.

02311. Lecoq, Anne-Marie. "La grand conjonction de 1524 demythifiée pour Louis de Savoi." Bibliotheque d'Humanisme et Renaissance 43 (1981):39-60.

02312. Markale, Jean. Anne de Bretagne. Paris: Hachette, 1980.

02313. Schlegel, Friedrich. Geschichte der Margaretha von Valois. Leipzig: Juniussischen Buchhandlung, 1803.

2. ECONOMIC

"Henceforth Charlotte Guillard, of a noble spirit, beyond that of herself, offered herself as the tailor, no matter what the sacrifice and took over business after the death of her husband."

Huchier

02314. Beech, Beatrice. "Charlotte Grillard: A Sixteenth Century Business Woman." Renaissance Quarterly 36 (Autumn 1983): 345-367.

02315. Davis, Natalie Zemon. "Women in the Arts Mécaniques in Sixteenth-Century Lyon." In Lyon et l'Europe.Hommes et sociétés. Melanges d'histoire offerts à Richard Gascon, pp. 139-167. Lyon: Presses et universitaires de Lyon, 1980. Also in Feminist Studies 8 (Spring 1982):46-80.

3. RELIGION

"In a word, there is no one [even the women not excepted] who has not been either killed or wounded."

Fr. Joachim Opser S.J.
about the St. Bartholomew's
Day Massacre, 1572

a) Saints/Religious Women

02316. Gabel, G. "La Sainteté dans le mariage. A propos de la 'Belle Acarie'" Année théologique 4 (1932):309-340.

02317. Garapon, Robert. "Marie de l'Incarnation, Ursuline de Québec, d'après sa correspondance." In Onze études sur l'image de la femme dans la littérature francaise du dix-septième siècle, edited by Wolfgang Weiner, pp. 51-66. Paris: Jean-Michel Place, 1978.

02318. Griguer, Thérèse. "La sainteté en Touraine au XVe siècle, la vie et le procès de canonisation de Jeanne-Marie de Maille." Annales de Bretagne 91 (1984); 27-37.

02319. Menthon, A. de. Les deux filles de Sainte-Chantal. Paris: n.p. 1872.

Also refer to #2336.

b) Francis de Sales

02320. Arnaud d'Angel, G. Les femmes d'après S. Francois de Sales. Paris: Plon, 1928.

02321. Schueller, T. "S. François de Sales et les femmes." Annales Salesiennes 55 (1959): 129-143.

02322. Vénard, Abbé André. "Deux contributions à l'histoire des pratiques contraceptives. I. Saint Fransois de Sales et Thomas Sanchez," Population 4 (1954):683-698.

c) Calvinism

02323. Blaisdell, Charmarie Jenkins. "Calvin's Letters to Women: The Courting of Ladies in High Places." Sixteenth Century Journal 13 (Fall 1982): 67-84.

02324. Bratt, John H. "The Role and Status of Women in the Writings of John Calvin." In Renaissance, Reformation, Resurgence, edited by Peter De Klerk, pp. 1-17. Grand Rapids, Mich.: Calvin Theological Seminary, 1976.

d) Witchcraft

02325. Febvre, Lucien. The Problem of Unbelief in the 16th Century. The Religion of Rabelais. Translated by Beatrice Gottlieb. Cambridge, Mass.: Harvard University Press, 1981.

4. SOCIAL

"It is proper, however, that . . . the speech of women never be made public.

Antoine du Moulin

a) Generic

02326. Davis, Natalie Zemon. The Return of Martin Guerre. Cambridge: Harvard University Press, 1983.

02327. Gonthier, N. "Délinquantes ou victimes, les femmes dans la société lyonnaise au XVe siècle." Revue historique 549 (January - March 1984): 25-46.

02328. Leclerq, Paulette. Un village de Provence dans la deuxième moitié du XVIe siècle. Paris: Ed. du CNRS, 1979.

b) Demography

02329. Aubry, Martine. "Les mortalités lilloises." Revue du Nord 65 (April-June 1983):327-342.

02330. Goubert, Pierre. "Recent Theories and Research in French Population between 1500 and 1700." In Population in History, edited by D.V. Glass and D.E.C. Eversley, pp. 457-473. Chicago: Aldine Publishing, 1965.

c) Family

02331. Zeller, Olivier. "L'espace et la famille à Lyon au XVIe et XVIIe siècles." Revue d'histoire moderne et contemporaine. 30 (October 1982): 587-596.

Also refer to #2316.

02332. ________. "Les structures familiales à Macon pendant la Ligue." Histoire, économie et societé 2 (1984):163-181.

d) Sex Life and Morals

02333. Rossiaud, Jacques. "Prostitution, Sex and Society in French Towns in the Fifteenth Century." In Western Sexuality, edited by Philippe Ariès and André Béjin, pp. 79-94. New York: Blackwell, 1979.

e) Fashion

02334. Anderson, Ruth Matilda. "Spanish Dress Worn by a Queen of France." Gazette des Beaux Arts 123 (December 1981): 215-222.

5. CULTURAL

"Mademoiselle, the harsh law of men no longer prevent women from applying themselves to the arts and sciences."
Louis Labé

a) Literature

(1) Women in Literature

02335. Bertaud, Madeleine. La jalousie dans la littérature au temps de Louis XIII: analyse littéraire et histoire des mentalités. Geneva:Droz, 1981.

02336. Beugnot, Bernhard. "Y-a-t-il une problématique féminine de la Retraite." In Onze études sur l'image de la femme dans la littérature francaise du dix-septième siècle, edited by Wolfgang Leiner, pp. 29-49. Paris: Jean-Michel Place, 1978.

02337. De Piaggi, Georgio. Società militaire e mondo femminile nell-opera di Brantôme. Salerno: Edizioni "Beta", 1970.

02338. Forestier, G. "Situation du personnage de la jeune fille dans la comédie francaise du XVIe siècle." Bibliotheque d'Humanisme et Renaissance 46 (1984):2-20.

02339. Guillerm-Curutchet, Luce, comp. La femme dans la littérature francaise et les traductions en francaise au 16e siècle. Lille: Université de Lille, 1971.

02340. Loupe, Laurence. "Paroles perdues au XVIe siècle." Art Press International 5 (March 1977): 18-19.

(2) Poetry

(a) Women in Poetry

02341. Bellenger, Yvonne. "La campagne et l'Anjou dans les 'Continuations des amours.'" Revue d'histoire littéraire de la France 76 (May - June 1976): 355-372.

02342. Mathieu-Castellani, Gisèle. "La Poésie amoureuse francaise à la fin du XVIe siècle d'après les Recueils Collectifs (1597-1600)." Revue d'histoire littèraire de la France 76 (January - February 1976): 3-19.

(b) Women Poets

(1) Louise Labé

02343. Ardouin, Paul. Maurice Sceve, Pernette du Guillet, Louise Labé. Paris: A.G. Nizet, 1981.

02344. Champdor, Albert. Louise Labé, son oeuvre et son temps. Trévoux: Edivions de Trévoux, 1981.

02345. Jones, Ann Rosalind. "Assimilation with a Difference: Renaissance Women poets and Literary Influence." Yale French Studies 62 (1981): 135-153.

02346. Kupisz, Casimir. "Louise Labé en Pologne." Cahiers d'histoire 11 (1966): 369-383.

02347. O'Connor, Dorothy. Louise Labé. 1926. Reprint. Geneva: Slatkine Reprints, 1972. Schollen-Jimack, Christine M. "Helisenne de Crenne, Octovien de Saint-Gelais and Virgil." Studi francesi 77 (March - April 1982): 197-210.

(2) Others

02348. Schollen-Jimack, Christine M. "Helisenne de Crenne, Octovien de Saint-Gelais and Virgil." Studi francesi 77 (March - April 1982):197-210.

(3) Prose

(a) Rabelais

02349. Freccero, Carla. "Damning haughty dames: Panurge and the Haulte Dame de Paris (Pantagrael, 14)." Journal of Medieval and Renaissance Studies 15 (Spring 1985): 57-67.

02350. Lefranc, Abel. "Le Tiers Livre de Pantagruel et la Querelle des femmes." In Rabelais études sur Gargantua, Pantagruel le Tiers Livre, pp. 263-315. Paris: A.Michel, 1953.

02351. Zegura, Elizabeth Chesney. "Toward a Feminist Reading of Rabelais." Journal of Medieval and Renaissance Studeis 15 (Spring 1985): 125-134.

Also refer to #2325.

b) Courtly Love

02352. Conley, Tom. "On the Birth of Death: An Arrest d'Amour of Martial D'Auvergne." In Gender and Literary Voice, Women and Literature, edited by Janet Todd, 1:248-257. New York: Holmes and Meier, 1980.

02353. Rebhorn, Wayne A. "Du Bellay's Imperial Mistress: Les Antiquités de Rome as Petrarchist Sonnet Sequence." Renaissance Quarterly 33 (Winter 1980):609-622.

D. THE GERMANIES

1. SURVEYS

"I'd rather marry a wise old man than a young fool."
Anna Maria of Braunschweig

02354. Fleischer, Manfred P. "'Are Women Human?' The Debate of 1595 Between Valens Acidalius and Simon Gediccus." Sixteenth Century Journal 12 (Summer 1981):107-121.

02355. Rebel, Hermann. Peasant Classes: The Bureaucratization of Property and Family Relations under the Habsburg Absolutism, 1511-1636. Princeton, N.J.: Princeton University Press, 1983.

2. POLITICAL

"Hence, if wives feel that their association and cohabitation with their husbands is injurious to their salvation as well of one as of the other...let them have recourse to the civil authority."

Martin Bucer
De Regno Christi

a) Legal

02356. Safley, Thomas Max. "Marital Litigation in the Diocese of Constance, 1551-1620." Sixteenth Century Journal 12 (Summer 1981): 61-78.

02357. ________. "To Preserve the Marital State: The Basler Ehegericht, 1550-1592." Journal of Family History 7 (Summer 1982): 162-179.

b) Political Roles

02358. Costello, Louise Stuart. Memoirs of Mary, the young Duchess of Burgundy and her Contemporaries. London: R. Bentley, 1853.

02359. Pognon, Edmond. "Une Femme qui a compté." Revue de Paris 75 (1968): 104-107.

02360. Seillière, Ernest. "Une favorite impériale au xvie siècle. La mère de Don Juan d'Autriche." Revue de la Renaissance 13 (1913): 223-234.

3. ECONOMIC

"Unskilled workers constituted the most economic group in the city, living from hand to mouth, a fact recognized by the municipal architects' habit of paying them their weekly wage on Saturday morning rather than just before quitting time in the evening so that their wives had some money for the weekend marketing."

Gerald Strauss
Nuremberg in the Sixteenth Century

02361. Wood, Merry Wiesner. "Paltry Peddlers or Essential Merchants? Women in the Distributive Trades in Early Modern Nuremberg." Sixteenth Century Journal 12 (Summer 1981): 3-14.

4. RELIGION

"And would to God that every town had a girls' school as well, where the girls would be taught the gospel for an hour every day either in German or in Latin."

Martin Luther
"To the Christian
Nobility of the German
Nation"

a) Generic

02362. Karant-Nunn, Susan C. "Continuity and Change: Some Effects of the Reformation on the Women of Zwickau." Sixteenth Century Journal 13 (Summer 1982): 16-42.

02363. Schneider, Annerose. "Frauen in den Flugschriften der frühen Reformationsbewegung." Jahrbuch für Geschichte Feudalismus 7 (1983): 247-264.

b) Lutheranism

02364. Lauterer-Pirner, Heidi. "Vom 'Frauenspiegel' zu Luthers Schrift 'Vom ehelichen Leben'. Das Bild der Ehefrau im Spiegel einiger Zeugnisse des 15. und 16. Jahrhunderts." In Frauen in der Geschichte III, edited by Annette Kuhn and Jörn Rüsen, pp. 63-85. Düsseldorf: Schwann-Bagel, 1983.

02365. Ozment, Steven. "Luther and the Family." Harvard Library Bulletin 32 (Winter 1984):36-53.

02366. Roper,Lyndal. "Luther: Sex, Marriage and Motherhood." History Today 33 (December 1983):33-38.

02367. Schwartz, Peter Hammond. "The Maternal Christ as Redeemer: Speech and Gender in the Thought of Martin Luther." Journal of Psychohistory 12 (Spring 1985):465-485.

c) Witchcraft

02368. Rauer, Brigitte. "Hexenwahn--Frauenverfolgung zu Beginn der Neuzeit--Ein Beitrag zur Frauengeschichte im Unterricht." In Frauen in der Geschichte II, edited by Annette Kuhn and Jörn Rüsen, pp.97-125. Düsseldorf: Schwann, 1982.

02369. Schade, Sigrid. Schadenzauber und die Magie des Körpers: Hexenbilder der frühen Neuzeit. Worms: Werner'sche Verlagsgesellschaft, 1983.

Also refer to #2376.

5. SOCIAL

"A mother's heart and love cannot forget her children--it is against her nature. She would go through fire for her children."

Martin Luther

a) Family

02370. Ozment, Steven. "The Family in Reformation Germany: The Bearing and Rearing of Children." Journal of Family History 8 (Summer 1983): 159-176.

Also refer to #2365, 2366.

b) Marriage

02371. Roper, Lyndal. "Going to Church and Street: Wedding in Reformation Augsburg." Past and Present 106 (February 1985):62-101.

02372. Safley, Thomas Max. Let no Man Put Asunder: The Control of Marriage in the German Southwest 1550-1600. Kirksville, Mo: Sixteenth Century Journal, 1984.

Also refer to #2356, 2357, 2364, 2366.

c) Sex Life and Morals

02373. Roper, Lyndal. "Discipline and Respectability: Prostitution and the Reformation in Augsburg." History Workshop 19 (Spring 1985): 3-28.

d) Health/Medical

02374. Assion, Peter. "Das Arzneibuch der Landgräfin Eleonore von Hessen-Darmstadt: Ein Beitrag zum Phänomen medizinischer caritas nach der Reformation." Medizinhistorisches Jahrbuch 17 (1982): 317-341.

6. CULTURAL

"Ever since I was ten years old I have been a student, much given to attending sermons. I have loved and frequented the company of learned men and conversed much with them about not worlds of pleasure but about the kingdom of God."

Katharine Zell, Letter to Rabus

02375. Guinsburg, Arlene Miller. "The Counterthrust to Sixteenth Century Misogyny: The Works of Agrippa and Paracelsus." Historical Reflections 8 (Spring 1981): 3-28.

02376. Hoak, Dale. "Art, Culture, and Mentality in Renaissance Society: The Meaning of Hans Baldung Grien's Bewitched Groom (1544)." Renaissance Quarterly 38 (Autumn 1985): 488-510.

02377. Moore, Cornelia Niekus. "Die adelige Mutter als Erzieherin: Erbauungsliteratur adeliger Mütter für ihre Kinder." In Europäische Hofkultur im 16. und 17. Jahrhundert, III, Wolfenbütteler Arbeiten zur Barockforschung, vol. 10, edited by August Buck, Georg Kauffmann, Blake Lee Spahr and Conrad Weidmann, pp. 505-510. Hamburg: Dr. Ernst Hauswedell, 1981.

02378. Schernberg, Dietrich. Ein schön Spiel von Frau Jutten, nach dem Eislebenen Druck von 1565. Berlin:Erich Schmidt, 1971.

Also refer to #2364, 2369.

E. IBERIA

1. POLITICAL

"God, the witness of hearts, knows that before my affections, I look first to the welfare of these kingdoms."
Isabella I

a) Feminism

02379. Matulka, Barbara. An Anti-Feminist Treatise of 15th Century Spain. New York:n.p., 1931.

b) Political Roles

1) Isabella I

02380. Brans, Jan. Isabel la Católica y el arte hispanoflamenco. Madrid: Ediciones Cultura Hispánica, 1952.

02381. Fernández Larraín, Sergio. Homenaje a los Reyes Católicos en el V i.e. quintos centenario de su proclamación en Segovia. Madrid: Cultura Hispánica 1975.

02382. Macía Serrano, Antonio. Los reyes y la corona. Alicante: Instituto de Estudios Alicantinos, 1978.

02383. Meseguer Fernández, Juan. "Isabel la Católica y las Franciscans." Archivo Ibero-Americano (July-September 1970): 265-310.

02384. Senior, Ray. The Crescent and Castile. A Historical Narrative on the Reign of Spain's Greatest Queen, Isabel of Castile. New York: Finch College, 1971.

02385. Val, Maria Isabel del. Isabel la Católica, princess. Valladolid: Instituto "Isabel la Católica," 1974.

2) Others

02386. Fernandez de Retana, Luis. Dona Juana de Austria. Madrid: Perpetual Socorro, 1955.

02387. Formica, Mercedes. Maria de Mendoza: solucion a un enigma amorosa. Madrid: Caro Raggio, 1979.

02388. Pfandl, Luis. Juana la loca. Madrid: Espasa-Calpe S.A., 1932.

2. RELIGION

"It is no small pity, and should cause us no little shame, that through our own fault, we do not understand ourselves or know who we are."

Teresa of Avila

a) Saints/Religious Women

1) Saint Theresa of Avila

02389. Alonso, Severino Maria. "Personalidad Humana de Santa Teresa de Jesús." Vida Religiosa 53 (1982): 331-342.

02390. Barton, Marcella B. "Saint Teresa of Avila: Did She Have Epilepsy?" Catholic Historical Review 68 (October 1982):581-598.

02391. Basdekis, Demetrios. "Unamuno y el estilo de Santa Teresa." Revista Hispanica Moderna 31 (1965): 54-56.

02392. Bernardo, Pablo M. Santa Teresa: la oración y la contemplación. Madrid: Ediciones Paulinas, 1977.

02393. Bertini, Giovanni Maria. "Teresa de Avila y el sentido de la naturaliza." Revista Hispanica Moderna 31 (1965): 71-77.

02394. De Sola, René. "La santa doctora Teresa de Jesus." Boletin Academia Nacional de la Historia 60 (January-March 1983):33-39.

02395. Egido, Teofanes. "Santa Teresa y su obra reformadora." Historia 16 (October 1982):43-50.

02396. Laguardia, Gari. "Santa Teresa and the Problem of Desire." Hispania 63 (September 1980): 523-531.

02397. Lincoln, Victoria. Teresa, a Woman: A Biography of Teresa of Avila. Albany, N.Y.: State University of New York Press, 1984.

02398. Poupard, Paul. "Sainte Thérèse d'Avila." Revue des deux mondes 8 (1983): 297-301.

02399. Romano, Catherine. "A Psycho-Spiritural History of Teresa of Avila: A Woman's Perspective." In Western Spirituality: Historical Roots, Ecumenical Routes, edited by Matthew Fox, pp. 261-295. Santa Fe, N.M.: Bear and Co., Inc., 1981.

Also refer to #2467.

2) Others

02400. Bilinkoff, Jodi. "The Holy Woman and the Urban Community in Sixteenth-Century Avila." In Women and the Structure of Society, edited by Barbara J. Harris and JoAnn McNamara, pp. 74-80. Durham, N.C.: Duke University Press, 1984.

3. SOCIAL

"The fundamentals of a home are the woman and the ox, the ox to plow and the woman to manage things."

The Perfect Wife
Fray Luís de Leon

a) Generic

02401. Bennassar, Bartolomé. Valladolid au Siécle d'Or: une ville de Castille et sa campagne au xvie siècle. Paris: Mouton and Co. 1967.

02402. Segura, Christina. Bases Socioeconómicas de la polación de Almeria(s.XV). Madrid: Editorial Peñagrande, 1979.

02403. Weisser, Michael R. "The Sense of Morality in the Montes." In The Peasants of the Montes, pp. 73-87. Chicago: University of Chicago Press, 1976.

b) Demography

02404. Maza Zorrilla, Elene. "Régimen demográfico de una villa castellana. La natalidad en Villalón de Campos durante los siglos XVI y XVII." Investigaciones Historicas 1 (1979): 69-97.

Also refer to #2322.

c) Family

02405. Rodriguez Sánchez, Angel. "La natalidad illegitima en Cáceres en el siglo XVI." Revista de Estudios Caceres 35 (1979): 123-164.

Also refer to #2422, 2423.

d) Fashion/Manners

02406. Souza, Alberto. O trajo popular em Portugal nos seculos XVI et XVII. Lisbon: n.p., 1925.

Also refer to #2334, 2408.

4. CULTURAL

"These birds were born
Singing for you;
Such softness imprisoned
Gives me much sorrow--
Yet no one weeps for me."
Florencia de Pinar
"To Some Partridges Sent to Her Alive"

a) Education

02407. Wayne, Valerie. "Some Sad Sentence: Vives' Instruction of a Christian Woman." In Silent but for the Word. Tudor Women as Patrons, Translators, and Writers of Religious Works, edited by Margaret P. Hannay, pp. 15-29. Kent, Ohio: Kent State University Press, 1985.

b) Literature

1) Women in Literature

02408. Goldberg, Harriet. "Clothing in Tirant-lo-Blanc: Evidence of 'Realismo vitalista' or of a New Unreality." Hispanic Review 52 (Summer 1984): 379-392.

02409. Salstad, M. Louise. The Presentation of Women in Spanish Golden Age Literature An Annotated Bibliography. Boston: G.K. Hall, 1980.

02410. Simms, Edna N. "Notes on the negative image of women in Spanish literature." CLA Journal 19 (June 1976): 468-483.

Also refer to #1941, 2069.

2) Women in Poetry

02411. Cirurgião, Antonio A. "O papel da beleza na Diana de Jorge de Montemor." Hispania 51 (September 1968): 402-407.

02412. Damiani, Bruno M. "Nature, Love and Fortune as Instruments of Didacticism in Montemayor's Diana." Hispanic Journal 3 (Spring 1982):7-19.

02413. Darst, David H. "Garcilaso's Love for Isabel Freire: The Creation of a Myth." Journal of Hispanic Philology 3 (Spring 1979): 261-268.

02414. Piper, Anson C. "The Feminine Presence in Os Lusiades." Hispania 57 (May 1974): 231-238.

02415. Rabassa, Clemintine C. "The Political Significance of Women in Canto III of the Lusiads." Luso-Brazilian Review 17 (Winter 1980):186-197.

02416. Ryan, James. "The Psychology of Love in the 'Cuestion de amor.'" Hispania 46 (March 1963): 61-65.

02417. Smith, John D. "Metaphysical Descriptions of Women in the First Sonnets of Gongora." Hispania 56 (April 1973): 244-248.

02418. Waley, Pamela. "Garcilaso, Isabel and Elena: the Growth of a Legend." Bulletin of Hispanic Studies 56 (January 1979): 11-15.

Also refer to #2077, 2085.

3. Prose

a) Cervantes

02419. Close, A.J. "Don Quixote's Love for Dulcinea: A Study of Cervantine Irony." Bulletin of Hispanic Studies 50 (1973): 237-255.

02420. Hughes, Gethin. "The Cave of Montesino: Don Quixote's Interpretation and Dulcinea's Disenchantment." Bulletin of Hispanic Studies 54 (April 1977): 107-114.

02421. ElSaffar, Ruth. Beyond Fiction: The Recovery of the Feminine in the Novels of Cervantes. Berkeley: University of California Press, 1985.

02422. Pabon, Thomas A. "Courtship and Marriage in El amante liberal: the Symbolic Quest for Self-Perfectibility." Hispanofilia 76 (September 1982): 47-52.

02423. Pabon, Thomas A. "The Symbolic Significance of Marriage in Cervantes' La espãnola inglesa." Hispanofilia 63 (May 1978): 59-66.

02424. Trachman, Sadie Edith. Cervantes' Women of Literacy Tradition. New York: Instituto de las Espanas en los Estados Unides, 1932.

b) Fernando de Rojas

02425. Barbera, Raymond E. "A Harlot, A Heroine (Celestina)." Hispania 48 (December 1965): 790-799.

02426. Herrero, Jawer. "Celestina's Craft: The Devil in the Skein." Bulletin of Hispanic Studies 61 (July 1984): 343-351.

02427. Moore, John A. "Ambivalence of Will in 'La Celestina.'" Hispania 47 (May 1964): 251-255.

c) Others

02428. Beysterveldt, Antony van. "El amor caballeresco de 'Amadis' y el 'Terante.'" Hispanic Review 49 (Autumn 1981): 407-425.

02429. _________. "Revisión de los debates feministas del siglo XV y las novelas de Juan de Flores." Hispania 64 (March 1981): 1-13.

02430. Davis, Barbara N. "Love and/or Marriage: The Surprising Revision of Jerónimo de Contreras' 'Selva de aventuras.'" Hispanic Review 50 (Spring 1982): 173-199.

02431. Chorpenning, Joseph F. "Rhetoric and Feminism in Cárcel de amor." Bulletin of Hispanic Studies 54 (January 1977): 1-8.

02432. Flightner, James A. "The Popularity of the 'Carcel de amor.'" Hispania 47 (September 1964): 475-478.

02433. Perez-Erdelyi, Mireya. La pícara y la dama: la imágen de las mujeres en las novelas picaresco cortesanas de María de Zayas y Sotomayor y Alonso del Castillo Solórzano. Miami, Fla: Edicione Universal, 1979.

02434. Whitbourn, Christine J. The 'Arcipreste de Talavera' and the Literature of Love. Hull: University of Hull, 1970.

Also refer to #2085, 4497.

c) Art

02435. Foster, David William. "Love and Death in an Early Spanish Ballad." *Papers on Language and Literature* 8 (Spring 1972): 127-134.

Also refer to #2380.

F. ITALY

1. SURVEYS

"You boast and publicly not merely wonder but indeed lament that I am said to possess as fine a mind as nature ever bestowed upon the most learned man."
Laura Cereta to Bibulus Sempronius

02436. Isolani, Carolina. *Donne di virtù nella baraonda bolognese del Settencento*. Bologna: N. Zanichelli, 1945.

02437. Lungo, Isidoro del. "La donna fiorentina ne Rinascimento e negli ultimi tempi della libertà." In *La vita italiana nel Rinascimento*, pp. 99-146. Milan: Fratelli Treves, Editori, 1925.

2. POLITICAL

"Young males because of their youth no less because of their nude knowledge...[are] equal to the vile females."
G. Cavalcanti
Tratto Politico-Morale

a) Feminism

02438. Conti Odorisio, Ginevra. *Donna e societá nel Seicento: Lucrezia Marinelli e Arcangela Tarabotti*. Rome: Bulzoni, 1979.

b) Political Roles

1) Women

02439. Cohn, Samuel K. Jr. "Donne in piazza e donne in tribunale a Firenze nel Rinascimento." *Studi Storici* 22 (July-September 1981): 515-533.

Also refer to #2300.

2) Individuals

a) Lucretia Borgia

02440. Nabonne, Bernard. *La Vie privée de Lucrèce Borgia*. Paris: Hachette, 1953.

02441. Villa-Urrutia, Wenceslao Ramírez de Villa Urrutia I, marques de. *Lucrecia Borja*. Madrid: Libreria Beltrán, 1943.

Also refer to #2300, 2506.

b) Margaret of France, duchess of Savoy

02442. Béné, Charles. "Marguerite de France et l'oeuvre de Du Bellay." In *Culture et pouvoir au temps de l'Humanisme et de la Renaissance*, pp. 223-241. Paris: Champion. 1978.

02443. Bentley-Cranch, Dana. "L'iconographie de Marguerite de Savoie (1523-1574)." In *Culture et pouvior au temps de l'Humanisme et de la Renaissance*, pp. 243-256. Paris: Champion, 1978.

02444. Margolin, Jean-Claude. "Une princesse d'inspiration érasmienne: Marguerite de France, duchesse de Berry, puis de Savoie." In *Culture et pouvoir au temps de l'Humanisme et de la Renaissance*, pp. 155-183. Paris: Champion, 1978.

02445. Pillorget, René. Le rôle universitaire de Marguerite de Savoie." In *Culture et pouvoir au temps de l'Humanisme et de la Renaissance*, pp. 207-222. Paris: Champion, 1978.

02446. Stegmann, André. " Les Cheminements spirituels de Marguerite de France, duchesse de Savoie." In *Culture et pouvoir au temps de l'Humanisme et de la Renaissance*, pp. 185-205. Paris: Champion, 1978.

c) Joanna I of Naples

02447. Baddeley, Welbore St. Clair. *Queen Joanna I of Naples, Sicily, and Jerusalem, Countess of Provence, Forcalquier and Piedmont*. London: W. Heinemann, 1893.

02448. De Feo, Italo. *Giovanna D'Angio regina di Napoli*. Naples: Fiorentino, 1968.

02449. Gleijeses, Vittorio. *Giovanna I d'Angio, regina di Napoli*. Naples: Societá Editrice napoletana, 1978.

02450. Stango, Nino. *Tutti gli uomini della regina*. Naples: Gallina, 1982.

3) Others

02451. Ady, Julia Mary. Christina of Denmark, Duchess of Milan and Lorraine, 1522-1590. 1913. Reprint. N.Y.: AMS Press, 1973.

02452. Benvenuti, Antonia Tissoni. "Il viaggio d'Isabella d'Este a Mantova nel giugno 1480 e la datazione dell' "Orfeo" del Poliziano." Giornale storico della letteratura italiana 158(1981): 368-383.

02453. Dina, Achille. "Isabella d'Aragon, Duchessa di Milan e di Bari." Archivio storico lambardo 5th ser. 48 (1921): 269-457.

02454. Kolsky, Stephen. "Images of Isabelle d'Este." Italian Studies 39 (1984): 47-62.

02455. Robbert, Louise Buenger. "Caterina Cornaro, Queen of Cyprus." In Female Scholars, edited by J.R. Brink, pp. 24-35. St. Albans, Vt.; Eden Press, 1980.

02456. Valentini, Norberto. Beatrice Cenci. Milan: Rusconi, 1981.

Also refer to #2506.

3. RELIGION

"Oh excellent gift of God! Oh virginity akin to the angels and consecrated in the Virgin Mother and in the Virgin's Son! You are the road to heaven, the enemy of demons, the ornament of the soul, the splendor and the crown of modesty."

Gregorio Correr

a) Generic

02457. Martin, John. "Out of the Shadow: Heretical and Catholic Women in Renaissance Venice." Journal of Family History 10 (Spring 1985): 21-33.

Also refer to #2494.

b) Saints/Religious Women

1) Catherine of Siena

02458. Champdor, Albert. Catherine de Sienne et son temps. Lyon: A. Guillot, 1982.

02459. Chéry, Henri Charles. Sainte Catherine de Sienne. Tours: Mame, 1962.

02460. Dore, Peppina. Santa Caterina de Siena. Turin: Soc. editrice internazionale, 1940.

02461. Giordani, Igino. Vita di santa Caterina da Siena, Boston: St. Paul Editions, 1975.

02462. Lavagna, Raffaello. Laudato sil mi' Signore. Milan: Massimo, 1968.

02463. Mondrone, Domenico. "Santa Caterina da Siena dottore della Chiesa Universale." Civiltà Cattolia (1970): 18-30.

02464. Nigg, Walter. Lehrmeister der Christenheit in verwirrter Zeit. Freiburg in Breisgau: Herder, 1981.

02465. Parks, Carola. "Social and Political Consciousness in the Letters of Catherine of Siena." In Western Spirituality: Historical Roots, Ecumenical Routes, edited by Matthew Fox, pp. 249-260. Santa Fe, N.M.: Bear and Co., Inc., 1981.

02466. Raymond of Capua. Vita Sanctae Catherinae Senensis. Ilkley, Eng.: Scolar Press, 1978.

02467. Rupp, Jean. Catherine et Thérèse. Paris: P. Lethielleux, 1971.

02468. Samore, Antonio. Caterina da Siena e il ritorno del papa da Avignone. Siena: Cantagalli, 1977.

Also refer to #1611, 2117, 2118, 2300.

2) Others

02469. Del Bo, Rinaldo. Caterina da Genova. Milan: All' insegna del pesce d'oro, 1978.

02470. Desaing, Marie-Petra. Angela Merici. Stein am Rhein: Christiana Verlag, 1976.

02471. Kaye-Smith, Sheila. Quartet in Heaven. Garden City, NY: Doubleday, 1962.

c) Mariology

02472. King, Georgiana Goddard. "The Virgin of Humility." Art Bulletin 17 (December 1935): 474-491.

02473. Meiss, Millard. "A 'Madonna' by Francesco Frami." Gazette des Beaux Arts 102 no. 2 (July-August 1960): 49-56.

02474. Pope-Hennessy, John, Sir. "The Altmann Madonna by Antonio Rossellino." Metropolitan Museum Journal 3 (1970): 133-148.

02475. Seymour, Charles Jr. and Swarzenski, Hanns. "A Madonna of Humility and Quercia's Early Style." Gazette des Beaux Arts 88 no. 2 (September 1946): 129-152.

02476. Valentiner, W.R. "The Madonna of the Scales." Gazette des Beaux Arts 99 no. 1 (March 1957): 129-148.

d) Monastic Life

02477. Brown, Judith C. Immodest Acts, the Life of a Lesbian Nun in Renaissance Italy. New York: Oxford University Press, 1985.

02478. Paschini, Pio. "I monasteri feminili." In Problemi di vita religiosa in Italia nel cinquecento. Atti del Convegno di storia della chiesa in Italia, pp. 31-60. Padua: Editrice Antenore, 1960.

02479. Weaver, Elissa. "Spiritual Fun: A Study of Sixteenth-Century Tuscan Convent Theater." In Women in the Middle Ages and the Renaissance Literary and Historical Perspectives, edited by Mary Beth Rose, pp. 173-205. Syracuse. N.Y.: Syracuse University Press, 1986.

e) Witchcraft

02480. Ginzburg, Carlo. The Night Battles, Witchcraft and Agrarian Cults in the Sixteenth and Seventeenth Centuries. Baltimore, MD: John Jopkins University Press, 1984.

02481. Monter, E. William. "Women and the Italian Inquisitions." In Women in the Middle Ages and the Renaissance Literary and Historical Perspectives, edited by Mary Beth Rose, pp. 73-87. Syracuse, N.Y.: Syracuse University Press, 1986.

4) SOCIAL

"Displeasing certainly to every honest eye, is paint in any lady, and more especially in beautiful and graceful virgins, whose property is the simplicity and dove-like purity that much delight and please."

Federico Luigini
The Book of Fair Women
1554

a) Generic

02482. Antonetti, Pierce. La vie quotidienne á Florence au temps de Dante. Paris: Hachette, 1979.

02483. Cohn, Samuel Kline. The Laboring Classes in Renaissance Florence. New York: Academic Press, 1980.

02484. Klapisch-Zuber, Christiane. Women, Family, and Ritual in Renaissance Italy. Chicago: University of Chicago Press, 1985.

b) Demography

02485. Cipolla, Carlo M. "The 'Bills of Mortality' of Florence." Population Studies 32 (November 1978): 543-548.

02486. Klapisch-Zuber, Christiane. "Célibat et service féminin dans la Florence du XVe siècle." Annales de démographie historique (1981): 289-302.

02487. Menzione, Andrea. "Schemi di matrimonio e mortalità dei sessi: una transizione fra medioevo ed eta moderna?" Società et Storia 12 (1981): 435-447.

02488. Pina, Marco Della. "Alcune reflessioni sull'evoluzione demografica della Toscana tra medioevo ed eta' moderna." Società et Storia 12 (1981): 423-433.

c) Family

02489. Caiati, Vito. "The Peasant Household under Tuscan Mezzadria: A Socioeconomic Analysis of some Sienese Mezzadri Households, 1591-1604." Journal of Family History 9 (Summer 1984):111-126.

02490. Chojnacki, Stanley. "Kinship Ties and Young Patricians in Fifteenth-Century Venice." Renaissance Quartely 38 (Summer 1985): 240-270.

02491. Guidoboni, Emanuela. "Terre, Villaggi e famiglie de Polesine di Casaglia fra XV e XVI secolo." Società et Storia 14 (1981): 793-848.

02492. Klapisch-Zuber, Christiane. "La mère cruelle': Maternité, veuvage et dot dans la Florence des XIV-XVe siècles." Annales: économies, sociétés civilisations 38 (September-October 1983): 1097-1109.

02493. Smith, Richard M. "The People of Tuscany and Their Families in the Fifteenth Century: Medieval or Mediterranean." Journal of Family History 6 (1981): 107-128.

02494. Swain, Elisabeth. "Faith in the Family: The Practice of Religion by the Gonzaga." Journal of Family History 8 (Summer 1983): 177-189.

Also refer to #2436, 2484, 2521.

d) Marriage

02495. Brucker, Gene. Giovanni and Lusanna, Love and Marriage in Reniassance Florence. Berkeley, Ca: University of California Press, 1986.

02496. Casa Giovanni della. [An uxor sit ducenda.] Prendine mille e una ma non sposarne alcuna. Naples: Guida, 1976.

02497. Della Casa, Giovanni. Prendine mille e una ma non sposarne alcuna. Naples: Guida, 1976.

02498. Klapisch-Zuber, Christiane. "Zacharie, ou le père évincé: les rites nuptiaux en Toscane." Annales: économies, sociétés, civilizations 34 (November-December 1979):1214-1243.

02499. ________. "Une ethnologie du mariage au temps de l'Humanisme." Annales: économies, sociétés, civilisations 36 (November-December 1981): 1016-1027.

02500. Rodocanachi, E. "Le Mariage en Italie a l'époque de la Renaissance." Revue des questions historique 76 (July 1904): 29-60.

Also refer to #2487, 2529.

e) Sex Life and Morals

02501. Livieri, Achillo. "Eroticism and Social Groups in Sixteenth-Century Venice: The Courtesan." In Western Sexuality, edited by Philippe Ariés and André Béjin, pp. 95-102. New York: Blackwell, 1985.

02502. Ruggiero, Guido. The Boundaries of Eros: Sex Crime and Sexuality in Renaissance Venice. Oxford: University Press, 1985.

02503. Trexler, Richard. "La prostitution florentine au XVe siècle." Annales: économies, sociéte´s, civilisations 36 (November-December 1981): 983-1015.

Also refer to #2477.

f) Fashion/Manners

02504. Herald, Jacqueline. Renaissance Dress in Italy, 1400-1500. Atlantic Highlands, N.J.: Humanities Press, 1981.

5. CULTURAL

"An eloquent woman is never chaste."
Said of Isotta Nogarola

a) Generic

02505. LaValva, Maria P. "Die Rolle der Frau für die italienische Sprache und Kultur im 16. Jahrhundert." In Europäische Hofkultur im 16. und 17. Jahrhundert, III, Wolfenbütteler Arbeiten zur Barockforschung, edited by August Buck, Georg Kauffman, Blake Lee Sparr and Conrad Wiedemann, 10:447-455. Hamburg: Dr. Ernst Hauswedell and Co., 1981.

02506. Prizer, W.F. "Isabella d'Este and Lucrezia Borgia as Patrons of Music: the frottola at Mantua and Ferrara." Journal of the American Musicological Society 38(1985):1-33.

Also refer to #2455.

b) Education

02507. Blade, Melinda. The Education of Italian Renaissance Women. Mesquite, Texas: Ide House, 1983.

02508. Jardine, Lisa. "Isotta Nogarola: Women Humanists - Education for What?" History of Education 12(1983):231-244.

c) Literature

1) Non-Specific

02509. King, Margaret L. and Rabil, Albert Jr. Her Immaculate Hand: Selected Works By and About the Women Humanists of Quattrocento Italy. Binghamton, New York: Center for Medieval and Early Renaissance Studies, 1982.

02510. Lopez, Maria Savi. "La donna italiana del trecento." In La donna italiana descritta da scrittici italianae, pp. 37-62. Florence: G. Civelli, 1890.

2) Drama

02511. Reiss, Timothy J. "Jodelle's Cléopâtre and the Enchanted Circle." Yale French Studies 47(1972):199-210.

02512. Terpening, R.H. "Between Lord and Lady: The Tyrant's Captain in Rucellai's Rosamunda and Dolce's Marianna." Forum italicum 15 (Fall-Winter 1981): 153-170.

Also refer to #2479.

3) Poetry

a) Women in Poetry

[1] Dante Alighieri

02513. Aprile, Giuseppe. _Dante, inferni dentro e fuori_. Palermo: Editrice de Il vespro, 1977.

02514. Gasti, Filippina Rossi. "Le donna nella Divina Comedia." In _La donna italiana descritta da scrittici italianae_, pp. 25-36. Florence: G. Civelli, 1890.

02515. Goyau, Luci (Faure). _Les Femmes dans l'oeuvre de Dante_. Paris: Perrin et cie, 1902.

02516. Klemp, P.J. "The Women in the Middle Layers of Love in Dante's _Vita Nuova_." _Italica_ 6(1984):185-194.

02517. Morand, Bernadette. "Béatrice." _Europe_ 427-428 (November-December 1964): 24-28.

02518. Paolucci, Anne. "Women in the Political Love-Ethic of the _Divine Comedy_ and the _Faerie Queene_." _Dante Studies with the Annual Report of the Dante Society_ 90(1972):139-153.

02519. Shapiro, Marianne. _Woman Earthly and Divine in the Comedy of Dante_. Lexington: University Press of Kentucky, 1975.

02520. Stock, Lorraine Kochanske. "Reversion for Conversion: Maternal Images in Dante's _Commedia_." _Italian Quarterly_ 23 (1982): 5-15.

[2] Others

02521. Benson, Pamela Joseph. "An Unrecognized Defender of Women in the _Orlando Furioso_." _Italica_ 57 (Winter 1980): 268-270.

02522. Ruffo-Fiore, Silvia. "A New Light on Suns and Lovers in Petrarch and Donne." _Forum italicum_ 8 (December 1974): 546-556.

02523. Tomalin, Margaret. "Bradamante and Marfisa: An Analysis of the Guerrier of the Orlando furioso." _Modern Language Review_ 71 (July 1976): 540-552.

02524. Tusiani, Joseph. "Charlotte, Queen of Cyprus, as a Partial Model for Tasso's Armida." _Forum italicum_ 9 (March 1975): 3-14.

02525. Vickerson, Nancy J. "Diana Described: Scattered Women and Scattered Rhyme." _Critical Inquiry_ 8 (Winter 1981): 265-279.

02526. Yoch, J.J. "The Limits of Sensuality: Pastoral Wilderness, Tasso's Aminta and the Gardens of Ferrara." Forum italicum 16 (Spring-Fall 1982): 60-81.

b) Women Poets

02527. Bassanese, Fiora A. Gaspara Stampa. Boston: Twayne Publishers, 1982.

02528. Brunamonti, Alinda Bonacci. "Beatrice Portinari e idealità della donna nei canti d'amore in Italia." In La donna italiana descritta da scrittici italianae, pp. 1-24. Florence: G. Civelli, 1890.

4) Prose

02529. Bonadeo, Alfredo. "Marriage and Adultery in the Decameron." Philological Quarterly 60 (1981): 287-303.

02530. Iannucci, A.A. "L'Elegia di Madonna Fiammetta and the First Book of the Arolani: The Eloquence of Unrequited Love." Forum italicum 10 (December 1976): 345-359.

02531. Kapp, Volker. "Frauentugend und Adelsethos in Boccaccio's Criselda-Novelle (Decameron X, 10). Archiv für das Studium der neueren Sprachen 219 (1982): 89-108.

02532. King, Margaret L. "Goddess and Captive: Antonio Loschi's Poetic Tribute to Maddalena Scrovegni (1389), Study and Text." Medievalia et Humanistica n.s. 10 (1980): 103-128.

02533. Luigini, Federico. The Book of Fair Women. Translated by Elsie M. Lang. New York: James Pott and Company, 1907.

02534. Pitkin, Hanna Fenichel. Fortune is a Woman: Gender and Politics in the Thought of Niccolo Machiavelli. Berkeley, Ca: University of California Press, 1984.

Also refer to #485, 1587, 2152.

d) Art and Artifacts

(1) Women in Art

02535. Ferrante, G.N. "Most beautiful woman of the Italian Renaissance." Arts and Decoration 35 (July 1931): 18-19.

02536. Groseclose, Barbara. " A Portrait Not by Guido Reni of a Girl Who is not Beatrice Cenci." Studies in Eighteenth Century Culture 11 (1982): 107-132.

02537. Keele, Kenneth D. "The Genesis of Mona Lisa." Journal of the History of Medicine 14 (April 1959): 135-159.

02538. Mambretti, Joel. "Neoplatonism and Botticelli's Primavera." Bucknell Review 21 (Spring 1973): 125-136.

02539. Richter, G.M. "Portrait of a lady by Giovanni Bellini may be identified as portrait of the famous Morosina." Burlington Magazine 69 (July 1936): 2-5.

Also refer to #2443, 2472-2476.

(2) Women Artists

(a) Painters/Sculptors

02540. Caroli, Flavio. "Antologia di artist; per Lucia Anguissola." Paragone 277 (1973): 69-73.

02541. Feinberg, Alice M. "Diana Ghisi-Italian Printmaker, 1530-1590." Feminist Art Journal 4 (Fall 1975): 28-30.

02542. Galli, Romeo. Lavinia Fontana, pittrice, 1552-1614. Imola: P. Galeati, 1940.

02543. Huntley, George Haydn. Andrea Sansovino, Sculptor and Architect of the Italian Renaissance. 1935. Reprint. Westport, Ct.; Greenwood Press, 1972.

02544. Schwartz, Theresa. "Catarina Vigri and Properzia de Rossi." Women's Studies 6 (1978): 13-21.

02545. Tietze-Conrat, E. "Marietta, fille du Tintoret: peintre de portraits." Gazette des Beaux-Arts 12 (December 1934): 258-262.

02546. Tufts, Eleanor. "Ms. Lavinia Fontana from Bologna: A Successful Sixteenth Century Portraitist." Art News 73 (February 1974): 60-64.

(b) Musicians

02547. Castleman, C. "Three Musical Virtuosi di Ferrara: Lucrezia Bendido, Laura Peperara and Tarquinia Molza." Anuario Musical 23 (1968): 191-198.

G. THE LOW COUNTRIES

1. POLITICAL

"All goes awry and lawless in the land, where power takes the place of justice...Quite possibly there will be whisperings, Nevertheless they'll not disturb my courage as long as I live."

Margaret of Austria

02548. Lacroix de Lavalette, Marie Josephe de. Charlotte de Bourbon. Paris: n.p., 1972.

2. CULTURAL

"They [Dutch women] are active with hand and tongue in affairs that properly pertain to men, and attend to them with such skill and energy that in many regions such as Holland and Zealand the men let their women settle everything."

Ludovico Guiccardini

a) Education

02549. Sowards, J. K. "Erasmus and the Education of Women." Sixteenth Century Journal 13 (1982): 77-89.

b) Art

1) Women in Art

02550. Alpers, Svetlana. "Art History and its Exclusions: The Example of Dutch Art." In Feminism and Art History: Questioning the Litany, edited by Norma Broude and Mary D. Garrard, pp. 182-199. New York: Harper and Row, 1982.

02551. Baldwin, Robert. "Marriage as a Sacramental Reflection of the Passion: The Mirror in Jan van Eyck's Arnolfini Wedding." Oud Holland 98 (1984): 57-75.

02552. Courtauld, S. "Three Portraits of Women: Holbein's Young Woman at The Hague Gallery, Rembrandt's Hendrickje Stoffels in the Louvre, and Lely's Ursula." Apollo 36 (December 1942): 141-142.

02553. O'meara, Carra Ferguson. "Isabelle of Portugal as the Virgin in Jan van Eyck's Washington 'Annunciation.'" Gazette des Beaux-Arts 123 (March 1981): 99-103.

02554. Vandenbroeck, Paul. "Verbeeck's Peasant Weddings: A Study of Iconography and Social Function. Simiolus 14 (1984): 79-124.

2) Women Artists

02555. Aulanier, Christiane. "Marguerite van Eyck et l'homme au turban rouge." Gazette des Beaux Arts 78 no. 2 (July-August 1936): 57-58.

02556. Bergmans, Simone. "The Miniatures of Levina Teerlinc." The Burlington Magazine 64 (1934): 232-236.

02557. _________. "Note complementaire à l'étude des De Hemessen, de van Amstel et du monogrammiste de Brunswick." Revue Belge d'Archéologie et d'histoire de l'art 27 (1958): 77-83.

02558. _________. " Le probléme Jan van Hemessen, monogrammiste de Brunswick." Revue Belge archéologie et d'histoire de l'art 23 (1955): 133-157.

V.
SEVENTEENTH CENTURY

A. GENERAL

1. BIBLIOGRAPHY

"I did dread marriage and shunned men's company as much as I could."

Margaret Cavendish

02559. Backscheider, Paula R.; Nussbaum, Felicity A.; and Anderson, Philip B. Annotated Bibliography of Twentieth Century Critical Studies of Women and Literature, 1660-1800. New York: Garland Publishing, Inc. 1977.

2. SURVEYS

"Thy lady's noble, fruitfull, chaste, withall His children thy great lord can call his owne; A fortune, in this age, but rarely knowne."

Ben Jonson
"To Penhurst"

02560. Ferguson, Margaret W., Quilligan, Maureen, and Wickers, Nancy, eds. Rewriting the Renaissance: The Discourses of Sexual Difference in Early Modern Europe. Chicago, Il: University of Chicago Press, 1986.

02561. Möbius, Helga. Woman of the Baroque Age. Translated by Barbara Chruscik Beedham. Montclair, New York: Abner Schram, 1984.

3. POLITICAL

"The decrees of the great princes are like the mysteries of the Holy Faith. It is not up to us to probe them."
Anne Marie Louis d'Orléans, _Mémoires_

02562. Stone, Elizabeth. [Menzies, Sutherland.] _Political women_. Port Washington, New York: Kennikat Press, 1970.

Also refer to #2143.

4. RELIGION

"A woman ought to read and meditate on the scriptures, and regulate her conduct by them, and to keep silence, agreeably to the command of St. Paul."
Anne Dacier

02563. Polman, Jean. _Le Chancre ou Couvre-sein Féminin ensemble le voile ou couvre-chef féminin_. 1635. Reprint. Geneva: J. Gay et Fils, 1868.

Also refer to #2142-2144, 2566.

5. SOCIAL

"Advise yee well, supreme Senat, if charity be thus excluded and expulst, how yee will defend the untainted honour of your own actions and proceedings: He who marries, intends as little to conspire his own ruine as he that swears Allegiance: and as a whole people is in proportion to an ill government, so is one man to an ill marriage."
Milton 1644

02564. Hajnal, J. "Two Kinds of Pre-Industrial Household Formation System." In _Family Forms in Historic Europe_, edited by Richard Wall, Jean Robin, and Peter Laslett, pp. 65-104. New York: Cambridge University Press, 1983.

02565. Köhler, Carl. "The Seventeenth Century." In _A History of Costume_, pp. 286-331. London: George Harrap and Co., 1928.

02566. Paris, Charles B. _Marriage in Seventeenth Century Catholicism_. Montreal: Bellarmin, 1975.

Also refer to #2563.

6. CULTURAL

"A girl should speak only when there is real need, with an air of doubt and deference."
Fénelon

02567. Hagstrum, Jean H. Sex and Sensibility: Ideal and Erotic Love from Milton to Mozart. Chicago: University Press, 1981.

02568. Kemp, Friedhelm. "Das himmlische Frauenzimmer." In Europäische Hofkultur im 16. und 17. Jahrhundert, III, Wolfenbütteler Arbeiten zur Barockforschung, edited by August Buck, Georg Kauffmann, Blake Lee Spahr, and Conrad Weidemann, 10:511-518. Hamburg: Dr. Ernst Hauswedell, 1981.

02569. Ramerick, Maureen. "The Woman Artist and the Art Academy: A Case Study in Institutional Prejudice." In New Research on Women at the University of Michigan, edited by Dorothy G. McGuigan, pp. 249-260. Ann Arbor, Mich: University of Michigan, Center for Continuing Education of Women 1974.

Also refer to #2151.

B. BRITISH ISLES

1. SURVEYS

"To whom thus Eve with perfect beauty adorned My Author and Disposer, what thou bidst Unargu'd I obey; so God ordains, God is thy Law, thou mine; to know no more woman's happiest knowledge and her praise."
Milton
Paradise Lost

02570. La Femme en Angleterre et dans les colonies américaines aux XVIIe et XVIIIe siècles: acte du Colloque tenu á Paris les 24 et 25 Octobre 1975. Villeneuve d'Ascqi: Publications de l'Université de Lille III, 1976.

02571. Fraser, Antonia. The Weaker Vessel, Woman's Lot in Seventeenth-Century England. New York: Vintage Books, 1984.

Also refer to #2158.

2. POLITICAL

"In a man's body, a woman's spirit."
Epitaph of Lady Eleanor

a) Criminal

02572. Sharpe, J. A. Crime in 17th-Century England, A County History. New York: Cambridge University Press, 1983.

b) Political Roles

02573. Adlard, John. "A Note on Nell Gwyn." Folklore 83 (Spring 1972): 61-67.

02574. Bevan, Bryan. Charles the Second's French Mistress. London: R. Hall, 1972.

02575. Cowles, Virginia. The Great Marlborough and His Duchess. New York: Macmillan, 1983.

02576. Cripps, Doreen. Elizabeth of the Sealed Knot. Kineton: Roundwood Press, 1975.

02577. Evans, N. E. "The Anglo-Russian Royal Marriage Negotiations of 1600-1603." Slavonic and East European Review 61 (July 1983): 363-387.

02578. Fraser, Antonia. "Mary Rich, Countess of Warwick." History Today 31 (June 1981): 48-51.

02579. Guizot, M. The Married Life of Rachel, Lady Russell. London: T. Bosworth, 1855.

02580. Higgins, Patricia. "The Reactions of Women, with Special Reference to Women Petitioners." In Politics, Religion and the English Civil War, edited by Brian Manning, pp.179-222. New York: St. Martin's Press, 1973.

02581. Hodgkin, Katharine. "The Diary of Lady Anne Clifford: A Study of Class and Gender in the Seventeenth Century." History Workshop 19 (Spring 1985): 148-161.

02582. Holmes, M. Proud Northern Lady: Lady Anne Clifford. London: Phillimore, 1977.

02583. Morrah, Patrick. A royal family: Charles I and his family. London: Constable, 1982.

3. ECONOMIC

"St. Paul sets it as the calling and the indispensable duty of the married women, that they guide the house. . .not thinking it a point of greatness to remit the manage of all domestic concerns to a mercenary housekeeper."
The Ladies Calling

02584. Willen, Diane. "Guildswomen in the City of York, 1560-1700." The Historian 46 (February 1984): 204-218.

Also refer to #2194, 2600.

4. RELIGION

". . .I could not take comfort in Husband or Children, House, or Lord, or any visibles, for want of the Marriage Union with the Lamb of God. . ."

Joan Vokins

a) Generic

02585. Smith, Steven R. "Religion and the Conception of Youth in Seventeenth-Century England." In Loving, Parenting and Dying, edited by Vivian C. Fox and Martin H. Quitt, pp. 334-353. New York: Psychohistory Press, Publishers, 1980.

b) Saints/Religious Women

02586. Smith, Catherine F. "Jane Lead: The Feminist Mind and Art of a Seventeeth-Century Protestant Mystic." In Women of Spirit, edited by Rosemary Ruether and Eleanor McLaughlin, pp. 183-203. New York: Simon and Schuster, 1979.

02587. _________. "Jane Lead: Mysticism and the Woman Clothed with the Sun." In Shakespeare's Sisters: Feminist Essays on Women Poets, edited by Sandra Gilbert and Susan Gubar, pp. 3-18. Bloomington, Ind.: Indiana University Press, 1981.

c) Prophets/Visionaries

02588. Burrage, Champlin. "Anna Trapnel's Prophecies." English Historical Review 26 (1911): 526-535.

02589. Cohen, Alfred. "Prophecy and Madness: Women Visionaries during the Puritan Revolution." Journal of Psychohistory 11 (Winter 1984): 411-430.

02590. Mack, Phyllis. "Women as Prophets during the English Civil War." Feminist Studies 8 (Spring 1982): 19-45.

02591. Nelson, Beth. "Lady Elinor Dawes: The Prophet as Publisher." Women's Studies International Forum 8 (1985):403-409.

02592. Spencer, Theodore. "The History of an Unfortunate Lady." Harvard Studies and Notes in Philology 20 (1938): 43-59.

d) Quakers

02593. Ford, Linda. "William Penn's Views on Women: Subjects of Friend-Ship." Quaker History 72 (Fall 1983): 75-102.

02594. Huber, Elaine C. "'A Woman Must Not Speak': Quaker Women in the English Left Wing." In Women of Spirit, edited by Rosemary Ruether and Eleanor McLaughlin, pp. 153-181. New York: Simon and Schuster, 1979.

02595. Scheffler, Judith. "Prison Writings of Early Quaker Women: We Were Stronger Afterward Than Before." Quaker History 73 (Fall 1984): 25-37.

e) Witchcraft

02596. Crossley, James, ed. Pott's Discovery of Witches in the County of Lancaster. 1613. Reprint. New York: Johnson Reprint Corporation, 1968.

02597. Fairfax, Edward. Daemonologia: A Discourse on Witchcraft. 1882. Reprint. New York: Barnes and Noble, 1971.

02598. Kingsbury, J. B. "The Last Witch of England." Folk-lore 61 (September 1950): 134-145.

02599. Rushton, Peter. "Crazes and Quarrels: The Character of Witchcraft in the North-East of England, 1649-80." Bulletin of the Durham County Local History Society 31 (December 1983): 2-40.

Also refer to #2215-2217.

5. SOCIAL

"Tis much easier, sure, to get a good fortune than a good husband; but whosoever marries without any consideration of fortune shall never be allowed to do it out of so reasonable an apprehension; the whole world (without any reserve) shall pronounce they did it merely to satisfy their giddy humour."

Dorothy Osborn
"Love Letter to William Temple"
(1652-1654)

a) Generic

(1) Non-Specific

02600. Chalklin, C. W. Seventeenth-Century Kent: A Social and Economic History. London: Longmans, 1965.

02601. McLysaght, E. Irish Life in the Seventeenth Century. Cork: University Press, 1950.

02602. Mather, Jean. "The Moral Code of the English Civil War." The Historian 44 (February 1982): 207-228.

02603. Wrightson, Keith. English Society, 1580-1680. New Brunswick, N.J.: Rutgers University Press, 1982.

2) Women

02604. Child, Lydia Maria (Francis). The Biographies of Lady Russell and Madame Guyn. Boston: Carter, Hendee and Co., 1932.

02605. Greville, Violet. "Some Seventeenth Century Housewives." Nineteenth Century and After 58 (November 1905): 796-814.

02606. Maurois, André. Trois Portraits de Femmes. La Duchesse de Devonshire, la Comtesse D'Albany, Henriette de France. Paris: Hachette, 1967.

02607. Woods, Margaret L. "The English Housewife in the 17th century." Fortnightly Review 94 (November 1910): 823-833.

b) Demography

02608. Chambers, J. D. "The Age at Marriage in England and its Implication." In Loving, Parenting and Dying, edited by Vivian C. Fox and Martin H. Quitt, pp. 126-132. New York: Psychohistory Press, Publishers, 1980.

02609. Cullen, L. M. "Population Trends in Seventeenth Century Ireland." The Economic and Social Review 6 (1975); 149-165.

02610. Forbes, Thomas Rogers. "Births and Deaths in a London Parish: The Record from the Registers, 1654-1693 and 1729-1743." Bulletin of the History of Medicine 55 (Fall 1981): 371-391.

02611. Goose, Nigel. "Household Size and Structure in Early-Stuart Cambridge." Social History 5 (October 1980): 347-385.

02612. Houston, R. A. "Parish Listing and Social Structure: Penninghame and Whirthon (Wigtownshire) in Perspective." Local Population Studies 23 (1979): 24-32.

02613. Laslett, Peter. "Infant Mortality." In Loving, Parenting and Dying, edited by Vivian C. Fox and Martin H. Quitt, pp. 258-260. New York: Psychohistory Press, Publishers, 1980.

02614. Schofield, Roger S. and Wrigley, Edward Anthony. "Remarriage Intervals and the Effect of Marriage Order on Fertility." In Marriage and Remarriage in Populations of the Past, edited by Jacques Dupâquier, et.al., pp. 211-227. New York: Academic Press, 1981.

02615. Wrigley, Edward Anthony and Schofield, Roger S. "English Population History from Family Reconstitution: 1600-1799." Population Studies 37 (July 1983): 157-184.

c) Family

(1) Non-specific

02616. Byard, Margaret M. "The Trade of Courtiership: The Countess of Bedford and the Bedford Memorials; a Family History 1585 to 1607." *History Today* 29 (January 1979): 20-28.

02617. Chrisman, Miriam. "Family and Religion in Two Noble Families: French Catholic and English Puritan." *Journal of Family History* 8 (Summer 1983): 190-210.

02618. Slater, Miriam. *Family Life in the Seventeenth Century: The Verneys of Claydon House*. London: Routledge and Kegan Paul, 1984.

Also refer to #2615, 2628.

(2) Childhood

02619. Illick, Joseph E. "English Childrearing in the Seventeenth Century." In *Loving, Parenting and Dying*, edited by Vivian C. Fox and Martin H. Quitt, pp. 277-289. New York: Psychohistory Press, Publishers, 1980.

02620. Johnson, Robert C. "The Transportation of Vagrant Children from London to Virginia, 1618-1622." In *Early Stuart Studies, Essays in Honor of David Harris Willson*, edited by Howard S. Reinmuth, Jr., pp. 137-151. Minneapolis: University of Minnesota Press, 1970.

02621. Schnucker, R. V. "Maternal Nursing and Wet-Nursing among English Puritans." In *Loving, Parenting and Dying*, edited by Vivian C. Fox and Martin H. Quitt, pp. 260-267. New York: Psychohistory Press, Publishers, 1980.

02622. Sommerville, C. John. "English Puritans and Children: a Socio-Cultural Explanation." *Journal of Psychohistory* 5 (Spring 1978): 113-137.

Also refer to #2585, 2613.

d) Marriage

02623. *Adultery and the Decline of Marriage: Three Tracts*. 1690 and 1700. Reprint. New York: Garland, 1984.

02624. Bonfield, Lloyd. *Marriage Settlements, 1601-1740*. Cambridge: University Press, 1983.

02625. Bonfield, Lloyd. "Marriage Settlements, 1660-1740: The Adoption of Strict Settlement in Kent and Northamptonshire." In _Marriage and Society Studies in the Social History of Marriage_, edited by R.B. Outhwaite, pp. 101-116. New York: St. Martin's Press 1981.

02626. Elliott, Vivien Brodsky. "Single Women in the London Marriage Market: Age, Status and Mobility, 1598-1619." In _Marriage and Society Studies in the Social History of Marriage_, edited by R.B. Outhwaite, pp. 81-100. New York: St. Martin's Press, 1981.

02627. Jordan, W. K. "Widows in London." In _Loving, Parenting and Dying_, edited by Vivian C. Fox and Martin H. Quitt, pp. 421-424. New York: Psychohistory Press, Publishers, 1980.

02628. Larmine, Vivienne. "Marriage and the Family: The Example of the Seventeenth-Century Newdigates." _Midland History_ 9 (1984): 1-22.

02629. Macfarlane, Alan. "The Informal Social Control of Marriage in Seventeenth-Century England: Some Preliminary Notes." In _Loving, Parenting and Dying_, edited by Vivian C. Fox and Martin H. Quitt, pp. 110-121. New York: Psychohistory Press, Publishers, 1980.

Also refer to #2577, 2608, 2614, 2631, 2661, 2663, 2667, 2683, 2686, 2691-2694.

e) Sex Life and Morals

02630. Goreau, Angeline. "Two English Women in the Seventeenth Century: Notes for an Anatomy of Feminine Desire." In _Western Sexuality_, edited by Philippe Ariès and André Béjin, pp. 103-113. New York: Blackwell, 1985.

02631. Nadelhaft, Jerome. "The Englishwoman's Sexual Civil War: Feminist Attitudes towards Men, Women, and Marriage, 1650-1740. _Journal of the History of Ideas_ 43 (October-December 1982): 555-579.

02632. Thompson, Roger. _Unfit for Modest Ears_. London: Macmillam, 1980.

f) Fashion/Manners

02633. Sichel, Marion. _Costume Reference 3. Jacobean and Stuart Restoration_. Boston: Plays Inc., 1977.

g) Health/Medical

02634. Crawford, P. "Attitudes to Menstruation in Seventeenth Century England." _Past and Present_ 91 (May 1981): 47-73.

02635. Erickson, Robert A." 'The Books of Generation': Some Observations on the Style of the English Midwife Books, 1671-1764." In Sexuality in Eighteenth-Century Britain, edited by Paul-Gabriel Boucé, pp. 74-94. Totowa, N.J.: Barnes and Noble. 1982.

02636. Eshleman, Michael K. "Diet During Pregnancy in the Sixteenth and Seventeenth Centuries." In Loving, Parenting and Dying, edited by Vivian C. Fox and Martin H. Quitt, pp. 225-237. New York: Psychohistory Press, Publishers, 1980.

02637. Keevil, J. J. "Elizabeth Alkin alias Parliament Joan." Bulletin of the History of Medicine 31 (January-February 1957): 17-28.

02638. MacDonald, Michael. Mystical Bedlam: Madness, Anxiety, and Healing in Seventeenth-Century England. New York: Cambridge University Press, 1981.

02639. Schnucker, R. V. "Childbearing among English Puritans." In Loving, Parenting and Dying, edited by Vivian C. Fox and Martin H. Quitt, pp.237-243. New York: Psychohistory Press, Publishers, 1980.

02640. Sisson, C. J. "Shakespeare's Helena and Dr. William Harvey." Essays and Studies n.s. 13 (1960): 1-20.

02641. Smith, Ginnie. "Thomas Tryon's Regimen for Women: Sectarian Health in the Seventeenth Century." In The Sexual Dynamics of History, edited by The London Feminist History Group, pp. 47-65. London: Pluto Press, 1983.

02642. Smith, Hilda, "Gynecology and Ideology in Seventeenth Century England." In Liberating Women's History: Theoretical and Critical Essays, edited by Berenice A. Carroll, pp. 97-114. Urbana, Ill.: University of Illinois Press, 1976.

02643. Spencer, Herbert Ritchie. The History of British Midwifery from 1650 to 1800: The Fitzpatrick Lectures for 1927 Delivered before the Royal College of Physicians in London. London: John Bale, Sons and Danielson, Ltd, 1927.

Also refer to #2144, 2242, 2610.

6. CULTURAL

"To make women learned and foxes tame had the same effect: to make them more cunning."

James I

a) Education

02644. Brink, J. R. "Bathsua Makin: Educator and Linguist." In Female Scholars, edited by J.R. Brink, pp. 86-100. St. Albans, Vt.: Eden Press, 1980.

02645. Grisar, Joseph, "Varii tentativi di Maria Ward di fondare scuole femminili a Napoli (1623-1628.)" In _Studi in onore di Riccardo Filangieri_, 2: 525-550. Naples: L'Arte tipographica, 1959.

b) Literature

(1) Non-specific

(a) Generic

02646. Foxon, David. _Libertine Literature in England, 1660-1743_. New York: University Books, 1965.

02647. Malekin, Peter. _Liberty and Love, English Literature and Society, 1640-88_. New York: St. Martin's, 1981.

02648. Spufford, Margaret. _Small Books and Pleasant Histories: Popular Fiction and its Readership in 17th-Century England_. London: Methuen, 1981.

(b) Women

02649. Berggren, Paula S. "'Womanish' mankind: Four Jacobean heroines." _International Journal of Women's Studies_ 1 (July-August 1978): 349-362.

02650. Crawford, Patricia. "Women's Published Writings 1600-1700." In _Women in English Society 1500-1800_, edited by Mary Prior, pp. 211-282. New York: Methuen, 1985.

02651. Day, Robert Adams. "Muses in the Mud: Wits Anthropologically Considered." _Women's Studies_ 7 no. 3 (1980): 61-74.

02652. Hampsten, Elizabeth. "Petticoat Authors: 1660-1720." _Women's Studies_ 7 nos. 1-2 (1980): 21-38.

02653. Mayer, Gertrude Townshend. _Women of Letters_. 1894. Reprint. New York: Arno Press, 1973.

02654. Smith, Hilda. _Reason's Disciples: Seventeenth Century English Feminists_. Urbana, Ill.: University of Illinois Press. 1982.

02655. Todd, Janet. _A Dictionary of British and American Women Writers, 1660-1800_. New York: Barnes and Noble, 1985.

(2) Philosophy

(a) Women in Philosophy

[1] Hobbes

02656. Stefano, Christine Di. "Masculinity as Ideology in Political Theory: Hobbesian Man Considered." Women's Studies International Forum 6 (1983): 633-644.

[2] Locke

02657. Butler, M. A. "Early Liberal Riots of Feminism: John Locke and the Attack on Patriarchy. American Political Science Review 72 (March 1978): 135-150.

02658. Clarke, Lorenne M. G. "Women and Locke: Who Owns the Apples in the Garden of Eden?" In The Sexism of Social and Political Theory: Women and Reproduction from Plato to Nietzsche, pp. 16-40. Toronto: University Press, 1979. Also in The Canadian Journal of Philosophy 7 (1977): 699-724.

02659. O'Donnell, Sheryl. "Mr. Locke and the Ladies: the Indelible Words on the Tabula rasa." Studies in Eighteenth Century Culture 8 (1979): 151-164.

02660. _________. "'My Idea in Your Mind' John Locke and Damaris Cudworth Masham." In Mothering the Mind, Twelve Studies of Writers and Their Silent Partners, edited by Ruth Perry and Martine Watson Brownley, pp. 26-46. New York: Holmes and Meier, 1984.

02661. Shanley, Mary Lyndon. "Marriage Contract and Social Contract in Seventeenth Century English Political Thought." In The Family in Political Thought, edited by Jean Bethke Elshtain, pp 80-95. Amherst, Mass.: University of Massachusetts Press, 1984.

(b) Women Philosophers

02662. Merchant, Carolyn. "The Vitalism of Anne Conway: Its Impact on Leibniz's Concept of the Monad." The Journal of the History of Philosophy 17 (July 1979): 255-270.

(3) Drama

(a) Women in Drama

[1] Non-specific

02663. Hume, Robert D. "Marital Discord in English Comedy from Dryden to Fielding." Modern Philology 74 (1977): 248-272.

02664. _________. "The Myth of the Rake in 'Restoration' Comedy." Studies in the Literary Imagination 10 (Spring 1977): 25-55.

02665. Leinwand, Theodore. "'This Gulph of Marriage': Jacobean City Wives and Jacobean City Comedy." Women's Studies 10 (1984):245-260.

[2] Individuals

[a] Thomas Middleton

02666. Cherry, Caroline L. The Most Unvaluedest Purchase: Women in the Plays of Thomas Middleton. Atlantic Highlands, N.J.: Humanities Press, Inc., 1973.

02667. Ewbank, Inga-Stina. "Realism and Morality in 'Women Beware Women.'" Essays and Studies n.s. 22 (1969): 57-70.

02668. Salingar, Leo. "'The Changling' and the Drama of Domestic Life." Essays and Studies n.s. 32 (1979): 80-96.

02669. Ure, Peter. "Patient Madmen and Honest Whore: The Middleton-Dekker Oxymoron." Essays and Studies n.s. 19 (1966): 18-40.

Also refer to #2258.

[b] William Wycherly

02670. Kaufman, Anthony. "Wycherly's The Country Wife and the Don Juan Character." Eighteenth-Century Studies 9 (Winter 1975-1976): 216-231.

02671. Morris, David B. "Language and Honor in The Country Wife." South Atlantic Bulletin 37 (November 1972): 3-10.

02672. Roper, Alan. "Sir Harbottle Grimstone and the Country Wife." Studies in the Literary Imagination 10 (Spring 1977): 109-123.

[c] Others

02673. Lord, J. M. "Duchess of Malfi: The Spirit of Greatness and of Women." Studies in English Literature 16 (Spring 1976): 305-317.

02674. Salingar, L. G. "Farce and Fashion in 'The Silent Woman.'" Essays and Studies n.s. 20 (1967): 29-46.

Also refer to #2258.

b) Women Dramatists

[1] Aphra Behn

02675. Armistead, J. M. Four Restoration Playwrights. Boston, Mass.: G.K. Hall, 1984.

02676. Cameron, W. J. New Light on Aphra Behn. 1961. Reprint. Darby, Pa.: Arden Library, 1978.

02677. Carver, Larry. "Aphra Behn: The Poet's Heart in a Woman's Body." Papers on Language and Literature 14 (1978):414-424.

02678. Gardiner, Judith Kegan. "Aphra Behn: Sexuality and Self-Respect." Women's Studies 7 nos. 1-2 (1980): 67-78.

02679. Goreau, Angeline. "Aphra Behn: A Scandal to Modesty (1640-1689)." In Feminist Theorists, edited by Dale Spender, pp. 8-27. New York: Pantheon Books, Random House, 1983.

02680. _________. Reconstructing Aphra: A Social Biography of Aphra Behn. Oxford: Oxford University Press, 1980.

02681. Guffey, George Robert. Two English Novelists, Aphra Behn and Anthony Trollope. Los Angeles, Ca.: William Andrews Clark Memorial Library, 1975.

02682. Link, Frederick M. Aphra Behn. New York: Twayne Publishers, 1968.

02683. Root, Robert L., Jr. "Aphra Behn, Arranged Marriage, and Restoration Comedy." Women and Literature 5 (Spring 1977): 3-14.

02684. Sackville-West, Victoria. Aphra Behn, the Incomparable Astrea. 1927. Reprint. New York: Russell and Russell, 1970.

[2] Elizabeth Cary, Viscountess Falkland

02685. Simpson, Richard. The Lady Falkland: Her Life. London: Catholic Publishing and Bookselling, 1861.

Also refer to #2207.

4) Poetry

(a) Women in Poetry

[1] Milton

02686. Couch, H. "Milton as Prophet: The Divorce Tracts and Contemporary Divorce Laws." Journal of Family Law 15 (1977): 569-581.

02687. Keplinger, Ann. "Milton: Polemics, Epic, and the Woman Problem, Again." Cithara 10 (1971): 40-52.

02688. Landy, Marcia. "Kinship and the Role of Women in Paradise Lost." Milton Studies 4 (1972): 3-18.

02689. LeComte, Edward. Milton and Sex. New York: Columbia University Press, 1978.

02690. Mollenkott, Virginia R. "Some Implications of Milton's Androgynous Muse." Bucknell Review 24 (Spring 1978): 27-36.

02691. Weinkauf, Mary S. "Dalila: The Worst of all Possible Wives." Studies in English Literature 13 (Winter 1973): 135-147.

02692. Willis, Gladys. The Penalty of Eve: John Milton and Divorce. New York: Peter Lang, 1984.

[2] Others

02693. Horne, William C. "'Between th' Petticoat and Breeches': Sexual Warfare and the Marriage Debate in Hudibras." Studies in Eighteenth Century Culture 11 (1982): 133-146.

02694. Wasserman, George R. "Hudibras and Male Chauvinism." Studies in English Literature 16 (1976): 351-361.

02695. Wilcoxon, Reba. "Rochester's Sexual Politics." Studies in Eighteenth-Century Culture 8 (1979): 137-149.

Also refer to #2523, 2892.

(b) Women Poets

02696. Rogers, Katharine. "Anne Finch, Countess of Winchilsea: An Augustan Woman Poet." In _Shakespeare's Sisters: Feminists Essays on Women Poets_, edited by Sandra M. Gilbert and Susan Gubar, pp. 32-46. Bloomington, Ind.: Indiana University Press, 1981.

Also refer to #2652.

(5) Satire

02697. Nussbaum, Felicity. _The Brink of All We Hate: English Satire on Women, 1660-1750_. Lexington, Ky: University Press of Kentucky, 1984.

(6) Prose

(a) Women in Novels

02698. Matlack, Cynthia S. "'Spectatress of the Mischief which She Made.': Tragic Woman Perceived and Perceiver." _Studies in Eighteenth Century Culture_ 6 (1977): 317-330.

(b) Women Novelists

[1] Mary Astell

02699. Kinnaird, Joan K. "Mary Astell: Inspired by Ideas (1668-1731)." In _Feminist Theorists_, edited by Dale Spender, pp. 28-39. New York: Pantheon Books, Random House, 1983. Also in _Journal of British Studies_ 19 (Fall 1979): 53-75.

02700. Perry, Ruth. "Mary Astell's Response to the Enlightenment." _Women and History_ 9 (Spring 1984): 13-40.

02701. __________. _Passionate Reason: The Life and Times of Mary Astell, 1666-1731_. Chicago, IL: University of Chicago Press, 1986.

02702. __________. "The Veil of Chastity: Mary Astell's Feminism." In _Sexuality in Eighteeth-Century Britain_, edited by Paul-Gabriel Boucé, pp. 141-158. Totowa, N.J.: Barnes and Noble, 1982. Also in _Studies in Eighteenth-Century Culture_ 9 (1980): 25-43.

02703. Upham, A. H. "Mary Astell as a Parallel for Richardson's Clarissa." _Modern Language Notes_ 28 (April 1913): 103-105.

Also refer to #3067.

[2] Others

02704. Bury, Samuel. Account of the Life and Death of Mrs Elizabeth Bury. Boston: Green Bushell and Allen, 1920.

02705. MacCarthy, Bridget G. Women Writers, Their Contribution to the English Novel, 1621-1744. 1946. Reprint. Norwood, Pa.: Norwood Editions, 1980.

02706. Mendelson, Sara Heller. "Stuart Women's Diaries and Occasional Memoirs." In Women in English Society 1500-1800, edited by Mary Prior, pp. 181-210. New York: Methuen, 1985.

02707. Paloma, Dolores. "Margaret Cavendish: Defining the Female Self." Women's Studies 7 nos. 1-2 (1980): 55-66.

02708. Pomerleau, Cynthia S. "The Emergence of Women's Autobiography in England." In Women's Autobiography, Essays in Criticism, edited by Estelle C. Jelinek, pp. 21-38. Bloomington, Ind: Indiana University Press, 1980.

Also refer to #2652.

c) Art

[1] Actresses/Directors

02709. Hook, Lucyle. "Portraits of Elizabeth Barry and Anne Bracegirdle." Theatre Notebook 15 (Summer 1961): 129-137.

02710. Milhous, Judith. "Elizabeth Bowtell and Elizabeth Davenport: Some Puzzles Solved." Theatre Notebook 39 (1985): 124-134.

02711. Price, Curtis A. "The Songs for Katherine Philips' Pompey (1663)." Theatre Notebook 33 (1979): 61-66.

02712. Schneider, Ben R. "The Coquette-Prude as an Actress's Line in Restoration Comedy during the Time of Mrs. Oldfield." Theatre Notebook 22 (Summer 1968): 143-156.

02713. Wilson, John Harold. "Biographical Note on Some Restoration Actresses." Theatre Notebook 18 (Winter 1963-1964): 43-47.

[2] Painters

02714. Walsh, Elizabeth. "'Mrs. Mary Beale, Paintress'." Connoisseur 131 (April 1953): 3-8.

02715. __________ and Jeffree, Richard. "The Excellent Mrs. Mary Beale": Catalogue of the Geffrey Museum Exhibition 13 October-21 December 1975. London: Inner Education Authority, 1975.

[3] Embroideress

02716. Ashton, Leigh. "Martha Edlin: A Stuart Embroideress." The Connoisseur 81 (August 1928): 215-223.

C. FRANCE

1. POLITICAL

"Some time you have to deceive the king for his own good."
Madame de Maintenon

a) Legal

02717. Portemer, Jean. "Réflexions sur les pouvoirs de la femme selon le droit français au XVIIe siècle." XVIIe siècle 36 (July-September 1984): 189-202.

02718. Ranum, Patricia M. "Mademoiselle de Guise, ou les défies de la quenouille." XVIIe siècle 36 (July-September 1984): 221-232.

b) Criminal

02719. Burnand, Robert. Vie et mort de la marquise de Brinvilliers. Paris: Tallandier, 1931.

c) Political Roles

(1) Women

02720. Cuénin, Micheline. "Les femmes aux affaires (1598-1661)." XVIIe siècle 36 (July-September 1984): 203-209.

02721. Dawson, Nelson. "Les filles du roi: des pollueuses? La France du XVIIe siècles." Historical Reflections/Réflexions historiques 12 (Spring 1985): 9-38.

02722. Hepp, Noémi. "Les pouvoirs féminins au XVIIe siécle." XVIIe Siècle 36 (July-September 1984): 187-188.

02723. Muhlstein, Anka. La Femme soleil: les femmes et le pouvoir: une relucture de Saint-Simon. Paris: Denoël-Gonthier, 1976.

(2) Individuals

(a) Madame de Maintenon

02724. Blennerhassett, Charlotte Julia (von Leyden). Louis XIV and Madame de Maintenon. London: G. Allen and Sons, 1920.

02725. Bury, Yetta de. "A Celebrated Frenchwoman." Fortnightly Review 55 (April 1893): 553-569.

02726. Chandernagor, Françoise. "Louis XIV a-t-il épousé Mme de Maintenon?" Historia 452 (July 1984): 64-75.

02727. Gelin, Henri. Francoise d'Aubigné. Niort: Bibliothèque du Mercure, 1899.

02728. R., Ernest. "Les témoins du mariage de Louis XIV et Mme de Maintenon." Chercheurs et Curieux 3 (November 1953): 517-518.

Also refer to #2782, 2784.

(b) Mazarin Family

02729. Olphe-Galliard, Jean-Raoul. "Le descendance des nièces de Mazarin." Chercheurs et Curieux 3 (November 1953): 519-520.

02730. Soissons, Guy Jean Raoul Eugène Charles Emmanuel de Savoie-Carignan, count de. The Seven Richest Heiresses of France. London: John Long Ltd., 1911.

02731. Vieuxbourg. "La descendance des nieces de Mazarin." Chercheurs et Curieux 3 (December 1953): 557-557.

(c) Elizabeth Charlotte, duchess d'Orléans

02732. Aretz, Gertrude. Liselotte von der Pfalz. eine deutsche Furstentochter in Frankreich. Stuttgart: J. Hoffman, 1924.

02733. Fürstenwald, Maria. "Liselotte von der Pfalz und der französische Hof." In Europäische Hofkultur im 16. und 17. Jahrhundert, III, Wolfenbütteler Arbeiten zur Barockforschung, edited by August Buck, Georg Kauffmann, Blake Lee Spahr, and Conrad Weidemann, 10:467-473. Hamburg: Dr. Ernst Hauswedell and Co., 1981.

02734. Lakebrink, Markus. "Ideologische Züge in Sainte-Beuves Porträt der Liselotte von der Pfalz." Germanisch-Romanische Monatsschrift n.s. 29 (1979): 87-94.

(d) Others

02735. Braux, Gustave. Louise de La Vallière. Paris: C.L.D., 1981.

02736. Duchêne, Roger. Ninon de Lenclos, la courtisane du Grand Siècle. Paris: Fayard, 1984.

02737. Dulong, Claude. "Anne d'Autriche maîtresse de Mazarin?" Historia 416 (July 1981): 41-55.

02738. Laulan, Robert. "La mort de Mlle. de Fontanges." Mercure de France 314 (April 1952): 731-734.

02739. Mallet-Joris, Francoise. Marie Mancini, le premier amour de Louis XIV. Paris: Hachette, 1964.

02740. Moyne, Christiane. Louise de La Vallière: ou, Le roi favori. Paris: Perrin, 1978.

02741. Yarrow, P. J. "Qui était la première femme de chambre de Madame." Dix-septième siècle. 35 (July 1983): 382-384.

Also refer to #2846.

2. RELIGION

"I am not the devil's because I fear God, and have at the bottom a principal of religion; then, on the other hand, I am not properly God's because His laws appears hard and irksome to me."

Madame de Sévigné

a) Saints/Religious Women

02742. Balsama, George. "Madame Guyon, Heterodox. . ." Church History 42 (September 1973):350-365.

02743. Borders, Hélène. "La Mise de Chantal, 'Maîtresse d'oraison.'" XVIIe siècle 36 (July-September 1984): 211-220.

02744. La Gorce Agnès de. "Madame Guyon á Blois, d'après des documents inédits." Etudes 310 (September 1961): 182-196.

02745. Mallet-Joris, Francoise. Jeanne Guyon. Paris: Flammarion, 1978.

02746. Ravier, André. Jeanne-Francoise Frémyot, baronne de Chantal. Paris: Labat, 1983.

Also refer to #2604.

b) Religious Orders

02747. Jegou, Marie-André. Les Ursulines du faubourg Saint-Jacques à Paris, 1607-1662. Paris: PUF, 1981.

02748. Leymont, H. de. Madame de Sainte-Beuve et les Ursulines de Paris, 1562-1630. Lyon: Vitte et Perussel, 1890.

c) Witchcraft

02749. Garrett, Clarke. "Witches and Cunning Folk in the Old Regime." Stanford French and Italian Studies 3 (1977): 53-64.

02750. Le Roy Ladurie, Emmanuel. Jasmin's Witch, A Case of Possession in Seventeenth-Century France. New York: Pantheon, 1985.

02751. Muchembled, Robert. Les dernièrs buchers: Un village de Flandre et ses sorcières sous Louis XIV. Paris: Ramsay, 1981.

3. SOCIAL

"She must do nothing against her husband, under whose will she is submitted by human and divine law."
Jean de Benedicti

a) Generic

(1) Non-Specific

02752. Bercé, Yves-Marie. La Vie quotidienne à l'Aquitaine du XVIIe siècle. Paris: Hachette, 1978.

02753. Bluche, Francois. La Vie quotidienne au temps de Louis XIV. Paris: Hachette, 1984.

02754. Deyon, Pierre. Amiens: capitale provinciale. Étude sur la société urbaine au 17e siècle. Paris: Mouton, 1967.

02755. Sagnac, Philippe. La Formation de la société francaise moderne. 2 vols. Paris: Presses universitaires de France, 1945.

02756. Saint-Germain, Jacques. La Vie quotidienne en France à la fin du Grand Siècle. Paris: Hachette, 1965.

02757. Saint-Jacob, Pierre de. Les Paysans de la Bourgogne du Nord au dernier siècle de l'Ancien Regime. Paris: Société Les Belles Lettres, 1960.

(2) Women

02758. Muchembled, Robert. "La Femme au village dans la region du Nord. (XVIIe-XVIIIe siècles)." Revue du Nord 58 (July-September 1981): 585-593.

02759. Platelle, Henri. "La Morale du temps (1700): Un traité antiféministe d'origine valenciennoise, conservé en manuscrit aux Facultés Catholiques de Lille." Revue du Nord 16 (April-September 1984):677-687.

02760. Rosso, Jeanette G. Études sur la féminité aux XVII et XVIIIe siècles. Pisa: Goliardica, 1984.

Also refer to #2606.

(b) Demography

02761. Bardet, Jean-Pierre. "Fécondité des premières mariées et des veuves remariées (l'exemple de Rouen et du Vexin Francais)." In Marriage and Remarriage in Populations of the Past, edited by Jacques Dupâquier et.al., pp. 533-546. New York: Academic Pess, 1981.

02762. Cabourdin, Guy. "Le remariage en France sous l'Ancien Régime (seizième--dix-huitième siècles)." In Marriage and Remarriage in Populations of the Past, edited by Jacques Dupâquier, et. al. pp. 273-285. New York: Academic Press, 1981.

02763. Derouet, Bernard. "Une démographie différentielle:cles pour un système auto-regulateur des populations rurales d'ancien régime." Annales: économies, sociétés, civilisations 35 (January-February 1980): 3-41.

02764. Dreyer-Roos, Suzanne. La population strasbourgeoise sous l'ancien régime. Strasbourg: Librairie Istra, 1969.

02765. Dupâquier, Jacques. "A Comparative Study of Data on Fertility in 25 Monographs Dealing with the Paris Basin at the End of the XVIIth Century and the Start of the XVIIIth." In Natural Fertility, edited by Henri Leridon and Jane Menken, pp. 409-439. Liège: Ordina Editions, 1979.

02766. ________. La population francaise aux XVIIe et XVIIIe siècles. Paris: P.U.F., 1979.

02767. ________. La population rurale de Bassin parisien á l'époque de Louis XIV. Paris: Editions de l'École des hautes études en sciences sociales, 1979.

02768. Gautier, Etienne and Henry, Louis. La Population de Crulai, paroisse normande. Paris: Presses universitaires de France, 1958.

02769. Houdaille, Jacques. "Les enfants issus des remariages des femmes de 1670 á 1789." In Marriage and Remarriage in Populations of the Past, edited by Jacques Dupâquier et. al. pp. 573-580. New York: Academic Press, 1981.

02770. Poussou, Jean-Pierre. "Les crises démographiques en milieu urbain: l'exemple de Bordeaux." Annales: économies, sociétés, civilisations 35 (March-April 1980): 235-252.

02771. Wiel, Philippe. "Une grosse paroisse du Cotentin aux XVIIe et XVIIIe siècles. Tamerville. Démographie. Société. Mentalité." Annales de démographie historique (1969): 136-189.

Also refer to #2329, 2330.

c) Family

02772. Chianea, Gerard. "La mère et l'enfant dans le Droit Dauphinois." Cahiers d'histoire 25 (1980): 258-279.

02773. Collomp, Alain. La Maison du père: Famillie et village en Haute-Provence aux XVIIe et XVIIIe siècles. Paris: Presses Universitaires de France, 1983.

02774. ________. "Tensions, Dissensions, and Raptures Inside the Family in Seventeenth- and Eighteenth-Century Haute Provence." In Interest and Emotion, Essays on the Study of Family and Kinship, edited by Hans Medick and David Warren Sabean, pp. 145-170. New York: Cambridge University Press, 1985.

02775. Darmon, Pierre, Le Mythe de la Procreation à l'âge baroque. Paris: Editions du Seuil, 1981.

02776. Phan, Marie-Claude. "Typologie d'aventures amoureuses d'après les déclarations de grossesse et les procédures criminelles enregistrées á Carcassonne de 1676 à 1786." In Aimer en France 1760-1860, edited by Paul Vialleneix and Jean Ehrard, 2:503-511. Clermont-Ferrand: Association des Publications de la Faculté des Lettres et Sciences Humaines de Clermont-Ferrand, 1980.

Also refer to #2331, 2617, 2820.

(d) Marriage

02777. Bontemps, Daniel. "La nuptualité dans la région de Canflans-en-Jarnesy (XVIIe-XVIIIe siècles.)" Annales de l'Est 5th ser. 33 (1981): 263-289.

02778. Burguière, André. "Réticences théoriques et intégration pratique du remariage dans la France d'Ancien Régime -- dix-septième-dix-huitième siècles." In Marriage and Remarriage in Population of the Past, edited by Jacques Dupâquier, et.al. pp. 41-48. New York: Academic Press, 1981.

Also refer to #2761, 2762, 2769, 2799.

e) Sex Life and Morals

02779. Couprie, Alain. "'Courtesanisme' et Christianisme au XVIIe siècle." _XVII[e] siècle_ 133 (October-December 1981): 371-391.

4. CULTURAL

"A book of hours is enough for a woman. Let her learn to embroider, to darn, to sew, and leave study to the men."
Alfonso, Belise's father
in _Les femmes savantes_

a) Education

02780. Alcover, Madeleine. "The Indecency of Knowledge." _Rice University Studies_ 64 (Winter 1978): 25-39.

02781. Fénélon, Francois de Salignac de la Mothe. _De l'education des filles_. Paris: Ed. d'aujourd'hui, 1983.

02782. Lavallée, Théophile. _Madame de Maintenon et la maison royale de Saint-Cyr_. Paris: Henri Plon, 1862.

02783. Piéron, Henri. "De L'influence sociale des principe cartésiens. Un Précurseur inconnu du féminisme et de la Révolution: Poulain de la Barre." _Revue de synthèse historique_ 2 (1902): 387-389.

02784. Prévot, Jacques. _La première institutrice de France: Madame de Maintenon_. Paris: Editions Belin, 1981.

02785. Zeller, Rosmarie. "Die Bewegung der Preziösen und die Frauenbildung im 17. Jahrhundert." In _Europäische Hofkultur im 16. und 17. Jahrhundert, III_, Wolfenbütteler Arbeiten zur Barockforschung, edited by August Buck, Georg Kauffmann, Blake Lee Spahr and Conrad Weidemann, 10:457-465. Hamburg: Dr. Ernst Hauswedell and Co., 1981.

b) Literature

(1) Non-specific

02786. Hepp, Noémi. "La notion d'Héroïne." In _Onze études sur l'image de la femme dans la littérature francaise du dix-septième siècle_, edited by Wolfgang Leiner, pp. 9-27. Paris: Jean-Michel Place, 1978.

02787. Leiner, Wolfgang, ed. _Onze études sur l'image de la femme dans la littérature francaise du dix-septième siècle_. Paris: Jean-Michel Place, 1978.

02788. Stanton, Domna C. "Fiction of préciosité and the fear of women." _Yale French Studies_ 62 (1981): 107-134.

(2) Drama

(a) Women in Drama

[1] Non-specific

02789. Baader, Horst. "Feminismus im Zwielicht der dramatischen Gattungen." In *Onze études sur l'image de la femme dans la littérature francaise du dix-septième siècle*, edited by Wolfgang Leiner, pp. 147-168. Paris: Jean-Michel Place, 1978.

02790. Baudin, M. "The Stateswomen in seventeenth-century French tragedy." *Modern Language Notes* 53 (1938): 319-327.

02791. Hilgar, Marie-France. "Théatralité du travestissement au XVIIe siècle." *XVIIe siècle* 130 (January-March 1981): 53-62.

02792. Scherer, Jacques. "Pour une sociologie des obstacles au mariage dans le théâtre francais du XVIIe siècle." In *Dramaturgie et société*, edited by Jean Jacquot, 1: 297-305. Paris: Editions du centre national de la recherche scientifique, 1968.

02793. Sharon D'Obremer, Marguerite. *Le rôle des femmes dans la comédie francaise de Molière à Marivaux*. Paris: E. Le Francais, 1941.

02794. Sweetser, Marie-Odile. "Women and Power: Reflections on Some Queens in French Classical Tragedy." *Proceedings of the Tenth Annual Meeting of the Western Society for French History* (1984): 60-67.

(2) Individuals

[a] Corneille

02795. Cloonan, William. "Women in *Horace*." *Romance Notes* 16 (Spring 1975): 647-652.

02796. Leiner, Wolfgang and Bayne, Sheila. "*Cinna* ou l'agenouillement d'Émile devant la Clémence d'Auguste." In *Onze études sur l'image de la femme dans la littérature francaise du dix-septième siècle*, edited by Wolfgang Leiner, pp. 195-219. Paris: Jean-Michel Place, 1978.

02797. Stanton, Domna C. "Power or Sexuality: The Bind of Corneille's Pulcherie." In *Gender and Literary Voice*, *Women and Literature*, edited by Janet Todd, 1:236-247. New York: Holmes and Meier, 1980.

[b] Molière

02798. Cazalbou, Jean and Sévely, Denise. *Les femmes savantes de Molière*. Paris: Editions Sociales, 1971.

02799. Duchêne, Roger. "La veuve au XVII[e] siècle." In *Onze études sur l'image de la femme dans la littérature francaise du dix-septième siècle*, edited by Wolfgang Leiner, pp. 221-242. Paris: Jean-Michel Place, 1978.

02800. Gossen, Emmett J., Jr. "'Les femmes savantes: Métaphore et mouvement dramatique." *French Review* 45 (October 1971): 37-45.

02801. Johnson, Barbara. "Teaching Ignorance: *L'Ecole des femmes*." *Yale French Studies* 63 (1983): 165-182.

02802. Molino, Jean. "'Les noeuds de la matière': l'unité des *Femmes savantes*." *XVIIe siècle* 113 (1976): 23-47.

02803. Rizza, Cecilia. "La condition de la femme et de la jeune fille dans les premières comédies de Corneille." In *Onze études sur l'image de la femme dans las littérature francaise du dix-septième siècle*, edited by Wolfgang Leiner, pp. 169-193. Paris: Jean-Michel Place, 1978.

02804. Rossat-Mignod, Suzanne. "Les femmes chez Molière." *Europe* 427-428 (November-December 1965): 35-41.

02805. Shaw, David. "*Les Femmes Savantes* and Feminism." *Journal European Studies* 14 (March 1984): 24-38.

02806. Suther, Judith D. "The Tricentennial of Molière's *Femmes savantes*." *French Review* 45 (Spring 1972): 31-38.

02807. Truchet, Jacques. "Molière et *Les Femmes Savantes*." In *Onze études sur l'image de la femme dans la littérature francaise du dix-septième siècle*, edited by Wolfgang Leiner, pp. 91-101. Paris: Jean-Michel Place, 1978.

[c] Racine

02808. Batache-Watt, Emy. *Profils des héroines raciniennes*. Paris: C. Klincksieck, 1976.

02809. Ubersfeld, Annie. "Racine et la peinture des femmes." *Europe* 427-428 (November-December 1964): 28-35.

(b) Women Dramatists

02810. Chevalley, Sylvie. "Les femmes auteurs dramatiques et la Comédie Francaise." *Europe* 427-428 (November-December 1964): 41-47.

(3) Poetry

02811. Berthaud, P.-L. "Une poétesse protestante inconnue. Suzon de Terson (1657-1684?)." Bulletin de la Société de l'histoire du protestantisme francais 100 (July-September 1954): 120-126.

02812. Pallister, Janis L. "Thisbe, martyred and Mocked." Romance Notes 16 (Autumn 1974): 124-133.

(4) Prose

(a) Novels

[1] Women in Novels

02813. Coulet, Henri. "Le pouvoir du charme féminin dans le roman au XVIIe siècle." XVIIe siècle 36 (July-September 1984): 249-260.

02814. Giraud, Yves. "Image et rôle de la femme dans Le Romant Comique de Scarron." In Onze études sur l'image de la femme dans la littérature francaise du dix-septième siècle, edited by Wolfgang Leiner, pp. 67-90. Paris: Jean-Michel Place, 1978.

02815. Ronzeaud, Pierre. "La femme dans le roman utopique de la fin du XVIIe siècle." In Onze études sur l'image de la femme dans la littérature francaise du dix-septième siècle, edited by Wolfgang Leiner, pp. 103-130. Paris: Jean-Michel Place, 1978.

[2] Women Novelists

((a)) Non-specific

02816. Varga, A. Kibédi. "Romans d'amour, romans de femmes, à l'époque classique." Revue des science humaines n.s. 168 (October-December 1977): 517-524.

((b)) Individuals

[[1]] Madame de Lafayette

02817. Chapco, Ellen J. "Women at Court in Seventeenth-Century France: Madame de Lafayette and the Concept of Honnêteté." Proceedings of the Western Society for French History 11 (1983): 122-129.

02818. Guetti, Barbara Jones. "'Travesty' and 'Usurpation' in Mme de Lafayette's Historical Fiction." Yale French Studies 69 (1985): 211-221.

02819. Haig, Sterling. Madame de Lafayette. New York: Twayne, 1970.

02820. Hirsch, Marianne. "A Mother's Discourse: Incorporation and Repetition in La Princesse de Cleves." Yale French Studies 62 (1981): 67-87.

02821. Landy, Bernard. "La vision tragique de Madame de La Fayette ou un jansénisme athée." Revue de l'institut de sociologie 42 (1969): 449-464.

02822. Mouligneau, Geneviéve. Madame de La Fayette, romancière? Brussels: Editions de l'Université de Bruxelles, 1980.

02823. Rieger, Dietmar. "Gattungstradition und historisch-soziale Realität. Madame de LaFayettes 'Zayde.'" Germanisch-Romanische Monatsschrift n.s. 26 (1976): 407-426.

02824. Virmaux, Odette. Les héroïnes romanesques de Madame de La Fayette. Paris: Klincksieck, 1981.

Also refer to #2944.

[[2]] Others

02825. Spahr, Blake Lee. "Ar(t)amene: Anton Ulrich und Fräulein von Scudéry." In Europäische Hofkultur im 16. und 17. Jahrhundert I. Wolfenbütteler Arbeiten zur Barockforschung, edited by August Buck, Georg Kauffman, Blake Lee Spahr and Conrad Wiedemann, 8:93-104. Hamburg: Dr. Ernst Hauswedell and Co., 1981.

(b) Other Works

02826. Morel, Jacques. "La place de la femme dans Les Caractères de La Bruyère." In Onze études sur l'image de la littérature francaise du dix-septième siècle, edited by Wolfgang Leiner, pp. 131-146. Paris: Jean-Michel Place, 1978.

02827. Vincent, Monique. "Le Mercure Galant témoin des pouvoirs de la femme du monde." XVIIe siècle 36 (July-September 1984): 241-248.

c) Salons

02828. Baxmann, Inge. "Von der Egalité im Salon zur Citoyenne--einige Aspekte der Genese des Bürgerlichen Frauenbildes." In Frauen in der Geschichte III, edited by Annette Kuhn and Jörn Rüsen, pp. 109-137. Düsseldorf: Schwann, 1983.

d) Intellectuals

(1) Madame de Sévigné

02829. Aubenas, Joseph Adolphe. Histoire de Madame de Sévigné, de sa famille et de ses amis. Paris: A. Allouard, 1842.

02830. Duchêne, Roger. Madame de Sévigné ou la chance d'être femme. Paris: Fayard, 1982.

02831. ________. Réalité vécue et art épistolaire: Madame de Sévigné et la lettre d'amour. Paris: Bordas, 1970.

02832. Guyard, Marius Francois. "Faut-il damner Madame de Sévigné." Études 280 (February 1954): 193-202.

02833. Harold, Ellen and Snitow, Ann. "Her Daughter was Her Muse." Aphra Magazine 2 (Autumn 1971): 35-40.

02834. Howard, Catherine Montfort. Les fortunes de Madame de Sévigné au XVIIème et au XVIIIème siècles. Tübingen: G. Narr Verlag, 1982.

02835. Mossiker, Frances. Madame de Sévigné: A Life and Letters. New York: Knopf, 1983.

02836. Ojala, Jeanne A. "Madame de Sévigné: Chronicler of an Age." In Female Scholars, edited by J.R. Brink, pp. 101-118. St. Albans, Vt.,: Eden Press, 1980.

(2) Others

02837. Mongrédien, Georges. "Une précieuse dévoté: Madame de Reval." XVIIe siècle 130 (January-March 1981): 9-23.

e) Art

02838. Boroff, Edith. An Introduction to Elisabeth-Claude Jacquet de la Guerre. Brooklyn: Institute of Medieval Music, 1966.

02839. La Force, Jerôme de. "Un opera francais représenté à la cour de Louis XIV en 1671 et 1672, Les Amours de Diane et d'Endymion, pastorale mise en musique par Sablières." XVIIe siècle 36 (January-March 1984): 37-46.

02840. Richtman, Jack. Adrienne Lecouvreur: the actress and the age, a biography. Englewood Cliffs, N.J.: Prentice-Hall, 1971.

02841. Rokseth, Yvonne. "Antonia Bembo, Composer to Louis XIV." Musical Quarterly 23 (April 1967): 147-169.

02842. Tourneux, Maurice. "Une exposition rétrospective d'art féminin." Gazette des Beaux-Arts 50.1 (April 1908): 290-300.

Also refer to #4554.

D. THE GERMANIES

1. POLITICAL

"Alas! The upright man had good cause to mourn his pregnant wife for she was captured by a band of imperial cavalry."
Grimmelshausen

a) Political Roles

(1) Elizabeth of Bohemia

02843. Hay, Marie. The Winter Queen. New York: Houghton Mifflin, 1910.

02844. Lenanton, Carola Mary Anima. Elizabeth of Bohemia. London: Hodder and Stoughton, 1964.

02845. Ross, Josephine. The Winter Queen, A Biography of Elizabeth of Bohemia. New York: St. Martin's, 1979.

(2) Others

02846. Chapman, Hester W. Privileged Persons, Four Seventeenth-Century Studies. New York: William Morrow and Co., 1966.

02847. Godfrey, Elizabeth. A Sister of Prince Rupert, Elizabeth Princess Palatine. London: John Lane, 1909.

02848. Leighton, Joseph. "Die Literarische Tätigkeit der Herzogin Sophie Elisabeth von Braunschweig-Lüneburg." In Europäische Hofkultur im 16. und 17. Jahrhundert, III, Wolfenbutteler Arbeiten zur Barockforschung, edited by August Buck, Georg Kauffman, Blake Lee Spahr and Conrad Weidemann, 10:483-488. Hamburg: Dr. Ernst Hauswedell, 1981.

02849. Palmblad, Wilhelm Fredeik. Aurora Königsmark, Leipzig: F.A. Brockhaus, 1848-53.

02850. Roloff, Hans-Gert. "Die höfischen Maskeraden der Sophie Elisabeth, Herzogin zu Braunscheig-Lüneburg." In Europäische Hofkultur im 16. und 17. Jahrhundert, III, Wolfenbütteler Arbeiten zur Barockforschung, edited by August Buck, Georg Kauffman, Blake Lee Spahr and Conrad Weidemann, 10:489-496. Hamburg: Dr. Ernst Hauswedell, 1981.

02851. Schmidt, Hans. "Zur Vorgeschichte der Heirat Kaiser Leopold I. mit Eleonore Magdalena von Pfalz-Neuburg." Zeitschrift für bayerische Landesgeschichte 45 (1982): 299-330.

02852. Ward, Adolphus William. "The Electress Sophia and the Hanoverian Succession." *English Historical Review* 1 (1886): 470-506.

2. RELIGION

"To us did Heavan grant this greatest good
So that the miracle grew all it could
In pure praise of faith and fame, not in sly power of the wise."

Katharine Regina von Greiffenberg,
"Why the Resurrection was Revealed to Women"

02853. Neveaux, Jean Baptiste. *Vie spirituelle et vie sociale entre Rhin et Baltique au XVIIe siècle*. Paris: Librairie C. Klincksieck, 1967.
[See especially pp. 717-735.]

Also refer to #2368.

3. SOCIAL

"My hand trembles,
The feather [pen] dances to its use
The paper vibrates and cannot bear the sorrowful words
These witnesses of my quiet suffering,
Of my sadness..."

Margaretha Susanna von Kuntsch,
Poem on the Death of her Fifth Born Son, Chrisander, 1686

a) Generic

02854. Benecke, Gerhard. "'Peasants, Procreation and Pensions' by Philip A. Neher: A Comment." *Journal of European Economic History* 2 (Fall 1973): 417-420.

b) Demography

02855. Bideau, Alain, and Perrenoud, Alfred. "Remariage et fécondité. Contribution à l'étude des mécanismes de récupération des populations anciennes." In *Marriage and Remarriage in Populations of the Past*, edited by Jacques Dupâquier, et. al., pp. 547-559. New York: Academic Press, 1981.

c) Family

02856. Mitterauer, Michael. "Vorindustrielle Familienformen: Zur Funktionsentlastung des 'ganzen Hauses' im 17. und 18. Jahrhundert." In Fürst, Bürger, Mensch, edited by Friedrich Engel-Janosi, Grete Klingenstein and Heinrich Lutz, pp. 123-185. Munich: Oldenbourg, 1975.

Also refer to #2356, 2377.

4. CULTURAL

"I never oppose opinions of any; but I must own that I never adopt them to the prejudice of my own."
Charlotte Bregy, Letters

a) Generic

02857. Otto, Karl F. "Die Frauen der Sprachgesellschaften." In Europäische Hofkultur im 16. und 17. Jahrhundert, III, Wolfenbütteler Arbeiten zur Barockforschung, edited by August Buck, Georg Kauffmann, Blake Lee Spahr and Conrad Weidemann, 10:497-503. Hamburg: Dr. Ernst Hauswedell, 1981.

Also refer to #2377.

b) Literature

02858. Dimler, G. Richard. "The Genesis and Development of Friedrich Spee's Love-Imagery in the Trutznachtigall." Germanic Review 48 (March 1973): 87-98.

02859. Jacobson, John W. "The Culpable Male: Grimmelshausen on Women." German Quarterly 39 (March 1966): 149-161.

c) Intelletuals

02860. Stalder, Xaver. Formen des barocken Stoizismus. Bonn: Grundmann, 1976.

d) Art

02861. Lendorff, Gertrude. Maria Sibylla Merian 1647-1717, ihr Leben und ihr Werk. Basel: Gute Schriften, 1955.

02862. Pfeiffer, M. A. Die Werke der Maria Sibylle Merian. Meissen: M. A. Pfeiffer, 1931.

02863. Quednau, Werner. Maria Sibylla Merian: der Lebensweg einer Künstlerin und Forscherin. Gutersloh: S. Mohn, 1966.

02864. Rücker, Elizabeth. Maria Sibylla Merian, 1647-1717. Nuremberg: Germanisches Nationalmuseum, 1967.

E. IBERIA

1. POLITICAL

"Let the world remain as it always was and know that women the vassals of men are born to be."

Christerna, in Afectos de odio y amor Pedro Calderón de la Barca

02865. Dória, Antonio Álvaro. A Rainha D. Maria Francisca de Saboia (1648-1683). Pôrto: Biblioteca Histórica, 1944.

02866. Raposa, Hipólito. D.Lvisa de Gvsmão. Lisbon: Empresa nacional de publicidade, 1947.

2. RELIGION

"[God] called me his trumpet and his carillon."

Madre Isabel de Jésus

02867. Arenal, Electa, "The Convent as Catalyst for Autonomy, Two Hispanic Nuns of the Seventeenth-Century." In Women in Hispanic Literature, Icons and Fallen Idols, edited by Beth Miller, pp. 147-183. Berkeley, Ca: University of California Press, 1983.

02868. Fitz-Darby, Delphine. "The Gentle Ribera, Painter of the Madonna and the Holy Family." Gazette des Beaux Arts 88 no. 1 (March 1946): 153-174.

02869. Flynn, Gerard Cox. "A Revision of the Philosophy of Sor Juana Inés de la Cruz." Hispania 43 (December 1960): 515-520.

02870. Gifford, Douglas. "Witchcraft and the Problem of Evil in a Basque Village." Folklore 90 (1979): 11-17.

02871. Henningsen, Gustav. The Witches' Adovcate: Basque Witchcraft and the Spanish Inquisition (1609-1614). Reno: University of Nevada Press, 1980.

Also refer to #2884.

3. SOCIAL

"It is vanity in a woman to spurn man, for when Aristotle stated that woman craved man as matter craves form, he intended the implication to be taken seriously."
Félix Lope de Vega Carpio,
La vengadora de la mujeres

02872. Berruezo, José. Catalina de Erauso, La Monja Alférez. San Sebastían: Caja de Ahorros Municipal, 1975.

02873. Castresana, Luis de. Catalina de Erauso; la monja alférez. Madrid: Aguado, 1968.

02874. Deleito y Pinuela, J. La Mala Vida en la Epoca de Felipe IV. Madrid: Espasa-culpa, 1948.

Also refer to #2403, 2404, 2882, 2883, 2885.

4. CULTURAL

"By all means do not love, but do not hate; by all means do not speak well of men, but do not slander them; even though your parents wanted you to be one. . .nature made you an imperfect man, a title given to woman by many philosophers."
Félix Lope de Vega Carpio
La vengadora de la mujeres

a) Literature

(1) Drama

(a) Women in Drama

[1] Non-specific

02875. Grant, Helen. "The 'mujer esquivo' - a measure of the feminist sympathies of seventeenth-century Spanish dramatists." Hispanic Review 40 (Spring 1972): 162-197.

02876. Kennedy, Ruth Lee. "Quiteria, Comediante Toledana: Her Importance for the Chronology of Quinones de Benavente and of other Dramatists." Revista Hispanica Moderna 37 (1972-1973): 1-28.

02877. McKendrick, Melveena. "Women Against Wedlock, The Reluctant Brides of Golden Age Drama." In Women in Hispanic Literature, Icons and Fallen Idols, edited by Beth Miller, pp. 115-146. Berkeley, Ca: University of California Press, 1983.

[2] Individuals

[a] Calderón

02878. Mujica, Barbara. "The Rapist and His Victim: Calderón's _No hay cosa como callar_." _Hispania_ 62 (March 1979): 30-46.

02879. Soufas, Teresa Scott. "Calderón's Melancholy Wife-Muderers." _Hispanic Review_ 52 (Spring 1984): 181-203.

02880. Sparks, Amy. "Honor in Hartzenbusch's 'Refundición' of Calderón's 'El medico de su honora.'" _Hispania_ 49 (September 1966): 410-413.

[b] Lope de Vega

02881. Collins, Marsha S. "Love in Absence: Lope's '_Rimas humanes_' _LXI_." _Hispanic Review_ 49 (Winter 1981): 107-118.

02882. Hesse, Everett W. "El conflicto entre madre e hijos en _Los melindres de Belisa_ de Lope." _Hispania_ 54 (December 1971): 837-843.

02883. ________. "The Perversion of Love in Lope de Vega's _El castigo sin venganza_." _Hispania_ 60 (September 1977): 430-435.

02884. Howe, Elizabeth Teresa. "Heavenly Defense: Dramatic Development of the Virgin Mary as Advocate." _Journal of Hispanic Philology_ 4 (Spring 1980): 189-202.

02885. McGrady, Donald. "The Comic Treatment of Conjugal Honor in Lope's _Las Ferias de Madrid_." _Hispanic Review_ 41 (Winter 1973): 33-42.

02886. ________. "Notes on Jerónima de Burgos in the Life and Work of Lope de Vega." _Hispanic Review_ 40 (Autumn 1972): 428-441.

02887. Zuckerman-Ingber, Alix. "Honor Reconsidered: _Los Comendadors de Cordoba_." _Journal of Hispanic Philology_ 4 (Autumn 1979): 59-75.

[c] Others

02888. Exum, Frances. "Role-Reversal and Parody in Moreto's _De Feura vendrá_." _Hispanofila_ 79 (September 1983): 1-9.

02889. Hesse, Everett W. "The Incest Motif in Tirso's 'La Venganza de Tarnar.'" _Hispania_ 47 (May 1964): 268-276.

02890. O'Connor, Thomas Austin. "Sexual Abberation and Comedy in Monroy y Silva's _El Caballero dama_." _Hispanofila_ 80 (January 1984): 17-39.

(2) Poetry

(a) Women in Poetry

[1] Quevedo

02891. Green, Otis H. Courtly Love in Quevedo. Boulder, Co.: University of Colorado Press, 1952.

02892. Hoover, L. Elaine. John Donne and Francisco de Quevedo, Poets of Love and Death. Chapel Hill, N.C.: University of North Carolina Press, 1978.

02893. Olivares, Julian, Jr. The Love Poetry of Francisco de Quevedo. Cambridge: Cambridge University Press, 1983.

(3) Prose

(a) Maria de Zaya de Sotomayor

02894. Felten, Hans. Maria de Zayas y Sotomayor: Zum Zusammenhang zwischen moralistischen Texten and Novellenliteratur. Frankfurt, A.M.: Vittorio Klostermann, 1978.

02895. Foa, Sandra M. Feminismo y forma narrative: Estudio de tema y las técnicas de Maria de Zayas. Valencia: Albatros Ediciones/Hispanofila, 1979.

02896. __________. "Maria de Zayas y Sotomayor: Sibyl of Madrid." In Female Scholars, edited by J.R. Brink, pp. 54-67. St. Albans, Vt.: Eden Press, 1980.

02897. Morby, Edwin. "The Difunta Pleiteada Theme in Maria de Zayas." Hispanic Review 16 (1948): 238-242.

02898. Place, Edwin. "Maria de Zayas. An Outstanding Woman Short-Story Writer of Seventeenth Century Spain." University of Colorado Studies 13 (1923): 26-30.

02899. Senabre, Ricardo. "La fuente de una novela de doña Maria de Zayas." Revista de Filologia Española 46 (1963): 163-172.

02900. Sylvania, Lena. Doña Maria de Zayas y Sotomayor. New York: AMS Press, 1966.

02901. Welles, Marcia L. "Maria de Zayas y Sotomayor and her novela cortesana: a reevaluation." Bulletin of Hispanic Studies 55 (October 1978): 301-310.

Also refer to #2433.

b) Art

(1) Louisa Ignacia Roldán

02902. Flack, Audrey. "Louisa Ignacia Roldán." Women's Studies 6 (1978): 23-33.

02903. Proske, Beatrice Gilman. "Luisa Roldán at Madrid." Connoisseur 155 (February-April 1964): 128-132, 199-203 and 269-273.

02904. Sanchez-Mesa Martín, Domingo. "Nuevas obras de Luisa Roldán y Jose Risueño en Londres y Granada." Archivo español de arte 157 (October 1967): 325-331.

(2) Others

02905. Sullivan, Edward J. "Josefa de Ayala--a woman painter of the Portuguese Baroque." Journal of the Walters Art Gallery 37 (1978): 22-35.

F. ITALY

1. RELIGION

"I have never been a witch, I am a benandante. ..I have never given my soul to the devil, never abjured my faith in Jesus Christ."

Maria Panzona, accused of witchcraft, 1618

02906. Tedeschi, John. "The Roman Inquisition and Witchcraft. An Early Seventeenth-Century "Instruction" on Court Trial Procedure." Revue de l'histoire des religions 200 (April-June 1983): 163-180.

Also refer to #2480, 2911.

2. SOCIAL

"...it is necessary that the lady, even if well born be draped in such [fine] clothes for her natural excellence and dignity and that the man be less adorned, as if a slave, born to serve."

Lucrezia Marinella, The Nobility and Excellence of Women Together with the Defects and Deficiencies of Men

a) Generic

02907. Léris, G. de. La comtesse de Verrue et la cour de Victor-Amédée II de Savoie. Paris: A. Quantan, 1888.

b) Demography

02908. Bellettini, Athos. "Aspetti e problemi della ripresa demografica nell'Italia del dettecento." Società et Storia 6 (1979): 817-838.

02909. ________. "Ricerche sulle crisis demografiche de seicento." Società et Storia 1 (1978): 35-64.

02910. Bonelli, Conenna Lucia. "Crisi economica e demografica dello stato Senese agli inizi del XVII secolo." Contadini e proprietari nella Toscana moderna 1 (1979): 495-533.

c) Family

02911. Stella, Pietro. "Strategie familiari e celibato sacro in Italia tra '600 e '700." Salesianum 41 (January-March 1979): 73-109.

3. CULTURAL

"I would rather lose my life before the desire to study."
Francesca Caccini, Letter to Michelangelo

a) Art

(1) Women in Art

02912. Rosand, David and Rosand, Ellen. "Barbara de Santa Sofia and Il Prete Benovese: on the Identity of a portrait by Bernardo Strozzi." Art Bulletin 63 (June 1981): 249-258.

(2) Women Artists

(a) Painters/Sculptors

[1] Fede Galizia

02913. Bottari, Stefano. "Fede Galizia." Arte antica e moderna 2 (1963): 309-360.

02914. ________. Fede Galizia pittrice (1578-1630). Trent: Collana Artisti Trentini, 1965.

[2] Artemesia Gentileschi

02915. Bissell, R. Ward. "Artemesia Gentileschi- A New Documented Chronology." Art Bulletin 50 (June 1968): 153-168.

02916. de Campos, R. Redig. "Una giuditta opera sconosciuta Gentileschi Nella Pinoteca Vaticana." Revista d'Arte 11 (July 1939): 311-323.

02917. Garrard, Mary D. "Artemesia and Susanna." In Feminism and Art History: Questioning the Litany, edited by Norma Broude and Mary D. Garrard, pp. 146-171. New York: Harper and Row, 1982.

02918. __________. "Artemesia Gentileschi's Self Portrait as the Allegory of Painting." Art Bulletin 62 (March 1980): 97-112.

02919. Levey, Michael. "Notes on the Royal Collection - - II: Artemisia Gentileschi's 'Self-Portrait' at Hampton Court." Burlington Magazine 104 (February 1962): 79-80.

02920. Longhi, Roberto. "Gentileschi padre e figlia." L'arte 19 (1916): 245-314.

[3] Elisabetta Sirani

02921. Edward, Evelyn Foster. "Elisabetta Sirani." Art in America 5 (August 1929): 242-246.

02922. Emiliani, Andrea. "Giovan Andrea ed Elisabetta Sirani." In Maestri della pittura del seicento emiliano, pp. 140-145. Bologna: Palazzo dell'archiginnasio, 1959.

(b) Musicians

02923. Arnold, Denis. "Orphans and Ladies: The Venetian Conservatories (1680-1790)." Proceedings of the Royal Music Association 89 (1962-1963): 31-47.

02924. Raney, Carol. "Francesca Caccini's Primo Libro." Music and Letters 48 (1967): 350-357.

G. THE LOW COUNTRIES

1. CULTURAL

"Woman has the same erect stance as man, the same ideals, the same love of beauty, honor, truth, the same wish for self-development."

Anna von Schurman

a) Literature

02925. Irwin, Joyce L. "Anna Maria van Schurman: The Star of Utrecht." In Female Scholars, edited by J.R. Brink, pp. 68-87. St. Albans, Vt.: Eden Press, 1980.

b) Art

(1) Women in Art

(a) Non-specific

02926. Smith, David Ross. Masks of Wedlock: Seventeenth-Century Dutch Marriage Portraiture. Ann Arbor, Mich: UMI Research Press, 1982.

(b) Individuals

[1] Rubens

02927. Burchard, L. "Genuesische Frauenbildnesse von Rubens." Jahrbuch der preussischen Kunstsammlungen 50 (1929): 319-349.

02928. Glück, G. "Einige Frauenbildnesse aus Rubens' anfängen." Jahrbuch der Kunsthistorischen Sammlungen 6 (1932): 157-168.

02929. Hofstede, Justus Müller. "Höfische und bürgerliche Damenporträts; Anmerkungen zu Rubens Antwerpener Bildnismalerei 1609-1620." Pantheon 41 (1983): 308-321.

[2] Others

02930. Friedlander, Walter. "La tintura delle rose by Titian." Art Bulletin 20 (June 1938): 320-324.

02931. Kahr, Madlyn Millner. "Vermeer's Girl Asleep. A Moral Emblem." Metropolitian Museum Journal 6 (1972): 115-132.

Also refer to #2550, 2552.

(2) Women Artists

02932. Harms, Juliana. "Judith Leyster, ihr Leben und ihr Werk." Oud-Holland 44 (1929): 88-96, 112-126, 145-154, 221-242, 275-279.

02933. Hofrichter, Frima Fox. "Judith Leyster's Proposition-Between Vice and Virtue." In Feminism and Art History: Questioning the Litany, edited by Norma Broude and Mary D. Garrard, pp. 172-181. New York: Harper and Row, 1982. Also in Feminist Art Journal 4 (Fall 1975): 22-26.

02934. Hofstede de Groot, Cornelis. "Judith Leyster." Jahrbuch der Königlichen preussischen Kunstsammlungen 14 (1893): 190-198, 232.

02935. Neurdenburg, Elisabeth. "Judith Leyster." Oud-Holland 46 (1929): 27-30.

VI.
EIGHTEENTH CENTURY

A. GENERAL

1. SURVEYS

"Men should not, properly speaking lie under any restraint of justice with regard to women."
Hume

02936. Bernier, Oliver. *The Eighteenth-Century Woman*. New York: Doubleday, 1982.

Also refer to #2559-2561.

2. SOCIAL

"What is not a Crime to Men is scandalous and unpardonable in Women."
Mary Delarivière Manley

a) Family

02937. Gouesse, Jean-Marie. "L'endogamie familiale dans l'Europe catholique au XVIII siècle." *Mélanges de l'École Francaise de Rome* 89 (1977):95-116.

02938. Matossian, Mary K. and Schafer, William D. "Family, Fertility and Violence 1700-1900." *Journal of Social History* 11 (Winter 1977): 137-178.

02939. Plakans, Andrejas. "The Study of Kinship in Modernizing Europe: Sources and Methods for a Comparative Inquiry." *Journal of Comparative Family Studies* 17 (Summer 1986): 161-172.

Also refer to #2564.

b) Sex Life and Morals

02940. Fletcher, Dennis. "The Oldest Profession: Some Eighteenth Century Views." Studies on Voltaire and the Eighteenth Century 190-193 (1980): 1042-1050.

02941. Rousseau, G.S. "Nymphomania, Bienville and the Rise of Erotic Sensibility." In Sexuality in Eighteenth-Century Britain, edited by Paul-Gabriel Boucé, pp. 95-119. Totowa, N.J.: Barnes and Noble, 1982.

02942. Tarczlyo, Théodore. Sexe et liberté au siècle des lumières. Paris: Presses de la Renaissance, 1983.

3. CULTURAL

"[She] had no feminine qualities. It was even one of her graces to not think of having any."
Marivaux,
about Mme. de Fécour

a) Generic

02943. Mack, Phyllis. "Women and the Enlightenment: Introduction." Women and History 9 (Spring 1984):1-12.

Also refer to #2567.

b) Literature

02944. Greene, Mildred. "'A chimera of her own creating': Love and Fantasy in Novels from Madame de Lafayette to Jane Austen." Studies on Voltaire and the Eighteenth Century 193(1980): 1940-1942.

02945. Gyenis, Vilmos. "Le Changement du rôle des femmes dans la vie littéraire au milieu du XVIII siècle." Studies on Voltaire and the Eighteenth Century 190-193 (1980): 2016-2027.

c) Art

(1) Painters

(a) Women in Art

02946. Spickernagel, Ellen. "Zur Anmut erzogen--Weibliche Körpersprache im 18. Jahrhundert." In Frauen in der Geschichte IV, edited by Ilse Brehmer et.al., pp. 305-319. Düsseldorf: Schwann, 1983.

(b) Women Painters

02947. Gaud, Roger. Les femmes peintres au XVIIIe siècle. Castres: Musée Goya, 1973.

02948. Goulinat, J.G. "Les femmes peintres au XVIIIe siècle." L'art et les artistes n.s. 13 (June 1926): 289-294.

02949. Paris. Galerie J. Charpentier. Exposition des femmes peintres du XVIIIe siècle. 1926.

Also refer to #2569.

(2) Music

02950. Grew, Sydney. Makers of Music. The Story of Singers and Instrumentalists. New York: The Dial Press, 1926.

B. ENGLAND

1. SURVEYS

"Because we men cannot resist temptation, is that a reason women ought not, when the whole of their education is caution and warning against our attempts? Do not their grandmothers give them one easy rule-Men are to ask- women are to deny?"

Richardson,
Clarissa, 1748

02951. Blackburne, Neville. Ladies' Chain. London: Falcon Press, 1952.

02952. Hill, Bridget. Eighteenth Century Women: An Anthology. Winchester, Ma.: Allen and Unwin, 1984.

02953. Jarrett, Derek. England in the Age of Hogarth. St. Alban's Herts: Paladin, 1976.

02954. Marshall, Dorothy, English People in the Eighteenth Century. New York: Longmans, Green, 1956.

02955. Rogers, Katharine M. "The View From England." In French Women and the Age of Enlightenment, edited by Samia I. Spencer, pp. 357-368. Bloomington, Indiana: Indiana University Press, 1984.

02956. Roscoe, Edward Stanley. The English Scene in the Eighteenth Century. New York: G.P. Putnam's Sons 1912.

Also refer to #2570.

2. POLITICAL

"By marriage, the husband and wife are one person in law; that is, the very being or legal existence of the woman is suspended during the marriage."
Blackstone

a) Legal

02957. Blackstone, William. Commentaries on the Laws of England. Philadephia: G.W. Childs, 1862. [See especially Vol. 1, chapter 15, "Of Husband and Wife."]

02958. Okin, Susan Moller. "Patriarchy and Married Women's Property in England: Questions About some Current Views." Eighteenth-Century Studies 17 (Winter 1983-1984): 121-155.

Also refer to #2624, 2625, 3034.

b) Criminal

02959. Campbell, Ruth. "Sentence of Death by Burning for Women." Journal of Legal History 5 (May 1984): 44-59.

02960. Doody, Margaret Anne. "'Those Eyes are Made so Killing': Eighteenth-Century Murderesses and the Law." Princeton University Library Chronicle 46 (Autumn 1984): 49-80.

02961. Mackaness, George. "Female Convicts: A Hell-Voyage to Botany Bay." American Book Collector 13 (October 1962):6-9.

02962. Wagner, Peter. "The Pornographer in the Courtroom: Trial Reports about Cases of Sexual Crimes and Delinquencies as a genre of Eighteenth-century Erotica." In Sexuality in Eighteenth-Century Britain, edited by Paul-Gabriel Boucé, pp. 120-140. Totowa, N.J.: Rowman and Littlefield, 1982.

c) Feminism

(1) Non-specific

02963. Rendall, Jane. The Origins of Modern Feminism: Women in Britain, France and the United States, 1780-1860. Houndmills:Macmillan, 1985.

02964. Rogers, Katharine M. Feminism in Eighteenth Century England. Urbana, Illinois: University of Illinois Press, 1982.

(2) Individuals

(a) Mary Wollstonecraft

02965. Barker-Benfield, G.J. "Mary Wollstonecraft's Depression and Diagnosis: The Relation between Sensibility and Women's Susceptibility to Nervous Disorders." The Psychohistory Review 13 (Spring 1985): 15-31.

02966. Brody, Miriam. "Mary Wollstonecraft: Sexuality and Women's Rights (1759-1797)." In Feminist Thoerists, edited by Dale Spencer, pp. 40-59. New York: Pantheon Books, Random House, 1983.

02967. Butler, Marilyn. "The Woman at the Window: Ann Radcliffe in the Novels of Mary Wollstonecraft and Jane Austen." In Gender and Literary Voice, Women and Literature, edited by Janet Todd, 1:128-148. New York: Holmes and Meier, 1980.

02968. Diurisi, Maria. Mary Wollstonecraft e la rivendicazione dei diritti della donna. Lecce: Messapica, 1975.

02969. Fawcett, Millicent Garrett. "A Pioneer of the Movement." The Case for Women's Suffrage, edited by Frederick John Shaw [Brougham Villars], pp. 164-189. London: T. Fisher Unwin, 1907.

02970. Kelly, Gary D. "Godwin, Wollstonecraft and Rousseau." Women and Literature 3 (Fall 1975): 21-26.

02971. __________. "Expressive style and 'the female mind': Mary Wollstonecraft's Vindication of the Rights of Woman." Studies on Voltaire and the Eighteenth Century 193(1980): 1942-1949.

02972. __________. "Mary Wollstonecraft as Vir Bonus." English Studies in Canada 5 (1979): 275-291.

02973. Myers, Mitzi. "Godwin's Memoirs of Wollstonecraft: The Shaping of Self and Subject." Studies in Romanticism 20 (1981):299-316.

02974. __________. "Mary Wollstonecraft's Letters Written in Sweden: Toward Romantic Autobiography." Studies in Eighteenth Century Culture 8 (1979): 165-185.

02975. __________. "Politics from the Outside: Mary Wollstonecraft's first Vindication." Studies in Eighteenth Century Culture 6 (1977): 113-132.

02976. __________. "Reform or Ruin: A Revolution in Female Manners." Studies in Eighteenth Century Culture 11 (1982): 199-216.

02977. Poovey, Mary. The Proper Lady and the Woman Writer: Ideology as Style in the Works of Mary Wollstonecraft, Mary Shelly, and Jane Austen. Chicago: University of Chicago Press, 1984.

02978. Ravetz, Alison. "The Trivialisation of Mary Wollstonecraft: A Personal and Professional Career Re-Vindicated." Women's Studies International Forum 6 (1983): 491-499.

02979. Roth, N. "The Roots of Mary Wollstonecraft's Feminism." Journal of the American Academy of Psychoanalysis 7 (1979) : 67-77.

02980. Thiébaux, Marcelle. "Mary Wollstonecraft in Federalist America, 1791-1802." In The Evidence of the Imagination: Studies in Interactions between Life and Art in English Romantic Literature, edited by Donald H. Reiman, Michael C. Jaye, and Betty T. Bennett, pp. 195-235. New York: New York University Press, 1978.

02981. Todd, Janet. "The female text--edited." Studies on Voltaire and the Eighteenth Century 193 (1980): 1949-1955.

02982. _________. "The Polwhelean Tradition and Richard Cobb." Studies in Burke and His Time 16 (1975)271-77.

02983. _________. "Reason and Sensibility in Mary Wollstonecraft's The Wrongs of Women." Frontiers 5 (Fall 1980): 17-20.

02984. Vlasopolos, Anca. "Mary Wollstonecraft's Mask of Reason in A Vindication of the Rights of Women." Dalhousie Review 60 (Autumn 1980): 462-471.

09285. Wollstonecraft, Mary. A Critical Edition of Mary Wollstonecraft's A Vindication of the Rights of Woman, with Strictures on Political and Moral Subjects. Troy, New York: Whitston Pub. Co., 1982.

Also refer to #3625.

(b) Others

02986. Locke, Don. A Fantasy of Reason: The Life and Thought of William Godwin. London: Routledge and Kegen Paul, 1980

02987. Marshall, Peter H. William Godwin: Philosopher, Novelist, Revolutionary. London: Yale University Press, 1984.

d) Political Roles

02988. Airlie, Mabell Frances Elizabeth (Gore) Ogilvy, Countess of. In Whig Society 1775-1818. New York: Hodder and Stoughton Ltd., 1921.

02989. Berry, Clarence Leo. _The Young Pretender's Mistress: Clementine Walkinshaw (Comtesse d'Albestroff; 1720-1802.)_ Edinburgh: Charles Skilton, 1976.

02990. Fitzgerald, Percy Hetherington. _The Good Queen Charlotte._ London: Downey, 1899.

02991. Fulford, Roger. _The Trial of Queen Caroline._ London:B.T. Batsford, 1967.

02992. MacGregor, Alexander. _The Life of Flora MacDonald._ Stirling, Eng.: E. MacKay, 1932.

02993. Pange, Victor de. _Le plus beau de boutes les fêtes._ Paris: Editions Klincksieck, 1980.

02994. Pearson, Norman. "An Eccentric Beauty of the 18th century." _Nineteenth Century and After_ 63 (May 1908): 771-786.

02995. Russell, Edward F.L. _Caroline, The Unhappy Queen._ London: Robert Hale, 1967.

Also refer to #2575.

3. ECONOMIC

". . . every person willing to work may find employment. It is vague assertion . . . of insensible indolence, when it relates to men/ but, with respect to women, I am sure of its fallacy, unless they submit to menial bodily labour; and even to be employed at hard labour is out of the reach of many, whose reputation misfortune or folly has tainted."

Mary Wollstonecraft
Maria or the Wrongs of Women

02996. Levine, David. "Industrialization and the Proletarian Family in England." _Past and Present_ 107 (May 1985): 168-203.

02997. Marchianò, Giovanna. "Tra famiglia e lavoro--Aspetti della condizione femminile in Inghilterra nell'età della rivoluzio-ne industraile." In _Esistere comme donna_, pp. 37-46. Milan: Mazzotta, 1983.

02998. Thwaites, W. "Women in the Market Place: Oxfordshire c. 1760-1800." _Midland History_ 9 (1984) : 23-42.

Also refer to #2194, 3035.

4. RELIGION

"Since GOD has given Women as well as Men intelligent souls, why should they be forbidden to improve them?"
Mary Astell

a) Saints/Religious Women

02999. Exell, Arthur Wallis. *Joanna Southcott at Blockley and the Rock Cottage Relics*. Shipston-on-Stour: P. Drinkwater, 1977.

03000. Hopkins, James K. *A Woman to Deliver Her People: Joanna Southcott and English Millenarian in An Era of Revolution*. Austin: University of Texas, 1982.

b) Methodists

03001. Brown, Earl Kent. *Women of Mr. Wesley's Methodism*. Lewiston, New York: Edwin Mellen Press, 1983.

03002. Keddie, Henrietta. *The Countess of Huntingdon and her Circle*. London: Pitman and Sons, 1907.

03003. Wallace, Charles, Jr. "Susanna Wesley's Spirituality: The Freedom of a Christian Woman." *Methodist History* 22 (April 1984): 158-173.

c) Witchcraft

03004. Gerish, W.B. *A Hertfordshire Witch; Or the Story of Jane Wenham, The "Wise Woman of Walkern"*. n.p. 1906.

03005. Guskin, Phyllis J. "The Context of Witchcraft: The Cast of Jane Wenham. (1712)." *Eighteenth-Century Studies* 15 (Fall 1981): 48-71.

Also refer to #2598.

5. SOCIAL

". . .night after night, like a poor submissive slave, have I laid my lordly master in his bed, intoxicated and indefensible; day after day I received blows and bruises for my reward: in short, I thought I had married a man, I found I had married a monster."

Catherine Jemmat

a) Generic

(1) Non-specific

03006. Maxwell, Constantin. Country and Town in Ireland under the Georges. Dundalk: W. Tempest, 1949.

03007. Plumb, J.H. Georgian Delights. Boston: Little Brown, 1980.

03008. Walton, John K. The English Seaside Resort: A Social History, 1750-1914. New York: St. Martin's, 1983.

(2) Women

03009. Arnold, Ralph. The Unhappy Countess and Her Grandson John Bowes. London: Constable, 1957.

03010. Duffy, Ian, ed. Women and Society in the Eighteenth Century. Bethlehem, Pa: Lawrence Henry Gipson Institute, 1983.

03011. Duhamel, Jean. "L'amour inconnu du Lady Hester Stanhope." Revue des deux mondes (15 November 1957): 297-309.

03012. Johnson, Joan. Excellent Cassandra: The Life and Times of the Duchess of Chandos. Atlantic Highlands, N.J.: Humanities Press, 1982.

03013. Masters, Brian. Georgiana: Duchess of Devonshire. North Pomfret, Vt.: Hamish Hamilton, 1981.

03014. Mavor, Elizabeth. Ladies of Llangollen. A Study in Romantic Friendship. Harmondsworth, Eng: Penguin Books, 1973.

03015. Napier, Priscilla (Hayter). The Sword Dance: Lady Sarah Lennox and the Napiers. New York: McGraw Hill, 1971.

03016. Spacks, Patricia M. "The Talent of Ready Utterance: Eighteenth-Century Female Gossip." In Women and Society in the Eighteenth Century, edited by Ian P.H. Duffy, pp. 1-14. Bethlehem, Pa.: Lawrence Henry Gibson Institute, 1983.

03017. Tipton, I.C. and Furlong, E.J. "Mrs. George Berkeley and her Washing Machine." Hermathena 101 (Autum 1965): 38-47.

Also refer to #2606

b) Demography

03018. Aldridge, Alfred Owen. "Population and Polygamy in Eighteenth Century Thought." _Journal of the History of Medicine_ 4 (Spring 1949): 129-148.

03019. Chambers, J.D. "Family Limitation in England." In _Loving, Parenting and Dying_, edited by Vivian C. Fox and Martin H. Quitt, pp. 215-225. New York: Psychohistry Press, Publishers, 1980.

03020. Wrigley, Edward Anthony. "The Growth of Population in 18th Century England: A Conundrum Resolved." _Past and Present_ 98 (February 1983): 121-150.

03021. ________. "Marriage, Fertility and Population Growth in 18th Century England." In _Marriage and Society Studies in the Social History of Marriage_, edited by R.B. Outhwaite, pp. 137-185. New York: St. Martin's Press, 1981.

Also refer to #2608, 2610, 2612, 2614, 1615.

c) Family

(1) Non-specific

03022. Hufton, Olwen. "Women Without Men: Widows and Spinsters in Britain and France in the Eighteenth Century." _Journal of Family History_ 9 (Winter 1984): 355-376.

03023. Lewis, Judith Schneid. _In the Family Way: Childbearing in the British Aristocracy, 1769-1860_. New Brunswick, N.J.: Rutgers University Press, 1985.

03024. Spring, Eileen. "The Family, Strict Settlement, and Historians." _Canadian Journal of History_ 18 (December 1983): 379-398.

03025. Stone, Lawrence. "Money, Sex and Murder in Eighteenth-Century England." In _Women and Society in the Eighteenth Century_, edited by Ian P.H. Duffy, pp. 15-27. Bethlehem, Pa:Lawrence Henry Gibson Institute, 1983.

Also refer to #2615, 2996, 2997, 3019.

(2) Childhood

03026. Camic, Charles. _Experience and Enlightenment. Socialization for Cultural Change in Eighteenth-Century Scotland_. Chicago: University of Chicago Press, 1983.

03027. Chambers, J.D. "The Chances of Life." In _Loving, Parenting and Dying_, edited by Vivian C. and Martin H. Quitt, pp. 156-157. New York: Psychohistory Press, Publishers, 1980.

03028. Hughes, Mary Joe. "Child-Rearing and Social Expectations in Eighteenth-Century England: The Case of the Colliers of Hastings." Studies in Eighteenth-Century Culture 13 (1984): 79-100.

03029. McClure, Ruth K. "Pediatric Practice at the London Foundling Hospital." Studies in Eighteenth Century Culture 10 (1981): 361-371.

03030. Plumb, J.H. "The New World of Children in Eighteenth-Century England." In Loving, Parenting and Dying, edited by Vivian C. Fox and Martin H. Quitt, pp. 299-312. New York: Psychohistory Press, Publishers, 1980. Also in Past and Present 67 (1975): 64-95.

d) Marriage

03031. Brown, Roger Lee. "The Rise and Fall of Fleet Marriages." In Marriage and Society. Studies in the Social History of Marriage, edited by R.B. Outhwaite, pp. 117-136. New York: St. Martin's Press, 1981.

03032. Dickson, Lance E. Treatise of Femme Coverts: Or the Lady's Law. 1732. Reprint. New York: Garland, 1978.

03033. Habbakuk, H.J. "Marriage Settlements in the 18th Century." In Loving, Parenting and Dying, edited by Vivian C. Fox and Martin H. Quitt, pp. 121-126. New York: Psychohistory Press, Publishers, 1980.

03034. Holmes, J. Derek. "Some Cases of Conscience, with Particular Reference to the Marriage Act of 1752," Recusant History 10 (October 1970): 350-355.

03035. Houston, R.A. "Marriage Formation and Domestic Industry: Occupational Endogamy in Kilmarnode, Ayrshire, 1697-1764." Journal of Family History 8 (Fall 1983): 215-229.

03036. Malcolmson, A.P.W. The Pursuit of the Heiress: Aristocratic Marriage in Ireland, 1750-1820. Belfast: Ulster Historical Foundation, 1982.

03037. Roberts, A. "Catholic Marriage in Eighteenth-Century Scotland." Innes Review 34 (1983): 9-16.

Also refer to #2608, 2614, 2624, 2625, 3018, 3021, 3025, 3152, 3153, 3173.

e) Sex Life and Morals

(1) Non-Specific

03038. Boucé, Paul-Gabriel, ed. Sexuality in Eighteenth-Century Britain. Totowa, New Jersey: Barnes and Noble, 1982.

03039. Boucé, Paul-Gabriel. "Some Sexual Beliefs and Myths in Eighteenth-Century Britain." In _Sexuality in Eighteenth-Century Britain_, edited by Paul-Gabriel Boucé, pp. 28-46. Totwa, N.J.: Barnes and Noble, 1982.

03040. Castle, Terry. "Eros and Liberty at the English Masquerade, 1710-1790." _Eighteenth Century Studies_ 17 (Winter 1983-1984): 156-176.

03041. Porter, Roy. "Mixed Feelings: The Enlightenment and Sexuality in Eighteenth-Century Britain." In _Sexuality in Eighteenth-Century Britain_, edited by Paul-Gabriel Boucé, pp. 1-27. Totowa, N.J.: Barnes and Noble, 1982.

03042. Smith, Norah. "Sexual Mores and Attitudes in Enlightenment Scotland." In _Sexuality in Eighteenth-Century Britain_, edited by Paul-Gabriel Boucé, pp. 47-73. Totwa, N.J.: Barnes and Noble, 1982.

03043. Trumbach, Randolph. "London's Sodomites: Homosexual Behavior and Western Culture in the Eighteenth-century." _Journal of Social History_ 11 (Fall 1977): 1-33.

Also refer to #2962, 3025, 3115-3118, 3169.

(2) Prostitutes

03044. Comston, Herbert Fuller Bright. _The Magdalen Hospital_. London: Society for the Promotion of Christian Knowledge, 1917.

03045. Coward, D.A. "Eighteenth-Century Attitudes to Prostitution." _Studies on Voltaire and Eighteenth-Century_ 189 (1980): 363-399.

03046. Nash, Stanley. "Prostitution and Charity: The Magdalen Hospital, A Case Study." _Journal of Social History_ 17 (Summer 1984): 617-628.

03047. Watson, Ross. "Portrait of a Courtesan." _Apollo_ 89 (March 1969): 184-187.

Also refer to #2631, 2643.

f) Fashion/Manners

03048. Sichel, Marion. _Costume Reference 4. The Eighteenth Century_. Boston: Plays Inc., 1977.

g) Health/Medical

03049. Erikson, R.A. "Mother Jewkes, Pamela and Midwives." _ELH_ 42 (December 1976): 500-501.

03050. Miller, Genevieve. "Putting Lady Mary in her Place: A Discussion of Historical Causation." Bulletin of the History of Medicine 55 (Spring 1981): 2-16.

03051. Peters, Dolores. "The Pregnant Pamela: Characterization and Popular Medical Attitudes in the Eighteenth Century." Eighteenth-Century Studies 14 (Summer 1981): 432-451.

03052. Schnorrenberg, Barbara Brandon. "Is Childbirth any Place for a Woman? The Decline of Midwifery in Eighteenth Century England." Studies in Eighteenth Century Culture 10 (1981): 393-408.

03053. Singer, Charles. "An Eighteenth century Naval Ship to accomodate Women Nurses." Medical History 4 (October 1960): 283-287.

Also refer to #2610, 2635, 2636, 3029, 3044, 3083, 3094.

h) Recreation

03054. Margetson, Stella. Leisure and Pleasure in the Eighteenth Century. London: Cassell, 1970.

6. CULTURAL

"Something is lika part o' thee
to praise, to love, I find
But dear as is thy form to me,
still dearer is thy mind."
Burns

a) Generic

03055. Brack, Gae. "English Literary Ladies and the Booksellers." Studies on Voltaire and the Eighteenth Century 193(1980): 1932-1939.

03056. Halsband, Robert. "Ladies of Letters in the Eighteenth Century." In The Lady of Letters in the Eighteenth Century, pp. 31-51. Los Angeles: Clark Library, 1969.

03057. Hunt, Margaret, et. al. Women and the Enlightenment. New York: Haworth Press, 1984.

03058. Jacob, Margaret. "Freemasonry, Women and the Paradox of the Enlightenment." Women and History 9 (Spring 1984):69-93.

b) Education

(1) Non-specific

03059. Ellis, Grace, A. A Memoir of Mrs. Anna Laetitia Barbauld with Many of her Letters. Boston: Osgood, 1874.

03060. Murch, Jerom. Mrs. Barbauld and her Contemporaries. London: Longmans, Green, 1877.

03061. Myers, Sylvia. "The Ironies of Education." Aphra Magazine 4 (Spring 1973): 61-72.

Also refer to #3155.

(2) Hannah More

03062. Agress, Lynne. "Hannah More: Female Messiah or Devil's Disciple?" University of Portland Review 32 (Fall 1980): 3-10.

03063. Knight, Helen C. A New Memoir of Hannah More; Or, Life in Hall and Cottage. New York: M.W. Dodd, 1851.

03064. More, Hannah. Essays on Various Subjects, Principally Designed for Young Ladies. London: Paternoster-Row, 1815.

03065. Pedersen, Susan. "Hannah More meets Simple Simon: Tracts, Chapbooks, and Popular Culture, in Late Eighteenth-Century England." Journal of British Studies 25 (January 1986): 84-113.

Also refer to #4072.

c) Literature

(1) Non-specific

03066. Goller, Karl Heinz. "The Emancipation of Women in Eighteenth-Century English Literature." Anglia 101 (1983): 78-98.

03067. Niklaus, Robert. "Étude comparée de la situation de la femme en Angleterre et en France." Studies on Voltaire and the Eighteenth Century 193 (1980): 1909-1918.

03068. Schnorrenberg, Barbara Brandon. "A Paradise like Eve's: Three eighteenth century English female Utopias." Women's Studies 9 (1982): 263-273.

03069. Todd, Janet M. Women's Friendship in Literature. New York: Columbia University Press, 1980.

Also refer to #2653, 2655.

(2) Philosophy

[a] Hume

03070. Battersby, Christine. "Enquiry concerning the Humean Woman." Philosophy 56 (July 1981): 303-312.

03071. __________. "An enquiry concerning the Humean woman." Studies on Voltaire and the Eighteenth Century 193 (1980): 1964-1967.

03072. Burns, Steve A. Macleod. "The Humean Female." In Sexism of Social and Political Theory: Woman and Reproduction from Plato to Nietzsche, edited by M.G. Clark and Lydia Lange, pp. 53-59. Toronto: University Press, 1979.

03073. Lacoste, Louise Michel. "Hume's Method in Moral Reasoning." In The Sexism of Social and Political Theory: Woman and Reproduction from Plato to Nietzsche, edited by M.G. Clark and Lydia Lange, pp. 60-73. Totono: University Press, 1979.

(3) Drama

03074. Dash, Irene. "A Penchant for Perdita on the Eighteenth-Century English Stage." Studies in Eighteenth Century Culture 6 (1977): 331-346.

03075. Lock, F.P. Susanna Centlivre. Boston: Twayne Publishers, 1979.

03076. Mattes, Eleanor. "The 'female virtuoso' in early eighteenth century English drama." Women and Literature 3 (Fall 1975): 3-9.

03077. Verdurmen, J. Peter. "Grasping for Permanence: Ideal Couples in The Country Wife and Aureng Zebe." Huntington Library Quarterly 42 (1979): 329-347.

Also refer to #3117.

(4) Poetry

[a] Women in Poetry

[1] Pope

03078. Delany, Shelia. "Sex and Politics in Pope's Rape of the Lock." In Writing Woman, pp. 93-112. New York: Schocken Books, 1983.

03079. Pollak, Ellen. The Poetics of Sexual Myth: Gender and Ideology in the Verse of Swift and Pope. Chicago, Il: University of Chicago Press, 1985.

03080. Pollak, Ellen. "Rereading The Rape of the Lock. Pope and the Paradox of Female Power. Studies in Eighteenth Century Culture 10 (1981): 429-444.

03081. Reynolds, Kelly. "The Rape of the Locke: Love Match-The 'Earthly Lover' vs. The 'Birth-night Beau!" Scholia Satyrica 6 (Summer-Autumn 1980): 3-11.

03082. Scruggs, Charles. "'Well our Power to Use': The Meaning of Clarissa's Speech in The Rape of the Lock." Tennessee Studies in Literature 25 (1980): 84-93.

03083. Sena, John F. "Belinda's Hysteria: The Medical Context of The Rape of the Lock." Eighteenth-Century Life 5, no. 4 (1979): 29-42.

03084. ________. "'The Wide Circumference around': The Context of Belinda's Petticoat in The Rape of the Lock." Papers on Language and Literature 16 (1980): 260-267.

Also refer to #3089.

[2] Others

03085. Murray, William James. "Robert Burns: the Poet as Liberationist." Studies on Voltaire and the Eighteenth Century 193 (1980): 1969-1980.

Also refer to #1715.

[b] Women Poets

03086. Lucas, E.V. A Swan and her Friends. London: Methuen, 1907.

03087. Stecher, Henry Fredrick. Elizabeth Singer Rowe, the Poetess on Frome. Bern: Herbert Lang, 1973.

(5) Prose

[a] Novels

[1] Women in Novels

((a)) Non-specific

03088. Blondel, Madeleine. Images de la femme dans le roman anglais de 1740 à 1771 2 vols. Lille: Reproduction des Thèses, Université Lille III, 1976.

03089. Brooks-Davies, Douglas. "The Mythology of Love: Venerean (and related) Iconography in Pope, Fielding, Cleland and Sterne." In Sexuality in Eighteenth-Century Britain, edited by Paul-Gabriel Boucé, pp. 176-197. Totowa, N.J.: Barnes and Noble, 1982.

03090. Howells, Coral Ann. Love, Mystery and Misery - Feeling in Gothic Fiction. London: Athlone Press, 1978.

03091. Kern, Jean B. "The Fallen Woman from the Perspective of Five Early Eighteenth century Women Novelists." Studies in Eighteenth Century Culture 10 (1981): 457-468.

03092. Miller, Nancy K. The Heroine's Text: Readings in the French and English Novel, 1722-1782. New York: Columbia University Press, 1980.

03093. Perry, Ruth. Women, Letters and the Novel. New York: AMS Press, 1980.

03094. Price, John Valdimir. "Patterns of Sexual Behavior in Some Eighteenth-Century Novels." In Sexuality in Eighteenth-Century Britain, edited by Paul-Gabriel Boucé, pp. 159-175. Totowa, N.J.: Barnes and Noble, 1982.

03095. Steeves, Edna L. "Pre-Feminism in Some Eighteenth Century Novels." Texas Quarterly 16 (Autumn 1973): 48-57.

[[1]] Richardson

03096. Blondel, Jacques. "L'Amour dans Pamela: de l'affrontement à la découverte de soi." In Études sur le XVIIIe siècle, edited by Jean Erhard, pp. 15-30. Clermont-Ferrand: Association pour les Publications de la Faculté des Lettres et Sciences Humaines, 1979.

03097. Brownstein, Rachel Mayer. "'An Examplar to Her Sex': Richardson's Clarissa." Yale Review 66 (1977): 30-47.

03098. Castle, Terry. Clarissa's Ciphers: Meaning and Disruption in Richardson's Clarissa. Ithaca, N.Y.: Cornell University Press, 1982.

03099. Doederlein, Sue Warrick. "Clarissa in the Hands of the Critics." Eighteenth-Century Studies 16 (Summer 1983): 401-414.

03100. Eagleton, Terry. The Rape of Clarissa: Writing, Sexuality, and Class Struggle in Samuel Richardson. Minneapolis, MN: University of Minnesota Press, 1982.

03101. Guilhamet, Leon M. "From Pamela to Grandison: Richardson's Moral Revolution in the Novel." In _Studies in Change and Revolution, Aspects of English Intellectual History, 1640-1800_, edited by Paul J. Korshin, pp. 191-210. Menston, Yorkshire: Scolar Press Ltd., 1972.

03102. Harvey, A.D. "_Clarissa_ and the Puritan Tradition." _Essays in Criticism_ 28 (1978): 38-51.

03103. Jabens, Sabine. "Das literarischen Frauenbild in der Mitte das 18. Jahrhunderts-Weibliche Bildung und Sexualität bei Richardson und Gellert." _Beiträge zur feministischen Theories und Praxis_ 5 (1981): 11-16.

03104. Kay, Carol. "Sympathy, Sex and Authority in Richardson and Hume." _Studies in Eighteenth Century Culture_ 12 (1983): 77-92.

03105. Klotman, Phyllis R. "Sin and Sublimation in the Novels of Samuel Richardson." _CLA Journal_ 20 (March 1977): 365-373.

03106. Laurence-Anderson, Judith. "Changing Affective Life in Eighteenth Century England and Samuel Richardson's _Pamela_." _Studies in Eighteenth Century Culture_ 10 (1981): 445-456.

03107. Rogers, Katharine. "Richardson's Empathy with Women." In _The Authority of Experience_, edited by Arlyn Diamond and Lee R. Edwards, pp. 118-136. Amherst: University of Massachusetts Press, 1977.

03108. Stevenson, John Allen. "The Courtship of the Family: Clarissa and the Harlows Once More." _Journal of English Literary History_ 48 (1981): 757-777.

03109. Trotter, W.A. "Richardson and the 'new lights': 'Clarissa' among the Victorians." _English_ 33 (Summer 1984): 117-125.

03110. Wilson, S. "Richardson's Pamela: an Interpretation." _PMLA_ 88 (January 1973): 79-81.

Also refer to #1715, 2703, 2944, 3153.

[[2]] Sterne

03111. Alter, R. "_Tristram Shandy_ and the Game of Love." _American Scholar_ 37 (1968): 316-323.

03112. Brady, F. "_Tristram Shandy_, Sexuality, Morality and Sensibility." _Eighteenth Century Studies_ 4 (1970-1971): 41-46.

03113. Cash, Arthur H. "The Birth of Tristram Shandy: Sterne and Dr. Burton." In _Sexuality in Eighteenth Century Britain_, edited by Paul-Gabriel Boucé, pp. 198-224. Totowa, N.J.: Barnes and Noble, 1982.

Also refer to #3089.

[[3]] Others

03114. Castle, Terry. "Matters not Fit to be Mentioned: Fielding's The Female Husband." _Journal of English Literary History_ 49 (Fall 1982): 602-622.

03115. Day, Robert Adams. "Sex Scatology, Smollett." In _Sexuality in Eighteenth-Century Britain_, edited by Paul-Gabriel Boucé, pp. 225-243. Totowa, NJ.: Barnes and Noble, 1982.

03116. Naumann, Peter. _Keyhole and Candle: John Cleland's "Memoirs of a Woman of Pleasure" und die Entstehung des pornographischen Romans in England_. Heidelberg: Carl Einter, 1976.

03117. Rogers, Pat. "The Breeches Part." In _Sexuality in Eighteenth-Century Britain_, edited by Paul-Gabriel Boucé, pp. 244-258. Totowa, N.J.: Barnes and Noble, 1982.

03118. Whitley, Raymond K. "The Libertine Hero and Heroine in the Novels of John Cleland." _Studies in Eighteenth Century Culture_ 9 (1980): 387-404.

Also refer to #3049, 3051, 3089.

[2] Women Novelists

((a)) Non-specific

03119. Rogers, Katharine M. "Dreams and Nightmares: Male Characters in the Feminine Novel of the Eighteenth Century." In _Men by Women, Women and Literature_, edited by Janet Todd, 2:9-24. New York: Holmes and Meier, 1981.

Also refer to #2705, 3093.

((b)) Individuals

[[1]] Fanny Burney

03120. Cutting, Rose Marie. "Defiant Women: The Growth of Feminism in Fanny Burney's Novels." _Studies in English Literature_ 17 (Summer 1977): 519-530.

03121. Cutting, Rose Marie. "A Wreath for Fammy Burney's Last Novel: The Wanderer's Contribution to Women's Studies." Illinois Quarterly 37 (1975): 45-64.

03122. Grau, Joseph A. Fanny Burney: An Annotated Bibliography. New York: Garland, 1981.

03123. Kilpatrick, Sarah. Fanny Burney. New York: Stein and Day, 1981.

03124. Marina Vessilli, Claudia. Cecilia tra i courtesy books e la Vindication of the Rights of women. Rome: Edizioni: dell'Ateneo Bizzarri, 1979.

03125. Overman, Antoinette Arnolda. An Investigation into the Character of Fanny Burney. 1933. Reprint. Philadelphia: R. West, 1977.

03126. Poovey, Mary. "Fathers and Daughters: The Trama of Growing Up Female." In Men by Women, Women and Literature, edited by Janet Todd, 2:39-58. New York: Holmes and Meier, 1982.

03127. Rogers, Katharine M. Fanny Burney: The Private Self and the Published Self." International Journal of Women's Studies 7 (March-April 1984): 111-117.

03128. Sparks, Patricia Meyer. "The Dynamics of Fear: Fanny Burney." In Imagining a Self, Autobiography and Novel in Eighteenth-Century England, pp. 158-192. Cambridge, Mass.: Harvard University Press, 1976.

[[2]] Others

03129. Ellis, Katherine. "Charlotte Smith's Subversive Gothic." Feminist Studies 3 (Spring-Summer 1976): 51-55.

03130. Pritcher, Edward W. "Maria Susanna Cooper (1738-1807): The 'Exemplary Mother' from Norfolk." American Notes and Queries 17 (1978): 35-36.

03131. Rogers, Katharine M. "Sensibility and Feminism: The Novels of Frances Brooke." Genre 11 (1978): 159-171.

03132. Schofield, Mary Ann. "Exposé of the Popular Heroine: The Female Protagonists of Eliza Haywood." Studies in Eighteenth Century Culture 12 (1983): 93-104.

03133. __________. Quiet Rebellion: The Fictional Heroines of Elizabeth Fowler Haywood. Washington: University Press of America, 1982.

03134. Schroeder, Natalie. "Regina Maria Roche, Popular Novelist, 1789-1834: The Rochean Canon." Papers of the Bibliographical Society of America 73 (1979): 462-468.

03135. Séjourné, Philippe. The Mystery of Charlotte Lennox. Aix-en-Provence: Publications des Annales de la Faculté des lettres, 1967.

03136. Todd, Janet. "Posture and Imposture: The Gothic Manservant in Ann Radcliffe's The Italian." In Men by Women, Women in Literature, edited by Janet Todd, 2:25-38. New York: Holmes and Meier, 1982.

[b] Periodicals

03137. Conroy, Peter V., Jr. "The Spectators' view of women." Studies on Voltaire and the Eighteenth Century 193 (1980): 1883-1890.

d) Intellectuals

(1) Individuals

(a) Daniel Defoe

03138. Bell, Robert H. "Moll's Grace Abounding." Genre 8 (December 1975): 267-282.

03139. Blewet, David. "Changing Attitudes toward Marriage in the Time of Defoe: The Case of Moll Flanders." Huntington Library Quarterly 44 (1981): 77-88.

03140. Borck, Jim Springer. "One Woman's Prospects: Defoe's Moll Flanders and the Ironies in Restoration Self-Image." Forum 17 (1979): 10-16.

03141. Bordner, Marsha. "Defoe's Androgynous Vision in Moll Flanders and Roxana." Gypsy Scholar 2 (Spring 1975): 76-93.

03142. Brooks, Douglas, "Moll Flanders: An Interpretation." Essays in Criticism 19 (1969): 46-59.

03143. Brown, Lloyd W. "Defoe and the Feminine Mystique." In Transactions of the Samuel Johnson Society of the Northwest, edited by Robert H. Carnie, 4: 4-18. Calgary, Alberta: Samuel Johnson Society of the Northwest, 1972.

03144. Byrd, Max. "The Madhouse, The Whorehouse and the Convent." Partisan Review 44 (1977): 268-278.

03145. Cohan, Steven. "Other Bodies: Roxana's Confession of Guilt." Studies in the Novel 8 (Winter 1976): 406-418.

03146. Curtis, Laura A. "A Case Study of Defoe's Domestic Conduct Manuals Suggested by The Family, Sex and Marriage in England 1500-1800. Studies in Eighteenth Century Culture 10 (1981): 409-428.

03147. Goestsch, Paul. "Defoes 'Moll Flanders' und der Leser." Germanisch-Romanische Monatsschrift n.s. 30 (1980): 271-288.

03148. Hartog, Curt. "Aggression, Femininity and Irony in Moll Flanders." Literature and Psychology 22 (1972): 121-138.

03149. Leranbaum, Miriam. "Moll Flanders: Woman on Her Own Account." In The Authority of Experience, edited by Arlyn Diamond and Lee R. Edwards, pp. 101-117. Amherst: University of Massachusetts Press, 1977.

03150. McCoy, Kathleen. "The Femininity of Moll Flanders." Studies in Eighteenth Century Culture 7 (1978): 413-422.

03151. McMaster, Juliet. "The Equation of Love and Money in Moll Flanders." Studies in the Novel 2 (1970): 131-144.

03152. Watson, T.G. "Defoe's Attitude towards Marriage and the Position of Women as revealed in Moll Flanders." The Southern Quarterly 3 (1964): 1-8.

03153. Wilson, Bruce L. "Sex and the Single Girl in the Eighteenth Century: An Essay on Marriage and the Puritan Myth." Journal of Women's Studies in Literature (179): 195-219.

(b) Samuel Johnson

03154. Brownley, Martine Watson. "'Under the Domination of Some Woman' The Friendship of Samuel Johnson and Hester Thrale." In Mothering the Mind, Twelve Studies of Writers and Their Silent Partners, edited by Ruth Perry and Martine Watson Brownley, pp 64-79. New York: Holmes and Meier, 1984.

03155. Wellington, Charmaine. "Dr. Johnson's Attitude towards the Education of Women." New-Rambler, ser. C, 18 (1977): 49-58.

(c) Jonathan Swift

03156. Carnochan, W.B. "The Secrets of Swift and Stella." In Mothering the Mind, Twelve Studies of Writers and Their Silent Partners, edited by Ruth Perry and Martine Watson Brownley, pp. 48-63. New York: Holmes and Meier, 1984.

03157. Ehrenpreis, Irvin. "Letters of Advice to Young Spinsters." In The Lady of Letters in the Eighteenth Century, pp. 3-27. Los Angeles: Clark Library, 1969.

Also refer to #3079.

(d) Hester Lynch Piozzi Thrale

03158. Brownley, Martine Watson. "Eighteenth-Century Women's Images and Roles: The Case of Hester Thrale Piozzi." Biography: An Interdisciplinary Quarterly 3 (1980): 65-76.

03159. Clifford, James L. "The Daily Diaries of Hester Lynch Piozzi." Columbia Library Columns 27 (1978): 10-17.

03160. Merritt, Percival. The True Story of the So-Called Love Letters of Mrs. Piozzi. Cambridge, Mass.: Harvard University Press, 1928.

03161. Rompkey, Ronald. "Mrs. Hester Thrale and The Pursuit of Her 'Nova Scotia Fortune.'" Dalhousie Review 58 (1978): 434-422.

Also refer to #3061.

(2) Others

03162. Brownley, Martine Watson. "'The Purest and Most Gentle Portion of the Human Species': Gibbon's Portrayals of Women in the Decline and Fall." South Atlantic Quarterly 77 (1978): 1-14.

03163. __________. "The Women in Clarendon's Life and Works." The Eighteenth Century: Theory and Practice 22 (1981): 153-174.

03164. Charles, B.G. "Peggy Owen and her Streatham friends." Cornhill Magazine 160 (1939): 334-351.

03165. Gold, Joel J. "'Buried Alive' Charlotte Forman in Grub Street." Eighteenth-Century Life 8 (October 1982): 28-45.

03166. Green, Mary Elizabeth. "Elizabeth Elstob: The Saxon Nymph." In Female Scholars, edited by J.R. Brink, pp. 137-160. St. Albans, Vt.: Eden Press, 1980.

03167. Halsband, Robert. "New Anecdotes of Lady Mary Wortley Montagu." In Evidence in Literary Scholarship: Essays in Memory of James Marshall Osborn, edited by Rene Wellek and Alvaro Ribeiro, pp. 241-246. Oxford: Clarendon Press, 1979.

03168. Leites, Edmund. "Good humor at home, good humor abroad: The intimacies of marriage and the civilities of social life in the ethic of Richard Steele." Social Sciences Information 20 (1981): 607-640.

03169. Smith, Norah. "Sexual Mores in the Eighteenth Century: Robert Wallace's 'Of Venery.'" Journal of the History of Ideas 39 (July-September 1978): 419-433.

03170. Wystrach, V.P. "Anna Blackburne (1726-1793) - A Neglected Patroness of Natural History." Journal of the Society for the Bibliography of Natural History 8 (1977): 146-168.

Also refer to #4350.

(3) Bluestockings

03171. Dobbs, Jeannine. "The Blue-Stockings: Getting It Together." Frontiers 1 (Spring 1976): 81-93.

e) Art

(1) Non-specific

03172. Sloan, Kim. "Drawing -- A 'Polite Recreation' in Eighteenth-century England." Studies in Eighteenth Century Culture 11 (1982): 217-240.

(2) Women in Art

03173. Cowley, Robert L.S. Hogarth's Marriage à-la mode. Ithaca, N.Y.: Cornell University Press, 1983.

(3) Women Artists

(a) Actresses/Critics

03174. Boader, James. The Life of Mrs. Jordan. London: Bell, 1831.

03175. Bushnell, George H. "The Original Lady Randolph." Theatre Notebook 13 (Summer 1959): 119-123.

03176. Fyvie, John. Comedy Queens of the Georgian Era. London: Constable, 1906.

03177. Hogan, Charles Beecher. "Eighteenth Century Actors in the D.N.B.: Additions and Corrections." Theatre Notebook 11 (July-September 1955): 103-111.

03178. __________. "Eighteenth Century Actors in the D.N.B.: Additions and Corrections." Theatre Notebook 6 (January-March 1952): 45-58; (April-June 1952): 66-71; (July-September 1952): 87-96.

03179. Jerrold (Nash), Clare. The Story of Dorothy Jordan. New York: Brentano's, 1914.

03180. Kelly, Linda. The Kemble Era: John Phillip Kemble, Sarah Siddons, and the London Stage. London: Bodley Head, 1980.

03181. Needham, Gwendolyn B. "Mrs. Frances Brooke: Dramatic Critic." Theatre Notebook 15 (Winter 1960-1961): 47-52.

03182. Pearce, Charles E. _Polly Peachum: The Story of Lavinia Fenton and the Beggar's Opera_. 1913. Reprint. New York: Blom, 1968.

03183. Vaughan, Anthony. _Born to Please_. London: Society for Theatre Research, 1979.

03184. Weinsheimer, Joel. "Mrs. Siddons, the Tragic Muse, and the Problem of _As_." _Journal of Aesthetics and Art Criticism_ 36 (1978): 317-328.

(b) Musicians/Singers

03185. Cook, D.R. "Francoise, Marguérite de l'Epine: The Italian Lady?" _Theatre Notebook_ 35 (1981): 58-73.

03186. Stookes, Sacha. "Some Eighteenth Century Women Violinists." _Monthly Musical Record_ 84 (January 1954): 14-17.

Also refer to #3645.

(c) Painters

[1] Diana Beauclerk

03187. Erskine, Beatrice Caroline Strong. _Lady Diana Beauclerk: Her Life and Work_. London: T.F. Unwin, 1903.

03188. __________. "Lady Di's Scrapbook." _Connoisseur_ 7 (1903): 32-37.

[2] Maria Cosway

03189. Scheerer, Constance. "Maria Cosway: Larger-than-Life Miniaturist." _Feminist Art Journal_ 5 (Spring 1976): 10-13.

03190. Williamson, George C. _Richard Cosway, R.A., His Wife and Pupils_. London: George Bell and Sons, 1905.

[3] Mary Delaney

03191. Hayden, R. _Mrs. Delaney. Her Life and Flowers_. London: British Museum, 1980.

03192. Johnson, R. Brimley. _Mrs. Delaney at Court and Among the Wits_. London: S. Paul, 1925.

03193. Symonds, Emily. _Mrs. Delaney_. London: G. Richards, 1900.

[4] Others

03194. Waterson, Merlin. "Elizabeth Ratcliff: An Artistic Lady's Maid." _Apollo_ 108 (July 1978): 56-63.

(d) Silversmiths

[1] Non-specific

03195. Wenham, Edward. "Women Silversmiths." Antiques 46 (October 1944): 200-202.

[2] Hester Bateman

03196. Gillingham, Harrold E. "Concerning Hester Bateman." Antiques 39 (February 1941): 76-77.

03197. Keys, Homer Eaton. "Hester Bateman, Silversmith." Antiques 20 (December 1931): 367-368.

03198. Shure, David. Hester Bateman: Queen of English Silversmiths. Garden City, N.Y.: Doubleday and Co., Inc., 1959.

03199. Walter, William. "New Light on Hester Bateman." Antiques 63 (January 1953): 36-39.

C. FRANCE

1. SURVEYS/BIBLIOGRAPHIES

"They [women] are an estate within the state."

Montesquieu

03200. Brehmer, Illse; Jacobi-Dittrich, Juliane; Kleinau, Elke; and Kuhn, Annette, eds. Frauen in der Geschichte IV "Wissen heisst leben ..." Beiträge zur Bildungsgeschichte von Frauen im 18. und 19. Jahrhundert. Geschichtsdidaktik, Studien Materialien, no. 18. Dusseldorf: Schwann, 1983.

03201. Ettori, Fernand. "La Découverte de la femme corse par les francais au XVIIIe siècle." In Femmes corses et femmes méditerranéennes, pp. 184-199. Provence: Centre d'Etudes Corses de l'Université de Provence, 1976.

03202. Jacobs, Eva et al., eds. Women and Society in Eighteenth Century France: Essays in Honour of John Stephenson Spink. Atlantic Highlands, N.J.: Humanities Press, 1979.

03203. Moses, Claire G. "Conclusion: The Legacy of the Eighteenth Century: A Look at the Future." In French Women and the Age of Enlightenment, edited by Samia I. Spencer, pp. 407-415. Bloomington, Indiana: Indiana University Press, 1984.

03204. Spencer, Samia I., ed. _French Women and the Age of Enlightenment_. Bloomington, Indiana: Indiana University Press, 1984.

2. POLITICAL

"The women reigned then."
Vigée LeBrun

a) Generic

03205. Conner, Susan P. "Sexual Politics and Citizenship: Women in Eighteenth-Century France." _Proceedings of the Tenth Annual Meeting of the Western Society for French History_ (1984): 264-273.

03206. __________. "Women and Politics." In _French Women and the Age of Enlightenment_, edited by Samia I. Spencer, pp. 49-63. Bloomington, Indiana: Indiana University Press, 1984.

b) Legal

03207. Castan, Nicole. _Justice et repression en Languedoc á l'époque des lumiéres_. Paris: Flammarion, 1980.

03208. Castan, Yves, "Ámor de luenh 'en Languedoc classique." In _Aimer en France 1760-1860_, edited by Paul Vialleneix and Jean Ehrard, 2: 445-452. 2 vols. Clermont-Ferrand: Association des Publications de la Faculté des Lettres et Sciences Humaines de Clermont-Ferrand, 1980.

03209. Rogers, Adrienne. "Women and the Law." In _French Women and the Age of Enlightenment_, edited by Samia I. Spencer, pp. 34-48. Bloomington, Indiana: Indiana University Press, 1984.

c) Criminal

03210. Castan, Nicole. _Les criminels de Languedoc, 1750-1790_. Toulouse: Association des publications de l'Université de Toulouse-Le Mirail, 1980.

03211. DePauw, Jacques. "Les filles-mères se marient-elles? L'example de Nantes au XVIIIe siècle." In _Aimer en France 1760-1860_, edited by Paul Vialleneix and Jean Ehrard, 2:525-531. 2 vols. Clermont-Ferrand: Association des Publications de la Faculté des Lettres et Sciences Humaines de Clermont-Ferrand, 1980.

03212. Gosselin, Louis Léon Théodore. _La Femme sans nom_. Paris: Perrin, 1925.

03213. Jeanfisher, Michèle. "Une erreur judiciaire. Le long martyre de Francoise Salmon." Historia 91 (June 1954): 743-750.

03214. Logette, Aline. "La Délinquance féminine devant la cour souveraine de Lorraine et Barrois." Annales de l'Est et du Nord 32 (1980): 133-160.

03215. Lüsebrink, Hans-Jürgen. "Les crimes sexuels dans les 'causes célèbres.'" XVIIIe siècle 12 (1980): 153-162.

03216. Millon, Patricia. "L'individu et la famille dans la région de Grasse, d'après les procedures criminelles de la Sénéchaussée (1748-1763)." Bulletin d'histoire économique et sociale de la Révolution francaise (1974): 43-62.

Also refer to #3314-3316.

d) Political Roles

1) Princess de Lamballe

03217. Decker, Michel de. La Princesses de Lamballe. Paris: Perrin, 1979.

03218. Flament, Albert. "Le destin de la Princesse de Lamballe." Historia 137 (April 1958): 415-423.

03219. Hardy, Blanche Christabel. The Princess de Lamballe: a Biography. New York: Appleton and Co., 1909.

03220. Sorel, Albert Emile. La princess de Lamballe, une amie de la Reine Maria-Antoinette. Paris: Hachette, 1933.

2) Marie Antoinette

03221. Asquith, Annunziata. Marie Antoinette. New York: Taplinger Publishers, 1976.

03222. Baumann, Emile. Marie-Antoinette et Axel Fersen. Paris: Crasset, 1931.

03223. Bernier, Olivier. The Secrets of Marie Antoinette. Garden City, NY: Doubleday, 1985.

03224. Blennerhassett, Charlotte Julia (von Leyden). Marie Antoinette, Königin von Frankreich. Bielefeld: Velhagen Klasing, 1917.

03225. Campan, I.-L.H. Genest, Mme. La Cour de Marie-Antoinette. Paris: Union générale d'éditions, 1971.

03226. Castelot, André. "La seconde prison de Madame Royale." Historia 368 (July 1977): 16-27.

03227. Coryn, M. Marie-Antoinette and Axel de Fersen. London: Butterworth, 1938.

03228. Cronin, Vincent. Louis and Antoinette. New York: Morrow, 1975.

03229. Furneaux, Rupert. The Last Days of Marie Antoinette and Louis XVI. New York: John Day Co., 1971.

03230. Girault de Coursac, Paul, and Girault de Coursac, Pierrette. "La vie conjugale de Louis XVI et Marie-Antoinette." Découverte 37 (1982): 3-25; 38 (1982): 3-30; 39 (1982): 13-45.

03231. Imbert de Saint-Armand, Arthur Léon. Les beaux jours de Marie Antoinette. Paris: E. Dentu, 1886.

03232. ________. La derniére année de Marie-Anntoinette. Paris: E. Dentu, 1888.

03233. Imbert de Saint-Armand, Arthur Léon. Marie Antoinette and the downfall of Royalty. Translated by Elizabeth Martin. New York: C. Scribner's Sons, 1906.

03234. ________. Marie Antoinette and the end of the old Regime. Translated by Thomas Sergeant Perry. New York: C. Scribner's Sons, 1892.

03235. Lescure, Mathurin Francois Adolphe de. La vraie Marie-Antoinette. Paris: Dupray de la Mahérie, 1863.

03236. Palache, John Garber. Marie Antoinette, the Player Queen. New York: Longmans, 1929.

03237. Ségur, Pierre Marie Maurice Henri, marquis de. Marie Antoinette. New York: E.P. Dutton and Company, 1928.

03238. Seward, Desmond. Marie Antoinette. London: Constable, 1981.

03239. Webster, Nesta. Marie-Antoinette intime. Paris: La Table ronde, 1981.

3) Madame de Pompadour

03240. Gallet, Danielle. Madame de Pompadour ou le pouvoir féminin. Paris: Fayard, 1985.

03241. Gordon, Katherine K. "Madame de Pompadour, Pigalle, and the Iconography of Friendship." Art Bulletin 50 (1968): 249-262.

03242. Labarre de Railicourt, D. "La 'petite chatte' ne veut pas trahir Mme de Pompadour." Historia 136 (March 1958): 262-264.

03243. Levron, Jacques. "Les débuts de Madame Pompadour." Historia 357 (December 1971): 102-113.

03244. Maurette, Marcelle. La Vie privée de Madame de Pompadour. Paris: Hachette, 1951.

Also refer to #3489.

4) The Regent

03245. Lescure, Mathurin Francois Adolphe. Les Maîtresses du Regent. Paris: E. Dentu, 1860.

03246. Ransan, André. "Le regent et ses maitresses." In Les Oeuvres libres, 206: 283-347. Paris: n.p., 1938.

03247. _________. La Vie privée du Régent. Paris: Hachette, 1938.

03248. Rat, Maurice. Les Femmes de la Régence. Paris: Berger-Levrault, 1961.

5) Others

03249. Andrieux, Maurice. Mademoiselle Aïssé. Paris: Plon, 1952

03250. Labracherie, Pierre. La Conspiration de Cellamare Paris: Del Duca, 1963.

03251. Levron, Jacques. Trois soeurs pour un roi ou la cour de Versailles au début du regne de Louis XV. Paris: Perrin, 1982.

03252. Maugras, Gaston. Le duc et la duchesse de Choiseul. Paris: Plon Nourrit et Cie., 1904.

03253. Stoeckl, Agnes (Barron) Baroness de. Mistress of Versailles: The Life of Madame du Barry. London: J. Murray, 1966.

03254. Stryienski, Casimir. La mère des trois derniers Bourbons, Marie-Josèphe de Saxe et la cour de Louis XV. Paris: Plon-Nourrit et Cie, 1902.

03255. Trouncer, Margaret. Madame Elizabeth; days at Versailles and in prison with Marie-Antoinette and her family. London: Hutchinson, 1955.

03256. Ward, Marion. The Du Barry Inheritance. New York: Crowell, 1968.

Also refer to #3484, 3491.

3. ECONOMIC

"Learn to know the value of money. This is a most essential point. The want of economy leads to the decay of powerful empires, as well as private families."
Jeanne Louise Campan

03257. Butel, Paul. "Comportements familiaux dans le négoce bordelais au XVIIIe siècle." Annales du Midi 88 (1976): 139-157.

03258. Fox-Genovese, Elizabeth. "Women and Work." In French Women and the Age of Enlightenment, edited by Samia I. Spencer, pp. 111-127. Bloomington, Indiana: Indiana University Press, 1984.

03259. Guignet, Phillippe. "The Lacemakers of Valenciennes in the Eighteenth Century: an Economic and Social Study of a Group of Female Workers under the Ancien Regime." Textile History 10 (1979): 96-113.

03260. Hafter, Daryl. "The Programmed Brocade Loom and the Decline of the Drawgirl." In Dynamos and Virgins Revisited, edited by Martha Moore Trescott, pp. 49-66. Metuchen, N.J.: Scarecrow Press, 1979.

03261. Hufton, Olwen. "Women, Work and Marriage in 18th century France." In Marriage and Society Studies in the Social History of Marriage, edited by R.B. Outhwaite, pp. 186-203. New York: St. Martin's Press, 1981.

03262. Lehning, James R. "Nuptuality and Rural Industry: Families and Labor in the French Countryside." Journal of Family History 8 (Winter 1983): 333-345.

03263. Maza, Sarah C. Servants and Masters in Eighteenth-Century France. Princeton: University Press, 1984.

03264. Poitrineau, Abel. "Communautés familiales agricoles et exploitation rurale en Berri et Auvergne au XVIIIe siècle: Point de vue économique et métaéconomique." Revue d' Auvergne 95 (1981): 41-51.

03265. Tarle, Evgenii Viktorovich. L'industrie dans les campagnes en France à la fin de l'ancien régime. Paris: E. Cornély et c[ie], 1910.

Also refer to #3302, 3304.

4. RELIGION

"Faith is a devout belief in what one does not understand."
Marie Anne du Deffand
Letter to d'Alembert

a) Generic

03266. Deprun, Jean. "'Pur amour' et supposition impossible chez quelques mystiques francais (1750-1850)." In Aimer en France 1760-1860, edited by Paul Vialleneix and Jean Ehrard, 2:323-329. 2 vols., Clermont-Ferrand: Association des Publications de la Faculté des Lettres et Sciences Humaines de Clermont-Ferrand, 1980.

03267. Graham, Ruth. "Women versus Clergy, Women pro Clergy." In French Women and the Age of Enlightenment, edited by Samia I Spencer, pp. 128-140. Bloomington, Indiana: Indiana University Press, 1984.

03268. Martin, Daniel. "Clergé et administration face à la débauche au XVIIIe siècle, l'exemple de l'Auvergne." In Aimer en France 1760-1860, edited by Paul Vialleneix and Jean Ehrard, 2: 461-469. 2 vols., Clermont-Ferrand: Association des Publications de la Faculté des Lettres et Sciences Humaines de Clermont-Ferrand, 1980.

03269. Queniart, J. Les hommes, l'église et dieu dans la France du XVIIIe siècle. Paris: Hachette, 1978.

03270. Vovelle, Michel. Piété baroque et déchristianisation en Provence au XVIIIe siècle. Paris: Seuil, 1978.

b) Jansenism

03271. Légier-Desgranges, Henry. Madame de Moysan et l'extravagante affaire de l'Hopital Général. 1749-1758: du jansénisme à la Révolution. Paris: Hachette, 1954.

Also refer to #2821.

c) Religious Orders

03272. Boquillon, Francoise. "Une carrière ecclésiastique féminin: Hyacinthe Céleste de Briery de Landres, chanoinesse de Remiremont (1731-1789)." Annales de l'Est n.s. 36 (1984): 3-15.

03273. __________. "Gabrielle de Spada, abbesse d'Epinal (1735-1784)." Annales de l'Est et du Nord 32 (1980): 243-258.

d) Canon Law

03274. Poitrineau, Abel. "Le mariage auvergnat, vu à travers les dispenses de consanguinité du diocése de Clermont, à la fin du XVIIIe siècle." In _Aimer en France 1760-1860_, edited by Paul Vialleneix and Jean Ehrard, 2: 435-444. 2 vols. Clermont-Ferrand: Association des Publications de la Faculté des Lettres et Sciences Humaines de Clermont-Ferrand, 1980.

5. SOCIAL

"And, indeed, where is the woman of delicacy and sensitivity who has not found misfortune in the very feeling [love] that promised her so much happiness? Do men ever appreciate the women they possess?"

Choderlos de Laclos
Les Liaisons Dangereuses

a) Generic

03275. Butel, Paul and Poussou, Jean-Pierre. _La vie quotidienne à Bordeaux au XVIIIe siècle_. Paris: Hachette, 1980.

03276. Castan, Nicole. "Inégalités sociales et différences de condition dans les liaisons amoureuses et les tentatives conjugales." In _Aimer en France 1760-1860_, edited by Paul Vialleneix and Jean Ehrard, 2: 513-524. 2 vols. Clermont-Ferrand: Association des Publications de la Faculté des Lettres et Sciences Humaines de Clermont-Ferrand, 1980.

03277. Chaussinand-Nogaret, Guy. _La noblesse au XVIIIe siècle_. Paris: Libraire Hachette, 1976.

03278. ________. _La vie quotidienne des francais sous Louis XV_. Paris: Hachette, 1979.

03279. Guibert, Elisabeth. "Barrières à l'amour, barrières à la circulation des richesses dans la société francaise d'Ancien Régime." In _Aimer en France 1760-1860_, edited by Paul Vialleneix and Jean Ehrard, 2: 453-459. 2 vols. Clermont-Ferrand: Association des Publications de la Faculté des Lettres et Sciences Humaines de Clermont-Ferrand, 1980.

03280. LeRoy Ladurie, Emmanuel. _Love, Death and Money in the Pays d'Oc_. London: Braziller, 1982.

03281. Meyer, Jean. _La noblesse bretonne au XVIIIe siècle_. Paris: S.E.V.P.E.N., 1966.

03282. Roche, Daniel. _Le peuple de Paris_. Paris: Aubier, 1981.

03283. Vialleneix, Paul and Ehrard, Jean, eds. Aimer en France 1760-1860. 2 vols. Clemont-Ferrand: Association des Publications de la Faculté des letres et Sciences Humaines de Clermont-Ferrand, 1980.

03284. Zoltowska, Maria Evelina. "Aimer en Pologne, mais à la francaise." In Aimer en France 1760-1860, edited by Paul Vialleneix and Jean Ehrard, 2: 541-552. 2 vols. Clermont-Ferrand: Association des Publications de la Faculté des Lettres et Sciences Humaines de Clermont-Ferrand, 1980.

Also refer to #2755, 2757, 2760.

b) Demography

03285. Deyon, P.-J. "A Propos des caractères démographiques de la Flandre rurale au XVIIIeme siècle." Revue du Nord 59 (1977): 101-103.

03286. Fine-Souriac, Agnès. "La limitation des naissances dans le sud ouest de la France. Fécondité allaitement et contraception au pays de Sault, au milieu du XVIIIe siècle à 1914." Annales du Midi 90 (April-June 1978): 155-188.

03287. Garden, Maurice. "L'attraction de Lyon à la fin de l'ancien regime." Annales de démographie historique 1970: 205-222.

03288. Lachiver, Marcel. "Une Étude et quelques esquisses." Annales de démographie historique 1969: 215-231.

03289. Lefebvre, Bernard and Thabaut, Louis. "Evolution démographique et développement industriel: Le Douaisis de 1750 à 1870." Revue du Nord 61 (1976): 165-169.

03290. Richards, Toni. "Weather, Nutrition and the Economy: Short-Run Fluctuations in Births, Deaths and Marriages, France 1740-1909." Demography 20 (May 1983): 197-212.

03291. Rollet, Catherine. "Varieté et mortalité des enfants au XVIIIe siècle." Cahiers d'histoire 23 (1978): 417-436.

03292. Terrisse, Michel. "Un Faubourg du Havre: Ingouville." Population 16 (April-June 1961): 285-300.

03293. Vincent, Paul E. "French Demography in the Eighteenth Century." Population Studies 1 (June 1947): 44-71.

Also refer to #2761-2766, 2678-2771.

c) Family

(1) Non-specific

03294. Augustin, Jean-Marie. Famille et société: Les substitutions fidei commissaires à Toulouse et en Haut-Languedoc au XVIIIe siècle. Paris: PUF, 1980.

03295. Denis, M. "Composition des familles à Bosselshausen au XVIIIe siècle." Revue des sciences sociales de la France de l'Est 7 (1978): 125-144.

03296. Fairchilds, Cissie. "Women and Family." In French Women and the Age of Enlightenment, edited by Samia I. Spencer, pp. 97-110. Bloomington, Indiana: Indiana University Press, 1984.

03297. Phillips, R. "Women's Emancipation, the Family and Social Change in Eighteenth Century France." Journal of Social History 12 (1979): 553-569.

03298. Scanlan, Timothy, M. "The Family as Depicted in the Encyclopédie." Trivium 14 (1979): 155-166.

Also refer to #2772-2776, 3359.

(2) Childhood

03299. Engrand, Charles. "Les abandons d'enfants à Amiens vers la fin de l'Ancien Régime." Revue du Nord 64 (January-March 1982): 73-92.

03300. Logette, Aline. "Naissances illégitimes en Lorraine dans la première moitié du XVIIIe siècle, d'après les déclarations de grossesses et la jurisprudence." Annales de l'Est 35 (1983): 91-126; 221-246.

03301. Pollet, Michelle. "Naissance illégitimes, filles-mères, et enfants trouvés à Grasse au XVIIIe siècle, 1751-1789." Bulletin d'Information de la Société de démographie historique 1979:5-21.

03302. Risler, Dominique. Nourrices et Meneurs de Paris au XVIIIe siècle. Paris: Bibliothèque Nationale microfiche, 1976.

03303. Senior, Nancy. "Aspects of Infant Feeding in Eighteenth-Century France." Eighteenth-Century Studies 16 (Summer 1983): 367-388.

03304. Sussman, George D. Selling Mother's Milk: Wet-Nursing Business in France 1715-1914. Urbana, Illinois: University of Illinois Press, 1982.

Also refer to #2772, 3259, 3262, 3264, 3422.

d) Marriage

03305. Flandrin, Jean-Louis. "Amour et mariage." Dix-huitième siècle 12 (1980): 163-176.

Also refer to #2761, 2762, 2769, 2778, 3261, 3262, 3274, 3290, 3359, 3436.

e) Sex Life and Morals

(1) Non-specific

03306. Brahimi, Denise. "La sexualité dans l'anthropologie humaniste de Buffon." XVIIIe siècle 12 (1980): 113-126.

03307. Delon, Michel. "La prétexte anatomique." XVIIIe siècle 12 (1980): 35-48.

03308. Goulemot, Jean Marie. "'Prêtons la main à la nature. . .' II. Fureurs utérines." XVIIIe siècle 12 (1980): 97-111.

03309. Guicciardi, Jean-Pierre. "Hermaphrodite et le prolétaire." XVIIIe siècle 12 (1980): 49-77.

03310. Masculin/Féminin: Discours sur le sexe et sexe du discours." In Aimer en France 1760-1860, edited by Paul Vialleneix and Jean Ehrard, 2: 295-306. 2 vols. Clermont-Ferrand: Association des Publications de la Faculté des Lettres et Sciences Humaines de Clermont-Ferrand, 1980.

03311. Peyronnet, Pierre. "Le péché philosophique." In Aimer en France 1760-1860, edited by Paul Vialleneix and Jean Ehrard, 2:471-478. 2 vols. Clermont-Ferrand: Association des Publications de la Faculté des Lettres et Sciences Humaines de Clermont-Ferrand, 1980.

03312. Tarczylo, Theodore. "'Prêtons la main à la nature. . .' I. L'Onanisme de Tisson." XVIIIe siècle 12 (1980): 79-96.

03313. Walter, Eric. "Le Complexe d'Abélard ou le célibat des gens de lettres." XVIIIe siècle 12 (1980): 127-152.

Also refer to #3362-3372, 3421, 3433, 3437, 3438.

(2) Prostitutes

03314. Aleil, Francois. "La prostitution à Clermont au XVIIIe siècle." In Aimer en France 1760-1860, edited by Paul Vialleneix and Jean Ehrard, 2:479-491. 2 vols. Clermont-Ferrand: Association des Publications de la Faculté des Lettres et Sciences Humaines de Clermont-Ferrand, 1980.

03315. Benabou, Erica-Marie. "'Amours vendues' à Paris à la fin de l'ancien régime: 'cleres libertins', police et prostituées." In Aimer en France 1760-1860, edited by Paul Vialleneix and Jean Ehrard, 2: 493-502. 2 vols. Clermont-Ferrand: Association des Publications de la Faculté des Lettres et Sciences Humaines de Clermont-Ferrand, 1980.

03316. Coward, D.A. "Restif de La Bretonne and the Reform of Prostitution." Studies on Voltaire and the Eighteenth Century 176 (1979): 343-383.

Also refer to #3045.

f) Fashions/Manners

03317. Bluche, Francois. "Quelques dates de costumes francais du XVIIIe siècle." Gazette des Beaux Arts 123 (November 1981): 151-154.

03318. Murphy, Michelle, ed. The Century of French Fashion. New York: Scribner's, 1950.

g) Health/Medical

03319. Birnbaum, Christine. "La vision médicale de l'amour dans l'Encyclopédie." In Aimer en France 1760-1860, edited by Paul Vialleneix and Jean Ehrard, 2: 307-314. 2 vols. Clermont-Ferrand: Association des Publications de la Faculté des Lettres et Sciences Humaines de Clermont-Ferrand, 1980.

03320. Hoffman, Paul. "Le discours médical sur les passions de l'amour, de Boissier de Sauvages à Pinel." In Aimer en France 1760-1860, edited by Paul Vialleneix and Jean Ehrard, 2: 345-356. 2 vols. Clermont-Ferrand: Association des Publications de la Faculté des Lettres et Sciences Humaines de Clermont-Ferrand, 1980.

03321. Jones, Colin and Sonenscher, Michael. "The Social Functions of the Hospital in Eighteenth Century France: The case of the Hôtel-Dieu of Nîmes." French Historical Studies 13 (Fall 1983): 172-214.

6. CULTURAL

"The bad education of women produces more evil than that of men...Women are unfortunately abandoned to themselves."

a) Generic

03322. Didier, Béatrice et al. "Le mot Amour." In _Aimer en France 1760-1860_, edited by Paul Vialleneix and Jean Ehrard, 1:117-129. 2 vols. Clermont-Ferrand: Association des Publications de la Faculté des Lettres et Science Humaines de Clermont-Ferrand, 1980.

03323. Runte, Roseann. "L'érotisme dévoilé ou l'autre côte de l'éventail." In _Aimer en France 1760-1860_, edited by Paul Vialleneix and Jean Ehrard, 1: 141-146. 2 vols. Clermont-Ferrand: Association des Publications de la Faculté des Lettres et Sciences Humaines de Clermont-Ferrand, 1980.

03324. ________. "Women as Muse." In _French Women and the Age of Enlightenment_, edited by Samia I. Spencer, pp. 143-154. Bloomington, Indiana: Indiana University Press, 1984.

Also refer to #2760.

b) Education

(1) Non-specific

03325. Fontainerie, de la F., ed. _French Liberalism and Education in the Eighteenth Century_. New York: McGraw Hill, 1932.

03326. Friedman, Leonard M. _Theories and Practices in the Education of Women during the Age of Enlightenment in France_. Pittsburgh: Chatham College, 1967.

03327. Laget, Mireille. "Petites écoles en Languedoc au XVIIIe siècle. "_Annales: économies, sociétés, civilisations_ 26 (1971): 1398-1418.

03328. Perrel, Jean. "Les écoles des filles dans la France d'Ancien Régime." _Historical Reflections_ 7 (Summer-Fall 1980): 75-84.

03329. Spencer, Samia I. "Women and Education." In _French Women and the Age of Enlightenment_, edited by Samia I. Spencer, pp. 83-96. Bloomington, Indiana: Indiana University Press, 1984.

03330. ________. "Women and Education in Eighteenth-Century France." _Proceedings of the Tenth Annual Meeting of the Western Society for French History_ 1984: 274-284.

03331. Viglieno, Laurence. "Le thème de l'education sentimentale.'" In Aimer en France, 1760-1860, edited by Paul Vialleneix and Jean Ehrard, 1: 131-139. 2 vols. Clermont-Ferrand: Association des Publications de la Faculté des Lettres et Sciences Humaines de Clermont-Ferrand, 1980.

(2) Individuals

[a] Madame de Genlis

03332. Diesbach, Ghislain de. "Madame de Genlis." Historia 409 (December 1980): 62-76.

03333. Grosperrin, Bernard. "Un manuel d'éducation noble "Adèle et Théodore" de Madame de Genlis." Cahiers d'historie 19 (1974): 343-352.

03334. Wyndham, Violet. Madame de Genlis: a Biography. London: Deutsch, 1958.

[b] Choderlos de Laclos

03335. Guetti, Barbara. "The Old Regime and the Feminist Revolution: Laclos' De l'education des femmes.'" Yale French Studies 63 (1983): 139-162.

03336. Laclos, Pierre Ambroise Francois de Choderlos. "De l'éducation des femmes, discours sur la question proposée par l'Académie de Châlons-sur-Marne; 'Quels seraient les meilleurs moyens de perfectionner l'éducation des femmes." In Oeuvres complètes pp. 427-482. Paris: Gallimard, 1951.

[c] Others

03337. Lambert, Mme. de. "Avis d'une mère à sa fille." In Oeuvres morales de Mme de Lambert, pp. 65-107. Paris: Librairie de Charles Gosselin, 1843.

03338. Montagu, Violette M. The Celebrated Madame Campan. Philadelphia, Pa.: J.B. Lippincott, 1914.

Also refer to #3443, 3445, 3447, 3448, 3452, 3455, 3462-3465.

c) Literature

(1) Non-specific

03339. Lee, Vera G. "The Edifying Examples." In French Women and the Age of Enlightenment, edited by Samia I. Spencer, pp. 345-354. Bloomington, Indiana: Indiana University Press, 1984.

03340. Runte, Roseann. "The Matron of Ephesus in Eighteenth-Century France: The Lady and the Legend." Studies in Eighteenth Century Culture 6 (1977): 361-375.

03341. Swiderski, Marie-Laure. "L'amour interdit ou la femme entre 'nature' et condition féminines." In Aimer en France 1760-1860, edited by Paul Vialleneix and Jean Ehrard, 1: 147-156. 2 vols. Clermont-Ferrand: Association des Publications de la Faculté des Lettres et Sciences Humaines de Clermont-Ferrand, 1980.

03342. Thomson, Ann. "L'art de jouir De La Mettrie à Sade." In Aimer en France 1760-1860, edited by Paul Vialleneix and Jean Ehrard, 2: 315-322. 2 vols. Clermont-Ferrand: Association des Publications de la Faculté des Lettres et Sciences Humaines de Clermont-Ferrand, 1980.

Also refer to #3067, 3069.

(2) Drama

[a] Women in Drama

[1] Marivaux

03343. Conroy, Peter V. Jr. "Marivaux's Feminist Polemic: La Colonie." Eighteenth-Century Life. n.s. 1 (1980): 43-66.

03344. Didier, Béatrice. "Structures temporelles dans la Vie de Marianne." Revue des sciences humaines n.s. 182 (April-June 1981): 99-113.

03345. Rossat-Mignod, Suzanne. "Les femmes chez Marivaux." Europe 427-428 (November-December 1964): 47-56.

03346. Trott, David A. "Des 'Amours déguisés' à la seconde 'Surprise de l'Amour': étude sur les avatars d'un lieu commun." Revue d'histoire littéraire de la France 76 (May-June 1976): 373-384.

03347. Whatley, Janet. "L'âge equivoque: Marivaux and the Middle-Aged Woman." University of Toronto Quarterly 46 (Fall 1976): 68-82.

03348. ________. "Nun's Stories: Marivaux and Diderot." Diderot Studies 20 (1981): 299-319.

Also refer to #3137.

[b] Women Dramatists

03349. Willen, Carol Kleiner. "Giving Madam Denis Her Due: The Mistaken Attribution of La Coquette punie." Harvard Library Bulletin 27 (1979): 192-208.

(3) Prose

(a) Novels

[1] Women in Novels

((a)) Non-specific

03350. Fein, P.L.-M. "The Role of Women in Certain Eighteenth-Century French libertin Novels." Studies on Voltaire and the Eighteenth Century 193 (1980): 1925-1932.

03351. Rustin, Jacques. "Idées sur les romans francais de l'année 1760 considérés du point de vue de l'amour." In Aimer en France 1760-1860, edited by Paul Vialleneix and Jean Erhard, 1: 159-167. 2 vols. Clermont-Ferrand: Association des Publications de la Faculté des Lettres et Sciences Humaines de Clermont-Ferrand, 1980.

03352. Simmons, Sarah. "Héroîne ou figurante? La femme dans le roman du XVIIIe siècle en France." Studies on Voltaire and the Eighteenth Century 193 (1980): 1918-1924.

03353. Tanner, Tony. Adultery in the Novel: Contract and Transgression. Baltimore: Johns Hopkins University Press, 1979.

03354. Thomas, Ruth P. "The Death of an Ideal: Female Suicides in the Eighteenth-Century French Novel." In French Women and the Age of Enlightenment, edited by Samia I. Spencer, pp. 321-331. Bloomington, Indiana: Indiana University Press, 1984.

Also refer to #3092.

((b)) Individuals

[[1]] Choderlos de Laclos

03355. Diaconoff, Suellen. Eros and Power in Les Liaisons dangereuses: A Study in Evil. Geneva: Droz, 1979.

03356. Hudon, E. Sculley. "Love and Myth in Les Liaisons dangereuses." Yale French Studies 11 (1953): 25-38.

03357. Stackelberg, Jürgen von. "Le féminisme de Laclos." In Themes et Figures du siècle des Lumières, edited by Raymond Trousson, pp. 271-284. Geneva: Libraire Droz, 1980.

[[2]] Antoine Francois Prévost

03358. Gossman, Lionel. "Prévost's Manon: Love in the New World." Yale French Studies 40 (1968): 91-102.

03359. Guiot, Jacqueline. "Images de la famille et du mariage étudiés d'après le vocabulaire de romans de l'abbé Prévost." In _Etudes sur le XVIIIe siècle_, edited by Jean Erhard, pp. 71-85. Clermont-Ferrand: Asociation pour les Publications de la Faculté des Lettres et Sciences Humaines, 1979.

03360. Lazzaro-Weis, Carol. "Feminism, Parody and Characterization in Prévost: The Example of the _Doyen de Killerine_." _Studies in Eighteenth-Century Culture_ 13 (1984): 143-154.

03361. Rabine, Leslie W. "History, Ideology, and Femininity in _Manon Lescaut_." _Stanford French Review_ 5 (1981): 65-83.

[[3]] Marquis de Sade

03362. Carter, Angela. _The Sadeian Woman and the Ideology of Pornography_. New York: Pantheon Books, 1978.

03363. Crocker, Lester G. "Au Coeur de la pensée de Sade. . ." In _Themes et Figures du siècle des lumières_, edited by Raymond Trousson, pp. 59-71. Geneva: Droz, 1980.

03364. Gallop, Jean. "The Immoral Teachers." _Yale French Studies_ 63 (1983): 117-128.

03365. Giraud, Raymond. "The First _Justine_." _Yale French Studies_ 35 (1965): 39-47.

03366. Klossowski, Pierce. "A Destructive Philosophy." _Yale French Studies_ 35 (1965): 61-79.

03367. Laborde, Alice M. "The Problem of Sexual Equality in Sadean Prose." In _French Women and the Age of Enlightenment_, edited by Samia I. Spencer, pp. 332-344. Bloomington, Indiana: Indiana University Press, 1984.

03368. __________. "Sade: La Dialectique du regard dans _La Marquise de Grange_." _Romanic Review_ 60 (February 1969): 47-53.

03369. McMahon, Joseph H. "Where Does Real Life Begin?" _Yale French Studies_ 35 (1965): 96-113.

03370. Pastoureau, Henri. "Sado-Masochism and the Philosophies of Ambivalence." _Yale French Studies_ 35 (1965): 48-60.

03371. Spruell, Shelby. "The Marquis de Sade-Pornography or Political Protest?" _Proceedings of the Western Society for French History_ 9 (1981): 238-249.

03372. Taylor, Robert E. "The SEXpressive S in Sade and Sartre." _Yale French Studies_ 11 (1953): 18-24.

Also refer to #3307.

[2] Women Novelists

((a)) Non-specific

03373. Stewart, Joan Hinde. "The Novelists and Their Fictions." In *French Women and the Age of Enlightenment*, edited by Samia I. Spencer, pp. 197-211. Bloomington, Indiana: Indiana University Press, 1984.

((b)) Individuals

[[1]] Isabelle de Charrière

03374. Courtney, C.P. *A Preliminary Bibliography of Isabelle Charrière Belle de Zuylen*. Oxfordshire: Cheney and Sons, 1980.

03375. Deguise, Alix. *Trois Femmes. Le Monde de Madame de Charrière*. Geneva: Editions Slatkine, 1981.

03376. Didier, Béatrice. "La femme à la recherche de son image: Mme de Charrière et l'écriture féminine dans la seconde moitié du XVIIIe siècle." *Studies on Voltaire and the Eighteenth Century* 193 (1980): 1981-1988.

03377. _________. "La nourriture dans les romans d'Isabelle de Charrière." *XVIIIe siècle* 15 (1983): 187-197.

03378. Farum, Dorothy. *The Dutch Divinity: A Biography of Madame de Charrière, 1740-1805*. London: Jarrolds, 1959.

03379. Kimstedt, Charlotte. *Frau von Charrière (1740-1805), ihre Gedankenwelt und ihre Beziehungen zur französischen und deutschen Literaturd*. Berlin: E. Eberling, 1938.

03380. Riccioli, Giovanni. *L''ésprit' di Madame de Charrière*. Bari: Adriatica Editrice, 1967.

[[2]] Marie Jeanne Riccoboni

03381. André, Arlette. "Le féminisme chez Madame Riccoboni." *Studies on Voltaire and the Eighteenth Century* 193 (1980): 1988-1995.

03382. Demay, Andrée. *Marie-Jeanne Riccoboni. De la pensée féministe chez une romancière du 18e siècle*. Paris: La Pensée Universelle, 1977.

03383. Piau, Collette. "L'écriture féminine? A propos de Marie-Jeanne Riccoboni." *XVIIIe siècle* 16 (1984): 369-385.

03384. Stewart, Joan-Hinde. "Aimer à soixante ans: les lettres de Madame Riccoboni à Sir Liston." In Aimer en France 1760-1860, edited by Paul Vialleneix and Jean Ehrard, 1: 181-189. 2 vols. Clermont-Ferrand: Association des Publications de la Faculté des Lettres et Sciences Humaines de Clermont-Ferrand, 1980.

(b) Periodicals

03385. Rimbaud, Caroline. "La presse féminine de langue francaise au XVIIIème siècle." In Le Journalisme d'Ancien Régime, edited by Pierre Retat, pp. 199-216. Lyons: Presses Universitaires de Lyon, 1982.

03386. Sullerot, Evelyne. "Lectrices et interlocutrices." Europe 427-428 (November-December 1964): 194-203.

03387. Van Dijk, Suzanne. "Femmes et journaux au XVIIIe siècle." Australian Journal of French Studies 18 (1981): 164-178.

03388. Wilkins, Kay. "Attitudes toward Women in Two Eighteenth-Century French Periodicals." Studies in Eighteenth Century Culture 6 (1977): 393-406.

d) Literary Salons

(1) Non-specific

03389. Clergue, Helen. The Salon: A Study of French Society and Personalities in the Eighteenth Century. New York: B. Franklin, 1971.

03390. Diderot, Denis. Salons. Vol. II: 1765. 2nd ed. Edited by Jean Seznec. Oxford: Clarendon Press, 1979.

03391. Foucaux, Marie. Quelques Salons de Paris au XVIIIe siècle. Paris: Société francaise d'editions d'art, 1898.

Also refer to #2828.

(2) Individuals

[a] Marie Anne du Deffand

03392. Claro, Elme-Marie. "Deux Types de femmes de l'autre siècle: Mme du Deffand, Mme Roland." Revue des deux mondes 92 (15 March, 1871): 256-273.

03393. Craveri, Benedetta. "Mme Du Deffand e Mme de Choiseul: un 'amicizia femminile'." Studies on Voltaire and the Eighteenth Century 193 (1980): 1956-1963.

[b] Madame de Graffigny

03394. Dainard, J.A. et al. "La correspondance de Madame de Graffigny." XVIIIe siècle 10 (1978): 379-395.

03395. Showalter, English, Jr. "The Beginnings of Madame de Graffigny's Literary Career: A Study in the Social History of Literature." In Essays on the Age of Enlightenment in Honor of Ira O. Wade, edited by Jean Macary, pp. 293-304. Geneva: Droz, 1977.

03396. ________. "Madame de Graffigny and Her Salon." Studies in Eighteenth Century Culture 6 (1977): 377-391.

03397. ________. Madame de Graffigny and Rousseau: Between the Two Discourses. No. 175 of Studies on Voltaire and the Eighteenth Century. Oxford: Voltaire Foundation, 1978.

[c] Julie de Lespinasse

03398. Castries, René de La Croix, duc de. Julie de Lespinasse: le drame d'un double amour. Paris: A. Michel, 1985.

03399. Dupont, Jacques. "De l'absence au chant. Sur les lettres à Guibert de Madame de Lespinasse." XVIIIe siècle 10 (1978): 395-404.

03400. Lacouture, Jean and Aragon, Marie Christine d'. Julie de Lespinasse: mourir d'amour. Paris: Ramsay, 1980.

03401. Pascal, Jean-Noël. "Une exemplaire mort d'amour, Julie de Lespinasse." In Aimer en France 1760-1860, edited by Paul Vialleneix and Jean Ehrard, 2: 553-563. 2 vols. Clermont-Ferrand: Association des Publications de la Faculté des Lettres et Sciences Humaines de Clermont-Ferrand, 1980.

03402. ________. "La rêve d'amour de d'Alembert." XVIIIe siècle 16 (1984): 163-170.

[d] Susan Necker

03403. Gambier-Parry, Mark. Madame Necker, Her Family and Her Friends, with some Account of Her Husband's Three Administrations. Edinburgh: W. Blackwood and Sons, 1913.

03404. Haussonville, Gabriel Paul Othenin de Cléron, comte d'. The Salon of Madame Necker. New York: Funk and Co., 1880.

[e] Others

03405. Herpin, Clara Adele Luce and Maugras, Gaston. Une femme du monde au XVIIIe siècle, 2 vols. Paris: Calmann Lévy, 1882, 1884.

03406. Masson, Pierre-Maurice. Madame de Tencin. (1682-1749) 1909. Reprint. Geneva: Slatkine, 1970.

03407. Parker, Alice. "Louise d'Epinay's Account of Female Epistemology and Sexual Politics." French Review 55 (1981): 43-51.

03408. Valentino, Henri. Mme. Epinay: Une femme d'esprit sous Louis XV. Paris: Perrin. 1952.

e) Intellectuals

(1) Enlightenment

(a) Non-specific

03409. Delon, Michel. "La Marquise et le philosophe." Revue des sciences humaines n.s. 182 (April-June 1981): 65-78.

03410. Dock, Terry Smiley. "The Encyclopédists' Woman." Proceedings of the Tenth Annual Meeting of the Western Society for French History 1984: 255-263.

03411. Malueg, Sara Ellen Procious. "Women and the Encyclopédie." In French Women and the Age of Enlightenment, edited by Samia I. Spencer, pp. 259-271. Bloomington, Indiana: Indiana University Press, 1984.

Also refer to #3298, 3319.

(b) Individuals

[1] Diderot

03412. Benrekassa, Georges. "L'article 'Jouissance' et l'idéologie érotique de Diderot." XVIIIe siècle 12 (1980): 9-34.

03413. Brady- Papadopoulou, Valentini. "Separation, Death and Sexuality: Diderot's La Religieuse and Rites of Initiation." Studies on Voltaire and the Eighteenth Century 190-193 (1980): 1199-1205.

03414. Chariter, Pierre. "Asmodée ou l'effraction." XVIIIe siècle 12 (1980): 209-218.

03415. Diderot, Denis. Ceci n'est pas un conte. Oeuvres complètes, 10: 151-171. Paris: Le club francais du livre, 1971.

03416. Diderot, Denis. Madame de La Carlière. Ouvres complètes, 10: 173-195. Paris: Le club francais du livre, 1971.

03417. _________. Le Rêve de d'Alembert. Oeuvres complètes, 8: 55-162. Paris: Le club francais du Livre, 1971.

03418. _________. Sur les femmes. Ouevres complètes, 10: 37-53. Paris: Le club francais du livre, 1971.

03419. Duchet, Michèle. "Du sexe des livres, à propos de l'essai Sur les Femmes de Diderot." Revue des sciences humaines 168 (October-December 1977): 525-536.

03420. Edmiston, William F. "Sacrifice and Innocence in La Religieuse." Diderot Studies 19 (1978): 67-84.

03421. Feigenbaum-Knox, Rena. "Aesthetics and Ethics: A Study of Sexuality in Denis Diderot's Art Criticism." Proceedings of the Western Society for French History 9 (1981): 226-237.

03422. Fellows, Otis. "The Facets of Illegitimacy in the French Enlightenment." Diderot Studies 20 (1981): 77-98.

03423. Hoffmann, Paul. "La Beauté de la femme selon Diderot." Dix-huitiéme siécle 9 (1977): 273-389.

03424. Laborde, Alice M. "Diderot: Amour et propriété." Stanford French Review 1 (1977): 367-378.

03425. _________. Diderot et l'amour. Saratoga, CA: Anna Libri, 1979.

03426. Leutrat, Jean-Louis. "L'histoire de Madame de la Pommeraye et le theme de la jeune veuve." Diderot Studies 18 (1975): 121-137.

03427. Lloyd, Caryl. "Illusion and Seduction: Diderot's Rejection of Traditional Authority in Works prior to Le Neveu de Rameau." Studies on Voltaire and the Eighteenth Century 228 (1984): 179-193.

03428. McLaughlin, Blandine L. "Diderot and Women." In French Women and the Age of Enlightenment, edited by Samia I. Spencer, pp. 296-308. Bloomington, Indiana: Indiana University Press, 1984.

03429. Rosso, Jeanette Geffriaud. "Jacques le fataliste": L'Amour et son image. Pisa: Libreria Goliardica Editrice, 1981.

03430. Russell, Lois Ann. "Challe and Diderot: Tales in Defense of Women." Proceedings of the Western Society for French History 9 (1981): 216-225.

03431. Sfragaro, Adriana. "La représentation de la femme chez Diderot." Studies on Voltaire and the Eighteenth Century 193 (1980): 1893-1899.

03432. Steinbrügge, Lieselotte. "Die Aufteilung der Menschen. Zur anthropologischen Bestimmung der Frau in Diderots Encyclopédie." In Frauen in der Geschichte IV, edited by Ilse Brehmer et.al., pp. 51-64. Düsseldorf: Schwann, 1983.

03433. Vartanian, Aram. "La Mettrie, Diderot, and Sexology in the Enlightenment." In Essays on the Age of the Enlightenment in Honor of Ira O. Wade, edited by Jean Macary, pp. 347-367. Geneva: Droz, 1977.

Also refer to #3207, 3348, 3390.

[2] Montesquieu

03434. Hunwick, Andrew. "Les femmes d'Usbeck et la Lettre persane XLVII." XVIIIe siècle 11 (1979): 427-428.

03435. Kra, Pauline. "Montesquieu and Women." In French Women and the Age of Enlightenment, edited by Samia I. Spencer, pp. 272-284. Bloomington, Indiana: Indiana University Press, 1984.

03436. Shanley, Mary Lyndon and Stillman, Peter G. "Political and Marital Despotism: Montesquieu's Persian Letters." In The Family in Political Thought, edited by Jean Bethke Elshtain, pp. 66-79. Amherst, Mass.: University of Massachusetts Press, 1982.

03437. Spruell, Shelby O. "The Metamorphical Use of Sexual Repression to Represent Political Oppression in Montesquieu's Persian Letters." Proceedings of the Annual Meeting of the Western Society for French History 8 (1980): 147-158.

03438. Vartanian, Aram. "Eroticism and Politics in the Lettres persanes." Romanic Review 60 (February 1969): 23-33.

03439. Yeatman, Anna. "Despotism and Civil Society: The Limits of Patriarchal Citizenship." In Women's Views of the Political World of Men, edited by Judith Hicks Stiehm, pp. 151-176. Dobbs Ferry, NY: Transnational Publishers Inc., 1984.

[3] Rousseau

03440. Aimery de Pierrebourg, Marguerite. Jean-Jacques Rousseau et les femmes. Paris: n.p. 1934.

03441. Blanc, André. "Le Jardin de Julie." XVIIIe siècle 14 (1982): 357-376.

03442. Christenson, Ron. "The Political Theory of Male Chauvinism: J.J. Rousseau's Paradigm." Midwest Quarterly 13 (Spring 1972): 291-299.

03443. DeJean, Joan. "La Nouvelle Héloïse, or the Case for Pedagogical Deviation." Yale French Studies 63 (1983): 98-116.

03444. Duckworth, Colin. "Georgiana Spencer in France: Or the Dangers of Reading Rosseau." Eighteenth-Century Life 7 (May 1983): 85-91.

03445. Ehrard, Jean. "Le Corps de Julie." In Themes et Figures du siècle des Lumières, edited by Raymond Trousson, pp. 95-106. Geneva: Droz, 1980.

03446. Ellis, Havelock. "Madame de Warens." Virginia Quarterly Review 9 (July 1933): 410-432.

03447. Garbe, Christine. "Sophie oder die heimliche Macht der Frauen. Zur Konzeption des Weiblichen bei J.-J. Rousseau." In Frauen in der Geschichte IV, edited by Ilse Brehmer et.al., pp. 65-87. Düsseldorf: Schwann, 1983.

03448. Hall, H. Gaston. "The Concept of Virtue in La Nouvelle Héloïse." Yale French Studies 28 (1961): 20-33.

03449. Lange, Lydia. "Rousseau: Women and the General Will." In The Sexism of Social and Political Theory: Women and Reproduction from Plato to Nietzsche, edited by M.G. Clark and Lydia Lange, pp. 41-52. Toronto: University Press, 1979.

03450. McMahon, Joseph H. "Madame de Warens." Yale French Studies 28 (1961): 97-105.

03451. Manfredi, G. L'Amore e gli amore in J.J. Rousseau, teorie della sessualità. Milan: Mazotta, 1978.

03452. Martin, Jane Roland. "Sophie and Emile: A Case Study of Sex Bias in the History of Educational Thought." Harvard Educational Review 51 (August 1981): 357-372.

03453. May, Gita. "Rousseau's 'Antifeminism' Reconsidered." In French Women and the Age of Enlightenment, edited by Samia I. Spencer, pp. 309-317. Bloomington, Indiana: Indiana University Press, 1984.

03454. Mead, William. "La Nouvelle Héloïse and the Public of 1761." Yale French Studies 28 (1961): 13-19.

03455. Misenheimer, Helen Evans. Rousseau on the Education of Women. Washington, D.C.: University Press of America, 1981.

03456. Monglond, Andrè. "Le Journal des Charmettes." Revue des deux mondes 8th ser. 14 (15 April 193): 896-926.

03457. Mugnier, Francois. Madame de Warens et Jean-Jacques Rosseau. Paris: Calmann-Lévy, 1891.

03458. Osmont, Robert. "Expérience vécue et création romanesque. Le sentiment de l'éphémére dans la _Nouvelle Helöise_." _XVIII^e siècle_ 7 (1975): 225-242.

03459. ________. "J.J. Rosseau and the Idea of Love." _Yale French Studies_ 28 (1961): 43-47.

03460. Piau-Gillot, Collette. "Le discours de Jean-Jacques Rousseau sur les femmes et sa réception critique." _XVIII^e siècle_ 13 (1981): 317-333.

03461. Schwartz, Joel. _The Sexual Politics of Jean-Jacques Rousseau_. Chicago: University of Chicago Press, 1984.

03462. Senior, Nancy. "Sophie and the State of Nature." _French Forum_ 2 (1977): 134-146.

03463. Tanner, Tony. "Julie and 'La Maison Paternellei: Another Look at Rousseau's _La Nouvelle Hélöise_." In _The Family in Political Thought_, edited by Jean Bethke Elshtain, pp. 96-124. Amherst, Mass: University of Massachussetts Press, 1982.

03464. Therrien, Madeleine B. "Morale sociale et éthique personnelle dans _La Nouvelle Héloïse_." _Revue des sciences humaines_ no. 161 (1976): 97-108.

03465. Vance, Christie. "_La Nouvelle Héloïse_: the Language of Paris." _Yale French Studies_ 45 (1970): 127-136.

[4] Voltaire

03466. Adams, D.J. _La femme dans les contes et les romans de Voltaire_. Paris: Nizet, 1974.

03467. Calin, William. "Love and War: Comic Themes in Voltaire's Pucelle." _French Forum_ 2 (1977): 34-46.

03468. Desvignes, Lucette. "Le théâtre de Voltaire et la femme victime." _Revue des sciences humaines_ n.s. 168 (October-December 1977): 537-551.

03469. Filstrup, Jane Merrill. "Cunégonde and Other Loathely Ladies." _Dalhousie Review_ 59 (1979): 239-249.

03470. Russo, Gloria M. "Voltaire and Women." In _French Women and the Age of Enlightenment_, edited by Samia I. Spencer, pp. 285-295. Bloomington, Indiana: Indiana University Press, 1984.

03471. Vaillot, René. _Madame du Châtelet_. Paris: A. Michel, 1978.

Also refer to #3349.

[5] Others

03472. Brookes, Barbara. "The Feminism of Condorcet and Sophie de Gouchy." Studies on Voltaire and the Eighteenth Century 189 (1980): 297-361.

03473. Bruit, Guy. "Restif de la Bretonne et les femmes." La Pensée 131 (January - February 1967): 117-126.

03474. Chadourne, Marc. "Eros and Restif." Yale French Studies 11 (1953): 12-17.

03475. Curtis, Judith. "The Epistolières." In French Women and the Age of Enlightenment, edited by Samia I. Spencer, pp. 226-241. Bloomington, Indiana: Indiana University Press, 1984.

03476. Fassioto, Mari-Jose. Madame de Lambert, 1647-1733, ou le féminisme moral. New York: P. Lang, 1985.

03477. Forno, Lawrence J. "Challe's Portrayal of Women." French Review 47 (April 1974): 865-873.

03478. Guillot, Gérard. "Restif de la Bretonne par et pour les femmes." Europe 427-428 (November-December 1964): 56-65.

03479. Hartman, Lydia-Claude. "A propos de Sophie Volland." Diderot Studies 12 (1969): 75-102.

03480. Kinsey, Susan R. "The Memorialists." In French Women and the Age of Enlightenment, edited by Samia I. Spencer, pp. 212-225. Bloomington, Indiana: Indiana University Press, 1984.

03481. Leroy Ladurie, Emmanuel. "Le Socialisme en familles." Cahiers Renaud Barrault 90 (1975): 19-22.

03482. Williams, David. "Boudier de Villemert: 'philosopher of the fair sex.'" Studies on Voltaire and the Eighteenth Century 193 (1980): 1899-1901.

03483. __________. "The Fate of French Feminism: Boudier de Villemert's Ami des Femmes." Eighteenth Century Studies 14 (Fall 1980): 37-55.

f) Art

(1) Women in Art

03484. Biebel, Franklin M. "Fragonard and Madame du Barry." Gazette des Beaux Arts 102 no. 2 (October 1960): 207-226.

03485. Cailleux, Jean. "Who was Boucher's Best Beloved?" Burlington Magazine 108 Supplement (February 1966): i-vi.

03486. Guicciardi, Jean-Pierre. "Formes et représentations de l'amour dans les livrets d'opéras (France, deuxième moitié du XVIIIe siècle)." In Aimer en France (1760-1860, edited by Paul Vialleneix and Jean Ehrard, 1: 169-180. 2 vols. Clermont-Ferrand: Association de Publications de la Faculté des Lettres et Sciences Humaines de Clermont-Ferrand, 1980.

03487. Guillerm, Alain. "Le système de l'iconographie galante." XVIIIe siècle 12 (1980): 177-194.

03488. Le Coat, Gérard. "La fonction dialectique de la représentation animale dans la peinture galante pré-révolutionnaire." In Aimer en France 1760-1860, edited by Paul Vialleneix and Jean Ehrard, 1: 45-53. 2 vols. Clermont-Ferrand: Association des Publications de la Faculté des Lettres et Sciences Humaines de Clermont-Ferrand, 1980.

03489. McInnes, Ian. Painter, King and Pompadour: Francois Boucher at the Court of Louis XV. London: F. Muller, 1965.

03490. Pupil, Francois. "Représentation de l'amour troubadour." In Aimer en France 1760-1860, edited by Paul Vialleneix and Jean Ehrard, 1: 57-65. 2 vols. Clermont-Ferrand: Association des Publications de la Faculté des Lettres et Sciences Humaines de Clermont-Ferrand, 1980.

03491. Roland-Michel, Marianne. "Fragonard illustrateur de l'amour." In Aimer en France 1760-1860, edited by Paul Vialleneix and Jean Ehrard, 1: 25-32. 2 vols. Clermont-Ferrand: Association des Publications de la Faculté des Lettres et Sciences Humaines de Clermont-Ferrand, 1980.

03492. Snoep-Reitsma, E. "Chardin and the Bourgeois Ideals of his time." Nederlands Kunsthistorisch Jaarboek 24 (1973): 153-156, 176-198, 219-229.

03493. Stewart, Philip. "Décence et dessin." In Aimer en France 1760-1860, edited by Paul Vialleneix and Jean Ehrard, 1: 35-43. 2 vols. Clermont-Ferrand: Association des Publications de la Faculté des Lettres et Sciences Humaines de Clermont-Ferrand, 1980.

(2) Women Artists

(a) Actresses/Dancers

03494. Avery, Emmett. "Two French Children on the English Stage." Philological Quarterly 73 (January 1934): 78-82.

03495. Beaumont, Cyril W. Three French dancers of the 18th century: Camargo, Sallé, Guimard London: Beaumont, 1934.

03496. Douglas, Robert Bruce. Sophie Arnould, Actress and Wit. Paris: C. Carrington, 1898.

03497. Dussane, Beatrix. Sophie Arnould: la plus spirituelle des bacchantes. Paris: A. Michel, 1938.

03498. Mittman, Barbara G. "Women and the Theatre Arts." In French Women and the Age of Enlightenment, edited by Samia I. Spencer, pp. 155-169. Bloomington, Indiana: Indiana University Press, 1984.

(b) Musicians

03499. Rempel, Ursula M. "Women and Music: Ornament of the Profession?" In French Women and the Age of Enlightenment, edited by Samia I. Spencer, pp. 170-180. Bloomington, Indiana: Indiana University Press, 1984.

(c) Painters/Sculptors

[1] Marie-Anne Collot

03500. Cournault, Charles. "Etienne-Maurice Falconet et Marie-Anne Collot." Gazette des Beaux-Arts 2nd ser. 2(1869): 117-144.

03501. Kosareva, Nina. "Masterpieces of Eighteenth-Century French Sculpture." Apollo 101 (June 1975): 446-447.

03502. Opperman, H.N. "Marie-Anne Collot in Russia: Two Portraits." Burlington Magazine 107 (August 1965): 408-415.

03503. Reau, Louis. "Les bustes de Marie-Anne Collot." Renaissance 14 (November 1931): 306-312.

03504. ________. "Une femme-sculpteur francaise au dix-huitième siècle, Marie-Anne Collot (Madame Falconet)." L'Art et les artistes (February 1923): 165-171.

[2] Adélaide Labille-Guiard

03505. Cailleux, Jean. "Royal Portraits of Mme. Vigée-LeBrun and Mme. Labille Guiard." The Burlington Magazine 3 supplement (March 1969): iii-vi.

03506. Passez, Anne Marie. Adélaide Labille-Guiard: biographie et catalogue raisonné de son oeuvre. Paris: Arts et métiers graphiques 1973.

03507. Portalis, Baron Roger. Adélaide Labille-Guiard (1749-1803). Paris: Georges Petit, 1902.

Also refer to #3525.

[3] Anne Vallayer-Coster

03508. Roland Michel, Marianne. "A Basket of Plums." Cleveland Museum Bulletin 60 (February 1973): 52-59.

03509. ________. Anne Vallayer-Coster 1744-1818. Paris: C.I.L., 1970.

03510. ________. "A propos d'un tableau retrouvé de Vallayer-Coster." Bulletin de la société de l'histoire de l'art francais (1965): 185-190.

[4] Elisabeth Louise Vigée LeBrun

03511. Baillio, Joseph. Elizabeth Louise Vigée LeBrun. Fort Worth, Tex.: Kimbell Art Museum, 1982.

03512. ________. "Identification de quelques portraits d'anonymes de Vigée le Brun aux États-Unis." Gazette des Beaux-Arts 122 (November 1980): 157-168.

03513. ________. "Quelques peintures réattribuées à Vigée-LeBrun." Gazette des Beaux-Arts 124 (January 1982): 13-26.

03514. Blum, André. Madame Vigée-LeBrun, peintre des grandes dames du XVIIIe siècle. Paris: H. Piazza, 1919.

03515. Bouchot, Henri. "Une artiste francaise pendant l'emigration, Madame Vigée-LeBrun." Revue de l'art ancien et moderne 1 (1898): 51-62, 219-230.

03516. Gallet, Michel. "La Maison de Madame Vigée-LeBrun, rue du gros-chenet." Gazette des Beaux-Arts 102 no. 2 (November 1960): 275-284.

03517. Hautecoeur, Louis. Mme Vigée-LeBrun. Paris: H. Laurens, 1914.

03518. Helm, William Henry. Vigée-LeBrun, Her Life, Works and Friendships. Boston: Small, Maynard and Co., 1915.

03519. Kamerick, Maureen. "The Woman Artist in the Eighteenth Century: Angelica Kauffman and Elizabeth Vigée-LeBrun." New Research on Women at the University of Michigan 1974: 14-22.

03520. Lucas, E.V. Chardin and Vigée-LeBrun. New York: George H. Doren Company, 1924.

03521. Macfall, Haldane. Vigée-LeBrun. New York: F.A. Stokes, Co, 1909.

03522. Mosser, Monique. "Le souper grec de Madame Vigée-LeBrun." XVIIIe siècle 15 (1983): 155-168.

03523. Nikolenko, Lada. "The Russian Portraits of Madame Vigée LeBrun." Gazette des Beaux Arts 109 no. 2 (July-August 1967): 91-120.

03524. Pillet, Charles. Madame Vigée-LeBrun. Paris: Librairie de l'Art, 1890.

03525. Rice, Danielle. "Vigée LeBrun vs. Labille-Guiard: A Rivalry in Context." Proceedings of the Western Society for French History 11 (1983): 130-138.

Also refer to #810, 3505.

[5] Others

03526. Auffret, Charles. Une Famille d'Art Brestois au dix-huitième siècle: Les Ozanne. Rennes: H. Caillière, 1891.

03527. Billioud, Joseph. "Un Peintre de types populaires: Francoise Duparc, de Marseilles (1726-1778)." Gazette des Beaux Arts 80 no. 2 (October 1938): 173-184.

03528. Moisy, Pierre. "A Pupil of Greuze: Genevieve Brossard de Beaulieu." Gazette des Beaux Arts 89 no. 2 (November - December 1947): 177-184.

Also refer to #2842.

(3) Patrons

03529. Rice, Danielle. "Women and the Visual Arts." In French Women and the Age of Enlightenment, edited by Samia I. Spencer, pp. 242-255. Bloomington, Indiana: Indiana University Press, 1984.

Also refer to #3489.

g) Science

03530. Gardiner, Linda. "Women in Science." In French Women and the Age of Enlightenment, edited by Samia I. Spencer, pp. 181-193. Bloomington, Indiana: Indiana University Press, 1984.

D. THE GERMANIES

1. SURVEYS

"For it may be that an action displeases us which would please us, if we knew its true aim and whole extent."
Margaret Klopstock
Letter to Samuel Richardson, 1758

03531. Joeres, Ruth-Ellen B. and Maynes, Mary Jo, ed. German Women in the Eighteenth and Nineteenth Centuries. Bloomington, Ind.: Indiana University Press, 1986.

03532. Prather, Charlotte C. "The View from Germany." In French Women and the Age of Enlightenment, edited by Samia I. Spencer, pp. 369-379. Bloomington, Indiana: Indiana University Press, 1984.

03533. Schultz, Hans Jürgen, ed. Frauen Porträts aus zwei Jahrhunderten. Stuttgart: Kreuz Verlag, 1981.

03534. Schwartz, Leon. "F.M. Grimm and the Eighteenth Century Debate on Women." French Review 58 (December 1984): 236-243.

Also refer to #3206.

2. POLITICAL

"Let us be honest: Every means by which human beings can distinguish themselves has been taken from the women."
Theodor Gottlieb von Hippel

a) Legal

03535. Cocalis, Susan L. "Der Vormund will Vormund sein: Zur Problematik der weiblichen Unmündigkeit im 18. Jahrhundert." Amsterdamer Beiträge zur neueren Germanistik 10 (1980): 33-55.

b) Feminism

03536. Dawson, Ruth P. "'And this shield is called--self-reliance.' Emerging Feminist Consciousness in the Late Eighteenth Century." In German Women in the Eighteenth and Nineteenth Centuries, edited by Ruth-Ellen B. Joeres and Mary Jo Maynes, pp. 157-174. Bloomington, Indiana: Indiana University Press, 1986.

03537. ________. "The Feminist Manifesto of Theodor Gottlieb von Hippel (1741-1796)." Amsterdamer Beiträge zur Neueren Germanistik 10 (1980): 13-32.

c) Political Roles

(1) Elizabeth Christine

03538. Adlersfeld, Eufemia Ballestrem di Castellengo. Elisabeth Christine, Königin von Preussen, Herzogin von Braunschweig-Lüneburg. Berlin: A. Schall, 1908.

03539. Hahnke, Friedrich Wilhelm. Elisabeth Christine, Königin von Preussen, Gemahlin Friedrichs der Grossen. Berlin: G. Reimer, 1848.

03540. Hurst, Catherine E. Elisabeth Christine, Wife of Frederick the Great. New York: Phillips and Hunt, 1880.

(2) Maria Theresa

03541. Frisi, Paolo. Elogio di Maria Teresa Imperatrice. Milan: Arti grafiche Fiorin, 1981.

03542. Fussenegger, Gertrud. Maria Theresia. Vienna: Molden, 1980.

03543. Heer, Friedrich. Der König und die Kaiserin, Friedrich und Maria Theresia, ein deutscher Konflikt. Munich: List, 1981.

03544. Maria Theresia und ihre Zeit. Vienna: Residenz Verlag, 1979.

03545. Pangels, Charlotte. Die Kinder Maria Theresias. Munich: Callwey, 1980.

03546. Slezak, Friedrich. "Maria Theresia und der Donauraum." Donauraum 25 (1980) 118-128.

03547. Suchenwirth, Richard. Maria Theresia: ein Kaiserleben. Leoni: am Starnbergersee: Druffel, 1975.

03548. Urbanski, Hans. Maria Theresia. Vienna: Prachner, 1980.

03549. Wandruszka, Adam. Maria Theresia. Göttingen: Muster-Schmidt, 1980.

3. SOCIAL

"The art of housekeeping is, as all my readers will know, the first and most important occupation of the female sex."
Marianne Ehrmann

a) Generic

03550. Handbuch Aller unter der Regierung Kaiser Joseph II für die K.K. Erblander Ergangenen Verordungen und Gesetze. 18 vols. Vienna: J. Georg Moesle, 1785-1790.

03551. Petschauer, Peter. "Growing up Female in Eighteenth Century Germany." _Journal of Psychohistory_ 11 (Fall 1983): 167-207.

03552. Taylor, Peter and Rebel, Hermann. "Hessian Peasant Women. Their Families, and the Draft: A Social-Historical Interpretation of Four Tales from the Grimm Collection." _Journal of Family History_ 6 (Winter 1981): 347-378.

Also refer to #2854, 3576.

b) Demography

03553. Gaede, Chr. E., et al., _Bevolkerungsbewegung und soziale Strukturen in Mainz zur Zeit des Pfälzischen Krieges (1680-1700). Eine historisch-demographische Fallstudie_. Wiesbaden: Franz Sterner Verlag, 1978.

03554. Knodel, John. "Child Mortality and Reproductive Behavior in German Village Populations in the Past: A Micro-Level Analysis of the Replacement Effect." _Population Studies_ 36 (July 1982): 177-200.

03555. _________ and Wilson, C. "The Secular Increase in Fecundity in German Village Populations: An Analysis of Reproductive Histories of Couples married 1750-1899." _Population Studies_ 35 (March 1981): 53-84.

03556. Sabean, David. "Household Formation and Geographical Mobility: A Family Register Study for a Württemberg Village 1760-1900." _Annales de démographie historique_ 1970: 275-294.

03557. Wicki, Hans. _Bevolkerung und Wirtschaft des Kantons Luzern im 18. Jahrhundert_. Munich: Rex Verlag, 1979.

Also refer to #3565.

c) Family

03558. Lindemann, Mary. "Love for Hire: The Regulation of the Wet-Nursing Business in Eighteenth-Century Hamburg." _Journal of Family History_ 6 (Winter 1981): 379-395.

03559. Mairbäurl, Gunda. _Die Familie als Werkstatt der Erziehung: Rollenbilder des Kindertheaters und soziale Realität im späten 18. Jahrhundert_. Munich: R. Oldenbourg, 1983.

03560. Medick, Hans. "Village Spinning Bees: Sexual Culture and Free Time Among Rural Youth in Early Modern Germany." In _Interest and Emotion, Essays on the Study of Family and Kinship_, edited by Hans Medick and David Warren Sabean, pp. 317-339. New York: Cambridge University Press, 1985.

03561. Mitterauer, Michael. "Familienformen und Illegitimität in ländlichen Gebieten Osterreichs." Archiv für Sozialgeschichte 19 (1979): 123-188.

03562. Schlumbohm, Juergen, ed. Kinderstuben. Wie Kinder zu Bauern, Burgern, Aristokraten wurden, 1700-1850. Munich: Deutschen Taschenbuch Verlag, 1983.

Also refer to #2856, 3551, 3552, 3554, 3556, 3569, 3583.

d) Marriage

03563. Hertz, Deborah. "Intermarriage in the Berlin Salons." Central European History 16 (December 1983): 303-346.

03564. Hippel, Theodor. Uber die Ehe. Sämtliche Werke, 5: 1-309. Berlin: G. Reimer, 1828.

03565. Knodel, John and Lynch, Katherine A. "The Decline of Remarriage: Evidence from German Village Populations in the Eighteenth and Nineteenth Centuries." Journal of Family History 10 (Spring 1985): 34-59.

03566. Perrenoud, Alfred. "Analyse des contrats de mariage génévois en 1749: une source pour l'étude des structures sociales." Cahiers d'histoire 12 (1967): 143-152.

Also refer to #3555.

e) Fashion/Manners

03567. Schmid, D.A. Trachtenfibel. The costumes of old Switzerland after the originals of D.A. Schmid. 1791-1861. Munich: Bruckmann, 1937.

f) Health/Medical

03568. Frevert, Ute. "Frauen und Ärzte im späten 18. und frühen 19. Jahrhundert--zur Sozialgeschichte eines Gewaltverhältnisses." In Frauen in der Geschichte II, edited by Annette Kuhn und Jörn Rüsen, pp. 177-210. Düsseldorf: Schwann, 1982.

03569. Lindemann, Mary. "Maternal Politics: The Principles and Practice of Maternity Care in Eighteenth-Century Hamburg." Journal of Family History 9 (Spring 1984): 44-63.

4. CULTURAL

"Our education teaches us to be entirely dependent on the judgment of others, makes applause and admiration the highest goal of our efforts and turns the effort to please into our primary duty."

Emilie Berlepsch

a) Generic

03570. Hoffmann, Volker. "Caratterizzazione dei sessi nei testi teorici e letterari dell'epoca Goethiana." *Studies on Voltaire and the Eighteenth Century* 193 (1980): 1901-1908.

03571. Nasse, Peter. *Kie Frauenzimmer-Bibliothek Hamburger 'Patrioten' von 1724*. Stuttgart: Akademischer Verlag Heinz, 1976.

b) Literature

(1) Non-specific

03572. Friedrichs, Elisabeth. *Die deutschsprachigen Schriftstellerinnen des 18. und 19. Jahrhunderts*. Stuttgart: Metzler, 1981.

03573. Grenz, Dagmar. *Mädchen literatur: Von dem moralisch-belehrenden Schriften im 18. Jahrhundert bis zur Herausbildung der Backfischliteratur im 19. Jahrhundert*. Stuttgart: Metzler, 1981.

03574. Mittner, L. "Freundschaft und Liebe in der deutschen Literatur des 18. Jahrhunderts." In *Stoffe, Formen, Strukturen*, edited by Albert Fuchs and Helmut Motekat, pp. 77-138. Munich: M. Hueber, 1962.

03575. Panke, Birgit. "Bürgerliches Frauenbild und Geschlectsrollenzuweisungen in der literarischen und brieflichen Produktion des 18. Jahrhunderts." *Beiträge zur feministischen Theorie und Praxis* 5 (March 1981): 6-10.

03576. Petschauer, Peter. "From *Hausmütter* to *Hausfrau*: Ideals and Realities in Late Eighteenth-Century Germany." *Eighteenth-Century Life* 8 (October 1982): 72-82.

03577. Reh, Albert M. "Wunschbild und Wirklichkeit. Die Frau als Leserin und als Heldin des Romans und des Dramas der Aufklärung." In *Die Frau als Heldin und Autorin*, edited by Wolfgang Paulsen, pp. 82-95. Munich: Francke Verlag, 1979.

03578. Weigel, Sigrid. "'. . . und führen jetzt die Feder statt der Nadel.' Vom Dreifachcharakter weiblicher Schreibarbeit--Emanzipation, Erwerb und Kunstanspruch." In _Frauen in der Geschichte IV_, edited by Ilse Brehmer et. al., pp. 347-367. Düsseldorf: Schwann, 1983.

Also refer to #3552.

(2) Drama

[a] Women in Drama

[[1]] Non-specific

03579. Prandi, Julie D. _Spirited Women Heroes: Major Female Characters in the Dramas of Goethe, Schiller and Kleist_. New York: Peter Lang, 1983.

03580. Tilton, Helga. "Virgins and Other Victims: Aspects of German Middle-Class Theatre." In _Female Studies IX: Teaching About Women in Foreign Languages_, edited by Sidonie Cassirer, pp. 180-188. Old Westbury, New York: Feminist Press, 1975.

[[2]] Individuals

[[a]] Goethe

03581. Fitzell, John. "Goethe's _Faust_: A Perspective on the Mirror-Image in 'Hexenküche' and on the Eternal Feminine." _Germanic Notes_ 8 (1977): 27-31.

03582. Heller, Peter. "Gretchen: Figur, Klischee, Symbol." In _Die Frau als Heldin und Autorin_, edited by Wolfgang Paulsen, pp. 175-189. Munich: Francke Verlag, 1979.

03583. Herzfeld, Marianne von. "Goethe's Images of Children." _German Life and Letters_ 25 (1971-1972) : 219-231.

03584. Knight, A.H.J. "Gretchen's Mother." _German Life and Letters_ 5 (July 1952): 243-248.

03585. Sjögren, Christine Oertel. "Pietism, Pathology, or Pragmatism in Goethe's _Bekenntnisse einer schönen Seele_." _Studies on Voltaire and the Eighteenth Century_ 193 (1980): 2009-2015.

03586. Timms, Edward. "The Matrix of Love: 'Warum gabst Du uns die tiefen Blicke.'" _German Life and Letters_ n.s. 36 (October 1982-January 1983): 49-65.

Also refer to #3596.

[[b]] Lessing

03587. Daemmrich, Horst S. "The Incest Motif in Lessing's *Nathan der Weise* and Schiller's *Braut von Messina*." *Germanic Review* 42 (May 1967): 184-196.

03588. Graham, Ilse Appelbaum. "The Currency of Love: A Reading of Lessing's 'Minna von Barnhelm.'" *German Life and Letters* 18 (1964-1965): 270-278.

03589. Hinck, Walter. "Lessings Minna: Armut und Geist, Kleine Komödien-Chronik zur Emanzipation der Frau. In *Festschrift für Rainer Gruenter*, edited by Bernhard Fabian, pp. 9-25. Heidelberg: Carl Winter, 1978.

03590. Labroisse, Gerd. "Zum Gestaltungsprinzip von Lessings *Miss Sara Sampson*." *Amsterdamer Beiträge zur neueren Germanistik* 1 (1972): 75-102.

03591. Rentschler, Robert. "Lissette, the Laugher." *Lessing Yearbook* 10 (1978): 46-64.

03592. Ryder, Frank G. "Emilia Galotti." *German Quarterly* 45 (March 1972): 329-347.

03593. Sjogren, Christine Oertel. "The Status of Women in several of Lessing's Dramas." *Studies in Eighteenth Century Culture* 6 (1977): 347-359.

03594. Van Ingen, Ferdinand. "Tugend bei Lessing. Bemerkungen zu *Miss Sara Sampson*." *Amsterdamer Beiträge zur neueren Germanistik* 1 (1972): 43-73.

03595. Wells, G.A. "What is Wrong with *Emilia Galotti*?" *German Life and Letters* n.s. 37 (April 1984): 163-173.

[[c]] Schiller

03596. Borchardt, Frank L. "Goethe, Schiller, Sphinx, Centaur and Sex." *Monatshefte* 64 (Fall 1972): 247-255.

03597. Bremner, G. "Millwood, Lady Milford and Maria Stuart." *German Life and Letters* 11 (1957-1958): 41-48.

03598. Heitner, Robert T. "Louise Millerin and the Schock Motif in Schiller's Early Dramas." *Germanic Review* 41 (January 1966): 27-44.

Also refer to #3621.

[b] Women Dramatists

03599. Richel, Veronica. "An Enlightened Jest: Luise Gottsched's *Horatii*." *Germanic Notes* 4 (1973): 50-52.

(3) Prose

[a] Novels

[1] Women in Novels

03600. Blackwell, Jeannine. "An Island of Her Own: Heroines of the German Robinsonades from 1720-1800." German Quarterly 58 (Winter 1985): 5-26.

03601. Boa, Elizabeth. "Sex and Sensibility: Wieland's Portrayal of Relationships between the Sexes in the Comische Erzählungen, Agathon, and Musarion." Lessing Yearbook 12 (1980): 189-218.

03602. Fritz-Grandjean, Sonia. Das Frauenbild im Jugendwerk von Ludwig Tieck als Mosaikstein zu seiner Weltanschauung. Las Vegas: Peter Lang, 1980.

03603. Menhennet, Alan. "The 'Galant' Novel as a School for Lovers: M.E. Franck's Rachgierige Fleurie." German Life and Letters n.s. 36 (April 1983): 266-276.

03604. Prather, Charlotte C. "Liberation and domesticity: two feminine ideals in the works of C.M. Wieland." Studies on Voltaire and the Eighteenth Century 193 (1980): 2002-2009.

03605. VanCleve, John. "A Countess in Name Only: Gellert's Schwedische Gräfin." Germanic Review 55 (Fall 1980): 152-155.

03606. Witte, Bernd. "Der Roman als moralische Anstalt. Gellerts 'Leben des schwedischen Gräfin von G. . .' und die Literatur des 18. Jahrhunderts." Germanisch-Romanische Monatsschrift n.s. 30 (1980): 150-169.

Also refer to #3103, 3353.

[2] Women Novelists

[[a]] Sophie La Roche

03607. Craig, Charlotte. "Mind and method: Sophie La Roche--a 'praeceptra filiarum Germaniae'?" Studies on Voltaire and the Eighteenth Century 193 (1980): 1996-2002.

03608. ________. "Sophie la Roche's Enlightened Anglophobia." Germanic Notes 8 (1977): 34-40.

03609. Joeres, Ruth-Ellen B. "'That girl is an entirely different character!' Yes, but is she a feminist? Observations on Sophie von la Roche's *Geschichte des Fräuleins von Sternheim*." In *German Women in the Eighteenth and Nineteenth Centuries*, edited by Ruth-Ellen B. Joeres and Mary Jo Maynes, pp. 135-156. Bloomington, Indiana: Indiana University Press, 1986.

03610. Milch, Werner. *Sophie La Roche: die Grossmutter der Brentanos*. Frankfurt a/Main: Societäts-Verlag, 1935.

03611. Petschauer, Peter. "Sophie von La Roche. Novelist between Reason and Emotion." *Germanic Review* 57 (Spring 1982): 70-77.

03612. Ridderhof, Kudo. *Sophie von La Roche und Wieland*. Hamburg: Lütcke und Wulff, 1907.

c) Intellectuals

03613. Bird, Alan. "Rahel Varnhagen von Ense and some English Assessments of her Character." *German Life and Letters* n.s. 26 (1972-1973): 183-192.

03614. Brinker-Gabler, Gisela. "Das weibliche Ich. Überlegungen zur Analyse von Werken weiblicher Autoren mit einem Beispiel aus dem 18. Jahrhundert: Sidonia Hedwig Zäunemann." In *Die Frau als Heldin und Autorin*, edited by Wolfgang Paulsen, pp. 55-65. Munich: Francke Verlag, 1979.

03615. Geiger, Ludwig. "Ernestine Reiske." In *Dichter und Frauen*, pp. 226-241. Berlin: Verlag von Gebrüder Paetel, 1899.

03616. __________. "Aus Therese Hubers Herzensleben." In *Dichter und Frauen*, pp. 1-82. Berlin: Verlag von Gebrüder Paetel, 1899.

03617. Gillies, Alexander. "Emilie von Berlepsch and her *Caledonia*." *German Life and Letters* n.s. 29 (October 1975): 75-90.

03618. Hertz, Deborah. "Hannah Arendt's Rahel Varnhagen." In *German Women in the Nineteenth Century*, edited by John C. Fout, pp. 72-87. New York: Holmes and Meier, 1984.

03619. Litvinoff, Barnet. "Rahel Levin--The Apex of a Triangle." *German Life and Letters* 1 (July 1948): 303-311.

03620. Nickisch, Reinhard M.G. "Die Frau als Briefschreiberin im Zeitalter der deutschen Aufklärung." *Wolfenbütteler Studien zur Aufklärung* 3 (1976): 29-66.

03621. Trainer, James. Caroline Schmidt and the Schillers." German Life and Letters 17 (1963-1964): 339-348.

Also refer to #3563, 4712.

d) Art

03622. Bartoschek, Gerd. Anna Dorothea Therbusch 1721-1782. Potsdam-Sanssouci: Kulturhaus Hans Marchwitza, 1971.

03623. Citron, Marcia J. "Corona Schröter: Singer, Composer, Actress." Music and Letters 61 (1980): 15-27.

03624. Harris, Edward P. "From Outcast to Ideal: The Image of the Actress in Eighteenth Century Germany." German Quarterly 54 (March 1981): 177-187.

03625. Rieger, Eva. "Die geistreichen aber verwahrlosten Weiber -- Sur musikalischen Bildung von Mädchen und Frauen." In Frauen in der Geschichte IV, edited by Ilse Brehmer, et al., pp. 397-406. Düsselforf: Schwann, 1983.

E. IBERIA

1. SOCIAL

"And we women, locked up in this narrow jail, can never go out anywhere, except to Mass."
L. Moratín's El viejo y la nina

03626. Dominguez Ortíz, Antonio. La Sociedad Española en el Siglo XVIII. 1955. Reprint. Barcelona: Editorial Ariel, 1976.

03627. McClendon, Carmen Chaves. "Idleness and the eighteenth-century Spanish woman." Studies on Voltaire and the Eighteenth Century 193 (1980): 2027-2028.

03628. Rudat, Eva M. Kahiluoto. "The View from Spain: Rococo Finesse and Esprit versus Plebeian Manners." In French Women and the Age of Enlightenment, edited by Samia I. Spencer, pp. 395-406. Bloomington, Indiana: Indiana University Press, 1984.

2. CULTURAL

"So long as they do not say what they feel, so long as they pretend to hate what they most desire, so long as they agree to pronounce on command a perjured, sacrilegious yes. . . they are indeed well reared, and an upbringing which inspires in the fear the silence, and astuteness of a slave is called excellent."

L. Moratín

03629. Carnero, Guillermo. "Francesca Ruiz de Larrea de Böhl de Faber y Mary Wollstonecraft." Hispanic Review 50 (Spring 1982): 133-142.

03630. Judicini, Joseph V. "The Problem of the Arranged Marriage and the Education of Girls in Goldoni's La figlia obbediente and Moratin's Et si las minas. Rivista di Letterature moderne e comparate 24 (Summer 1971): 208-222.

03631. Kish, Kathleen. "A School for Wives, Women in Eighteenth-Century Spanish Theater. In Women in Hispanic Literature, Icons and Fallen idols, edited by Beth Miller, pp. 184-200. Berkeley, Ca.: University of California Press, 1983.

F. ITALY

1. POLITICAL

"You may be sure that I know that there is a world, men, and bread beyond the lagoons [of Venice] . . . my journeys shall be only to my easel."

Rosalba Carriera

03632. Beauriez, L. de Une fille de France. Paris: Perrin et Cie, 1887.

03633. Farina, Rachele and Sillano, Maria Teresa. "La pastorella d'Arcadia contesta. . . Il Settecento femminista in Italia." In Esistere comme donna, pp. 27-36. Milan: Mazzata, 1983.

2. SOCIAL

"No one loves gayety more than I do: I try to have it at home, and to carry it wherever I go. Diversion and amusements are the best and universal remedy for our ills."

Rosalba Carriera

a) Generic

03634. Cazzoli, Carla Pellandra. "Dames et sigisbées: Un Début d'émancipation féminine?" Studies on Voltaire and the Eighteenth Century 193 (1980): 2028-2035.

b) Demography

03635. Bigi, Patrizia; Ronchi, Anna; and, Zambruno, Elisabetta. "Demografia differenziale di un villaggio alessandrino: dall'analisi quantitativa alle storie di famiglia." Quaderni storici 46 (April 1981): 11-59.

03636. Delille, Gerard; Villani, Pasquale; and, Grendi, Edoardo. "Sulle strutture demografiche del Regno di Napoli tra '700 et '800." Società et Storia 8 (1980): 413-432.

03637. Rofrano, Anna Maria. "Strutture demografiche e socio-professionali della parrocchia della SS.MA Trinità di Potenza nel 1753." In Studi di stora sociale e religiosa Scritti in onore di Gabriele de Rosa, pp. 1407-1437. Naples: Editrici Ferraro, 1980.

c) Marriage

03638. Corsini, Carlo A. "Why is Remarriage a Male Affair? Some Evidence from Tuscan Villages during the Eighteenth Century." In Marriage and Remarriage in Populations of the Past, edited by Jacques Dupâquier, et. al., pp. 385-395. New York: Academic Press, 1981.

03639. Giacomini, Mariuccia. Sposi a Belmonte mel Settecento. Milan: A Giuffrè, 1981.

Also refer to #2911.

3. CULTURAL

"I should not be mistress of my own will, and whenever I might have a fancy not to sing, the people would insult, perhaps misuse me: it is better to remain unmolested, were it even in a prison."

Caterina Gabrielle

a) Literature

03640. Anzoletti, Lujsa. "La donna italiana nel secolo XVIII." In La donna italiana da scrittici italianae, pp. 101-124. Florence: G. Civelli, 1890.

03641. Petrini, Mario. Le commedie popolari del Goldone. Padua: Liviana, 1976.

Also refer to #3630.

b) Art

(1) Women in Art

03642. Busiri Vici, Andrea. _La 'donne' del Batoni_. Lucca: Nuova grafica lucchese, 1968.

(2) Women Artists

[a] Musicians/Singers

03643. Anzoletti, L. _Maria Caetana Agnesi_. Milan: L.F. Cogliati, 1900.

03644. Constable, M.V. "The _Figlie del Goro_: Fiction and Fact." _Journal of European Studies_ 11 (June 1981): 111-139.

03645. Scott, Marion M. "Maddalena Lombardini, Madame Syrmen." _Music and Letters_ 14 (n.d.): 149-163.

Also refer to #2923, 3186.

[b] Painters

[1] Rosalba Carriera

03646. Cessi, F. _Rosalba Carriera_. Milan: I. Meastri di Colore, 1967.

03647. Gatto, Gabrielle. "Per la cronologia di Rosalba Carriera." _Art veneta_ 25 (1971): 182-193.

03648. Hoerschelmann, Emilie von. _Rosalba Carriera, Die Meisterin der Pastellmalerie und Bilder aus der Kunst und Kulturgeschichte des 18. Jahrhunderts_. Leipzig: Klinkhardt and Biermann, 1908.

03649. Malamini, Vittorio. _Rosalba Carriera_. Bergamo: Instituto d'arti grafiche, 1910.

03650. Wilhelm, Jacques. "Le Protrait de Watteau par Rosalba Carriera." _Gazette des Beaux Arts_ 95 no. 2 (November 1953): 235-246.

[2] Angelica Kauffman

03651. Bregenz. Vorarlberger Landesmuseum. _Angelica Kauffman und ihre Zeitgenossen_. Bregenz, 1968.

03652. Busiri Vici, Andrea. "Angelica Kauffman and the Bariatinskis." _Apollo_ 77 (March 1963): 201-208.

03653. Gerard, Frances A. Angelica Kauffman. A Biography. London: Ward and Downey, 1893.

03654. Hughes, G. Bernard. "Angelica Kauffman." Apollo 34 (October 1941), 100-103.

03655. Kauffmann, Angelica. Angelika Kauffmann und ihre Zeit. Düsseldorf, C.G. Boerner, 1979.

03656. Mayer, Dorothy Moulton. Angelica Kauffman. Atlantic Highlands, N.J.: Humanities Press, Inc., 1978.

03657. Poensgen, Georg. "Ein Kunstlerbildnis von Angelika Kauffmann." Pantheon 3 (1973: 294-297.

03658. Rossi, Giovanni Gherado de. Vita di Angelica Kauffman, pittrice. Florence: Landi e comp, 1810.

03659. Sleigh, Sylvia. "Angelica Kaufmann." Women's Studies 6 (1978): 35-41.

03660. Smidt-Dörrenberg, Irmgard. Angelika Kauffmann. Goethes Freundin in Rom. Vienna: Bergland Verlag, 1968.

03661. Sparrow, Walter Shaw. "Angelica Kauffman's Amazing Marriage." Connoisseur 92 (1933): 242-248.

Also refer to #3519.

[3] Giulia Lama

03662. Pallucchini, R. "Per la conoscenza di Giulia Lama." Arte veneta (1970): 161-172.

03663. Ruggeri, Ugo. Dipinti e disegni di Giulia Lama. Bergamo: Monumenta Bergmensia, 1973.

G. THE LOW COUNTRIES

1. SOCIAL

". . .it had long been the custom and whoever offered to break it would have banded against him not only all the women of the town, but all the men too that were governed by their wives, which would be too great a party to oppose."

Hendrik Hooft
Dutch Mayor

03664. Bougard, Jean-Paul. "La fécondité au Borinage au XVIIIe et au début du XIXe siècle." Population et famille 46 (1979): 109-146.

03665. Buijnsteis, P.J. "The Tutor/Governess between Nobility and Bourgeoisie: Some Considerations with Reference to an Essay of 1734 by Justus van Effen." _Studies on Voltaire and the Eighteenth Century_ 216 (1983): 164-166.

2. CULTURAL

"So lengthy and brilliant a career is not given to many women."

R. Renraw,
about Rachel Reysch

03666. Grant, Maurice H. _Rachel Huysch 1664-1750_. Leigh-on-Sea: F. Lewis, 1956.

03667. Renraw, R. "The Art of Rachel Ruysch." _The Connoisseur_ 92 (1933): 397-399.

03668. Timm, Werner. "Bemerkungen zu einem Stilleben von Rachel Ruysch." _Oud-Holland_ 77 (1972): 137-138.

03669. Tremaine, George. "A Queen of Flower Painters: Rachel Ruysch." _Garden Design_ 22 (1935): 52-54.

VII.
NINETEENTH CENTURY
(c. 1789-1914)

A. GENERAL

1. SURVEYS

"Woman wants to become self-reliant, and for that reason she is beginning to enlighten men about 'woman as such': _this_ is one of the worst developments of the general _uglification_ of Europe."

Friedrich Nietzsche
Beyond Good and Evil

03670. Branca, Patricia and Stearns, Peter. _Modernization of Women in the Nineteenth Century_. Saint Louis, Mo.: Forum Press, 1981.

2. POLITICAL

"International Law does not prevent a State from sending a female as diplomatic envoy. But under the present circumstances many States would refuse to receive her."

Oppenheim, 1912

a) Marxism and Socialism

03671. Hobsbawm, Eric. "Uomo e donna nell' iconografia socialista." _Studi storici_ 20 (October-December 1979): 705-723.

03672. Mullaney, Marie Marmo. "Gender and the Socialist Revolutionary Role, 1871-1921: A General Theory of the Female Revolutionary Personality." _Historical Reflections_ 11 (Summer 1984): 99-151.

03673. Pieroni Bortolotti, Franca. "Donne e socialismo: I. Congressi femminili della 2ª Internazionale." Rivista storica italiana 92 (1980): 482-505.

03674. Taylor, Barbara. "Socialist Feminism: Utopian or Scientific." In People's History and Socialist Theory, edited by Raphael Samuel, pp. 158-163. Boston: Routledge and Kegan Paul, 1981.

b) Legal

03675. Makarov, A.N. "La Nationalité de la femme mariée." Recueil des Cours 60 (1937): 111-241.

c) Feminism

03676. Acerbi, Susanna. "L'epopea suffragista." In Esistere comme donna, pp. 179-188. Milan: Mazzotta, 1983.

03677. Farina, Rachele. "Le grandi protagoniste del femminismo europeo." In Esistere comme donna, pp. 167-178. Milan: Mazzotta, 1983.

03678. Sherrick, Rebecca L. "Toward Universal Sisterhood." Women's Studies International Forum 5 (1982): 655-661.

Also refer to #3674.

d) International Congress

03679. "The International Congress of Women." Englishwoman's Review 30 (1899): 153-162.

03680. The International Congress of Women, London 1899. 7 vols. Edited by the Countess of Aberdeen. London: T. Fisher Unwin, 1900.

Also refer to #3673.

3. SOCIAL

"The extension of rights to women is the basis of all social progress."

Fourier

a) Family

03681. Mitterauer, Michael. Ledige Mütter Zur Geschichte unehelicher Geburten in Europa. Munich: C.H. Beck, 1983.

03682. Taylor, Karen J. "Veneral Disease in Nineteenth-Century Children." Journal of Psychohistory 12 (Spring 1985): 431-463.

Also refer to #2938, 2939, 3675.

b) Sex Life and Morals

03683. Bristow, Edward. Prostitution and Prejudice: The Jewish Fight Against White Slavery 1870-1939. New York: Schocken, 1983.

03684. Faderman, Lillian. "The Morbidification of Love Between Women by Nineteenth Century Sexologists." Journal of Homosexuality 4 (Fall 1978): 73-90.

03685. Meyers, Jeffrey. Homosexuality and Literature, 1890-1930. London: Athlone Press, 1977.

c) Fashion/Manners

03686. Hinks, Peter. Nineteenth-Century Jewelry. London: Faber and Faber, 1975.

03687. Lecompte, Hippolyte. Costumes européens. Paris: Delpech, 1817-1819.

03688. Steele, Valerie. Fashion and Eroticism, Ideals of Feminine Beauty from the Victoria Age to the Jazz Age. New York: Oxford University Press, 1985.

d) Health/Medical

03689. Duffin, Lorna. "Social and Cultural Contradictions: Women and Medicine in the Nineteenth Century." Bulletin of the Society for the Social History of Medicine 21 (1977): 24-26.

03690. Mackenzie, Charlotte. "Women and Psychiatric Professionalization, 1780-1914." In The Sexual Dynamics of History, edited by The London Feminist History Group, pp. 107-119. London: Pluto Press, 1983.

03691. Schultze, Caroline. Female Physicians in the Nineteenth Century. Leipzig: Peter Hobbing, 1889.

03692. Schwarz, Gudrun. "'Mannweiber' in Männertheorien." In Frauen suchen ihre Geschichte, Historische Studien zum 19. und 20. Jahrhundert, edited by Karin Hausen, pp. 62-80. Munich: Verlag C. H. Beck, 1983.

Also refer to #3682.

4. CULTURAL

> "Deliberately, women are given a deplorable education. . . While man frees himself from constraining civil and religious bonds, he is only to glad to have woman hold tightly to the Christian principle of suffering and keeping her silence."
>
> George Sand
> Letters to Marcie, 1837

a) Literature

03693. Gerrard, Lisa. "Romantic Heroines in the Nineteenth Century Novel: A Feminist View." International Journal of Women's Studies 7 (January-February 1984): 10-16.

03694. Higonnet, Margaret. "Suicide: Representations of the Feminine in the Nineteenth Century." Poetics Today 6 (1985): 103-118.

Also refer to #3685.

b) Art

03695. Bade, Patrick. Femme Fatale: Images of Evil and Fascinating Women. New York: Mayflower Books, 1979.

03696. Callen, Anthea. Women Artists of the Arts and Crafts Movement, 1870-1914. New York: Pantheon Books, 1979.

03697. Catalogue d'une collection unique de dessins, gravures et eaux-fortes composés ou executés par des femmes. Amsterdam: Frederik Muller & Co., [1884?].

03698. Lewen, J. Mewburn. "Santley and Some Famous Singers of His Time." Proceedings of the Royal Music Association 69 (1942-1943): 83-104.

Also refer to #2950, 3671.

B. BRITAIN

1. SURVEYS

> "Work and not drudgery, but work is the great beautifier. Activity of brain, heart and limb gives health and beauty."
>
> Barbara Leigh Smith

03699. Alexander, Sally. "Women, Class and Sexual Differences in the 1830s and 1840s: Some Reflections on the Writing of Feminist History." History Workshop 17 (Spring 1984): 125-149.

03700. Bailey, Susan F. _Women and the British Empire_. New York: Garland Publishing, 1983.

03701. Peterson, M. Jeanne. "No Angels in the House: The Victorian Myth and the Paget Women." _American Historical Review_ 89 (June 1984): 677-709.

03702. Tweedsmuir, Susan. _The Edwardian Lady_. London: Gerald Duckworth and Co., 1966.

Also refer to #2957.

2. POLITICAL

"By marriage, the husband and wife are one person in law; that is, the very being, or legal existence of the woman is suspended during the marriage or least is incorporated and consolidated into that of the husband. . . ."

William Blackstone
Commentaries on the Laws of England, 1793

a) Generic

03703. Balfour, Lady Betty. "Motherhood and the State." _New Statesman_ 2 Spec. Supp. (1 November 1913): xii-xiii.

03704. Jones, David. "Women and Chartism." _History_ 68 (February 1983): 1-21.

03705. Robb, Janet Henderson. _The Primrose League, 1883-1906_. New York: Columbia University Press, 1942.

03706. Rowan, Caroline. "'Mothers, Vote Labour!' The State the Labour Movement and Working-Class Mothers, 1900-1918." In _Feminism, Culture and Politics_, edited by Rosalind Brunt and Caroline Rowan, pp. 59-84. London: Wishart, 1982.

03707. Thomis, Malcolm I. and Grimmett, Jennifer. _Women in Protest, 1800-1850_. New York: St. Martin's Press, 1982.

03708. Tyrrell, Alex. "'Women's Mission' and Pressure Group Politics in Britain (1825-60)." _Bulletin of the John Rylands Library_ 63 (1982): 194-230.

b) Marxism and Socialism

(1) Non-specific

03709. Kendall, Walter. _The Revolutionary Movement in Britain, 1900-1921_. London: Weidenfeld and Nicolson, 1969.

03710. Reeves, Magdalen Stuart (Maud Pember Reeves). Round About a Pound a Week. 1913. Reprint. London: Virago, 1979.

03711. Shaw, George Bernard. Women as Councillors. Fabian Tract no. 93. London: Fabian Society, 1900.

03712. Taylor, Barbara. Eve and the New Jerusalem. Socialism and Feminism in the Nineteenth Century. New York: Pantheon Books, 1983.

03713. Women in Rebellion--1900: Two Views on Class, Socialism and Liberation. Square One Pamphlet no. 6. Leeds: Independent Labour Party Square One Publication, 1973.

Also refer to #3788.

(2) Beatrice and Sydney Webb

03714. Britain, Ian. Fabianism and Culture: A Study in British Socialism and the Arts. New York: Cambridge University Press, 1982.

03715. Caine, Barbara. "Beatrice Webb and Her Diary." Victorian Studies 27 (Autumn 1983): 81-90.

03716. ______________. "Beatrice Webb and the 'Woman Question.'" History Workshop 14 (1982): 23-43.

03717. Longford, Elizabeth. "Beatrice Webb's 'Other Self'." History Today 33 (February 1983): 28-32.

03718. Nord, Deborah Epstein. The Apprenticeship of Beatrice Webb. Amherst, Mass.: University of Massachusetts Press, 1985.

03719. Radice, Lisanne. Beatrice and Sidney Webb. New York: St. Martin's Press, 1984.

Also refer to #3897, 4631.

(3) Others

03720. Wallis, Lena. The Life and Letters of Carolyn Martyn. London: Labour Leader Publishing, 1898.

c) Legal

03721. Black, Clementina. "The Coming Factory Act." Contemporary Review 59 (1891): 710-717.

03722. Browne, George and Powles, L.D. The Law and Practice in Divorce and Matrimonial Causes. 5th ed. London: Sweet and Maxwell, 1889.

03723. "Conference on the National Insurance Bill." National Union of Women Workers. Occasional Paper 55 (July 1911): 13-28.

03724. Great Britain. Royal Commission on Divorce and Matrimonial Causes. The Minority Report of the Divorce Commission, Signed by Archbishop of York, Sir William R. Anson, and Sir Lewis T. Dibdin. London: H.M. Stationery Office, 1912.

03725. ____________. Report. London: H.M. Stationery Office, 1912.

03726. Holcombe, Lee. Wives and Property: Reform of the Married Women's Property Law in Nineteenth-Century England. Buffalo: University of Toronto Press, 1983.

03727. Horstman, Allen. Victorian Divorce. New York: St. Martin's Press, 1985.

03728. Hutchins, Elizabeth Leigh, and Harrison, Amy. A History of Factory Legislation. 1926. Reprint. London: Frank Cass & Co., 1966.

03729. John, Angela V. "Colliery Legislation and Its Consequences: 1842 and the Women Miners of Lancashire." Bulletin of the John Rylands Library 61 (1979): 78-114.

03730. Minor, Iris. "Working Class Women and Matrimonial Law Reform, 1890-1914." In Ideology and the Labour Movement, edited by David E. Martin, pp. 103-124. London: Croom Helm, 1979.

03731. Savage, Gail L. "The Operation of the 1857 Divorce Act, 1860 1910. A Research Note." Journal of Social History 16 (Summer 1983): 103-110.

03732. Shanley, Mary Lyndon. "One Must Ride Behind: Married Women's Rights and the Divorce Act of 1857." Victorian Studies 25 (1982): 355-376.

03733. Thane, Pat. "Women and the Poor Law in Victorian and Edwardian England." History Workshop 6 (Autumn 1978): 29-51.

03734. Zaborsky, Dorothy E. "'Domestic Anarchy and the Destruction of the Family': Caroline Norton and the Custody of Infants Bill." International Journal of Women's Studies 7 (November-December 1984): 397-411.

Also refer to #3751, 3787, 3840, 3859, 3878, 4047, 4053, 4303.

d) Criminal

03735. Bell, Clark. Criminal Abortion and the New English Criminal Evidence Act. New York: n.p., 1898.

03736. Clark, Anna K. "Rape or Seduction? A Controversy Over Sexual Violence in the Nineteenth Century." In The Sexual Dynamics of History, edited by The London Feminist History Group, pp. 13-27. London: Pluto Press, 1983.

03737. Taylor, Bernard. Cruelly Murdered: Constance Kent and the Killing at Read Hill House. London: Souvenir House, 1979.

03738. Walkowitz, Judith R. "Jack the Ripper and the Myth of Male Violence." Feminist Studies 8 (Fall 1982): 543-574.

e) Feminism

(1) Non-specific

03739. Banks, Olive. The Biographical Dictionary of British Feminists. Vol. I: 1800-1930. New York: University Press, 1985.

03740. Black, Eugene C. Feminists, Liberalism, and Morality. London: LLRS Publications, 1981.

03741. Black, Naomi. "The Mothers' International, the Women's Co-operative Guild and Feminist Pacifism." Women's Studies International Forum 7 (1984): 467-476.

03742. Caine, Barbara. "Feminism, Suffrage and the Nineteenth-Century English Women's Movement." Women's Studies International Forum 5 (1982): 537-550.

03743. Forster, Margaret. Significant Sisters: The Grassroots of Active Feminism, 1839-1939. New York: Alfred A. Knopf, 1985.

03744. Moore, Lindy. "Feminists and Femininity: A Case Study of WSPU Propaganda and Local Response at a Scottish By-Election." Women's Studies International Forum 5 (1982): 675-684.

03745. Trollope, Joanna. Britannia's Daughters: Women of the British Empire. London: Hutchinson, 1983.

Also refer to #2963, 3914.

(2) Individuals

(a) Frances Power Cobbe

03746. Bauer, Carol and Ritt, Lawrence. "'A Husband is a Beating Animal' "Frances Power Cobbe Confronts the Wife-Abuse Problem in Victorian England." International Journal of Women's Studies 6 (March-April 1983): 99-118.

03747. Bauer, Carol and Ritt, Lawrence. "Wife Abuse, Late Victorian Feminists and the Legacy of Frances Power Cobbe." International Journal of Women's Studies 6 (May-June 1983): 195-207.

(b) John Stuart Mill

03748. Annas, Julia. "Mill and the Subjection of Women." Philosophy 52 (1977): 179-194.

03749. Collini, Stefan. "John Stuart Mill on the Subjection of Women." History Today 34 (December 1984): 34-39.

03750. Krouse, Richard W. "Patriarchal Liberalism and Beyond: From John Stuart Mill to Harriet Taylor." In The Family in Political Thought, edited by Jean Bethke Elshtain, pp. 145-172. Amherst, Mass.: University of Massachusetts Press, 1982.

03751. Pateman, Carole. "The Shame of the Marriage Contract." In Women's Views of the Political World of Men, edited by Judith Hicks Stiehm, pp. 67-97. Dobbs Ferry, N.Y.: Transnational Publishers Inc., 1984.

(c) Others

03752. Ball, Terence. "Utilitarianism, Feminism, and the Franchise: James Mill and His Critics." History of Political Thought 1 (Spring 1980): 91-115.

03753. Bradbrook, Muriel Clara. Barbara Bodichon, George Eliot and and the Limits of Feminism. Oxford: Somerville College, 1975.

03754. Herstein, Sheila R. A Mid-Victorian Feminist: Barbara Leigh Smith Bodichon. New Haven, Ct.: Yale University Press, 1986.

03755. Kersley, Gillian. Darling Madame: Sarah Grand and Devoted Friend. London: Virago, 1983.

03756. Matthews, Jacquie. "Barbara Bodichon: Integrity in Diversity (1827-1891)." In Feminist Theorists, edited by Dale Spender, pp. 90-123. New York: Pantheon Books, Random House, 1983.

03757. Oakley, Ann. "Millicent Garrett Fawcett: Duty and Determination (1847-1929)." In Feminist Theorists, edited by Dale Spender, pp. 184-202. New York: Pantheon Books, Random House, 1983.

Also refer to #2969, 3760, 3765.

f) Suffrage

(1) Non-specific

(a) Contemporary

03758. National Union of Women's Suffrage Societies. _Women Workers and Women's Votes_, n.d.

03759. Prothero, Rowland E. _Women's Suffrage_. London: National Union of Women's Suffrage Societies, n.d.

Also refer to #3713.

(b) Secondary

03760. Billington, Rosamund. "Ideology and Feminism: Why the Suffragettes were 'Wild Women.'" _Women's Studies International Forum_ 5 (1982): 663-674.

03761. Blewett, Neal. "The Franchise in the United Kingdom." _Past and Present_ 32 (December 1965): 27-56.

03762. Bostick, Theodora. "The Press and the Launching of the Women's Suffrage Movement, 1866-1867." _Victorian Periodicals Newsletter_ 13 (Winter 1980): 125-131.

03763. ________________. "Women's Suffrage, the Press, and the Reform Bill of 1867." _International Journal of Women's Studies_ 3 (1980): 373-390.

03764. Butler, Melissa A. and Templeton, Jacqueline. "The Isle of Man the First Votes for Women." _Women and Politics_ 4 (Summer 1984): 33-47.

03765. Garner, Les. _Stepping Stones to Women's Liberty: Feminist Ideas in the Women's Suffrage Movement, 1900-1918_. Rutherford, N.J.: Fairleigh Dickinson University Press, 1984.

03766. Hamilton, Margaret. "Opposition to Woman Suffrage in England, 1865-1888." _Victorian Institute Journal_ 4(1975): 59-73.

03767. Hirshfield, Claire. "The Actresses' Franchise League and the Campaign for Women's Suffrage 1908-1914." _Theatre Research International_ 10 (Summer 1985): 129-153.

03768. Hume, Leslie Parker. _The National Union of Women's Suffrage Societies 1897-1914_. New York: Garland Publishing Inc., 1982.

03769. Liddington, Jill. "Rediscovering Suffrage History." _History Workshop_ 4 (1977): 192-202.

03770. Moore, Lindy. "The Women's Suffrage Campaign in the 1907 Aberdeen By-Election." Northern Scotland 5 (1983): 155-178.

Also refer to #3741, 3752, 3867, 3892.

(2) The Pankhursts

03771. Franchini, Silvia. Sylvia Pankhurst, 1912-1924. Pisa: ETS Università, 1980.

03772. Noble, Iris. Emmeline and Her Daughters: The Pankhurst Suffragettes. New York: J. Messner, 1971.

03773, Sarah, Elizabeth. "Christabel Pankhurst: Reclaiming Her Power (1880-1958)." In Feminist Theorists, edited by Dale Spender, pp. 256-284. New York: Pantheon Books, Random House, 1983.

03774. Spacks, Patricia Meyer. "Selves in Hiding." In Women's Autobiography, Essays in Criticism, edited by Estelle C. Jellinek, pp. 112-132. Bloomington, Ind.: Indiana University Press, 1980.

(g) Political Roles

03775. Bennett, Anthony. "Broadsides on the Trial of Queen Caroline: A Glimpse at Popular Song in 1820." Proceedings of the Royal Music Association 107 (1980-1981): 79-85.

03776. Bloom, Ursula. The Great Queen Consort. London: Hale, 1976.

03777. Clarke, W. The Authentic and Impartial Life of Mrs. Mary Ann Clarke. London: T. Kelly, 1809.

03778. Duff, David. Alexandra: Princess and Queen. London: Collins, 1980.

03779. Fisher, G. and Fisher, H. Bertie and Alex. Anatomy of a Royal Marriage. London: R. Hale, 1974.

03780. Keppel, Sonia. The Sovereign Lady. A Life of Elizabeth Vassal, Third Lady Holland With Her Family. London: Hamilton, 1974.

03781. Laqueur, Thomas W. "The Queen Caroline Affair: Politics as Art in the Reign of George IV." Journal of Modern History 54 (September 1982): 417-466.

03782. Pratt, Linda Ray. "Maud Gonne: 'Strange Harmonies Amid Discord'." Biography 6 (Summer 1983): 189-208.

03783. Richardson, Joanna. "Queen Adelaide: A Portrait." History Today 28 (March 1978): 188-193.

03784. ________________. Victoria and Albert: A Study of a Marriage. New York: Quadrangle, 1977.

03785. Wakeford, G. Three Consort Queens: Adelaide, Alexandra, and Mary. London: Hale, 1971.

Also refer to #4310, 4314.

3. ECONOMIC

"The ranks of sufferers from want of work and of women left dependent on themselves are recruited from the higher classes where work is not a duty until it becomes a necessity."

Art Journal, 1872

a) Generic

03786. Bosanquet, Helen. The Standard of Life, and Other Reprinted Essays. 2d ed. London: Macmillan, 1906.

03787. British Association for Labour Legislation. Report on the Administration of Labour Laws in the United Kingdom. London: Twentieth Century Press, 1908.

03788. Harben, Henry D. The Endowment of Motherhood. Fabian Tract no. 149. London: Fabian Society, 1910.

03789. Holley, J. C. "The Two Family Economies of Industrialism Factory Workers in Victorian Scotland." Journal of Family History 6 (1981): 57-69.

03790. Hopkins, Eric. "The Decline of the Family Work Unit in Black Country Nailing." International Review of Social History 22 (1977): 184-197.

03791. Humphries, Jane. "Class Struggle and the Persistence of the Working Class Family." Cambridge Journal of Economics 1 (1977): 241-258.

03792. McQuillan, Kevin. "Economic Factors and Internal Migration: The Case of Nineteenth-Century England." Social Science History 4 (Fall 1980): 479-499.

03793. Porter, G. R. The Progress of the Nation in Its Various Social and Economic Relations From the Beginning of the Nineteenth Century. London: Methuen, 1912.

03794. Roberts, Elizabeth. "Working-Class Standards of Living in Barrow and Lancaster, 1890-1914." Economic History Review 2nd ser. 30 (1977): 306-319.

03795. Roberts, Elizabeth. "Working-Class Standards of Living in Three Lancashire Towns, 1890-1914." _International Review of Social History_ 27 (1982): 43-65.

03796. Ross, Ellen. "Survival Networks: Women's Neighborhood Sharing in London Before World War One." _History Workshop_ 15 (Spring 1983): 4-27.

03797. Rowntree, B. Seebohm. _Poverty: A Study of Town Life_. 2nd ed. London: Macmillan, 1902.

03798. ____________________ and Kendall, May. _How the Labourer Lives, A Study of the Rural Labor Problem_. London: Thomas Nelson & Sons, 1913.

03799. Samuelson, James. _The Lament of the Sweated_. London: P.S. King & Son, 1908.

03800. Storch, Robert D. "Popular Festivity and Consumer Protest: Food Price Disturbances in the Southwest and Oxfordshire in 1867." _Albion_ (Winter 1982): 209-234.

03801. Vicinus, Martha. _Independent Women: Work and Community for Single Women, 1850-1920_. Chicago: University of Chicago Press, 1985.

03802. Winter, James. "Widowed Mothers and Mutual Aid in Early Victorian Britain." _Journal of Social History_ 17 (Fall 1983): 115-125.

Also refer to #2996, 3707, 3723, 3726, 3733, 3982.

b) Women's Employment

(1) Non-specific

03803. Adler, N., and Tawney, R. H. _Boy and Girl Labour_. London: Women's Industrial Council, 1909.

03804. Black, Clementina. _Married Women's Work_. 1915. Reprint. London: Virago, 1983.

03805. "Enquirers into Women's Work." _Englishwoman's Review_ 30 (1899): 14-18.

03806. Gittins, Diana. _Fair Sex: Family Size and Structure in Britain, 1900-1939_. New York: St. Martin's Press, 1982.

03807. Great Britain. Board of Trade. _Report by Miss Collet on the Statistics of Employment of Women and Girls_. Parliamentary Papers, 1894, lxxxi, part 2, C 7564.

03808. Great Britain. Royal Labour Commission. _Reports on the Employment of Women by the Lady Assistant Commissioners_. Parliamentary Papers, 1893-94, xxxvii, C6894.

03809. Harris, Lillian. Abolition of Overtime for Women. Women's Co-operative Guild, Investigative Papers, no. 2. London: Women's Co-operative Guild, 1896.

03810. Higgs, Mary. Glimpses into the Abyss. London: n.p., 1906.

03811. Hutchins, Elizabeth Leigh. "Some Aspects of Women's Life and Work." Women's Trades Unions Review, no. 74 (July 1909): 6-12.

03812. Jones, T. Spencer. The Moral Side of Living-In. London: Shop Assistant Publishing Co., 1907.

03813. Lewis, Jane. "Dealing with Dependency: State Practices and Social Realities, 1870-1945." In Women's Welfare, Women's Rights, pp. 17-37. London: Croom Helm, 1983.

03814. Low, Barbara. Some Considerations Concerning Women in the Labour Market. London: P. S. King & Son, 1914.

03815. McFeely, Mary Drake. Women's Work in Britain and America From the Nineties to World War I, An Annotated Bibliography. Boston, Mass: G.K. Hall & Co., 1982.

03816. Nash, Mrs. Vaughan. Reduction of Hours of Work for Women. Women's Co-operative Guild Investigation Papers no. 1. London: The Guild, 1896.

03817. Oliver, Thomas, ed. Dangerous Trades. London: John Murray, 1902.

03818. Phillipps, Leonora. A Dictionary of Employments Open to Women, With Details of Wages, Hours of Work, and Other Information, London: The Women's Institute, 1898.

03819. "Reports on Skilled Employments for Women." Charity Organization Review n.s. 7 (June 1900): 325-328; 8 (July 1900): 47-49; 9 (February 1901): 101-140; 10 (November 1901): 276-277; 12 (July 1902): 54-55.

03820. Scott, W.R. Report on Home Industries in the Highlands and Islands. Edinburgh: HMSO, 1914.

03821. Wohl, Anthony S. "Working Women or Healthy Homes: The Late Victorian Controversy." Bulletin of the Society for the Social History of Medicine 21 (1977): 20-24.

03822. Women's Co-operative Guild. Report of Investigations into the Conditions of Women's Work. London: Women's Co-operative Guild, 1896.

03823. Zimmern, Alice. Unpaid Professions for Women. London: Guardian Office, 1906.

Also refer to #2997.

(2) Domestic

03824. Aberdeen, Ishbel. "Household Clubs: An Experiment." _Nineteenth Century_ 31 (1892): 391-398.

03825. "The Coming Domestic Evolution." _Chambers's Edinburgh Journal_ 81 (9 April 1904): 289-291.

03826. "The Domestic Tyrant." _Chambers's Edinburgh Journal_ 82 (29 July 1905): 545-548.

03827. Ebery, Mark, and Preston, Brian. _Domestic Service in Late Victorian and Edwardian England, 1871-1914_. Geographical Papers, no. 42. Reading, Pa.: Department of Geography, University of Reading, 1976.

03828. Higgs, Edward. "Domestic Servants and Households in Victorian England." _Social History_ 8 (May 1983): 201-210.

03829. Lewis, Elizabeth. "A Reformation of Domestic Service." _Nineteenth Century_ 38 (January-June 1893): 128-138.

03830. McCall, Dorothy Home. "Another Aspect of the Servant Problem." _National Review_ 60 (1912): 969-973.

03831. Webb, Catherine. "An Unpopular Industry." _Nineteenth Century_ 43 (January-June 1903): 989-1001.

03832. Willoughby de Broke, Marie. "The Pros and Cons of Domestic Service." _National Review_ 60 (1912): 452-460.

Also refer to #4079.

(3) Industrial

03833. Bosanquet, Helen. "Report of the Special Committee on the Industrial Employment of Women." _Charity Organization Review_ 8 (December 1900): 407-408.

03834. Boucherett, E. Jessie. "Lead Poisoning in Pottery Work." _Englishwomen's Review_ 30 (15 April 1899): 98-102.

03835. Bythell, Duncan. _The Sweated Trades: Outwork in Nineteenth Century Britain_. London: Botsford, 1978.

03836. Dilke, Emilia F.S. _The Industrial Position of Women_. London: Women's Trade Union League, n.d.

03837. Ford, Isabella O. _Industrial Women and How to Help Them_. London: Humanitarian League, 1894.

03838. Galton, Frank W., ed. _Workers on Their Industries_. London: Swann Sonnenschein, 1895.

03839. Great Britain. Board of Trade. *Report on Changes in the Employment of Women and Girls in Industrial Centres*. Part I. *Flax and Jute Centres*. By C.E. Collet. Parliamentary Papers, 1898, lxxxviii, C.8794.

03840. Harrison, Amy. *Women's Industries in Liverpool*. London: Williams & Norgate, 1904.

03841. Haslam, James. "Female Labour in the Potteries." *Englishwoman* 3 (July-September 1909): 61-73.

03842. ___________. "Sweating in the Irish Linen Industry." *Englishwoman* 9 (January-March 1911): 137-146.

03843. Haslam, James. "Women Workers in the Linen Industry." *Enlishwoman* 9 (January-March 1911): 32-40.

03844. Irwin, Margaret H. *Women's Work in Tailoring and Dressmaking: Report of an Inquiry Conducted for the Scottish Council for Women's Trades*. Glasgow: The Council, 1900.

03845. Lambertz, Jan. "Sexual Harassment in the Nineteenth Century English Cotton Industry." *History Workshop* 19 (Spring 1985): 29-61.

03846. Lown, Judy. "Not so much a Factory, More a Farm of Patriarchy: Gender and Class During Industrialization." In *Gender, Class and Work*, edited by Eva Gamarnikow, et al., pp. 28-45. London: Heinemann, 1983.

03847. Mallet, C. *Dangerous Trades for Women*. The Humanitarian Leagues; Publications no. 9. London: William Reeves, 1893.

03848. Mappen, Ellen. *Helping Women at Work: The Women's Industrial Council, 1889-1914*. London: Hutchinson in association with the Explorations in Feminism Collective affiliated to the Women's Research and Resources Center, 1985.

03849. Meyer, Adele, and Black, Clementina. *Makers of Our Clothes: A Case for Trade Boards: Being the Results of a Year's Investigation into the Work of Women in London in the Tailoring Dressmaking, and Underclothing Trades*. London: Duckworth & Co., 1909.

03850. Mudie-Smith, Richard, comp. *Sweated Industries: Being a Handbook of the "Daily News" Exhibition*. London: Daily News Office, 1906.

03851. Muirhead, M.T. "Women Workers in the Printing and Stationery Trades in Birmingham." *Women Workers* (Birmingham) 9 (September 1901): 31-33.

03852. Papworth, Lucy Wyatt, and Zimmern, Dorothy M. *Clothing and Textile Trades: Summary Tables*. London: Women's Industrial Council, 1912.

03853. "Report on the Millinery Trade." Women's Industrial News n.s. 34 (March 1906): 535-541.

03854. Robertson, John. Report on Industrial Employment of Married Women and Infantile Mortality. Birmingham: City of Birmingham Health Department, 1910.

03855. Satre, Lowell J. "After the Match Girls' Strike: Bryant and May in the 1890's." Victorian Studies 26 (Autumn 1982): 7-31.

03856. Schmeichen, James Andres. Sweated Industries and Sweated Labor: The London Clothing Trades, 1867-1914. Champaign, Ill.: University of Illinois Press, 1983.

03857. Scottish Council for Women's Trades. Report of the National Conference on Sweated Industries. Glasgow: The Council, 1907.

03858. Tuckwell, Gertrude M. "The Industrial Position of Women." Independent Review (August 1904): 365-376.

03859. Wilson, Mona. Our Industrial Laws: Working Women in Factories, Workshops, Shops and Laundries, and How to Help Them. Edited and with a preface by Mrs. H.J. Tennant. Issued by the Industrial Law Committee. London: Duckworth & Co., 1899.

03860. Women's Co-operative Guild. Women Employees in Co-operative Stores and Factories. Oxford: Women's Co-operative Guild, 1910.

03861. Women's Trade Union Association. How Women Work, Being Extracts from Evidence Given Before Group C of the Labour Commission in Regard to Women Working in the Ropemaking and Other Trades in London. London: The Association, n.d.

Also refer to #3721, 3728, 3729, 3939, 3946.

(4) Agricultural

03862. Breen, Richard. "Farm Servanthood in Ireland, 1900-1940." Economic History Review 36 (February 1983): 87-102.

03863. Fitzpatrick, David. "Irish Farming Families Before the First World War." Comparative Studies in Society and History 25 (April 1983): 339-374.

03864. Horn, Pamela. Labouring Life in the Victorian Countryside. Dublin: Gill & Macmillan, 1976.

03865. Miller, C. "The Hidden Workforce: Female Field Workers in Gloucestershire, 1870-1901." Social History 6 (1984): 139-161.

(5) Retail

03866. Bondfield, Margaret G. "Conditions Under Which Shop Assistants Work." _Economic Journal_ 9 (1899): 227-286.

03867. ____________________. _Shop Workers and the Vote_. London: The People's Suffrage Federation, 1911.

03868. ____________________. "What Shop Workers Want from Parliament." _Women's Trade Union Review_, 70 (July 1908): 12-17.

03869. "Report on the Condition of Female Shop Assistants in London." In _Women's Industrial Council, Annual Report_, pp. 17-19. 3rd ed. London: The Council, 1896-1897.

(6) Other Forms of Employment

03870. Ford, Isabella O. _Women as Factory Inspectors and Certifying Surgeons_. Investigation Papers, no. 4, Manchester: Women's Cooperative Guild, 1898.

03871. Greenwood, M. "Women in Dust Yards." _Englishwoman's Review_ 31 (1900): 158-161.

03872. Irwin, Margaret H. _Home Work in Ireland: Report of an Inquiry Conducted for the Scottish Council for Women's Trades_. 2nd ed. Glasgow: The Council, 1913.

03873. Joint Committee on the Employment of Barmaids. _Women as Barmaids_. London: P.S. King, 1905.

03874. Langley, Herbert Hunt. "The Typists' Sex War." _Socialist Review_ 3 (1909): 308-312.

03875. Leslie, Anita and Chapman, Pauline. _Madame Tussaud_. London: Hutchinson, 1978.

03876. Liverpool Women's Industrial Council. _Report on Homework in Liverpool_. Liverpool: The Council, 1908.

03877. Malcolmson, Patricia E. "Laundresses and the Laundry Trade in Victorian England." _Victorian Studies_ 24 (Summer 1981): 439-462.

03878. "Of the Admission of Women to the Legal Profession a Word in Favour, by a Solicitor." _Englishwoman_ 9 (January-March 1911): 293-300.

03879. Spencer, Edward. "Women and the Handicrafts." _Englishwoman_ 12 (October-December 1911): 56-67.

03880. Twining, Louisa. "Official Work of Women." _Englishwoman's Review_ 30 (1899): 81-85.

03881. Twining, Louisa. "Women as Official Inspectors." _Nineteenth Century_ (March 1894): 489-494.

03882. ______________. "Women as Public Servants." _Nineteenth Century_ (December 1890): 950-958.

03883. Walten, John K. _The Blackpool Landlady: A Social History_. Manchester: University Press, 1978.

03884. Webber, Nigel. "Prospect and Prejudice: Women and Librarianship, 1880-1914." _Library History_ 6 (1984): 153-162.

03885. Women's Institute, London. _The Women's Institute_. London: The Institute, 1897.

(7) Vocational Training/Apprenticeship

03886. Apprenticeship and Skilled Employment Association. _Trades for London Girls and How to Enter Them_. London: Longmans Green, 1914.

03887. Women's Industrial Council. _Technical Education for Girls in England and Elsewhere_. London: Women's Industrial Council, 1897.

03888. _________________________. _Technical Education for Women and Girls at Home and Abroad_. London: Women's Industrial Council, 1905.

(8) Wages

03889. Bosanquet, Helen. "The Economics of Women's Work and Wages." _National Liberal Club, Political and Economic Circle. Transactions_, vol. 5, part 14. London: P.S. King, 1907.

03890. _______________. "A Study in Women's Wages." _Economic Journal_ 12 (March 1902): 42-49.

03891. _______________. "Wages and Housekeeping." In _Methods of Social Advance_, edited by C.S. Loch, pp. 131-146. London: Macmillan, 1904.

03892. Hamilton, Mary Agnes. "Women's Wages and the Vote." _Englishwoman_ 7 (July-September 1910): 41-47, 139-146.

03893. John, Angela V., ed. _Unequal Opportunities. Women's Employment in England 1800-1918_. New York: Basic Blackwell, 1986.

03894. Jones, Dora. "The Cheapness of Women." _Englishwoman's Review_ 40 (1909): 235-243.

03895. MacDonald, Margaret, et al. _Wage Earning Mothers_. London: Women's Labour League, n.d.

03896. National Anti-Sweating League. Report of Conference on a Minimum Wage, Held at the Guildhall. London: Co-operative Printing Society, 1907.

03897. Webb, Sidney. "The Alleged Differences of the Wages Paid to Men and Women for Similar Work." Economic Journal 1 (1891): 635-662.

03898. Williamson, Jeffrey G. "Earnings Inequality in Nineteenth-Century Britain." Journal of Economic History 40 (1980): 457-476.

03899. Women's Co-operative Guild. A Minimum Wage Scale for Co-operative Women and Girl Employees. Manchester: Co-operative Wholesale Society's Printing Works, 1910.

03900. Women's Industrial Council. "Report of the National Conference on the Unemployment of Women Dependent on Their Own Earnings, Held in the Council Chamber of the Guildhall, London, E.C., on Tuesday, October 15th, 1907." Women's Industrial News 41 (December 1907): 669-705.

03901. ________. Women's Wages in England in the Nineteenth Century. London: Women's Industrial Council, 1906.

c) Trade Unions

03902. Dilke, Emilia Frances Strong. Trades Unions for Women. London: Women's Trade Union League, n.d.

03903. Glage, Liselotte. Clementina Black: A Study in Social History and Literature. Heidelberg: Winter, 1981.

03904. ________. "Clementina Black: Ein Beitrag zur Geschichte der englischen Arbeiterinnenbewegung." Englisch-Amerikanische Studien 2 (1980): 214-222.

03905. Muirhead, M.T. "Report on the Pen Trade in Birmingham." Women Workers. (Birmingham) 11 (September 1901): 34-37.

Also refer to #3892.

d) Housing for Working Women

03906. "Bow and Spear: Women's Lodging Houses and the Woman Worker." Englishwoman 8 (1910): 139.

03907. Higgs, Mary. "Housing of the Women Workers." Progress 4 (1909): 167-174.

03908. ________. "A Visit to the Manchester Municipal Women's Lodging House." Progress 8 (1913): 163-168.

03909. Higgs, Mary. "Women's Lodging Homes in London." Progress 6 (1911): 248-255.

03910. Meredith, Maud. "Housing of Educated Women Workers." Englishwoman 9 (January-March 1911): 159-164.

03911. Reinherz, H. "The Housing of the Educated Working Woman." Englishwoman's Review 31 (1900): 7-11.

03912. Zimmern, Alice. "Ladies' Dwellings." Contemporary Review 77 (1900): 96-104.

4. RELIGION

> "Though religion is indispensably necessary to both sexes, and in every possible character and station, yet a woman seems, more peculiarly to need its enlivening support."
>
> John Bennett, Letters to a Young Lady on a Variety of Useful and Interesting Subjects 1789

a) Generic

03913. Bramwell-Booth, Catherine. Catherine Booth; The Story of Her Loves. London: Houder and Stoughton, 1973.

03914. Burfield, Diana. "Theosophy and Feminism: Some Explorations in Nineteenth-Century Biography." In Women's Religious Experience, edited by Pat Holden, pp. 27-56. Totowa, N.J.: Barnes and Noble Books, 1983.

03915. Creighton, Louise. Women's Work for the Church and for the State. Pan-Anglican papers, no. 7, London: Society for Promoting Christian Knowledge, 1907.

03916. Ducrocq, Francoise. "The London Biblewomen and Nurses Mission, 1857-1880: Class Relations/Women's Relations." In Women and the Structure of Society, edited by Barbara J. Harris and JoAnn McNamara, pp. 98-107. Durham, N.C.: Duke University Press, 1984.

03917. Healey, Charles J. "Maude Petre: Her Life and Significance." Recusant History 15 (May 1979): 23-42.

03918. Heeney, Brian. "Women's Struggle for Professional Work and Status in the Church of England, 1900-1930." Historical Journal 26 (June 1983): 329-347.

03919. Holden, Pat, ed. Women's Religious Experience. Totowa, N.J.: Barnes and Noble Books, 1983.

03920. Hutch, William D. Mrs. Ball: Foundress of the Institution of the Blessed Virgin Mary in Ireland and the British Colonies. London: James Duffy, 1879.

03921. Kerr, Anabel. *Sister Chatelain, or Forty Years Work in Westminister*. London: Catholic Truth Society, 1900.

03922. McLeod, Hugh. *Class and Religion in the Late Victorian City*. Hamden, Conn.: Archon Books, 1974.

03923. Malmgreen, Gail. "Anne Knight and the Radical Subculture." *Quaker History* 71 (Fall 1982): 100-113.

03924. Meade, Marion. *Madame Blavatsky: The Woman Behind the Myth*. New York: Putnam, 1980.

03925. Murdoch, Norman H. "Female Ministry in the Thought of Catherine Booth." *Church History* 53 (September 1984): 348-362.

03926. Skultans, Vieda. "Mediums, Controls and Eminent Men." In *Women's Religious Experience*, edited by Pat Holden, pp. 15-26. Totowa, N.J.: Barnes and Noble, 1983.

03927. Valenze, Deborah M. "Pilgrims and Progress in Nineteenth-Century England." In *Culture, Ideology and Politics*, edited by R. Samuel and G. Stedman Jones, pp. 113-125. London: Routledge and Kegan Paul, 1983.

03928. ________________. *Prophetic Sons and Daughters, Female Preaching and Popular Religion in Industrial England*. Princeton, N.J.: Princeton University Press, 1985.

b) Missionaries

03929. Christian, Carol and Plummer, Gladys. *God and One Redhead: Mary Slessor of Calabar*. Grand Rapids, Mich.: Zondervan Publishing, 1970.

03930. Giberne, Agnes. *A Lady of England: The Life and Letters of Charlotte Maria Tucker*. London: Hodder and Stoughton, 1896.

03931. Livingstone, William Pringle. *Mary Slessor of Calabar, Pioneer Missionary*. Grand Rapids, Mich.: Zondervan Publishing House, 1984.

Also refer to #3916.

5. SOCIAL

"Much is expected of the housewife, in that she should remain good-tempered, patient and calm amid the cares and worries of domestic life. Controlling a family with various temperaments, interests and problems, calls for great sympathy, affection and humour . . . "

Mrs. Beeton's Cookery and Household Management 1860

a) Generic

(1) Non-specific

03932. Adburgham, Alison. Silver Fork Society: Fashionable Life and Literature from 1814-1840. London: Constable, 1983.

03933. Anderson, Michael. "The Social Position of Spinsters in Mid-Victorian Britain." Journal of Family History 9 (Winter 1984): 377-393.

03934. Beaver, Patrick. The Spice of Life: Pleasures of the Victorian Age. London: Elm Tree, 1979.

03935. Beck, Jane C. "The White Lady of Great Britain and Ireland." Folk-lore 81 (Winter 1970): 292-306.

03936. Brennan, E.R.; James, A.V; and Morrill, W.T. "Inheritance, Demographic Structure and Marriage: A Cross-Cultural Perspective." Journal of Family History 7 (Fall 1982): 282-298.

03937. Ford, Colin and Harrison, Brian. A Hundred Years Ago: Britain in the 1880's in Words and Photographs. Cambridge: Harvard University Press, 1983.

03938. Jalland, Patricia. "Victorian Spinsters: Dutiful Daughters, Desperate Rebels and the Transition to the New Woman." In Exploring Women's Past, edited by Patricia Crawford, et al., pp. 129-170. Boston: George Allen and Unwin, 1983.

03939. John, Angela V. Coalmining Women: Victorian Lives and Campaigns. New York: Cambridge University Press, 1984.

03940. Kanner, S. Barbara. Victorian Women in English Social History. New York: Garland Publishing, 1986.

03941. Maas, Barbara. "Idealisierung und Domestikation: Das bürgerliche Frauenbild in der frühviktorianischen Publizistik." In Frauen in der Geschichte III, edited by Annette Kuhn and Jörn Rüsen, pp. 139-166. Dusseldorf: Schwann, 1983.

03942. McKibbin, Ross I. "Social Class and Social Observation in Edwardian England." Transactions of the Royal Historical Society 5th ser. 28 (1978): 175-199.

03943. O'Neill, Kevin. Family and Farm in Pre-Famine Ireland: The Parish of Killashandra. Madison: University of Wisconsin Press, 1984.

03944. Osborn, Christabel. "Rowton Houses for Women." Contemporary Review 99 (June 1911): 707-717.

03945. Roberts, Elizabeth. A Woman's Place, An Oral History of Working-Class Women 1890-1940. New York: Basil Blackwell, 1986.

03946. Treble, James H. Urban Poverty in Britain, 1830-1914. London: Batsford, 1979.

03947. Wingfield-Stratford, Esme. The Victorian Tragedy. London: George Routledge and Sons, 1930.

Also refer to #3008, 3883.

(2) Women

(a) Individuals

03948. Askwith, Betty. Piety and Wit: A Biography of Harriet, Countess Granville, 1785-1862. London: Collins, 1982.

03949. Freeman, Sarah. Isabella and Sam: The Story of Mrs. Beeton. New York: Coward, McCann and Geoghegan, 1978.

03950. Legge, Sylvia. Affectionate Cousins: T. Sturge Moore and Maria Appia. New York: Oxford University Press, 1980.

03951. Nicholson, Nigel. Mary Curzon. New York: Harper, 1977.

03952. Powell, Violet. Margaret, Countess of Jersey, A Biography. London: Heinemann, 1978.

03953. Sturt, George. Lucy Bettesworth. Firle, Sussex: Caliban Books, 1978.

03954. Thomas, Hilary M. Grandmother Extraordinary: Mary de la Beche Nicholl, 1839-1922. Barry: Stewart Williams, 1979.

03955. Westwater, Martha. The Wilson Sisters, A Biographical Study of Upper Middle-Class Victorian Life. Athens, Ohio: Ohio University Press, 1984.

03956. Young, Percy M. Alice Edgar: Enigma of a Victorian Lady. London: Dobson, 1978.

(b) Travellers

03957. Armstrong, Martin D. Lady Hester Stanhope. New York: Viking Press, 1928.

03958. Glynn, Stephen Lucius. *Life of Mary Kingsley*. London: Macmillan, 1933.

03959. Hall, Richard S. *Lovers on the Nile: The Incredible African Journeys of Sam and Florence Baker*. New York: Random House, 1980.

03960. Heussler, Robert. "Imperial Lady: Gertrude Bell and the Middle East, 1889-1926." *British Studies Monitor* 9 (1979): 3-22.

03961. Howard, C. *Mary Kingsley*. London: Hutchinson, 1957.

03962. Scott, D.F.S. "Sarah Austin and Germany: 'An Interpreter Between the Mind of Britain and the Mind of Germany." *German Life and Letters* 2 (January 1949): 138-148.

03963. Scott, J.M. "An Explorer's Wife." *Blackwood's Magazine* 328 (1980): 324-334, 496-508.

03964. Williams, W.H. *The Romance of Isabel, Lady Burton*. New York: Dodd Mead, 1897.

(c) Migration

03965. Macdonald, Charlotte J. "Ellen Silk and Her Sisters: Female Emigration to the New World." In *The Sexual Dynamics of History*, edited by The London Feminist History Group, pp. 66-86. London: Pluto Press, 1983.

b) Demography

03966. Clarkson, L.A. "Marriage and Fertility in 19th Century Ireland." In *Marriage and Society: Studies in the Social History of Marriage*, edited by R.B. Outhwaite, pp. 237-255. New York: St. Martin's Press, 1981.

03967. Connolly, S.J. "Illegitimacy and Pre-Nuptial Pregnancy in Ireland Before 1864: The Evidence of Some Catholic Paris Registers." *Irish Economic and Social History* 6 (1979): 5-23.

03968. Crafts, N.F.R. "Illegitimacy in England and Wales in 1911." *Population Studies* 36 (July 1982): 327-331.

03969. Firsch, Rose E. "Some Further Notes on Population, Food Intake and Natural Fertility." In *Natural Fertility*, edited by Henri Leridon and Jane Menken, pp. 135-147. Liege: Ordina Editions, 1979.

03970. Friedlander, Dov. "Demographic Responses and Socioeconomic Structure: Population Processes in England and Wales in the Nineteenth Century." *Demography* 20 (August 1983): 249-272.

03971. Friedlander, Dov; Schellekens, Jona; Ben-Moshe, E.; and Keysar, Arula. "Socioeconomic Characteristics and Life Expectancies in Nineteenth-Century England:--a District Analysis." Population Studies 39 (March 1985): 137-152.

03972. Haines, Michael R. "Age Specific and Differential Fertility in Durham and Easington Registration Districts, England 1851 and 1861." Social Science History 2 (Fall 1977): 23-52.

03973. Ledbetter, Rosanna. A History of the Malthusian League, 1877-1927. Columbus: Ohio State University Press, 1976.

03974. Teitelbaum, Michael S. The British Fertility Decline, Demographic Transition in the Crucible of the Industrial Revolution. Princeton: Princeton University Press, 1984.

03975. Woods, R.I. and Smith, C.W. "The Decline of Marital Fertility in the Late Nineteenth Century: The Case of England and Wales." Population Studies 37 (July 1983): 207-226.

Also refer to #3993, 4008.

c) Family

03976. Anderson, Nancy F. "No Angel in the House: The Psychological Effects of Maternal Death." The Psychohistory Review 11 (Fall 1982): 20-46.

03977. Banks, Joseph A. Victorian Values: Secularism and the Size of Families. London: Routledge and Kegan Paul, 1981.

03978. Bell, Florence [Lady Bell]. At the Works, A Study of a Manufacturing Town. 1907. Reprint. New York: Augustus M. Kelley, 1969.

03979. Martin, Anna. "The Mother and Social Reform." Nineteenth Century (1913): 1060-1079; 1235-1255.

03980. Mills, Dennis. "Residential Propinquity of Kin in a Cambridgeshire Village, 1841." Journal of Historical Geography 4 (July 1978): 265-276.

03981. Mintz, Stephen. A Prison of Expectations: The Family in Victorian Culture. New York: New York University Press, 1983.

03982. Nash, Roy. "Family and Economic Structure in Nineteenth-Century Wales: Llangernyw and Gwytherin in 1871." Welsh History Review 11 (December 1982): 135-149.

03983 Smelser, Neil. "The Victorian Family." In Families in Britain, pp. 59-74. Boston: Routledge and Kegan Paul, 1983.

03984. Varley, Anthony. "The Stem Family in Ireland. Reconsidered." Comparative Studies in Society and History 25 (April 1983): 381-392.

Also refer to #2996, 2997, 3703, 3734, 3788-3791, 3802, 3806, 3854, 3895, 3936, 3967, 3968, 3974, 4084, 4088, 4161, 4198, 4213, 4241, 4585.

d) Marriage

(1) Contemporary

03985. "Domestic Harmony." Chambers's Edinburgh Journal 57 (7 February 1880): 93-95.

03986. "Matrimony by Advertisement." Chambers's Edinburgh Journal 47 (26 November 1870): 753-756.

03987. Oliphant, Margaret. "Anti-Marriage League." Blackwood's Magazine 324 (1978): 132-140.

03988. W.C. "The Matrimonial." Chambers's Edinburgh Journal 56 (1 November 1879): 689-692.

(2) Secondary

03989. Crafts, N.F.R. "Average Age at First Marriage for Women in Mid-Nineteenth Century England and Wales: A Cross-Section Study." Population Studies 32 (1978): 21-25.

03990. Herbert, Christopher. "'He Knew He Was Right', Mrs. Lynn Linton, and The Duplicities of Victorian Marriage." Texas Studies in Literature and Language 25 (Fall 1983): 448-469.

03991. Ross, Ellen. "'Fierce Questions and Taunts'" Married Life in Working-Class London, 1870-1914." Feminist Studies 8 (Fall 1982): 575-602.

03992. Trustam, Myna. Women of the Regiment. Marriage and the Victorian Army. Cambridge: University Press, 1984.

03993. Woods, R.I. and Hinde, P.R.A. "Nuptuality and Age at Marriage in Nineteenth Century England." Journal of Family History 10 (Summer 1985): 119-144.

Also refer to #3722, 3724-3727, 3730-3732, 4080, 4081.

e) Sex Life and Morals

(1) Non-specific

03994. Brome, Vincent. Havelock Ellis: Philosopher of Sex. New York: Routledge and Kegan Paul, 1979.

03995. Chaloner, W.H. "How Immoral Were the Victorians? A Bibliographical Reconsideration." Bulletin of the John Rylands Library 60 (1978): 362-375.

03996. Jeffreys, Sheila. "'Free From All Uninvited Touch of Man': Women's Campaigns Around Sexuality, 1880-1914." Women's Studies International Forum 5 (1982): 629-645. Also in The Sexuality Papers, edited by Lal Coveney et al., pp. 22-44. London: Hutchinson, 1984.

03997. Maynard, John. "The Worlds of Victorian Sexuality: Work in Progress." In Sexuality and Victorian Literature, edited by Don Richard Cox, pp. 251-266. Knoxville, Tenn.: University of Tennessee Press, 1984.

03998. Weeks, Jeffrey. Coming Out: Homosexual Politics in Britain From the Nineteenth Century to the Present. New York: Quartet Books, 1977.

03999. ____________. "'Sins and Diseases': Some Notes on Homosexuality in the Nineteenth Century." History Workshop 1 (1976): 211-219.

Also refer to #4052, 4054, 4077, 4078, 4082, 4089, 4286, 4289.

(2) Prostitutes/Courtesans

(a) Generic

04000. Engel, Arthur J. "'Immoral Intentions': The University of Oxford and the Problem of Prostitution, 1827-1914." Victorian Studies 23 (Autumn 1979): 79-107.

04001. Unsworth, Madge. Maiden Tribute a Study in Voluntary Social Service. London: Salvationist Publishing and Supplies, 1949.

04002. Walkowitz, Judith R. "Male Vice and Female Virtue: Feminism and the Politics of Prostitution in Nineteenth-Century Britain." In Class, Race and Sex: The Dynamics of Control, edited by Amy Swerdlow and Hanna Lessinger, pp. 10-30. Boston: G.K. Hall and Co., 1983. Also in History Workshop 13 (Spring 1982): 77-93.

Also refer to #3044, 3993.

(b) Josephine Butler

04003. Fawcett, Millicent Garrett. "Josephine Butler." *Contemporary Review* 133 (April 1928): 442-446.

04004. Spencer, Anna Garlin. "Josephine Butler and the English Crusade." *Forum* 49 (June 1913): 711-716.

04005. Uglow, Jenny. "Josephine Butler: From Sympathy to Theory (1828-1906)." In *Feminist Theorists*, edited by Dale Spender, pp. 146-164. New York: Pantheon Books, Random House, 1983.

Also refer to #4001.

f) Fashion/Manners

04006. Buck, Anne. *Women's Costume 1870-1900*. Manchester: Gallery of English Costume, 1953.

04007. __________. *Women's Costume 1900-1930*. Manchester: Gallery of English Costume, 1956.

04008. Davies, Mel. "Corsets and Conception: Fashion and Demographic Trends in the Nineteenth Century." *Comparative Studies in Society and History* 24 (October 1982): 611-641.

04009. Gernsheim, Alison. *Victorian and Edwardian Fashion*. New York: Dover, 1981.

04010. Ginsburg, Madeleine. *Victorian Dress in Photographs*. New York: Holmes and Meier, 1982.

04011. Gitter, Elisabeth G. "Power of Women's Hair in the Victorian Imagination." *Proceedings of the Modern Language Association* 99 (October 1984): 936-954.

04012. Monro, D.H. "Godwin, Oakeshott and Mrs. Bloomer." *Journal of the History of Ideas* 35 (October-December 1974): 611-624.

04013. Sichel, Marion. *Costume Reference 5. The Regency*. Boston: Plays Inc., 1978.

04014. __________. *Costume Reference 6. The Victorians*. Boston: Plays Inc., 1978.

04015. Stevenson, Pauline. *Edwardian Fashion*. London: Ian Allan, 1980.

g) Philanthropy

(1) Non-specific

04016. Checkland, Olive. *Philanthropy in Victorian Scotland: Social Welfare and the Voluntary Principle*. Atlantic Highlands, N.J.: Humanities Press, 1980.

04017. Evans, Neil. "Urbanization, Elite Attitudes and Philanthropy: Cardiff, 1850-1914." *International Review of Social History* 27 (1982): 290-323.

Also refer to #3916.

(2) Women

(a) Individuals

[1] Angela Burdett-Coutts

04018. Healey, Edna. *Lady Unknown: The Life of Angela Burdett-Coutts* London: Sidgwick and Jackson, 1984.

04019. Orton, Diana. *Made of Gold: A Biography of Angela Burdett Coutts*. North Pomfret, Vt.: David and Charles, 1980.

(b) Others

04020. Allen, Herbert Warner. *Lucy Houston, D.B.E*. London: Constable, 1947.

04021. Allen, Vivien. *Lady Trader: A Biography of Mrs. Sarah Heckford*. London: Collins, 1979.

04022. Biller, Sarah. *Memoir of the Late Hannah Kilham*. London: Darton and Harvey, 1837.

04023. Craven, Pauline. *Lady Georgiana Fullerton*. Paris: Perrin, 1889.

04024. "A Group of Female Philanthropists." *London Quarterly Review* 57 (1881): 49-81.

h) Social Reform

04025. Blunden, Margaret. *The Countess of Warwick*. London: Cassell, 1967.

04026. Cohen, L. *Lady de Rothschild and Her Daughters*. London: Murray, 1935.

04027. Fitzpatrick, Kathleen. *Lady Henry Somerset*. London: J. Cape, 1923.

04028. Hilton, John Deane. _Marie Hilton: Her Life and Work_. London: Isbister and Co., 1897.

04029. Jackaman, Peter. "Books for Blockade Men: The Concerns of Mistress Fry." _Library Review_ 31 (Summer 1982): 111-120.

04030. Jones, E. Huws. _Margery Fry: The Essential Amateur_. New York: Oxford University Press, 1966.

04031. Lang, T. _My Darling Daisy_. London: M. Joseph, 1966.

04032. Lloyd, Mary Anne. _Susanna Meredith: A Record of a Vigorous Life_. London: Hodder & Stoughton, 1903.

04033. Martin, Frances. _Elizabeth Gilbert and Her Work for the Blind_. New York: Macmillan, 1891.

04034. Metcalfe, Ethel E. _Memoir of Rosamond Davenport Hill_. London: Longmans and Green, 1904.

Also refer to #4071, 4072.

i) Health/Medical

(1) Birth Control/Abortion

04035. Mortimer, Joanne Stafford. "Annie Besant and India, 1913-1917." _Journal of Contemporary History_ 18 (January 1983): 61-78.

Also refer to #3973.

(2) Women in Medicine

(a) Doctors

04036. Baker, Rachel. _The First Woman Doctor_. London: G.G. Harrap, 1946.

04037. Lutzker, Edythe. _Women Gain a Place in Medicine_. New York: McGraw Hill, 1969.

04038. Morantz, Regina Markell. "Feminism, Professionalism, and Germs: The Thought of Mary Putnam Jacobi and Elizabeth Blackwell." _American Quarterly_ 34 (Winter 1983): 459-478.

04039. Murray, Flora. "The Position of Women in Medicine and Surgery." _New Statesman_ 2 Spec. Supp. (1 November 1913): xvi-xvii.

04040. Riddell, George Allardice. _Dame Louisa Aldrich-Blake_. London: Hodder and Stoughton, 1926.

04041. Stoddart, Anna M. _Elizabeth Pease Nichol_. New York: E.P. Dutton, 1899.

Also refer to #3743, 3870, 3914, 4083.

(b) Nurses

04042. Barlow, May S. "Report of an Enquiry into the Supply of and Demand for Nurses for Little Children." _Women's Industrial News_ 55 (1911): 95-104.

04043. Bishop, William and Goldie, Sue. _A Bio-Bibliography of Florence Nightingale_. London: Dawsons of Pall Mall for the International Council of Nurses, 1962.

04044. Smith, F. B. _Florence Nightingale: Reputation and Power_. New York: St. Martin's, 1982.

04045. Summers, Anne. "Images of the Nineteenth-Century Nurse." _History Today_ 34 (December 1984): 40-42.

04046. ____________. "Pride and Prejudice: Ladies and Nurses in the Crimean War." _History Workshop_ 16 (Autumn 1983): 33-56.

Also refer to #3743, 3914.

(c) Midwives

04047. Van Blarcom, Carolyn Conant. _The Midwife in England: Being a Study in England of the Working of the English Midwives Act of 1902_. Philadelphia: William F. Fell Co., 1913.

(d) Medical School

04048. Gordon, William M. "The Right of Women to Graduate in Medicine-Scottish Judicial Attitudes in the Nineteenth Century." _Journal of Legal History_ 5 (September 1984): 136-151.

04049. Great Britain. General Council of Medical Education and Registration. _Special Education for Women_. London: W.J. and S. Goldburn, 1873.

04050. Thorne, Mrs. Isabel. _Sketch of the Foundation and Development of the London School of Medicine for Women_. London: G. Sharrow, 1905.

04051. Wilson, Robert. "Aesculapia Victrix." _Fortnightly Review_ n.s. 39 (January-June 1886): 18-33.

(3) Women and Health

04052. Banks, Joseph A. "The Attitude of the Medical Profession to Sexuality in the Nineteenth Century." _Bulletin of the Society for the Social History of Medicine_ 22 (1978): 9-10.

04053. Edwards, Susan. "Femina Sexualis: Medico-Legal Controversies in Victoriana." _Bulletin of the Society for the Social History of Medicine_ 28 (1981): 17-20.

04054. Lansbury, Coral. "Gynaecology, Pornography, and the Antivivisection Movement." _Victorian Studies_ 28 (Spring 1985): 413-437.

04055. Lewis, Judith Schneid. "Maternal Health in the English Aristocracy: Myths and Realities 1790-1840." _Journal of Social History_ 17 (Fall 1983): 97-114.

04056. Oddy, D.J. "Urban Famine in Nineteenth-Century Britain: The Effect of the Lancashire Cotton Famine on Working Class Diet and Health." _Economic History Review_ 2nd ser. 36 (February 1983): 68-86.

04057. Peterson, M. Jeanne. "The Victorian Medical Profession, the Family, and Social Mobility." _Bulletin of the Society for the Social History of Medicine_ 21 (1977): 19-20.

04058. Trustram, Myna. "Distasteful and Derogatory? Examining Victorian Soldiers for Venereal Disease." In _The Sexual Dynamics of History_, edited by The London Feminist History Group, pp. 154-164. London: Pluto Press, 1983.

Also refer to #3821, 3998, 3999.

j) Recreation

04059. Bailey, Peter. _Leisure and Class in Victorian England: Rational Recreation and the Contest for Control, 1830-1885_. London: Routledge, 1978.

04060. McCrone, Kathleen E. "Play Up! Play Up! And Play the Game! Sport at the Late Victorian Girls' Public School." _Journal of British Studies_ 23 (Spring 1984): 106-134.

04061. Rubinstein, David. "Cycling in the 1890's." _Victorian Studies_ 21 (Autumn 1977): 47-71.

6. CULTURAL

"Mental powers so highly developed in women are in some measure abnormal and involve a physiological cost which the feminine organization will not bear without injury more or less profound."

Constance Naden

a) Education

(1) Non-specific

04062. Blunden, Gill. "'Our Women are Expected to Become. . .': Women and Girls in Further Education in England at the Turn of the Century." In _The Sexual Dynamics of History_, edited by the The London Feminist History Group, pp. 87-102. London: Pluto Press, 1983.

04063. Bulley, Agnes Amy. _Middle Class Education in England: Its Influence on Commercial Pursuits_. London: Marshall and Company, 1881.

04064. Bryant, Margaret. _The Unexpected Revolution: A Study of the History of the Education of Women and Girls in the 19th Century_. London: Institute of Education, 1979.

04065. Hind, Robert J. "The Loss of English Working-Class Parents' Control Over Their Children's Education: The Role of Property-Holders." _Historical Reflections/Reflexions Historiques_ 12 (Spring 1985): 77-108.

04066. Low, Florence B. "The Educational Ladder and the Girl." _Nineteenth Century and After_ 62 (September 1907): 395-405.

04067. Prentice, Alison. "The Education of 19th Century British Women." _History of Education Quarterly_ 22 (Summer 1982): 215-219.

04068. Vicinus, Martha. "One Life to Stand Beside Me: Emotional Conflicts in First Generation College Women in England." _Feminist Studies_ 8 (Fall 1982): 603-628.

Also refer to #3886-3888.

(2) Education as a Profession

04069. Bergen, Barry H. "Only a Schoolmaster: Gender, Class and the Effort to Professionalize Elementary Teaching in England 1870-1910." _History of Education Quarterly_ 22 (1982): 1-22.

04070. Carpenter, J. Estlin. _The Life and Work of Mary Carpenter_. London: Macmillan, 1879.

04071. Manton, Jo. _Mary Carpenter and the Children of the Streets_. London: Heinemann, 1976.

04072. Tabor, Margaret Emma. Pioneer Women; Second Series: Hannah More, Mary Carpenter, Octavia Hill, Agnes Jones. London: Sheldon Press, 1927.

04073. Turnbull, Annmarie. "'So Extremely Like Parliament': The Work of the Women Members of the London School Board, 1870-1904." In The Sexual Dynamics of History, edited by The London Feminist History Group, pp. 120-133. London: Pluto Press, 1983.

04074. Widdowson, Frances. Going Up Into the Next Class: Women and Elementary Teacher Training 1840-1914. London: Women's Research and Resources Center Publications, 1980.

Also refer to #3753.

b) Literature

(1) Non-specific

(a) Women in Literature

04075. Auerbach, Nina. Woman and the Demon: The Life of Victorian Myth. Cambridge, Mass.: Harvard University Press, 1982.

04076. Blake, Kathleen. Love and the Woman Question in Victorian Literature. New York: Barnes and Noble, 1983.

04077. Calder, Jenni. "Cash and the Sex Nexus." In Sexuality and Victorian Literature, edited by Don Richard Cox, pp. 40-53. Knoxville, Tenn.: University of Tennessee Press, 1984.

04078. Cox, Don Richard, ed. Sexuality and Victorian Literature. Knoxville, Tenn.: University of Tennessee Press, 1984.

04079. Elbert, Sarah and Glastonbury, Marion. Inspiration and Drudgery: Notes on Literature and Domestic Labour in the Nineteenth Century. London: Women's Research and Resource Centre Publications, 1978.

04080. Foster, Shirley. "Female Januses: Ambiguity and Ambivalence Towards Marriage in Mid-Victorian Women's Fiction." International Journal of Women's Studies 6 (May-June 1983): 216-229.

04081 ____________. Victorian Women's Fiction, Marriage, Freedom, and the Individual. New York: Barnes and Noble, 1985.

04082. Fulweiler, Howard. "'Here a Captive Heart Busted': From Victorian Sentimentality to Modern Sexuality." In Sexuality and Victorian Literature, edited by Don Richard Cox, pp. 234-250. Knoxville, Tenn.: University of Tennessee Press, 1984.

04083. Gregg, Hilda C. "The Medical Woman in Fiction." Blackwood's Magazine 164 (1898): 94-109.

04084. Grylls, David. Guardians and Angels: Parents and Children in Nineteenth Century Literature. Boston: Faber and Faber, 1978.

04085. Homans, Margaret. Bearing the Word: Language and the Female Experience in Nineteenth-Century Women's Writing. Chicago, Il.: University of Chicago Press, 1986.

04086. Hughes, Judith M. "Self-Suppression and Attachment: Mid-Victorian Emotional Life." Massachusetts Review 19 (1978): 541-555.

04087. Keating, P.J. The Working Class in Victorian Fiction. London: Routledge & Kegan Paul, 1971.

04088. Knoepflmacher, U.C. "The Balancing of Child and Adult: An Approach to Victorian Fantasies for Children." Nineteenth-Century Fiction 37 (March 1983): 497-530.

04089. McCalman, Iain. "Unrespectable Radicalism: Infidels and Pornography in Early Nineteenth Century London." Past and Present 104 (August 1984): 74-110.

04090. MacPike, Loralee. "The Fallen Woman's Sexuality: Childbirth and Censure." In Sexuality and Victorian Literature, edited by Don Richard Cox, pp. 54-71. Knoxville, Tenn.: University of Tennessee Press, 1984.

04091. Newton, Judith L. Women, Power and Subversion: Social Strategies in British Fiction, 1778-1860. Athens, Ga.: University of Georgia Press, 1981.

04092. Rose, Phyllis. Parallel Lives: Five Victorian Marriages. New York: Knopf, 1983.

04093. Slater, Michael. "The Bachelor's Pocket Book for 1851." In Sexuality and Victorian Literature, edited by Don Richard Cox, pp. 128-140. Knoxville, Tenn.: University of Tennessee Press, 1984.

04094. Strauss, Sylvia. "Women in 'Utopia'." South Atlantic Quarterly 75 (1976): 115-131.

04095. Watt, George. The Fallen Woman in the 19th Century English Novel. Totowa, N.J.: Barnes and Noble, 1984.

Also refer to #3932, 4011.

(b) Women Authors

04096. Huff, Cynthia. British Women's Diaries: A Descriptive Bibliography of Selected Nineteenth-Century Women's Manuscript Diaries. New York: AMS Press, 1985.

(2) Drama

04097. Coxhead, Elizabeth. J.M. Synge and Lady Gregory. London: Longmans Green, 1962.

04098. Johnson, Wendell Stacy. "Fallen Women, Lost Children: Wilde and the Theatre of the Nineties." In Sexuality and Victorian Literature, edited by Don Richard Cox, pp. 196-211. Knoxville, Tennessee: University of Tennessee Press, 1984.

04099. Kohlfeldt, Mary Lou. Lady Gregory. The Woman Behind the Irish Renaissance. New York: Atheneum, 1985.

04100. McGhee, Richard D. Marriage Duty and Desire in Victorian Poetry and Drama. Lawrence: Regents Press of Kansas, 1980.

04101. Marcus, Jane Connor. "Salome: The Jewish Princess Was a New Woman." Bulletin of the New York Public Library 78 (Fall 1974): 95-113.

04102. Vicinus, Martha. "Helpless and Unfriended, Nineteenth Century Domestic Melodrama." New Literary History 13 (Autumn 1981): 127-143.

(3) Poetry

(a) Poets

[1]Individuals

[a] The Brownings

04103. Gelpi, Barbara Charlesworth. "Aurora Leigh: The Vocation of the Woman Poet." Victorian Poetry 19 (1981): 35-48.

04104. Mermin, Dorothy. "The Domestic Economy of Art Elizabeth Barrett and Robert Browning." In Mothering the Mind, Twelve Studies of Writers and Their Silent Partners, edited by Ruth Perry and Martine Watson Brownley, pp. 82-101. New York: Holmes & Meier, 1984.

Also refer to #4149.

[b] The Rossettis

04105. Armytage, A.J. Green. "C.G. Rossetti." In Maids of Honour, pp. 273-302. London: Blackwood, 1906.

04106. Birkhead, Edith. Christina Rossetti and Her Poetry. London: Harrap, 1930.

04107. Crump, Rebecca W. Christina Rossetti: A Reference Guide. Boston: G.K. Hall, 1976.

04108. Grebanier, Frances. Poor Splendid Wings: The Rossettis and Their Circle. Boston: Little, Brown, 1933.

04109. Homans, Margaret. "'Syllables of Velvet': Dickinson, Rossetti and the Rhetoric of Sexuality." Feminist Studies 11 (Fall 1985): 569-593.

04110. Hueffer, Ford Madox. "Christina Rossetti." Fortnightly Review 95 (March 1911): 422-429.

04111. ________. "Christina Rossetti and Pre-Raphaelite Love." In Ancient Lights, pp. 54-69. London: Chapman and Hall, 1911. Also in Memories and Impressions: A Study in Atmosphere, pp. 60-77. New York: Harper and Row, 1911.

04112. Kaplan, Cora. "The Indefinite Disclosed: Christina Rossetti and Emily Dickinson." In Women Writing and Writing About Women, edited by Mary Jacobus, pp. 61-79. New York: Barnes and Noble, 1979.

04113. Oliva, Gina, ed. I Rossetti tra Italia e Inghilterra: atti del convegno internazionale di studi. Rome: Bulzoni, 1984.

04114. Sandars, Mary F. The Life of Christina Rossetti. London: Hutchinson, 1930.

04115. Shove, Fredegond. Christina Rossetti: A Study. Reprint. 1931. Folcroft, Pa.: Folcroft Library Editions, 1974.

04116. Stuart, Dorothy Margaret. Christina Rossetti. London: Macmillan, 1930.

04117. Symons, Arthur. "Christina G. Rossetti: 1830-1894." In The Poets and the Poetry of the Nineteenth Century, edited by Alfred H. Miles, 9: 1-16. New York: E.P. Dutton, 1907.

04118. Weintraub, Stanley. Four Rossettis: A Victorian Biography. New York: Weybright and Talley, 1977.

[c] Algernon Swinburne

04119. Harrison, Anthony H. "'Love Strong as Death and Valour Strong as Love' Swinburne and Courtly Love." Victorian Poetry 18 (1980): 61-73.

04120. Harrison, Anthony H. "The Swinburnian Woman." Philological Quarterly 58 (1979): 90-102.

04121. McGhee, Richard. "'Swinburne Planteth, Hardy Watereth': Victorian Views of Pain and Pleasure in Human Sexuality." In Sexuality and Victorian Literature, edited by Don Richard Cox, pp. 83-107. Knoxville, Tenn.: University of Tennessee Press, 1984.

Also refer to #4208.

[d] Alfred Tennyson

04122. Hair, Donald S. Domestic and Heroic in Tennyson's Poetry. Toronto: University of Toronto Press, 1981.

04123. Hoeveler, Diane Long. "Manly-Women and Womanly-Men in Tennyson's Androgynous Ideal in The Princess and In Memoriam." Michigan Occasional Papers in Women's Studies 19 (1981).

04124. Story, Kenneth E. "Theme and Image in The Princess." Tennessee Studies in Literature 20 (1975): 50-59.

04125. Wimsatt, W.K., Jr. "Prufrock and Maud: From Plot to Symbol." Yale French Studies 9 (1952): 84-92.

Also refer to #3875, 4139.

[e] The Wordsworths

04126. Brownstein, Rachel Meyer. "The Private Life: Dorothy Wordsworth's Journal." Modern Language Quarterly 34 (1973): 48-63.

04127. Gittings, Robert and Manton, Jo. Dorothy Wordsworth. New York: Oxford University Press, 1985.

04128. Gunn, Elizabeth. A Passion for the Particular, Dorothy Wordsworth: A Portrait. London: Victor Gollancz, 1981.

04129. Homans, Margaret. Women Writers and Poetic Identity: Dorothy Wordsworth, Emily Brontë, and Emily Dickinson. Princeton, N.J.: Princeton University Press, 1980.

04130. Ketcham, Carl H. "Dorothy Wordsworth's Journals, 1824-1835." The Wordsworth Circle 9 (Winter 1978): 3-16.

04131. Lee, Edmund. Dorothy Wordsworth. The Story of a Sister's Love. London: J. Clarke, 1894.

04132. Manley, Seon. Dorothy and William Wordsworth: The Heart of a Circle of Friends. New York: Vanguard, 1974.

04133. Taylor, Elisabeth Russell. "Dorothy Wordsworth: Primary and Secondary Sources." _Bulletin of Bibliography_ 40 (December 1983): 254-257.

04134. Vogler, Thomas A. "'A Spirit, Yet a Woman Too!' Dorothy and William Wordsworth." In _Mothering the Mind, Twelve Studies of Writers and Their Silent Partners_, edited by Ruth Perry and Martine Watson Brownley, pp. 238-259. New York: Holmes & Meier, 1984.

[2] Others

04135. Diehl, Joanne Feit. "'Come Softly-Eden': An Explanation of Women Poets and Their Muse." _Signs_ 3 (1978): 572-587.

04136. Kestner, Joseph. "Everyone Knows Her Ryhme, But Who Remembers Jane?" _Smithsonian_ 14 (October 1983): 172-186.

04137. Murray, E.B. "Thel, _Thelphthora_, and the Daughters of Albion." _Studies in Romanticism_ 20 (1981): 275-297.

04138. Punter, David. "Blake, Trauma and the Female." _New Literary History_ 15 (Spring 1984): 475-490.

04139. Stephenson, Harold William. _The Author of Nearer, My God, To Thee_. London: Lindsey Press, 1922.

Also refer to #4100, 4225.

(4) Prose

(a) Women in Novels

04140. Barickman, Richard. _Corrupt Relations: Dickens, Thackeray, Trollope, Collins, and the Victorian Sexual System_. New York: Columbia, 1982.

04141. Gribble, Jennifer. _The Lady of Shalott in the Victorian Novel_. Salem: N.H.: Salem House, 1984.

04142. Kennard, Jean E. _Victims of Convention_. Hamden, Ct.: Archon Books, 1978.

04143. Maly-Schlater, F. _The Puritan Element in Victorian Fiction: With Special Reference to the Works of George Eliot, Dickens and Thackeray_. Zurich: A.G. Gebr. Leeman and Company, 1940.

04144. Mussell, Kay J. "Beautiful and Damned: The Sexual Woman in Gothic Fiction." _Journal of Popular Culture_ 9 (1975): 84-89.

04145. Patteson, Richard F. "Manhood and Misogyny in the Imperialist Romance." Rocky Mountain Review of Language and Literature 35 (1981): 3-12.

04146. Putzell-Korab, Sara. "Passion Between Women in the Victorian Novel." In Sexuality and Victorian Literature, edited by Don Richard Cox, pp. 180-195. Knoxville, Tenn.: University of Tennessee Press, 1984.

04147. Williams, Merryn. Women in the English Novel 1800-1900. New York: St. Martin's, 1985.

04148. Wilt, Judith. "The Laughter of Maidens, the Cackle of Matriarchs: Notes on the Collision Between Comedy and Feminism." In Gender and Literary Voice, Women and Literature, vol. 1: 173-196. New York: Holmes and Meier, 1980.

Also refer to #3090.

(b) Novelists

[1] Non-specific

04149. Armstrong, Nancy. "The Rise of Feminine Authority in the Novel." Novel 15 (1982): 127-145.

04150. Bonnell, Henry Houston. Charlotte Brontë, George Eliot, Jane Austen: Studies in Their Works. New York: Longmans, Green and Co., 1902.

04151. Gilbert, Sandra M. and Gubar, Susan. The Madwoman in the Attic: A Study of Women and the Literary Imagination in the Nineteenth Century. New Haven, Ct.: Yale University Press, 1980.

04152. Green, Roger Lancelyn. "The Golden Age of Children's Books." Essay and Studies n.s. 15 (1962): 59-73.

04153. Kestner, Joseph. "Men in Female Condition of England Novels." In Men by Women, Women and Literature, edited by Janet Todd, 2: 77-100. New York: Holmes and Meier, 1982.

04154. ______________. Protest and Reform The British Social Narrative by Women, 1827-1867. Madison, Wis.: University of Wisconsin Press, 1984.

Also refer to #3976.

[2] Individuals

[a] Jane Austen

((1)) Biographies

04155. Halperin, John. The Life of Jane Austen. Baltimore, Md.: Johns Hopkins University Press, 1984.

04156. Kirkham, Margaret. Jane Austen, Feminism and Fiction. New York: Barnes and Noble, 1983.

04157. Mitton, Geraldine E. Jane Austen and Her Times. London: Methuen and Co., 1905.

04158. Smith, Leroy W. Jane Austen and the Drama of Women. London: Macmillan, 1983.

Also refer to #2944, 2967, 4148, 4150.

((2)) Views on Society

04159. Hardy, J.P. Jane Austen's Heroines: Intimacy in Human Relationships. London: Routledge and Kegan Paul, 1984.

04160. Leimberg, Inge. "'Humble Independence.' Das Thema und seine dichterische Verwirklichung in Jane Austen's 'Emma.'" Germanisch-Romanische Monatsschrift n.s. 30 (1980): 395-422.

04161. MacDonald, Susan Peck. "Jane Austen and the Tradition of the Absent Mother." In The Lost Tradition Mothers and Daughters in Literature, edited by Cathy N. Davidson and E.M. Broner, pp. 58-69. New York: Ungar, 1980.

04162. Nardin, Jane. Those Elegant Decorums, The Concept of Propriety in Jane Austen's Novels. Albany, N.Y.: State University of New York Press, 1973.

04163. Olshin, Toby A. "Jane Austen: A Romantic, Systematic or Realistic Approach to Medicine." Studies in Eighteenth Century Culture 10 (1981): 313-326.

04164. Thompson, James. "Jane Austen's Clothing: Things, Property, and Materialism in Her Novels." Studies in Eighteenth-Century Culture 13 (1984): 217-231.

04165. Wilt, Judith. "Jane Austen's Men: Inside/Outside 'The Mystery.'" In Men and Women, Women and Literature, edited by Janet Todd, 2: 59-76. New York: Holmes and Meier, 1982.

[b] Mary Elizabeth Braddon

04166. Casey, Ellen Miller. "'Other People's Prudery': Mary Elizabeth Braddon." In Sexuality and Victorian Literature, edited by Don Richard Cox, pp. 72-82. Knoxville, Tenn.: University of Tennessee Press, 1984.

04167. Wolff, Robert Lee. Sensational Victorian: The Life and Fiction of Mary Elizabeth Braddon. New York: Garland, 1979.

[c] The Brontës

((1)) Non-specific

04168 Braithwaite, William Stanley. The Bewitched Parsonage: The Story of the Brontës. New York: Coward-McCann, 1950.

04169. Chadwick, Esther Alice. In the Footsteps of the Brontës. London: Sir I. Pitman and Sons, 1914.

04170. Crump, Rebecca W. Charlotte and Emily Brontë, 1846-1915, A Reference Guide. Boston: H.K. Hall and Co., 1982.

04171. Duthie, Enid L. The Brontës and Nature. New York: St. Martin's Press, 1986.

04172. Hinkley, Laura L. The Brontës: Charlotte and Emily. New York: Hastings House, 1945.

04173. Leyland, Francis A. The Brontë Family With Special Reference to Patrick Branwell Brontë. 2 vols. London: Hurst and Blackett, 1886.

04174. Passel, Anne. Charlotte and Emily Brontë: An Annotated Bibliography. New York: Garland, 1979.

04175. Pinion, F.B. A Brontë Companion: Literary Assessment, Background, and Reference. London: Macmillan Press, 1975.

04176. Pollard, Arthur. "The Brontës and Their Father's Faith." Essays and Studies n.s. 37 (1984): 46-61.

04177. Sinclair, May. The Three Brontës. New York: Houghton and Mifflin, 1914.

((2)) Anne Brontë

04178. Hale, Will Taliafero. Anne Brontë, Her Life and Writing. 1929. Reprint. New York: Folcroft, 1974.

04179. Raymond, Ernest. "Exiled and Harassed Anne." Brontë Society Transactions 11 (1949): 225-236.

04180. Schofield, Guy. "The Gentle Anne." Brontë Society Transactions 16 (1971): 1-10.

((3)) Charlotte Brontë

((a)) Biographies

04181. Birrell, Augustine. Life of Charlotte Brontë. 1887. Reprint. Ann Arbor, Mich.: Finch Press, 1972.

04182. Crompton, Margaret. Passionate Search: A Life of Charlotte Brontë. London: Cassel, 1955.

04183. Goldring, Maude. Charlotte Brontë: The Woman. 1915. Reprint. New York: R. West, 1974.

04184. Parkison, Jami. "Charlotte Brontë: A Bibliography of Nineteenth Century Criticism." Bulletin of Bibliography 35 (April-June 1978): 73-83.

04185. Reid, T. Wemyss. Charlotte Brontë: A Monograph. New York: Scribner, Armstrong and Co., 1877.

Also refer to #3976, 4149, 4150.

((b)) Views on Society

04186. Baines, Barbara J. "Villette, A Feminist Novel." Victorian Institute Journal 5 (1976): 51-59.

04187. Bledsoe, Robert. "Snow beneath Snow: A Reconsideration of the Virgin of Vilette." In Gender and Literary Voice, Women and Literature, edited by Janet Todd, 1: 214-222. New York: Holmes and Meier, 1980.

04188. Fulton, E. Margaret. "Jane Eyre: The Development of a Female Consciousness." English Studies in Canada 5 (1980): 432-447.

04189. Griffin, Gail B. "The Humanization of Edward Rochester." In Men by Women, Women and Literature, edited by Janet Todd, 2: 118-129. New York: Holmes and Meier, 1982.

04190. Harrison, Rachel. "Shirley: Relations of Reproduction and Ideology of Romance." In Women Take Issue: Aspects of Women's Subordination, pp. 176-196. London: Hutchinson, 1978.

04191. Jacobus, Mary. "The Buried Letter: Feminism and Romanticism in Villette." In Women Writing and Writing About Women, edited by Mary Jacobus, pp. 42-60. New York: Barnes and Noble, 1979.

Also refer to #5839.

((4)) Emily Brontë

((a)) Biographies

04192. Hopkins, Marie M. Emily Brontë. Chicago: J. Lipton, 1903.

04193. Kavanagh, James. Emily Brontë. New York: Basil Blackwell, 1985.

04194. Simpson, Charles Walter. Emily Brontë. 1929. Reprint. Folcroft, PA: Folcroft Library Editions, 1977.

((b)) Views on Society

04195. Paris, Bernard J. "'Hush, hush! He's a human being.': A Psychological Approach to Heathcliff." In Men by Women, Women and Literature, edited by Janet Todd, 2: 101-117. New York: Holmes and Meier, 1982.

[d] Frances Hodgson Burnett

04196. Burnett, Vivian. The Romantick Lady (Frances Hodgson Burnett). New York: Scribner, 1927.

04197. Thwaite, A. Waiting for the Party: The Life of Frances Hodgson Burnett. New York: Scribner, 1974.

[e] Lewis Carroll

04198. Auerbach, Nina. "Falling Alice, Fallen Women, and Victorian Dream Children." English Language Notes 20 (December 1982): 46-64.

04199. Clark, Anne. The Real Alice: Lewis Carroll's Dream Child. London: Joseph, 1981.

04200. Rackin, Donald. "Love and Death in Carroll's Alice." English Language Notes 20 (December 1982): 1-25.

[f] Wilkie Collins

04201. Frick, Patricia. "The Fallen Angels of Wilkie Collins." International Journal of Women's Studies 7 (September-October 1984): 343-351.

04202. Meckier, Jerome. "Wilkie Collins's The Woman in White. Providence against the Evils of Propriety." Journal of British Studies 22 (Fall 1982): 104-126.

Also refer to #4140.

[g] De la Rameé, Marie Louise

04203. Bigland, Eileen. Ouida. New York: Duell, Sloan and Pearce, 1950.

04204. Ffrench, Yvonne. Ouida, A Study in Ostentation. New York: D. Appleton-Century, Co., 1938.

04205. Phillips, Celia G. "Ouida and Her Publishers: 1874-1880." Bulletin of Research in the Humanities 81 (1978): 210-215.

04206. Stirling, Monica. The Fine and the Wicked: The Life and Times of Ouida. London: Victor Gollancz, 1957.

[h] Charles Dickens

04207. Blain, Virginia. "Double Vision and the Double Standard in Bleak House: A Feminist Perspective." Literature and History 11 (Spring 1985): 31-46.

04208. Carter, Geoffrey, "Sexuality and the Victorian Artist: Dickens and Swinburne." In Sexuality and Victorian Literature, edited by Don Richard Cox, pp. 141-160. Knoxville, Tenn.: University of Tennessee Press, 1984.

04209. Clark, Robert. "Riddling the Family Firm: The Sexual Economy in Dombey and Son." Journal of English Literary History 51 (Spring 1984): 69-84.

04210. Kennedy, G. E. "Women Redeemed: Dickens's Fallen Women." Dickensian 73 (1978): 42-47.

04211. Rose, Phyllis. "A Victorian Marriage: Catherine Hogarth and Charles Dickens." Yale Review 72 (Summer 1983): 481-521.

04212. Slater, Michael. Dickens and Women. London: Dent, 1983.

04213. Spilka, Mark. "On the Enrichment of Poor Monkeys by Myth and Dream; or How Dickens Rousseauisticized and Pre-Freudianized Victorian Views of Childhood." In Sexuality and Victorian Literature, edited by Don Richard Cox, pp. 161-179. Knoxville, Tenn.: University of Tennessee, 1984.

04214. Wilson, Angus. "The Heroes and Heroines of Dickens." In Dickens: A Collection of Critical Essays, edited by Martin Price, pp. 16-23. Englewood Cliffs, N.J.: Prentice Hall, 1967.

Also refer to #4140, 4143.

[i] George Eliot

((1)) Biographies

04215. Fulmer, Constance Marie. George Eliot: A Reference Guide. Boston: G. K. Hall, 1977.

04216. Jarmuth, Sylvia. George Eliot-Nineteenth-Century Novelist. New York: Excelsior Publishing Company, 1968.

04217. May, James Lewis. George Eliot. London: Cassel, 1930.

04218. Speaight, Robert. George Eliot. London: Arthur Barker, 1968.

Also refer to #3753, 3976, 4148, 4150, 4233, 5051.

((2)) Views on Society

04219. Beer, Gillian. "Beyond Determinism: George Eliot and Virginia Woolf." In Women Writing and Writing About Women, edited by Mary Jacobus, pp. 80-99. New York: Barnes and Noble, 1979.

04220. Bennett, James R. "Scenic Structure of Judgement in 'Middlemarch.'" Essays and Studies n.s. 37 (1984): 62-74.

04221. Blake, Kathleen. "Middlemarch and the Woman Question." Nineteenth-Century Fiction 31 (1976): 285-312.

04222. Fernando, Lloyd. "George Eliot, Feminism and Dorothea Brooke." Review of English Literature 4 (1963): 76-90.

04223. Fisher, Philip. Making up Society: The Novels of George Eliot. Pittsburgh: University of Pittsburgh Press, 1982.

04224. Foltinek, Herbert. "George Eliot und der unwissende Erzähler." Germanisch-Romanische Monatsschrift n.s. 33 (1983): 167-178.

04225. Knoepflmacher, U. C. "On Exile and Fiction The Leweses and the Shelleys." In Mothering the Mind, Twelve Studies of Writers and Their Silent Partners, edited by Ruth Perry and Martine Watson Brownley, pp. 102-121. New York: Holmes and Meier, 1984.

04226. ________________. "Unveiling Men: Power and Masculinity in George Eliot's Fiction." In Men by Women, Women and Literature, edited by Janet Todd, 2: 130-146. New York: Holmes and Meier, 1982.

04227. Martin, Carol A. "No Angel in the House: Victorian Mothers and Daughters in George Eliot and Elizabeth Gaskell." Midwest Quarterly 24 (Spring 1983): 297-314.

04228. Trilling, Diana. "The Liberated Heroine." Partisan Review 45 (1978): 501-522.

04229. Woolson, Abba Goold. George Eliot and Her Heroines. New York: Harper and Brothers, 1886.

04230. Zimmerman, Bonnie. "'The Mother's History' in George Eliot's Life, Literature and Political Ideology." In The Lost Tradition: Mothers and Daughters in Literature, edited by Cathy N. Davidson and E. M. Broner, pp. 81-94. New York: Ungar, 1980.

[j] Elizabeth Gaskell

((1)) Biographies

04231. Easson, Angus. Elizabeth Gaskell. Boston: Routledge and Kegan, Paul, 1979.

04232. Ffrench, Yvonne. Mrs. Gaskell. Denver: Allan Swallow, 1949.

04233. Gilbert, Thomas. "Mrs. Gaskell and George Eliot: A Study in Contrast." Chambers' Journal 121 (1944): 631-634.

04234. Payne, George Andrew. Mrs. Gaskell: A Brief Biography. Manchester, England: Sherrat and Hughes, 1929.

04235. Sanders, Gerald DeWitt. Elizabeth Gaskell. New Haven, Ct.: Yale University Press, 1930.

04236. Selig, Robert L. Elizabeth Gaskell: A Reference Guide. Boston, Mass.: G. K. Hall and Company, 1977.

04237. Welch, Jeffrey. Elizabeth Gaskell: An Annotated Bibliography, 1929-1975. New York: Garland, 1977.

04238. Whitfield, Archie Stanton. Mrs. Gaskell, Her Life and Works. 1929. Reprint. Folcroft, Penn.: Folcroft Library Editions, 1973.

Also refer to #3976, 4149, 4153, 4227.

((2)) Views on Society

04239. Berke, Jacqueline and Berke, Laura. "Mothers and Daughters in Wives and Daughters: A Study of Elizabeth Gaskell's Last Novel." In The Lost Tradition Mothers and Daughters in Literature, edited by Cathy N. Davidson and E. M. Broner, pp. 95-111. New York: Ungar, 1980.

[k] George Gissing

04240. Eakin, D. B. Gissing and the Feminist Critics." Gissing Newsletter 15, no. 4 (1979): 16-19.

04241. Halperin, John. "Gissing, Marriage, and Women's Rights: The Case of Denzil Quarrier." Gissing Newsletter 15, Supplement (1979): 1-10.

04242. Harrison, J. "The Emancipated: Gissing's Treatment of Women and Religious Emancipation." Gissing Newsletter 17, no. 2 (1981): 1-10.

04243. Lansbury, C. "Gissing and the Female Surrogate. Gissing Newsletter 15, Supplement (1979): 11-16.

04244. Zaborszky, Dorothy E. "Victorian Feminism and Gissing's The Odd Women: 'Why Are Women Redundant?'" Women's Studies International Forum 8 (1985): 489-496.

[l] Thomas Hardy

04245. Beegel, Susan. "Bathsheba's Lovers: Male Sexuality in Far from the Madding Crowd." In Sexuality and Victorian Literature, edited by Don Richard Cox, pp. 108-127. Knoxville, Tenn.: University of Tennessee Press, 1984.

04246. Blake, Kathleen. "Sue Bridehead, 'The Woman of the Feminist Movement!" Studies in English Literature 18 (1978): 703-726.

04247. Boumelha, Penny. Thomas Hardy and Women: Sexual Ideology Narrative Form. Totowa, N.J.: Barnes and Noble, 1982.

04248. Gifford, Henry. "Thomas Hardy and Emma." Essays and Studies n.s. 19 (1966): 106-121.

04249. Gittings, Robert and Manton, Jo. The Second Mrs. Hardy. Seattle, Wash.: University of Washington Press, 1979.

04250. Goode, John. "Sue Bridehead and the New Woman." In Women Writing About Women, edited by Mary Jacobus, pp. 100-113. New York: Barnes and Noble, 1979.

04251. Kay-Robinson, Denys. The First Mrs. Thomas Hardy. New York: St. Martin's, 1979.

Also refer to #4121.

[m] George Meredith

04252. Belken, Roslyn. "According to Their Age: Older Women in George Meredith's The Egoist." International Journal of Women's Studies 7 (January-February 1984): 37-46.

04253. Williams, David. George Meredith: His Life and Lost Love. London: Hamish Hamilton, 1977.

Also refer to #4252, 4253.

[n] Mary Shelley

04254. Church, Richard. Mary Shelley (1797-1851). London: Gerald Howe, 1928.

04255. Dunn, Jane. Moon in Eclipse: A Life of Mary Shelley. New York: St. Martin's, 1978.

04256. Frank, Frederick S. "Mary Shelley's Frankenstein: A Register of Research." Bulletin of Bibliography 40 (September 1983): 163-188.

04257. Harris, Janet. The Woman Who Created Frankenstein: A Portrait of Mary Shelley. New York: Harper and Row, 1979.

04258. Laszlo, Pierre. "Extase sublime et declin de la nature (Note sur le Frankenstein de Mary Shelley)." Revue des sciences humaines n.s. 188 (October-December 1982): 89-92.

04259. Neumann, Bonnie Rayford. Lonely Muse: A Critical Biography of Mary Wollstonecraft Shelley. Salzburg: Institut fur Anglistik und Amerikanistik, 1981.

Also refer to #3126, 3976.

[o] Bram Stoker

04260. Johnson, Alan P. "'Dual Life': The Status of Women in Stoker's Dracula." In Sexuality and Victorian Literature, edited by Don Richard Cox, pp. 20-39. Knoxville, Tenn.: University of Tennessee Press, 1984.

04261. Senf, Carol A. "'Dracula': Stoker's Response to the New Woman." Victorian Studies 26 (Autumn 1982): 33-49.

[p] Charlotte Elizabeth Tonna

04262. Fryckstedt, Monica Correa. "Charlotte Elizabeth Tonna: A Forgotten Evangelical Writer." Studia Neophilologica 52 (1980): 79-102.

04263. Kovačević, Ivanka and Kanner, S. Barbara. "Blue Book into Novel: The Forgotten Industrial Fiction of Charlotte Elizabeth Tonna." Nineteenth Century Fiction 25 (September 1970): 152-173.

Also refer to #4153.

[q] Anthony Trollope

04264. Halperin, John. "Trollope and Feminism." South Atlantic Quarterly 77 (1978): 179-188.

04265. Wijesinha, Rajiva. The Androgynous Trollope: Attitudes to Women Amongst Early Victorian Novelists. Washington, D.C.: University Press of America, 1982.

Also refer to #4140, 4290.

[r] Frances Trollope

04266. Heineman, Helen. Frances Trollope. Boston: Twayne, 1984.

04267. ______________. Mrs. Trollope: The Triumphant Feminine in the Nineteenth Century. Athens: Ohio University Press, 1979.

04268. Johnston, Joanna. The Life, Manners, and Travels of Fanny Trollope: A Biography. New York: Hawthorn, 1978.

Also refer to #4153.

[s] Charlotte Yonge

04269. Battiscombe, Georgina. Charlotte Mary Yonge: The Story of an Uneventful Life. London: Constable and Company, Ltd., 1944.

04270. Coleridge, Christobel Rose. Charlotte Mary Yonge: Her Life and Letters. 1903. Reprint. Detroit: Gale Research Company, 1969.

04271. Sturrock, June. "A Personal View of Women's Education, 1883-1900: Charlotte Yonge's Novels." Victorian Institute Journal 7 (1979): 7-18.

[3] Others

04272. Baker, Margaret Joyce. Anna Sewell and Black Beauty. London: Harrap, 1956.

04273. Crabbe, John K. "The Harmony of Her Mind: Peacock's Emancipated Women." Tennessee Studies in Literature 23 (1978): 75-86.

04274. Cullinan, Mary. Susan Ferrier. Boston: Twayne Publishers, 1984.

04275. Freeman, Gillian. The Schoolgirl Ethics: The Life and Work of Angela Brazil. London: Allen Lane, 1976.

04276. Frerichs, Sarah C. "Feminine and Feminist Values in a 'High Minded and Spirited Authoress'." English Review 29 (1978): 5-7.

04277. Gérin, Winifred. Anne Thackeray Ritchie: A Biography. New York: Oxford University Press, 1981.

04278. Howe, S. Geraldine Jewsbury. London: Allen and Unwin, 1935.

04279. Lane, Margaret. Flora Thompson. London: J. Murray, 1976.

04280. Lee, H. Elizabeth Bowen. New York: Barnes and Noble, 1981.

04281. Mitchell, Sally. Dinah Mulock Craik. Boston: Twayne Books, 1983.

04282. Powell, Violet. Flora Annie Steel: Novelist of India. London: Heinemann, 1981.

04283. Sharpe, Henrietta. A Solitary Woman: A Life of Violet Trefusis. London: Constable, 1981.

04284. Sloan, Barry. "Mrs. Hall's Ireland." Éire-Ireland 19 (Fall 1984): 18-30.

Also refer to #3755, 3976, 4094, 4140, 4143.

(c) Periodicals

04285. Behnken, E. M. "The Feminine Image in the English Woman's Journal." Ball State University Forum 19 (1978): 71-75.

04286. Boyle, Thomas F. "'Morbid Depression Alternating with Excitement': Sex in Victorian Newspapers." In Sexuality and Victorian Literature, edited by Don Richard Cox, pp. 212-233. Knoxville, Tenn.: University of Tennessee Press, 1984.

04287. Myerson, Joel. "Ann Stephens, the London Journal, and Anglo-American Copyright in 1854." Manuscripts 35 (Fall 1983): 281-286.

04288. Nestor, Pauline. "A New Departure in Women's Publishing: The English Woman's Journal and The Victoria Magazine." Victorian Periodicals Review 15 (Fall 1982): 93-106.

04289. Palmegiano, E. M. "The Propaganda of Sexuality: Victorian Periodicals and Women." Victorian Institute Journal 6 (1978): 21-30.

04290. Rinehart, Nana. "'The Girl of the Period' Controversy." Victorian Periodicals Review 13 (Spring-Summer 1980).

04291. Stone, James S. "More Light on Emily Faithful and the Victoria Press." Library 33 (1978): 63-67.

04292. Van Arsdel, Rosemary T. "Mrs. Florence Fenwick-Miller and The Woman's Signal 1859-1899." Victorian Periodicals Review 15 (Fall 1982): 107-118.

Also refer to #3976, 3990.

(5) Intellectuals

(a) Harriet Martineau

04293. Courtney, Janet Elizabeth (Hogarth). Freethinkers of the Nineteenth Century. 1920. Reprint. Philadelphia, Penn.: R. West, 1977.

04294. Martineau, Harriet. Harriet Martineau on Women. Edited by Gayle Graham Yates. New Brunswick, N.J.: Rutgers University Press, 1985.

04295. Myers, Mitzi. "Harriet Martineau's Autobiography: The Making of a Female Philosopher." In Women's Autobiography, Essays in Criticism, edited by Estelle C. Jelinek, pp. 53-70. Bloomington, Ind.: Indiana University Press, 1980.

04296. ___________. "Unmothered Daughter and Radical Reformer: Harriet Martineau's Career." In The Lost Tradition Mothers and Daughters in Literature, edited by Cathy N. Davidson and E. M. Broner, pp. 70-80. New York: Ungar, 1980.

04297. Nevill, John Cranstoun. Harriet Martineau. 1943. Reprint. Norwood, Penn.: Norwood, 1976.

04298. Thomas, Gillian. Harriet Martineau. Boston: Twayne, 1985.

04299. Weiner, Gaby. "Harriet Martineau: A Reassessment (1802-1876)." In Feminist Theorists, edited by Dale Spender, pp. 60-74. New York: Pantheon Books, Random House, 1983.

(b) Others

04300. Badini, June. The Slender Tree: A Life of Alice Meynell. Cornwell: Tabb House, 1980.

04301. Bruce, Mary Louisa. Anna Swanwick. London: T. F. Unwin, 1903.

04302. Burdett, Osbert. The Two Carlyles. London: Faber and Faber, 1930.

04303. Casper, Dale. "Caroline Nortion: Her Writings." Bulletin of Bibliography 40 (June 1983): 113-116.

04304. Eastlake, Elizabeth. Mrs. Grote. London: J. Murray, 1880.

04305. Fryckstedt, Monica Correa. "The Hidden Rill: The Life and Career of Maria Jane Jewsbury: I." Bulletin of the John Rylands Library 66 (Spring 1984): 177-203.

04306. Garmonsway, G. N. "Anna Gurney: Learned Saxonist." Essays and Studies n.s. 8 (1955): 40-57.

04307. Gray, T. S. "Herbert Spencer on Women: A Study in Personal and Political Disillusion." International Journal of Women's Studies 7 (May-June 1984): 217-231.

04308. Hall, Trevor H. The Strange Story of Ada Goodrich Freer. London: Duckworth, 1980.

04309. Hamburger, Lotte and Hamburger, Joseph. Troubled Lives: John and Sarah Austin. Toronto: University of Toronto Press, 1985.

04310. Lee, Amice. Laurels and Rosemary: The Life of William and Mary Howitt. New York: Oxford University Press, 1955.

04311. Van Thal, Herbert. Eliza Lynn Linton: The Girl of the Period. Boston: George Allen and Unwin, 1979.

04312. Wagenknecht, Edward. Daughters of the Covenant: Portraits of Six Jewish Women. Amherst: University of Massachusetts Press, 1983.

04313. Williams, David. Genesis and Exodus: A Portrait of the Benson Family. London: Hamish Hamilton, 1979.

04314. Woodring, Carl Ray. Victorian Samplers: William and Mary Howitt. Lawrence, Kan.: University of Kansas Press, 1952.

Also refer to #3743, 3962, 3976, 3990, 4094, 4290, 4303, 4311.

(c) Art/Artifacts

(1) Women in Art

04315. Dearden, James S. "The Portraits of Rose la Touche." Burlington Magazine 120 (1978): 92-96.

04316. Kestner, Joseph. "Edward Burne-Jones and Nineteenth Century Fear of Women" Biography 7 (Spring 1984): 95-122.

04317. Powell, Violet. "Love in Victorian Painting." Apollo 111 (June 1980): 448-453.

(2) Women Artists

(a) Non-specific

04318. Marsh, Jan. The Pre-Raphaelite Sisterhood. New York: St. Martin's Press, 1985.

04319. Yeldham, Charlotte. Women Artists in Nineteenth-Century France and England. New York: Garland, 1984.

(b) Actresses/Stage Managers

04320. Armstrong, William A. "Madame Vestris: A Centenary Appreciation." Theatre Notebook 11 (October-December 1956): 11-18.

04321. Barker, Kathleen M.D. "The Terrys and Godwin in Bristol." Theatre Notebook 22 (Autumn 1967): 27-43.

04322. Booth, Michael R. "Ellen Terry's Rehearsal Copy of King Lear." Theatre Notebook 33 (1979): 23-29.

04323. Donahue, Joseph W., Jr. "Kemble and Mrs. Siddons in Macbeth: The Romantic Approach to Tragic Character." Theatre Notebook 22 (Winter 1967-1968): 65-86.

04324. Foulkes, Richard. "'Measure for Measure': Miss Hornimann and Mr. Poel at the Gaiety." Theatre Quarterly 10 (Spring-Summer 1981): 43-46.

04325. Gates, Joanne E. "Elizabeth Robins and the 1891 Production of Hedda Gabler." Modern Dance 28 (December 1985): 611-619.

04326. Hadjipantazis, Theodore. "A Footnote to the Memoirs of Leonora Whiteley." Theatre Notebook 37 (1983): 131-136.

04327. Irvin, Eric. "Laura Keene and Edwin Booth in Iydney." Theatre Notebook 23 (Spring 1969): 95-102.

04328. __________. "The Mrs. Siddons of Sydney (Part I)." Theatre Notebook 25 (Spring 1971): 97-103.

04329. __________. "The Mrs. Siddons of Sydney (Part II)." Theatre Notebook 25 (Summer 1971): 122-131.

04330. Kahan, Gerald. "Fanny Kemble Reads Shakespeare: Her First American Tour, 1849-50." Theatre Survey 24 (1983): 77-98.

04331. Mullin, David, ed. Victorian Actors and Actresses in Review: A Dictionary of Contemporary Views of Representative British and American Actors and Actresses, 1837-1901. Westport, Ct.: Greenwood Press, 1983.

04332. Murray, Christopher. "Macready, Helen Faucit and Acting Style." Theatre Notebook 23 (Autumn 1968): 21-25.

04333. Pogson, Rex. Miss Horniman and the Gaiety Theatre. London: Roehcliff, 1952.

04334. Rao, V. "Vivie Warren in the Blakean World of Experience." Shaw Review 22 (1979): 123-124.

04335. Ransome, Eleanor. The Terrific Kemble. London: H. Hamilton, 1978.

04336. Thorndike, Sybil. Lilian Baylis. London: Chapman and Hall, 1938.

Also refer to #3767.

(c) Painters/Sculptors

04337. Kiger, William, ed. Kate Greenaway. Pittsburgh: Carnegie Mellon University, 1980.

04338. Parkin Gallery. The Sickert Women and the Sickert Girls. London, 1974.

(d) Musicians

04339. Dean-Smith, Margaret. "The Work of Anne Geddes Gilchrist, G.B.E., F.S.A., 1863-1954." Proceedings of the Royal Music Association 84 (1957-1958): 43-53.

04340. Farson, Daniel. Marie Lloyd and Music Hall. London: Tom Stacey, Ltd., 1972.

04341. Jacob, Naomi Ellington. Our Marie. A Biography. 1936. Reprint. Bath: Cedric Chivers, 1972.

04342. Klein, Hermann. The Reign of Patti. 1920. Reprint. New York: Da Capo Press, 1978.

04343. Mackenzie-Grieve, Averil. Clara Novello, 1818-1908. 1955. Reprint. New York: Da Capo Press, 1980.

04344. Rockstro, W. S. Jenny Lind the Artist. London: J. Murray, 1893.

04345. Stratton, Stephen S. "Woman in Relation to Musical Art." Proceedings of the Royal Music Association 9 (1882-1883): 115-146.

04346. Swinburne, J. "Women and Music." Proceedings of the Royal Music Association 46 (1919-1920): 21-42.

d) Science

04347. Alaya, Flavia. "Victorian Science and the 'Genius of Women.'" Journal of the History of Ideas 38 (1977): 261-280.

04348. Love, Rosaleen. "'Alice in Eugenics-Land': Feminism and Eugenics in the Scientific Careers of Alice Lee and Ethel Eldersten." Annals of Science 36 (1979): 145-158.

04349. Patterson, Elizabeth Chambers. Mary Somerville and the Cultivation of Science, 1815-1840. Boston: Nijhoff, 1983.

04350. Shteir, Ann B. "Linnnaeus's Daughter: Women and British Botany." In Women and the Structure of Society, edited by Barbara J. Harris and JoAnn K. McNamara, pp. 67-73. Durham, N.C.: Duke University Press, 1984.

C. FRANCE

1. SURVEYS

"If the path of civilization is closed to one sex, it is also closed to the other."
Fourier

04351. Aron, Jean-Paul. Miserable et glorieuse: La Femme du XIXe siecle. Paris: Ed Complexe, 1984.

04352. Beretti, Francis. "La femme corse vue par les voyageurs victoriens." In Femmes corses et femmes méditerranéennes, pp. 200-208. Provence: Centre d'Etudes Corses de l'Universite de Provence, 1976.

04353. Hildenbrand, Suzanne. "Researching Women's History in Paris: The Bibliotheque Marguerite Durand." Journal of Library History, 20 (Winter 1985): 70-80.

04354. Offen, Karen. "The Beginnings of 'Scientific' Women's History in France, 1830-1848. Proceedings of the Western Society for French History 11 (1983): 255-264.

04355. Sewell, William H. Jr. Structure and Mobility: The Men and Women of Marseille, 1820-1870. New York: Cambridge University Press, 1984.

04356. Smith, Bonnie G. "The History of Women's History in Nineteenth-Century France." Proceedings of the Western Society for French History 11 (1983): 265-271.

2. POLITICAL

"The first revolution did indeed give women the 'citizen' but not the rights. They were excluded from liberty and equality."
La sociale, 1871

a) Generic

04357. Hause, Steven C. and Kenney, Anne R. Women's Suffrage and Social Politics in the French Third Republic. Princeton: Princeton University Press, 1984.

04358. Offen, Karen. "Depopulation, Nationalism, and Feminism in Fin-de-Siecle France." American Historical Review 89 (June 1984): 648-676.

04359. Parturier, Françoise and Armingeat, Jacqueline. Liberated Women (Bluestockings and Socialist Women). New York: Vilo Inc., 1982.

b) Marxism and Socialism

04360. Delpla, François. "Les communistes français et la sexualité." Le Mouvement social 91 (April-June 1975): 121-152.

04361. Fremder, Lara and Lejeune, Paule. "La voce delle donne nella Francia prima di Marx." In Esistere comme donna, pp. 89-96. Milan: Mazzotta, 1983.

04362. Goldstein, Leslie F. "Feminism in St. Simonians and Fourier." Journal of the History of Ideas 43 (January-March 1982): 91-108.

04363. Marotin, François. "De l'amour au mariage ou l'enracinement dans l'absolu (aspects de la penseé proudhonienne)." In Aimer en France 1760-1860, edited by Paul Vialleneix and Jean Ehrard, 2: 389-399. Clermont-Ferrand: Association des Publications de la Faculté des Lettres et Sciences Humaines de Clermont-Ferrand, 1980.

04364. Moon, S. Joan. "The Saint-Simonian Association of Working-Class Women, 1830-1850." Proceedings of the Fifth Annual Meeting of the Western Society for French History 5 (1978): 274-281.

04365. ________. "The Saint-Simoniennes and the Moral Revolution." Proceedings of the Consortium on Revolutionary Europe (1976): 162-174.

04366. Strumingher, Laura S. "The Legacy of Flora Tristan." International Journal of Women's Studies 7 (May-June 1984): 232-247.

Also refer to #4359, 4456, 4459.

c) Legal

04367. La Femme au XIXe siècle, littérature et idéologie. Lyon: Presses universitaires de Lyon, 1979.

Also refer to #4452, 4454.

d) Criminal

04368. Martin, Benjamin F. "Sex, Property and Crime in the Third Republic: A Statistical Introduction." Historical Reflections/Réflexions historiques 11 (Fall 1984): 323-349.

04369. O'Brien, Patricia. "The Kleptomania Diagnosis: Bourgeois Women and Theft in Late Nineteenth-Century France." Journal of Social History 17 (Fall 1983): 65-78.

04370. Vallaud, Dominique. "Le crime d'infanticide et l'indulgence des cours d'assize en France au XIXe siècle." Social Science Information 21 (1982): 475-498.

Also refer to #4457-4460.

e) Feminism

04371. Alméras, Henri d. "Les femmes de 1848. Les Vesuviennes George Sand." In La vie parisienne sous la république de 1848, pp. 127-158. Paris: Albin Michel, 1921.

04372. Bei, Neda and Schwarz, Ingeborg. "Olympe de Gouges: Les droits de la Femme. A la Reine. -- Die Frauenrechte. An die Königin. Widergabe und Übersetzung des Textes aus 1791." In Das ewige Klischee, zum Rollenbild und Selbstverständnis bei Männern und Frauen, pp. 45-75. Vienna: Hermann Böhlaus, 1981.

04373. Blanc, Olivier. Olympe de Gouges. Paris: Syros, 1981.

04374. Boxer, Marilyn. "'First Wave' Feminism in Nineteenth-century France: Class, Family and Religion." Women's Studies International Forum 5 (1982): 551-559.

04375. Evans, Richard J. "Feminism and Anticlericalism in France, 1870-1922." Historical Journal 25 (December 1982): 947-952.

04376. Goliber, Sue Helder. "Marguerite Durand: A Study in French Feminism." International Journal of Women's Studies 5 (November-December 1983): 402-412.

Also refer to #4353.

04377. Hause, Steven C. and Kenney, Anne R. The Political Rights of French Women: Feminism, Social Politics and Women's Suffrage in the Third Republic. Princeton, N.J.: Princeton University Press, 1984.

04378. Moses, Claire G. French Feminism in the Nineteenth Century. Albany, N.Y.: State University of New York Press, 1984.

04379. Rebérioux, Madeleine; Dufrancatel, Christiane; and Slama, Beatrice. "Hubertine Auclert et la question des femme à l'immortel congrès (1879)." Romantisme 13-14 (1976): 123-142.

04380. Tilly, Louise A. "Women's Collective Action and Feminism in France, 1870-1914." In Class Conflict and Collective Action, edited by Louise A. Tilly and Charles Tilly, pp. 207-231. Beverly Hills, Calif.: Sage, 1981.

Also refer to #2963.

f) Political Roles

(1) French Revolution

(a) Generic

04381. Applewhite, Harriet B. and Levy, Darline Gay. "Responses to the Political Activism of Women of the People in Revolutionary Paris, 1789-1793." In Women and the Structure of Society, edited by Barbara J. Harris and JoAnn McNamara, pp. 215-231. Durham, N.C.: Duke University Press, 1984.

04382. ________________. "Women, Democracy, and Revolution in Paris, 1789-1794." In French Women and the Age of Englightenment, edited by Samia I. Spencer, pp. 64-79. Bloomington, Ind.: Indiana University Press, 1984.

04383. Conner, Susan P. "Les Femmes Militaires: Women in the French Army, 1792-1815." Proceedings of the Consortium on Revolutionary Europe (1982): 290-302.

04384. ________. "A Woman's View of War: On Campaign with the Grande Armeé, 1810-1811." Laurels 53 (Fall 1982): 99-109.

04385. Farina, Rachele. "Le francesi prendono la parola--Donne e Rivoluzione francese." In Esistere comme donna, pp. 49-62. Milan: Mazzotta, 1983.

04386. Legouvé, Jean-Baptiste-Gabriel. Le Mérite des femmes. Paris: Camuzeaux, Librarie-Editeur, 1837.

(b) Individuals

04387. Castelot, André. "Talleyrand et les femmes." Historia 413 (1981): 52-61.

04388. Escoffier, Françoise. "Mme de Staël et la Révolution." Revue des deux mondes (April 1984): 95-100.

04389. Gelfand, Elissa. "A Response to the Void: Madame Roland's Mémoires particuliers and Her Imprisonment." Romance Notes 20 (1979): 75-80.

04390. Girod de l'Ain, Gabriel. Désireé Clary; d'après sa correspondance inédite avec Bonaparte, Bernadotte et sa famille. Paris: Hachette, 1959.

04391. Mullaney, Marie Marmo. "Madame Roland: The Paradoxical Feminism of an Eighteenth-Century 'Loophole Woman.'" Maryland Historian 14 (Spring/Summer 1983): 1-10.

(2) Charles X

04392. Imbert de Saint-Armand, Arthur Léon. La duchesse de Berry et la cour de Charles X. Paris: Dentu et Cie, 1888.

04393. ________________. La duchesse de Berry et la Vendee. Paris: E. Dentu, 1892.

(3) July Monarchy

04394. Clarke, M. L. "Mme de Genlis and Louis Philippe." History Today 27 (October 1977): 673-678.

(4) Second Republic and Second Empire

04395. Alba, Duque de. "La Emperatriz Eugenia." Boletin de la Real Academia de la Historia Madrid 110 (April-June 1942): 197-221.

04396. ________. "La Emperatriz Eugenia." Boletin de la Real Academia de la Historia Madrid 120 (January-March 1947): 71-101.

04397. Bannour, Wanda. "Eugénie et Maurice de Guérin." Historia 439 (June 1983): 82-87.

04398. Lacour-Gayet, G. "L'Imperatrice Eugénie avant son règne." Revue de Paris 31 (15 December 1924): 879-892.

04399. Llanos y Torrigla, Félix de. - "Emperatriz Eugenia en el archivo de Palacio de Leria." Boletin de la Real Academia de la Historia Madrid 106 (April-June 1935): 443-478.

(5) Third Republic

04400. Jouan, Lucienne. "Autre visage de Louise Michel [Commundarde.]." Nouveaux Cahiers Second Empire 12 (1985): 19-20.

04401. Lejeune, Paule. "Le donne della Comune di Parigi." In Esistere comme donna, pp. 97-108. Milan: Mazzotta, 1983.

04402. Schulkind, Eugene. "Socialist Women During the 1871 Paris Commune." Past and Present 106 (February 1985): 124-163.

04403. Thomas, Edith. Louise Michel. Montreal: Black Rose Books, 1983.

3. ECONOMIC

"They live only by privation, even in industry."
Fourier

a) Generic

04404. Fauve-Chamoux, Auboinette. "The Importance of Women in an Urban Environment: The Example of the Rheims Household at the Beginning of the Industrial Revolution." In Family Forms in Historic Europe, edited by Richard Wall, Jean Robin, and Peter Laslett, pp. 475-492. New York: Cambridge University Press, 1983.

04405. Gough, Austin. "French Workers and Their Wives in the Mid-Nineteenth Century." Labour History (1982): 74-82.

04406. Grubitzsch, Helga. "Women's Projects and Co-Operatives in France at the Beginning of the 19th Century." Women's Studies International Forum 8 (1935): 279-386.

04407. Heywood, Colin. "The Market for Child Labour in Nineteenth Century France." History 66 (1981): 34-49.

04408. Lehning, James R. "Developpement économique et mutation familiale. Le ménage paysan dans un village de la region Stephanoise au XIXe siècle." Cahiers d'histoire 23 (1978): 275-291.

04409. McDougall, Mary Lynn. "Protecting Infants: The French Campaign for Maternity Leaves 1890s-1913." French Historical Studies 13 (Spring 1983): 79-105.

04410. Moch, Leslie Page and Tilly, Louise A. "Joining the Urban World: Occupation, Family, and Migration in Three French Cities." Comparative Studies in Society and History 27 (January 1985): 33-56.

04411. Smith, Harvey. "Family and Class: The Household Economy of Languedoc Winegrowers, 1830-1870." Journal of Family History 9 (Spring 1984): 64-87.

04412. Tilly, Louise A. "Linen was Their Life: Family Survival Strategies and Parent-Child Relations in Nineteenth Century France." In _Interest and Emotion, Essays on the Study of Family and Kinship_, edited by Hans Medick and David Warren Sabean, pp. 300-316. New York: Cambridge University Press, 1985.

04413. ______________. "Rich and Poor in a French Textile City." In _Essays on the Family and Historical Change_, edited by Leslie Page Moch and Gary D. Stark, pp. 65-90. College Station: Texas A&M University Press, 1983.

b) Women's Employment

04414. Bachrach, Susan Dimlich. _Dames Employeés: The Feminization of Postal Work in Nineteenth-Century France_. New York: Haworth Press, 1984.

04415. Cottereau, Alain. "Usure au travail, destins masculins et destins féminins dans les cultures ouvrières, en France, au XIXe siècle." _Mouvement social_ 124 (July 1983): 71-112.

04416. Guilbert, Madeleine. "Le travail des femmes." _Revue française du travail_ 1 (November 1946): 663-670.

04417. Guiral, Pierre and Thuiller, Guy. _La vie quotidienne des domestiques en France au XIXe siècle_. Collection la vie quotidienne. Paris: Hachette, 1978.

04418. Hilden, Patricia. "Class and Gender: Conflicting Components of Women's Behavior in the Textile Mills of Lille, Roubaix, and Tourcoing, 1880-1914." _Historical Journal_ 27, no. 2 (June 1984): 361-385.

04419. McDougall, Mary Lynn. "The Meaning of Reform: The Ban on Women's Night Work, 1892-1914." _Proceedings of the Western Society for French History_ 10 (1984): 404-417.

04420. Sowerwine, Charles. "Workers and Women in France before 1914: The Debate over the Coureau Affair." _Journal of Modern History_ 55 (September 1983): 411-441.

04421. Tilly, Louise A. "Structure de l'emploi, travail des femmes et changements démographiques dans deux villes industrielles, Anzin et Roubais, 1872-1906." _Le mouvement social_ 105 (October-December 1978): 33-58.

Also refer to #4451.

c) Trade Unions

04422. Deremeyez, Jean-William, and Griveau, Léon. "Marie Guillot et le syndicat des instituteurs de Saone-et-Loire (premier tiers du XXe siècle): un document inedit." Mouvement social 127 (April 1984): 89-109.

04423. Tristan, Flora. The Worker's Union. Translated and introduced by Beverly Livingston. Urbana, Ill.: University of Illinois Press, 1983.

4. RELIGION

"My heart once captured (by religion), I deliberately and, with a sort of frantic joy, showed reason the door. I accepted everything, I believed everything, without a struggle."

George Sand
The Story of My Life

04424. Jacquement, Gerard. "Dechristianisation, structures familiales et anticlericalisme. Belle-ville au XIX siecle." Archives de sciences sociales des religions 29 (January-March 1984): 69-82.

04425. Langlois, Claude. "Le Catholicisme au féminin." Archives des sciences sociales des religions 29 (January-March 1984): 29-53.

04426. Maitre, J. "Entre femmes. Notes sur und filière du mysticisme catholique." Archives de sciences sociales des religions 28 (January-March 1983): 105-137.

Also refer to #4375, 4479.

5. SOCIAL

"Women! Do you want to be republicans? . . .Be simple in your dress, hardworking in your homes, never go to the public assemblies."

Moniteur, 17 November 1793

a) Generic

04427. Bernos, Marcel. "De l'influence salutaire ou pernicieuse de la femme dans la famille et la société." Revue d'histoire moderne et contemporaine 29 (July-September 1982): 453-461.

04428. Bonnebault, Armand. Les groupements professionnels féminins. Leur passé, leur présent, leur avenir. Paris: Rousseau, 1910.

04429. De Lamotte, A., La femme en ville et a la campagne. Salaires et conditions diverses. Angoulême: M. Despujois, 1909.

04430. Faitrop, Anne Christine. "Une comtesse bretonne à Rome en 1874." Annales de Bretagne 90 (1983): 593-601.

04431. Fleury, Comte de and Sonolet, Louis. La société du Second Empire Paris: Librairie Albin Michel, 1911.

04432. Huertas, Monique de and Polasteron, Louise de. Le Grand amour du comte d'Artois. Paris: Perrin, 1983.

04433. Lampérière, Anna. La femme et son pouvoir. Paris: V. Giard et E. Brière, 1909.

04434. Leleu, Thierry. "Scenes de la vie quotidienne: les femmes de la valleé de la Lys (1870-1920)." Revue du Nord 58 (July-September 1981): 637-666.

04435. Moch, Leslie Page. "Adolescence and Migration: Nîmes, France, 1906." Social Science History 5 (Winter 1981): 25-51.

04436. ________________. "Infirmities of the Body and Vices of the Soul: Migrants, Family, and Urban Life in Turn-of-the-Century France." In Essays on the Family and Historical Change, edited by Leslie Page Moch and Gary D. Stark, pp. 35-64. College Station: Texas A&M University Press, 1983.

04437. Roussy, Baptiste. Education domestique de la femme et renovation sociale. Paris: Delagrave, 1914.

Also refer to #3284.

b) Demography

04438. Barbier, Frédéric. "Les caractères généraux de la démographie de Valenciennes au XIXe siècle." Revue du Nord 65 (July-September 1983): 567-579.

04439. Bourdelaise, Patrice. "Le poid démographique des femmes seules en France [1851-1896]." Annales de démographie historique (1981): 215-227.

04440. Ganiage, Jean G. "Aux confins de la Normandie: structures de la natalité dans cinq villages du Beauvaisis." Annales de Normandie 23 (1973): 57-90.

04441. Hunter, John C. "The Problem of the French Birth Rate on the Eve of World War I." French Historical Studies 2 (Fall 1962): 490-503.

04442. Spagnoli, Paul G. High Fertility in Mid-Nineteenth Century France: A Multivariate Analysis of Fertility Patterns in the Arrondissement of Lille. Vol. 2 of Research in Economic History. London: Jai Press, 1977.

04443. _______________. "Industrialization, Proletarianization and Marriage: A Reconsideration" Journal of Family History 8 (Fall 1983): 230-247.

04444. Vouloir, Marie-Christine. "Les naissance illégitimes à Saint-Germain-en Laye, 1810-1874." Bulletin d'information de la société de démographie historique 28 (1979): 3-12.

Also refer to #3286, 3289, 3290, 4421.

c) Family

(1) Non-specific

04445. Collomp, Alain. "Conflits familiaux et groupes de residence en Haute-Provence." Annales: économies, sociétés, civilisations 36 (May 1981): 408-425.

04446. Garaud, Marcel and Szamkiewicz, Romauld. La Révolution francaise et la famille. Paris: Presses Universitaires de France, 1979.

04447. Segalen, Martine. Love and Death in the Peasant Family, Rural France in the Nineteenth Century. Chicago: University of Chicago Press, 1983.

Also refer to #4370, 4408-4413, 4424, 4427, 4435, 4436, 4453.

(2) Childhood

04448. Fuchs, Rachel Ginnis. Abandoned Children Foundlings and Child Welfare in Nineteenth-Century France. Albany, N.Y.: State University of New York Press, 1983.

04449. Loux, Françoise. Le jeune enfant et son corps dans la médecine traditionelle. Paris: Flammarion, 1978.

04450. Martin-Fugier, Anne. "La fin des nourrices." Le mouvement social 105 (October-December 1978): 11-32.

04451. Perrot, Michelle. "De la nourrice a l'employee . . . Travaux des femmes dans la France du XIXe siecle." Le Mouvement social 105 (October-December 1978): 3-10.

Also refer to #4407, 4409, 4412, 4444.

d) Marriage

04452. Dessertine, Dominique. "Le divorce à l'époque révolutionnaire et impériale. Etude socio-démographique des divorces lyonnais." Bulletin du centre d'histoire économique et sociale de la région lyonnaise 4 (1978): 37-54.

04453. Huussen, Arend. "La 'crise' du mariage et de la famille pendant la Révolution française." In Aimer en France 1760-1860, edited by Paul Vialleneix and Jean Ehrard, 2:331-343. Clermont-Ferrand: Association des Publications de la Faculté des Lettres et Sciences Humaines de Clermont-Ferrand, 1980.

04454. Kelly, Edmond. The French Law of Marriage and the Conflict of Laws that Arises Therefrom. 1885. Reprint. Littleton, Co.: F. B. Rothman and Company, 1985.

04455. Sardon, Jean-Paul. "Mariage et révolution dans une petite ville de vignerons: Argenteuil (1780-1819)." Population 34 (1979): 1162-1167.

Also refer to #3290, 4363, 4443, 4494.

e) Sex Life and morals

(1) Non-specific

04456. Devance, Louis. "L'éthique de la sexualité dans le socialisme romantique en France: De la loi du désir et du désir de loi." In Aimer en France 1760-1860, edited by Paul Vialleneix and Jean Ehrard, 2:367-376. Clermont-Ferrand: Association des Publications de la Faculté des Lettres et Sciences Humaines de Clermont-Ferrand, 1980.

Also refer to #3310, 3311, 4485.

(2) Prostitutes

04457. Frey, Michel. "Hypothèses sur les comportements concubins au sein des classes populaires à Paris en 1846-1847: le rôle des prostituées et des femmes logeant en garnis." In Aimer en France 1760-1860, edited by Paul Vialleneix and Jean Ehrard, 2:565-585. Clermont-Ferrand: Association des Publications de la Faculté des Lettres et Sciences Humaines de Clermont-Ferrand, 1980.

04458. Harsin, Jill. The Policing of Prostitution in Nineteenth Century Paris. Princeton: Princeton University Press, 1985.

04459. Michaud, Stéphane. "La prostitution comme interrogation sur l'amour chez les socialistes romantiques (1830-1840)." In Aimer en France 1760-1860, edited by Paul Vialleneix and Jean Ehrard, 2:377-388. Clermont-Ferrand: Association des Publications de la Faculté des Lettres et Sciences Humaines de Clermont-Ferrand, 1980.

04460. Vissière, Jean-Louis. "Un témoin de l'évolution des moeurs au XVIIIe siècle: l'avocat Fournel." In Aimer en France 1760-1860, edited by Paul Vialleneix and Jean Ehrard, 2:533-539. Clermont-Ferrand: Association des Publications de la Faculté des Lettres et Sciences Humaines de Clermont-Ferrand, 1980.

Also refer to #4488, 4514, 4520.

f) Fashion/Manners

04461. Delpierre, Madeleine. Modes de la Belle Epoque. Costumes francais 1890-1910 et portraits. Paris: Musee du costume de la Ville de Paris, 1961.

04462. ________ and Vanier, Henriette. Elegantes parisiennes au temps de Marcel Proust 1890-1910. Paris: Musee du costume de la Ville de Paris, 1968.

04463. Saunders, Edith. The Age of Worth, Couturier to the Empress Eugenie. Bloomington, Ind.: Indiana University Press, 1955.

Also refer to #3318, 4496.

g) Health/Medical

04464. Bartin, Celia. Marie Bonaparte. New York: Harcourt Brace Jovanovich, 1982.

04465. Bollenot, Gilles. "Les fous à Lyon au XIXe siècle." Cahiers d'histoire 26 (1981): 231-258.

04466. Calbo, Philippe. "Medecins en Sarthe dans seconde moitie de XIXe siècle." Annales de Bretagne et des Pays de L'Ouest 92 (1985): 209-224.

04467. Isambert, Emilie. The Medical Role of Women. Paris: Joel Cherbuliez, 1871.

04468. Knibiehler, Yvonne. "Le Discours médical sur la femme: Constantes et ruptures." Romantisme 13-14 (1976): 41-55.

04469. ________. "Les medecins et 'l'amour conjugal' au XIXe siècle." In Aimer en France 1760-1860, edited by Paul Vialleneix and Jean Ehrard, 2:357-366. Clermont-Ferrand: Association des Publications de la Faculté des Lettres et Sciences Humaines de Clermont-Ferrand, 1980.

04470. Quartararo, Anne T. "Clean and Decent Students: Health Care Practices Inside Women's Normal Schools, 1830-1900." Proceedings of the Society for French History 10 (1984): 394-403.

Also refer to #3320, 4449.

6. CULTURAL

"Women are proving just now not only that the domain of art should be open to them as freely as it is to men, on the grounds of right and reason, but also that they are specially gifted. . . . "

Léonce Bénédite

a) Education

04471. Clark, Linda. "The Primary Education of French Girls: Pedagogical Prescriptions and Social Realities, 1880-1940." History of Education Quarterly 21 (Winter 1981): 411-428.

04472. ________. "The Socialization of Girls in the Primary Schools of the Third Republic." Journal of Social History 15 (Summer 1982): 685-697.

04473. Gildea, Robert. Education in Provincial France, 1800-1914. Oxford: Oxford University Press, 1983.

04474. Grubitzsch, Helga. "'Wissen heisst leben...' /Der Kampf der Frauen um die Bildung zu Beginn des 19. Jahrhunderts (Frankreich)." In Frauen in der Geschichte, edited by Ilse Brehmer, et al., pp. 171-204, Dusseldorf: Schwann, 1983.

04475. Mayeur, Françoise. "L'enseignement secondaire des jeunes filles 1867-1924." Le Mouvement social 96 (July-September 1976): 103-110.

04476. Offen, Karen. "The Second Sex and the Baccalaureat in Republican France, 1880-1924." French Historical Studies 13 (Fall 1983): 252-286.

04477. Peron, Françoise. "La femme cultivatrice au XIXe siècle." Cahiers Iroise 29 (1982): 88-102.

04478. Schuyten, M.C. L'éducation de la femme. Paris: O. Doin, 1908.

04479. Secondy, Louis. "L'education des filles en milieu catholique au XIXe siècle." Cahiers d'histoire 26 (1981): 337-352.

Also refer to #3331, 4470.

b) Literature

(1) Non-specific

04480. Gautier, Jean-Maurice. "Amours romantique, amours frenetiques." In _Aimer en France 1976-1860_, edited by Paul Vialleneix and Jean Ehrard, 1:217-225. Clermont-Ferrand: Association des Publications de la Faculté des Lettres et Sciences Humaines de Clermont-Ferrand, 1980.

04481. Guiot-Lauret, Jacqueline. "Amour et tabous linguistiques dans quelques romans et nouvelles des années 1833-1836." In _Aimer en France 1760-1860_, edited by Paul Vialleneix and Jean Ehrard, 1;205-215. Clermont-Ferrand: Association des Publications de la Faculté des Lettres et Sciences Humaines de Clermont-Ferrand, 1980.

04482. Palacio, Jean de. "La féminité dévorante. Sur quelques images de la manducation dans la littérature décadente." _Revue des sciences humaines_ n.s. 168 (October-December 1977): 601-618.

04483. Pich, Edgard. "Littérature et codes sociaux: L'antiféminisme sous le Second Empire." _Romantisme_ 13-14 (1976): 167-182.

04484. Ridga, George Ross. "Metamorphoses of the Vampire: Modern Woman and the Femme Fatale." In _The Hero in French Decadent Literature_, pp. 141-162. Athens: University of Georgia Press, 1961.

04485. Saint-Gérand, Jacques-Philippe. "L'amour: érotisme, pornographie et normes littéraires (1815-1845)." In _Aimer en France 1760-1860_, edited by Paul Vialleneix and Jean Ehrard, 1:191-204. Clermont-Ferrand: Association des Publications de la Faculté des Lettres et Sciences Humaines de Clermont-Ferrand, 1980.

04486. Schor, Naomi. _Breaking the Chain: Women Theory and French Realist Fiction_. New York: Columbia University Press, 1985.

Also refer to #4367.

(2) Drama

04487. Ihrig, Grace Pauline. _Heroines in French Drama of the Romantic Period, 1829-1848._ New York: King's Crown Press, 1950.

04488. Millstone, Amy. "French Feminist Theatre and the Subject of Prostitution." In _The Image of the Prostitute in Modern Literature_, edited by Pierre Liltorn and Mary Beth Pringle, pp. 19-27. New York: F. Ungar, 1984.

(3) Poetry

04489. Ahearn, Edward J. "'Simplifier avec gloire la femme': Syntax, Synechdoche, Subversion in a Mallarmé Sonnet." French Review 58 (February 1985): 349-359.

04490. Smith, Madeleine M. "Mallarmé and the Chimeres." Yale French Studies 11 (1953): 59-72.

04491. Whiteside, Anna. "Poèmes du guerre et d'amour, ou la doube chevauchée d'Apollinaire." French Review 54 (May 1981): 804-809.

(4) Prose

(a) Novelists

[1] Individuals

[a] Balzac

04492. Feldman, Shoshana. "Rereading Femininity." Yale French Studies 62 (1981): 19-44.

04493. Frappier-Mazur, Lucienne. "Le regime de l'aveu dans 'Le lys la vallée'." In Aimer en France 1760-1860, edited by Paul Vialleneix and Jean Ehrard, 1:241-252. Clermont-Ferrand: Association des Publications de la Faculté des Lettres et Sciences Humaines de Clermont-Ferrand, 1980.

04494. Michel, Arlette. Le Mariage et l'amour dans l'oeuvre romanesque d'Honoré de Balzac. Paris: Champion, 1976.

Also refer to #3331, 4533.

[b] Flaubert

04495. Aprile, Max L. "Aveugle et sa signification dans 'Madame Bovary.'" Revue d'histoire littéraire de la France 76 (May-June 1976): 385-392.

04496. Festa-McCormick, Diana. "Emma Bovary's Masculinization: Convention of Clothes and Morality of Conventions." In Gender and Literary Voice, Women and Literature, edited by Janet Todd 1: 223-235. New York: Holmes and Meier, 1980.

04497. Kovács, Katherine S. "The Bureaucraticization of Knowledge and Sex in Flaubert and Vargas Llosa." Comparative Literature Studies 21 (Spring 1984): 30-51.

04498. Lajoux, Alexandra Reed. "From Emma to Félicité: The Use of Hagiography in the Works of Gustave Flaubert." Studi Medievali 2 (Spring 1983): 35-50.

04499. Oliver, Hermia. Flaubert and an English Governess: The Quest for Julia Herbert. Oxford: Clarendon Press, 1980.

04500. Pace, Jean. "Flaubert's Image of Woman." Southern Review 13 (1977): 114-130.

04501. Riggs, Larry W. "La Banqueroute des idéaux reçus dans Madame Bovary." In Aimer en France 1760-1860, edited by Paul Vialleneix and Jean Ehrard, 1:253-262. Clermont-Ferrand: Association des Publications de la Faculté des Lettres et Sciences Humaines de Clermont-Ferrand, 1980.

[c] Judith Gautier

04502. Barthou, Louis. "Richard Wagner et Judith Gautier." La Revue de Paris 39 (August 1932): 481-498.

04503. Brody, Elaine. "Letters from Judith Gauthier to Chalmers Clifton." French Review 58 (April 1985): 670-674.

04504. Camacho, M. Dita. Judith Gautier, sa vie et son oeuvre. Paris: E. Droz, 1939.

[d] George Sand

((1)) Biographies

04505. Barry, Joseph. George Sand ou le Scandale de la liberté. Paris: Editions du Seuil, 1982.

04506. Biermann, Karlheinrich. "George Sand und die soziale Republik (1848-1851)." Lendemains 7 (no. 28, 1982): 45-51.

04507. Manifold, Gay. George Sand's Theatre Career. Ann Arbor, Mich.: UMI Research Press, 1985.

04508. Schor, Naomi. "Female Fetishism: The Case of George Sand." Poetics Today 6 (1985): 301-310.

04509. Thomson, Patricia. George Sand and the Victorians: Her Influence and Reputation in Nineteenth-Century England. New York: Columbia University Press, 1976.

Also refer to #4371.

((2)) Views on Society

04510. Brahimi, Denise. "Ecriture--Féminité--Féminisme. Réflexions sur trois romans de George Sand." Revue des sciences humaines n.s. 168 (October-December 1977): 577-588.

04511. Cornell, Kenneth. "George Sand: Emotion and Idea." Yale French Studies 13 (1954): 93-97.

04512. Didier, Beatrice. "Femme/Identité/Ecriture. A propos de l'Histoire de ma vie de George Sand." Revue des sciences humaines n.s. 168 (October-December 1977): 561-576.

04513. Marix-Spire, Thérèse. "George Sand Le Marquise de Villemer." Europe 427-428 (November-December 1964): 77-81.

04514. Schor, Naomi. "Female Paranoia: The Case for Psychoanalytic Feminist Criticism." Yale French Studies (1981): 204-219.

04515. Sivert, Eileen Boyd. "Lélia and Feminism." Yale French Studies 62 (1981): 45-66.

04516. Toesca, Maurice. "Un diner chez George Sand." Revue des deux mondes (August 1983): 340-344.

[e] Emile Zola

04517. Kaminskas, Jenate D. "Thérèse Racquin et Manet: harmonie en gris." French Review 57 (February 1984): 309-319.

04518. Mitterand, Henri. "The Calvary of Catherine Maheu: The Description of a Page in Germinal." Yale French Studies 42 (1969): 115-125.

04519. Warren, Jill. "Zola's View of Prostitutes." In The Image of the Prostitute in Modern Literature, edited by Pierre Liltorn and Mary Beth Pringle, pp. 29-41. New York: Ungar, 1984.

Also refer to #4521.

[2] Others

04520. Bailbe, Joseph-Marc. "Autour de La Dame aux Camelias: présence et signification du thème de la courtisane dans le roman français (1830-1850)." In Aimer en France 1760-1860, edited by Paul Vialleneix and Jean Ehrard, 1:227-239. Clermont-Ferrand: Association des Publications de la Faculté des Lettres et Sciences Humaines de Claremont-Ferrand, 1980.

04521. Bernheimer, Charles. "Huysmans: Writing Against (Female) Nature." Poetics Today 6 (1985): 311-324.

04522. Brombert, Victor H. "Stendhal, Analyst or Amorist?" Yale French Studies 11 (1953): 39-48.

04523. Escoube, Paul. La femme et le sentiment de l'amour chez Remy de Gourmont. Paris: Mercur de France, 1923.

04524. Field, Trevor J. "Imagery of Fecundity and Sterility in the Works of Maurice Barres." Degré second 2 (June 1978): 115-136.

04525. Gaudefroy-Demombynes, Lorraine. La Femme dans l'oeuvre de Maupassant. Paris: Mercure de France, 1943.

04526. Herz, Micheline. "The Angelism of Madame de Ségur." Yale French Studies 27 (1961): 12-21.

04527. Morcos, Saad. Juliette Adam. Beirut: Dar-al-Maaref-Liban, 1962.

04528. Mozet, Nicole. "Féminité et pouvoir après 1830: Le cas étrange de Félicité des Touches (Béatrix.)" Revue des sciences humaines n.s. 168 (October-December 1977): 553-560.

04529. Rabaut, Jean. "Droits de la femme: Victor Hugo féministe!" Histoire 40 (1981): 79-81.

04530. Wallace, Albert Harlan. "Philogyny as an Element in Maupassant's Work." University of North Carolina: Studies in the Romance Languages and Literatures 124 (1972): 177-195.

Also refer to #4858.

(b) Periodicals

04531. Adler, Laure. A l'aube du féminisme: les premieres journalistes: 1830-1850. Paris: Payot, 1979.

04532. Bernheim, Nicole. "'La presse féminine': une affaire importante." Europe 427-428 (November-December 1964): 203-206.

c) Literary salons

(1) Madame Récamier

04533. Lamartine, Alphonse de. Portraits et salons romantiques. Paris: Le Goupy, 1927.

04534. Ledoux-Labard, René; Ledoux-Labard, Guy; and, Ledoux-Labard, Christian. "La Décoration et l'ameublement de la chambre de Madame Récamier sous le Consulat. I."" Gazette des Beaux Arts 94 no. 2 (October 1952): 175-192.

04535. ____________. "La Decoration et l'ameublement de la Chambre de Madame Récamier sous le Consulat, II." Gazette des Beaux Arts 97 no. 1 (May-June 1955): 299-312.

(2) Madame de Staël

(a) Biographies

04536. Balayé, Simone. "Madame de Staël." Europe 427-428 (November-December 1964): 65-69.

04537. Benjamin, Constant. Madame de Staël et le Groupe de Coppet. Oxford: Voltaire Foundation, 1982.

04538. Diesbach, Ghislain de. Madame de Staël. Paris: Perrin, 1983.

04539. Godechot, Jacques. Madame de Staël. Considérations sur la Révolution française. Paris: Hachette, 1983.

04540. Larg, David Glass. Madame de Staël. La vie dans l'oeuvre (1766-1800); essai de biographie morale et intellectuelle. Paris: E. Champion, 1924.

Also refer to #4388.

(b) Views on Society

04541. Balayé, Simone. "Corinne et Rome: ou le Chant du Cygne." In Themes et Figures du siècle des Lumières, edited by Raymond Trousson, pp. 45-58. Geneva: Droz, 1980.

04542. Gibelin, J. "Notes sur le protestantisme de Mme de Staël." Bulletin de la Société de l'histoire du Protestantisme français 100 (July-September 1954): 111-119.

04543. Kohn, Hans. "Madame de Staël, Liberal and Nationalist." Forum 111 (February 1949): 81-85.

04544. Morros, Lucy. "The Impact of German Thought and Culture on Madame de Staël's Thinking About Women." In Women in German Studies, edited by Kay Goodman and Ruth H. Sandars, pp. 5-23. Oxford, Ohio: Miami University, 1977.

04545. Zemek, Théodora. "Madame de Staël et l'esprit national." XVIIIe siècle 14 (1982): 89-101.

(3) Others

04546. Leflaive, Anne, ed. Ce merveilleux troisième âge. Madame Swetchine. Paris: Tequi, 1984.

04547. Pouquet, Jeanne Simone. The Last Salon: Anatole France and His Muse. Translated by Lewis Galantiere. New York: Harcourt, Brace, 1927.

d) Intellectuals

04548. Kaplan, Edward K. Michelet's Poetic Vision, A Romantic Philosophy of Nature, Man, and Woman. Amherst, Mass.: University of Massachusetts, 1977.

Also refer to #4359.

e) Art/Artifacts

(1) Women in Art

04549. Agulhon, Maurice. Marianne au combat: l'imagerie et la symbolique republicaines de 1789 à 1880. Paris: Flammarion, 1979.

04550. Berthoud, Dorette. "Léopold Robert et Charlotte Bonaparte." Gazette des Beaux Arts 77 no. 2 (July-December 1935): 17-35.

04551. Hardouin-Fugier, Elisabeth. "Aimer à Lyon: Virginitas (vers 1850)." In Aimer en France 1760-1860, edited by Paul Vialleneix and Jean Ehrard, 1:81-88. Clermont-Ferrand: Association des Publications de la Faculté des Lettres et Sciences Humaines de Clermont-Ferrand, 1980.

04552. Lesko, Diane. "From Genre to Allegory in Gustave Courbet's Les Demoiselles de Village." Art Journal 38 (Spring 1978): 171-177.

04553. Pintorno, Giuseppe. "Largo alle donne! Si salvi chi puo!--L'ironica risposta maschile." In Esistere comme donna, pp. 109-114. Milan: Mazzotta, 1983.

04554. Tsiakma, Katia. "Cézanne's and Poussin's Nudes." Art Journal 37 (Winter 1977-1978): 120-132.

04555. Weisberg, Gabriel P. Images of Women: Printmakers from 1830-1930. Salt Lake City: Museum of Fine Arts, 1977.

(2) Women Artists

(a) Actresses/Dancers

04556. Beaumont, Cyril W. Three French Dancers of the Nineteenth Century: Duvernay, Livry, Beaugrand. London: Beaumont, 1935.

04457. Guest, Ivor. The Ballet of the Second Empire. London: Pitman Publishing, 1974.

04558. Poinsot, Edmond Antoine. Rachel d'après sa correspondence. Paris: Librairie des bibliophiles, 1882.

04559. Richardson, Joanna. Sarah Bernhardt and Her World. New York: Putnam, 1977.

04560. Richardson, Joanna. "Sarah Bernhardt and Politics." History Today 26 (1976): 591-597.

04561. Salmon, Eric, ed. Bernhardt and the Theatre of Her Time. Westport, Ct.: Greenwood Press, 1984.

04562. Senelick, Laurence. "Rachel in Russia: The Shchepkin-Annenkov Correspondence." Theatre Reserch International 3 (February 1978): 93-114.

Also refer to #1017, 1811.

(b) Painters

04563. Jean, René. "Madame de Mirbel." Gazette des beaux-arts 3rd ser. 35 (1906): 131-146.

04564. Radychi, J. Diane. "Life of Lady Art Students; Changing Art Education at the Turn of the Century." Art Journal 42 (Spring 1982): 9-13.

04565. Rey, Jean Dominique. Berthe Morisot. Naefels, Switzerland: Bonfini Press, 1982.

Also refer to #4320.

f) Science

04566. Giroud, Françoise. An Honorable Woman, Marie Curie-Sklodowska. New York: Holmes and Meier, 1984.

D. THE GERMANIES

1. BIBLIOGRAPHIES

"The assertion that housekeeping and child-rearing is women's natural sphere is as intelligent as the assertion that there must always be kings, because there have been kings as long as there has been history."

August Bebel

04567. Fout, John C. "Current Research on German Women's History in the Nineteenth Century." In German Women in the Nineteenth Century, a Social History, edited by John C. Fout, pp. 3-54. New York: Holmes & Meier, 1984.

2. SURVEYS

"As long as it is said man _will_ and woman _shall_, we live in a state governed by might and not by right."
Hedwig Dohm
"The Rights of Women's Suffrage," 1876

04568. Fout, John C., ed. _German Women in the Nineteenth Century, a Social History_. New York: Holmes and Meier, 1984.

04569. Pols, Werner, ed. _Deutsche Sozialgeschichte Dokumente und Skizzen. Band I: 1815-1870_. Munich: Beck, 1973.

04570. Ritter, Gerhard A. and Kocka, Jurgen, eds. _Deutsche Sozialgeschichte Dokumente und Skizzen. Band II: 1870-1914_. Munich: Beck, 1974.

Also refer to #3531, 3533.

3. POLITICAL

"There is now a species of men who call themselves Social Democrats; they want to destroy marriage and family life. . . ."
Die Post

a) Generic

04571. Altmann-Gottheiner, Elisabeth. "Die deutschen politischen Parteien und ihre Stellung zur Frauenfrage." _Zeitschrift fur Politik_ 3 (1910): 581-598.

04572. Pierard, Richard V. "The Transportation of White Women to German Southwest Africa, 1898-1914." _Race_ 12 (January 1971): 317-322.

04573. Secci, Lia. "German Women Writers and the Revolution of 1848." In _German Women in the Nineteenth Century, A Social History_, edited by John C. Fout, pp. 151-171. New York: Holmes & Meier, 1984.

Also refer to #4665.

b) Marxism and Socialism

(1) Non-specific

04574. Albrecht, Willy; Boll, Friedhelm; Bouwer, Beatrix W; and, Leuschen-Sippel, Rosemarie. "Frauenfrage und deutsche Sozialdemocratie vom Ende des 19. Jahrhunderts bis zum Beginn der zwanziger Jahre." _Archiv für Sozialgeschichte_ 19 (1979): 459-510.

04575. Kleinau, Elke. "Über den Einfluss bürgerlicher Vorstellungen von Beruf, Ehe und Familie auf die sozialistische Frauenbewegung." In Frauen in der Geschichte IV, edited by Ilse Brehmer, et. al, pp. 145-168. Düsseldorf: Schwann, 1983.

04576. Lichey, Margarete. Sozialismus und Frauenarbeit: Ein Beitrag zur Entwicklung des deutschen Sozialismus von 1869 bis 1921. Breslau, n.p., 1927.

04577. Niggemann, Heinz. Emanzipation zwischen Sozialismus und Feminismus: die sozialdemokratische Frauenbewegung im Kaiserreich. Wuppertal: Peter Hammer, 1981.

(2) Individuals

(a) Rosa Luxemburg

04578. Badia, Gilbert. "Note à propos de Rosa Luxemburg." Allemagnes d'Aujourd'hui n.s. 58 (May-June 1977): 48-52.

04579. Laschitza, Annelies. "Was die Marxistin Rosa Luxemburg auszeichnete." Zeitschrift für Geschichtswissenschaft 32 (1984): 99-109.

04580. Mullaney, Marie Marmo. "Gender and Revolution: Rosa Luxemburg and the Female Revolutionary Personality." Journal of Psychohistory 11 (Spring 1984): 463-476.

04581. Pfeifer, Eleanora. "Rosa Luxemburgs Kulturkonzeption: Zur Entwicklung der Kulturauffassung in der revolutionaren deutschen Arbeiterbewegung Anfang des 20. Jahrhunderts. Zeitschrift für Geschichtswissenschaft 32 (1984): 700-705.

04582. Raulet, Gerard. "Rosa Luxemburg et-ou (?) la gauche communiste allemande." Allemagnes d'Aujourd'hui n.s. 56 (January-February 1977): 27-34.

04583. Roth, Frederike. "Rosa Luxemburg (1871-1919)." In Frauen Porträts aus zwei Jahrhunderten, edited by Hans Jürgen Schultz, pp. 280-292. Stuttgart: Kreuz Verlag, 1981.

(b) Karl Marx and Friedrich Engels

04584. Clark, Lorenne M. G. "Consequences of Seizing the Reins in the Household: A Marxist-Feminist Critique of Marx and Engels." In Women's Views of the Political World of Men, edited by Judith Hicks Stiehm, pp. 177-204. Dobbs Ferry, N.Y.: Transnational Publishers, Inc., 1984.

04585. Humphries, Jane. "The Working Class Family: A Marxist Perspective." In The Family in Political Thought, edited by Jean Bethke Elshtain, pp. 197-222. Amherst, Mass.: University of Massachusetts Press, 1982.

04586. Jagger, Alison M. and McBride, William L. "'Reproduction' as Male Ideology." Women's Studies International Forum 8 (1985): 185-196.

(c) Clara Zetkin

04587. Elsner, Gisela. "Clara Zetkin (1857-1933)." In Frauen Porträts aus zwei Jahrhunderten, edited by Hans Jurgen Schultz, pp. 158-171. Stuttgart: Kreuz Verlag, 1981.

04588. Haferkorn, Katja. "Clara Zetkin in Paris (1882-1898)." Beiträge zur Geschichte der deutschen Arbeiterbewegung 26 (1984): 184-196.

04589. ________________. "Clara Zetkin und die Bolschewiki." Beiträge zur Geschichte der deutschen Arbeiterbewegung 24 (1982): 334-347.

c) Legal

04590. Dedekind, Adolf, comp. Das protestantische Ehescheidungsrecht und Verwandtes; Zusammenstellung neuerer Entscheidungen der braunschweigischen Obergerichte. Braunschweig: F. Wreden, 1872.

04591. Dohm, Hedwig. Emanzipation. Zurich: Ala-Verlag, c1977.

04592. Heindl, Waltraud. "Ehebruch und Strafrecht. Zur bürgerlichen Moral in Österreich um 1900." In Das ewige Klischee, zum Rollenbild und Selbstverständnis bei Mannern und Frauen, pp. 155-178. Vienna: Hermann Böhlaus, 1981.

04593. ________________. "Frau und bürgerliches Recht. Bemerkungen zu den Reformvorschlagen österreichische Frauenvereine vor dem Ersten Weltkrieg." In Politik und Gesellschaft im alten und neuen Österreich, edited by Isabella Ackerl, Walter Hummelberger, and Hans Mommsen, pp. 133-149. Munich: R. Oldenbourg Verlag, 1981.

04594. Kraut, Wilhelm Theodor. Die Vormundschaft nach den Grundsätzen des deutschen Rechts. Göttingen: Dietrich, 1835-1859.

04595. Schubert, Werner. "Die preussischen Regierungsinitiativen zur Reform des Ehescheidungs-und Eheschliessungsrechts in der Nachmarzzeit (1854-1861)." Zeitschrift der Savigny-Stiftung fur Rechtsgeschichte 70 (1984): 301-338.

d) Criminal

04596. Bergstrom, Randolph E. and Johnson, Eric A. "The Female Victim, Homicide and Women in Imperial Germany." In German Women in the Nineteenth Century, A Social History, edited by John C. Fout, pp. 345-367. New York: Holmes & Meier, 1984.

e) Feminism

(1) Bibliographies

04597. Arendt, Hans-Jürgen. "Frauenfrage und Frauenbewegung in Deutschland 1871 bis 1945: Bürgerliche und sozialreformistische Publikationen seit Anfang der siebziger Jahre." Zeitschrift für Geschichtswissenschaft 32 (1984): 141-149.

04598. Duelli-Klein, Renate. "Accounts of 'First Wave' Feminism in Germany by German Feminists." Women's Studies International Forum 5 (1982): 691-696.

(2) Non-specific

04599. Allen, Ann Taylor. "Spiritual Motherhood: German Feminists and the Kindergarten Movement, 1848-1911." History of Education Quarterly 22 (Fall 1982): 319-339.

04600. Evans, Richard J. "The Concept of Feminism. Notes for Practicing Historians." In German Women in the Eighteenth and Nineteenth Centuries, edited by Ruth-Ellen B. Joeres and Mary Jo Maynes, pp. 247-268. Bloomington, Ind.: Indiana University Press, 1986.

04601. Freier, Anna-Elisabeth. "Dimensionen weiblichen Erlebens und Handelns innerhalb der proletarischen Frauenbewegung." In Frauen in der Geschichte III, edited by Annette Kuhn and Jorn Rusen, pp. 195-218. Düsseldorf: Schwann, 1983.

04602. Gerhard, Ute. "A Hidden and Complex Heritage: Reflections on the History of Germany's Women's Movements." Women's Studies International Forum 5 (1982): 561-567.

04603. ____________. "Über die Änfange der deutschen Frauenbewegung um 1848. Frauenpresse, Frauenpolitik und Frauenvereine." In Frauen suchen ihre Geschichte, Historische Studien zum 19. und 20. Jahrhundert, edited by Karin Hausen, pp. 196-220. Munich: Verlag C. H. Beck, 1983.

04604. Hein, Hilde. "Comment on Max Scheler's 'Concerning the Meaning of the Feminist Movement.'" Philosophical Forum 9 (Fall 1977): 55-59.

Also refer to #4608.

04605. Kaplan, Marion A. "Prostitution, Morality Crusades and Feminism: German-Jewish Feminists and the Campaign Against White Slavery.: Women's Studies International Forum 5 (1982): 619-627.

04606. ______________. "Sisterhood under Siege: Feminism and Anti-Feminism in Germany, 1904-1938." In When Biology Became Destiny Women in Weimar and Nazi Germany, edited by Renate Bridenthal, et al., pp. 174-196. New York: Monthly Review Press, 1984.

04607. Richebächer, Sabine. Uns fehlt nur eine Kleinigkeit: deutsche proletarische Frauenbewegung 1890-1914. Frankfurt am Main: Fischer Taschenbuch Verlag, 1982.

04608. Scheler, Max. "Concerning the Meaning of the Feminist Movement." Philosophical Forum 9 (Fall 1977): 42-54.

Also refer to #4604.

04609. Secci, Lia and Gargano, Antonella, et al. Dal salotto al partito: scrittrici tedesche tra la rivoluzione borghese e il diritto di voto (1848-1918). Milan: Savelli, 1982.

04610. Stoehr, Irene. "'Organisierte Mütterlichkeit.' Zur Politik der deutschen Frauenbewegung um 1900." In Frauen suchen ihre Geschichte, Historische Studien zum 19. und 20. Jahrhundert, edited by Karin Hausen, pp. 221-249. Munich: Verlag C. H. Beck, 1983.

Also refer to #4577, 4640.

(3) Individuals

(a) Lily Braun

04611. Meyer, Alfred G. The Feminism and Socialism of Lily Braun. Bloomington, Ind.: Indiana University Press, 1985.

04612. ______________. "The Radicalization of Lily Braun." In German Women in the Nineteenth Century, edited by John C. Fout, pp. 218-233. New York: Holmes & Meier, 1984.

04613. Stolten, Inge. "Lily Braun (1865-1916)." In Frauen Porträts aus zwei Jahrhunderten, edited by Hans Jürgen Schultz, pp. 212-224. Stuttgart: Kreuz Verlag, 1981.

Also refer to #4660.

(b) Hedwig Dohm

04614. Duelli-Klein, Renate. "Hedwig Dohm: Passionate Theorist (1833-1919)." In _Feminist Theorists_, edited by Dale Spender, pp. 165-183. New York: Pantheon Books, Random House, 1983.

04615. Joeres, Ruth-Ellen Boetcher. "The Ambiguous World of Hedwig Dohm." _Amsterdamer Beiträge zur neueren Germanistik_ 10 (1980): 255-276.

04616. Plessen, Elisabeth. "Hedwig Dohm (1833-1919)." In _Frauen Portrats aus zwei Jahrhunderten_, edited by Hans Jürgen Schultz, pp. 128-141. Stuttgart: Kreuz Verlag, 1981.

Also refer to #4660.

(c) Helene Lange

04617. Brehmer, Ilse. "Von geistigen Müttern und anderen Bildern der Mütterlichkeit in Helene Langes Autobiographie." In _Frauen in der Geschichte IV_, edited by Ilse Brehmer, et al., pp. 88-98. Düsseldorf: Schwann, 1983.

04618. Brick, Barbara. "Die Mutter der Nation--zu Helene Langes Begrundung einer 'weiblichen Kultur.'" In _Frauen in der Geschichte IV_, edited by Ilse Brehmer, et al., pp. 99-132. Dusseldorf: Schwann, 1983.

04619. Frandsen, Dorothea. _Helene Lange. Ein Leben fur das volle Burgerrecht der Frau_. Vienna: Herder, 1980.

04620. Jochimsen, Luc. "Helene Lange (1848-1930)." In _Frauen Porträts aus zwei Jahrhunderten_, edited by Hans Jurgen Schultz, pp. 142-156. Stuttgart: Kreuz Verlag, 1981.

Also refer to #4660, 4691.

(d) Rosa Mayreder

04621. Reiss, Mary-Ann. "Rosa Mayreder: Pioneer of Austrian Feminism." _International Journal of Women's Studies_ 7 (May-June 1984): 207-216.

04622. Schnedl-Bubenicek, Hanna. "Grenzgängerin der Moderne. Studien zur Emanzipation in Texten von Rosa Mayreder." In _Das ewige Klischee, zum Rollenbild und Selbstverständnis bei Männern und Frauen_, pp. 179-205. Vienna: Hermann Böhlaus, 1981.

(e) Others

04623. Adler, Hans. "On a Feminist Controversy. Louise Otto vs. Louise Aston." In _German Women in the Eighteenth and Nineteenth Centuries_, edited by Ruth-Ellen B. Joeres and Mary Jo Maynes, pp. 193-214. Bloomington, Ind.: Indiana University Press, 1986.

04624. Drewitz, Ingeborg. "Gertrud Bäumer (1873-1954)." In _Frauen Porträts aus zwei Jahrhunderten_, edited by Hans Jürgen Schultz, pp. 244-260. Stuttgart: Kreuz Verlag, 1981.

04625. Kohlhagen, Norgard. "Louise Otto-Peters (1819-1895)." In _Frauen Porträts aus zwei Jahrhunderten_, edited by Hans Jürgen Schultz, pp. 102-126. Stuttgart: Kreuz Verlag, 1981.

04626. Schenk, Herrad. "Anita Augspurg (1857-1943)." In _Frauen Porträts aus zwei Jahrhunderten_, edited by Hans Jürgen Schultz, pp. 172-184. Stuttgart: Kreuz Verlag, 1981.

Also refer to #4660, 4662, 4712.

f) Political Roles

04627. Corti, Egon Cäsar Conte. _Metternich und die Frauen_. Zurich: Europa Verlag, 1948-1949.

04628. Day, Diane. "Lola Montez and Her American Image." _History of Photography_ 5 (October 1981): 339-353.

04629. Hamann, Brigitte. _Elisabeth Kaiserin wider Willen_. Vienna: Amalthea, 1981.

04630. ______________. "Kaiserin Elisabeth von Österreich." _Zeitschrift für bayerische Landesgeschichte_ 44 (1981): 397-412.

04631. Klöhn, Sabine. _Helene Simon (1862-1947). Deutsche und britische Sozialreform und Sozialgesetzgebung im Spiegel ihrer Schriften und ihr Wirken als Sozialpolitikerin im Kaiserreich und in der Weimärer Republik_. Frankfurt: Peter Lang, 1982.

04632. Sinclair, Andrew. _The Other Victoria: The Princess Royal and the Great Game of Europe_. London: Weidenfeld, 1981.

04633. Thomas, Daniel H. "Dorothea Lieven: Princess of Diplomacy and Intrigante Extraordinaire." _New England Social Studies Bulletin_ 40 (Fall 1982): 11-21.

04634. ______________. "Princess Lieven's Last Diplomatic Confrontation [Crimean War]." _International History Review_ 5 (November 1983): 550-560.

04635. Wickert, Christl; Hamburger, Brigitte; and Lienau, Marie. "Helene Stocker and the Bund für Mutterschutz. (The Society for the Protection of Motherhood)." Women's Studies International Forum 5 (1982): 611-618.

04636. Zucker, Stanley. "Female Political Opposition in Pre-1848 Germany, The Role of Kathinka Zitz-Halein." In German Women in the Nineteenth Century, A Social History, edited by John C. Fout, pp. 133-150. New York: Holmes & Meier, 1984.

4. Economic

"Difference of age and sex have no longer any distinctive social validity for the working class. . . ."
Marx and Engels

a) Women's Employment

(1) Non-specific

04637. Albisetti, James. "Women and the Professions in Imperial Germany." In German Women in the Eighteenth and Nineteenth Centuries, edited by Ruth-Ellen B. Joeres and Mary Jo Maynes, pp. 94-109. Bloomington, Ind.: Indiana University Press, 1986.

04638. Fout, John C. "The Viennese Enquête of 1896 on Working Women." In German Women in the Eighteeenth and Nineteenth Centuries, edited by Ruth-Ellen B. Joeres and Mary Jo Maynes, pp. 42-60. Bloomington, Ind.: Indiana University Press, 1986.

04639. Goodman, Kay. "Motherhood and Work. The Concept of the Misuse of Women's Energy, 1895-1905." In German Women in the Eighteenth and Nineteenth Centuries, edited by Ruth-Ellen B. Joeres and Mary Jo Maynes, pp. 110-134. Bloomington, Ind.: Indiana University Press, 1986.

04640. Kaiser, Annette. "'Frauenemancipation' wider Willen--Die pragmatische Politik des Lette-Vereins 1866-1876." In Frauen in der Geschichte III, edited by Annette Kuhn and Jörn Rüsen, pp. 167-194. Dusseldorf: Schwann, 1983.

04641. Meyer, Sibylle. "Die mühsame Arbeit des demonstrativen Müssigangs. Uber die häuslichen Pflichten der Beamtenfrauen im Kaiserreich." In Frauen suchen ihre Geschichte, Historische Studien zum 19. und 20. Jahrhundert, edited by Karin Hausen, pp. 172-194. Munich: Verlag C. H. Beck, 1983.

04642. Möhrmann, Renate. "Women's Work as Portrayed in Women's Literature." In German Women in the Eighteenth and Nineteenth Centuries, edited by Ruth-Ellen B. Joeres and Mary Jo Maynes, pp. 61-77. Bloomington, Ind.: Indiana University Press, 1986.

04643. Quataert, Jean H. "Social Insurance and the Family Work of Oberlausitz Home Weavers in the Late Nineteenth Century." In German Women in the Nineteenth Century, A Social History, edited by John C. Fout, pp. 270-294. New York: Holmes & Meier, 1984.

04644. _______________. "Teamwork in Saxon Homeweaving Families in the Nineteenth Century. A Preliminary Investigation Into the Issue of Gender Work Roles." In German Women in the Eighteenth and Nineteenth Centuries, edited by Ruth-Ellen B. Joeres and Mary Jo Maynes, pp. 3-23. Bloomington, Ind.: Indiana University Press, 1986.

04645. Silbermann, J. "Die Frauenarbeit nach den beiden letzten Berufszählungen." Schmollers Jahrbuch für Gesetzgebung, Verwaltung und Volkswirtschaft im Deutschen Reiche 35 (1911): 721-759.

(2) Domestic

04646. Schlegel, Katharina. "Mistress and Servant in Nineteenth Century Hamburg: Employer/Employee Relationships in Domestic Service, 1880-1914." History Workshop 15 (Spring 1983): 60-77.

04647. Wierling, Dorothee. "'Ich hab meine Arbeit gemacht--was wollte sie mehr?' Dienstmädchen im städtischen Haushalt der Jahrhundertwende." In Frauen suchen ihre Geschichte, Historische Studien zum 19. und 20. Jahrhundert, edited by Karin Hausen, pp. 144-171. Munich: Verlag C. H. Beck, 1983.

(3) Industrial

04648. Beier, Rosmarie. "Zur Geschichte Weiblicher Lebenschancen--Alltagsleben, gewerkschaftliche Organisation und Streik Berliner Bekleidungsarbeiterinnen 1870-1914." In Frauen in der Geschichte II, edited by Annette Kuhn and Jörn Rüsen, pp. 211-244. Düsseldorf: Schwann, 1982.

04649. Ehmer, Josef. "Frauenarbeit und Arbeiterfamilie in Wien. Vom Vormärz bis 1934." Geschichte und Gesellschaft 7 (1981): 438-473.

04650. Ellerkamp, Marlène and Jungmann, Brigitte "Le travail et la santé: la vie des ouvrières d'une usine textile de Brême entre 1888 et 1914." Le Mouvement Social 124 (July-September 1983): 113-130.

04651. _______________. "Unendliche Arbeit. Frauen in der 'Jutespinnerei und -weberei Bremen' 1888-1914." In Frauen suchen ihre Geschichte, Historische Studien zum 19. und 20. Jahrhundert, edited by Karin Hausen, pp. 128-143. Munich: Verlag C.H. Beck, 1983.

04652. Franzoi, Barbara. *At the Very Least She Pays the Rent: Women and German Industrialization, 1871-1914.* Westport, Ct.: Greenwood Press, 1985.

04653. ______________. "Domestic Industry, Work Options and Women's Choices." In *German Women in the Nineteenth Century, A Social History*, edited by John C. Fout, pp. 256-269. New York: Holmes & Meier, 1984.

04654. Orthmann, Rosemary. "Labor Force Participation, Life Cycle, and Expenditure Patterns. The Case of Unmarried Female Factory Workers in Berlin (1902)." In *German Women in the Eighteenth and Nineteenth Centuries*, edited by Ruth-Ellen B. Joeres and Mary Jo Maynes, pp. 24-41. Bloomington, Ind.: Indiana University Press, 1986.

04655. Quataert, Jean H. "Combining Agrarian and Industrial Livelihood: Rural Households in the Saxon Oberlausitz in the Nineteenth Century." *Journal of Family History* 10 (Summer 1985): 145-162.

04656. ______________. "A Source Analysis in German Women's History: Factory Inspectors' Reports and the Shaping of Working-Class Lives, 1878-1914." *Central European History* 16 (June 1983): 99-121.

04657. Schneck, Peter. "Die gesundheitliche Verhältnisse der Fabrikarbeiterinnen. Ausgewählte Aspekte der Situation in der sächisischen Oberlausitz im ausgehenden 19. Jahrhundert." *Jahrbuch für Wirtschaftgeschichte* 3 (1975): 53-72.

(4) Agricultural

04658. Lee, W.R. "The Impact of Agrarian Change on Women's Work and Child Care in Early-Nineteenth-Century Prussia." In *German Women in the Nineteenth Century, A Social History*, edited by John C. Fout, pp. 234-255. New York: Holmes & Meier, 1984.

04659. Schulte, Regina. "Bauernmägde in Bayern am Ende des 19. Jahrhunderts." In *Frauen suchen ihre Geschichte, Historische Studien zum 19. und 20. Jahrhundert*, edited by Karin Hausen, pp. 110-127. Munich: Verlag C.H. Beck, 1983.

Also refer to #4655.

5. SOCIAL

"The weakness of their reasoning faculty also explains why it is that women show more sympathy for the unfortunate than men do, and so treat them with more kindness and interest . . . ."

Arthur Schopenhauer
"Of Women" in Studies in Pessimism

a) Generic

04660. Jacobi-Dittrich, Juliane. "Growing Up Female in the Nineteenth Century." In German Women in the Nineteenth Century, edited by John C. Fout, pp. 197-217. New York: Holmes and Meier, 1984.

04661. Kocka, Jürgen; Ditt, K.; Mooser, J; Reif, H; and Schüren, R. Familie und soziale Plazierung. Studien zum Verhältnis von Familie, sozialer Mobilität und Heiratsverhalten an westfälischen Beispielen im spaten 18. und 19. Jahrhundert. Opladen: Westdeutscher Verlag, 1980.

04662. Prelinger, Catherine M. "Prelude to Consciousness, Amalie Sieveking and the Female Association for the Care of the Poor and the Sick." In German Women in the Nineteenth Century, A Social History, edited by John C. Fout, pp. 118-132. New York: Holmes & Meier, 1984.

04663. Simmel Georg. Georg Simmel on Women, Sexuality and Love. New Haven, Ct.: Yale University Press, 1984.

04664. Weber-Kellermann, Ingeborg. Frauenleben in 19. Jahrhundert: Empire und Romantik, Biedermeier, Gründerzeit. Munich: C.H. Beck, 1983.

04665. Wychgram, Jakob and Müller, Paula. Ziel und Grenzen der Frauentätigkeit nach evangelischen Grundsätzen. Leipzig: B.G. Teubner, 1908.

b) Demography

04666. Fischer, Eugen. "Report on Muckermann's Studies of the Differential Fertility Within Certain Social Groups in Germany (Abstract)." In Problems of Population. Report of the Proceedings of the Second General Assembly of the International Union for the Scientific Investigation of Population Problems, edited by G.H.L.F. Pitt-Rivers, pp. 105-107. Port Washington, N.Y.: Kennikat Press, 1932.

04667. Fischer, Eugen. "Untersuchungen über die Differenzierte Fortpflanzung am deutschen Volk nach Hermann Muckermann." In Problems of Population. Report of the Second General Assembly of the International Union for the Scientific Investigation of Population Problems, edited by G.H.L.F. Pitt-Rivers, pp. 108-111. Port Washington, N.Y.: Kennikat Press, 1932.

04668. Knodel, John. "Town and Country in Nineteenth Century Germany: A Review of Urban-Rural Differentials in Demographic Behavior." Social Science History 1 (Spring 1977): 356-382.

04669. Kocka, Jurgen. "Family and Class Formation: Intergenerational Mobility and Marriage Patterns in Nineteenth-Century Westphalian Towns." Journal of Social History 17 (Spring 1984): 411-435.

Also refer to #3554-3556, 3565.

c) Family

04670. Bajohr, Stefan. "Uneheliche Mütter im Arbeitermilieu: Die Stadt Braunschweig 1900-1930." Geschichte und Gesellschaft 7 (1981): 474-506.

04671. Fout, John C. "The Woman's Role in the German Working-Class Family in the 1890s from the Perspective of Women's Autobiographies." In German Women in the Nineteenth Century, A Social History, edited by John C. Fout, pp. 295-319. New York: Holmes & Meier, 1984.

04672. Kintner, Hallie J. "Trends and Regional Differences in Breastfeeding in Germany from 1871 to 1937." Journal of Family History 10 (Summer 1985): 163-182.

04673. Prelinger, Catherine M. "The Nineteenth-Century Deanconessate in Germany. The Efficacy of a Family Model." In German Women in the Eighteenth and Nineteenth Centuries, edited by Ruth-Ellen B. Joeres and Mary Jo Maynes, pp. 215-229. Bloomington, Ind.: Indiana University Press, 1986.

04674. Sabean, David Warren. "Young Bees in an Empty Hive: Relations Between Brothers-in-Law in a South German Village Around 1800." In Interest and Emotion, Essays on the Study of Family and Kinship, edited by Hans Medick and David Warren Sabean, pp. 171-186. New York: Cambridge University Press, 1985.

04675. Schulte, Regina. "Infanticide in Rural Bavaria in the Nineteenth Century." In Interest and Emotion, Essays on the Study of Family and Kinship, edited by Hans Medick and David Warren Sabean, pp. 77-102. New York: Cambridge University Press, 1985.

04676. Wiesbauer, Elisabeth. *Das Kind als Objekt der Wissenschaft.* Vienna: Loecker Verlag, 1982.

Also refer to #3554, 3556, 3561, 3562, 4575, 4585, 4594, 4599, 4617, 4636, 4639, 4643, 4644, 4649, 4661, 4689, 4723, 4724.

d) Marriage

04677. Borscheid, Peter. "Lebensstandard und Familie: Partnerwahl und Ehezyklus in einer württembergischen Industriestadt im 19. Jahrhundert." *Archiv für Sozialgeschichte* 22 (1982): 227-262.

04678. Kaplan, Marion A. "For Love or Money--the Marriage Strategies of Jews in Imperial Germany." *Leo Baeck Institute Yearbook* 28 (1983): 263-300. Also in *The Marriage Bargain: Women and Dowries in European History*, edited by Marion A. Kaplan, pp. 121-164. New York: Harrington Books, 1985.

04679. "A Rural Wedding in Lorraine." *Folk-Lore Record* 3 (1880): 258-274.

Also refer to #3555, 3565, 4575, 4590, 4592, 4595, 4661, 4669, 4753.

e) Sex Life and Morals

(1) Non-specific

04680. Deleuze, Gilles. *Présentation de Sacher-Masoch, Le froid et le cruel.* Paris: Editions de Minuit, 1967.

04681. Palmier, Jean-Michel. "Névrose et antiféminisme: *Sex et caractère* d'Otto Weiniger." In *Les femmes et leur maîtres*, edited by Maria Antonietta Macciocchi, pp. 59-61. Paris: C. Bourgeois, 1979.

(2) Prostitutes

04682. Bristow, Edward. "The German Jewish Fight Against White Slavery." *Leo Baeck Institute Yearbook* 28 (1983): 301-328.

Also refer to #4605.

f) Fashion/Manners

04683. *Les habitants de Tyrol. Abbildungen der Einwohner von Tirol.* Vienna: Stöckl, [1820].

04684. Kirchebner, Alois. *Neueste Volkstrachten aus Tirol in 12 Blättern.* Innsbruck: Schopf, mid 19th century.

04685. Opitz, Georg Emanuel. _52 Szenen aus dem Volks-und Strassenleben des Francisceischen Wien_. Vienna: Eder, c. 1801-1814.

Also refer to #3567.

g) Health/Medical

(1) Birth Control

04686. Bergmann, Anneliese. "Frauen, Männer, Sexualität und Geburtenkontrolle. Zue 'Gebärstreikdebatte' der SPD 1913." In _Frauen suchen ihre Geschichte, Historische Studien zum 19. un 20. Jahrhundert_, edited by Karin Hausen, pp. 81-108. Munich: Verlag C.H. Beck, 1983.

(2) Women in Medicine

04687. Albisetti, James C. "The Fight for Female Physicians in Imperial Germany." _Central European History_ 15 (June 1982): 99-123.

04688. Holmes, Madelyn. "Go to Switzerland, Young Woman, If You Want to Study Medicine." _Women's Studies International Forum_ 7 (1984): 243-245.

(3) Women and Health

04689. Carter, K. Codell. "Infantile Hysteria and Infantile Sexuality in Late Nineteenth-Century German-Language Medical Literature." _Medical History_ 27 (April 1983): 186-196.

04690. Frevert, Ute. "The Civilizing Tendency of Hygiene, Working-Class Women Under Medical Control in Imperial Germany." In _German Women in the Nineteenth Century, A Social History_, edited by John C. Fout, pp. 320-344. New York: Holmes & Meier, 1984.

Also refer to #3568.

6. CULTURAL

". . .I have written one quite tiny piece, but I do not know what I shall call it. I have a particular aversion to showing you anything that I have composed: I am always ashamed."

Clara Wieck Schumann
Letter to her husband,
Robert Schumann, 1839

a) Education

04691. Albisetti, James C. "Could Separate Be Equal? Helen Lange and Women's Education in Imperial Germany.? History of Education Quarterly 22 (Fall 1982): 301-317.

04692. ________________. "The Reform of Female Education in Prussia, 1899-1908: A Study in Compromise and Containment." German Studies Review 8 (February 1985): 11-41.

04693. Bernstein, George and Bernstein, Lottelore. "The Curricula for German Girls' Schools, 1870-1914." Paedagogica Historica 18 (1979): 275-295.

04694. Jacobi-Dittrich, Juliane. "'Hausfrau, Gattin und Mutter.' Lebensläufe und Bildungsgänge von Frauen im 19. Jahrhundert.'" In Frauen in der Geschichte IV, edited by Ilse Brehmer, et al, pp. 262-281. Düsseldorf: Schwann, 1983.

04695. Ladj-Teichmann, Dagmar. "Weibliche Bildung im 19. Jahrhundert: Fesselung von Kopf, Hand und Herz?" In Frauen in der Geschichte IV, edited by Ilse Brehmer, et al., pp. 219-243. Düsseldorf: Schwann, 1983.

04696. Martin, Marie. Aus der Welt der deutschen Frau. Berlin: C. A. Schwetschke und Sohn, 1906.

04697. ____________. Die höhere Mädchenschule in Deutschland. Leipzig: B. G. Teubner, 1905.

04698. ____________. Lehrbuch der Mädchenerziehung für Lehrerinnenbildungsanstalten und zum Selbstunterricht. Leipzig: Dürr'sche Buchhandlung, 1903.

04699. ____________. Wahre Frauenbildung. Tübingen: J.C.B. Mohr, 1905.

04700. ____________. Die weibliche Bildungsbedürfnisse der Gegenwart. Berlin: Trowitzsch und Sohn, 1906.

04701. Möhrmann, Renate. "The Reading Habits of Women in the Vormärz." In German Women in the Nineteenth Century, A Social History, edited by John C. Fout, pp. 104-117. New York: Holmes and Meier, 1984.

04702. Riemann, Ilka and Simmel, Monika. "Bildung zur Weiblichkeit durch soziale Arbeit." In Frauen in der Geschichte IV, edited by Ilse Brehmer, et al., pp. 133-144. Düsseldorf: Schwann, 1983.

04703. Schlüter, Anne. "Wissenschaft fur die Frauen? -- Frauen fur die Wissenschaft! Zur Geschichte der ersten Generation von Frauen in der Wissenschaft." In Frauen in der Geschichte IV, edited by Ilse Brehmer, et al., pp. 244-261. Düsseldorf: Schwann, 1983.

04704. Schneider, Joanne. "Enlightened Reforms and Bavarian Girls' Education, Tradition Through Innovation." In German Women in the Nineteenth Century, A Social History, edited by John C. Fout, pp. 55-71. New York: Holmes and Meier, 1984.

04705. ________________. "Das Schulerlebnis der bayerischen Mädchen." In Frauen in der Geschichte IV, edited by Ilse Brehmer, et al., pp. 205-219. Düsseldorf: Schwann, 1983.

04706. Schneider, Karl. Bildungsziel und Bildungswege fur unsere Tochter. Berlin, n.p., 1888.

04707. Wychgram, Jakob. Frauenbildung. Berlin: B.G. Teubner, 1902.

04708. ______________. Vorträge und Aufsätze zur Madchenschulwesen. Leipzig: B.G. Teubner, 1907.

Also refer to #4688.

b) Literature

(1) Non-specific

(a) Women in Literature

04709. Finney, Gail. "Self-Reflexive Siblings: Incest as Narcissism in Tieck, Wagner and Thomas Mann." German Quarterly 56 (March 1983): 243-256.

04710. Grenz, Dagmar. "'Das eine sein und das andere auch sein . . .' Über die Widersprüchlichkeit des Frauenbildes am Beispiel der Madchenliteratur." In Frauen in der Geschichte IV, edited by Ilse Brehmer, et al., pp. 282-301. Düsseldorf: Schwann, 1983.

04711. Hanlin, Tood C. "Demonic Eroticism in Jugendstil" Jahrbuch für Internationale Germanistik 14 no. 2 (1982): 31-54.

04712. Joeres, Ruth-Ellen Boetcher. "Self-Conscious Histories, Biographies of German Women in the Nineteenth Century." In _German Women in the Nineteenth Century, A Social History_, edited by John C. Fout, pp. 172-196. New York: Holmes and Meier, 1984. Also in _Frauen in der Geschichte IV_, edited by Ilse Brehmer et al., pp. 320-346. Dusseldorf: Schwann, 1983.

04713. Lorenz, Dagmar C.G. "Weibliche Rollenmodelle bei Autoren des 'Jungen Deutschland' und des 'Biedermeier.'" _Amsterdamer Beiträge zur neueren Germanistik_ 10 (1980): 155-184.

04714. Sagarra, Eda. "'Echo ohne Antwort' Die Darstellung der Frau in der deutschen Erzählporse 1815-1848." _Geschichte und Gesellschaft_ 7 (1981): 394-411.

Also refer to #3572, 3573, 3578, 4642.

(b) Fairy Tales

[1] Grimm Brothers

04715. Bottigheimer, Ruth B. "Tale Spinners: Submerged Voices in Grimm's Fairy Tales." _New German Critique_ 27 (1982): 141-150.

04716. ________________. "The Transformed Queen: A Search for the Origins of Negative Female Archetypes in Grimm's Fairy Tales." _Amsterdamer Beiträge zur neueren Germanistik_ 10 (1980): 1-12.

Also refer to #3552.

[2] E.T.A. Hoffmann

04717. McGlathery, James M. "'Bald Dein Fall ins Ehebett?' A New Reading of E.T.A. Hoffmann's _Goldner Topf_." _Germanic Review_ 53 (Summer 1978): 106-114.

03718. ________________. _Mysticism and Sexuality. E.T.A. Hoffmann. Part I. Hoffmann and His Sources_. Las Vegas: Peter Lang, 1981.

04719. Weiss, Hermann F. "'The Labyrinth of Crime.' A Reinterpretation of E.T.A. Hoffmann's _Das Fraulein von Scuderi_." _Germanic Review_ 51 (May 1976): 181-189.

(c) Women Authors

04720. Herminghouse, Patricia. "Women and the Literary Enterprise in Nineteenth-Century Germany." In _German Women in the Eighteenth and Nineteenth Centuries_, edited by Ruth-Ellen B. Joeres and Mary Jo Maynes, pp. 78-93. Bloomington, Ind.: Indiana University Press, 1986.

(2) Philosophy

(a) Georg Hegel

04721. Ernst, Ulla. "Hegels Idealisierung von Mann und Frau." In _Das ewige Klischee, zum Rollenbild und Selbstverständnis bei Männern und Frauen_, pp. 108-313. Vienna: Hermann Böhlaus, 1981.

04722. Fuchs, Jo-Ann Pilardi. "On the War Path and Beyond: Hegel, Freud and Feminist Theory." _Women's Studies International Forum_ 6 (1983): 565-572.

04723. Landes, Joan B. "Hegel's Conception of the Family." In _The Family in Political Thought_, edited by Jean Bethke Elshtain, pp. 125-144. Amherst, Mass.: University of Massachusetts Press, 1982.

Also refer to #3751.

(b) Friedrich Nietzsche

04724. Strong, Tracy B. "Oedipus as Hero: Family and Family Metaphors in Nietzsche." In _The Family in Political Thought_, edited by Jean Bethke Elshtain, pp. 173-196. Amherst, Mass.: University of Massachusetts Press, 1982.

04725. Thomas, R. Hinton. "Nietzsche, Women and the Whip." _German Life and Letters_ n.s. 34 (October 1980): 117-125.

(3) Drama

04726. Baker, Christa Suttner. "Structure and Imagery in Grillparzer's _Sappho_." _Germanic Review_ 48 (January 1973): 44-55.

04727. Barlow, D. "Marianne's Motives in Hebbel's 'Herodotus and Marianne.'" _Modern Language Review_ 55 (April 1960): 213-220.

04728. Bossinade, Johanna. "'Wenn es aber . . . bei mir anders wäre.' Die Frage der Geschlechterbeziehungen in Arthur Schnitzlers _Reigen_." _Amsterdamer Beiträge zur neueren Germanistik_ 18 (1984): 273-328.

04729. Driver, Beverley R. "Arthur Schnitzler's Frau Berta Garlan: A Study in Form." Germanic Review 46 (November 1971): 285-298.

04730. Harris, Edward P. "The Liberation of the Flesh from Stone: Pygmalion in Frank Wedekind's Erdgeist." Germanic Review 52 (January 1977): 44-56.

04731. Hoverland, Lilian. "Heinrich von Kleist and Luce Irigaray: Visions of the Feminine." Amsterdamer Beiträge zur neueren Germanistik 10 (1980): 57-82.

04732. Krispyn, E. "Grillparzer and his Ahnfrau." Germanic Review 38 (May 1963): 209-225.

04733. Paulen, Harry W. "Kohlhaas and Family." Germanic Review 52 (May 1977): 171-182.

04734. Schroeder, Sabine. "Anna Mahr in Gerhart Hauptmann's Einsame Menschen-- The 'Emancipated Woman' Re-Examined." Germanic Review 54 (Summer 1979): 125-130.

(4) Poetry

(a) Women in Poetry

04735. Feuerlicht, Ignace. "Mörike's 'Jilted Girl." Germanic Review 55 (Winter 1980): 22-26.

(b) Poets

[1] Annette von Droste-Hülshoff

04736. Brender, Irmela. "Annette von Droste-Hülshoff (1791-1848)." In Frauen Porträts aus zwei Jahrhunderten, edited by Hans Jürgen Schultz, pp. 60-71. Stuttgart: Kreuz Verlag, 1981.

04737. Guder, G. "Annette von Droste-Hülshoff's Conception of Herself as Poet." German Life and Letters 11 (1957-1958): 13-24.

04738. Maurer, Doris. Annette von Droste-Hülshoff: Ein Leben zwischen Auflehnung und Gehorsam. Bonn: Keil, 1982.

04739. Morgan, Mary Elizabeth. Annette von Droste-Hülshoff: A Biography. New York: Lang, 1984.

04740. Pickar, Gertrud Bauer. "Annette von Droste-Hülshoff's 'Reich der goldnen Phantasie.'" Amsterdamer Beiträge zur neueren Germanistik 10 (1980): 109-123.

04741. Plachta, Bodo. "Die Sage von der schönen Rosamunde und das literarische Umfeld des Droste-Gedichts 'Rosamund.'" Michigan Germanic Studies 11 (Spring 1985): 34-49.

[2] Else Lasker-Schüler

04742. Bänsch, Dieter. Else Lasker-Schüler Zur Kritik einer etablierten Bildes. Stuttgart: J.B. Mitzlerische Verlagsbuchhandlung, 1971.

04743. Bauschinger, Sigrid. Else Lasker-Schüler: Ihr Werk und ihre Zeit. Heidelberg: Lothar Stiehm Verlag, 1980.

04744. Guder, G. "The Significance of Love in the Poetry of Else Lasker-Schüler." German Life and Letters 18 (1964-1965): 177-188.

[3] Rainer Maria Rilke

04745. Belmore, Herbert W. "Sexual Elements in Rilke's Poetry." German Life and Letters 19 (1965-1966): 252-261.

04746. Rossi, Dominick. "Rainer Maria Rilke and the Metamorphosis of Women's Liberation." Germanic Notes 4 (1973): 34-36.

04747. Weinhold, Ulrike. "Die Renaissancefrau des Fin de Siècle. Untersuchungen zum Frauenbild der Jahrhundertwende am Beispiel vom R.M. Rilke's Die weisse Furstin und H. von Hofmannsthals Die Frau im Fenster." Amsterdamer Beiträge zur neueren Germanistik 18 (1984): 235-271.

[4] Others

04748. Geiger, Ruth-Esther. "Louise Aston(1818-1871)." In Frauen Porträts aus zwei Jahrhunderten, edited by Hans Jürgen Schultz, pp. 88-101. Stuttgart: Kreuz Verlag, 1981.

04749. Raynaud, Franziska. "Alma Johanna Koenig (1887-1942): Leben und Dichten einer Wienerin." Bulletin of the Leo Baeck Institute 64 (1983): 29-54.

04750. Rey, William H. "'Arthur Schnitzler und Ich': Das Vermachtnis der Clara Katharina Pollaczek." Germanic Review 41 (March 1966): 120-135.

(5) Prose

(a) Novelists

[1] Theodor Fontane

04751. Bormann, Alexander von. "Glücksanspruch und Glücksverzicht. Zu einigen Frauengestalten Fontanes." Amsterdamer Beiträge zur neueren Germanistik 10 (1980): 205-233.

04752. Riechel, Donald C. "Effi Briest and the Calendar of Fate." Germanic Review 48 (May 1973): 189-211.

04753. Robinson, Alan R. "Problems of Love and Marriage in Fontane's Novels." German Life and Letters 5 (July 1952): 279-285.

[2] Others

04754. Bröhan, Margrit. Die Darstellung der Frau bei Wilhelm Raabe und ein Vergleich mit liberalen Positionen zur Emanzipation der Frau im 19. Jahrhundert. Bern: Lang, 1981.

04755. Byrnes, John. "Emil Marriot Bibliography." Modern Austrian Literature 12 Nos. 3-4 (1979): 58-76.

04756. ___________. "An Introduction to Emil Marriot." Modern Austrian Literature nos. 3-4 (1979): 45-57.

04757. De Groot, Cegienas. "Das Bild der Frau in Gottfried Kellers Prosa." Amsterdamer Beiträge zur neueren Germanistik 10 (1980): 185-204.

04758. Hibberd, J. "Dorothea Schlegel's Florentin and the Precarious Idyll." German Life and Letters n.s. 30 (April 1977): 198-207.

04759. Joeres, Ruth-Ellen Boetcher. "The Triumph of the Woman: Johanna Kinkel's Hans Ibeles in London (1860)." Euphorion 70 (1976): 187-197.

04760. Johnson, Richard L. "Men's Power over Women in Gabriele Reuter's Aus guter Familie." Amsterdamer Beiträge zur neueren Germanistik 10 (1980): 235-253.

04761. Lloyd, Danuta A. Dorf und Schloss: The Socio-Political Image of Austria as Reflected in Marie von Ebner-Eschenbach's Work." Modern Austrian Literature 12 no. 3-4 (1979): 25-44.

04762. Raebling, Irmgard. "Liebe und Variationen zu einer biographischen Konstante in Storms Prosawerk." Amsterdamer Beiträge zur neueren Germanistik 17 (1983): 99-130.

Also refer to #6239.

04763. Sjogren, Christine Oertel. "Klotilde's Journey into the Depths. A Probe into a Psychological Landscape in Stifter's Der Nachsommer." Germanic Notes 2 (1971): 50-52.

04764. Stephan, Inge. "Richarda Huch (1864-1947)." In Frauen Porträts aus zwei Jahrhunderten, edited by Hans Jürgen Schultz, pp. 198-211. Stuttgart: Kreuz Verlag, 1981.

Also refer to #3353, 4712.

(b) Others

04765. Jacobi-Dittrich, Juliane. "The Struggle for an Identity. Working-Class Autobiographies by Women in Nineteenth-Century Germany." In German Women in the Eighteenth and Nineteenth Centuries, edited by Ruth-Ellen B. Joeres and Mary Jo Maynes, pp. 321-345. Bloomington, Ind.: Indiana University Press, 1986.

04766. Maynes, Mary Jo. "Gender and Class in Working-Class Women's Autobiographies." In German Women in the Eighteenth and Nineteenth Centuries, edited by Ruth-Ellen B. Joeres and Mary Jo Maynes, pp. 230-246. Bloomington, Ind.: Indiana University Press, 1986.

04767. Wedel, Gudrun. "'. . . nothing more than a German woman.' Remarks on the Biographical and Autobiographical Tradition of the Women of One Family." In German Women in the Eighteenth and Nineteenth Centuries, edited by Ruth-Ellen B. Joeres and Mary Jo Maynes, pp. 305-320. Bloomington, Ind.: Indiana University Press, 1986.

04768. Wulfing, Wulf. "On Travel Literature by Women in the Nineteenth Century. Malwida von Meysenbug." In German Women in the Eighteenth and Nineteenth Centuries, edited by Ruth-Ellen B. Joeres and Mary Jo Maynes, pp. 289-304. Bloomington, Ind.: Indiana University Press, 1986.

c) Intellectuals

(1) Fanny Lewald

04769. Brinker-Gabler, Gisela. "Fanny Lewald (1811-1889)." In Frauen Porträts aus zwei Jahrhunderten, edited by Hans Jürgen Schultz, pp. 72-87. Stuttgart: Kreuz Verlad, 1981.

04770. Venske, Regula. "Discipline and Daydreaming in the Works of a Nineteenth-Century Woman Author: Fanny Lewald." In German Women in the Eighteenth and Nineteenth Centuries, edited by Ruth-Ellen B. Joeres and Mary Jo Maynes, pp. 175-192. Bloomington, Ind.: Indiana University Press, 1986.

04771. ______________. "'Ich hätte ein Mann sein müssen oder eines grossen Mannes Weib!'--Widerspruche im Emanzipationsverständnis der Fanny Lewald." In Frauen in der Geschichte IV, edited by Ilse Brehmer, et al., pp. 368-396. Dusseldorf: Schwann, 1983.

(2) Lou Andreas Salomé

04772. Guéry, François. "Lou Salomé, rencontre de Nietzsche." Allemagnes d'Aujourd'hui n.s. 62 (March-April 1978): 116-121.

04773. Hamburger, Käte. "Lou Andreas-Salomé (1861-1937)." In Frauen Porträts aus zwei Jahrhunderten, edited by Hans Jürgen Schultz, pp. 186-197. Stuttgart: Kreuz Verlag, 1981.

(3) Others

04774. Gerhardt, Marlis. "Franziska zu Reventlow (1871-1918)." In Frauen Porträts aus zwei Jahrhunderten, edited by Hans Jürgen Schultz, pp. 225-243. Stuttgart: Kreuz Verlag, 1981.

04775. Hoock-Demart, Marie-Claire. "Les écrits sociaux de Bettina von Arnim ou les débuts de l'enquête sociale dans le Vormärz prussien." Le Mouvement social 110 (January-March 1980): 5-33.

04776. Jensen, Gwendolyn E. "Henriette Schleiermacher: A Woman in a Traditional Role." In German Women in the Nineteenth Century, edited by John C. Fout, pp. 88-103. New York: Holmes and Meier, 1984.

04777. McCort, Dennis. "Lena Dahme contra Psychobiographical Character Assassination: Towards the Rehabilitation of Frau Betsy Meyer." German Life and Letters n.s. 36 (April 1983): 294-300.

04778. Stern, Carola. "Caroline Schlegel-Schelling (1763-1809)." In Frauen Porträts aus zwei Jahrhunderten, edited by Hans Jürgen Schultz, pp. 8-19. Stuttgart: Kreuz Verlag, 1981.

04779. Vischer, Eduard. "Briefe von Frau Dore Hensler geb. Behrens an Staatsrat L. Nicolovius." Archiv für Kulturgeschichte 62-63 (1980-1981): 301-349.

04780. Wolf, Christa. "Bettina von Arnim (1785-1859)." In Frauen Porträts aus zwei Jahrhunderten, edited by Hans Jürgen Schultz, pp. 48-59. Stuttgart: Kreuz Verlag, 1981.

Also refer to #4712.

d) Art

(1) Women in Art

04781. Fitzell, John. "'Jeder schau der Nachbarin in die Augensterne' Das Frauenerlebnis im Busch-Gedicht." German Studies Review 8 (May 1985): 203-215.

04782. Mannoni, Gérard. "Création à l'Opera de Paris de 'La femme sans ombre' (Die Frau ohne Schatten)." Allemagnes d'Aujourd'hui n.s. 35 (November-December 1972): 80-81.

04783. Montandon, Alain. "La répresentation de l'amour dans la peinture romantique allemande." In Aimer en France 1760-1860, edited by Paul Vialleneix and Jean Ehrard, 1:69-78. Clermont-Ferrand: Association des Publications de la Faculté des Lettres et Sciences Humaines de Clermont-Ferrand, 1980.

(2) Women Artists

04784. Bardua, Wilhelmine. Jugendleben der Malerin Caroline Bardua. Breslau; R. Hoffmann, 1874.

04785. Berger, Renate. "Auf der Suche nach Kunstlerinnen." In Frauen in der Geschichte IV, edited by Ilse Brehmer, et al., pp. 407-428. Düsselforf: Schwann, 1983.

04786. Chissell, Joan. Clara Schumann, A Dedicated Spirit: A Study of Her Life and Work. London: W. Hamilton, 1983.

04787. Haslip, Joan. The Emperor and the Actress: The Love Story of Emperor Franz Josef and Katharina Schratt. New York: Dial Press, 1982.

04788. Reich, Nancy B. Clara Schumann: The Artist and the Woman. Ithaca, New York: Cornell University Press, 1985.

04789. Zeller, Eva. "Paula Mördersohn-Becker (1876-1907)." In Frauen Porträts aus zwei Jahrhunderten, edited by Hans Jürgen Schultz, pp. 262-279. Stuttgart: Kreuz Verlag, 1981.

Also refer to #3625, 4346, 4564, 4709.

E. IBERIA

1. SURVEYS

" . . . I have woven in this book the humble lives of women, obscure, tormented lives, filled with sorrow and abnegation, which aroused deep echoes in my heart. Perhaps you would prefer happier stories, and joyous inventions, sunny romances of some fortunate land, where flowers never cease to bloom. But I have already told you that I am recounting the lives of women."

Concha Espina,
about her novels.

04790. Ellis, Havelock. "The Women of Spain." In The Soul of Spain, pp. 61-105. London: Constable and Company, Limited, 1926.

04791. Nash, Mary. Mujer, familia y trabajo en Espana (1875-1936). Barcelona: Anthropos, 1983.

2. POLITICAL

"A delightful but scandalously unchaste queen."
Gerald Brenan

04792. Abad, Juan Jose and Trigo, Lorenzo. La monarquía isabelina. Madrid: Circulo de Amigos de la Historia, 1979.

04793. Aróstegui, Julio, Martínez, Jesus A., and De La Torre, Rosario. "La regencia de María Cristina (1833-1840)." Historia 16, no. 9 (June 1984): 33-56.

04794. Sierra Nava, Luis. La reaccion del episcopado espanol ante les decretos de matrimonios del ministro Urquijo de 1799 a 1813. Balboa: Universidad de Deusto, 1964.

04795. Soto, Monica. La España Isabelina. Madrid: Altalena, 1979.

Also refer to #4799.

3. RELIGION

"I tried at various times to approach Maria Rasario. It was useless: she divined my intentions and cautiously and noiselessly defeated them with her eyes lowered and her hands crossed on the conventual scapular she was already wearing."
Ramón de Valle-Inclan
Sonata of Spring

04796. Alfieri, J.J. "Images of the 'Sacra Familia' in Galdos' Novels.' Hispanofilia 74 (January 1982): 25-40.

04797. Vales y Failde, Francisco Javier. La protection des jeunes filles en Espagne. Madrid: Impr. de "Arch., bibl. y museos," 1912.

Also refer to #4794.

4. SOCIAL

"Marriage is a necessary evil from which much good can be derived. . . . For me there is no difference between matrimony guaranteed in the customary way and matrimony guaranteed solely by the reciprocal faith of the betrothed."
Gertrudis Gomez de Avellaneda

a) Demography

04798. Abelson, Andrew. "Inheritance and Population Control in a Basque Valley Before 1900." Peasant Studies 7 (Winter 1978): 11-27.

b) Marriage

04799. Burgos Segui, Carmen de. El divorcio en España. Madrid: Viuda de M. Romero, impressor, 1904.

Also refer to #4794, 4856.

5. CULTURAL

"This woman is quite a man."
Said of Gertrudis Gómez de Avellaneda

a) Literature

(1) Bibliographies

04800. Zubatsky, David S. "An Annotated Bibliography of Nineteenth-Century Catalan, Galician and Spanish Author Bibliographies." Hispania 65 (May 1982): 212-224.

(2) Non-specific

(a) Women in Literature

04801. Nickel, Catherine. "The Secret of La Marquesa Rosalinda: From the Physical to the Metaphysical." Hispanic Journal 5 (Spring 1984): 75-88.

(3) Drama

04802. Engler, Kay. "Amor, muerte y destino: la psicologia de Eros en Los amantes de Tervel." Hispanofilia 70 (September 1980): 1-15.

04803. Ibarra, Fernando. "Clarín y la liberación de la mujer." Hispanofilia 51 (May 1974): 27-33.

04804. O'Connor, Patricia W. "Spain's First Successful Woman Dramatist: Maria Martinez Sierra." Hispanofilia 66 (May 1979): 87-108.

04805. Sedwick, Frank. "Unamundo and Womanhood: His Theater." Hispania 43 (September 1960): 309-313.

(4) Poetry

(a) Rosalie de Castro

04806. Albert Robatto, Matilde. Rosalía de Castro y la condicion femenina. Madrid: Partenon, 1981.

04807. Da Cal, Ernesto G. "Siete ensayos sobre Rosalie." Revista hispanica moderna 20 (October 1954): 328-329.

04808. Palley, Julian. "Rosalia de Castro: Two Mourning Dreams." Hispanofilia 82 (September 1984): 20-27.

04809. Rivero, Eleana Suarez. "Machado y Rosalia: Dos almas gemelas." Hispania 49 (December 1966): 748-754.

(b) Others

04810. Diez Taboada, Juan Maria. La mujer ideal. Aspectos y fuentes de las rimas de G.A. Becquer. Madrid: Consejo superior de investigaciones cientificas, 1965.

04811. Rosenberg, S.L. Millard. "Concha Espina: Poet-Novelist of the Montaña." Modern Language Forum 18 (April 1933): 76-81.

04812. Woolsey, Wallace. "La mujer inalcanzable como tema en ciertas leyendas de Becquer." Hispania 47 (May 1964): 277-281.

(5) Prose

(a) Women in Novels

04813. Lowe, Elizabeth. "Love as Liturgy and Liturgy as Love: The Satirical Subversion of Worship and Courtship in Eca de Queiroz." Hispania 61 (December 1978): 912-918.

04814. Risco, Antonio. "La mujer en la novela de Azorin. Cuadernos hispanoamericanos 385 (July 1982): 172-191.

04815. Smith, Paul. "Juan Valera and the Illegitimacy Motif." Hispania 51 (December 1968): 804-811.

(b) Novelists

[1] Fernan Caballero

[a] Biographies

04816. Asencio, José María. Fernán Caballero y la novela contemporánea. Madrid: Rivadeneyra, 1893.

04817. Coloma, Luis. Recuerdos de Fernán Caballero. Bilbao: El Mensajero del Corazón de Jesus, 1928.

04818. Heinerman, Theodor. Cecilia Bohl de Faber y Juan Eugenio Hartzenbusch. Madrid: Espasa, 1944.

04819. Herrero, Gabriel. Fernán Caballero: Nuevo planteamiento. Madrid: Gredos, 1963.

04820. Hespelt, E. Herman. "Francisca de Larrea, A Spanish Feminist of the Early Century." Hispania 13 (May 1930): 173-186.

04821. Klibbe, Lawrence Hadfield. Fernán Caballero. New York: Twayne, 1973.

04822. Montesinos, Jose. Fernán Caballero: Ensayo de justitficación. Mexico City: El Colegio de Mexico, 1961.

04823. Morel-Fatio, Alfred. "Fernán Caballero d'apres sa correspondance avec Antoine de Latour." Bulletin Hispanique 3 (1901): 252-294.

04824. Pitollet, Camille. "Deux Mots encore sur Fernán Caballero." Bulletin Hispanique 34 (1932): 153-160.

[b] Views on Society

04825. Hespelt, E. Herman. "The Genesis of La familia Alvareda." Hispanic Review 2 (July 1934): 179-201.

04826. Pitollet, Camille. "Les Premiers Essais littêraires de Fernân Caballero." Bulletin Hispanique 9 (1907): 67-86; 286-302.

04827. ______________. "Les Premiers Essais littéraires de Fernán Caballero." Bulletin Hispanique 10 (1908): 286-305; 378-396.

04828. ______________. "A propos de Fernán Caballero." Bulletin Hispanique 33 (1931): 335-340.

[2] Concha Espina

04829. Bretz, Mary Lee. Concha Espina. New York: Twayne Publishers, Inc., 1980.

04830. Cano, Juan. "La mujer en la novela de Concha Espina." Hispania 22 (February 1939): 51-60.

04831. Douglas, Frances. "Concha Espina: A New Star Ascendant." Hispania 7 (March 1924): 111-120.

04832. ______________. "Recent Works by Concha Espina." Hispania 6 (May 1923): 185-187.

04833. Fria Lagoni, Mauro. Concha Espina y sus criticos. Toulouse: Editions Figarola Maurin, 1929.

04834. Rosenberg, S.L. Millard. "Concha Espina." Hispania 10 (November 1927): 321-329.

Also refer to #4811.

[3] Benito Perez Galdos

04835. Blanco, Louise S. "Origin and History of the Plot of 'Marianela.'" Hispania 48 (September 1965): 463-467.

04836. Bly, Peter A. "Sex, Egotism and Social Regeneration in Galdos's El Caballero encantador." Hispania 62 (March 1979): 20-29.

04837. Huidobro, Matías Montes. "El Audaz: Desdoblamientos de un ritual sexorevolucionario." Hispania 63 (September 1980): 487-497.

04838. Kirsner, Robert. Veinte años de matrimonio en novela de Galdos. New York: Eliseo Torres, 1983.

04839. Livingstone, Leon. "The Law of Nature and Women's Liberation in Tristana." Anales Galosianos 7 (1972): 93-100.

04840. Lowe, Jennifer. "Ángel Guerra and Halma: A Study of Two Love-Relationships." Hispanofilia 71 (January 1981): 53-61.

04841. ______________. "Galdos' Presentation of Rosalia in La de Bringas." Hispanofilia 50 (January 1974): 49-65.

04842. Penuel, Arnold M. "Narcissism in Galdos' Doña Perfecta." Hispania 62 (May-September 1979): 282-288.

04843. Turner, Harriet. "Family Ties and Tyrannies: A Reassessment of Jacinta." Hispanic Review 51 (Winter 1983): 1-22.

04844. Wellington, Marie A. "Marianela: nuevas dimensiones." Hispania 51 (September 1968): 38-48.

Also refer to #4796, 6368.

[4] Gertrudis Gomez de Avellaneda

04845. Bravo-Villasante, Carmen. Une vida romantica: La Avellaneda. Barcelona: Editora y Distribuidora Hispano Americana, 1967.

04846. Cotareo y Mori, Emilio. La Avellaneda y sus obras: Ensayo biográfico y crítico. Madrid: Tipografía de Archivos, 1930.

04847. Figarola-Caneda, Domingo and Boxhorn, Emilia. Gertrudis Gomez de Avellaneda. Madrid: Sociedad General Española de Libreria, 1929.

04848. Miller, Beth. "Gertrude the Great Avellaneda, Nineteenth-Century Feminist." In Women in Hispanic Literature, Icons and Fallen Idols, pp. 201-214. Berkeley, Calif.: University of California Press, 1983.

04849. Williams, Edwin B. The Life and Dramatic Works of Gertrudis Gomez de Avellaneda. Philadelphia: Publications of the University of Pennsylvania, 1924.

[5] Emila Pardo Bazán

[a] Biographies

04850. Barja, Cesar. Emilia Pardo Bazán. Madrid: Editorial Molino, 1925.

04851. Bravo-Villasante, Carmen. "El patriotismo de dona Emilia Pardo Bazán." Cuadernos hispanoamericanos 49 (February 1962): 243-252.

04852. Clémessy, Nelly. Emilia Pardo Bazán Como novelista (de la teoria a la practica). Translated by Irene Gambra. Madrid: Fundacion Universitaria Española, 1981.

04853. Cook, Teresa A. "Emilia Pardo Bazán y la educacion como elemento primordial en la liberación de la mujer." Hispania 60 (May 1977): 259-265.

04854. Gonzales Lopez, Emilio. Emilia Pardo Bazán. Novelista de Galicia. New York: Hispanic Institute of the United States, 1944.

04855. Hilton, Ronald. "Emilia Pardo Bazán et le mouvement féministe en Espagne." Bulletin Hispanique 54 (1952): 153-164.

Also refer to #4803.

[b] Views on Society

04856. Bieder, May Ellen. "Capitulation: Marriage, not Freedom-A Study of Emilia Pardo Bazán's Memorias de un solteron and Galdos' Tristana." Symposium 30 (1976): 93-109.

04857. Charnon-Deutsch, Lou. "Naturalism in the Short Fiction of Emilia Pardo Bazán." Hispanic Journal (Fall 1981): 73-85.

04858. DeCoster, Cyrus C. "Maupassant's Une Vie and Pardo Bazán's Los Pazos de Ulloca." Hispania 56 (September 1973): 586-592.

04859. Feeny, Thomas. "Illusion and the Don Juan Theme in Pardo Bazán's Cuentos de amor." Hispanic Journal 1 (Spring 1980): 67-71.

04860. Feeny, Thomas. "Pardo Bazán's Pessimistic View of Love as Revealed in Cuentos de amor." Hispanofilia 64 (September 1978): 7-14.

04861. Giles, Mary E. "Feminism and the Feminine in Emilia Pardo Bazán's Novels." Hispania 63 (May 1980): 356-367.

04862. Hilton, Ronald. "Pardo Bazán's Analysis of the Social Structure of Spain." Bulletin of Hispanic Studies 19 (1952): 1-15.

04863. ____________. "Pardo Bazán and the Spanish Problem." Modern Language Quarterly 13 (1952): 292-298.

04864. Kirby, Harry L., Jr. "Pardo Bazán, Darwinism and 'La madre naturaleza.'" Hispania (December 1964): 733-737.

04865. ________________. "Pardo Bazán's Use of the Cantar de los cantares in La madre naturaleza." Hispania 61 (December 1978): 905-911.

04866. Lopez, Mariano. "Moral y estetica fin de siglo en La Quimera de Pardo Bazán." Hispania 62 (March 1979): 62-70.

04867. ____________. "A propósito de La madre naturaleza de Emilia Pardo Bazán." Bulletin Hispanique 83 (January-June 1981): 79-108.

04868. ____________. "En torno a la segunda manera de Pardo Bazán" Una cristiana y La prueba." Hispanofilia 63 (May 1978): 67-78.

b) Art

04869. Wilson, Robert E. "Calatayud and the Dolores Legend: The Story of a Song." Hispania 49 (September 1966): 395-403.

F. ITALY

1. POLITICAL

"In every way. . . I aimed at an order of things very different from what we had in favor of women."
Gualberti Beccari

a) Generic

04870. Farina, Rachele and Sillano, Maria Teresa. "Tessitrici dell'Unità escluse dal Risorgimento." In Esistere comme donna, pp. 79-88. Milan: Mazzotta, 1983.

04871. Orlandi, Giuseppe. Le campagne modenesi fra rivoluzione e restaurazione, 1790-1815. Modena: Aedes muratoriana, 1967.

b) Legal

04872. Pierantoni, Augusto. Gli atti di matrimonio: ricevuti all' estero dagli agenti diplomatici o consolari. Rome: Tip. Elzeviriana, 1901.

c) Criminal

04873. Gibson, Mary. "The Female Offender and the Italian School of Criminal Anthropology." Journal of European Studies 12 (September 1982): 155-165.

d) Feminism

04874. Cecchin, Francesco Maria. Il Femminismo cristiano: la questione femminile nella prima Democrazia Cristiana, 1898-1912. Rome: Riuniti, 1979.

04875. Giovannini, Claudio. "L'emancipazione della donna nell' Italia postunitaria: una questione Borghese?" Studi storici 23 (April-June 1982): 355-381.

04876. Nobile, Caterina Eva. "Aspetti problematica ed associativi della question femminile a Reggio Calabria attraverso i giornale cattolici locali (1869-1918)." In Studi di storia sociale et religiosa Scritti in onore di Gabriele de Rosa, pp. 329-368. Naples: Editrici Ferraro, 1980.

04877. Roggero, Maria Pia. "L'emancipazione della donna nel pensiero italiano dai 'Lumi' a Mazzini." Risorgimento 35 (1983): 149-164.

04878. Tanara, Maria Grazia. "Femminismo cristiano--Le donne cattoliche e la sfida del lavoro." In Esistere comme donna, pp. 143-152. Milan: Mazzotta, 1983.

e) Suffrage

04879. Cerilli, Romualdo. La donna elettrice: studio sul diritto di suffragio in rapporto alla questione femminile. Turin: Unione tip. editrice, 1900.

f) Political Roles

04880. Alfieri, Vittorio Enzo. "Bianca Ceva combattente per la liberta." Risorgimento 34 (1982): 165-171.

04881. Brombert, Beth Archer. Cristina, Portraits of a Princess. Chicago: University of Chicago Press, 1982.

04882. Camerani, Sergio. "L'ultima Granduchessa di Toscana." In Studie in onore di Riccardo Filangieri, 3: 509-519. Naples: L'arte tipografica, 1959.

04883. Cavalli, Iudi Faini and Farina, Rachele. "La Mozzoni, la Kuliscioffe e tante altre." in Esistere comme donna, pp. 159-166. Milan: Mazzotta, 1983.

04884. Vigezzi, Brunelle. Il PSI, le riforme e la rivoluzione: Filippo Turati e Anna Kuliscioff dai fatti del 1898 alla prima guerra mondiale. Florence: Sansoni, 1981.

2. ECONOMIC

"No one of us (tailoresses) can by twelve hours of work earn a living while wages remain at their present absurd rate. We are thus compelled to work 'double,' supplementing our labor in the workshop by labor at home, if we wish to gain an honest livelihood."

Chamber of Labor, Union of Tailoresses, Dressmakers and Allied Trades, Turin 1903

04885. Schneider, Jane. 'Trousseau as Treasure: Some Contradictions of Late Nineteenth-Century Change in Sicily." In The Marriage Bargain: Women and Dowries in European History, edited by Marion A. Kaplan, pp. 81-120. New York: Harrington Park, 1985.

04886. Sellin, Volker. "Die Sorge um Erhaltung des Subjekts des ökonomischen Gesetzes: die Beschrankung der Kinderarbeit." In Die Anfänge staatlicher Sozialreform im liberalen Italien, pp. 87-105. Stuttgart: Ernst Klett Verlag, 1971.

04887. Zappi, Elda Gentili. "'If Eight Hours Seem Few to You. . . .': Women Workers' Strikes in Italian Rice Fields, 1910-1906." In Women and the Structure of Society, edited by Barbara J. Harris and JoAnn McNamara, pp. 206-214. Durham, N.C.: Duke University Press, 1984.

Also refer to #4878, 4890.

3. SOCIAL

"Above all, I felt myself stirred to rebellion when I learned of some brutal husband who had beaten his wife."

Gualberta Beccari

a) Demography

04888. Gattei, Giorgio. "Per una storia de comportamento amoroso dei Bolognese; le nascite dall' Unita fascismo." Societa̒ et Storia 9 (1980): 613-640.

04889. Schiaffino, Andrea. "Fecondità e vita conjugale a Bologna nell'ultimo secolo: analisi longitudinale delle discendenze." Instituto di Statistica-Quaderno 3 (1979): 199-275.

Also refer to #3636.

b) Family

04890. Kertzer, David I. Family Life in Central Italy, 1880-1910: Sharecropping Wage Labor, and Coresidence. New Brunswick, N.J.: Rutgers University Press, 1984.

04891. Peruta, Franco Della. "Infanzia e famiglia nella prima meta dell'Ottocento." Studi storici 20 (July-September 1979): 473-491.

Also refer to #4872, 4885, 4886, 4889.

4. CULTURAL

"I know nothing, nothing! I have everything to learn. Twelve years ago, when I left the theatre, I did so with no regrets. I was tired of living for others; I wanted to live for myself and learn and learn."

Eleanora Duse

04892. Bonifazi, Neuro. "La donna di Leopardi." Forum italicum 11 (June-September 1977): 192-217.

04893. Dodi, Luisa. "Una figura diversa di intellettuale impegnata." In Esistere comme donna, pp. 135-142. Milan: Mazzotta, 1983.

04894. Jeffries, Giovanna Miceli. "Una donna: Singolare e radicale esperienza di ricerca e liberazione di una coscienza." Forum italicum 15 (Spring 1981): 31-51.

04895. Nozzoli, Anna. Tabù et coscienza. La condizione femminile nella lettatura italiano del Novecento. Florence: La Nuova Italia, 1978.

Also refer to #4553.

G. THE LOW COUNTRIES

1. POLITICAL

"There is no happiness for women to be found outside the affection of a family and the accomplishment of duty."
Zoé Gatti de Gamond

a) Feminism

04896. Boël, Marthe (de Kerchove de Dentergehm) and Duchène, Christiana. _La féminisme en Belgique, 1892-1914_. Brussels: Editions du conseil national des femmes belges, 1955.

04897. Continho-Wiggelendam, Anneke. "Women's Emancipation Around the Turn of the Century and the Opposition to It." _Netherlands Journal of Sociology_ 19 (1983): 113-131.

04898. Desmed, Roger, "Examen du problème de l'émancipation de la femme par la Loge 'Les Amis Philanthrophes' vers 1860." _Revue de l'Université de Bruxelles_ 3-4 (1977): 386-413.

04899. Polasky, Janet L. "Utopia and Domesticity: Zoé Gatti de Gamond." _Proceedings of the Western Society for French History_ 11 (1983): 273-281.

b) Hortense

04900. Castries, René de La Croix, duc de. "La Reine Hortense." _Revue des deux mondes_ (February 1984): 313-320.

04901. ______________________________. _La Reine Hortense_. Paris: Tallandier, 1983.

04902. ______________________________. "Un des plus mauvais mariages de l'histoire: Hortense et Louis Bonaparte." _Historia_ 448 (March 1984): 10-19.

2. ECONOMIC

"Here they [the men] lounge about,
where all year long the stout
Fishers' dames
sell, from their wooden frames,
herrings and anchovies. . . ."
Emile Verhaeren
"A Corner of the Quay"

04903. Alter, George. "Work and Income in the Family Economy: Belgium 1853 and 1891." _Journal of Interdisciplinary History_ 15 (Autumn 1984): 255-276.

04904. Desama, Claude. "La population active à Verviers pendant la revolution industrielle. 1. Inactivite et sousemploi." Population et famille 47 (1979): 45-68.

04905. ______________. "La population active à Verviers pendant la revolution industrielle. 2. Les actifs: Reparation economique et structures démographiques." Population et famille 47 (1979): 69-76.

Also refer to #4911.

3. SOCIAL

"The union of the sexes is not for pleasure; it can cause the arrival of a child. The child has a right to its father's care, not only for his material well being, but for his moral upbringing as well. Therefore, do not let passion cloud your judgment."

Madame Van Kol
Sex Education 1905

a) Demography

04906. Danhieux, Luc. "The Evolving Household: The Case of Lampernisse, West Flanders." In Family Forms in Historic Europe, edited by Richard Wall, Joan Robin, and Peter Laslett, pp. 409-420. New York: Cambridge University Press, 1983.

04907. Duchêne, J., and Lesthaeghe, R. "Essai de reconstitution de la population belge sous la régime française: quelques caracteristiques demographiques de la population féminine." Population et famille 36 (1975): 1-47.

04908. Leboutte, Rene. "Demographie et industrialisation: la population de Herstal en 1812." Cahiers de Clio 55 (1978): 30-56.

b) Family

04909. Janssens, Angelique. "Industrialization Without Family Change? The Extended Family and the Life Cycle in a Dutch Industrial Town 1880-1920." Journal of Family History 11 (1986): 1-24.

04910. Wall, Richard. "The Composition of Household in a Population of 6 Men to 10 Women: South-East Bruges in 1814." In Family Forms in Historic Europe, edited by Richard Wall, Jean Robin, and Peter Laslett, pp. 421-474. New York: Cambridge University Press, 1983.

04911. Wall, Richard. "Does Owning Real Property Influence the Form of the Household? An Example from Rural West Flanders." In _Family Forms in Historic Europe_, edited by Richard Wall, Jean Robin, and Peter Laslett, pp. 379-407. New York: Cambridge University Press, 1983.

Also refer to #4903.

c) Marriage

04912. LaPage, Yvan. "Cent vingt années de choix du conjoint à Alle-sur-Semois." _Population_ 34 (November-December 1979): 1152-1161.

d) Fashion/Manners

04913. Maaskamp, E. _Representations of Dresses, Morals and Customs in the Kingdom of Holland at the Beginning of the Nineteenth Century_. Amsterdam: Maaskamp, 1808.

04914. Semple. _Costumes of the Netherlands After Drawings Made from Nature, by Miss Semple_. London: Ackermann's Repository of Arts, 1817.

4. CULTURAL

> "The favorite subject among the women were children and the rainy weather: aside from gossip there was talk of little else. The men . . . were inclined to consider the women who talked as chatterboxes."
>
> Isabel Anderson
> _The Spell of Belgium_

04915. Despy-Meyer, Andrée and Becquevort, Jacques. _Les femmes et l'enseignement supérieur. L'Université libre de Bruxelles de 1880 à 1914_. Brussels: Université libre de Bruxelles, 1980.

04916. Wynants, Paul. "L'école des femmes. Les catholiques belges et l'enseignement primaire féminin (1842-1860)." _Revue Nouvelle_ 77 (1983): 69-76.

VIII. EARLY TWENTIETH CENTURY, 1914–1945

A. GENERAL

1. POLITICAL

"The bourgeois women's movement is a serious dangerous power of the counter-revolution. . . . It must be beaten down, so that the proletarian world revolution may be victorious."
Clara Zetkin

a) Feminism

04917. Aubenas-Bastié, Jaqueline. "Introduction. Le champ des femmes." In Les femmes et leur maîtres, edited by Maria-Antonietta Macciocchi, pp. 9-14. Paris: C. Bourgeois, 1979.

04918. Costin, Lela B. "Feminism, Pacifism, Internationalism and the 1915 International Congress of Women." Women's Studies International Forum 5 (1982): 301-315.

04919. Riley, Denise. "Feminist Thought and Reproductive Control: The State and 'the Right to Choose.'" In Women in Society, edited by the Cambridge Women's Studies Group, pp. 185-199. London: Virago Press, 1981.

Also refer to #3677.

b) Political Roles

04920. Farina, Rachele and Lejeune, Paule. "Guerra alla guerra." In Esistere comme donna, pp. 189-198. Milan: Mazzotta, 1983.

04921. Seidler, Franz W. Frauen zu den Waffen-Markettenderinnen, Helferinnen, Soldatinnen. Bonn: Wehr and Wissen, 1978.

04922. Singer, Kurt. Spies and Traitors of World War II. New York: Prentice-Hall, 1945.

04923. Wiltsher, Anne. Most Dangerous Women Feminist Peace Campaigners of the Great War. Boston: Pandora, 1985.

2. ECONOMIC

"Birth Control and the use of Contraceptives, Marriage Laws, the treatment of sexual offences and abnormalities, the economic position of the family,--in all these matters the existing state of the Law and of orthodoxy is still mediaeval--altogether out of touch with civilised opinion and civilised practice. . . ."

John Maynard Keynes
Essays in Persuasion

04924. International Labour Office. "Convention Concerning the Employment of Women Before and After Childbirth" Official Bulletin 1 (1920): 359-360.

04925. ______________________. "Employment of Women during the War" International Labour Review 40 (December 1939): 795-807.

Also refer to #4930.

3. SOCIAL

"A mother is only brought unlimited satisfaction by her relation to a son; this is altogether the most perfect, the most free from ambivalence of all human relationships. A mother can transfer to her son the ambition which she has been obliged to suppress in herself. . . ."

Sigmund Freud
New Introductory Lectures on Psychoanalysis

a) Demography

04926. Caldwell, John C. "Toward a Restatement of Demographic Transition Theory." Population and Development Review 2 (September-December 1976): 321-366.

04927. Hankins, Frank H. "Has the Reproductive Power of Western Peoples Declined?" In Problems of Population. Report of the Second General Assembly of the International Union for the Scientific Investigation of Population Problems, edited by G.H.L.F. Pitt-Rivers, pp. 181-188. Port Washington, N.Y.: Kennikat Press, 1932.

04928. Kirk, Maurice; Livi Bacci, Massimo; and Szabady, Egon, eds. Law and Fertility in Europe. Liege: Oudina Editions, 1976.

04929. Zimmerman, Anthony. Catholic Viewpoint on Overpopulation. Garden City, N.Y.: Hanover House, 1961.

b) Family/Marriage

04930. Chester, Robert and Kooy, Gerritt, eds. Divorce in Europe. Leiden: Martinus Nijhoff Social Sciences Division, 1977.

04931. Kuo, Eddie Chen-Yu. "Industrialization and the Family Type: An Integrated Overview." International Journal of Sociology of the Family 4 (Spring 1974): 75-90.

Also refer to #3675.

c) Sex Life and Morals

04932. Newman, Frances and Cohen, Elizabeth. "Historical Perspectives on Prostitution." International Journal of Women's Studies 8 (January-February 1985): 80-86.

Also refer to #3683, 3686.

4. CULTURAL

" . . . the progressive women are in the city centers. . . . In the country districts, especially in the south, there is much general illiteracy and the position of women is unaltered in attainment or vision."

Elizabeth Hazelton Haight
Italy Old and New, 1922.

a) Art

(1) Women in Art

04933. Gauthier, Xavière. Surréalisme et sexualité. Paris: Gallimard, 1969.

[See especially pp. 71-194.]

04934. Haskell, Molly. From Reverence to Rape: The Treatment of Women in the Movies. New York: Holt, Rinehart and Winston, 1974.

04935. Sullerot, Evelyne. "La femme au cinéma." Europe 427-428 (November-December 1964): 177-181.

04936. Vismara, Mariarosa. "La donna nei fumetti." In Esistere comme donna, pp. 247-256. Milan: Mazzotta, 1983.

(2) Women Artists/Critics

04937. Heck-Rabi, Louise. Women Filmmakers: A Critical Reception. Metuchen, N.J.: Scarecrow Press, 1984.

04938. LePage, Jane Weiner. Women Composers, Conductors, and Musicians of the Twentieth Century: Selected Biographies. Metuchen, N.J.: Scarecrow Press, 1980.

04939. McCreadle, Marsha. Women on Film: The Critical Eye. New York: Praeger, 1983.

04940. Mulvey, Laura. "Feminism, Film and the Avant-Garde." In Women Writing and Writing About Women, edited by Mary Jacobus, pp. 177-195. New York: Barnes and Noble, 1979.

04941. Rasponi, Lanfranc. The Last Prima Donnas. New York: Knopf, 1982.

B. BRITAIN

1. SURVEYS

"We must recognize that these ideals of 'the wife' and 'the mother' do not cover the whole number of female beings . . . ."

George Bernard Shaw

04942. The Six Point Group. In Her Own Right. London: Harrap, 1968.

2. POLITICAL

"She was the product of her age: full of steel and guts."

James Margach
said of Ellen Wilkinson

a) Generic

04943. Byles, Joan Montgomery. "Women's Experience of World War One: Suffragists, Pacifists and Poets." Women's Studies International Forum 8 (1985): 473-487.

04944. Hornsby-Smith, Pat. "Women in Public Life." In In Her Own Right, edited by The Six Point Group, pp. 133-146. London: Harrap, 1968.

04945. Rasmussen, Jorgen A. "The Political Integration of British Women: The Response of a Traditional System to a Newly Emergent Group." Social Science History 7 (Winter 1983): 61-95.

04946. Rodgers, Silvia. "Women's Space in a Men's House: The British House of Commons." In Women and Space Ground Rules and Social Maps, edited by Shirley Ardener, pp. 50-71. New York: St. Martin's Press, 1981.

04947. Smith, Harold L. "Sex vs. Class: British Feminists and the Labour Movement, 1919-1929." The Historian 47 (November 1984): 19-37.

04948. Stacey, Margaret. Women, Power and Politics. New York: Tavistock, 1981.

b) Marxism and Socialism

04949. Cresswell, D'Arcy. Margaret McMillan: A Memoir. London: Hutchinson and Company, 1948.

04950. Hughes, Billy. "In Defense of Ellen Wilkinson." History Workshop 7 (Spring 1979): 157-160.

04951. Rubinstein, David. "Ellen Wilkinson Reconsidered." History Workshop 7 (Spring 1979): 161-169.

Also refer to #3709, 4958.

c) Feminism

04952. Davin, Anna. "Feminism and Labour History." In People's History and Socialist Theory, edited by Raphael Samuel, pp. 176-181. Boston: Routledge and Kegan Paul, 1981.

04953. Doughan, David. Lobbing for Liberation: British Feminism 1918-1968. London: City of London Polytechnic, 1980.

04954. Hunkins-Hallinan, Hazel. "A Revolution Unfinished." In In Her Own Right, edited by The Six Point Group, pp. 9-17. London: Harrap, 1968.

04955. Jeffreys, Sheila. "Sex Reform and Anti-Feminism in the 1920s." In The Sexual Dynamics of History, edited by The London Feminist History Group, pp. 177-202. London: Pluto Press, 1983.

04956. Jeger, Lena. "Power in Our Hands." In In Her Own Right, edited by The Six Point Group, pp. 147-158. London: Harrap, 1968.

04957. Laski, Marghanita. "The Cult of Servility." In In Her Own Right, edited by The Six Point Group, pp. 18-22. London: Harrap, 1968.

04958. Linklater, Andro. An Unhusbanded Life: Charlotte Despard: Suffragette, Socialist, and Sinn Feiner, London: Hutchinson, 1980.

04959. McKillen, Beth. "Irish Feminism and Nationalist Separatism, 1914-1923." Eire-Ireland 17 (Winter 1982): 72-90.

04960. Mellown, Muriel. "Vera Brittain: Feminist in a New Age. (1896-1970)." In Feminist Theorists, edited by Dale Spender, pp. 314-334. New York: Pantheon Books, Random House, 1983.

04961. Spender, Dale. There's Always Been a Women's Movement This Century. Boston: Pandora Press, 1983.

04962. ___________. Time and Tide Wait for No Man. Boston, Mass.: Pandora Press, 1984.

Also refer to #551, 3739, 3943, 4947.

d) Political Roles

04963. Birmingham, Stephen. Duchess: The Story of Wallis Warfield Windsor. Boston: Little, Brown, 1981.

04964. Duff, David. George and Elizabeth: A Royal Marriage. London: Collins, 1983.

04965. Izard, Molly. A Heroine in Her Time: A Life of Dame Helene Gwynne-Vaughan 1879-1967. London: Macmillan, 1969.

04966. Warwick, Christopher. King George VI and Queen Elizabeth: A Portrait. New York: Beaufort Books, 1985.

Also refer to #3785.

e) Military/World Wars

04967. Clark-Kennedy, Archibald Edmund. Edith Cavell: Pioneer and Patriot. New York: Hillary House, 1965.

04968. Gilbert, Sandra M. "Soldier's Heart: Literary Men and Literary Women and the Great War." Signs 8 (Spring 1983): 422-450.

04969. Leslie, J.H. An Historical Roll With Portraits of Those Women of the British Empire to Whom the Military Medal Has Been Awarded During the War. Sheffield: W.C. Long, 1919-1920.

04970. Mason, Ursula Stuart. The Wrens 1917-1977. Reading, England: Educational Explorers, 1977.

04971. Robertson, James C. "Dawn (1928): Edith Cavell and Anglo-German Relations." Historical Journal of Film, Radio and TV 4 (March 1984): 15-28.

04972. Wadge, D. Collett, ed. Women in Uniform. London: S. Low Marston, 1947.

04973. Ward, Irene. F.A.N.Y. Invicta. London: Hutchinson, 1940.

04974. Webster, N.H. Britain's Call to Arms: An Appeal to Our Women. London: Rees, 1914.

Also refer to #4966.

3. ECONOMIC

"But this greater [industrial] capacity does exist. It is to be attributed mainly to three factors--the ever-increasing technical efficiency of our industry, the greater economic output of women, and the larger proportion of the population which is at the working period of life."

John Maynard Keynes
Essays in Pursuasion

a) Generic

04975. Holme, Anthea. "Woman in Her Two Roles." In In Her Own Right, edited by The Six Point Group, pp. 60-77. London: Harrap, 1968.

Also refer to #5000.

b) Women's Employment

04976. Bedford, John Robert Russell. The Flying Duchess. London: Macdonald and Company, 1968.

04977. Dunning, J.H. "Employment for Women in the Development Areas, 1935-51." Manchester School of Economic and Social Studies 21 (September 1953): 271-277.

04978. Garside, W.R. "Unemployment and the School-Leaving Age in Inter-War Britain." International Review of Social History 26 (1981): 159-170.

04979. Mitchell, Margaret. "The Effects of Unemployment on the Social Condition of Women and Children in the 1930s." History Workshop 19 (Spring 1985): 105-127.

04980. Seear, Nancy. "The World of Work." In In Her Own Right, edited by The Six Point Group, pp. 44-59. London: Harrap, 1968.

04981. Zimmeck, Meta. "Strategies and Strategems for the Employment of Women in the British Civil Service, 1919-1939." Historical Journal 7 (December 1984): 901-924.

Also refer to #3806, 3813, 3862.

c) Work and the War Effort

04982. Abbott, Edith. "The War and Women's Work in England." Journal of Political Economy (July 1917): 641-678.

04983. Allen, Margaret. "The Domestic Ideal and the Mobilization of Woman Power in World War II." Women's Studies International Forum 6 (1983): 401-412.

04984. Smith, Harold L. "The Womanpower Problem in Britain During the Second World War." Historical Journal 27 (December 1984): 925-945.

04985. Summerfield, Penelope. Women Workers in the Second World War. London: Croom Helm, 1984.

04986. Usborne, H.M. Women's Work in War Time: A Handbook of Employments. London: T. Werher Laurie, 1917.

4. RELIGION

> " . . . it's a fine thing to be the mother of a young fellow going on for the Church. It must make you very contented in yourself when you think of all the Masses he will say for you . . . ."
>
> Brinsley MacNamara
> The Valley of the Squinting Windows

04987. Burgess, Alan. The Small Woman. New York: Dutton, 1957.

04988. Chamberlain, Elsie. "The World in Which We Worship." In In Her Own Right, edited by The Six Point Group, pp. 121-132. London: Harrap, 1968.

04989. Mitchell, Carol. "The 20th Century Witch in England and the United States: An Annotated Bibliography." Bulletin of Bibliography 39 (June 1982): 69-83.

5. SOCIAL

> "Abortion must be the key to a new world for women, not a bulwark for things as they are, economically or biologically."
>
> Stella Browne

a) Generic

04990. Cowles, Virginia. The Astors: The Story of a Transatlantic Family. New York: Knopf, 1979.

04991. Coxhead, Elizabeth. Constance Spry, A Biography. London: Luscombe, 1975.

04992. Gower, Pauline. Women with Wings. London: J. Long, 1938.

04993. Marwick, Arthur. The Deluge: British Society and the First World War. Boston: Little, Brown, 1965.

04994. Messum, D. The Life and Work of Lucy Kemp-Welch. London: Antique Collector's Club, 1976.

04995. Payne, Geoff; Payne, Judy; and Chapman, Tony. "Trends in Female Social Mobility." In Gender, Class and Work, edited by Eva Gamarnikow et al., pp. 61-76. London: Heinemann, 1983.

04996. Stuart, Denis. Dear Duchess: Millicent Duchess of Sutherland 1867-1955. London: Gollancz, 1982.

Also refer to #3945, 4957.

b) Demography

04997. Haskey, John. "Marital Status Before Marriage and Age at Marriage: Their Influence on the Chance of Divorce." Population Trends 32 (Summer 1983): 4-14.

04998. Pamuk, Elsie R. "Social Class Inequality in Mortality from 1921 to 1972 in England and Wales." Population Studies 39 (March 1985): 17-31.

04999. Werner, Barry, "Family Size and Age at Childbirth: Trends and Projections." Population Trends 33 (Autumn 1983): 4-13.

c) Family

05000. Summerfield, Penelope. "Women, Work and Welfare: A Study of Child Care and Shopping in Britain in the Second World War." Journal of Social History 17 (Winter 1983): 248-269.

Also refer to #3806, 4975, 4999, 5079, 5080.

d) Marriage

05001. Holtzman, Ellen M. "The Pursuit of Married Love: Women's Attitude Toward Sexuality and Marriage in Great Britain, 1918-1939." Journal of Social History 16 (Winter 1982): 39-51.

05002. Stone, Olive. "The World of Wedlock." In In Her Own Right, edited by The Six Point Group, pp. 78-105. London: Harrap, 1968.

Also refer to #4997, 5019.

e) Sex Life and Morals

05003. Jackson, Margaret. "Sexology and the Social Construction of Male Sexuality (Havelock Ellis)." In _The Sexuality Papers_, edited by Lal Coveney et al., pp. 45-68. London: Hutchinson, 1984.

05004. ________________. "Sexual Liberation or Social Control? Some Aspects of the Relationship Between Feminism and the Social Constriction of Sexual Knowledge in the Early Twentieth Century." _Women's Studies International Forum_ 6 (1983): 1-17.

Also refer to #3998, 5001, 5084, 5085.

f) Philanthropy

05005. Blunt, W.J.W. _Lady Muriel Paget, Her Husband and Her Philanthropic Work in Central and Eastern Europe_. London: Methuen, 1962.

05006. White, Evelyne. _Winifred Holtby as I Knew Her_. London: Collins, 1938.

05007. Wilson, Francesca M. _Rebel Daughter of a Country House_. London: Allen and Unwin, 1967.

g) Health/Medical

05008. Brookes, Barbara. "The Illegal Operation: Abortion, 1919-1939." In _The Sexual Dynamics of History_, edited by The London Feminist History Group, pp. 165-176. London: Pluto Press, 1983.

05009. Lawrence, Marilyn. "Education and Identity: Thoughts on the Social Origins of Anorexia." _Women's Studies International Forum_ 7 (1984): 201-209.

05010. Simms, Madeleine. "The Choice of Motherhood." In _In Her Own Right_, edited by The Six Point Group, pp. 106-120. London: Harrap, 1968.

05011. Thurstan, Violetta. _Field Hospital and Flying Column_. London: G.P. Putnam, 1915.

05012. Wahl, Charles William. "Ella Freeman Sharpe, 1875-1947. The Search for Empathy." In _Psychoanalytic Pioneers_, edited by Franz Alexander, Samuel Eisenstein, and Martin Grotjohn, pp. 265-271. New York: Basic Books, 1966.

Also refer to #4967, 4971.

6. CULTURAL

"The indifference of the world which Keats and Flaubert and other men of genius have found so hard to bear was in her [a woman's] case not indifference but hostility. The world did not say to her as it said to them, write if you choose; it makes no difference to me. The world said with a guffaw, Write? What's the good of your writing?"

Virginia Woolf
A Room of One's Own, 1929

a) Education

05013. Bradbrook, Muriel Clara. "'My Cambridge.'" In Women and Literature 1779-1982. The Collected Papers of Muriel Brad-Brook 2: 113-123. Totowa, N.J.: Barnes and Noble, 1983.

05014. Deneke, Helena Clara. Grace Hadow. London: Oxford University Press, 1946.

05015. Drotner, Kirsten. "Schoolgirls, Madcaps and Air Aces: English Girls and Their Magazine Reading Between the Wars." Feminist Studies 9 (Spring 1983): 33-52.

05016. Gillott, Jacky. "The World of Learning." In In Her Own Right, edited by The Six Point Group, pp. 23-43. London: Harrap, 1968.

05017. Great Britain. Board of Education. The Adult Education Committee, The Development of Adult Education for Women. London: His Majesty's Stationery Office, 1922.

05018. Great Britain. Board of Education. Consultative Committee. Report on the Consultative Committee on Differentiation of the Curriculm for Boys and Girls Respectively in Secondary Schools. London: His Majesty's Stationery Office, 1923.

05019. Oram, Alison M. "Serving Two Masters? The Introduction of a Marriage Bar in Teaching in the 1920s." In The Sexual Dynamics of History, edited by The London Feminist History Group, pp. 134-148. London: Pluto Press, 1983.

Also refer to #4949, 5009.

b) Literature

(1) Poetry

05020. Bradbrook, Muriel Clara. "'The Lyf So Short, The Craft So Long To Lerne': Kathleen Raine." In Women and Literature 1779-1982. The Collected Papers of Muriel Bradbrook, 2: 132-151. Totowa, N.J.: Barnes and Noble Books, 1983.

05021. Brooke, Nicholas. "Crazy Jane and 'Byzantium.'" Essays and Studies n.s. 27 (1974): 68-83.

05022. Kline, Gloria C. The Last Courtly Lover: Yeats and the Idea of Woman. Ann Arbor, Mich.: UMI Research Press, 1983.

05023. Laity, Cassandra. "W.B. Yeats and Florence Farr: The Influence of the 'New Woman' Actress on Yeats' Changing Images of Women." Modern Drama 28 (December 1985): 620-637.

05024. Willy, Margaret. "The Poetry of Lilian Bowes Lyon." Essays and Studies n.s. 5 (1952): 52-63.

(2) Prose

(a) Non-fiction

05025. Bradbrook, Muriel Clara. "Queenie Leavis: The Dynamics of Rejection." In Women and Literature 1779-1982. The Collected Papers of Muriel Bradbrook 2: 124-131. Totowa, N.J.: Barnes and Noble Books, 1983.

05026. Chisholm, A. Nancy Cunard: A Biography. New York: Knopf, 1979.

05027. Fielding, Daphne. Emerald and Nancy: Lady Cunard and Her Daughter. London: Eyre and Spottiswoode, 1968.

(b) Novelists

[1] Agatha Christie

05028. Bardell, Eunice Bonow. "Dame Agatha's Dispensary." Pharmacy History 26 (1984): 13-19.

05029. Keating, H.R.F. Agatha Christie, First Lady of Crime. New York: Holt, Rinehart and Winston, 1977.

05030. Morgan, Janet. Agatha Christie: A Biography. New York: Knopf, 1985.

05031. Osborne, Charles. The Life and Crimes of Agatha Christie. London: Collins, 1982.

05032. Ramsey, Gordon C. Agatha Christie, Mistress of Mystery. London: Collins, 1968.

05033. White, William. "Agatha Christie: Additions to Secondary Sources." Bulletin of Bibliography 40 (June 1983): 84-89.

05034. ______________. "Agatha Christie: A First Checklist of Secondary Sources." Bulletin of Bibliography 36 (January-March 1979): 14-17, 49.

[2] James Joyce

05035. Reynolds, Mary T. "Joyce and Miss Weaver." James Joyce Quarterly 19 (Summer 1982): 373-403.

05036. Scott, Bonnie Kime. Joyce and Feminism. Bloomington: Indiana University Press, 1984.

[3] D.H. Lawrence

05037. Apter, T.E. "Let's Hear What the Male Chauvinist is Saying: The Plumed Serpent." In Lawrence and Women, edited by Anne Smith, pp. 156-177. New York: Barnes and Noble, 1978.

05038. Blanchard, Lydia. "Mother and Daughters in D.H. Lawrence: The Rainbow and Selected Shorter Works." In Lawrence and Women, edited by Anne Smith, pp. 75-100. New York: Barnes and Noble, 1978.

05039. Davies, Rosemary Reeves. "Lawrence, Lady Cynthia Asquith, and 'The Rocking-Horse Winner'." Studies in Short Fiction 20 (Spring-Summer 1983): 121-126.

05040. Hardy, Barbara N. "Women in D.H. Lawrence's Works." In D.H. Lawrence; Novelist, Poet, Prophet. pp. 90-121. New York: Harper and Row, 1973.

05041. Heath, Jane. "Helen Corke and D.H. Lawrence: Sexual Identity and Literary Relations." Feminist Studies 11 (Summer 1985): 317-342.

05042. Kinkead-Weekes, Mark. "Eros and Metaphor: Sexual Relationship in the Fiction of Lawrence." In Lawrence and Women, edited by Anne Smith, pp. 101-121. New York: Barnes and Noble, 1978.

05043. Malraux, Andre. "D.H. Lawrence and Eroticism: Concerning Lady Chatterly's Lover." Yale French Studies 11 (1953): 55-58.

05044. Moore, Harry T. "Bert Lawrence and Lady Jane." In Lawrence and Women, edited by Anne Smith, pp. 178-188. New York: Barnes and Noble, 1978.

05045. Moynahan, Julian. "Lawrence, Woman, and the Celtic Fringe." In Lawrence and Women, edited by Anne Smith, pp. 122-135. New York: Barnes and Noble, 1978.

05046. Pullin, Faith. "Lawrence's Treatment of Women in Sons and Lovers." In Lawrence and Women, edited by Anne Smith, pp. 49-74. New York: Barnes and Noble, 1978.

05047. Smith, Anne, ed. Lawrence and Women. New York: Barnes and Noble, 1978.

05048. Smith, Anne. "A New Adam and a New Eve--Lawrence and Women: A Biographical Overview." In _Lawrence and Women_, edited by Anne Smith, pp. 9-48. New York: Barnes and Noble, 1978.

05049. Spilka, Mark. "On Lawrence's Hostility to Wilful Women: The Chatterly Solution." In _Lawrence and Women_, edited by Anne Smith, pp. 189-212. New York: Barnes and Noble, 1978.

05050. Tristram, Philippa. "Eros and Death (Lawrence, Freud and Women)." In _Lawrence and Women_, edited by Anne Smith, pp. 136-155. New York: Barnes and Noble, 1978.

[4] Katherine Mansfield

05051. Citati, Pietro. _Vita breve di Katherine Mansfield_. Milan: Rizzoli, 1980.

05052. Clarke, Isabel Constance. _Katherine Mansfield: A Biography_. 1944. Reprint. Philadelphia: R. West, 1977.

05053. Eustace, Cecil Johnson. "The Genius: Katherine Mansfield." In _An Infinity of Questions_, pp. 53-78. 1946. Reprint. New York: Longmans, 1969.

05054. Kaplan, Sydney Janet. "'A Gigantic Mother': Katherine Mansfield's London." In _Women Writers and the City: Essays in Feminist Literary Criticism_, edited by Susan M. Squier, pp. 161-175. Knoxville, Tenn.: University of Tennessee Press, 1984.

05055. Mantz, Ruth Elvish and Murray, J. Middleton. _The Life of Katherine Mansfield_. 1933. Reprint. Norwood, Pa.: Norwood Editions, 1977.

05056. Meyers, Jeffrey. _Katherine Mansfield: A Biography_. New York: New Directions Pub. Corp., 1980.

05057. Moore, James. _Gurdjieff and Mansfield_. Boston: Routledge and Kegan Paul, 1980.

[5] George Orwell

05058. Nielsen, Joyce McCarl. "Women in Dystopia/Utopia: _1984_ and Beyond." _International Journal of Women's Studies_ 7 (March-April 1984): 144-154.

05059. Patai, Daphne. "Orwell's Despair, Burdekin's Hope: Gender and Power in Dystopia." _Women's Studies International Forum_ 7 (1984): 85-95.

[6] Virginia Woolf

((a)) Biographies

05060. Black, Naomi. "Virginia Woolf: The Life of Natural Happiness (1882-1941)." In _Feminist Theorists_, edited by Dale Spender, pp. 296-313. New York: Pantheon Books, Random House, 1983.

05061. De Salvo, Louise A. "Lighting the Cave: The Relationship Between Vita Sackville-West and Virginia Woolf." _Signs_ 8 (Autumn 1982): 195-214.

05062. Gordon, Lyndall. _Virginia Woolf, a Writer's Life_. New York: Oxford University Press, 1984.

05063. Klein, Kathleen Gregory. "Virginia Woolf and Women Writers: Knowing and Understanding." _South Atlantic Quarterly_ 82 (Autumn 1983): 359-369.

05064. Lilienfeld, Jane. "Reentering Paradise: Cather, Colette, Woolf and Their Mothers." In _The Lost Tradition Mothers and Daughters in Literature_, edited by Cathy N. Davidson and E.M. Broner, pp. 160-175. New York: Ungar, 1980.

05065. Meisel, Peter. _The Absent Father: Virginia Woolf and Walter Pater_. New Haven: Yale University Press, 1980.

((b)) Feminist Perspective

05066. Dash, Irene G; Kushner, Deena Dash; and Moore, Deborah Dash. "How Light a _Lighthouse_ for Today's Women?" In _The Lost Tradition Mothers and Daughters in Literature_, edited by Cathy N. Davidson and E.M. Broner, pp. 176-188. New York: Ungar, 1980.

05067. Marcus, Jane, ed. _New Feminist Essays on Virginia Woolf_. Lincoln: University of Nebraska Press, 1981.

((c)) Views on Society

05068. Bradbrook, Muriel Clara. "Notes on the Style of Mrs. Woolf." In _Women and Literature 1799-1982. The Collected Papers of Muriel Bradbrook_, 2: 152-157. Totowa, N.J.: Barnes and Noble Books, 1983.

05069. ______. "_To the Lighthouse_." In _Women and Literature 1779-1982. The Collected Papers of Muriel Bradbrook_ 2: 158-164. Totowa, N.J.: Barnes and Noble Books, 1983.

05070. Erzgraber, Willi. "Zur Asthetik des Augenblicks bei Virginia Woolf." _Germanisch-Romanische Monatsschrift_ n.s. 34 (1984): 133-148.

05071. Gillespie, Diane. "Virginia Woolf and the 'Reign of Error'." Washington State University. Research Studies 43 (1975): 222-234.

05072. McNaron, Toni A.H. "Echoes of Virginia Woolf." Women's Studies International Forum 6 (1983): 501-507.

05073. Marcus, Jane, ed. Virginia Woolf: A Feminist Slant. Lincoln: University of Nebraska Press, 1983.

05074. ___________. "Virginia Woolf and Her Violin: Mothering, Madness, and Music." In Mothering the Mind, Twelve Studies of Writers and Their Silent Partners, edited by Ruth Perry and Martine Watson Brownley, pp. 180-201. New York: Holmes & Meier, 1984.

05075. Spivak, Gayatri Chaikravorty. "Unmaking and Making in To the Lighthouse." In Women and Language in Literature and Society, edited by Sally McConnel-Ginet, et al., pp. 310-327. New York: Praeger, 1980.

05076. Squier, Susan Merrill. "Tradition and Revision: The Classic City Novel and Virginia Woolf's Night and Day." In Women Writers and the City: Essays in Feminist Literary Criticism, pp. 114-133. Knoxville, Tenn.: University of Tennessee Press, 1984.

Also refer to #1900, 4219.

[7] Others

05077. Auerbach, Nina. "Dorothy Sayers and the Amazons." Feminist Studies 3 (1975): 55-62.

05078. Bargainnier, Earl F., ed. Ten Women of Mystery. Bowling Green, Ohio: Bowling Green State University, 1981.

05079. Fromm, Gloria G. "What Are Men to Dorothy Richardson?" In Men by Women, Women and Literature, edited by Janet Todd, 2: 168-188. New York: Holmes and Meier, 1982.

05080. Gregory, Horace. Dorothy Richardson: An Adventure in Self Discovery. New York: Holt, Rinehart and Winston, 1967.

05081. Marcus, Jane. "A Wilderness of One's Own: Feminist Fantasy Novels of the Twenties: Rebecca West and Sylvia Townsend Warner." In Women Writers and the City: Essays in Feminist Literary Criticism, pp. 134-160. Knoxville, Tenn.: University of Tennessee Press, 1984.

05082 Powell, Violet Georgiana. The Constant Novelist: A Study of Margaret Kennedy. London: Heinemann, 1983.

05083. Quigley, Isabel. Pamela Hansford Johnson. London: Longmans Green, 1968.

05084. Roberts, Richard Ellis. Portrait of Stella Benson. London: Macmillan, 1939.

05085. Ruehl, Sonja. "Inverts and Experts: Radclyffe Hall and the Lesbian Identity." In Feminism, Culture and Politics, edited by Rosalind Brunt and Caroline Rowan, pp. 15-36. London: Wishart, 1982.

05086. Ziegler, Gilette. "Les femmes et le roman policier." Europe 427-428 (November-December 1964): 103-108.

c) Intellectuals

05087. Alsop, Susan Mary. Lady Sackville: A Biography. New York: Doubleday, 1978.

05088. Blackett, Monica. The Mark of the Maker: A Portrait of Helen Waddell. London: Constable, 1973.

05089. DeSalvo, Louise A. "Every Woman is an Island: Vita Sackville-West, the Image of the City, and the Pastoral Idyll." In Women Writers and the City: Essays in Feminist Literary Criticism, edited by Susan M. Squier, pp. 97-113. Knoxville, Tenn.: University of Knoxville Press, 1984.

05090. Turcon, Sheila. "A Quaker Wedding: The Marriage of Bertrand Russell and Alys Pearsall Smith." Russell 3 (Winter 1983-1984): 103-128.

Also refer to #5061.

d) Art

(1) Women Artists

(a) Actresses/Dancers

05091. Adlard, Eleanor. Edy. London: Muller, 1949.

05092. Forbes, Bryan. Ned's Girl: The Authorized Biography of Dame Edith Evans. London: Elm Tree Books, 1977.

05093. Hippel, Peter. "Jennie Alexander." Theatrephile 1 (September 1984): 42-43.

05094. Keown, Eric. Margaret Rutherfod. London: Rockcliff, 1956.

05095. Morley, Sheridan. Gertrude Lawrence. New York: McGraw Hill, 1981.

05096. ______________. Gladys Cooper, a Biography. London: Heinemann, 1979.

05097. Peters, Margot. _Mrs. Pat: The Life of Mrs. Patrick Campbell._ New York: Alfred A. Knopf, 1984.

05098. Sprigge, Elizabeth. _Sybil Thorndike Casson._ London: Gollancz, 1971.

05099. Trewin, John Courtenay. _Edith Evans._ London: Rockcliff, 1954.

Also refer to #5023.

(b) Musicians

05100. Gower, Herschel and Porter, James. "Jeannie Robertson: The Lyric Songs." _Scottish Studies_ 21 (1977): 55-103.

(c) Painters/Potters

05101. Bruce, George. _Anne Redpath._ Edinburgh: University Press, 1974.

05102. Hale, Sheila. "Simple Genius. Lucie Rie's Pots are High Art." _Connoisseur_ 881 (June 1985): 127-130.

05103. Spalding, Frances. _Vanessa Bell._ New Haven, Ct.: Ticknor and Fields, 1983.

(d) Architects

05104. Johnson, Stewart. _Eileen Gray._ London: Debrett, 1979.

05105. Massingham, B. _Gertrude Jekyll._ Aylesbury: Shire Publications, 1975.

C. FRANCE

1. SURVEYS

". . . man is defined as a human being and woman is defined as female. Whenever she tried to behave as a human being she is accused of trying to emulate the male."

Simone de Beauvoir

05106. Clark, Francis I. _The Position of Woman in Contemporary France._ 1937. Reprint. Westport Ct.: Hyperion Press, 1981.

05107. Machard, Raymonde. _Les Françaises._ Paris: Flammarion, 1945.

05108. Tinayre, Marcelle. "French Women After the War." Yale Review 75 (February 1986): 200-209.

Also refer to #4353.

2. POLITICAL

> The Constituent Assembly was to be elected by a secret ballot "by all French men and French women with the exception of those judged incompetent under laws already in force."
>
> Charles de Gaulle, 1944

a) Generic

05109. Coudert, Marie-Louise. Elles, la Resistance. Paris: Messidor/Temps actuels, 1984.

05110. Francos, Ania. Il etait des femmes dans la Resistance. Paris: Stock, 1978.

05111. Prost, Antoine. "L'evolution de la politique familiale en France de 1938 a 1981." Le mouvement social 129 (October-December 1984): 7-28.

05112. Rossiter, Margaret L. Women in the Resistance. Westport, Ct.: Greenwood Press, 1985.

05113. Weitz, Margaret Collins. "As I Was Then: Women in the French Resistance." Contemporary French Civilization 10 (Fall-Winter 1986): 1-19.

Also refer to #4357.

b) Legal

05114. Bates, Lindell Theodore. The Divorce and Separation of Aliens in France. New York: Columbia University Press, 1929.

05115. Caunes, Magdeleine. Les Mesures juridique propres à faciliter la présence de la mère au foyer ouvrier. Paris: A Pedone, 1938.

05116. Foyer, Jacques. "French Law." In Reform of Family Law in Europe: The Equality of the Spouses, Divorce, Illegitimate Children, edited by A.G. Chloros, pp. 75-109. Boston: Kluwer, 1978.

05117. Gouazé, Jean, et al. Stratégies de la presse et du droit: la loi de 1920 et l'avortement au procès de Bobigny. Lyon: Presses universitaires de Lyon, 1979.

Also refer to #4368.

c) Feminism

05118. Dallery, Arleen B. "Sexual Embodiment: Beauvoir and French Feminism (ecriture feminine)." Women's Studies International Forum 8 (1985): 197-202.

05119. Finel-Honigman, Irene. "American Misconceptions of French Feminism." Contemporary French Civilization 5 (Spring 1981): 317-325.

05120. Rollet, Henri. Andrée Butillart et le féminisme chrétien. Paris: Spes, 1960.

Also refer to #4377, 5180-5195.

d) Political Roles

05121. Dienesch, Marie-Madeleine. "Marie Noël et al vie politique." Revue des deux mondes (May 1984): 328-333.

05122. Kingcaid, Renée A. "Charlotte Delbo's Auschwitz et après: The Struggle for Signification." French Forum 9 (January 1984): 98-109.

3. ECONOMIC

"It is a great prejudice to believe that women's work is something bad and that it brings you down."

Le PEM
13 January 1918

05123. Colin, Madeleine. Ce n'est pas d'aujourd'hui. Femmes, syndicats, luttes de classes. Paris: Editions sociales, 1975.

05124. Guillaumen, Collette and Mathieu, Nicole. "Données statistiques sur le travail professionnel et les conditions de vie des femmes, suivies d'une bibliographie sommaire sur le travail féminin." In La Femme dans la société, edited by Paul-Henry Chombart de Lauwe and Marie-Jose Chomart de Lauwe, pp. 411-429. Paris: Centre National de la Recherche Scientifique, 1963.

05125. Maack, Mary Niles. "Women Librarians in France: The First Generation." Journal of Library History 14 (Fall 1983): 407-449.

05126. Robert, Jean-Louis. "La CGT et la famille ouvriere, 1914-1918: premiere approche." Le Mouvement social 116 (July-September 1981): 47-66.

05127. Sohn, Anne-Marie. Féminisme et syndicalisme. Les institutrices de la Federation universitaire de l'enseignement de 1919 à 1935. Nanterre: n.p., 1973.

05128. Touraine, A. La civilisation industrielle (de 1914 à nos jours). Paris: Nouvelle Librarie de France, 1961.

05129. Werner, Francoise. "Du ménage à l'art menager: l'évolution du Travail ménager et son echo dans la presse féminine française de 1919 à 1939." Le Mouvement social 129 (October-December 1984): 61-87.

Also refer to #4422, 5115.

4. RELIGION

> "The Cross of wood is heavy enough, do not let us overweight it with a casting of lead. I have 'discovered,' then, that man has a reserve of unsuspected strength . . . Can one doubt it when we see what is achieved by mothers at the bedside of a sick child, or by soldiers in the trenches or by saints every day of their lives."
>
> France Pastorelli
> Strength Out of Suffering

05130. Dubois, Emile. Une Mission prophétique: Helen Villefranche, fondatrice des Auxiliaires du Cur de Jesus, 1879-1951. Montsors: Resiac, 1976.

05131. Education et images de la femme chrétienne en France au début du XXeme siècle. Lyon: Hermes, 1980.

05132. Hackel, Sergei. Pearl of Great Price: The Life of Mother Maria Skobtsova 1891-1945. Crestwood, N.Y.: St. Vladimir's Seminary Press, 1982.

Also refer to #4416, 4422, 5176.

5. SOCIAL

> "Until now, women were beautiful and architectural, like the prow of a ship. Now they resemble undernourished telephone operators."
>
> Paul Poiret, about
> Coco Chanel's designs

a) Generic

05133. Charles-Roux, Edmond E. Chanel and Her World. New York: Vendome Press, 1981.

05134. Cobb, Richard. French and Germans, Germans and French: A Personal Interpretation of France Under Two Occupations, 1914-1918/1940-1944. Hanover, N.H.: University Press of New England, 1983.

05135. Gennep, Arnold Van. Manuel de folklore français contemporain. Paris: Picard, 1938 and 1943-1953.

05136. Tomlinson, Richard; Ogden, Philip E.; and Huss, Marie-Monique. "France in Peril: The French Fear of Denatalité." History Today 35 (April 1985): 24-31.

b) Health/Medical

05137. Nacht, S. "Marie Bonaparte, 1882-1963." International Journal of Psycholanalysis 44 (1963): 516-517.

05138. Stein-Mando, Claude. "Marie Bonaparte, 1882-1962. The Problem of Female Sexuality." In Psychoanalytic Pioneers, edited by Franz Alexander, Samuel Eisenstein and Martin Grotjohn, pp. 399-414. New York: Basic Books, 1966.

05139. Stevens, Gwendolyn and Gardner, Sheldon. "Outcast Among Aristocrats; Aristocrat of Outcasts Marie Bonaparte (1882-1962)." In The Women of Psychology, 1: 208-210. Cambridge, Mass.: Schenkman Publishing Company, Inc., 1982.

6. CULTURAL

"She does not wish to become a woman completely since she loathes women. She wants to be a man-woman: a woman when she is passive, a man when she acts."

Jean-Paul Sartre
Saint Genet

a) Education

05140. Thamin, Raymond. "L'Education des filles après la guerre." Revue des deux mondes (October 1919): 512-532 and (November 1919): 120-160.

Also refer to #4471, 4472, 4475, 4476, 5131.

b) Literature

(1) Poetry

05141. Charpier, Jacques. "Saint-John Perse and the Fertile Woman." Yale French Studies 11(1953): 101-105.

05142. Labry, Suzanne. "La femme, l'amour, la poésie au XXe siècle." Europe 427-428 (November-December 1964): 65-93.

05143. Vigée, Claude. "The Interplay of Love and the Universe in the Work of Lucien Becker." Yale French Studies 21 (1958): 23-29.

05144. Walzer, P.O. "The Physiology of Sex." Yale French Studies 44 (1970): 215-230.

05145. Whiting, Charles. "Femininity in Valery's Early Poetry." Yale French Studies 9 (1952): 74-83.

(2) Prose

(a) Women in Literature

05146. Bugliani,Ann. Women and the Feminine Principle in the Works of Paul Claudel. Madrid: Ediciones Jose Porruda Turanzas, S.A., 1977.

Also refer to #4480.

(b) Novelists

[1] Colette

05147. Brodin, Pierre. "Colette." In Présences contemporaines, 2: 195-211. Paris: Editions Debresse, 1955.

05148. Cothran, Ann. "The Pure and the Impure: Codes and Constructs." Women's Studies 8 (1981): 335-357.

05149. Dormann, Genevieve. Colette: A Passion for Life. New York: Abbeville Press, 1985.

05150. Fargue, Léon-Paul. "Colette et la sensibilité féminine française." In Portraits de famille, pp. 19-27. Paris: J.B. Janin, 1947.

05151. Harris, Elaine. L'approfondessement de sensualité dans l'oeuvre romanesque de Colette. Paris: Nizet, 1973.

05152. Lilienfeld, Jane. "The Magic Spinning Wheel: Straw to Gold--Colette, Willy, and Sido." In Mothering the Mind, Twelve Studies of Writers and Their Silent Partners, edited by Ruth Perry and Martine Watson Brownley, pp. 164-178. New York: Holmes & Meier, 1984.

05153. Michel, Jacqueline. "Montherlant et Colette . . . reflexions sur un 'eloge.'" Revue d'histoire litteraire de la France 76 (May-June 1976): 412-427.

05154. Miller, Nancy K. "D'une solitude à l'autre: vers un intertexte féminine." French Review 54 (May 1981): 797-803.

05155. ______________. "Women's Autobiography in France: For a Dialectics of Indentification." In Women and Language in Literature and Society, edited by Sally McConnel-Ginet, pp. 258-273. New York: Praeger, 1980.

05156. Norell, Donna. "The Novel as Mandola: Colette's _Break of Day_." _Women's Studies_ 8 (1981): 313-333.

05157. Relyea, Suzanne. "The Symbolic in the Family Factory: _My Apprenticeships_." _Women's Studies_ 8 (1981): 273-297.

05158. Richardson, Joanna. _Colette_. New York: Franklin Watts, 1984.

05159. Spencer, Sharon. "The Lady of the Beasts: Eros and the Transformation in Colette." _Women's Studies_ 8 (1981): 298-312.

05160. Stewart, Joan Hinde. "Colette's Gynaceum: Regression and Revewal." _French Review_ 53 (April 1980): 662-669.

05161. Stockinger, Jacob. "Impurity and Sexual Politics in the Provinces: Colette's Anti-idyll in 'The Patriarch.'" _Women's Studies_ 8 (1981): 359-366.

Also refer to #5051, 5064.

[2] Natalie Sarraute

05162. Besser, Gretchen. _Nathalie Sarraute_. Boston: Twayne, 1979.

05163. Cohn, Ruby. "A Diminishing Difference." _Yale French Studies_ 27 (1961): 99-105.

05164. Goitein, Denise. "Nathalie Sarraute as Dramatist." _Yale French Studies_ 46 (1971): 101-112.

05165. Minor, Anne. "Nathalie Sarraute: _Le Planetarium_." _Yale French Studies_ 24 (1959): 96-100.

05166. Roudiez, Leon S. "A Glance at the Vocabulary of Nathalie Sarraute." _Yale French Studies_ 27 (1961): 90-98.

05167. Sartre, Jean-Paul. "The Anti-Novel of Nathalie Sarraute." _Yale French Studies_ 16 (1955-1956): 40-44.

[3] Others

05168. Albeaux-Fernet, Michel. "Jean Giraudoux et ses heroines." _Revue des Deux Mondes_ (January 1983): 104-114.

05169. Evans, Martha Noel. "La mythologie de l'ecriture dans 'La Batarde' de Violette Leduc." _Litterature_ 46 (May 1982): 82-92.

05170. Friedman, Melvin. "Valery Larbaud: The Two Traditions of Eros." _Yale French Studies_ 11 (1953): 91-100.

05171. Girard, Rene. "The Role of Eroticism in Malraux's Fiction." _Yale French Studies_ 11 (1953): 49-54.

05172. Gossel, Alfred F. "Clara Malraux's Le bruit de nos pas: Biography and the Question of Women in the 'Case of Malraux.'" Biography 7 (Summer 1984): 213-232.

05173. Herz, Micheline. "Woman's Fate." Yale French Studies 18 (1957): 7-19.

05174. Houston, John. "The Memoirs of Hadrian by Marguerite Yourcenar." Yale French Studies 27 (1061): 140-141.

05175. May, Georges. "Marriage Versus Love in the World of Giraudoux." Yale French Studies 11 (1953): 106-115.

05176. Tobin, Michael. "Thérèse de Lisieux and Bernanos' First Novel." French Forum 10 (January 1985): 84-96.

Also refer to #5086.

c) Intellectuals

(1) Individuals

(a) André Breton

05177. Clébert, Jean Paul. "Traces de Nadja." Revue des sciences humaines n.s. 184 (October-December 1981): 79-94.

05178. Decottignies, Jean. "Le Poète et la statue." Revue des sciences humaines n.s. 184 (October-December 1981): 95-117.

05179. Leroy, Claude. "L'Amour fou, même." Revue des sciences humaines n.s. 184 (October-December 1981): 119-124.

(b) Simone de Beauvoir

05180. Bays, Gwendolyn. "Simone de Beauvoir: Ethics and Art." Yale French Studies 1 (1948): 106-112.

05181. Ehrmann, Jacques. "Simone de Beauvoir and the Related Destinies of Woman and Intellectual." Yale French Studies 27 (1961): 26-32.

05182. Evans, Mary. "Simone de Beauvoir: Dilemmas of a Feminist Radical (1908-1986)." In Feminist Theorists, edited by Dale Spender, pp. 348-365. New York: Pantheon Books, Random House, 1983.

05183. Ferguson, Ann. "Lesbian Identity: Beauvoir and History." Women's Studies International Forum 8 (1985): 203-208.

05184. Girard, René. "Memoirs of a Dutiful Existentialist." Yale French Studies 27 (1961): 41-46.

05185. Hirschman, Sarah. "Simone de Beauvoir, Lycee Teacher." Yale French Studies 22 (1958-1959): 79-82.

05186. Jones, Judith Zykofsky and Reinelt, Janelle. "Simone de Beauvoir as Dramatist: Les Bouches Inutiles." Modern Drama 26 (December 1983): 528-535.

05187. Lazar, Lillane. "Conversation avec Simone de Beauvoir." Contemporary French Civilization 8 (Spring 1984): 368-374.

05188. Patterson, Yolanda Astarita. "Entretien avec Simone de Beauvour (20 juin 1979)." French Review 52 (April 1979): 745-754.

05189. Reck, Rima Drell. "Les Mandarins: Sensibility, Responsibility." Yale French Studies 27 (1961): 33-40.

05190. Siegfried, Charlene Haddock. "Gender-Specific Values." Philosophical Forum 15 (Summer 1984): 425-442.

05191. ________________. "Second Sex: Second Thoughts." Women's Studies International Forum 8 (1985): 219-229.

05192. Simons, Margaret A. "The Silencing of Simone de Beauvoir Guess What's Missing from The Second Sex." Women's Studies International Forum 6 (183): 559-564.

05193. Singer, Linda. "Interpretation and Revival: Rereading Beauvoir." Women's Studies International Forum 8 (1985): 213-238.

05194. Tucker, William R. "Simone de Beauvoir and the French Right 1929-1955." Proceedings of the Fifth Annual Meeting of the Western Society for French History 5 (1978): 331-339.

05195. Zephir, Jacques C. "Neo-Féminisme et Socialisme selon Simone de Beauvoir." Contemporary French Civilization 7 (Spring 1983): 293-315.

Also refer to #4586, 5120.

(c) Simone Weil

05196. Cook, Bradford. "Simone Weil: Art and the Artist Under God." Yale French Studies 12 (1953): 73-80.

05197. Dunaway, John M. Simone Weil. Boston: Twayne, 1984.

05198. Goldschlager, Alain. "Quelques objections de Simone Weil a l'Eglise catholique." Revue de l'Institute de Sociologie (1982): 509-525.

05199. Hellman, John. Simone Weil: An Introduction to Her Thought. Waterloo, Canada: Wilfred Laurier University Press, 1982.

05200. Scattigno, Anna. "Simone Weil. La volonta di conoscere." Memoria 5 (November 1982): 5-22.

(d) Others

05201. Champigny, Robert. "Way of Flesh." Yale French Studies 11 (1953): 73-79

05202. Quinn, Bernard J. "The Authentic Woman in the Theatre of Sartre." Language Quarterly 10 (1972): 39-44.

05203. Sohn, Anne-Marie. "La Garçonne face à l'opinion publique: type littéraire ou type social des années 20?" Le Mouvement social 80 (July-September 1972): 3-27.

Also refer to #3372, 5129.

e) Art

(1) Women Artists

(a) Sculptors/Animators

[1] Camille Claudel

05204. Camille Claudel (1864-1943). Paris: Musée Rodin, 1984.

05205. Kuthy, Sandor. Camille Claudel-Auguste Rodin, Dialogues d'artistes-résonances. Berne: Musée des Beaux-Arts, 1985.

05206. Paris, Reine-Marie. Camille Claudel (1864-1943). Paris: Gallimard, 1984.

05207. Wernick, Robert. "Camille Claudel's Tempestuous Life of Art and Passion." Smithsonian 16 (September 1985): 56-65.

[2] Others

05208. Grémillot-Cadet, Marion. "Sylvie animatrice." Europe 427-428 (November-December 1964): 188-193.

05209. Guth, Paul. "Encounter with Germaine Richier." Yale French Studies 19-20 (1957-1958): 78-84.

05210. Lippard, Lucy R. "Louise Bourgeois: From the Inside Out." In From the Center Feminist Essays on Women's Art, pp. 238-249. New York: H.P. Dutton, 1976.

05211. Marandel, J. Patrice. "Louise Bourgeouis." Art International 15 (20 December 1971): 46-47, 73.

D. THE GERMANIES

1. SURVEYS

"Women are no class and what their movement would like to attain is in no way a form of special interest. Women simply want to find a useful place for their unrecognized power/talents in everyday life."

Gertrud Baumer
1933

05212. Bridenthal, Renate; Grossmann, Atina; and, Kaplan, Marion A. "Introduction." In _When Biology Became Destiny. Women in Weimar and Nazi Germany_, pp. 1-29. New York: Monthly Review Press, 1984.

05213. ________________, eds. _When Biology Became Destiny. Women in Weimar and Nazi Germany_. New York: Monthly Review Press, 1984.

05214. Mason, Tim. "Women in Nazi Germany." _History Workshop_ 1 (1976):74-113 and 2 (1976):5-32.

2. POLITICAL

"Our displacement of women from public life occurs solely to restore their essential dignity to them."

Goebbels

a) Generic

05215. Bridenthal, Renate and Koonz, Claudia. "Beyond _Kinder_, _Küche_, _Kirche_: Weimar Women in Politics and Work." In _When Biology Became Destiny. Women in Weimar and Nazi Germany_, edited by Renate Bridenthal et al., pp. 33-65. New York: Monthly Review Press, 1984.

05216. Fessenden, Patricia K. "More than A Question of Numbers: Woman Deputies in the German National Constituent Assembly and the Reichstag, 1919-1933." In _Women in German Studies_, edited by Kay Goodman and Ruth H. Sanders, pp. 80-98. Oxford, Ohio: Miami University, 1977.

05217. Grossmann, Atina. "Crisis, Reaction and Resistance: Women in Germany in the 1920s and 1930s." In _Class, Race and Sex: The Dynamics of Control_, edited by Amy Swerdlow and Hanna Lessinger, pp. 60-74. Boston: G.K. Hall and Company, 1983.

05218. Hausen, Karin. "Mother's Day in the Weimar Republic." In _When Biology Became Destiny. Women in Weimar and Nazi Germany_, edited by Renate Bridenthal, et al., pp. 131-152. New York: Monthly Review Press, 1984.

05219. Hausen, Karin. "Mothers, Sons and the Sale of Symbols and Goods: The 'German Mother's Day' 1923-33. In Interest and Emotion, Essays on the Study of Family and Kinship, pp. 371-413. New York: Cambridge University Press, 1985. Also in Memoria 4 (June 1982): 5-29.

05220. Kaufmann, Doris. "Vom Vaterland zum Mutterland. Frauen im katholischen Milieu der Weimarer Republik." In Frauen suchen ihre Geschichte, Historische Studien zum 19. und 20. Jahrhundert, edited by Karin Hausen, pp. 250-275. Munich: Verlag C.H. Beck, 1983.

05221. Kipfmuller, Berta. "Helene von Forster." In Lebensläufe aus Franken, edited by Anton Chroust, 3: 166-176. Wurzburg: C. J. Becker, 1927.

b) Legal

05222. Grossmann, Atina. "Abortion and Economic Crisis: The 1931 Campaign Against Paragraph 218." In When Biology Became Destiny Women in Weimar and Nazi Germany, edited by Renate Bridenthal et al., pp. 66-86. New York: Monthly Review Press, 1984. Also in New German Critique 14 (Spring 1978): 119-138.

05223. Schneider, Petra. Weg mit dem 218. Die Massenbewegung gegen das Abtreibungsverbot in der Weimarer Republik. Berlin: Oberbaumverlag, 1975.

05224. Scheffler, Dr. Erna. Die Stellung der Frau in Familie und Gesellschaft im Wandel der Rechtsordnung seit 1918. Berlin: Alfred Metzner Verlag, 1970.

Also refer to #5255.

c) Feminism

05225. Bridenthal, Renate. "'Professional' Housewives: Stepsisters of the Women's Movement." In When Biology Became Destiny. Women in Weimar and Nazi Germany, edited by Renate Bridenthal, et al., pp. 153-173. New York: Monthly Review Press, 1984.

05226. Carroll, Bernice A. "Feminist Politics and Peace." In The Role of Women in Conflict and Peace: Papers, edited by Dorothy McGuigan, pp. 61-70. Ann Arbor, Mich.: University of Michigan, 1977.

05227. Hackett, Amy. "Helene Stöcker: Left-Wing Intellectual and Social Reformer." In When Biology Became Destiny. Women in Weimar and Nazi Germany, edited by Renate Bridenthal, et al., pp. 109-130. New York: Monthly Review Press, 1984.

05228. Peyser, Dora. *Alice Salomon, die Begründerin des sozialen Frauenberufs in Deutschland.* Berlin: Carl Heymanns Verlag, 1958.

Also refer to #4597, 4598, 5234, 5257.

d) Military/World Wars

05229. Holland, Carolsue and Garett, G.R. "The 'Skirt' of Nessus: Women and the German Opposition to Hitler." *International Journal of Women's Studies* 6 (September-October 1983): 363-387.

05230. Jacob, Katharina. "Comrade-Woman-Mother--Resistance Fighter." In *When Biology Became Destiny. Women in Weimar and Nazi Germany*, edited by Renate Bridenthal, et al., pp. 349-362. New York: Monthly Review Press, 1984.

05231. Scholl, Inge. *The White Rose: Munich, 1942-1943.* Middletown, Ct.: Wesleyan University Press, 1983.

05232. Vinke, Herman. *The Short Life of Sophie Scholl.* New York: Harper and Row, 1984.

e) Nazism

05233. Bock, Gisela. "Racism and Sexism in Nazi Germany: Motherhood, Compulsory Sterilization and the State." In *When Biology Became Destiny Women in Weimar and Nazi Germany*, edited by Renate Bridenthal, et al., pp. 271-296. New York: Monthly Review Press, 1984. Also in *Signs* 8 (Spring 1983): 400-421.

05234. Classen, Brigitte and Goettle, Gabriele. "Le juif nous a vole la femme." In *Les femmes et leur maîtres*, edited by Maria-Antonietta Macciocchi, pp. 17-23. Paris: C. Bourgeois, 1979.

05235. Hermand, Jost. "*All Power to the Women:* Nazi Concepts of Matriarch." *Journal of Contemporary History* 19 (October 1984): 649-668.

05236. Hervé, Florence. "Les femmes et le national-socialisme." *Allemagnes d'Aujourd'hui* n.s. 66 (January-February 1979): 72-78.

05237. Koonz, Claudia. "The Competition for Women's *Lebensraum*, 1928-1934." In *When Biology Became Destiny. Women in Weimar and Nazi Germany*, edited by Renate Bridenthal, et al., pp. 199-236. New York: Monthly Review Press, 1984.

05238. Milton, Sybil. "Women and the Holocaust: The Case of German and German-Jewish Women." In When Biology Became Destiny. Women in Weimar and Nazi Germany, edited by Renate Bridenthal, et al., pp. 297-333, New York: Monthly Review Press, 1984.

05239. Nebel, Ruth. "The Story of Ruth." In When Biology Became Destiny. Women in Weimar and Nazi Germany, edited by Renate Bridenthal, et al., pp. 334-348. New York: Monthly Review Press, 1984.

05240. Palmier, Jean-Michel. "Romantisme et bestialite: quelques remarques sur la representation de la femme dans l'ideologie et l'art sous le IIIe Reich." In Les femmes et leur maîtres, edited by Maria-Antonietta Macciocchi, pp, 25-57. Paris: C. Bourgeois, 1979.

05241. Pauwels, Jacques R. "German Women University Students, National Socialism and the War, 1939-1945." In Women in German Studies, edited by Kay Goodman and Ruth H. Sanders, pp. 99-113. Oxford, Ohio: Miami University, 1977.

05242. Pommerin, Reiner. "The Fate of Mixed Blood Children in Germany." German Studies Review 5 (October 1982): 315-324.

05243. Ringelheim, John Miriam. "The Unethical and the Unspeakable: Women and the Holocaust." Simon Wiesenthal Center Annual 1 (1984): 69-87.

05244. Smith, Arthur L. Jr. Die "Hexe von Buchenwald": Der Fall Ilse Koch. Cologne: Böhlau, 1983.

05245. Stephenson, Jill. "Middle-class Women and National Socialist Service." History 67 (February 1982): 32-44.

05246. Thompson, Larry V. "Lebensborn and the Eugenics Policy of the Reichsführer SS." Central European History 4 (March 1971): 54-77.

3. ECONOMIC

"At 6:30 the siren signals the beginning of work. . .I remove all the stains from clothes which are to be taken for cleaning. This is not so simple as one might think; one has to watch that the material is not damaged through brushing . . . ."

H.H.B.
My Workday--
My Weekends: 150
Reports from Textile Workers

a) Generic

05247. Hardach, Karl. "The Economy of the Third Reich, 1933-1945." In The Political Economy of Germany in the Twentieth Century, pp. 53-89. Los Angeles, Ca.: University of California Press, 1980.

Also refer to #5223.

b) Women's Employment

05248. Bessel, Richard. "'Eine nicht allzu grosse Beunruhigung Arbeitermarktes.' Frauenarbeit und Demobilmachung in Deutschland nach dem Ersten Weltkrieg." Geschichte und Gesellschaft 9 (1983): 211-229.

05249. Hirsch, Max. Die Gefahren der Frauenerwerbsarbeit für Schwangerschaft, Geburt, Wochenbett und Kindesaufzucht mit besonderer Berücksichtigung der Textilindustrie. Leipzig: C. Kabitzsch, 1925.

Also refer to #4649, 5215, 5225.

c) Nazism and Women's Work

05250. Stephenson, Jill. "Women's Labor Service in Nazi Germany." Central European History 15 (September 1982): 241-265.

05251. Tröger, Annemarie. "The Creation of a Female Assembly-Line Proletariat." In When Biology Became Destiny. Women in Weimar and Nazi Germany, edited by Renate Bridenthal, et al., pp. 237-270. New York: Monthly Review Press, 1984.

05252. ________________. "Die Planung des Rationalisierungs-proletariats. Zur Entwicklung der geschlechtsspezifischen Arbeitsteilung und des weiblichen Arbeitsmarktes im Nationalsozialismus.' In Frauen in der Geschichte II, edited by Annette Kuhn and Jörn Rüsen, pp. 245-313. Dusseldorf: Schwann, 1982.

4. SOCIAL

"The outstanding and highest calling of women is always that of wife and mother and it would be an unfortunate misfortune to be turned away from this point of view."

Joseph Goebbels

a) Generic

05253. Von Eckardt, Wolf and Gelman, Sandar L. Bertolt Brecht's Berlin. A Scrapbook of the Twenties. Garden City, N.Y.: Anchor Press, 1975.

b) Demography

05254. Stephenson, Jill. "'Reichsbund der Kinderreichen': the League of Large Families in the Population Policy of Nazi Germany." European Studies Review 9 (July 1979): 351-375.

Also refer to #4666, 4667.

c) Family/Marriage

05255. Schoen, Robert and Baj, John. "Cohort Marriages and Divorce in Twentieth Century Switzerland." Journal of Marriage and the Family 46 (November 1984): 963-969.

Also refer to #4649, 5224, 5233, 5235, 5242, 5246, 5249, 5254, 5305, 5309, 5311.

d) Sex Life and Morals

05256. Grossmann, Atina. "The New Woman and the Rationalization of Sexuality in Weimar Germany." In Powers of Desire: The Politics of Sexuality, edited by Ann Snitow, Christine Stansell, and Sharon Thompson, pp.51-73. New York: Pergamon Press, 1983.

05257. Meyer-Renschhausen, Elisabeth. "The Bremen Morality Scandal." In When Biology Became Destiny. Women in Weimar and Nazi Germany, edited by Renate Bridenthal, et al., pp. 87-108. New York: Monthly Review Press, 1984.

Also refer to #4682, 5218, 5219, 5288.

e) Fashion

05258. Geramb, Victor von. Zeitgemässe Steirertrachten. Graz: Styria, 1936.

05259. Julien, Rose. Die Deutschen Volkstrachten zu beginn des 20. Jahrhunderts. Munich: Bruckmann, 1912.

05260. Pesendorfer, Gertrud. _Lebendige Tracht in Tirol_. Innsbruck: Wagner, 1966.

05261. ____________________ and Karasek, Gretel. _Neue deutsche Bauerntrachten_. Munich, 1938.

f) Health/Medical

(1) Psychology

(a) Freud

05262. Decker, Hannah S. "Freud and Dora: Constraints on Medical Progress." _Journal of Social History_ 14 (Spring 1981): 445-464.

05263. Ellenberger, Henri F. "The Story of 'Anna O.': A Critical Review of New Data." _Journal of the History of the Behavioral Sciences_ 8 (July 1972): 267-279.

05264. Freeman, Lucy and Strean, Herbert S. _Freud and Women_. New York: Frederick Ungar Publishing Company, 1981.

05265. Gearhart, Suzanne. "The Scene of Psychoanalysis: The Unanswered Questions of Dora." _Diacritics_ 9 (Spring 1979): 114-126.

05266. Hunter, Dianne. "Hysteria, Psychoanalysis, and Feminism: The Case of Anna O." _Feminist Studies_. 9 (Fall 1983): 464-488.

05267. Kittay, Eva Feder. "Rereading Freud on 'Femininity' or Why not _Womb_ Envy?" _Women's Studies International Forum_ 7 (1984): 385-391.

05268. Kofman, Sarah. _The Enigma of Woman: Woman in Freud's Writings_. Translated by Catherine Porter. Ithaca, N.Y.: Cornell University Press, 1985.

Also refer to #4722.

(b) Others

05269. Briehl, Marie. "Helene Deutsch: The Maturation of Women." In _Psychoanalytic Pioneers_, edited by Franz Alexander, Samuel Eisenstein, and Martin Grotjohn, pp. 282-298. New York: Basic Books, 1966.

05270. Lantos, Barbara. "Kate Friedländer 1903-1949: Prevention of Juvenile Delinquency." In _Psychoanalytic Pioneers_, edited by Franz Alexander, Samuel Eisenstein and Martin Grotjohn, pp. 508-518. New York: Basic Books, 1966.

05271. Lauter, Estella and Rupprecht, Carol Schreier. *Feminist Archetypal Theory: Interdisciplinary Re-Visions of Jungian Thought*. Knoxville, Tenn.: University of Tennessee, 1985.

05272. Lindon, John Arnold. "Melanie Klein: Her View of the Unconscious." In *Psychoanalytic Pioneers*, edited by Franz Alexander, Samuel Eisenstein and Martin Grotjohn, pp. 360-372. New York: Basic Books, 1966.

05273. Main, T.F. "Melanie Klein." *British Journal of Medical Psychology* 34 (1961): 163-166.

05274. Marschak, Marianne. "One Year among the Behavioral Scientists: In Memory of Frieda Fromm-Reichmann." *Psychiatry* 23 (August 1960): 303-309.

05275. Natterson, Joseph M. "Karen Horney--The Cultural Emphasis." In *Psychoanalytic Pioneers*, edited by Franz Alexander, Samuel Eisenstein, and Martin Grotjohn, pp. 450-456. New York: Basic Books, 1966.

05276. Peters, Uwe Henrik. *Anna Freud: A Life Dedicated to Children*. New York: Schocken Books, 1984.

05277. Pumpian-Mindlin, Eugene. "Anna Freud and Erik H. Erickson." In *Psychoanalytic Pioneers*, edited by Franz Alexander, Samuel Eisenstein, and Martin Grotjohn, pp. 519-533. New York: Basic Books, 1966.

05278. Roazen, Paul. "Helene Deutsch's Feminism." *The Psychohistory Review* 13 (Winter 1985): 26-32.

05279. Stevens, Gwendolyn and Gardner, Sheldon. "The Dowdy Child Analyst who was Freud's Favorite Hermine von Hug Hellmuth (-1924.)" In *The Women of Psychology* 1: 132-133. Cambridge, Mass.: Schenkman Publishing Company, Inc. 1982.

05280. ————————. "Explorer of the Inner World of Childhood Melanie Reizes Klein (1882-1960.)" In *The Women of Psychology* 1: 168-176. Cambridge, Mass.: Schenkman Publishing Company, Inc., 1982.

05281. ————————. "Perhaps the Greatest, Karen Horney (1885-1952).)" In *The Women of Psychology* 1: 144-159. Cambridge, Mass.: Schenkman Publishing Company, Inc., 1982.

05282. ————————. "An Unconventional Orthodox Psychoanalyst Helene Rosenback Deutsch (1884-)." In *The Women of Psychology* 1: 186-193. Cambridge, Mass.: Schenkman Publishing Company, Inc., 1982.

05283. ————————. "You Don't Need to Be Afraid. Frieda Fromm-Reichmann (1889-1957.)" In *The Women of Psychology* 1: 205-208. Cambridge, Mass.: Schenkman Publishing Company, Inc., 1982.

05284. Weigert, Edith. "In Memoriam. Frieda Fromm-Reichmann, 1889-1957." Psychiatry 21 (February 1958): 91-95.

5. CULTURAL

"The work in the Day Care Centers demands female kindergarten teachers, aids and youth leaders, who know about and appreciate the importance of the Folk Community and who approach life with a clear and positive approach."

Hildegard Kownatzki
"Die Kindertagesstatten des NSV."
Das junge Deutschland, 1936

a) Education

05285. Pauwels, Jacques R. Women, Nazis, and Universities: Female University Students in the Third Reich, 1933-1945. Westport, Ct.: Greenwood Press, 1984.

b) Literature

(1) Biographical Sketches

05286. "Kleines Lexikon deutschsprachiger Autorinnen der Gegenwart." In Neue Literatur der Frauen, edited by Heinz Puknus, pp. 273-342. Munich: C.H. Beck, 1980.

(2) Drama

(a) Brecht

05287. Bryant-Bertail, Sarah. "Women, Space, Ideology: Mutter Courage und ihre Kinder." Brecht Yearbook 12 (1983): 43-61.

05288. Case, Sue-Ellen. "Brecht and Women: Homosexuality and the Mother." Brecht Yearbook 12 (1983): 65-74.

05289. Eisler-Fischer, Louise. "Brecht et les femmes." Allemagne d'aujourd'hui n.s. (January-February 1974): 101-102.

05290. Nussbaum, Laureen. "The Evolution of the Feminine Principle in Brecht's Work: Beyond the Feminist Critique." German Studies Review 8 (May 1985): 217-244.

05291. Voris, Renate. "Inszenierte Ehrlichkeit: Bertolt Brechts 'Weiber-Geschichten.'" Brecht Yearbook 12 (1983): 79-95.

Also refer to #5253.

(b) Others

05292. Blumenthal, Bernhardt. "Claire Goll's Prose." Monatshefte 75 (Winter 1983): 358-368.

05293. Jäger, Georg. "Kokoschkas 'Mörder Hoffnung der Frauen.' Die Geburt des Theaters der Grausamkeit aus dem Geist der Wiener Jahrhundertwende." Germanisch-Romanische Monatsschrift n.s., 32 (1982): 215-233.

05294. Knapp, Bettina L. "Oskar Kokoschka's Murderer Hope of Womankind: An Apocalyptic Experience." Theatre Journal 35 (May 1983): 179-194.

05295. Wegener, Adolph. "Ernst Wiechert's Mater Dolorosa." Germanic Notes 3 (1972): 26-28.

(3) Poetry

(a) Nelly Sachs

05296. Berendsohn, Walter A. Nelly Sachs Einführung in das Werk der Dichterin jüdischen Schicksals. Darmstadt: Agora Verlag, 1974.

05927. ____________________. "Nelly Sachs, der künstlerische Aufstieg der Dichterin jüdischen Schicksals." In Nelly Sachs, Dichter und Denker unserer Zeit, pp. 5-30. Dortmund: Städtische Volksbüchereien, 1962-1963.

05928. Bieber, Hedwig. "Nelly Sachs Bibliographie." In Nelly Sachs, Dichter und Denker unserer Zeit, pp. 31-38. Dortmund: Städtische Volksbuchereien, 1962-1963.

05299. Rey, William H. "Zum Tode der Dichterin Nelly Sachs." Germanic Review 45 (November 1970): 273-288.

(b) Others

05300. Eben, Michael C. "Gertrud Kolmar: An Appraisal." German Life and Letters n.s. 37 (April 1984): 197-210.

05301. Schoolfield, G.C. "Paula von Prezadovic--An Introduction." German Life and Letters 7 (July 1954): 285-292.

05302. Wallmann, Jürgen P. "Rose Ausländer." In Neue Literatur der Frauen, edited by Heinz Puknus, pp. 25-29. Munich: C.H. Beck, 1980.

(4) Prose

(a) Women in Literature

[1] General

05303. Harrigan, Renny. "Die Sexualität der Frau in der deutschen Unterhaltungsliteratur 1918-1933." Geschichte und Gesellschaft 7 (1981): 412-437.

05304. ______________. "The Stereotype of the Emancipated Woman in the Weimar Republic." In Women in German Studies, edited by Kay Goodman and Ruth H. Sanders, pp. 47-79. Oxford, Ohio: Miami University, 1977.

05305. Kamenetsy, Christa. Children's Literature in Hitler's Germany: The Cultural Policy of National Socialism. Athens, Ohio: Ohio University Press, 1984.

05306. King, Lynda J. "Probable or Possible: The Issue of Women's Emancipation in German Literature of the 1920s." Rocky Mountain Review 35 (1981): 138-153.

05307. ____________. "The Woman Question and Politics in Austrain Interwar Literature." German Studies Review 6 (February 1983): 75-100.

05308. Wittmann, Livia Z. "Der Stein des Anstosses. Zu einem Problemkomplex in berühmten Romanen der Neuen Saclichkeit." Jahrbuch für Internationale Germanistik 14 no. 2 (1982): 56-78.

Also refer to #4709.

[2] Individuals

((a)) Franz Kafka

05309. Bödeker, Karl-Gernhard. Frau und Familie im erzählerischen Werk Franz Kafkas. Frankfurt: Peter Lang, 1974.

05310. Böhme, Hartmut. "'Mutter Milena': Zum Narzissmus-Problem bei Kafka." Germanisch-Romanische Monatsschrift n.s. 28 (1978): 50-69

05311. Glass, James. "Kafka and Laing on the Trapped Consciousness: The Family as Political Life." In The Family in Political Thought, edited by Jean Bethke Elshtain, pp. 269-287. Amherst, Mass.: University of Massachusetts Press, 1982.

((b)) Gertrud von Le Fort

05312. Eschbach, Maria. Die Bedeutung Gertrud von Le Forts in unserer Zeit. Warendorf: J. Schnell, 1948.

05313. Hilton, I. "Gertrud le Fort--a Christian Writer." German Life and Letters n.s. 15 (1961-1962): 300-308.

05314. ________. "'Hålfte des Lebens': Gertrud le Forts." German Life and Letters n.s. 20 (1966-1967): 117-118.

05315. Kampmann, Theodorich. Gertrud von Le Fort. Die Welt der Dichterin. Munich: Kosel und Pustet, 1935.

05316. Neuschaffer, W. "The World of Gertrud von Le Fort." German Life and Letters 8 (1954-1955): 30-36.

((c)) Robert Musil

05317. Appignanesi, Lisa. "Femininity and Robert Musil's 'Die Vollendung der Liebe.'" Monatshefte 65 (Spring 1973): 14-26.

05318. Braun, Wilhelm. "Musil's Vinzenz und die Freundin bedeutender Manner." German Review 37 (March 1962): 121-134.

05319. Kirchberger, Lida. "Musil's Trilogy: An Approach to 'Drei Frauen.'" Monatshefte 55 (April-May 1963): 167-182.

((d)) Others

05320. Chedin, Renate, "'L'ordre froid' ou la 'Neue Sachlichkeit' dans les premiers romans d'Irmgard Keun." Allemagnes d'Aujourd'hui n.s. 82 (October-December 1982): 90-108.

05321. Endres, Elisabeth. "Marie Luise Kaschnitz." In Neue Literatur der Frauen, edited by Heinz Puknus, pp. 20-24. Munich: C.H. Beck, 1980.

05322. Hoffmeister, Donna. "Growing Up Female in the Weimar Republic: Young Women in the Seven Stories by Marieluise Fleisser." German Quarterly 56 (May 1983): 396-407.

05323. Kane, B.M. "Scenes from Family Life: The Novels of Walter Kempowski." German Life and Letters n.s. 28 (July 1975): 418-426.

05324. King, Lynda J. "The Image of Fame: Vicki Baum and Weimar Germany." German Quarterly 58 (Summer 1985): 375-393.

05325. Nelson, Donald F. "Hermann Hesse's Demian and the Resolution of the Mother-Complex." Germanic Review 59 (Spring 1984): 57-62.

05326. Roloff, Gerd. "Irmgard Keun: Vorláufiges zu Leben und Werk." Amsterdamer Beitråge zur neueren Germanistic 6 (1977): 45-68.

05327. Tewarson, Heidi Thomann. "Von der Frauenfrage zum Geschlechterkampf: Der Wandel der Prioritaten im Fruhwerk Alfred Doblins." German Quarterly 58 (Spring 1985): 208-222.

05328. ______________________. "The Woman Question in the Early Work of Alfred Doblin." In Women in German Studies, edited by Kay Goodman and Ruth H. Sanders, pp. 24-46. Oxford, Ohio: Miami University , 1977.

05329. Weisstein, Ulrich. "Heinrich Mann's Madame Legros--not a Revolutionary Drama." Germanic Review 35 (February 1960): 39-49.

c) Art

05330. Bergstrom, Janet. "Sexuality at a Loss: The Films of F.W. Murnau." Poetics Today 6 (1985): 185-203.

Also refer to #4709, 5240.

05331. Evers, Ulrika. Deutsche Künstlerinnen des 20. Jahrhunderts: Malerei, Bildhauerei, Tapisserie. Hamburg: L. Schultheis, c. 1983.

05332. Formann, Wilhelm. "Hedwig Bleibtreu (1869-1959), Sechs Jahrzehnte am Burgtheater." In Oberosterreicher Lebensbilder zur Geschichte Oberosterreichs, edited by Alois Zauner and Harry Slapnicka, pp. 147-155. Linz: Oberösterreichischer Landesverlag, 1981.

05333. Monson, Karen. Alma Mahler, Muse to Genius: From Fin-de-siècle Vienna to Hollywood's Heyday. Boston: Houghton Mifflin, 1983.

05334. Muller, Agathe, ed. Vierzig jahre Club Hrotsvit: [1932-1972]. Lucerne: Club Hrotsvit/Kunst & Frau, Schweizerischer Verein fur Kulturelle Tatigkeit, 1975.

05335. Neue Galerie der Stadt Linz, Wolfgang-Gurlitt-Museum. Vier Frauen. Gisela Frank, Frida Schubert-Steingraeber, Juliane Stoklaska, Brigitte Johanna Wasmeyer. Linz: Neue Galerie der Stadt Linz, 1970.

05336. Wutzel, Otto. "Margret Bilger (1904-1979), Kunst und Mystik." In Oberösterreicher, Lebensbilder zur Geschichte Oberösterreichs, edited by Alois Zauner and Harry Slapnicka, pp. 224-236. Linz: Oberösterreichischer Landesverlag, 1981.

Also refer to #4709, 5240.

E. IBERIA

1. SURVEYS

"She [my daughter] prepares the bread at three, when the morning star shines. She never speaks. She is soft as wool, embroiders all kinds of fancy work and can cut a strong cord with her teeth."

Federico Garcia Lorca
Blood Wedding

05337. Coates, Mary Weld. "The Spanish Woman." Hispania 13 (May 1930): 213-217.

05338. "Women and the New Spain." Spain 5 (1 April 1940): 15-16.

2. POLITICAL

"A woman was carrying a child, a little girl scarcely two years old, whose lower jaw was missing. . . . Another woman crossed the street; the child in her arms was headless."

André Malraux
Man's Hope

05339. Bernard, Maria-Dolorès. "Le Franquisme et les femmes." In Les femmes et leur maîtres, edited by Maria-Antonietta Macciocchi, pp. 159-187. Paris: C. Bourgeois, 1979.

05340. Capmany, María Aurélia. La Dona i la II Republica. Barcelona: La Gaia Ciencia, 1977.

05341. DiFebo, Giuliana. Resistencia y movimiento de mujeres en España 1936-1976. Barcelona: ICARIA, 1979.

05342. Rita Lopes, Teresa. "Les femmes et le fascisme: hier, aujourd'hui." In Les femmes et leur maîtres, edited by Maria-Antonietta Macciocchi, pp. 189-200. Paris: C. Bourgeois, 1979.

05343. Salvacão, A. de Paes. Concordata: dois milhoes de filhos ilegítimos e duzentas mil pessoas sem direita ao amor. Lisbon: Agência Portuguesa de Revistas, 1974.

05344. Silva, Regina Tavares da. Feminismo em Protugal na voz de mulheres escritoras do inicío bo sec. XX. Lisbon: Commissao da Condícão feminina, 1982.

05345. Willis, Liz. Women in the Spanish Revolution. London: Solidarity, 1975.

Also refer to #5346, 6329.

3. RELIGION

"Women in church shouldn't look at any man but the priest --and him only because he wears skirts."

Bernarda Alba in
The House of Bernarda Alba,
Federico Garcia Lorca

05346. Lopes, Virgílio. Divórcio em Portugal. Lisbon: Editorial Aster, 1978.

4. SOCIAL

"Try to be affectionate with your wife, and if you notice her acting conceited or stubborn, caress her in a way that will cause her a bit of pain: a strong embrace, a bite followed by a soft kiss . . . enough to let her know that you are the macho, the one who gives the orders."

Federico Garcia Lorca

05347. Saez, Armand, "La fécondité en Espagne depuis le début de siècle." Population 34 (1979): 1007-1021.

Also refer to #5344.

5. CULTURAL

". . . breaking upon the silence of the house is heard the sweet and languorous sound of a harpsichord; it is Alisa, who is making music. Ere long upon the garden-paths . . . it is Alisa walking amid the trees."

Azorin
Clouds

a) Literature

(1) Drama

05348. Burton, Julianne. "The Greatest Punishment, Female and Male in Lorca's Tragedies." In Women in Hispanic Literature, Icons and Fallen Idols, edited by Beth Miller, pp. 259-279. Berkeley, Calif.: University of California Press, 1983.

05349. Busette, Cedric. "Mariana Pineda as Religious Martyr." Revista de estudios hispanicos 18 (January 1984): 115-121.

05350. Goldfaden, Bruce M. "'Boclas de Sangre' and 'La Donna del Alba.'" Hispania 44 (May 1961): 234-236.

05351. Knapp, Bettina L. "Federico García Lorca's The House of Bernarda Alba: A Hermaphroditic Matriarchate." Modern Drama 27 (September 1984): 382-394.

(2) Poetry

05352. Havard, Robert G. "Pedro Salinas and Courtly Love. The 'Amada' in La voz a ti debida: Woman, Muse and Symbol." Bulletin of Hispanic Studies 56 (April 1979): 123-144.

05353. Rogers, Timothy J. "Tensive Language and the Paradox of Love in Miguel Hernandez's El Rao que non cesa." Hispania 62 (December 1979): 647-654.

05354. Schyfter, Sara E. "The Rebellious Beloved in La voz a ti debida." Hispanofilia 68 (January 1980): 57-71.

(3) Prose

(a) Women in Literature

05355. Feeny, Thomas. "Maternal-paternal Attitudes in the Fiction of Ramon Perez de Ayala." Hispanofilia 62 (January 1978): 77-86.

05356. Levine, Linda Gould. "The Censored Sex. Woman as Author and Character in Franco's Spain." In Women in Hispanic Literature. Icons and Fallen Idols, edited by Beth Miller, pp. 289-315. Los Angeles: University of California Press, 1983.

05357. Ouimette, Victor. "Instincto etico y moralidad social en Aurora Roja." Hispanic Journal 6 (Fall 1984): 81-100.

(b) Women Novelists

05358. Chown, Linda E. "American Critics and Spanish Women Novelists, 1942-1980." Signs 9 (Autumn 1983): 4-28.

05359. Mayers, Eunice. "Estacion, ida y vuelta: Rosa Chacel's Apprenticeship Novel." Hispanic Journal 4 (Spring 1983): 77-84.

05360. Sayers, Raymond S. "Irene Lisboa as a Writer of Fiction." Hispania 45 (May 1962): 224-232.

Also refer to #5356.

b) Art

05361. Flint, Weston. "Wax Figures and Mannequins in Solana." Hispania 46 (December 1963): 740-747.

F. ITALY

1. POLITICAL

"The Italian public spirit and the tendency of our policy offer no preconceived opposition to the enfranchisement of women."

Benito Mussolini
12 May 1923

a) Marxism and Socialism

05362. Kertzer, David I. "The Liberation of Evelina Zaghi: The Life of an Italian Communist." Signs 8 (Autumn 1982): 45-67.

b) Legal

05363. Maroi, Fulvio. "Gli approti di lavoro della donna nel matrimonio secondo il progetto de Codice Civile Italiano." In Scritti Guiridica, 1: 23-49. Milan: A. Giuffre, 1956.

c) Fascism

05364. Detragiache, Denise. "Un aspect de la politique démographique de l'Italie fasciste: la répression de l'avortement." Mélanges de l'école française de Rome. Moyen age-temps moderne 92 (1980): 691-735.

05365. ________________. "Il fascismo femminile da San Sepolcro all'affare Matteotti (1919-1925). Storia contemporanea 14 (1983): 211-251.

05366. Macciocchi, Maria-Antonietta. "Sept thèses sur la sexualité féminine dans l'idéologie fascite." In Les femmes et leur maîtres, pp. 65-93. Paris: C. Bourgeois, 1979.

05367. Mariani, Laura. "Mogli e madri per la patria." In Esistere comme donna, pp. 199-210. Milan: Mazzotta, 1983.

05368. ____________. "Nel fascismo all'opposizione." In Esistere comme donna, pp. 211-222. Milan: Mazzotta, 1983.

05369. Ostenc, Michel. "La conception de la femme fasciste." Resorgimento (Belgium) 4, no. 3 (1983): 155-174.

d) Resistance

05370. Gadola, Giuliana Beltrami and Bruzzone, Anna Maria. "La Resistenza sulle spalle." In Esistere comme donna, pp. 223-236. Milan: Mazzotta, 1983.

Also refer to #5368.

2. ECONOMIC

I had been a "bizarre feminist of the type who spent her days making life pleasant for her companion, and not only for love, but as the woman of the house . . . all an unpaid, anonymous task . . . ."

Sibilla Aleramo

05371. Bravo, Anna. "Donne contadine e prima guerra mondial." Società et Storia 19 (1980): 843-862.

05372. Cornelio, Giuliana. "Sebben che siamo donne . . .--La contadina italiana dall'Unità alla Prima guerra mondiale." In Esistere comme donna, pp. 115-122. Milan: Mazzotta, 1983.

05373. Federici, Nora. "Evolution et caractéristique de travail féminin en Italie." Cahiers de l'Institut de Science Economique Appliquée 122 (February 1962): 43-76.

05374. Torcellan, Nanda. "Se otto ore vi sembran poche . . . La lavoratrice italiana dall'Unità alla Prima guerra mondiale." In Esistere comme donna, pp. 123-134. Milan: Mazzotta, 1983.

3. CULTURAL

"Sicilian parents of the well-to-do classes do not aim, as a rule, at the higher education of their daughters; they are apt to think that they have done all that is necessary to prepare a girl for life when they have seen to it that she is instructed in the use of a musical instrument and has attained a certain proficiency in some foreign language."

Cicely Hamilton
Modern Italy 1932

a) Education

05375. Standing, E. Mortimer. Maria Montessori: Her Life and Work. New York: New American Library, 1962.

05376. Stevens, Gwendolyn and Gardner, Sheldon. "A Tough, Intelligent Woman, Maria Montessori (1870-1952)." In The Women of Psychology 1: 105-115. Cambridge, Mass.: Schenkman Publishing Company, Inc., 1982.

b) Literature

05377. Melandri, Lea. "La spudoratezza. Vita e opere di Sibilla Aleramo." Memoria 8 no. 2 (1983): 5-23.

c) Art

05378. Weller, Simona. Il complesso di Michelangelo: ricerca sul contributo dato dalla donna all'arte italiana del Novecento. Pollenza: La nuova Foglio, 1976.

G. THE LOW COUNTRIES

1. POLITICAL

"One of the strongest forces for the prevention of war will be the combined influence of the women of all countries."

Aletta Jacobs

05379. Collin, Françoise. "No Man's Land: Réflexions sur l'esclavage volontaire des femmes." In Les femmes et leur maîtres, edited by Maria Antonietta Macciocchi, pp. 141-158. Paris. C. Bourgeois, 1979.

05380. Peemans-Poullet, Hedwige. "Crise et antiféminisme." In Les femmes et leur maîtres, edited by Maria Antonietta Macciocchi, pp. 103-139. Paris. C. Bourgeois, 1979.

Also refer to #5384.

2. SOCIAL

". . . when birth control becomes the subject of discussion in any country, when the women of any nation begin to make maternity a real boon instead of the burden it so often is, the same old objections are raised."

Aletta Jacobs

a) Demography

05381. Baudhuin, Fernand. "L'avenir de la population Belge." In Problems of Population. Report of the Second Genral Assembly of the International Union for the Scientific Investigation of Population Problems, edited by G.H.L.F. Pitt-Rivers, pp. 239-253. Port Washington, N.Y.: Kennikat Press, 1932.

05382. Methorst, H.W. "Research on Income, Natality and Infant Mortality in Holland." In Problems of Population. Report of the Proceedings of the Second General Assembly of the International Union for the Scientific Investigation of Population Problems, edited by G.H.L.F. Pitt-Rivers, pp. 137-141. Port Washington, N.Y.: Kennikat Press, 1932.

b) Family/Marriage

05383. Dupreel, M. Eugene. "Premiers Resultats de l'Enquête Belge sur les conditions de vie des familles nombreuses." In _Problems of Population. Report of the Proceedings of the Second General Assembly of the International Union for the Scientific Investigation of Population Problems_, edited by G.H.L.F. Pitt-Rivers, pp. 129-133. Port Washington, N.Y.: Kennikat Press, 1932.

05384. Schoen, Robert; Baj, John; and Woodrow, Karen. "Marriage and Divorce in Twentieth Century Belgian Cohorts." _Journal of Family History_ 9 (1984): 88-103.

Also refer to #4909, 4912, 5382.

c) Health/Medical

05385. Davis, Kathy. "Women as Patients: A Problem for Sex Differences Research." _Women's Studies International Forum_ 7 (1984): 211-217.

IX. TWENTIETH CENTURY, SINCE 1945

A. GENERAL

1. SURVEYS

"The so-called women question is a whole person question. . . . The creation of a new woman of necessity demands the creation of a new man. . . ."
Sheila Rowbotham

05386. Chaton, Jeanne H. "The UNESCO Long-Range Program for the Advancement of Women." Annals of the American Academy of Political and Social Science 375 (January 1968): 145-153.

05387. Hottel, Althea Kratz, ed. Women Around the World. Annals of the American Academy of Political and Social Science, no. 375. Philadelphia: The American Academy of Political and Social Science, 1968.

05388. Kuhn, Annette. "Das Geschlecht--eine historische Kategorie? Gedanken zu einem aus der neueren Geschichtswissenschaft verdrängten Begriff." In Frauen in der Geschichte IV, edited by Ilse Brehmer et al., pp. 29-50. Düsseldorf: Schwann, 1983.

05389. Roberts, Joan I. Beyond Intellectual Sexism: A New Woman, a New Reality. New York: David McKay, 1976.

05390. Steiner, Shari. The Female Factor: Women in Western Europe. Chicago: Intercultural Press, 1977.

05391. Van Hemeldonck, Marijke. "Changing European Structures in Order to Change Mentality." Memo From Belgium spec. no. (1979): 97-101.

05392. Women for Europe. European Women About Europe: Views and Ideas. Brussels: Ministry of Foreign Affairs, External Trade and Cooperation in Development, 1979.

2. POLITICAL

> "We are trying to create together a new society with totally new relationships where no human being ever looks to another to find her identity or to use another to acquire an identity. A society without cultural heroes or leaders."
>
> Statement by Collettivo Lotta Feminista, quoted by Bonnie Charles Bluh, in Woman to Woman

a) Generic

05393. Bashevkin, Sylvia. "Introduction: Women in Politics in Western Europe." Western European Politics 8 (October 1985): 1-4.

05394. Choisez, Anne. "Time for a European Foreing Policy." Memo from Belgium spec. no. (1979): 77-83.

05395. Enloe, Cynthia H. "Women in NATO Militaries: A Conference Report." Women's Studies International Forum 5 (1982): 329-334.

05396. Grote, Jacqueline de and Thys, Christiane. "Electoral Strategy and Tactics." Memo from Belgium spec. no. (1979): 41-47.

05397. Jennings, M. Kent and Farah, Barbara G. "Ideology, Gender and Political Action. A Cross-National Survey." British Journal of Political Science 10 (April 1980): 219-240.

05398. Krouwel-Vlam, Annie. "Women, Society and Politics." Memo from Belgium spec. no. (1979): 62-67.

05399. LaValle, Fausta Deshormes. "The 'Women's Press and Organizations': Department of the EEC Commission." Memo from Belgium spec. no. (1979): 48-52.

05400. Loeb-Mayer, Nicole. "The Political Parties of Europe: Prospects of Renewal." Memo from Belgium spec. no. (1979): 25-34.

05401. Maes, Nelly. "Europe: A Necessity, But . . ." Memo from Belgium spec. no. (1979): 53-58.

05402. Mayer, Lawrence C. and Smith, Roland E. "Feminism and Religiosity: Female Electoral Behavior in Western Europe." Western European Politics 8 (October 1985): 38-49.

05403. Norris, Peppa. "Women's Legislative Participation in Western Europe." Western European Politics 8 (October 1985): 90-101.

05404. Rabier, J.R. "Men and Women Citizens Facing Europe and the Proposed Election of the European Parliament." Memo from Belgium spec. no. (1979): 59-61.

b) Marxism and Socialism

05405. Lizin, Anne-Marie. "A Difficult Road to Travel: The European Outlook in the Union of Socialist Parties." Memo from Belgium spec. no. (1979): 35-40.

05406. Women's Liberation and the Workers' Revolution. London: International Communist League, 1977.

c) Legal

05407. L'Aborto nelle sentenze delle corti costizionali: USA, Austria, Francia e Repubblica federale tedesca. Milan: A. Guiffre, 1976.

05408. Ansay, Tugrul. "Problems of Migrant Workers in Europe." In Reform of Family Law in Europe: The Equality of the Spouses, Divorce, Illegitimate Children, edited by A.G. Chloros, pp. 323-338. Boston: Kluwer, 1978.

05409. Chloros, A.G., ed. The Reform of Family Law in Europe: The Equality of the Spouses, Divorce, Illegitimate Children. Boston: Kluwer, 1978.

05410. Le Divorce en droit international privé: allemand, français et suisse: actes du Colloque des 11-12 mai 1979. Paris: Librairie générale de droit et de jurisprudence, 1980.

05411. Dumusc, Daniel. Le Divorce par consentement mutuel dans les législations européenes. Geneva: Droz, 1980.

05412. Grave, Eugen Dietrich. "The Rights of Surviving Spouses Under Private International Law." American Journal of Comparative Law 15 (1966-1967): 164-194.

05413. Juenger, Friedrich. "Recognition of Foreign Divorces--British and American Perspectives." American Journal of Comparative Law 20 (Winter 1972): 1-37.

05414. Kellogg, Edmund H. and Stepan, Jan. "Legal Aspects of Sex Education." American Journal of Comparative Law 26 (Fall 1978): 573-608.

05415. Krause, Harry D. "Bastards Abroad--Foreign Approaches to Illegitimacy." American Journal of Comparative Law 15 (1966-1967): 726-751.

05416. Laroque, Pierre. "Women's Rights and Widows' Pensions." In Women Workers and Society. International Perspectives, pp. 79-88. Geneva: International Labor Office, 1976. Also in International Labour Review 106 (July 1972): 1-10.

05417. Neumayer, K.H. "General Introduction." In The Reform of Family Law in Europe: The Equality of the Spouses, Divorce, Illegitimate Children, edited by A.G. Chloros, pp. 1-17. Boston: Kluwer, 1978.

05418. Nielsen, Ruth. Equality Legislation in a Comparative Perspective: Towards State Feminism. Copenhagen: Women's Research Center in Social Science, 1983.

05419. Overbeck, Alfred E. von. "Private International Law." In The Reform of Family Law in Europe: The Equality of the Spouses, Divorce, Illegitimate Children, edited by A.G. Chloros, pp. 282-322. Boston: Kluwer, 1978.

05420. Philip, Allan. "Hague Draft Convention on Matrimonial Property." American Journal of Comparative Law 24 (Spring 1976): 307-318.

05421. Reese, Willis L.M. "The Hague (draft) Convention on the Recognition of Foreign Divorces. A Comment." American Journal of Comparative Law 14 (1965-1966): 692-700.

05422. Schwelb, Egon. "Marriage and Human Rights." American Journal of Comparative Law 12 (Summer 1963): 337-383.

05423. Steiner, J.M. "Sex Discrimination Under UK and EEC Law: Two Plus Four Equals One." International Comparative Law Quarterly 32 (1983): 399-423.

05424. Stepan, Jan and Kellogg, Edmund H. "The World's Laws on Contraceptives." American Journal of Comparative Law 22 (Fall 1974): 615-651.

05425. Tsai, Pi-song. Ehescheidung, Anerkennung ausländischer Ehescheidungen und Wiederverheiratung im internationalen Privatrecht: eine rechtsvergleichende Studie des schweizerischen, des deutschen, des englischen Rechtes und des Haager Abkommens uber Anerkennung der Scheidungen und der Trennungen vom 1. Juni 1970. Zurich: Schulthess, 1975.

Also refer to #4928, 5455, 5462, 5507, 5509.

d) Feminism

05426. Bradshaw, Jan, ed. The Women's Liberation Movement: Europe and North America. New York: Pergamon Press, 1982.

05427. Bunch, Charlotte; Carrillo, Roxana; and Guinee, Ied. "Feminist Perspectives: Report on the Feminist Perspectives Working Group to the Closing Plenary." *Women's Studies International Forum* 8 (1985): 243-247.

05428. Cixous, Hélène. "Entretien avec Françoise van Rossum-Guyon." *Revue des sciences humaines* n.s. 168 (October-December 1977): 479-493.

05429. Femmes pour l'Europe. *Europäerinnen sprechen über Europa*. Brussels: Ministerium fur Auswärtige Angelegenheiten, für Aussenhandel und Entwicklungszusammenarbeit, 1979.

05430. Flax, Jane. "The Family in Contemporary Feminist Thought: A Critical Review." In *The Family in Political Thought*, edited by Jean Bethke Elshtain, pp. 223-253. Amherst, Mass.: University of Massachusetts Press, 1982.

05431. Haas, Lu. "Love and Guilt: Normative Orientations and Their Implications for Accommodation and Resistance Among Women." *Women's Studies International Forum* 8 (1985): 335-342.

05432. Itzin, Catherine. "Margaret Thatcher is My Sister. Counseling on Divisions Between Women." *Women's Studies International Forum* 8 (1985): 73-83.

05433. Jelpke, Ulla, ed. *Das Höchste Glück auf Erden: Frauen in linken Organisationen*. Hamburg: Buntbuch-Verlag, 1981.

05434. Jenson, Jane. "Struggling for Identity: The Women's Movement and the State in Western Europe." *Western European Politics* 8 (October 1985): 5-18.

05435. Kelly, Joan. "The Doubled Vision of Feminist Theory." In *Women, History and Theory: The Essays of Joan Kelly*, pp. 51-64. Chicago: The University of Chicago Press, 1984.

05436. Lartéguy, Jean. *Lettre ouverte aux bonnes femmes*. Paris: Albin Michel, 1972.

05437. LeMoncheck, Linda. *Dehumanizing Women: Treating Persons as Sex Objects*. Totowa, N.J.: Rowman and Allanheld, 1985.

05438. Linnhoff, Ursula. *Die neue Frauenbewegung; USA-Europa seit 1968*. Cologne: Kiepenheuer & Witsch, 1974.

05439. Macciocchi, Maria-Antonietta. "Le post-féminisme." In *Les femmes et leur maîtres*, pp. I-XIII. Paris: C. Bourgeois, 1979.

05440. Morgan, Robin. "Planetary Feminism: The Politics of the 21st Century." In *Sisterhood is Global*, pp. 1-37. Garden City, N.Y.: Anchor Press, Doubleday, 1984.

05441. __________ ed. *Sisterhood is Global*. Garden City, N.Y.: Anchor Press, Doubleday, 1984.

05442. Rowland, Robyn. "Women Who Do and Women Who Don't, Join the Women's Movement." Women's Studies International Forum (1985): 249-254.

05443. Spender, Dale. "Modern Feminist Theorists: Reinventing Rebellion." In Feminist Theorists, pp. 366-380. New York: Pantheon Books, Random House, 1983.

05444. Young, Iris Marion. "Humanism, Gynocentrism and Feminist Politics." Women's Studies International Forum 8 (185) 173-183.

3. ECONOMIC

"One of the worst aspects of night work for women is that, whereas men on night work can often come home in the morning and go straight to bed, women start to do a 'bit of tidying or washing' and then found they only had time for a few hours' sleep."

Lynn Stevens as quoted in Sheila Rowbotham Woman's Consciousness, Man's World

a) Generic

05445. Gelber, Sylva M. "Society, Security, and Women: A Partisan's View." In Women Workers and Society International Perspectives, pp. 65-78. Geneva: International Labour Office, 1976. Also in International Labour Review 112 (July- December 1975): 431-444.

05446. Granrut, Claude de. "Professional Guidance and Training in the Countries Forming the European Community." Memo from Belgium spec. no. (1979): 166-172.

05447. Lavalle, Fausta Deshormes. "Le donne nella Comunità economica europea." In Esistere comme donna, pp. 277-279. Milan: Mazzotta, 1983.

05448. Scott, Hilda. Working Your Way to the Bottom: The Feminization of Poverty. London: Pandora Press, 1984.

05449. Vital, Jane. "The Saga of the Fund and Some Women." Memo from Belgium spec. no. (1979): 141-144.

Also refer to #5416.

b) Women's Employment

(1) Non-Specific

05450. "Appendix: Texts Concerning Women Workers Adopted by the 60th Session of the International Labor Conference, 4-25 June 1975." In _Women Workers and Society International Perspectives_, pp. 199-211. Geneva: International Labour Office, 1976.

05451. Davidson, Marilyn J. and Cooper, Cary L., eds. _Working Women An International Survey_. New York: John Wiley and Sons, 1984.

05452. Gubbels, Robert. "The Female Labor Force in Western Europe." In _Women in the World: A Comparative Study_, edited by Lynne B. Iglitzen and Ruth Ross, pp. 149-162. Santa Barbara, Calif.: Clio Books, 1976.

05453. International Labour Office, "Women in the Labor Force." _International Labour Review_ 77 (March 1958): 254-272.

05454. Kottis, Athena Petraki. "Female-Male Earnings Differentials in the Founder Countries of the European Economic Community. An Economic Investigation." _Economist_ 132 (1984): 204-223.

05455. Landau, C.E. "Recent Legislation and Case Law in the EEC on Sex Equality in Employment." _International Labour Review_ 123 (1984): 53-70.

05456. Marzolf, Marion. "View from Europe." In _Up from the Footnote: A History of Women Journalists_, pp. 266-297. New York: Hastings House, 1977.

05457. Morgan, Florence. "Equal Treatment for Men and Women--Thanks to Europe?" _Memo from Belgium_ spec. no. (1979): 114-116.

05458. NATO Symposium on Women and the World of Work. _Women and the World of Work_. Brussels, 1982.

05459. Seguret, Marie Claire. "Women and Working Conditions: Prospects for Improvement?" _International Labour Review_ 122 (May-June 1983): 295-311.

05460. United Nations. Economic Commission for Europe. _The Economic Role of Women in the EEC Region_. New York: United Nations, 1980.

(2) Equal Pay Issue

05461. Antoine, Bernadette. "Equal Pay: A Right to be Enforced." _Memo from Belgium_ spec. no. (1979): 102-105.

05462. Morgenstern, Felice. "Women Workers and the Courts." In Women Workers and Society International Perspectives, pp. 51-63. Geneva: International Labour Office, 1976. Also in International Labour Review 112 (July-December 1975): 15-27.

05463. Pettman, Barrie O., ed. Equal Pay for Women: Progress and Problems in Seven Countries. Washington: Hemisphere, 1977.

05464. Sullerot, Evelyne. "Equality of Remuneration for Men and Women in the Member States of the EEC." In Women Workers and Socity International Perspectives, pp. 89-110. Geneva: International Labour Office, 1976. Also in International Labour Review 112 (July-December 1975): 87-108.

Also refer to #5455.

c) Trade Unions and Organizations

05465. Brunfaut, Emilienne. "Women Workers in European Trade Unions." Memo from Belgium spec. no. (1979): 173-182.

05466. Cook, Alice H.; Lorwin, Val R.; and Daniels, Arlene Kaplan, eds. Women and Trade Unions in Eleven Industrialized Countries. Philadelphia: Temple University Press, 1984.

4. RELIGION

"The Lord is not my shepherd. I shall want."
May Sarton
Mrs. Stevens Hears the Mermaids Singing, 1965

a) Generic

05657. Bussman, Magdalene. "Anliegen und Ansatz feministischer Theologie." In Die Frau im Urchristentum, edited by Gerhard Dautzenberg, et al., pp. 339-358. Freiburg: Herder, 1983.

05468. Goldenberg, Naomi R. Changing of the Gods: Feminism and the End of Traditional Religions. Boston: Beacon Press, 1979.

05469. Starhawk. "Ethics and Justice in Goddess Religion." In The Politics of Women's Spirituality, edited by Charlene Spretnak, pp. 415-422. Garden City, N.Y.: Doubleday and Company, Inc., Anchor Press, 1982.

Also refer to #5402.

b) Christianity

05470. Carmody, Denise Lardner and Carmody, John Tully. "Contemporary Feminist Theology." In Christianity: An Introduction, pp. 217-233. Belmont, Calif.: Wadsworth Publishing Co., 1983.

05471. Carr, Anne. "Is a Christian Feminist Theology Possible?" Theological Studies 43 (June 1982): 279-297.

05472. Hallett, Garth L. "Contraception and Prescriptive Infallibility." Theological Studies 43 (December 1982): 629-650.

05473. Rinser, Luise. Zölibat und Frau. Würzburg: Echter-Verlag, 1967.

05474. World Council of Churches' Conference. The Community of Women and Men in the Church. Philadelphia: Fortress Press, 1983.

c) Women as Priests

05475. Carroll, Elizabeth. "Women in the Life of the Church." In Women Priests, A Catholic Commentary on the Vatican Declaration, edited by Leonard Swidler and Arlene Swidler, pp. 61-64. New York: Paulist Press, 1977.

05476. Cooke, Bernard and Turner, Pauline. "Women in the Sacramental Priesthood." In Women Priests, A Catholic Commentary on the Vatican Declaration, edited by Leonard Swidler and Arlene Swidler, pp. 249-250. New York: Paulist Press, 1977.

05477. Irvin, Dorothy. "Omni Analogia Claudet." In Women Priests, A Catholic Commentary on the Vatican Declaration, edited by Leonard Swidler and Arlene Swidler, pp. 271-277. New York: Paulist Press, 1977.

05478. Kirkman, Maggie and Grieve, Norma. "Women, Power and Ordination: A Psychological Interpretation of Objections to the Ordination of Women to the Priesthood." Women's Studies International Forum 7 (1984): 487-494.

05479. LeBlanc, Paul J. "Substantive Changes in the Sacraments?" In Women Priests, A Catholic Commentary on the Vatican Declaration, edited by Leonard Swidler and Arlene Swidler, pp. 216-220. New York: Paulist Press, 1977.

05480. Morrisey, Francis G. "The Juridical Significance of the Declaration." In Women Priests, A Catholic Commentary on the Vatican Declaration, edited by Leonard Swidler and Arlene Swidler, pp. 19-24. New York: Paulist Press, 1977.

05481. Prusak, Bernard P. "Use the Other Door; Stand at the End of the Line." In Women Priests, A Catholic Commentary on the Vatican Declaration, edited by Leonard Swidler and Arlene Swidler, pp. 81-84. New York: Paulist Press, 1977.

05482. Stuhlmueller, Carroll. "Internal Indecisiveness." In Women Priests, A Catholic Commentary on the Vatican Declaration, edited by Leonard Swidler and Arlene Swidler, pp. 23-24. New York: Paulist Press, 1977.

05483. Swidler, Leonard. "Introduction: Roma Locuta, Causa Finita?" In Women Priests, A Catholic Commentary on the Vatican Declaration, edited by Leonard Swidler and Arlene Swidler, pp. 3-18. New York: Paulist Press, 1977.

05484. Wright, Helen M. "Diversity of Roles and Solidarity in Christ." In Women Priests, A Catholic Commentary on the Vatican Declaration, edited by Leonard Swidler and Arlene Swidler, pp. 244-248. New York: Paulist Press, 1977.

d) Witchcraft

05485. Goldenberg, Naomi R. "Feminist Witchcraft: Controlling Our Own Inner Space." In The Politics of Women's Spirituality, edited by Charlene Spretnak, pp. 213-218. Garden City, N.Y.: Doubleday and Company, Inc., Anchor Press, 1982.

05486. Monter, E. William. "The Historiography of European Witchcraft." The Journal of Interdisciplinary History 2 (Spring 1972): 435-451.

5. SOCIAL

> "An inescapable conclusion from the many recent studies of women's experiences in trying to reconcile the claims of marriage, motherhood, and work is the existence of a traditional and firmly rooted double standard of occupational morality."
>
> Law Commission, 1980

a) Generic

05487. Banissoni, Maria. Bibliografia sulla condizione femminile: articoli, saggi, ricerche psicologico-sociali. Rome: Bulzoni, 1978.

05488. Basham, Richard. "Machismo." Frontiers 1 (Spring 1976): 127-143.

05489. Bastin, Max. "Loisirs, culture et promotion feminine." In La femme et la société contemporaine, pp. 127-151. Brussels: Les Editions vie ouvrière, 1967.

05490. Hobson, Dorothy. "Housewives: Isolation as Oppression." In Women Take Issue: Aspects of Women's Subordination, pp. 79-95. London: Hutchinson, 1978.

05491. Lowe, Marian and Hubbard, Ruth. "Social Effects of Some Contemporary Myths about Women." In Women's Nature: Rationalizations of Inequality, pp. 1-8. New York: Pergamon Press, 1983.

05492. McRobbie, Angela. "Working Class Girls and the Culture of Femininity." In Women Take Issue: Aspects of Women's Subordination, pp. 96-108. London: Hutchinson, 1978.

05493. Padrun, Ruth. "Immigrant Women--Our Sister." Memo from Belgium spec. no. (1979): 189-194.

b) Demography

05494. Bourguignon, Odile. "La famille et la mort des enfants." Social Science Information 23 (1984): 325-340.

05495. Britton, Malcolm. "Birth Intervals: Recent Changes in Birth Intervals." Population Trends 18 (Winter 1979): 8-16.

05496. Calot, Gérard and Thompson, Jean. "The Recent Up-Turn in Fertility in England and Wales, France and West Germany." Population Trends 24 (Summer 1981): 8-9.

05497. Davis, Norman. "Population Trends: A European Overview." Population Trends 12 (Summer 1978): 10-12.

05498. Festy, Patrick. The Demographic Prospects of Southern European Countries and Ireland. Strasbourg: Council of Europe, 1983.

05499. Gray, Ronald H. "Biological Factors Other than Nutrition and Lactation Which May Influence Natural Fertility: A Review." In Natural Fertility, edited by Henri Leridon and Jane Menken, pp. 217-251. Liège: Ordina Editions, 1979.

05500. Weatherall, J.A.C. "Infant Mortality: International Difference." Population Trends 1 (Autumn 1975): 9-12.

Also refer to #4926, 4928.

c) Family

05501. Bolognese-Leuchtenmuller, Birgit. "Zwischen Anforderung, Anpassung und Alternativen--Uberlegungen zur gegenwartigen Rollenverteilung in der Familie." In Das ewige Klischee, zum Rollenbild und Selbstverstandnis bei Mannern und Frauen, pp. 132-154. Vienna: Hermann Bohlaus, 1981.

05502. Cooper, David Graham. The Death of the Family. New York: Pantheon Books, 1971.

05503. Fogarty, Michael and Rodgers, Barbara. "Family-Policy--International Perspectives." In Families in Britain, pp. 3-55. Boston: Routledge and Kegan Paul, 1983.

05504. Newton, Niles: "Birth Rituals in Cross-Cultural Perspective: Some Practical Applications." In Being Female: Reproduction, Power and Change, edited by Dana Raphael, pp. 37-41. The Hague: Mouton, 1975.

05505. Ong, Bie Nio. "Understanding Child Abuse: Ideologies of Motherhood." Women's Studies International Forum 8 (1985): 411-419.

05506. Pollock, Scarlet. "Fathers' Rights, Women's Losses." Women's Studies International Forum 8 (1985): 593-599.

Also refer to #5408, 5409, 5415, 5417, 5419, 5430, 5494, 5500.

d) Marriage

05507. Autorino Stanzione, Gabriella. Divorzio e tutela della persona: l'esperanza francese italiana e tedesca. Naples: Edizioni scientifiche italiane, 1981.

05508. Béjin, André. "The Extra-marital Union Today." In Western Sexuality, edited by Philippe Aries and Andre Bejin, pp. 158-167. New York: Blackwell, 1985.

05509. International Research Group on Divorce. Le divorce en Europe occidentale. 2 vols. Paris: Documentation francaise, c. 1975-1978.

Also refer to #4929, 5409-5413, 5416, 5420-5422, 5425.

e) Sex Life and Morals

05510. Jackson, Margaret. "Sexology and the Universalization of Male Sexuality (from Ellis to Kinsey, and Masters and Johnson)." In The Sexuality Papers, edited by Lal Coveney et al., pp. 69-84. London: Hutchinson, 1984.

Also refer to #4932, 5414, 5431.

f) Health/Medical

(1) Birth Control/Abortion

05511. Ethical Aspects of Abortion: Some European Views. London: International Planned Parenthood Federation, Europe Region, 1978.

05512. L'Interruption volontaire de grossesse dans l'Europe des Neuf: journée d'étude du 23 octobre 1979. Paris: Presses universitaires de France, 1981.

05513. Mies, Maria. "'Why Do We Need All This?' A Call Against Genetic Engineering and Reproductive Technology." Women's Studies International Forum 8 (1985): 553-560.

Also refer to #5407, 5424, 5472.

(2) Women in Medicine

05514. Abrams, Frederick R. "Rejoinder to 'Medicine as Patriarchal Religion.'" Journal of Medicine and Philosophy 9 (August 1984): 313-318.

05515. ________________. "Response to Professor Rawlinson." Journal of Medicine and Philosophy 9 (August 1984): 325-326.

05516. Rawlinson, Mary C. "Women, Medicine and Religion: A Response to Raymond and Abrams." Journal of Medicine and Philosophy 9 (May 1984): 321-325.

05517. Raymond, Janice G. "Letter to the Editors: A Response to Abrams." Journal of Medicine and Philosophy 9 (May 1984): 319-320.

05518. ________________. "Medicine as Patriarchal Religion." Journal of Medicine and Philosophy 7 (May 1982): 197-216.

6. CULTURAL

"How, as women, can we go to the theatre without lending complicity to the sadism directed against women, or being asked to assume, in the patriarchal family structure that the theatre reproduces ad infinitum, the position of victim."

Hélène Cixous

a) Education

05519. Boeykins, Lily. "Education for Girls in EEC Countries." Memo from Belgium spec. no. (1979): 147-165.

05520. Bree, Germaine. "Women's Voices in Cross-Cultural Exchange." Contemporary French Civilization 5 (Spring 1981): 403-410.

05521. Diem-Wille, Gertraud. "Ausbildung und weibliche Indentitat. Exemplarisch dargestellt in der Ausbildung zur Gruppendynamik-Trainerin." In Das ewige Klischee, zum Rollenbild un Selbstverständnis bei Männern und Frauen, pp. 253-275. Vienna: Hermann Böhlaus, 1981.

05522. Heyniger, Line Robillard. "The International Conference on Research and Teaching Related to Women." Women's Studies International Forum 8 (1985): 157-160.

05523. Koussoula-Pantazopoulou, Eleutheria. "The Requirements of Physical Training and Sport in Female Education." Prospects 9 (1979): 458-462.

05524. Saunders, Fay E. "Sex Roles and the Schools." Prospects 5 (1975): 362-371.

05525. Schmuck, Patricia. "Women as Educators in the Western World: A Summary of the Issues." Women's Studies International Forum 8 (1985): 395-397.

Also refer to #5414.

b) Literature

05526. Ezergailis, Inta. Women Writers: The Divided Self: Analysis of Novels by Christa Wolf, Ingeborg Bachmann, Doris Lessing and Others. Bonn: Bouvier Verlag Herbert Grundmann, 1982.

05527. Schemen, Naomi. "Individualism and the Objects of Psychology." In Discovering Reality, Feminist Perspectives on Epistemology, Metaphysics, Methodology, and Philosophy of Science., edited by Sandra Harding and Merrill B. Hintikka, pp. 225-244. Boston: D. Reidel Publishing Co., 1983.

05528. Showalter, Elaine. "Towards a Feminist Poetics." In Women Writing and Writing About Women, edited by Mary Jacobus, pp. 22-41. New York: Barnes and Noble, 1979.

c) Art

(1) Women in Art

05529. Boersman, Dee. "A Report on the United Nations Commission on the Status of Women and the Mass Media." Journal of the University Film Association 26 (1974): 3-4.

Also refer to #4933-4936.

(2) Women Artists

05530. Arrandon, Monique. "La conquête esthétique des mondes nouvaux." Europe 427-428 (November-December 1964): 167-170.

05531. Lippard, Lucy R. "The Pains and Pleasures of Rebirth: European and American Women's Body Art." In From the Center: Feminist Essays on Women's Art, pp. 121-138. New York: H.P. Dutton, 1976.

05532. Lippard, Lucy R. "Sweeping Exchanges: The Contribution of Feminism to the Art of the 1970s." Art Journal 40 (1980): 362-365.

Also refer to #4937-4941.

B. BRITAIN

1. SURVEYS

"The home may be the centre of woman's life, but it should not be the boundary."
Dame Patricie

05533. General Household Survey Unit. "The Changing Circumstances of Women." Population Trends 13 (Autumn 1978): 17-22.

05534. Morgan, Elaine. Women and Society. London: British Broadcasting Corporation, 1975.

05535. Ross, Ruth. "Tradition and the Role of Women in Great Britain." In Women in the World: A Comparative Perspective edited by Lynne B. Iglitzin and Ruth Ross, pp. 163-174. Santa Barbara, Calif.: Clio Books, 1976.

05536. Tansey, Jean, "Ireland and the UN Decade for Women." Women's Studies International Forum 8 (1985): 145-146.

Also refer to #4942.

2. POLITICAL

"When times get bad, people turn to a hard line because it seems to offer protection. As Britain gets poorer and more violent and its future more frightening, . . . feminists are starting to go for conformity and get a thrill from 'leadership.'"
Amanda Sebestyen

a) Generic

05537. Beazley, Christine and Knight, Jill. To Be, or Not to Be? London: Conservative Political Centre, 1974.

05538. Brown, Rosemary. Going Places. Women in the Conservative Party. London: Conservative Political Centre, 1980.

05539. Ireland, Women's Representative Committee. Progress Report on the Implementation of the Recommendations in the Report of the Commission on the Status of Women: A Report. Dublin: Stationery Office, 1976.

05540. Keyworth, Florence,. "Invisible Struggles: The Politics of Ageing." In Feminism, Culture and Politics, edited by Rosalind Brunt and Caroline Rowan, pp. 131-142. London: Wishart, 1982.

05541. Labour Party. Women in Society: Second Class Citizens Today, But What About Tomorrow?: An Analysis. London: Labour Party, 1975.

05542. Randall, Vicky. Women and Politics. London: Macmillan Press, Ltd., 1982.

05543. Rasmussen, Jorgen, S. "Women's Role in Contemporary British Politics: Impediments to Parliamentary Candidature." Parliamentary Affairs 36 (Summer 1983): 300-315.

05544. Smyth, Ailbhe. "Women and Power in Ireland: Problems, Progress and Practice." Women's Studies International Forum 8 (1985): 255-262.

05545. ___________. Women's Rights in Ireland. Dublin: Ward River Press, 1983.

05546. Vallance, Elizabeth. "Women Candidates in the 1983 General Election." Parliamentary Affairs 37 (Summer 1984): 301-309.

Also refer to #4944-4946, 4948.

b) Marxism and Socialism

05547. Davis, Tricia. "'What Kind of Woman is She?' Women and Communist Party Politics, 1941-1955." In Feminism, Culture and Politics, edited by Rosalind Brunt and Caroline Rowan, pp. 85-108. London: Wishart, 1982.

05548. Fighting for Women's Rights. London: Relocrest Ltd., 1979.

05549. McIntosh, Mary. "The Family in Socialist-Feminist Politics." In Feminism, Culture and Politics, edited by Rosalind Brunt and Caroline Rowan, pp. 109-130. London: Wishart, 1982.

05550. Richardson, Joanna. Women, Sexism, and Socialism. London: National Organization of Labour Students, 1977.

05551. Rowbotham, Sheila. "The Women's Movement and Organizing for Socialism." In Beyond the Fragments: Feminism and the Making of Socialism, pp. 21-155. Boston: Alyson Pub., 1981.

05552. ________________;Segal, Lynne; and Wainwright, Hilary. Beyond the Fragments: Feminism and the Making of Socialism. Boston: Alyson Pub., 1981.

05553. Segal, Lynne. "A Local Experience." In Beyond the Fragments: Feminism and the Making of Socialism, pp. 157-209. Boston, Alyson Pub., 1981.

Also refer to #5614, 5646, 5811.

c) Legal

05554. Atkins, Susan and Hoggett, Brenda. Women and the Law. New York: Blackwell, 1984.

05555. Baker, Barrington, et al. The Matrimonial Jurisdiction of Registrars: The Exercise of the Matrimonial Jurisdiction by Registrars in England and Wales. Oxford: Centre for Socio-Legal Studies, Social Science Research Council, 1977.

05556. Brayshaw, A.J. Public Policy and Family Life. London: Policy Studies Institute, 1980.

05557. Bromley, Peter Mann and Passingham, Bernard. Divorce Law Reform in Northern Ireland: Matrimonial Causes (N.I.) Order 1978: The Text of Addresses Delivered on 18th February 1978 to a Conference Held at Queen's University, Belfast. Belfast: Northern Ireland Legal Quarterly Inc., 1978.

05558. Brown, George Gordon. Brown on Divorce. London: Shaw and Sons, 1974.

05559. ____________________. The New Divorce Laws Consolidated. London: Shaw and Sons, 1970.

05560. Camp, Georges. Die Reform des englischen Scheidungsrechts. Zurich: Juris-Verlag, 1974.

05561. Cartwright, Ann and Waite, Marjorie. General Practitioners and Abortion: Evidence to the Committee on the Working of the Abortion Act. London: Journal of the Royal College of General Practitioners, 1972.

05562. Carvell, Ian George. Divorce Law and Practice. Guildford: College of Law, 1978.

05563. Chiswell, P.G. Divorce, Maintenance and Legal Aid: Recent Changes of Law and Practice. Guildford: The College of Law, 1977.

05564. Dew, Edward Roderick. Divorce Law and Practice; Refresher Lecture Delivered by E.R. Dew, 1966. London: Law Society, 1967.

05565. Dickens, Bernard Morris. Abortion and the Law. London: MacGibbon & Kee, 1966.

05566. Forbes, Thayne. Divorce Law. 2nd edition. London: MacDonald & Evans, 1972.

05567. Friedman, Gil. How to Conduct Your Own Divorce in England and Wales, and a Guide to the Divorce Laws. 2nd edition. London: Wildwood House, 1978.

05568. Great Britain, Committee on the Working of the Abortion Act. The Abortion Act Inquiry: Summary of Conclusions, Some of Its Findings, List of Recommendations from Report of the Committee on the Working of the Abortion Act. St. Albans: Abortion Law Reform Association, 1974.

05569. Great Britain, Committee on the Working of the Abortion Act. Report of the Committee on the Working of the Abortion Act. London: H.M.S.O., 1974.

05570. Great Britain, Parliament, House of Commons, Select Committee on the Abortion (Amendment) Bill. Special Reports and Minutes of the Select Committee on the Abortion (Amendment) Bill, Session 1974-1975, Together with the Proceedings of the Committee. London: H.M.S.O., 1976.

05571. A Guide to the Abortion Act 1967. London: Abortion Law Reform Association, 1968.

05572. Hickey, Owen. Law and Laxity. London: Times Newspapers, 1970.

05573. Hindell, Keith and Simms, Madeleine. Abortion Law Reformed. London: Own, 1971.

05574. Hussain, S. Jaffer. Marriaeg [sic] Breakdown and Divorce Law Reform in Contemporary Society: A Comparative Study of U.S.A., U.K., and India. New Delhi: Concept, 1983.

05575. Hutter, Bridget and Williams, Gillian, ed. Controlling Women, the Normal and the Deviant. London: Croom Helm, 1981.

05576. International Labour Office. "Proposed Charter to Promote Equality." Social and Labour Bulletin (September 1982): 411.

05577. Irvine, James. The Law of Divorce. London: Church Literature Association, 1978.

05578. Jenkins, Alice. Law for the Rich. London: V. Gollancz, 1964.

05579. Latey, William et al. The Law and Practice in Divorce and Matrimonial Causes. 15th ed. London: Longman, 1973.

05580. Lee, Bong Ho. Divorce Law Reform in England. London: Owen, 1974.

05581. Legge, Jerome S., Jr. Abortion Policy: Consequences for Maternal and Infant Health. Albany: State University of New York Press, 1985.

05582. Lowe, Robert. Marriage, Divorce and Cohabitation. Guildford: The College of Law, 1978.

05583. McGuinness, J. Louise and O'Connor, Gabrielle J. Divorce and Family Law in a Nutshell: With Test Questions. London: Sweet & Maxwell, 1971.

05584. Marsh, David and Chambers, Joanna. Abortion Politics. London: Junction Books, 1981.

05585. Medical Defence Union. Memoranda on the Abortion Act 1967, and the Abortion Regulations 1968. London: Medical Defense Union, 1968.

05586. Meehan, Elizabeth. "Equal Opportunity Policies: Some Implications for Women of Contrasts Between Enforcement Bodies in Britain and the USA." In Women's Welfare, Women's Rights, edited by Jane Lewis, pp. 170-192. London: Croom Helm, 1983.

05587. Murch, Mervyn. Justice and Welfare in Divorce. London: Sweet and Maxwell, 1980.

05588. Owen, Aron. The New Divorce Law: A Note for Jewish Marriage Education Counsellors. London: Jewish Marriage Education Council, 1970.

05589. Passingham, Bernard. Divorce Law and Practice. London: Law Society, 1969.

05590. ________________. The Divorce Reform Act 1969. London: Butterworths, 1970.

05591. Ramos Bossini, Francisco. La indisolubilidad matrimonial en el Derecho anglicano. Granada: Instituto de Historia del Derecho, Universidad, 1977.

05592. Robinson, John Arthur Thomas. Abortion: Beyond Law Reform, Lecture Delivered by the Bishop of Woolwich on October 22nd 1966 to a Meeting of the Abortion Law Reform Association. London: Abortion Law Reform Association, 1966.

05593. Smart, Carol. The Ties That Bind: Law, Marriage, and the Reproduction of Patriarchal Relations. Boston: Routledge & Kegan Paul, 1984.

05594. Tarnesby, Herman Peter. Abortion Explained: A Sunday Times Guide to Abortion Within the Law. London: Sphere Books, 1969.

05595. Thomson, Joseph M. "English Law." In The Reform of Family Law in Europe: The Equality of the Spouses, Divorce, Illegitimate Children, edited by A.G. Chloros, pp. 43-71. Boston: Kluwer, 1978.

05596. Tolstoy, Dimitry. The Law and Practice of Divorce and Matrimonial Causes, Including Proceedings in Magistrates' Courts. 5th edition. London: Sweet & Maxwell, 1963.

05597. Veitch, Edward and Tracey, R.R.S. "Abortion in the Common Law World." American Journal of Comparative Law 22 (Fall 1974): 652-696.

05598. Virdi, P.K. The Grounds for Divorce in Hindu and English Law: A Study in Comparative Law. Delhi: Motilal Banarsidass, 1972.

05599. Wasoff, Frances. "Legal Protection from Wifebeating: The Processing of Domestic Assaults by Scottish Persecutors and Criminal Courts." International Journal of the Sociology of Law 10 (1982): 187-204.

05600. A Woman's Right to Choose Organization. A Woman's Right to Choose Action Guide. London: Abortion Law Reform Association, 1975.

Also refer to #5758, 5764-5766, 5768, 5774, 5776-5783, 5790.

d) Criminal

05601. Carlen, Pat. Women's Imprisonment: A Study in Social Control. London: Routledge and Kegan Paul, 1983.

05602. Griffiths, A. "Some Battered Women in Wales: An Interactionist View of Their Legal Problem." Family Law 11 (1981): 25-29.

05603. Howells, Kevin; Shaw, Fiona; Greasley, Mark; Robertson, Jane; Gloster, Denise; and Metcalfe, Nicholas. "Perceptions of Rape in a British Sample: Effects of Relationship, Victim Status, Sex, and Attitudes to Women." British Journal of Social Psychology 23 (February 1984): 35-40.

05604. Maidment, Susan. "Civil v. Criminal: The Use of Legal Remedies in Response to Domestic Violence in England and Wales." Victimology 8 (1983): 172-187.

Also refer to #5758.

e) Feminism

05605. Ashworth, Georgina. "Changing the World: Time, Space and Perceptions." Women's Studies International Forum 8 (1985): 153-156.

05606. Barrett, Michèle. "Feminism and the Definition of Cultural Politics." In Feminism, Culture and Politics, edited by Rosalind Brunt and Caroline Rowan, pp. 37-58. London: Wishart, 1982.

05607. Feminist Anthology Collective, ed. *No Turning Back, Writings from the Women's Liberation Movement 1975-1980*. London: Women's Press, 1981.

05608. McCafferty, Nell. "Ireland(s): Coping with the Womb and the Border." In *Sisterhood is Global*, edited by Robin Morgan, pp. 347-352. Garden City, N.Y.: Anchor Press, Doubleday, 1984.

05609. Richards, Janet Radcliffe. *The Sceptical Feminist: A Philosophical Enquiry*. Boston: Routledge and Kegan Paul, 1982.

05610. Rowbotham, Sheila. *Dreams and Dilemmas: Collected Writings*. London: Virago, 1983.

05611. Rowe, Marsha, ed. *The Spare Rib Reader*. New York: Penguin Books, 1982.

05612. Sebestyen, Amanda. "Britain: The Politics of Survival." In *Sisterhood is Global*, edited by Robin Morgan, pp. 94-99. Garden City, N.Y.: Anchor Press, Doubleday, 1984.

05613. Thompson, Jane L. *Learning Liberation: Women's Response to Men's Education*. London: Croom Helm, 1983.

05614. Wainwright, Hilary. "Moving Beyond Fragments" in *Beyond the Fragments: Feminism and the Making of Socialism*, edited by Sheila Rowbotham et al., pp. 211-253. Boston: Alyson Pub., 1981.

05615. Winship, Janice. "A Woman's World: Woman: An Ideology of Femininity." In *Women Take Issue: Aspects of Women's Subordination*, pp. 133-154. London: Hutchinson, 1978.

05616. *Women's Liberation in Britain and Ireland*. Belfast: British and Irish Communist Organisation, 1974.

Also refer to #4952-4954, 4956, 4957, 4961, 4962.

f) Political Roles

(1) Mrs. Thatcher

05617. Burch, Martin. "Mrs. Thatcher's Approach to Leadership in Government: 1979 - June 1983." *Parliamentary Affairs* 36 (Autumn 1983): 399-416.

05618. Junor, Penny. *Margaret Thatcher: Wife, Mother, Politician*. London: Sidgwich and Jackson, 1983.

05619. Lewis, Russell. *Margaret Thatcher: A Personal and Political Biography*. Boston: Routledge and Kegan Paul, 1984.

(2) Others

05620. Longford, Elizabeth. _The Queen: The Life of Elizabeth II._ New York: Knopf, 1983.

05621. Toole, M. _Mrs. Bessie Braddock, MP._ London: R. Hale, 1957.

05622. Warwick, Christopher. _Princess Margaret._ London: Weidenfeld and Nicolson, 1983.

g) Irish Nationalism

05623. Deutsch, Richard. _Mairead Corrigan, Betty Williams._ Woodbury, N.Y.: Barron's, 1977.

h) Family Allowances and Policy

05624. Bottomley, Peter. "Family Policy Targets." In _Family Matters; Perspectives on the Family and Social Policy_, edited by Alfred White Franklin, pp. 175-179. New York: Pergamon Press, 1983.

05625. Bradshaw, Jonathan. "Tax and Benefit Policy for the Family." In _Family Matters; Perspectives on the Family and Social Policy_, edited by Alfred White Franklin, pp. 87-94. New York: Pergamon Press, 1983.

05626. Cooper, Joan D. "A Family Service?" In _Family Matters; Perspectives on the Family and Social Policy_, edited by Alfred White Franklin, pp. 105-112. New York: Pergamon Press, 1983.

05627. Decks, Elsa. "A Family Perspective in Policies for the Under Fives?" In _Family Matters; Perspectives on the Family and Social Policy_, edited by Alfred White Franklin, pp. 125-136. New York: Pergamon Press, 1983.

05628. Dowling, Sue. "Question of Inter-Agency Collaboration for Family Health." In _Family Matters; Perspectives on the Family and Social Policy_, edited by Alfred White Franklin, pp. 113-123. New York: Pergamon Press, 1983.

05629. Franklin, Alfred White, ed. _Family Matters; Perspectives on the Family and Social Policy._ New York: Pergamon Press, 1983.

05630. Goody, Esther. "Family Policy in a Multi-Culture Society." In _Family Matters; Perspectives on the Family and Social Policy_, edited by Alfred White Franklin, pp. 43-48. New York: Pergamon Press, 1983.

05631. Hutchence, Pamela. "Housing Problems of the Inner City Family: The Practical Outcome of Governmental Policy." In Family Matters; Perspectives on the Family and Social Policy, edited by Alfred White Franklin, pp. 63-69. New York: Pergamon Press, 1983.

05632. Karn, Valene and Henderson, Jeff. "Housing Atypical Households: Understanding the Practices of Local Government Housing Departments." In Family Matters; Perspectives on the Family and Social Policy, edited by Alfred White Franklin, pp. 71-86. New York: Pergamon Press, 1983.

05633. Land, Hilary. "Who Still Cares for the Family? Recent Developments in Income Maintenance, Taxation and Family Law." In Women's Welfare, Women's Rights, edited by Jane Lewis, 64-85. London: Croom Helm, 1983.

05634. Lister, Ruth. "Income Maintenance for Families with Children." In Families in Britain, pp. 432-446. Boston: Routledge and Kegan Paul, 1983.

05635. Parker, Roy. "Family and Social Policy: An Overview." In Families in Britain, pp. 357-371. Boston: Routledge and Kegan Paul, 1983.

05636. Rimmer, Lesley. "Changing Family Patterns: Some Implications for Policy." In Family Matters; Perspectives on the Family and Social Policy, edited by Alfred White Franklin, pp. 11-18. New York: Pergamon Press, 1983.

05637. Wicks, Malcolm. "Does Britain Need a Family Policy?" In Family Matters; Perspectives on the Family and Social Policy, edited by Alfred White Franklin, pp. 165-173. New York: Pergamon Press, 1983.

05638. ______________. "A Family Cause? Voluntary Bodies, Pressure Groups and Politics." In Families in Britain, pp. 459-472. Boston: Routledge & Kegan Paul, 1983.

3. ECONOMIC

> "Since the early days of industrialization women have constituted both a significant proportion of the country's labour force and a main source of cheap labour."
>
> Law Commission, 1980

a) Generic

05639. Barr, N.A. "The Taxation of Married Women's Income-I." British Tax Review 5 (1980): 398-412.

05640. _________. "The Taxation of Married Women's Income-II." British Tax Review 6 (1980); 478-490.

05641. Breen, Richard. "Status Attainment or Job Attainment? The Effects of Sex and Class on Youth Unemployment." British Journal of Sociology 35 (September 1984): 363-386.

05642. Duckworth, Peter. Matrimonial Property and Finance. London: Oyez, 1980.

05643. International Labour Office. "Women Pay Cost of a Caring Society." Social and Labour Bulletin (June 1982): 270-271.

05644. Jackson, Joseph. Matrimonial Finance and Taxation. London: Butterworths, 1972.

05645. Kroll, Una. Flesh of My Flesh. London: Darton, Longman and Todd, 1975.

05646. Marshall, Kate. Real Freedom: Women's Liberation and Socialism. London: Junius, 1982.

05647. Matrimonial Finance and Costs. Guildford: The College of Law, 1981.

05648. Moss, Peter. "Work and the Family." In Family Matters; Perspectives on the Family and Social Policy, edited by Alfred White Franklin, pp. 95-104. New York: Pergamon Press, 1983.

05649. Seear, Nancy. "Families and Unemployment." In Families in Britain, pp. 382-415. Boston: Routledge and Kegan Paul, 1983.

05650. Wacjman, Judy. "Work and the Family: Who Gets 'The Best of Both Worlds'?" In Women in Society, edited by the Cambridge Women's Studies Group, pp. 9-24. London: Virago Press, 1981.

05651. Wilson, Harriett. "Families in Poverty." In Families in Britain, pp. 252-262. Boston: Routledge and Kegan Paul, 1983.

Also refer to #4975, 5586.

b) Women's Employment

(1) Non-specific

05652. All Work and No Pay: Women, Housework and the Wages Due. Bristol: The Power of Women Collective and The Falling Wall Press, 1975.

05653. Attwood, Margaret and Hatton, Frances. "'Getting On.' Gender Differences in Career Development: A Case Study in the Hairdressing Industry." In *Gender, Class and Work*, edited by Eva Gamarnikow et al., pp. 115-130. London: Heinemann, 1983.

05654. *Employment Policy in the United Kingdom and the United States: A Comparison of Efficiency and Equity*. London: John Martin, 1980.

05655. Frank, Peter. "Women's Work in the Yorkshire Inshore Fishing Industry." *Oral History* 4 (1976): 57-72.

05656. Great Britain. *Women and Work: Review*. London: Her Majesty's Stationery Office, 1975.

05657. Great Britain. House of Commons. *The Employment of Women*. London: Her Majesty's Stationery Office, 1973.

05658. Hadjifotiu, Nathalie. *Women and Harassment at Work*. London: Pluto Press, 1983.

05659. Lockwood, Betty and Knowles, Wilf. "Women at Work in Great Britain." In *Working Women: An International Survey*, edited by Marilyn J. Davidson and Cary L. Cooper, pp. 3-38.. New York: John Wiley and Sons, 1984.

05660. Lonsdale, Susan. *Work and Inequality*. London: Longmans, 1985.

05661. Murdoch, Henry. "Women at Work in Ireland." In *Working Women An International Survey*, edited by Marilyn J. Davidson and Cary L. Cooper, pp. 39-62. New York: John Wiley and Sons, 1984.

05662. Pollert, Anna. "Women, Gender Relations and Wage Labour." In *Gender, Class and Work*, edited by Eva Gamarnikow et al., pp. 96-114. London: Heinemann, 1983.

05663. Read, Sue. *Sexual Harassment at Work*. Feltham, Middlesex: Mamlyn Paperbacks, 1982.

05664. Siltanen, Janet. "A Commentary on Theories of Female Wage Labour." In *Women in Society*, edited by the Cambridge Women's Studies Group, pp. 25-40. London: Virago Press, 1981.

05665. Taylor, J. "Hidden Female Labour Reserves." *Regional Studies* 2 (November 1968): 221-231.

05666. Wacjman, Judy. *Women in Control: Dilemmas of a Workers' Co-operative*. New York: St. Martin's Press, 1983.

05667. Walby, Sylvia. "Patriarchal Structures: The Case of Unemployment." In Gender, Class and Work, edited by Eva Gamarnikow et al., pp. 149-166. London: Heinemann, 1983.

05668. Williams, Gwyn A. "Women Workers in Wales, 1968-82." Welsh Historical Review 11 (December 1983): 530-548.

Also refer to #4977, 4980, 5641, 5704, 5705, 5731, 5748, 5749, 5775.

(2) Equal Pay Issue

05669. Chiplan, B. and Sloane, P.J. "Equal Pay in Great Britain." In Equal Pay for Women: Progress and Problems in Seven Countries, edited by Barrie O. Pettman, pp. 9-34. Washington: Hemisphere, 1977.

05670. ______________. "Male-Female Earning Difference: A Further Analysis." British Journal of Industrial Relations 14 (March 1976): 77-81.

05671. Meehan, Elizabeth. Women's Rights at Work: Campaigns and Policy in Britain and the United States. London: Macmillan, 1985.

05672. "Unequal Pay: Britain, France." Women at Work 2 (1979): 9-10.

Also refer to #5645, 5660.

c) Trade Unions and Organizations

05673. Charles, Nicola. "Trade Union Censorship." Women's Studies International Forum 6 (1983): 525-533.

05674. Cunnison, Sheila. "Participation in Local Union Organization. School Meals Staff: A Case Study." In Gender, Class and Work, edited by Eva Gamarnikow et al., pp. 77-95. London: Heinemann, 1983.

05675. Heritage, John. "Feminisation and Unionization: A Case Study from Banking." In Gender, Class and Work, edited by Eva Gamarnikow et al., pp. 131-148. London: Heinemann, 1983.

05676. King, Deborah Schuster. "Ireland." In Women and Trade Unions in Eleven Industrialized Countries, edited by Alice H. Cook, Val R. Lorwin, and Arlene Daniels Kaplan, pp. 162-183. Philadelphia: Temple University Press, 1984.

05677. Lorwin, Val R. and Boston, Sarah. "Great Britain." In Women and Trade Union in Eleven Industrialized Countries, edited by Alice H. Cook, Val R. Lorwin, and Arlene Daniels Kaplan, pp. 140-161. Philadelphia: Temple University Press, 1984.

4. RELIGION

"It is the creative potential itself in human beings that is the image of God."
Mary Daly
Beyond God the Father

05678. Church of England, Commission on the Christian Doctrine of Marriage. *Marriage, Divorce and the Church: The Report of a Commission Appointed by the Archbishop of Canterbury to Prepare a Statement on the Christian Doctrine of Marriage*. London: S.P.C.K., 1972.

05679. Church of England Moral Welfare Council. *Marriage, Divorce, and the Royal Commission: A Study Outline of the Report of the Royal Commission on Marriage and Divorce, 1951-1955*. Westminster: Published for the Church of England Moral Welfare Council by the Church Information Board, 1956.

05680. Fisher, Geoffrey Francis. *The Church and Marriage: Evidence Presented to the Royal Commission on Marriage and Divorce*. Westminster: Church Information Board, 1954.

05681. Maitland, Sara. *A Map of the New Country. Women and Christianity*. Boston: Routledge and Kegan Paul, 1983.

05682. O'Donovan, Oliver. *Principles in the Public Realm: The Dilemma of Christian Moral Witness*. Oxford: Clarendon Press, 1984.

05683. Porter, Mary Cornelia and Venning, Corey. "Catholicism and Women's Role in Italy and Ireland." In *Women in the World: A Comparative Study*, edited by Lynne B. Iglitzin and Ruth Ross, pp. 81-103. Santa Barbara, Ca.: Clio Books, 1976.

Also refer to #4988, 4989, 5761, 5786.

5. SOCIAL

"The passage to parenthood is instant, ferocious and irrefutable; it comes on like being winded . . . This is not to say that it is love alone. The new world inspires rage and fear as well. The exhaustion of the first few weeks is hallucinatory."
Marina Warner
"New-born Mother"
The Guardian, 1977

a) Generic

05684. Britten, Nicky and Heath, Anthony. "Women, Men and Social Class." In *Gender, Class and Work*, edited by Eva Gamarnikow et al., pp. 46-60. London: Heinemann, 1983.

05685. Finch, Janet and Groves, Dulcie. "By Women for Women: Caring for the Frail Elderly." Women's Studies International Forum 5 (1982): 427-438.

05686. Murcott, Anne. "Women's Place: Cookbooks' Images of Technique and Technology in the British Kitchen." Women's Studies International Forum 6 (1983): 33-39.

05687. Musgrave, Beatrice and Menell, Zoe, eds. Change and Choice, Women and Middle Age. London: Peter Owen, 1980.

Also refer to #4995, 5575.

b) Demography

05688. Acheson, Roy and Sanderson, Colin. "Strokes: Social Class and Geography." Population Trends 12 (Summer 1978): 13-17.

05689. Bone, Margaret. "Recent Trends in Sterilisation." Population Trends 13 (Autumn 1978): 13-16.

05690. Britton, Malcolm. "Recent Trends in Births." Population Trends 20 (Summer 1980): 4-8.

05691. Brown, Audrey. "Estimating Fertility from Household Composition Data in the Census: The 'Own-Child' Approach." Population Trends 29 (Autumn 1982): 15-19.

05692. Bulusu, Lak and Alderson, Michael. "Suicides 1950-1982." Population Trends 35 (Spring 1984): 11-17.

05693. Bytheway, William R. "The Variation with Age of Age Differences in Marriage." Journal of Marriage and the Family 43 (November 1981): 923-927.

05694. Campbell, Rona; Davies, Isobel Macdonald; and Macfarlane, Alison. "Perinatal Mortality and Place of Delivery." Population Trends 28 (Summer 1982): 9-12.

05695. Chilvers, Clair. "Cancer Mortality: The Regional Pattern." Population Trends 12 (Summer 1978): 4-9.

05696. Corsini, Carlo A. "Is Fertility Reducing-Effect of Lactation Really Substantial?" In Natural Fertility, edited by Henri Leridon and Jane Menken, pp. 195-215. Liege: Ordina Editions, 1979.

05697. Davies, Isobel Macdonald. "Perinatal and Infant Deaths: Social and Biological Factors." Population Trends 19 (Spring 1980): 19-21.

05698. Hellier, Jackie. "Perinatal Mortality 1950 and 1973." Population Trends 10 (Winter 1977): 13-15.

05699. Kiernan, Kathleen E. and Diamond, I. "The Age at Which Childbearing Starts--A Longitudinal Study." *Population Studies* 37 (November 1983): 363-380.

05700. King, J.R. "Immigrant Fertility Trends and Population Growth in Leeds." *Environment and Planning* 6 (September-October 1974): 509-546.

05701. Lambert, P. "Perinatal Mortality: Social and Environmental Factors." *Population Trends* 4 (Summer 1976): 4-8.

05702. Leete, Richard. "Adoption Trends and Illegitimate Births, 1951-1977." *Population Trends* 14 (Winter 1978): 9-16.

05703. ______________. "Changing Marital Composition." *Population Trends* 10 (Winter 1977): 16-21.

05704. McDowall, Michael. "Measuring Women's Occupational Mortality." *Population Trends* 34 (Winter 1983): 25-29.

05705. ________________; Goldblatt, Peter O.; and Fox, John. "Employment during Pregnancy and Infant Mortality." *Population Trends* 26 (Winter 1981): 12-15.

05706. Macfarlane, Alison. "Child Deaths from Accidents 2: Place of Accident." *Population Trends* 15 (Spring 1979): 10-15.

05707. __________________ and Fox, John. "Child Deaths from Accidents and Violence." *Population Trends* 12 (Summer 1978): 22-27.

05708. Macfarlane, Alison and Thew, Pat. "Births: The Weekly Cycle." *Population Trends* 13 (Autumn 1978): 23-24.

05709. Pearce, David. "Births and Family Formation: Current Patterns and Increasing Childlessness in Early Marriage." *Population Trends* 1 (Autumn 1975): 6-8.

05710. _____________ and Britton, Malcolm. "The Decline of Births: Some Socioeconomic Aspects." *Population Trends* 7 (Spring 1977): 9-14.

05711. Population Statistics Division. "Recent Population Growth and the Effect of the Decline in Births." *Population Trends* 27 (Spring 1982): 18-24.

05712. Thompson, Jean. "The Age at Which Childbearing Starts." *Population Trends* 21 (Autumn 1980): 10-13.

05713. ______________. "Fertility and Abortion Inside and Outside Marriage." *Population Trends* 5 (Autumn 1976): 3-8.

05714. Werner, Barry. "Fertility and Family Background: From the O.P.C.S. Longitudinal Study." *Population Trends* 35 (Spring 1984): 5-10.

05715. Werner, Barry. "Recent Trends in Illegitimate Births and Extramarital Conception." Population Trends 30 (Winter 1982): 9-15.

Also refer to #4997-4999, 5739, 5767, 5772, 5773, 5791

c) Family

(1) Bibliographies

05716. "Bibliography." In Families in Britain, pp. 500-538. Boston: Routledge and Kegan Paul, 1983.

(2) Non-specific

05717. Aldgate, Jane. "Foster and Adoptive Families." In Families in Britain, pp. 303-321. Boston: Routledge and Kegan Paul, 1983.

05718. Ballard, Roger. "South Asian Families." In Families in Britain, pp. 179-204. Boston: Routledge and Kegan Paul, 1983.

05719. Barrow, Jocelyn. "West Indian Families: An Insider's Perspective." In Families in Britain, pp. 220-232. Boston: Routledge and Kegan Paul, 1983.

05720. Bliss, Kathleen; Bessey, Gordon S.: Tait, Marjorie; and, Jones, R. Huws. "Forum on Family Relationships." In The Family. British National Conference on Social Welfare, pp. 30-47. London: National Council of Social Service, 1953.

05721. Bowlby, John. "Problem Families, Neglectful Parents, the Broken Home and Illegitimacy." In The Family. British National Conference on Social Welfare, pp. 22-29. London: National Council of Social Service, 1953.

05722. Brown, Muriel. "Deprivation, Disadvantage and the Family in Britain." In Family Matters; Perspectives on the Family and Social Policy, edited by Alfred White Franklin, pp. 49-56. New York: Pergamon Press, 1983.

05723. Burgoyne, Jacqueline and Clark, David. "Re-Constituted Families." In Families in Britain, pp. 286-302. Boston: Routledge and Kegan Paul, 1983.

05724. Collins, Michael and Strelitz, Ziona. "Families and Leisure." In Families in Britain, pp. 418-431. Boston: Routledge and Kegan Paul, 1983.

05725. Dominion, Jack. "Families in Divorce." In Families in Britain, pp. 263-285. Boston: Routledge and Kegan Paul, 1983.

05726. Driver, Geoffrey. "West Indian Families: An Anthropological Perspective." In Families in Britain, pp. 205-219. Boston: Routledge and Kegan Paul, 1983.

05727. Eekelaar, John M. Family Security and Family Breakdown. Harmondsworth: Penguin, 1971.

05728. Eversley, David and Bonnerja, Lucy. "Social Change and Indicators of Diversity." In Families in Britain, pp. 75-94. Boston: Routledge and Kegan Paul, 1983.

05729. Families in Britain. Boston: Routledge and Kegan Paul, 1983.

05730. Franklin, Alfred White. "The Family as Patient." In Family Matters; Perspectives on the Family and Social Policy, pp. 25-31. New York: Pergamon Press, 1983.

05731. Gowler, D. and Legge, K. "Dual-Worker Families." In Families in Britain, pp. 138-158. Boston: Routledge and Kegan Paul, 1983.

05732. Great Britain. Committee on One-Parent Families. Report of the Committee on One-Parent Families: Presented to Parliament by the Secretary of State for Social Service by Command of Her Majesty July 1974. London: H.M.S.O., 1974.

05733. Jackson, Brian. "Single-Parent Families." In Families in Britain, pp. 159-177. Boston: Routledge and Kegan Paul, 1983.

05734. Johnson, Daphne. "Families and Educational Institutions." In Families in Britain, pp. 372-386. Boston: Routledge and Kegan Paul, 1983.

05735. Jones, E.M. Gresford. "A Biblical View of the Family and Some Assessment of the Strength and Weakness of the Family Today in Light of the Bible." In The Family. British National Conference on Social Welfare, pp. 84-90. London: National Council of Social Service, 1953.

05736. Jordan, Bill. "Families and Personal Social Services." In Families in Britain, pp. 447-458. Boston: Routledge and Kegan Paul, 1983.

05737. Leach, Edmund. "Are There Alternatives to the Family?" In Family Matters; Perspectives on the Family and Social Policy, edited by Alfred White Franklin, pp. 3-10. New York: Pergamon Press, 1983.

05738. Leete, Richard. "New Directions in Family Life." Population Trends 15 (Spring 1979): 4-9.

05739. ____________. "One-Parent Families: Numbers and Characteristics." Population Trends 13 (Autumn 1978): 4-9.

05740. McCulloch, Andrew. "Alternative Households." In *Families in Britain*, pp. 322-337. Boston: Routledge and Kegan Paul, 1983.

05741. Nissell, Muriel. "Families and Social Change since the Second World War." In *Families in Britain*, pp. 95-119. Boston: Routledge and Kegan Paul, 1983.

05742. Oakley, Ann. "Conventional Families." In *Families in Britain*, pp. 123-137. Boston: Routledge and Kegan Paul, 1983.

05743. Oakley, Robin. "Cypriot Families." In *Families in Britain*, pp. 233-251. Boston: Routledge and Kegan Paul, 1983.

05744. Rapoport, Robert and Rapoport, Rhona. "British Families in Transition." In *Families in Britain*, pp. 475-499. Boston: Routledge and Kegan Paul, 1983.

05745. Strathern, Marilyn. *Kinship at the Core: An Anthropology of Elmdon, a Village in North-west Essex in the Nineteen-sixties*. Cambridge: Cambridge University Press, 1981.

05746. Titmuss, Richard M. "The Family as Social Institution." In *The Family. British National Conference on Social Welfare*, pp. 8-20. London: National Council of Social Service, 1953.

05747. Venvell, Don. "The Primary School and the Family." In *Family Matters; Perspectives on the Family and Social Policy*, edited by Alfred White Franklin, pp. 137-143. New York: Pergamon Press, 1983.

05748. Vickers, Geoffrey and Wynne, N. "The Family and Work." In *The Family. British National Conference on Social Welfare*, pp. 48-57. London: National Council of Social Service, 1953.

05749. Westwood, Sallie. *All Day, Every Day, Factory and Family in the Making of Women's Lives*. Champaign, Ill.: University of Illinois, 1985.

05750. Wolkind, Stephen; Kruk, Susan; and, Hall, Fae. "The Family Research Unit's Study of Women from Broken Homes: What Conclusions Should We Draw?" In *Family Matters; Perspectives on the Family and Social Policy*, edited by Alfred White Franklin, pp. 33-42. New York: Pergamon Press, 1983.

Also refer to #4975, 4999, 5549, 5556, 5583, 5595, 5624-5638, 5648-5651.

(3) Childhood

05751. Freeman, Michael. "Child-Rearing: Parental Autonomy and State Intervention." In _Family Matters; Perspectives on the Family and Social Policy_, edited by Alfred White Franklin, pp. 145-164. New York: Pergamon Press, 1983.

05752. Osborn, A.F.; Butler, N.R.; and Morris, A.C. _The Social Life of Britain's Five-Year-Olds. A Report of the Child Health and Education Study_. Boston: Routledge and Kegan Paul, 1984.

05753. Pringle, Mia Kellmer. "The Needs of Children and their Implications for Parental and Professional Care." In _Family Matters; Perspectives on the Family and Social Policy_, edited by Alfred White Franklin, pp. 19-24. New York: Pergamon Press, 1983.

05754. Willmott, Phyllis, and Willmott, Peter. "Children and Family Diversity." In _Families in Britain_, pp. 338-354. Boston: Routledge and Kegan Paul, 1983.

Also refer to #5395, 5697, 5702, 5705-5707, 5715, 5769, 5785.

(4) Motherhood

05755. Antonis, Barbie. "Motherhood and Mothering." In _Women in Society_, edited by the Cambridge Women's Studies Group, pp. 55-74. London: Virago Press, 1981.

Also refer to #5809.

(5) Battered Wives

05756. Binney, Val. "Domestic Violence: Battered Women in Britain in the 1970s." In _Women in Society_, edited by the Cambridge Women's Studies Group, pp. 115-126. London: Virago Press, 1981.

05757. Dobash, R. Emerson and Dobash, Russell P. _Wife Abuse, the Women's Movement and the State: A Cross-Cultural Comparison of Britain, the United States and Scandinavia_. Stirling, Scotland: International Sociological Association, 1982.

05758. Owens, David. "Battered Wives: Some Social and Legal Problems." _British Journal of Law and Society_ 2 (1975): 201-211.

d) Marriage

(1) Non-specific

05759. Fennell, Nuala. Irish Marriage--How Are You! Dublin: Mercier Press, 1974.

05760. Harrison, G.A. and Palmer, C.D. "Husband-Wife Similarities Among Oxfordshire Villagers." Man 16 (March 1981): 130-134.

05761. Haskey, John. "Marriages--Trends in Church, Chapel and Civil Ceremonies." Population Trends 22 (Winter 1980): 19-24.

05762. ___________. "Social Class Patterns of Marriage." Population Trends 34 (Winter 1983): 12-19.

05763. ___________. "Widowhood, Widowerhood and Remarriage." Population Trends 30 (Winter 1982): 15-20.

Also refer to #4997, 5002, 5555, 5557-5560, 5562-5564, 5566, 5567, 5574, 5577, 5579, 5580, 5582, 5583, 5587-5591, 5593, 5595, 5596, 5598, 5647, 5678-5680, 5725.

(2) Divorce

05764. Chiswell, P.G. Marriage Breakdown. Guildford: College of Law, 1979.

05765. Consumer's Association. Getting a Divorce. Edited by Edith Rudinger. London: The Association, 1976.

05766. Gordon, Augusta. Turn Off the Peas, I'm Leaving. London: Tom Stacey Ltd., 1972.

05767. Great Britain. Office of Population Censuses and Surveys. Marriage and Divorce Statistics, 1974. London: H.M. Stationery Office, 1974.

05768. Hart, Nicky. When Marriage Ends: A Study in Status Passage. London: Tavistock Publications, 1976.

05769. Haskey, John. "Children of Divorcing Couples." Population Trends 31 (Spring 1983): 20-26.

05770. ___________. "The Proportion of Marriages Ending in Divorce." Population Trends (Spring 1982): 4-7.

05771. Itzin, Catherine, ed. Splitting Up: Single Parent Liberation. London: Virago, 1980.

05772. Leete, Richard. "Marriage and Divorce: Trends and Patterns." Population Trends 3 (Spring 1976): 3-8.

05773. Leete, Richard and Anthony, Susan. "Divorce and Remarriage. A Record Linkage Study." Population Trends 16 (Summer 1969): 5-11.

05774. Macy, Christopher, ed. Marriage--and Divorce; Based on a Series of Articles which First Appeared in "The Guardian." London: Pemberton, 1969.

05775. Martin, Anna. Working Women and Divorce/The Women's Co-operative Guild, The Married Working Woman. New York: Garland, 1980.

05576. Morris, David Elwyn. The End of Marriage. London: Cassell, 1971.

05777. Mortlock, Bill. The Inside of Divorce: A Critical Examination of the System. London: Constable, 1972.

05778. Murphy, M.J. "Marital Breakdown and Socio-Economic Status: A Reappraisal of the Evidence from Recent British Sources." British Journal of Sociology 36 (March 1985): 81-93.

05779. Rakusen, Michael L. and Hunt, D. Peter. Distribution of Matrimonial Assets on Divorce. Boston: Butterworths, 1979.

05780. Rees, David Perronet. Rees's Divorce Handbook. Part 2 of Rees's Probate and Divorce Handbook, by B.P. Tickle and L.T.L. Carne. 3rd ed. London: Butterworths, 1963.

05781. Sanctuary, Gerald and Whitehead, Constance. Divorce -- And After. London: Gollancz, 1970.

05782. Search, Gay. Surviving Divorce: A Handbook for Men. London: Elm Tree Books, 1983.

05783. Sell, Kenneth D. and Sell, Betty H. Divorce in the United States, Canada, and Great Britain: A Guide to Information Sources. Detroit: Gale Research Co., 1978.

05784. Thornes, Barbara and Collard, Jean. Who Divorces? Boston: Routledge and Kegan Paul, 1979.

05785. Wilkinson, Martin. Children and Divorce. Oxford: Blackwell, 1981.

05786. Winnett, Arthur Robert. The Church and Divorce. London: Mowbray, 1968.

Also refer to #5557-5560, 5562-5564, 5566, 5567, 5574, 5577, 5579, 5580, 5582, 5583, 5587-5591, 5593, 5595, 5596, 5598, 5642, 5644, 5678-5680, 5703, 5709, 5713, 5715.

e) Sex Life and Morals

05787. Brunt, Rosalind. "'An Immense Verbosity': Permissive Sexual Advice in the 1970's." In _Feminism, Culture and Politics_, edited by Rosalind Brunt and Caroline Rowan, pp. 143-170. London: Wishart, 1982.

05788. Coveney, Lal; Kay, Leslie; and Mahony, Pat. "Theory into Practice: Sexual Liberation or Social Control? (_Forum_ Magazine 1968-81)." In _The Sexuality Papers_, edited by Lal Coveney et al., pp. 85-103. London: Hutchinson, 1984.

05789. Scheper-Hughes, Nancy. "From Anxiety to Analysis: Rethinking Irish Sexuality and Sex Roles." _Women's Studies_ 10 (1983): 147-160.

Also refer to #3998, 5814.

f) Health/Medical

(1) Birth Control/Abortion

05790. _The Abortion Act 1967: Proceedings of a Symposium Held by the Medical Protection Society, in Collaboration with the Royal College of General Practitioners, at the Royal College of Obstetricians and Gynaecologists, London, 7 February 1969_. London: Pitman Medical, 1969.

05791. _Abortion Statistics_. Office of Population Censuses and Surveys. London: H.M.S.O., 1980.

05792. Aitken-Swan, Jean. _Fertility Control and the Medical Profession_. London: Croom Helm, 1977.

05793. Benn, Melissa and Richardson, Ruth. "Uneasy Freedom: Women's Experiences of Contraception." _Women's Studies International Forum_ 7 (1984): 219-225.

05794. Christopher, Elphis. _Sexuality and Birth Control in Social and Community Work_. London: Temple Smith, 1980.

05795. Ferris, Paul. _The Nameless: Abortion in Britain Today_. Harmondsworth: Penguin, 1967.

05796. Gardner, Reginald Frank Robert. _Abortion, the Personal Dilemma: A Christian Gynaecologiest Examines the Medical, Social and Spiritual Issues_. Exeter: Paternoster Press, 1972.

05797. Greenwood, Victoria and Young, Jock. _Abortion on Demand_. London: Pluto Press, 1976.

05798. Langford, Christopher. "Attitudes to Abortion in Britain: Trends and Changes." _Population Trends_ 22 (Winter 1980): 11-13.

05799. Litchfield, Michael and Kentish, Susan. Babies for Burning. London: Serpentine Press, Ltd., 1974.

05800. Munoz-Perez, F. "Douze ans d'avortement légal en Angleterre-Galles." Population 36 (1981): 1105-1138.

05801. Peel, John. "Contraception and the Medical Profession." Population Studies 18 (November 1964): 133-146.

05802. Potts, Malcolm; Diggory, Peter; and Peel, John. Abortion. New York: Cambridge University Press, 1977.

05803. Society for the Protection of the Unborn Child, Dunedin Branch. A Statement Issued by the Society for the Protection of the Unborn Child. Dunedin: Society for the Protection of the Unborn Child, 1973.

05804. Williams, Jean Morton, and Hindell, Keith. Abortion and Contraception: A Study of Patients' Attitudes. London: P.E.P., 1972.

Also refer to #5011, 5561, 5565, 5568-5571, 5573, 5578, 5581, 5584, 5585, 5592, 5594, 5597, 5600, 5713.

(2) Women in Medicine

05805. Great Britain. National Council of Nurses of the United Kingdom. A Reform of Nursing Education: First Report of a Special Committee on Nurse Education. London: Royal College of Nursing, 1964.

05806. Leeson, Joyce and Gray, Judith. Women and Medicine. London: Tavistock Publications, 1978.

05807. Medical Women's Federation. Careers Symposium, Women in Medicine 1979, What is Our Future? [London]: The Federation, [1979?].

(3) Women and Health

05808. Blaxter, Mildred and Paterson, Elizabeth. Mothers and Daughters. A Three Generational Study of Health Attitudes and Behavior. London: Heinemann Educational Books, 1982.

05809. Breen, Dana. "The Mother and the Hospital." In Tearing the Veil, Essays on Femininity, edited by Susan Lipshitz, pp. 15-33. London: Routledge and Kegan Paul, 1978.

05810. Laws, Sophie. "The Sexual Politics of Pre-Menstrual Tension." Women's Studies International Forum 6 (1983): 19-31.

05811. Oakley, Ann. "Women and Health Policy." In Women's Welfare, Women's Rights, edited by Jane Lewis, pp. 103-129. London: Croom Helm, 1983.

05812. Orbach, Susie and Eichenbaum, Luise. _What do Women Want?_ London: Michael Joseph, 1983.

Also refer to #5009, 5575, 5688, 5694, 5695, 5730.

(4) Psychology

05813. Coward, Rosalind. "Sexual Politics and Psychoanalysis: Some Notes on Their Relation." In _Feminism, Culture and Politics_, edited by Rosalind Brunt and Caroline Rowan, pp. 171-188. London: Wishart, 1982.

Also refer to #5750.

6. CULTURAL

"It is unusual too that in natural science anyone, still less a woman, should receive an honorary degree without any degree already from any university."

Oxford University, 1968
degree to Miriam Rothschild

a) Education

05814. David, Miriam E. "The New Right, Sex Education and Social Policy: Towards a New Moral Economy in Britain and the USA." In _Women's Rights, Women's Welfare_, edited by Jane Lewis, pp. 193-218. London: Croom Helm, 1983.

05815. Great Britain, Department of Education and Science. _Curricular Difference for Boys and Girls_. London: Her Majesty's Stationery Office, 1975.

05816. London, University of, Institute of Education. _Women in Higher Education_. London, 1975.

05817. Mahony, Pat. "'Silence is a Woman's Glory': The Sexist Content of Education." _Women's Studies International Forum_ 5 (1982): 463-473.

05818. Newson, John. _The Education of Girls_. London: Faber and Faber, 1948.

05819. Weiner, Gaby, ed. _Just a Bunch of Girls: Feminist Approaches to Schooling_. Philadelphia: Open University Press, 1985.

Also refer to #5009, 5016, 5734, 5747, 5805.

b) Literature

(1) Drama

05820. Dunderdale, Sue. "The Status of Women in the British Theatre." Drama, The Quarterly Theatre Review 152 (1984): 9-11.

05821. Forsas-Scot, Helena. "Life and Love and Serjeant Musgrave: An Approach to Arden's Play." Modern Drama 26 (March 1983): 1-11.

05822. Hall, Linda. "Sex and Class in John Osborne's Look Back in Anger." Women's Studies International Forum 7 (1984): 505-510.

05823. Wandor, Michelene. "'The Fifth Column' Feminism and the Theatre." Drama, The Quarterly Review 152 (1984): 5-9.

(2) Prose

(a) Women in Literature

05824. Ruthven, K.K. Feminist Literary Studies: An Introduction. New York: Cambridge University Press, 1984.

05825. Suleiman, Susan Rubin. "(Re) writing the Body: The Politics and Poetics of Female Eroticism." Poetics Today 6 (1985): 43-65.

Also refer to #5615.

(b) Novelists

[1] Ivy Compton-Burnett

05826. Baldanza, Frank. Ivy Compton-Burnett. New York: Twayne Publishers, 1964.

05827. Burkhart, Charles. I. Compton-Burnett. London: Gollancz, 1965.

05828. Greig, Cicely. Ivy Compton-Burnett: A Memoir. London: Garnstone Press, 1972.

05829. Huff, Kathy M. "Ivy Compton-Burnett: A Bibliography." Bulletin of Bibliography 35 (July-September 1978): 132-142.

05830. Johnson, Pamela Hansford. I. Compton-Burnett. London: Longmans, 1951.

05831. Spurling, Hilary. Ivy When Young: The Early Life of I. Compton-Burnett 1884-1919. London: Gollancz, 1974.

05832. Spurling, Hilary. Ivy: The Life of I. Compton-Burnett. New York: Knopf, 1984.

[2] Doris Lessing

05833. Christ, Carol P. and Spretnak, Charlene. "Images of Spiritual Power in Women's Fiction." In The Politics of Women's Spirituality, edted by Charlene Spretnak, pp. 327-343. Garden City, N.Y.: Doubleday and Company, Inc., Anchor Press, 1982.

05834. Cohen, Mary. "Out of the Chaos, a New Kind of Strength: Doris Lessing's The Golden Notebook." In The Authority of Experience, edited by Arlyn Diamond and Lee R. Edwards, pp. 178-193. Amherst: University of Massachussetts Press, 1977.

05835. Fishburn, Katherine. "The Nightmare Repetition: The Mother-Daughter Conflict in Doris Lessing's Children of Violence." In The Lost Tradition: Mothers and Daughters in Literature, edited by Cathy N. Davidson and E.M. Broner, 207-216. New York: Ungar, 1980.

05836. Knapp, Mona. Doris Lessing. New York: Frederick Ungar Publishing Co., 1984.

[3] Others

05837. Cohan, Steven. "From Subtext to Dream Text: The Brutal Egoism of Iris Murdoch's Male Narrators." In Men by Women, Women and Literature, edited by Janet Todd,2: 222-242. New York: Holmes and Meier, 1982.

05838. Diamond, Elin. "Refusing the Romanticism of Identity: Narrative Interventions in Churchill, Benmussa and Duras." Theatre Journal 37 (October 1985): 273-286.

05839. Ezell, Margaret J.M. "'What Shall We Do With Our Old Maids?': Barbara Pym and the 'Women Question.'" International Journal of Women's Studies 7 (November-December 1984): 450-465.

05840. Kane, Marie. "Maeve Kelly and New Irish Women Writing." Women's Studies International Forum 5 (1982): 393-400.

05841. Sellery, J. Elizabeth Bowen, a Bibliography. Austin, Tx.: University of Texas, 1981.

05842. Whittier, Gayle. "Mistresses and Madonnas in the Novels of Margaret Drabble." In Gender and Literary Voice, Women and Literature, edited by Janet Todd, 1: 197-213. New York: Holmes and Meier, 1980.

Also refer to #4280, 5078, 5086.

c) Intellectuals

05843. Richardson, Joanna. Enid Starkie. New York: Macmillan, 1974.

d) Art

(1) Women Artists

(a) Actresses/Directors

05844. Dent, A. Vivien Leigh--A Bouquet? London: Hamilton, 1969.

05845. Edwards, A. Vivien Leigh. New York: Simon and Schuster, 1977.

05846. Venables, Claire. "Woman Director in the Theatre." Theatre Quarterly 10 (Summer 1980): 3-7.

(b) Dancers

05847. Anthony, Gordon. Margot Fonteyn. London: Phoenix House, Ltd., 1951.

05848. Crowle, Eileen Georgina. Moira Shearer, Portrait of a Dancer. New York: Pitman Publishing Co., 1951.

(c) Musicians/Singers

05849. Ferrier, Winifred. Kathleen Ferrier: Her Life. Harmondsworth, Middlesex: Penguin Books, 1955.

(d) Painters

05850. Buchanan, William. Joan Eardley. Edinburgh: Edinburgh University Press, 1976.

e) Science

05851. McCullough, David. "A Rothschild Who is Known as the Queen of the Fleas." Smithsonian 16 (June 1985): 139-154.

C. FRANCE

1. SURVEYS

"In the so-called History, women appear only as mistresses, intrigantes, poisoners. The History of women unfolds in bed, is read in the horizontal."
Annie and Anne, MLF

05852. Caisson, Max. "La femme corse à Marseilles." In Femmes corses et femmes méditerranéennes, pp. 358-367. Provence: Centre d'Etudes corses de l'Universite de Provence, 1976.

05853. Les Femmes s'entêtent. Paris: Gallimard, 1975.

05854. Giroud, Francoise. "The Second Sex." Yale French Studies 27 (1961): 22-25.

05855. Juillard, Joelle Rutherford. "Women in France." In Women in the World: A Comparative Study, edited by Lynne B. Iglitzin and Ruth Ross, pp. 115-128. Santa Barbara, Ca.: Clio Books, 1976.

05856. Lacoste, Christiane. La femme et le bon sens. Paris: Centurion/Grasset, 1974.

05857. Makward, Christiane. "Les Editions des femmes: historique, politique et impact." Contemporary French Civilization 5 (Spring 1981): 347-355.

05858. Toussaint-Samat, Maguelonne. La Femme de 40 ans. Paris: Centurion-Grasset, 1973.

Also refer to #5108.

2. POLITICAL

"It seems to me interesting to note that when, for the first time, four women are members of the French government, what responsibility is committed to them? Hospitals, children, prisoners, and women. Nothing in short that might frighten men and bring them to think that women may invade their territory."
Francoise Giroud

a) Generic

05859. Bersani, C. "Femme et la fonction publique." Droit sociale 8 (1976): 51-55.

05860. Faure, Christian. "Women and Politics in France Until the Accession of Francois Mitterand's Socialist Government." Cultures 8, no. 4 (1982): 103-120.

05861. Flaitz, Jeffra and Northcutt, Wayne. "Women and Politics in Contemporary France: The Electoral Shift to the Left in the 1981 Presidential and Legislative Elections." Contemporary French Civilization 7 (Winter 1983): 183-198.

05862. Guide des droits des femmes. Paris: La documentation française, 1983.

05863. Mossuz-Lavau, Janine and Sineau, Mariette. Enquête sur les femmes et la politique en France. Paris: P.U.F., 1983.

05864. Northcutt, Wayne and Flaitz, Jeffra. "Women, Politics and the French Socialist Government." Western European Politics 8 (October 1985): 50-70.

Also refer to #5111.

b) Marxism and Socialism

05865. Bouchardeau, Huguette; Goueffic, Suzanne; Thouvenot, Geneviève, and Gresset, Monique. Pour une politique des femmes, par les femmes, pour les femmes: les propositions du P.S.U. Paris: Syros, 1981.

05866. Les Cahiers du Communisme, Les femmes dans la France aujourd'hui. Paris: Les Cahiers du Communisme, 1969.

c) Legal

05867. Boigeol, Anne, et al. Le Divorce et les français. Paris: Presses universitaires de France, 1974-1975.

05868. Brown, L. Neville. "The Reform of French Matrimonial Property Law." American Journal of Comparative Law 14 (Spring 1965): 308-321.

05869. Carbonneau, Thomas E. "The New Article 310 of the French Civil Code for International Divorce Actions." American Journal of Comparative Law 26 (Summer 1978): 446-460.

05870. Chevalier, Michèle. Avortement: une loi en procès; l'affaire de Bobigny, Sténotypie intégrale des débats du Tribunal de Bobigny (8 Nov. 1972). Paris: Gallimard, 1973.

05871. Choain, C.; Descamps, J.; and Royer, J.P. Le Divorce et la separation de corps: la pratique recente. Paris: De Vecchi, 1979.

05872. Dourien-Rollier, Anne Marie and Holstein, Colette. Le divorce à la carte. Paris: Le Centurion, 1976.

05873. Dupont Delestraint, Pierre. La réforme du divorce et dispositions annexes. Paris: Dalloz, 1976.

05874. France. Ministère des droits de la femme. Les Femmes en France dans une société d'inegalité . Paris: La Documentation française, 1982.

05875. Futé, Robert. Ces enfants pris en otages: le racket judiciaire. Paris: la Pensée universelle, 1976.

05876. Gorny, Violette. Le divorce en 10 leçons: [et tout pour defendre vos enfants et vos interets]. Paris: Hachette, 1975.

05877. Jarrier, Bernard. Guide du nouveau divorce. Paris: Stock, 1976.

05878. Libmann, Jean. Le nouveau divorce. Tournai: Casterman, 1976.

05879. Lindon, Raymond. La nouvelle législation sur le divorce et le recouvrement public des pensions alimentaires: lois du 11 juillet 1975. Paris: Librairies techniques, 1975.

05880. ______________ and Bertin, Philippe. Divorce 1976. Paris: Librairies techniques, 1976.

05881. Lombard, Paul. Divorcer. Paris: La Table ronde, 1975.

05882. Maillard, Claude. Avortement: les pièces du dossier. Paris: R. Laffont, 1974.

05883. Marcelli, Daniel. Comment leur dire?: L'enfant face au couple en crise. Paris: Hachette, 1979.

05884. Nakache, Yves and Beaupuis, Gerard de. Marriage et divorce. Paris: Larousse, 1977.

05885. Pagès, Fanchon and Mareillou, Valerie. Guide pratique de l'avortement légal et de la contraception. Paris: Mercure de France, 1976.

05886. Parti socialiste, Secrétariat national à l'action féminine. Femmes en lutte: pour le droit a l'information sexuelle a la contraception et a l'interruption de grossesse. Paris: Parti socialiste, 1979.

05887. Peyret, Claude and Brisset, Claire. Avortement: pour une loi humaine. Paris: Calmann-Lévy, 1974.

05888. Poullot, Genevieve. Pilate ou Herode?: de l'indifference au massacre. Paris: Editions Saint-Paul, 1981.

05889. Prévot, Floriane. Le divorce: législation, procédure et conseils pratiques. Montreal: A.D.P., 1979.

05890. Schuberl, Waltraud. Die neue Ehescheidungstatbestände in Frankreich seit dem Gesetz vom 11. Juli 1975 und ihre Aufnahme durch die Gerichte. Frankfurt am Main: Verlag für Standesamtswesen, 1982.

05891. Stetson, Dorothy M. "Abortion Law Reform in France." Journal of Comparative Family Studies 17 (Autumn 1986): 277-290.

05892. Vellay, Pierre. Le vécu de l'avortement. Paris: Editions universitaires, 1972.

05893. Weyl, Monique. Divorce: liberálisme ou liberté. Paris: Editions sociales, 1975.

Also refer to #5116, 5860, 5862, 5949-5951.

d) Criminal

05894. Cahiers sur la femme et la criminalité. Paris: Editions du CNRS, 1979.

05895. Cherbit, Jacqueline and Mermoz, Monique. "S.O.S. Femmes battues." Victimology 8 (1983): 270-274.

Also refer to #5944, 5945.

e) Feminism

05896. Beauvoir, Simone de. "France: Feminism--Alive, Well, and in Constant Danger." In Sisterhood is Global, edited by Robin Morgan, pp. 229-235. Garden City, N.Y.: Anchor Press, Doubleday, 1984.

05897. Dhavernas, Odile. Petite soeur née --- Prépare suicide. Paris: Seuil, 1981.

05898. Falconnet, Georges and Lefaucheur, Nadine. La fabrication des males: du sexisme ordinaire aux pièges de la libération sexuelle. Paris: Seuil, 1975.

05899. Les Femmes de Nice. Les babarotes. Paris: Editiones des femmes, 1978.

05900. García Guadilla, Naty. Libération des femmes le M.L.F. Paris: Presses universitaires de France, 1981.

05901. Gennari, Geneviève. Le dossier de la femme. Paris: Librairie Academique Perrin, 1965.

05902. Jardine, Alice. "Pre-Texts for the Transatlantic Feminist." Yale French Studies 62 (1981): 220-236.

05903. Kaufmann-McCall, Dorothy. "Politics of Difference: The Women's Movement in France from May 1968 to Mitterand." Signs 9 (Winter 1983): 282-293.

05904. LeBrun, Annie. Lâchez-tout. Paris: Sagittaire, 1977.

05905. Leger, Danièle. Le féminisme en France. Paris: Le Sycomore, 1982.

05906. Lesperance, Emmanuel. L'ère de la femme moderne: essai sur le féminisme. Brive: Nouvelle Maugein, 1970.

05907. Manceaux, Michèle. Les femmes de Gennevilliers. Paris: Mercure de France, 1974.

05908. Ozzello, Yvonne Rochette and Marks, Elaine. "Mignonnes allons voir sous la rose: Socialism, Feminism and Misogyny in the France of Yvette Roudy: May 1981-May 1983." Contemporary French Civilization 8 (Fall-Winter 1983-1984): 202-227.

05909. Pellaumail, Marcelle Maugin. Le masochisme "dit" féminin. Paris: Stanké, 1979.

05910. Sauter-Bailliet, Theresia. "The Feminist Movement in France." In The Women's Liberation Movement, edited by Jan Bradshaw, pp. 409-420. New York: Pergamon Press, 1982.

05911. Spivak, Gayatri Chakravorty. "French Feminism in an International Framework." Yale French Studies 62 (1981): 154-184.

05912. Wolinski, Georges. Lettre ouverte à ma femme. . . . Paris: A. Michel, 1978.

Also refer to #5118, 5119.

f) Political Roles

05913. Cauvin, Claire and Poncet, Dominique. Les femmes de Giscard. Paris: Téma, 1975.

05914. Spencer, Samia I. "The Female Cabinet Members of France and Quebec: Token Women." Contemporary French Civilization 9 (Spring-Summer 1985): 166-181.

05915. Vines, Lois. "Une femme remarquable: Interview avec Françoise Giroud." Contemporary French Civilization 7 (Fall 1982): 74-81.

3. ECONOMIC

"Unionised women do not join in to merge quietly in a male union movement. . . They ask _other_ questions, propose other forms of militancy, formulate other struggle objectives."

Margaret Maruani
Les Syndicats a l'epreuve du feminisme

a) Generic

05916. Aumont, Michèle. _Les dialogues de la vie ouvrière_. Paris: Spes, 1953.

Also refer to #5128, 5868, 5935, 5946.

b) Women's Employment

05917. Allauzen, Marie. _La paysanne française aujourd'hui_. Paris: Denoël/Gonthier, 1967.

05918. Ambassade de France, Service de Presse et d'Information. _The French Working Women_. No. 66. New York, 1974.

05919. Fraisse, Geneviève. _Femmes toutes mains: essai sur le service domestique_. Collection libre à elles. Paris: Seuil, 1979.

05920. Klatzmann, Joseph. _Le Travail à domicile dans l'industrie parisienne de vetement_. Paris: A. Colin, 1957.

05921. Lantier, Francoise, et al. _La structure de l'emploi féminin dans trois regions: La Rochelle, Limoges et Montlucon_. Paris: Ministère du Travail, 1971.

05922. Peslouan, Genevieve de. _Qui sont les femmes ingénieurs en France?_ Paris: P.U.F., 1974.

Also refer to #5124, 5125, 5672.

c) Trade Unions and Organizations

05923. Maruani, Margaret. "France." In _Women and Trade Unions in Eleven Industrialized Countries_, edited by Alice H. Cook, Val R. Lorwin, and Arlene Daniels Kaplan, pp. 120-139. Philadelphia: Temple University Press, 1984.

05924. Simon, Catherine. _Syndicalisme au féminin_. Paris: Etudes et documentation internationales, 1981.

Also refer to #5123.

4. RELIGION

"St. Joan's International Alliance re-affirms its loyality and filial devotion and expresses its conviction that should the Church in her wisdom and in her good time decide to extend to women the dignity of the priesthood, women would be willing and eager to respond."
St. Joan's International Alliance

05925. Andezian, Sossie. "Pratiques féminines de l'Islam en France." Archives de sciences sociales des religions 28 (January-March 1983): 53-66.

05926. Duchêne, Gilbert and Defois, Gérard. Faire vivre: l'Eglise catholique et l'avortement: un dossier. Paris: Centurion, 1979.

Also refer to #5948.

5. SOCIAL

"She began to think about her friends' happy tranquility, of their affection, of their two non-problem children: the boy wasn't on drugs; the girl wasn't a nymphomaniac; they weren't even quarrelsome. The kind of children nobody had any more."
Genevieve Antoine-Dariaux
The Fall Collection, 1973

a) Generic

05927. Carlier-Mackiewicz, Nicole. Les veuves et leurs familles dans la société d'aujourd'hui: étude sociologique. Paris: Caisse Nationale des Allocations Familiales, 1970.

05928. Fabre, Claudine. "Cuisine et rôles sexuels en Languedoc Montagnard." In Femmes corses et femmes méditerranéennes, pp. 20-47. Provence: Centre d'Etudes Corses de l'Universite de Provence, 1976.

05929. Gros, Brigitte. Les Paradisiennes. Paris: Robert Laffont, 1973.

05930. Lavoisier, Bénédicte. Mon corps, ton corps, leur corps: le corps de la femme dans la publicité. Paris: Seghers, 1978.

05931. Le Garrec, Evelyne. Un lit à soi: itinéraires des femmes. Paris: Seuil, 1979.

05932. Lemoine-Luccioni, Eugénie. Partage des femmes. Paris: Seuil, 1976.

05933. Leroy, Suzanne. C'est dur la solitude. Collection Une Femme et son Metier. Paris: Robert Laffont, 1972.

05934. Massip, Renee. La femme et l'amitié. Paris: Centurion/ Grasset, 1970.

05935. Rocard, Geneviève and Gutman, Collette. Sois belle et achète: la publicité et les femmes. Paris: Denoel/Gonthier, 1968.

b) Demography

05936. Dupâquier, Jacques. "La contre-offensive de la mortalité dans le dernier quart du XXe siècle." Histoire, économie et société 3 (1984): 473-490.

05937. Leridon, Henri. "Sterilité, hypofertilité, et infecondité en France." Population 37 (July 1982): 807-836.

05938. Rallu, Jean-Louis. "Evolution du nombre et de la composition des familles françaises entre 1975 et 1979." Population 36 (May-June 1981): 629-633.

Also refer to #5136, 5867.

c) Family

05939. Gérôme, Noëlle. "Les formules du bonheur: 'Parents' 1969-1976; l'information des familles par la grande presse." Le Mouvement social 129 (October-December 1984): 89-115.

05940. Larrive, Hélène. Les creches: des enfants à la consigne? Paris: Seuil, 1978.

05941. Pitrou, Agnès. La famille dans la vie de tous les jours. Toulouse: Privat, 1972.

05942. Ribeaud, Marie-Cathérine. Les enfants des exclus. Paris: Stock, 1976.

05943. ______________________. La maternité en milieu sous-proletariat. Paris: Stock, 1979.

05944. Sebbar, Leïla. On tue les petites filles. Paris: Stock, 1978.

05945. ____________. Le pédophile et la maman: l'amour des enfants. Paris: Stock, 1980.

05946. Segalen, Martine. "'Avoir sa Part': Sibling Relations in Partible Inheritance Brittany." In Interest and Emotion Essays on the Study of Family and Kinship, edited by Hans Medick and David Warren Sabean, pp. 129-144. New York: Cambridge University Press, 1985.

05947. Tabard, Nicole. Enquête sur les besoins et aspirations des familles et des jeunes. Paris: Centre de Recherche et de Documentation sur la Consommation/Caisse Nationale d'Allocations Familiale, 1974.

05948. Villain, Pierre. 130,000 familles prennent la parole. Paris: Cerf, 1973.

Also refer to #5116, 5875, 5883, 5927, 5938, 5949.

d) Marriage

05949. Commaille, Jacques. "Divorce and the Child's Status: The Evolution in France." Journal of Comparative Family Studies 14 (Spring 1983): 97-116.

05950. The French Embassy. "Women and Divorce in France." International Journal of Family Therapy 3 (Spring 1981): 62-82.

05951. Roussel, Louis. "Situations domestiques de la population divorcée--non remariée en France." Population 36 (1981): 403-409.

05952. Segalen, Martine. Mari et femmes dans la société paysanne. Paris: Flammarion, 1980.

Also refer to #5867-5869, 5871-5873, 5883, 5884, 5889, 5890, 5893.

e) Sex Life and Morals

05953. Belladonna, Judith. Folles femmes de leurs corps: les prostituees. Paris: Recherches, 1977.

05954. Coninck, Christine and Coninck, Barbara. La partagée. Paris: Editions de Minuit, 1977.

05955. Lafont, Hubert. "Changing Sexual Behaviour in French Youth Gangs." In Western Sexuality, edited by Philippe Ariès and Andre Béjin, pp. 168-180. New York: Blackwell, 1985.

05956. Rogers, Susan Carol. "Gender Definitions in the Latin Quarter: A Personal Account." Women's Studies 10 (1983): 179-201.

05957. Tomeh, Aida K. and Gallant, Clifford J. "The Structure of Sex-Role Attitudes in a French Student Population: A Factoral Analysis." Journal of Marriage and the Family 45 (November 1983): 975-983.

f) Health/Medical

(1) Birth Control/Abortion

05958. L'Avortement: histoire d'un débat. Paris: Flammarion, 1975.

05959. Comité pour la liberté de l'avortement et de la contraception. Liberons l'avortement. Paris: F. Maspero, 1973.

05960. Isambert, François André. Contraception et avortement: dix ans de débat dans la presse, 1965-1974. Paris: Centre national de la recherche scientifique, 1979.

05961. Mouvement pour la liberté de l'avortement et de la contraception Rouen-Centre. Paris: F. Maspero, 1975.

05962. Parmain, Jean Michel. L'Enfant désiré ou le contrôle des naissances. Paris: De Vecchi, 1975.

Also refer to #5870, 5882, 5885-5888, 5891, 5892, 5926.

(2) Psychology

05963. Rose, Jacqueline and Mitchell, Juliet, eds. Feminine Sexuality: Jacques Lacan and the Ecole Freudienne. New York: Macmillan, 1982.

6. CULTURAL

> "A woman's prose can only be subversive, because it pushes volcano-like against an immobile crust [of traditional male-dominated literature]."
>
> Hélène Cixious
> From the French, 1975

a) Education

05964. Ambassade de France, Service de Presse et d'Information. French Women and Education, no. 64. New York, 1974.

05965. Decroux-Masson, Annie. Papa lit, maman coud. Paris: Denoël/Gonthier, 1979.

b) Literature

(1) Non-specific

05966. Auburtin, Graziella. Tendenzen der zeitgenössischen Frauenliteratur in Frankreich. Ein Beitrag zum literärischen Aspekt der weiblichen Identitätsfindung. Frankfurt a Main: Haag und Herchen, 1979.

05967. Hoog, Armand. "Today's Woman--Has She a Heart?" Yale French Studies 27 (1961): 66-73.

05968. Jones, Ann Rosalind. "Writing the Body: Toward an Understanding of L'Ecriture feminine." Feminist Studies 7 (Summer 1981): 247-263.

05969. Peyre, Henri. "Contemporary Feminine Literature in France." Yale French Studies 27 (1961): 47-65.

(2) Drama

05970. Feral, Josette. "Ecriture et deplacement: la femme au theatre." French Review 56 (December 1982): 281-292.

05971. ____________. "Writing and Displacement: Women in Theatre." Modern Drama 27 (December 1984): 549-563.

05972. Savona, Jeannette Laillou. "French Feminism and Theatre: An Introduction." Modern Drama 27 (December 1984): 540-545.

(3) Poetry

05973. Hubert, Renée Rises. "Three Women Poets: Renee Rivet, Joyce Mansour, Yvonne Caroutch." Yale French Studies 21 (1958): 40-48.

05974. Schaettel, Marcel. "Quelques images de la femme dans la poésie de Charles Cros." Revue des sciences humaines n.s. 168 (October-December 1977): 589-600.

(4) Prose

(a) Women in Literature

05975. Gillman, Linda. "The Looking-Glass Through Alice." In Gender and Literary Voice, Women and Literature, edited by Janet Todd 1: 12-23. New York: Holmes and Meier, 1980.

05976. Homans, Margaret. "'Her Very Own Hovel': The Ambiguities of Representation in Recent Women's Fiction." Signs 9 (Winter 1983): 186-205.

Also refer to #5825.

(b) Novelists

[1] Marguerite Duras

05977. Bree, Germaine. "An Interview with Marguerite Duras." Contemporary Literature 13 (Autumn 1972): 401-422.

05978. Cismaru, Alfred. Marguerite Duras. New York: Twayne Publishers, 1971.

05979. Cixous, Hélène and Foucault, Michel. "A propos de Marguerite Duras." Cahiers Renaud Barrault 89 (1975): 8-22.

05980. Cottenet-Hage, Madeleine. "Magnetic Fields II: From Breton to Duras." French Review 58 (March 1985): 540-550.

05981. Gauthier, Xavière. "La danse, Le desir." Cahiers Renaud Barrault 89 (1975): 23-32.

05982. Guicharnaud, Jacques. "The Terrorist Marivaudage of Marguerite Duras." Yale French Studies 46 (1971): 113-124.

05983. ____________________. "Woman's Fate: Marguerite Duras." Yale French Studies 27 (1961): 106-113.

05984. Hoog, Armand. "The Itinerary of Marguerite Duras." Yale French Studies 24 (1959): 68-73.

05985. Husserl-Kapet, Susan. "An Interview with Marguerite Duras." Signs 1 (Winter 1975): 423-434.

05986. Knapp, Bettina L. "Interviews avec Marguerite Duras et Gabriel Cousin." French Review 44 (March 1971): 653-664.

05987. Kneller, John W. "Electric Empathies and Musical Affinities." Yale French Studies 27 (1961): 114-120.

05988. Marini, Marcelle. Territoires du féminin avec Marguerite Duras. Paris: Les Editions de Minuit, 1977.

05989. Montrelay, Michele. L'Ombre et le nom. Paris: Minuit, 1977.

05990. Murphy, Carol J. Alienation and Absence in the Novels of Marguerite Duras. Lexington, Ky.: French Forum, Publishers, 1982.

05991. Schuster, Marilyn R. "Fiction et folie dans l'oeuvre de Marguerite Duras." In Ethique et esthetique dans la littérature française du XXe siècle, Stanford French and Italian Studies, no. 10, edited by Maurice Cagnon, pp. 123-132. Saratoga, Calif.: Anma Libri, 1978.

05992. Vircondelet, Alain. Marguerite Duras ou les temps de detruire. Paris: Editions Seghers, 1972.

Also refer to #5838.

[Others]

05993. Bieber, Konrad. "Ups and Downs in Elsa Triolet's Prose." Yale French Studies 27 (1961): 81-85.

05994. Delattre, Genevieve. "Mirrors and Masks in the World of Françoise Mallet-Joris." _Yale French Studies_ 27 (1961): 121-126.

05995. Desanti, Dominique. _Les Clés d'Elsa: Aragon-Triolet romanvrai_. Paris: Editions Ramsay, 1983.

05996. Hoffman, Leon-François. "Notes on Zoe Oldenbourg's _Destiny of Fire_." _Yale French Studies_ 27 (1961): 127-130.

05997. McCarty, Mari. "Possessing Female Space: 'The Tender Shoot." _Women's Studies_ 8 (1981): 367-374.

05998. McMahon, Joseph H. "What Rest for the Weary?" _Yale French Studies_ 27 (1961): 131-139.

05999. Pflaum-Vallin, Marie-Monique. "Elsa Triolet and Aragon: Back to Lilith." _Yale French Studies_ 27 (1961): 86-89.

06000. Reck, Rima Drell. "Françoise Mallet-Joris and the Anatomy of Will." _Yale French Studies_ 24 (1959): 74-79.

06001. Veza, Lorette. "A Tentative Approach to Some Recent Novels." _Yale French Studies_ 27 (1961): 74-80.

06002. Wenzel, Helene Vivienne. "The Text as Body/Politics. An Appreciation of Monique Wittig's Writings in Context." _Feminist Studies_ 7 (Summer 1981): 264-287.

06003. Willis, Sharon. "Hélène Cixous's _Portrait de Dora_: The Unseen and the Unscene." _Theatre Journal_ 37 (October 1985): 287-301.

Also refer to #5086, 5835, 5976.

(c) Press

06004. Bernheim, Nicole. "Histoire d'un magazin feminin serieux." _Europe_ 427-428 (November-December 1964): 207-212.

06005. Spencer, Samia I. and Millman, Mary M. "French and American Women in the Feminine Press: A Cross-Cultural Look." _Contemporary French Civilization_ 5 (Winter 1981): 179-203.

c) Intellectuals

06006. Burke, Carolyn. "Irigaray Through the Looking Glass." _Feminist Studies_ 7 (Summer 1981): 288-306.

d) Art

06007. Crosland, Margaret. _Piaf_. New York: Putnam, 1985.

06008. Il n'y a pas a proprement parler une histoire: Maison de la culture de Rennes . . . du 26 fevrier au 20 mars 1983. Rennes: La Maison, 1983.

06009. Kerien, Wanda. "La comedienne avec et sans maquillage." Europe 427-428 (November-December 1964): 181-188.

D. THE GERMANIES

1. SURVEYS

"The women in our society have the same rights and opportunities as do men, but they have one additional option, to be taken care of by a man."

Reinold Thiel

06010. German Democratic Republic. Women in the GDR: Facts and Figures. Berlin: Staatsverlag, 1975.

06011. Germany (West). Bundestag. Enquette-Kommission Frau und Gesellschaft. Frau und Gesellschaft. Bonn: Das Presse- und Informationszentrum, 1981.

06012. Lemke, Christiane. "Social Change and Women's Issues in the GDR: Problems of Women in Leadership Positions." In Studies in GDR Culture and Society 2, Proceedings of the Seventh Annual Symposium on the German Democratic Republic, edited by Margy Gerber, et al., pp. 251-259. Washington, D.C.: University Press of America, Inc., 1982.

06013. Merkl, Peter H. "The Politics of Sex: West Germany." In Women in the World: A Comparative Study, edited by Lynne B. Iglitzin and Ruth Ross, pp. 129-147. Santa Barbara, Ca.: Clio Books, 1976.

06014. Meyer, Sibylle and Schulze, Eva. Wie wir das alles geschafft haben: Alleinstehende Frauen berichten über ihr Leben nach 1945. Munich: C.H. Beck, 1984.

06015. Norden, Peter. Das Recht der Frau auf zwei Männer. Kempfenhausen (am Starnberger See): Schulz, 1974.

06016. Pickle, Linda Schelbitzki. "Unreserved Subjectivity as a Force for Social Change: Christa Wolf and Maxie Wander's Guten Morgen, du Schöne." In Studies in GDR Culture and Society 2, Proceedings of the Seventh Annual Symposium on the German Democratic Republic, edited by Margy Gerber, et al., pp. 217-230. Washington, D.C.: University Press of America, Inc., 1982

06017. Roubitschek, Walter. Die Gleichberechtigung der Frau in unserem Staat: Festrede bei 8. März 1973. Halle: Martin-Luther-Universität Halle-Wittenberg, 1973.

06018. Das schöne Geschlecht und die Gleichberechtigung in der DDR. East Berlin: Aus erster Hand, 1970.

06019. Shaffer, Harry G. "The Status and Position of Women in the German Democratic Republic." Studies in GDR Culture and Society 3 (1983):57-69.

Also refer to #5286.

2. POLITICAL

"Men and women have equal rights. All laws and decrees contrary to women's equality are repealed."
1949 GDR Constitution

a) Generic

06020. Fiedeler, Beate, and Ladwig, Ulrike. "Women and the Peace Movement in the Federal Republic of Germany." Frontiers 8, no. 2 (1985): 59-64.

06021. Hervé, Florence. "Les femmes et le politique en RFA." Allemagnes d'aujourd'hui n.s. 57 (March-April 1977): 66-79.

06022. Kreisky, Eva, et al. "Frauenforschung und Frauenpolitik in Österreich [symposium]." Österreichische Zeitschrift fur Politikwissenschaft 13, no. 4 (1984): 395-493.

06023. Metzker, Maria. "Die Frau in der Sozialpolitik." In Arbeitswelt und Sozialstaat, edited by Oswin Martinek, Josef Cerny, and Josef Weidenholzer, pp. 35-39. Vienna: Europaverlag, 1980.

06024. Struck, Karin. Zwei Frauen. Münster: Tende, 1982.

b) Marxism and Socialism

06025. Austria, Kommunistische Partei. Protokoll der Konferenz der KPÖ, 30 Nov. 1974, Wien. Vienna: Kommunistische Partei Österreichs, 1975.

06026. Einhorn, Barbara. "Socialist Emancipation: The Women's Movement in the German Democratic Republic." In The Women's Liberation Movement, edited by Jan Bradshaw, pp. 435-452. New York: Pergamon Press, 1982.

06027. Konze, Marianne and Mies, Herbert. Mit der DKP Preise stoppen, Arbeitsplatze sichern, für die Rechte der Frauen kämpfen. Düsseldorf: Parteivorstand der DKP, Referat Offentlichkeitsarbeit, 1974.

06028. Ligue marxiste revolutionnaire. Femmes: de l'oppression a la révolution. Lausanne: CEDIPS, 1975.

06029. Ligue marxiste révolutionnaire. _Von der Unterdrückung zur Befreiung_. Zurich: Veritas-Verlag, 1975.

06030. _Nur mit der proletarischen Frau wird der Sozialismus siegen_. Hamburg: Verlag Arbeiterkampf, 1976.

c) Legal

06031. Alberndt, A. _Ehe und Ehescheidung_. Berlin: de Gruyter, 1977.

06032. Arndt, Claus; Erhard, Benno; and Funcke, Liselotte, eds. _Der Paragraph 218 StGB vor dem Bundesverfassungsgericht_. Karlsruhe: Muller, Juristischer Verlag, 1979.

06033. Bastian, Günther, et al. _EheRG: Das neue Ehe- und Scheidungsrecht: Kommentar_. Mainz: Kohlhammer, 1977.

06034. Beckel, Albrecht, ed. _Abtreibung in der Diskussion. Medizinische, psychologische, ethische und politische Aspekte der Reform des Paragraphen 218_. Münster: Regensberg, 1972.

06035. Becker, Christa. _Problem 218. Wie es die anderen machen: Schweden, Danemark, Finnland. Wie man es nicht machen sollte: Bundesrepublik Deutschland_. Frankfurt a.M.: Fischer Taschenbuchverlag, 1972.

06036. Becker, Friedemann. _Versorgungsausgleichs-Verträge_. Königstein/Ts.: Athenaum, 1983.

06037. Belchaus, Gunter. _Familien- und Eherecht in der Bundesrepublik Deutschland: mit dem neuen Scheidungs- und Scheidungsfolgenrecht, dem ab 1. Januar 1980 geltenden neuen elterlichen Sorgerecht und einem Überblick über die Zuständigkeit der Gerichte_. Karlsruhe: Müller, Juristischer Verlag, 1980.

06038. Bergschneider, Ludwig. _Die Ehescheidung und ihre Folgen: Grundriss mit vielen praktischen Beispielen und Gesetzestexten_. Munich: Rehm, 1981.

06039. ____________________. _Wir lassen uns scheiden: Beispielen_. Bergisch Gladbach: Bastei-Lübbe, 1978.

06040. Bönitz, Dieter. _Zur Psychologie der Abtreibung: legale und illegale Schwangerschaftsabbrüche im Vergleich_. Gottingen: Vandenhoeck und Ruprecht, 1979.

06041. Bork, Dagmar et al. _Scheidungsratgeber: von Frauen für Frauen_. Münster: Verlag Frauenpolitik, 1978.

06042. Diederichsen, Uwe. _Das Recht der Ehescheidung und Scheidungsfolgesachen in der anwaltlichen Praxis: aktuelle Probleme, Erfahrungen, praktische Hinweise_. Cologne: Tagungs- und Verlagsgesellschaft, 1982.

06043. Diederichsen, Uwe. *Vermögensauseinandersetzung bei der Ehescheidung*. Cologne: Kommunikationsforum Recht, Wirtschaft, Steuern, 1983.

06044. Dietz, Klaus. *Die Pille: Wirkung und Nebenwirkung; Geburtenplanung, Schwangerschaftsunterbrechung oder Schwangerschaftsverhütung?* Berlin: Verlag Volk und Gesundheit, VEB, 1973.

06045. Dürr, Rudolf. *Verkehrsregelungen gemass Paragraph 1634 BGB*. Stuttgart: Kohlhammer, 1977.

06046. Edlinger, Gertrude. *Dokumentation der politischen Geschichte zur Reform des [Paragraphen] 144 STG.* Vienna: Ludwig-Boltzmann-Institut fur Kriminalsoziologie, 1981.

06047. Ehmke, Horst. *Die Fristenregelung und das Grundgesetz*. Bonn-Bad Godesberg: Verlag Neue Gesellschaft, 1975.

06048. European Commission of Human Rights. *The Brüggemann and Scheuten Case*. Strasbourg: Council of Europe, 1978.

06049. Forster, Christoph. *Geburtenregelung und Abtreibung; ein Diskussionsbeitrag zu ihrer strafrechtlichen Abgrenzung unter Berücksichtigung neuer medizinischer Erkenntnisse*. Munich: Leidig-Druck, 1968.

06050. Frauenaktion Dortmund. *Schwangerschaft und der neue Paragraph 218. Handbuch für Frauen. Abtreibung in der BRD: Praxis und Möglichkeiten: Handbuch für Frauen*. Cologne: Pahl-Rugenstein, 1976.

06051. Fuchs, Andreas. *Das neue Scheidungsrecht*. Munich: Heyne, 1976.

06052. Füllemann, Dieter. *Verschulden und Zerrüttung in rechtsvergleichender Sicht*. Bern: Stämpfli, 1982.

06053. Germany (West). Bundesministerium der Justiz. *Zur Reform des Paragraphen 218*. Bonn-Bad Godesberg: Bundesministerium der Justiz, Referat Presse- und Öffentlichkeitsarbeit, 1973.

06054. Germany (West). Bundesverfassungsgericht. *The Abortion Decision of February 25, 1975 of the Federal Constitutional Court, Federal Republic of Germany*. Washington: Library of Congress, Law Library, 1975.

06055. Giesen, Dieter. "German Law." In *The Reform of Family Law in Europe: The Equality of the Spouses, Divorce, Illegitimate Children*, edited by A.G. Chloros, pp. 111-138. Boston: Kluwer, 1978.

06056. Glockner, Rainer; Bohmer, Christof; and Klein, Michael. *Versorgungsausgleich bei Scheidung unter Berücksichtigung der verschiedenen Versorgungsformen*. Heidelberg: Verlagsgesellschaft Recht und Wirtschaft, 1981.

06057. Göppinger, Horst. Vereinbarungen anlässlich der Ehescheidung Die vertragliche Regelung der zivilsteuer- und sozialrechtlichen Folgen. Munich: Beck, 1977.

06058. Gropp, Walter. Der straflose Schwangerschaftsabbruch: die rechtliche Einordnung der Straffreiheit zu 218 StGB. Tübingen: Mohr, 1981.

06059. Gutzwiller, Peter Max. Jurisdiktion und Anerkennung auslandischer Entscheidungen im schweizerischen internationalen Ehescheidungsrecht auf der Grundlage der Rechtsprechung. Bern: Stämpfli, 1969.

06060. Harmsen, Hans, ed. Zur Entwicklung des Gesundheitswesens in der DDR. Bonn: Gesamtdeutsches Institut, 1975.

06061. Hartman-Hilter, Hannes. Der Ehevertrag auf der Grundlage des neuen Scheidungsrechts. Munich: Wirtschaftsverlag Langen-Muller-Herbig, 1978.

06062. Haslimann-Izbicki, Marianne. Die Unzumutbarkeit zur Fortsetzung der ehelichen Gemeinschaft und das Zerrüttungsprinzip: eine rechtspolitische Betrachtung von Art, 142 Abs. 1 ZGB. Diessenhofen: Ruegger, 1977.

06063. Hepp, Hermann and Schmitt, Rudolf. Zur Reform des 218. St.GB. Paderborn: Schöningh, 1974.

06064. Hinderling, Hans. Das schweizerisch Ehescheidungsrecht, unter besonderer Berücksichtigung der Rechtsprechung. Zurich: Schulthess, 1981.

06065. Hirsch, G. and Weissauer, W., eds. Rechtliche Probleme des Schwangerschaftsabbruchs. Erlangen: Perimed-Verlag Straube, 1977.

06066. Hofmann, Dieter, ed. Schwangerschaftsunterbrechung: aktuelle Uberlegungen zur Reform der section 218. Frankfurt am Main: Suhrkamp, 1974.

06067. International Labour Office. "Equal Rights for Men and Women -- Current Inequalities in Federal Laws and Proposals for Eliminating Them." Social and Labour Bulletin (December 1982): 553-555.

06068. ________________. "Juridical Decision in the Field of Labour Law." International Labour Review 91 (March 1965): 210-229.

06069. Kehl-Zeller, Robert and Kehl, Dieter. Die Abänderrung und Ergänzung von Scheidungs- und Trennungsurteilen gemäss Artikel 153 und 157 ZGB. Zurich: Roke-Verlag, 1973-1975.

06070. Knöfer, Günter, et al. Modellprogramm: "Beratungsstellen" 218: wissenschaftliche Begleitung: Schlussbericht. Stuttgart: Kohlhammer, 1982.

06071. Köhler, Hans, ed. *Ehescheidungsrecht*. Vienna: Druck und Verlag d. Osterrichische Staatsdruckerei, 1978.

06072. König, Uta. *Gewalt uber Frauen*. Hamburg: Gruner and Jahr, 1980.

06073. Komitee für Straffreie Abtreibung. *Meinungen, Argumente, Stellungnahmen zur Abtreibungsfrage*. Vienna: Olga Makomaski, 1975.

06074. Kommers, Donald P. "Abortion and Constitution: United States and West Germany." *American Journal of Comparative Law* 25 (Spring 1977): 255-285.

06075. Lambelet, Jean-Christian. *Une analyse statistique de la votation fédérale du 25 septembre 1977, sur l'initiative populaire "pour la solution du délai."* Lausanne: Centre de recherches économiques appliquées, 1978.

06076. Leisner, Walter and Goerlich, Helmut. *Das Recht auf Leben: Untersuchungen zu Artikel 2,2 des Grundgesetzes für die Bundesrepublik Deutschland*. Hanover: Niedersächsische Landeszentrale für Politische Bildung, 1976.

06077. Lin-Liu, Chu-Chi. *Die Tätigkeit der Vormundschaftsgerichte nach der Auflösung der Ehe: eine empirische Untersuchung*. Taipei: San Min Books Company, 1980.

06078. Loehr, Hardo G. *Das Unterhaltsrecht geschiedener Ehegatten in Deutschland und der Schweiz*. Zürich: Schulthess, 1982.

06079. Lucke, Doris. *Die angemessene Erwerbstätigkeit im neuen Scheidungsrecht: zur soziologischen Interpretation unbestimmter Rechtsbegriffe*. Baden-Baden: Nomos, 1982.

06080. Lynker, Hilmar. *Das neue Scheidungsrecht: Hinweise und Muster für die Anwaltspraxis*. Berlin: Heymann, 1977.

06081. Maier, Kurt. *Härteregelungen zum Versorgungsausgleich: Text und Erlauterungen zum Gesetz zur Regelung von Harten im Versorgungsausgleich*. Frankfurt/M.: Verband Deutscher Rentenversicherungstrager, 1983?.

06082. Mühll, Georg Vonder. *Der Scheidungsgrund des Artikel 142 ZGB, nach der Praxis der Basler Gerichte (1957-1968)*. Bern: Herbert Lang, 1974.

06083. Münch, Eva Marie von. *Eheschliessung, Eheführung, Ehescheidung*. Munich: Goldmann, 1977.

06084. ____________________. *Die Scheidung nach neuem Recht*. Munich: Deutscher Taschenbuch-Verlag, 1983.

06085. Oeter, Karl and Nohke, Anke. *Der Schwangerschaftsabbruch: Gründe, Legitimationen, Alternativen*. Stuttgart: W. Kohlhammer, 1982.

06086. Oswald, Denis. *L'Opposition au divorce: application et réforme de l'article 142, alinéa 2, du Code civil suisse.* Neuchâtel: Ides et Calendes, 1977.

06087. Paczensky, Susanne von, ed. *Wir sind keine Mörderinnen!: Streitschrift gegen eine Einschüchterungskampagne.* Reinbek bei Hamburg: Rowohlt, 1980.

06088. Pap, Tibor. "Socialist Law." In *The Reform of Family Law in Europe: The Equality of the Spouses, Divorce, Illegitimate Children*, edited by A. G. Chloros, pp. 227-254. Boston: Kluwer, 1978.

06089. Pawlowski, Harald. *Krieg gegen die Kinder? Für und wider die Abtreibung.* Limburg: Lahn-Verlag, 1971.

06090. Pro Familia Bremen, ed. *Wir wollen nicht mehr nach Holland fahren. Nach der Reform des Paragraphen 218. Betroffene Frauen ziehen Bilanz.* Reinbek bei Hamburg: Rowohlt, 1978.

06091. Pross, Helge. *Abtreibung. Motive und Bedenken. Mit einem Exkurs uber die Abtreibung in der DDR.* Stuttgart: Kohlhammer, 1971.

06092. *Reform des Abtreibungsparagraphen: ein Überblick zur sachgerechten Diskussion.* Munich: Bund der deutschen Katholischen Jugend, Landsstelle Bayern, 1973.

06093. Rolland, Walter, *Gesetz zur Regelung von Härten im Versorgungsausgleich (HRG): Kommentar.* Neuwied: Luchterhand, 1983.

06094. Rüffer, Wilfried. *Die formelle Rechtskraft des Scheidungsausspruchs bei Ehescheidung im Verbundverfahren.* Bielefeld: Gieseking, 1982.

06095. Rüpke, Giselher. *Schwangerschaftsabbruch und Grundgesetz.* Frankfurt: Suhrkamp, 1975.

06096. Ruland, Franz, and Tiemann, Burkhard. *Versorgungsausgleich und steuerliche Folgen der Ehescheidung.* Munich: Beck, 1977.

06097. Rummler, Thomas. *Die Aufteilung des ehelichen Gebrauchsvermögens und der ehelichen Ersparnisse: ein Vergleich der vermogensrechtlichen Folgen der Ehescheidung nach dem gesetzlichen ehelichen Güterrecht in Osterreich und der Bundesrepublik Deutschland.* Cologne: FM-Druck, 1982.

06098. Runte, Klaus-Peter. *Paragraph 218 nach der Reform: Erfahrungsbericht eines Arztes.* Cologne: Kiepenheuer und Witsch, 1978.

06099. Schmalhofer, Rudolf, *Versorgungsausgleich für offentliche Bedienstete.* Munich: Verlag für Verwaltungspraxis Rehm, 1978.

06100. Schröder, Friedrich-Christian, ed. Abtreibung. Reform des ___ 218. Berlin: de Gruyter, 1972.

06101. Schunk Ursula. Die Umgangsregelung gemäss 1634 BGB bei gescheiterter Ehe. Dortmund: Modernes Lernen, 1981.

06102. Schwab, Dieter. Handbuch des Scheidungsrechts. Munich: Vahlen, 1977.

06103. ____________. Neue Rechtsprechung zum Ehescheidungsrecht. Cologne: Kommunikationsforum Recht, Wirtschaft, Steuern, 1981.

06104. Stolz, Dieter. Ein Lehrstück und sechs Thesen: Zur Reform des 218. Munich: Kaiser, 1976.

06105. Tallen, Hermann. Die Auseinandersetzung über 218 StGB. Zu einem Konflikt zwischen der SPD und der Katholischen Kirche. Vienna: Schöningh, 1977.

06106. ____________. Paragraph 218: Zwischenbilanz einer Reform. Dusseldorf: Patmos-Verlag, 1980.

06107. Vespermann, Hans-Joachim. Scheidungs- und Scheidungsverbundverfahren. Munich: Beck, 1980.

06108. Weck, Bernhard. Die Scheidung. Zurich: Im Selbstverlag, 1976.

06109. Weg mit dem ___ 218. Hamburg: Verlag Arbeiterkampf, 1976.

06110. Werdt, Josef Duss von and Fuchs, Armin., eds. Scheidung in der Schweiz; eine wissenschaftliche Dokumentation. Stuttgart: P. Haupt, 1980.

06111. Wilkens, Erwin, comp. Section 218 Dokumente und Meinungen zur Frage des Schwangerschaftsabbruchs. Gutersloh: Gutersloher Verlagshaus Mohn, 1973.

Also refer to #5224, 6162.

d) Feminism

06112. Altbach, Edith H. et al., eds. German Feminism: Readings in Politics and Literature. Albany, New York: State University of New York Press, 1984.

06113. Benard, Cheryl and Schlaffer, Edit. "Austria: Benevolent Despotism Versus the Contemporary Feminist Movement." In Sisterhood is Global, edited by Robin Morgan, pp. 72-76. Garden City, N.Y.: Anchor Press, Doubleday, 1984.

06114. Benz-Burger, Lydia, et al. Schweizerischer Frauenkongress, 4th, Bern, 1975. Die Schweiz im Jahr der Frau Kongressbericht, 17.-19.1.1975. Zurich: ARGE, [1975].

06115. Berger, Renate; Kolb, Ingrid; and Janssen-Jurreit, Marielouise. "Germany (West; FRG): Fragmented Selves (A Collage)." In Sisterhood is Global, edited by Robin Morgan, pp. 248-254. Garden City, N.Y.: Anchor Press, Doubleday, 1984.

06116. Borgmann, Grete. Freiburg und die Frauenbewegung. Baden: Stückle, 1973.

06117. Bund Demokratischer Frauen Osterreichs. Programm. Vienna: Bund Demokratischer Frauen Osterreichs, 1975.

06118. Centre des femmes de Brokenheim. "'Bye! Bye Baby! Appel à toutes les femmes pour inventer le bonheur." In Les femmes et leur maîtres, edited by Maria-Antonietta Macciocchi, pp. 297-307. Paris: C. Bourgeois, 1979.

06119. Feuersenger, Marianne. Die garantierte Gleichberechtigung: ein umstrittener Sieg der Frauen. Vienna: Herder, 1980.

06120. Frauengruppe. Frauengruppe im Revolutionären Kampf. Frankfurt: Sozialistische Druckerei, 1973?.

06121. Gabriel, Nicole. "Féminisme à Berlin-Ouest." Allemagnes d'aujourd'hui n.s. 78 (October-December 1981): 53-72.

06122. Hellwig, Renate. Frauen verändern die Politik: eine gesellschaftspolitische Streitschrift. Stuttgart: Verlag Bonn Aktuell, 1975.

06123. Hervé, Florence. "Le mouvement feminin en RFA." Allemagnes d'aujourd'hui n.s. 78 (October-December 1981): 35-52.

06124. ______________. "Le mouvement feminin en RFA." Allemagnes d'aujourd'hui n.s. 56 (January-February 1977): 51-61.

06125. ______________ and Konze, Marianne. Frauen kontra Männer, Sackgasse oder Ausweg? Frankfurt am Main: Verlag Marxistische Blatter, 1977.

06126. Jaeckel, Monika. "Feminist Catch-as-Catch Can." Women's Studies International Forum 8 (1985): 5-8.

06127. Klein, Renatel Duelli; Cora, Gena; and Hubbard, Ruth. "German Women say NO to Gene and Reproductive Technology: Reflections on a Conference in Bonn, West Germany, April 19-21, 1985." Women's Studies International Forum Feminist Forum 8 no. 3(1985): i-vi.

06128. Morgner, Irmtraud. "Germany (East; GDR): Witch Wilmma's Invention of Speech-Swallowing (A Parable)." In Sisterhood is Global, edited by Robin Morgan, pp. 242-244. Garden City, N.Y.: Anchor Press, Doubleday, 1984.

06129. Nationaler Frauenkongress, Munich, Germany. Nationaler Frauenkongress: am 5.-6.3.77 in München. Munich: Frauenoffensive, 1977.

06130. Schork, Erika. Eine Frau ist kein Mann. Die Grenzen der Emanzipation. Berlin: Herbig, 1977.

06131. Stern, Carola, ed. Was haben die Parteien für die Frauen getan? Reinbek bei Hamburg: Rowohlt, 1976.

06132. Wecker, Regina, ed. Frauen in der Schweiz: von den Problemen einer Mehrheit. Zug: Klett und Balmer, 1983.

06133. Wiggershaus, Renate. Geschichte der Frauen und der Frauenbewegung. In der Bundesrepublik Deutschland und in der DDR nach 1945. Wuppertal: Hammer, 1979.

Also refer to #5226, 5234, 6025, 6029, 6030, 6163, 6164.

3. ECONOMIC

"Women are forced, for example in the workplace, more and more to adapt to the male cultural model."
Brigitte Wartmann

a) Generic

06134. Höllwarth, Georg. Steuerfolgen der Ehescheidung. Vienna: Industrieverlag, P. Linde, 1976.

06135. Rosenberg, Dorothy. "On Beyond Superwomen: The Conflict between Work and Family Roles in GDR Literature." Studies in GDR Culture and Society 3 (1983): 87-100.

06136. Rueschemeyer, Marilyn. Professional Work and Marriage: An East-West Comparison. New York: St. Martin's Press, 1985.

Also refer to #6069.

b) Women's Employment

06137. Addison, J.F. "Gleichberechtigung--The German Experience." In Equal Pay for Women: Progress and Problems in Seven Countries, edited by Barrie O. Pettman, pp. 99-128. Washington: Hemisphere, 1977.

06138. Hesse, Beate. "Women at Work in the Federal Republic of Germany." In Working Women: An International Survey, edited by Marilyn J. Davidson and Cary L. Cooper, pp. 63-81. New York: John Wiley and Sons, 1984.

06139. International Labour Office. "Girls in Industrial Training." Social and Labour Bulletin (March 1982): 128-129.

06140. Koch, Ursula. "Living Conditions in Rural Areas of the GDR." In Studies in GDR Culture and Society 2, Proceedings of the Seventh Annual Symposium on the German Democratic Republic, edited by Margy Gerber, et al., pp. 279-292. Washington, D.C.: University Press of America, Inc., 1982.

06141. Kutsch, Marlie. Die Frau im Berufsleben. Vienna: Herder, 1979.

06142. Lange, Inge. Aktuelle Probleme der Arbeit mit den Frauen bei der weiteren Verwirklichung der Beschlüsse des VIII. Parteitages der SED. Berlin: Dietz, 1974.

06143. Lestrade, Brigitte. "La situation du salariat féminin en Republique federale." Allemagnes d'aujourd'hui n.s. 41 (January-February 1974): 81-100.

06144. Lusset, Felix. "Les femmes et la vie professionnelle en RFA." Allemagnes d'aujourd'hui n.s. 66 (January-February 1979): 79-85.

06145. Wex, Helga and Kollenberg, Udo. Frau und Industriegesellschaft: Pladoyer für die freiheitliche Alternative Partnerschaft. Cologne: Deutscher Instituts-Verlag, 1979.

06146. Woll-Schumacher, Irene. "Der Hausfrauenberuf als Enklave der Leistungsgesellschaft." Hamburger Jahrbuch für Wirtschaft-und Gesellschaftspolitik 18 (1973): 343-353.

Also refer to #6010, 6068, 6151, 6167.

c) Trade Unions and Organizations

06147. Cook, Alice H. "Federal Republic of Germany." In Women and Trade Unions in Eleven Industrialized Countries, edited by Alice H. Cook, Val R. Lorwin, and Arlene Daniels Kaplan, pp. 63-94. Philadelphia: Temple University Press, 1984.

06148. Gabriel, Nicole. "Syndicalisme au féminin." Allemagnes d'aujourd'hui n.s. 79 (January-March 1982): 68-84.

06149. Krebs, Edith. "Women Workers and the Trade Unions in Austria: An Interim Report." In Women Workers and Society International Perspectives, pp. 185-198. Geneva: International Labour Office, 1976. Also in International Labour Review 112 (July-December 1975): 256-265.

4. RELIGION

"Catholics in the Eastern zone are affected the same way as the Protestants, with participation in church services handicapping men and women in obtaining jobs and hindering their advancement if they have employment."

Harry W. Flannery and
Gerhart Seger
Which Way Germany, 1968

06150. Wegan, Martha. *Ehescheidung: Auswege mit der Kirche*. Graz: Verlag Styria, 1983.

5. SOCIAL

"Why is it of all the mothers in the world this one is mine--we approach one another like enemy soldiers and destroy each other and then run away."

Helga Novak
Die Eisheiligen

a) Generic

06151. Pust, Carola; Reichert, Petra; and Wenzel, Anne. *Frauen in der BRD: Beruf, Familie, Gewerkschaften, Frauenbewegung*. Hamburg: VSA-Verlag, 1983.

06152. Rosenberg, Dorothy. "The Emancipation of Women in Fact and Fiction: Changing Roles in GDR Society and Literature." In *Women, State, and Party in Eastern Europe*, edited by Sharon L. Wolchik and Alfred G. Meyer, pp. 344-361. Durham, N.C.: Duke University Press, 1985.

06153. *Women in the GDR*. Dresden: Zeit im Bild, 1978.

Also refer to #6122.

b) Demography

06154. Gouazé, Serge L. "L'evolution démographique en RFA." *Allemagnes d'aujourd'hui* n.s. 64-65 (September-December 1978): 97-117.

06155. ______________. "L'évolution démographique en FRA (IIe partie)." *Allemagnes d'aujourd'hui* n.s. 66 (January-February 1979): 52-71.

c) Family

(1) Non-specific

06156. Freier, Anna-Elizabeth; Kuhn, Annette; and Schubert, Doris. "Frauen suchen nach neuen Formen der Selbstverwirklichung und des menschlichen Zusammenlebens. Überlegungen zur Kontinuität von Ehe und Familie nach 1945." In _Frauen in der Geschichte III_, edited by Annette Kuhn and Jörn Rüsen, pp. 233-273. Düsseldorf: Schwann, 1983.

06157. Helwig, Gisela. _Frau und Familie in beiden deutschen Staaten_. Cologne: Wissenschaft und Politik, 1982.

06158. Schultz, Wolfgang; Weiss, Hilde; and Strodl, Robert. _Ehe- und Familienleben heute: Einstellungen und Bewertungen_. Vienna: Federal Ministry for Finances, 1980.

Also refer to #5224, 6055, 6086, 6088, 6135, 6136, 6180.

(2) Childhood

06159. Ende, Aurel. "Damit's kein Prachtkind wird- Kindheit in Deutschland." _Psychologie heute_. (December 1980): 37-42.

06160. _________. "The Psychohistorian's Childhood and the History of Childhood: A Personal Experience." _Journal of Psychohistory_ 9 (Fall 1981): 173-177.

06161. Williamson, Robert C. "A Partial Replication of the Kohn-Geca-Nye Thesis in a German Sample." _Journal of Marriage and the Family_ 46 (November 1984): 971-979.

Also refer to #6180.

d) Marriage

06162. Bauer, Erich. _Neues Ehescheidungsrecht_. Stuttgart: Fachverlag für Wirtschafts- und Steuerrecht Schäffer, 1977.

06163. Hoesch-Daffis, Renate. _Ehe und Scheidung. Neue Entwicklungen in der Zweierbeziehung_. Munich: Kindler, 1980.

06164. Switzerland, Eidgenössisches Statistisches Amt. _Zur Entwicklung der Scheidungshäufigkeit in der Schweiz_. Bern: Bundesamt für Statistik, 1979.

06165. Szinovacz, M.E. "Another Look at Normative Resource Theory: Contributions from Austrian Data." _Journal of Marriage and the Family_ 40 (May 1978): 413-421.

06166. Wiegmann, Barbelies. *Ende der Hausfrauenehe: Plädoyer gegen eine trügerische Existenzgrundlage*. Reinbek bei Hamburg: Rowohlt, 1980.

Also refer to #6031, 6033, 6036-6039, 6041-6043, 6045, 6051, 6052, 6056, 6057, 6059, 6061, 6062, 6064, 6069, 6071, 6077-6084, 6086, 6093, 6094, 6096, 6097, 6099, 6101-6103, 6107, 6109, 6110, 6134, 6150, 6158.

e) Sex Life and Morals

06167. Schlei, Marie and Brück, Dorothea. *Wege zur Selbstbestimmung: Sozialpolitik als Mittel der Emanzipation*. Frankfurt am Main: Europaische Verlagsanstalt, 1976.

f) Health/Medical

(1) Birth Control/Abortion

06168. Becker, Michael. *Politik an der Schwelle des Lebens*. Erlangen: VLE-Verlags-GmbH, 1972.

06169. Brot und Rosen. *Frauenhandbuch*. Berlin: Verlag Frauen, 1974.

06170. Duda, Gunther. *Abtreibung, ja oder nein?* Pahl: Verlag Hohe Warte von Bebenburg, 1973.

06171. Gaillard, Ursula and Mahaim, Annik. *Retards de règles: attitudes devant le contrôle des naissances et l'avortement en Suisse du début du siècle aux années vingt*. Lausanne: Editions d'En bas, 1983.

06172. Jürgens, Hans W. and Pieper, Ursula. *Demographische und sozialmedizinische Auswirkungen der Reform des 218*. Stuttgart: Kohlhammer, 1975.

06173. Legge, Jerome S., Jr. "Predictors of Abortion Attitudes in the Federal Republic of Germany." *Journal of Politics*, 45 (August 1983): 759-766.

06174. Mikocki, Alfred. *Rettet das Leben--Gemeinschaft zum Schutz der Ungeborenen*. Vienna: n.p., 1966.

06175. Neubauer, Erika. *Schwangerschaftsabbruch als soziales und personales Problem: eine empirische Untersuchung zur Soziologie der Frau*. Weinheim: Beltz, 1982.

06176. Pohl, Katharina. *Familie, Planung oder Schicksal: sozio-demographische und innerfamiliäre Aspekte der Einstellung deutscher Ehefrauen zu Familienplanung und Schwangerschaftsabbruch*. Boppard am Rhein: Boldt, 1980.

06177. Schöpf, Elfi von. Unerwünscht schwanger, was tun? Dokumentation über den Schwangerschaftsabbruch in der Schweiz. Basel: Z-Verlag, 1977.

06178. Sozialwissenschaftliche Arbeitsgemeinschaft. Vom Volksbergehren zum Schutz des menschlichen Lebens. Vienna: Sozialwissenschaftliche Arbeitsgemeinschaft, 1975.

06179. Wilkitzki, Peter and Lauritzen, Christian. Schwangerschaftsabbruch in der Bundesrepublik Deutschland. Heidelberg: Kriminalistik-Verlag, 1981.

Also refer to #6032, 6034, 6035, 6040, 6044, 6046-6050, 6053, 6054, 6058, 6060, 6063, 6065, 6066, 6070, 6072-6076, 6085, 6087, 6089-6092, 6095, 6098, 6100, 6104-6106, 6109, 6111.

(2) Women and Health

06180. Greenberg, Robert A. "Maternal and Child Health Care in the German Democratic Republic." In Studies in GDR Culture and Society 2, Proceedings of the Seventh Annual Symposium on the German Democratic Republic, edited by Margy Gerber, et al., pp. 261-278. Washington, D.C.: University Press of America, 1982.

(3) Psychology

06181. Wodak, Ruth, "Geschlechtsspezifische Strategien in einer therapeutischen Gruppe: Aspekte einer sozio- und psycholinguistischen Untersuchung." In Das ewige Klischee, zum Rollenbild und Selbstverständnis bei Männern und Frauen, pp. 232-252. Vienna: Hermann Böhlaus, 1981.

6. CULTURAL

"Men and women must commit themselves to giving up their masculine and feminine roles and together learn about human roles and partnership."
Luise Rinser
Undeveloped Land-Woman, 1970

a) Education

06182. Brehmer, Ilse, ed. Lehrerinnen: Zur Geschichte eines Frauenberufes. Munich: Urban and Schwarzenberg, 1980.

06183. Pronay, Inge. "Denk- und Merkwürdigkeiten zum Bild der Frau in österreichischen Schulbüchern." In Das ewige Klischee, zum Rollenbild und Selbstverstandnis bei Männern und Frauen, pp. 276-304. Vienna: Hermann Böhlaus, 1981.

Also refer to #6139.

b) Literature

(1) Non-specific

06184. Cella, Ingrid. "'Das Rätsel Weib' und die Literatur. Feminismus, feministische Ästhetik und die neuen Frauenliterature in Österreich." Amsterdamer Beiträge zur neueren Germanistik 14 (1982): 189-228.

06185. Romero, Christiane Zehl. "Vertreibung aus dem Paradies: Zur neuen Frauenliteratur in der DDR." Studies in GDR Culture and Society 3 (1983): 71-85.

Also refer to #6152.

(2) Philology

06186. Tromel-Plötz, Senta. "Frauen und Sprache: Unterschied und Unterdruckung." Jahrbuch fur Internationale Germanistik 14 no. 2 (1982): 79-97.

(3) Drama

06187. Cosentino, Christine. "Frau und Staatsbürger in Volker Braun's Schauspiel 'Tinka'." In Women in German Studies, edited by Kay Goodman and Ruth H. Sanders, pp. 114-120. Oxford, Ohio: Miami University, 1977.

06188. Drewitz, Ingeborg. "Gerlind Reinshagen." In Neue Literatur der Frauen, edited by Heinz Puknus, pp. 102-109. Munich: C.H. Beck, 1980.

06189. Jäschke, Bärbel. "Ingeborg Drewitz." In Neue Literatur der Frauen, edited by Heinz Puknus, pp. 69-74. Munich: C.H. Beck, 1980.

06190. Kumar, Doris Marianne. "Hope, Despair and Resignation in Gunter Eich's Mädchen von Viterbo." Germanic Notes 7 (1976): 40-44.

06191. Vanovitch, Katherine. Female Roles in East German Drama 1949-1977. A Selective History of Drama in the GDR. Frankfurt: Lang, 1982.

06192. Wilson, Rodger Edward. "The Devouring Mother: Analysis of Dürrenmatt's Besuch der alten Dame." Germanic Review 52 (November 1977): 274-288.

06193. Zipes, Jack D. "Die Funktion der Frau in den Komödien der DDR." In Die Deutsche Komödie im zwanzigsten Jahrhundert, edited by Wolfgang Paulsen, pp. 187-205. Heidelberg: Stiehm, 1976.

(4) Poetry

(a) Hilde Domin

06194. Raulet, Gérard. "La poésie lyrique en 1975. Un nouveau bilan: La reedition de 'Wozu Lyrik Heute?' de Hilde Domin." _Allemagnes d'aujourd'hui_ n.s. 53 (May-June 1976): 61-65.

06195. ______. "La résistance en poésie: l'unité de la théorie et de la pratique poétique chez Hilde Domin." _Allemagnes d'aujourd'hui_ n.s. 54 (September-October 1976): 86-100.

06196. Schaumann, Lore. "Hilde Domin." In _Neue Literatur der Frauen_, edited by Heinz Puknus, pp. 29-33. Munich: C.H. Beck, 1980.

(b) Sarah Kirsch

06197. Armster, Charlotte E. "Merkwürdiges Beispiel weiblicher Entschlossenheit'--A Woman's Story--by Sarah Kirsch." In _Studies in GDR Culture and Society 2_, Proceedings of the Seventh Annual Symposium on the German Democratic Republic, edited by Margy Gerber, et al., p. 243-250. Washington, D.C.: University Press of America, Inc., 1982.

06198. Behn-Liebherz, Manfred. "Sarah Kirsch." In _Neue Literatur der Frauen_, edited by Heinz Puknus, pp. 158-165. Munich: C.H. Beck, 1980.

06199. Cosentino, Christine. "Die Lyrikerin Sarah Kirsch im Spiegel ihrer Bilder." _Neophilologus_ 3 (1979): 418-429.

06200. ______. "Privates und Politisches: Zur Frage des offenen Spielraums in der Lyrik Sarah Kirschs." _Germanic Notes_ 10 no. 2 (1979): 17-20.

06201. ______. "Sarah Kirschs Lyrikband 'Drachensteigen': Eine Neuorientierung?" _Michigan Germanic Studies_ 9 (Spring 1983): 63-74.

06202. ______. "Von 'italienischen Amseln' und 'provenzalischen Eulen': Sara Kirschs westliche Dichtungen _Drachensteigen_ und _La Pagerie_." In _Studies in GDR Culture and Society 2_, Proceedings of the Seventh Annual Symposium on the German Democratic Republic, edited by Margy Gerber, et al., pp. 87-98. Washington, D.C.: University Press of America, Inc., 1982.

06203. Meyer-Krentler, Eckardt. "Littérature d'une subjectivité engagée: Sarah Kirsch." _Allemagnes d'aujourd'hui_ n.s. 63 (May-June 1978): 88-96.

(c) Others

06204. Frederiksen, Elke. "Verena Stefan." In Neue Literature der Frauen, edited by Heinz Puknus, pp. 208-213. Munich: C.H. Beck, 1980.

06205. Lindemann, Gisela. "Friederike Mayröcker." In Neue Literatur der Frauen, edited by Heinz Puknus, pp. 51-54. Munich: C.H. Beck, 1980.

06206. Ozana, Anna. "Gertrud Leutenegger." In Neue Literatur der Frauen, edited by Heinz Puknus, pp. 236-240. Munich: C.H. Beck, 1980.

06207. Wischenbart, Rudiger. "Karin Kiwus." In Neue Literatur der Frauen, edited by Heinz Puknus, pp. 240-243. Munich: C.H. Beck, 1980.

Also refer to #5526, 6212-6218, 6226-6230, 6247, 6266.

(5) Prose

(a) Women in Novels

06208. Bronsen, David. "Böll's Women: Patterns in Male-Female Relationships." Monatshefte 57 (November 1965): 291-300.

06209. Clason, Synnöve. "Wie progressiv ist 'progressive' Literatur? Männliche Schweirigkeiten mit der Gleichberechtigung. Am Beispiel des DDR und Hermann Kants Roman 'Das Impressum.'" Jahrbuch für Internationale Germanistik 14 no. 1 (1982): 37-52.

06210. Critchfield, Richard. "From Abuse to Liberation: On Images of Women in Peter Handke's Writing of the Seventies." Jahrbuch fur Internationale Germanistik 14 no. 1 (1982): 27-36.

06211. Fehervary, Helen. "Women and the Aesthetic of the Positive Hero in the GDR." In Women in German Studies, edited by Kay Goodman and Ruth H. Sanders, pp. 121-132. Oxford, Ohio: Miami University, 1977.

(b) Novelists

[1] Individuals

[a] Ingeborg Bachmann

06212. Casanova, Nicole. "Ingeborg Bachmann ou le 'drame cardinal'." Allemagnes d'aujourd'hui n.s. 33 (May-June 1972): 40-53.

06213. Casey, T.J. "The Collected Works of Ingeborg Bachmann." German Life and Letters n.s. 34 (April 1981): 315-336.

06214. Dierick, Augustinus P. "Eros and Logos in Ingeborg Bachmann's _Simultan_." _German Life and Letters_ n.s. 35 (October 1981): 73-84.

06215. Frieden, Sandra. "Bachmann's _Malina_ and _Todesarten_: Subliminal Criminals." _German Quarterly_ 56 (January 1983): 61-73.

06216. Horsley, Ritta Jo. "Ingeborg Bachmann's 'Ein Schritt nach Gomorrha': A Feminist Appreciation and Critique." _Amsterdamer Beiträge zur neueren Germanistik_ 10 (1980): 277-293.

06217. Jurgensen, Manfred. _Ingeborg Bachmann: Die neue Sprache_. Bern: Lang, 1981.

06218. Witte, Bernd. "Ingeborg Bachmann." In _Neue Literatur der Frau_, edited by Hanz Punkus, pp. 33-43. Munich: C.H. Beck, 1980.

Also refer to #5526.

[b] Irmtraud Morgner

06219. Nordmann, Ingeborg. "Die halbierte Geschichtsfähigkeit der Frau. Zu Irmtraud Morgners Roman _Leben und Abenteuer der Trobadora Betriz nach Zeugnissen ihrere Spielfrau Laura_." _Amsterdamer Beiträge zur neueren Germanistik_ 11-12 (1981): 419-462.

06220. Obermüller, Klara. "Irmtraud Morgner." In _Neue Literatur der Frauen_ edited by Heinz Puknus, pp. 178-185. Munich: C.H. Beck, 1980.

[c] Anna Seghers

06221. Andrews, R.C. "An East German Novelist: Anna Seghers." _German Life and Letters_ 8 (1954-1955): 121-129.

06222. Greener, Bernhard. "'Suject Barre' und Sprache des Begehrens. Die Autorschaft 'Anna Seghers.'" _Amsterdamer Beiträge zur neueren Germanistik_ 17 (1983): 319-351.

06223. Kolb, Christine. "Anna Seghers 1900-1983. De la fidélité critique au silence." _Allemagnes d'aujourd'hui_ n. s. 86 (October-December 1983): 96-114.

06224. ______________. "Bibliographie -- Anna Seghers." _Allemagnes d'aujourd'hui_ n.s. 86 (October-December 1983): 115-116.

06225. Romero, Christiane Zehl. "The Rediscovery of Romanticism in the GDR: A Note on Anna Seghers' Role." In Studies in GDR Culture and Society 2, Proceedings on the Seventh Annual Symposium on the German Democratic Republic, edited by Margy Gerber, et al., pp. 19-29. Washington, D.C.: University Press of America, Inc., 1982.

[d] Gabriele Wohmann

06226. Knapp, Gerhard P. and Knapp, Mona. Gabriele Wohmann. Königstein: Athenäum, 1981.

06227. Knapp, Mona. "Zwischen den Fronten: Zur Entwicklung der Frauengestalten in Erzähltexten von Gabriele Wohmann." Amsterdamer Beitrage zur neuren Germanistik 10 (1980): 295-317.

06228. Kraft, Helga W. and Kosta, Barbara. "Mother-Daughter Relationships: Problems of Self-Determination in Novak, Henrich and Wohmann." German Quarterly 56 (January 1983): 74-88.

06229. Schloz, Gunther. "Gabriele Wohmann." In Neue Literatur der Frauen, edited by Heinz Punkus, pp. 79-87. Munich: C.H. Beck, 1980.

06230. Waidson, H.M. "The Short Stories and Novels of Gabriele Wohmann." German Life and Letters n.s. 26 (1972-1973): 214-227.

[e] Christa Wolf

06231. Cicora, Mary A. "Language, Identity and the Woman in Nachdenken über Christa T.: A Post-Structuralist Approach." Germanic Review 57 (Winter 1982): 16-22.

06232. Clausen, Jeanette. "The Difficulty of Saying 'I' as Theme and Narrative Technique in the Works of Christa Wolf." Amsterdamer Beiträge zur neueren Germanistik 10 (1980): 319-333.

06233. Hill, Linda. "Loyalism in Christa Wolf's Nachdenken über Christa T." Michigan Germanic Studies 7 (Fall 1981): 249-261.

06234. Hilzinger, Sonja. Kassandra: über Christa Wolf. Frankfurt/Main: Haag und Herchen, 1982.

06235. Jackson, Neil and Saunders, Barbara. "Christa Wolf's Kindheitsmuster: An East German Experiment in Political Autobiography." German Life and Letters n.s. 33 (July 1980): 319-329.

06236. Kolb, Christine. "Repères biographiques sur C. Wolf et son oeuvre." _Allemagnes d'aujourd'hui_ n.s. 91 (January-March 1985): 73-79.

06237. Krogmann, Werner. "Moralischer Realismus -- Ein Versuch uber Christa Wolf." _Amsterdamer Beiträge zur neueren Germanistik_ 7 (1978): 233-261.

06238. Lennox, Sara. "Christa Wolf and the Women Romantics." In _Studies in GDR Culture and Society 2_, Proceedings of the Seventh Annual Symposium on the German Democratic Republic, edited by Margy Gerber, et al., pp. 31-43. Washington, D.C.: University Press of America, Inc., 1982.

06239. McGauran, Fergus. "'Gebrochene Generation': Christa Wolf und Theodor Storm." _German Life and Letters_ n.s. 31 (July 1978): 328-335.

06240. Parkes, K.S. "An All-German Dilemma: Some Notes on the Presentation of the Theme of the Individual and Society in Martin Walser's _Halbzeit_ and Christa Wolf's _Nachdenken über Christa T._" _German Life and Letters_ n.s. 28 (October 1974): 58-64.

06241. Sevin, Dieter. "The Plea for Artistic Freedom in Christa Wolf's 'Lesen und Schreiben' and _Nachdenken über Christa T._ Essay and Fiction as Mutually Supportive Genre Forms." In _Studies in GDR Culture and Society 2_, Proceedings of the Seventh Annual Symposium on the German Democratic Republic, edited by Margy Gerber, et al., pp. 45-58. Washington, D.C.: University Press of America, Inc., 1982.

06242. Stephan, Alexander. "Christa Wolf." In _Neue Literatur der Frauen_, edited by Heinz Puknus, pp. 149-158. Munich: C.H. Beck, 1980.

Also refer to #5526, 6016.

[2] Others

06243. Behn-Liebherz, Manfred. "Brigitte Reimann." In _Neue Literatur der Frauen_, edited by Heinz Puknus, pp. 165-171. Munich: C.H. Beck, 1980.

06244. Beth, Hanno. "Elfriede Jelinek." In _Neue Literatur der Frauen_, edited by Heinz Puknus, pp. 133-138. Munich: C.H. Beck, 1980.

06245. Botzat, Tatjana. "Sigrid Brunk." In _Neue Literatur der Frauen_, edited by Heinz Puknus, pp. 130-133. Munich: C.H. Beck, 1980.

06246. Dietze, Gabriele. "Birgit Pausch." In _Neue Literatur der Frauen_, edited by Heinz Puknus, pp. 190-192. Munich: C.H. Beck, 1980.

06247. Dietze, Gabriele. "Hannelies Taschau." In *Neue Literatur der Frauen*, edited by Heinz Puknus, pp. 98-102. Munich: C.H. Beck, 1980.

06248. Drewitz, Ingeborg. "Elisabeth Plessen." In *Neue Literatur der Frauen*, edited by Heinz Puknus, pp. 224-230. Munich: C.H. Beck, 1980.

06249. Endres, Elisabeth. "Ilse Aichinger." In *Neue Literatur der Frauen*, edited by Heinz Puknus, pp. 44-50. Munich: C.H. Beck, 1980.

06250. Fecht, Friederike. "Jutta Heinrich." In *Neue Literatur der Frauen*, edited by Heinz Puknus, pp. 214-216. Munich: C.H. Beck, 1980.

06251. ________________. "Maria Erlenberger." In *Neue Literatur der Frauen*, edited by Heinz Puknus, pp. 216-220. Munich: C.H. Beck, 1980.

06252. Frederiksen, Elke. "Luise Rinser." In *Neue Literatur der Frauen*, edited by Heinz Puknus, pp. 55-61. Munich: C.H. Beck, 1980.

06253. Gerhardt, Marlis. "Gisela Elsner." In *Neue Literatur der Frauen*, edited by Heinz Puknus, pp. 88-94. Munich: C.H Beck, 1980.

06254. Jäger, Manfred. "Bemerkungen zu Brigitte Reimanns *Franziska Linkerhand*." *Amsterdamer Beiträge zur neueren Germanistik* 11-12 (1981): 407-417.

06255. Jäschke, Bärbel. "Margarete Hannsmann." In *Neue Literatur der Frauen*, edited by Heinz Puknus, pp. 65-69. Munich: C.H. Beck, 1980.

06256. Kempf, Marcelle. "Elfriede Jelinek, féministe malgré elle?" *Allemagnes d'aujourd'hui* n.s. 57 (March-April 1977): 86-95.

06257. Kindl, Ulrike. "Barbara Frischmuth." In *Neue Literatur der Frauen*, edited by Heinz Puknus, pp. 144-148. Munich: C.H. Beck, 1980.

06258. Kurz, Paul Konrad. "Karin Struck." In *Neue Literatur der Frauen*, edited by Heinz Puknus, pp. 193-200. Munich: C.H. Beck, 1980.

06259. Laurien, Ingrid. "Angelika Mechtel." In *Neue Literatur der Frauen*, edited by Heinz Puknus, pp. 116-125. Munich: C.H. Beck, 1980.

06260. McInnes, Edward. "Luise Rinser and the Religious Novel." *German Life and Letters* n.s. 32 (October 1978): 40-45.

06261. Melzer, Gerhard. "Marianne Fritz." In Neue Literatur der Frauen, edited by Heinz Puknus, pp. 220-224. Munich: C.H. Beck, 1980.

06262. Puknus, Heinz. "Brigitte Schwaiger." In Neue Literatur der Frauen, pp. 230-236. Munich: C.H. Beck, 1980.

06263. Pulver, Elsbeth. "Erica Pedretti." In Neue Literatur der Frauen, edited by Heinz Puknus, pp. 138-143. Munich: C.H. Beck, 1980.

06264. Schafroth, Heinz F. "Hanna Johansen." In Neue Literatur der Frauen, edited by Heinz Puknus, pp. 251-254. Munich: C.H. Beck, 1980.

06265. Schwarz, Waltraut. "Barbara Frischmuth--Rebellion und Ruckkehr." Amsterdamer Beiträge zur neueren Germanistik 14 (1982): 229-253.

06266. Smith, Stephen W. "Renate Rasp." In Neue Literatur der Frauen, edited by Heinz Puknus, pp. 94-98. Munich: C.H. Beck, 1980.

06267. Stromberg, Kyra. "Annemarie Weber." In Neue Literatur der Frauen, edited by Heinz Puknus, pp. 74-79. Munich: C.H. Beck, 1980.

06268. Tanner, Josef. "Anna Ozana." In Neue Literatur der Frauen, edited by Heinz Puknus, pp. 62-65. Munich: C.H. Beck, 1980.

06269. Zander, Jürgen. "Helga M. Novak." In Neue Literatur der Frauen, edited by Heinz Puknus, pp. 125-130. Munich: C.H. Beck, 1980.

06270. Zeller, Konradin. "Christa Reinig." In Neue Literatur der Frauen, edited by Heinz Puknus, pp. 200-208. Munich: C.H. Beck, 1980.

Also refer to #6228.

(c) Short Stories

06271. Allenstein, Bernd. "Elke Erb." In Neue Literatur der Frauen, edited by Heinz Puknus, pp. 243-246. Munich: C.H. Beck, 1980.

06272. Fiedler, Marion. "Friederike Roth." In Neue Literatur der Frauen, edited by Heinz Puknus, pp. 249-251. Munich: C.H. Beck, 1980.

06273. Hammerschmidt, Volker and Oettel, Andreas. "Helga Schubert." In Neue Literatur der Frauen, edited by Heinz Puknus, pp. 175-178. Munich: C.H. Beck, 1980.

06274. Hammerschmidt, Volker and Oettel, Andreas. "Helga Schütz." In _Neue Literatur der Frauen_, edited by Heinz Puknus, pp. 171-174. Munich: C.H. Beck, 1980.

06275. Mechtel, Angelika. "Katja Behrens." In _Neue Literatur der Frauen_, edited by Heinz Puknus, pp. 246-248. Munich: C.H. Beck, 1980.

06276. Petersen, Karin. "Ursula Krechel." In _Neue Literatur der Frauen_, edited by Heinz Puknus, pp. 185-190. Munich: C.H. Beck, 1980.

Also refer to #6197.

(d) Non-fiction

06277. Bellan, Monika. "La revue 'Alternative' juillet 1976: Mouvement des femmes, langage, psychanalyse." _Allemagnes d'aujourd'hui_ n.s. 54 (September-October 1976): 35-36.

06278. Smith, Stephen W. "Erika Runge." In _Neue Literatur der Frauen_, edited by Heinz Puknus, pp. 109-116. Munich: C.H. Beck, 1980.

06279. Wagener, Mary L. "Berta Zuckerkandl. Viennese Journalist and Publicist of Modern Art and Culture." _European Studies Review_ 12 (October 1982): 425-444.

c) Art

(1) Women in Art

06280. Verzola, Laurence. "Margarethe von Trotta _L'Age de Plomb_. 'A la recherche d'une soeur.'" _Allemagnes d'aujourd'hui_ n.s. 79 (January-March 1982): 111-118.

Also refer to #5330.

(2) Women Artists

(a) Non-specific

06281. Christ, Dorothea and Suter, Margrit, eds. _Schweizer Künstlerinnen heute_. Zurich: Gesellschaft Schweizerischer Malerinnen, Bildhauerinnen und Kunstgewerblerinnen, 1984?.

06282. Klemke, Rainer E., ed. _Karl-Hofer-Symposion. Frau, Raum, Zeit_. Berlin: Colloquium, 1983.

06283. Künstlergilde. _Malerei, Graphik, Plastik: eine Ausstellung der Künstlergilde zum Jahr der Frau_. Regensburg: Die Galerie, 1975.

06284. Rosenbach, Ulrike, ed. Beispiel einer autonomen Kulturarbeit. Cologne: Schule für Kreativen Feminismus, 1980.

06285. Türe, Anna, ed. Körper, Liebe, Sprache: über weibliche Kunst, Erotik. Berlin (West): Elefanten Press, 1982.

Also refer to #5331, 5335.

(b) Actresses/Directors

06286. Hervo, Brigitte. "Entretien avec Lotte Eisner." Allemagnes d'aujourd'hui n.s. 66 (January-February 1979): 118-125.

06287. ______________. "Hommages a Lotte Eisner." Allemagnes d'aujourd'hui n.s. 81 (July-September 1982): 124-125.

06288. Verzola, Laurence. "'Allemagne, Mere Blaforde' de Helgma Sandars Brahms." Allemagnes d'aujourd'hui n.s. 77 (July-September 1981): 128-132.

(c) Musicians/Singers

06289. Mannoni, Gerard. "Léonie Rysanek." Allemagnes d'aujourd'hui n.s. 48 (May-June 1975): 90-93.

(d) Painters

06290. Lippard, Lucy R. "Eva Hesse: The Circle." In From the Center Feminist Essays on Women's Art, pp. 155-166. New York: H.P. Dutton, 1976.

E. IBERIA

1. SURVEYS

"I'm only a woman, and that's enough with a goat
and an old car, a "Praise the Lord" every morning,
and a lecherous fool running the show."

Gloria Fuertes
I'm Only a Woman

06291. Barbosa, Madelena. "Women in Portugal." In The Women's Liberation Movement, edited by Jan Bradshaw, pp. 477-480. New York: Pergamon Press, 1982. Also in Women's Studies International 4 (1981): 477-480.

06292. Calheiros, Pedro. "Fado et Fatima: femmes portugaises." In Les femmes et leur maîtres, edited by Maria-Antonietta Macciocchi, pp. 201-218. Paris: C. Bourgeois, 1979.

06293. Krogbaumker, Beate. Portugiesische Landfrauen zwischen Kirche und Kapital: Bewusstseinsbildung des Gral in Portugal. Fort Lauderdale: Verlag Breitenbach, 1980.

06294. Miguel, Amando de. Sexo: mujer y natalidad en Espana. Madrid: EDICUSA, 1975.

2. POLITICAL

"There have been women here who were feminists and no one knows about it. It's as if feminism were suddenly a new fashion. . ."

Charo Ema

a) Legal

06295. Abella Santamaria, Jaime. Ley del divorcio. Madrid: Instituto Nacional de Prospectiva, 1980.

06296. Alberdi, Cristina; Cerrillos, Angela; and Abril, Consuelo. Ahora divorcio. Barcelona:Bruguera, 1977.

06297. Aradillas Agudo, Antonio. Divorcio, recta final. Barcelona:Ediciones Actuales, 1977.

06298. ______________________. Divorcio 77. Madrid: Sedmay Ediciones, 1976.

06299. Arza Arteaga, Antonio. Remedios juridicos a los matrimonios rotos: (nulidad, separacion, divorcio). Bilbao: Universidad de Deusto, 1982.

06300. Barja Quiroga, Juan. El divorcio en Espana: critica de la nueva ley. Madrid: Forja, 1982.

06301. Bastos, Jacinto Fernandes Rodrigues. Codigo civil Portugues, actualizacao legislativa. Lisbon: Bastos, 1976.

06302. Caballero Gea, Jose Alfredo. La ley del divorcio, 1981. Pamplona: Aranzadi, 1982.

06303. Delgado, Abel Pereira. O divorcio: apontamentos para uma troca de impressoes com candidatos a juizes de direito, no Centro de Estudos Judiciarios. Lisbon: Livraria Petrony, 1980.

06304. Fosar Benlloch, Enrique. La separacion y el divorcio en el derecho espanol vigente. Barcelona: Bosch, c1982.

06305. Gafo, Javier. El aborto ante la conciencia y la ley. Madrid: PPC, [1982?].

06306. Garcia Vitoria, Aurora. El tipo basico de aborto. Pamplona:Aranzadi, 1981.

06307. Guerra Campos, Jose. La ley de divorcio y el episcopado espanol, 1976-1981. Madrid: ADUE, 1981.

06308. Hervada, J. et al. Divorcio. Pamplona: EUNSA, 1977.

06309. Huerta Tocildo, Susana. Aborto con resultado de muerte o lesiones graves. Madrid: Publicaciones del Instituto de Criminologia de la Universidad Complutense, 1977.

06310. Jiménez Butragueno, De Los Angeles, María. "Protective Legislation and Equal Opportunity and Treatment for Women in Spain." International Labour Review 121 (March-April 1982): 185-198.

06311. Landrove Diaz, Gerardo. Politica criminal del aborto. Barcelona: Bosch, c1976.

06312. Lezcano, Ricardo. El divorcio en la Segunda Republica. Madrid: Akal, [c1979].

06313. Lopez Alarcon, Mariano. El nuevo sistema matrimonial espanol: nulidad, separacion y divorcio. Madrid: Tecnos, 1983.

06314. Metrass, Célia; Medeiros, Helena de Sa; and Horta, Maria Teresa. Aborto: direito ao nosso corpo. Lisbon: Editorial Futura, 1975.

06315. Mir, Santiago, ed. La Despenalizacion del aborto. Bellaterra: Universidad Autonoma de Barcelona, 1983.

06316. Narbona Gonzalez, Francisco. Un cierto divorcio. Barcelona: Espana: Planeta, 1980.

06317. ____________________________. El divorcio viaja a España. Torrejon de Ardoz: A.Q. Ediciones, 1974.

06318. Para Martin, Antonio. Divorcio, separacion y declaracion de nulidad: la crisis matrimonial ante el derecho. Barcelona: Humanitas, [1983?].

06319 Pinto, Fernando Brand ao Ferreira. Causas do divórcio: doutrina, legislação, jurisprudencia: Portugal e Brasil. Coimbra: Livraria Almedina, 1980.

06320. Santos, Eduardo dos. Divórcio e separação judicial de pessoas e bense simples separação judicial de bens, declaração de nulidade d dissolução do casamento católico. Amadora: Livraria Bertrand, 1975.

06321. ____________________. A nova lei do divórcio: divórcio, separação judicial de pessoas d bens e simples separação judicial de bens, dissolução do casamento católico e separação de leito, mesa e habitação. Lisbon: Liber, 1979.

06322. Sauquillo, Francisco, ed. Spain. Ley de divorcio: texto integro. Madrid: E. Escolar, [1981?].

06323. Valladares Rascon, Etelvina. Nulidad, separacion, divorcio: commentarios a la ley de reforma del matrimonio. Madrid: Civitas, 1982.

06324. Vega Sala, Francisco. Sintesis practica sobre la regulacion del divorcio en España. Barcelona: Praxis, 1982.

06325. Zarraluqui, Luis. El divorcio, defensa del matrimonio. Barcelona: Bruguera, 1980.

Also refer to #5346, 6355.

b) Criminal

06326. Falcón, Lidia. En el infierno: Ser mujer en las carceles de España. Barcelona: Ediciones de Feminismo S.A., 1977.

c) Feminism

06327. ____________. "Spain: Women Are the Conscience of Our Country." In Sisterhood is Global, edited by Robin Morgan, pp. 626-631. Garden City, N.Y.: Anchor Press, Doubleday, 1984.

06328. Hurtado, Amparo. "Phalange et phallocratie." In Les femmes et leur maîtres, edited by Maria-Antonietta Macciocchi, pp. 345-364. Paris: C. Bourgeois, 1979.

06329. Levine, Linda Gould and Waldman, Gloria Feeman. Feminismo ante el franquismo. Florida: Ediciones Universal, 1980.

06330. Pintasilgo, Maria de Lourdes. "Portugal: Daring to Be Different." In Sisterhood is Global, edited by Robin Morgan, pp. 571-575. Garden City, N.Y.: Anchor Press, Doubleday, 1984.

06331. Rague-Arias, Maria-Jose. "Spain: Feminism in Our Time." In The Women's Liberation Mouvement, edited by Jan Bradshaw, pp. 471-476. New York: Pergamon Press, 1982.

3. ECONOMIC

"Spain is still a country without academic scholarships for older women or support for working wives, with an insufficient system of day-care centers, schools, clinics . . . Spanish women also are the free labor force that the State counts on to care for the sick, the retarded. . . ."

Lidia Falcon

a) Generic

06332. Silva, Regina Tavares de. A imagem da mulher na publidade. Lisbon: Presidencia do Consleho de Ministros, Comissao da Condicao Feminina, 1970.

06333 Teran Alvarez, Manuel. "El presupuesto familiar de ingresos y gastos en Espana," <u>Estudios Geograficos</u> 21 (August 1960): 408-413.

b) Women's Employment

06334. International Labour Office. "Spanish Women and Work." <u>Social and Labour Bulletin</u> (December 1982): 552-553.

06335. Masur, Jenny. "Women's Work in Rural Andalusia." <u>Ethnology</u> 23 (January 1984): 25-38.

06336. Miguel, Amando de. "El trabajo de la mujer." In <u>Manuel de estructura social de Espana</u>, pp. 270-299. Madrid: Editorial Tecnos, 1974.

06337. Nunes, Maria do Carmo. "Women at Work in Portugal." In <u>Working Women An International Survey</u>, edited by Marilyn J. Davidson and Cary L. Cooper, pp. 209-233. New York: John Wiley and Sons, 1984.

06338. <u>Portugal--der Kampf der arbeitenden Frau</u>. Hamburg: Verlag Arbeitskampf, 1975.

4. SOCIAL

"How to tell a woman in this day and age; make a bridge, as once upon a time she was told: make me a son."
First Leter V
<u>The Three Marias</u>

a) Generic

06339. Aceves, Joseph B. <u>Social Change in a Spanish Village</u>. Cambridge, Mass.: Schenkman, 1971.

06340. Buechler, H. C. and Buechler, Judith-Maria Hess. "Los Suizos: Galician Migration to Switzerland." In <u>Migration and Development</u>, edited by Helen I. Safa and Brian M. du Toit, pp. 17-29. The Hague: Mouton, 1975.

06341. Freeman, Susan Tax. <u>The Pasiegos. Spaniards in No Man's Land</u>. Chicago: University of Chicago Press, 1979.

06342. Miguel, Amando de. <u>Manual de estructura social de España</u>. Madrid: Editorial Tecnos, 1974.

b) Demography

06343. Campo Urbano, Salustiano del. <u>La poblacion de España</u>. Paris: C.I.C.R.E.D., 1975.

06344. Gregory, David. "Migration and Demographic Change in Andalucia." In _The Changing Faces of Rural Spain_, edited by Joseph B. Aceves and William A. Douglass, pp. 63-96. New York: Schenkman Publishing Company, 1976.

06345. Stycos, J. Mayone. "The Timing of Spanish Marriages: A Socio-Statistical Study." _Population Studies_ 37 (July 1983): 227-238.

Also refer to #5347.

c) Marriage

06346. Aradillas Agudo, Antonio. _Matrimonios rotos_. Madrid: Sedmay Ediciones, 1975.

06347. Catholic Church. Conferencia Episcopal Espanola. _Divorcio, ensenanza y misiones: documentos de la XXXII Asamblea Plenaria del Episcopado Espanol_. Madrid: PPC, c1980.

06348. Diaz Eledo, Loloes and Pabon, Maria, eds. _El Divorcio-a lo clara_. Madrid: Editorial Popular, 1981.

06349. Fraser, Ronald. "Men and Women: Engagement, Marriage and Parenthood." In _Tajos The Story of a Village on the Costa del Sol_, pp. 163-180. New York: Pantheon Books, Random House, 1973.

06350. Osborne, Raquel and Luis Recio, Juan. _Hacia el divorcio_. Madrid: Taller do Sociologia, 1979.

Also refer to #5346, 6295-6304, 6308, 6312, 6313, 6316-6325, 6345.

d) Sex Life and Morals

06351. Cela, Camil José. _Izas, Rabizas y Colipoterras. Drama con acompañamiento da cachondeo y dolor de corazon_. Barcelona: Editorial Lumen, 1964.

e) Health/Medical

06352. Alberdi, Cristina and Sendon, Victoria. _Aborto_. Barcelona: Bruguera, 1977.

06353. Blazquez, Niceto. _Le dictadura del aborto_. Madrid: Edica, D.L., 1978.

06354. CERP. _Aborto, uma questão social: depoimento para uma reflexao alargada_. Lisbon: distribuicao, Livraria Multinova, 1974?

06355. Garcia Marin, José Maria. *El aborto criminal en la legislación y la doctrine (pasado y presente de una polemica).* Madrid: Edit. de Derecho Reunidas, 1980.

Also refer to #6305, 6306, 6309, 6311, 6314, 6315.

5. CULTURAL

> "For men and women, things are arranged in different perspectives of interest, valuation, or importance, constituting different perspectives of reality, different real worlds. . . .not only do man and woman need different things to be happy, but they are happy in different senses."
>
> Julian Marias
> *Metaphysical Anthropology*

a) Literature

(1) Drama

06356. Burgers, Ronald D. "Enigma, Paradox and Dramatic Movement in *La Dama del Alba*." *Hispania* 68 (March 1985): 29-34.

06357. Giuliano, William. "The Role of Man and of Woman in Buero Vallejo's Plays." *Hispanofilia* 39 (May 1970): 21-28.

06358. Jordan, Barry. "Patriarchy, Sexuality and Oedipal Conflict in Buero Vallejo's *El concierto de San Ovidio*." *Modern Drama* 28 (September 1985): 431-450.

06359. Podol, Peter L. "The Theme of Honor in Two Plays of Buero Vallejo: *Las palabras en la arena* and *La tejedora de suenos*." *Hispanofilia* 68 (January 1980): 37-46.

(2) Poetry

06360. Long, Ada. "Introduction." In *Off the Map. Selected Poems By Gloria Fuertes*, edited and translated by Philip Levine and Ada Long, pp. 3-8. Middletown, Ct.: Wesleyan University Press, 1984.

06361. Pinet, Carolyn. "The Sacramental View of Poetry and the Religion of Love in Jorge Guillen's *Cantico*." *Hispania* 62 (March 1979): 47-55.

(3) Prose

(a) Women in Novels

06362. Boring, Phyllis Zatlin. "Deblibes' Two Views of the Spanish Mother." *Hispanofilia* 63 (May 1978): 79-87.

06363. Ortega, José. "La frustracion femenina en Los Mercadres de Ana Maria Matute." Hispanofilia 54 (May 1975): 31-38.

06364. Planells, Antonio. "Represión sexuel, frigidez y maternidad frustrada: 'Verano' de Julio Cortazar." Bulletin of Hispanic Studies 56 (July 1979): 233-237.

(b) Novelists

06365. Jones, Margaret W. "Religious Motifs and Biblical Allusions in the Works of Ana Marie Matute." Hispania 51 (September 1968): 416-423.

06366. Winecoff, Janet. "Existentialism in the Novels of Elena Soriano." Hispania 47 (May 1964): 309-315.

06367. ______________. "Style and Solitude in the Works of Ana Maria Matute." Hispania 49 (March 1966): 61-69.

Also refer to #5357.

b) Art

06368. Miller, Beth. "From Mistress to Murderess, The Metamorphosis of Bunuel's Tristana." In Women in Hispanic Literature, Icons and Fallen Idols, pp. 340-359. Berkeley, Calif.: University of California Press, 1983.

06369. Riley, E.C. "The Story of Ana in El espiritu de la colmena." Bulletin of Hispanic Studies 61 (October 1984): 491-497.

F. ITALY

1. SURVEYS

"Women are less respectable and autonomous human beings in bourgeois Italy today, with all its commerce and modernity . . ."

Jean-François Reval
As For Italy, 1958

06370. Bielli, Carla. "Some Aspects of the Condition of Women in Italy." In Women in the World: A Comparative Study, pp. 105-113. Santa Barbara, Calif.: Clio Books, 1976.

06371. Fontanes, Monique de. "La situation de la femme en Italie meridionale." In Femmes corses et femmes méditerranéennes, pp. 98-113. Provence: Centre d'Etudes Corses de l'Universite de Provence, 1976.

2. POLITICAL

> " . . . it is necessary that a democratically organized women's movement be able to exercise on a political level, all its power, and therefore have the strength to initiate not only economic and social changes, but also civil and cultural ones."
>
> Italian Communist Party
> 15th National Congress

a) Generic

06372. Ergas, Yasmine. "1968-1972--Feminism and the Italian Party System: Women's Politics in a Decade of Turmoil." Comparative Politics 14 (April 1982): 253-279.

b) Legal

06373. Aborto: norme per la tutela sociale della maternita e sull'interruzione volontaria della gravidanza. Rome: Edizioni delle autonomie, [1978].

06374. Aborto quando come e dove: la Legge 22 maggio 1978, n. 194. Milan: Teti, 1978.

06375. Ballestrero, Maria Vittoria. "Women at Work in Italy: Legislation--Evolution and Prospects." In Working Women: An International Survey, edited by Marilyn J. Davidson and Cary L. Cooper, pp. 103-122. New York: John Wiley and Sons, 1984.

06376. Berlinguer, Giovanni. La legge sull'aborto. Rome: Editori riuniti, 1978.

06377. Berutti, Mario. Il divorzio in Italia. Milano: Edizioni di Comunita, 1964.

06378. Bonetti, Alberto and Monducci, Mario. Dodici maggio '74 fine dell'ipoteca clericale. Cronaca di un referendum. Manduria: Lacaita, 1974.

06379. Burke, Cormac, et al. Aborto no.. Milan: Ares, [1975].

06380. Cali, Rita, ed. La nuova disciplina dell aborto: commento articolo per articolo della L. 22-5-1978, n. 194 concernente norme per la tutela sociale della maternita e sulla interruzione volontaria della gravidanza. Naples: Simone, 1978.

06381. Carettoni, Tullia and Gatto, Simone. L'aborto: problemi e leggi. Palermo: Palumbo, 1973.

06382. Casini, Carlo and Cieri, Francesco. La nuova disciplina dell'aborto: (commento alla legge 22 maggio 1978 n 194). Padua: CEDAM, 1978.

06383. Cigoli, Vittorio. *Separazione, divorzio e affidamento die figli: tecniche e criteri della perizia e del trattamento*. Milan: Giuffre, 1983.

06384. Cipriani, Nicola. *La nuova disciplina giuridica sull'aborto*. Rimini: Maggioli Editore, 1978.

06385. Coccia, Franco. *Le conseguenze patrimoniali dello scioglimento del matrimonio*. Milan: Giuffre, 1981.

06386. Colombo, Bernardo. *La diffusione degli aborti illegali in Italia*. Milan: Vita e pensiero. 1977.

06387. Concetti, Gino J. *Il diritto alla vita. Alternative all'aborto*. Rome: Logos, 1984.

06388. Conti, Laura. *Il tormento e lo scudo: un compromesso contro le donne*. Milan: G. Mazzotta, c1981.

06389. *Declaratio de abortu procurato*. Vatican: Libreria Editrice Vaticana, 1974.

06390. De Francesco, Romano. *Io raschio, tu raschi, ella rischia*. Naples: SEN, 1979.

06391. *Dibattito sull'aborto*. Rome: Apes, 1984.

06392. *La difesa del diritto alla nascita*. *Atti* (*Roma 1972*). Milan: Giuffre, 1975.

06393. Fleig, Walther. *Die Ehescheidung im italienischen Recht*. Bielefeld: E. und W. Gieseking, 1975.

06394. Fusaro, Carlo and Conciani, Giorgio. *Aborto libero, ecco perche*. Livorno: La nuova frontiera, 1975.

06395. Galeotti, Serio. *Esigenza e problemi del referendum*. Milan: A. Giuffre, 1970.

06396. ______________, et al. *Tavola rotonda sul tema per la determinazione ope legis della nuova data del referendum sul divorzio*, *Rome*, *1972*. Rome, Centro studi di scienze sociali, 1972.

06397. Galli, Guido, ed. *L'Interruzione volontaria della gravidanza:* (*commento alla legge 22 maggio 1978, n. 194: norme per la tutela sociale della maternita e sull'interruzione volontaria della gravidanza*). Milan: Giuffre, 1978.

06398. Gallini, Clara and Pinna, Luca. *Il referendum sul divorzio in Sardegna*. Cagliari: EDES, 1975.

06399. Galoppini, Annamaria, ed. *Commentario sul divorzio*. Milan: A. Giuffre, 1980.

06400. Grassi, Lucio and Grassi, Paolo. Il divorzio nella giurisprudenza: rasegna critica delle sentenze costituzionali, di legittimita e di merito sulla Legge 898/1970. Naples: Jovene, 1978.

06401. Legge aborto e consultori familiari. Milan: Pirola, 1979.

06402. Legge sull'aborto. Norme per la tutela sociale della maternità e sull'interruzione volontaria della gravidanza. Milan: Pirola, 1979.

06403. Legislazione sull'aborto: prospettive di una riforma. Atti (dal 20 al 21 febbraio 1975). Naples: Jovene, 1975.

06404. Liberalizzare l'aborto? Assisi: Cittadella, n.d.

06405. Libro bianco sull'aborto. Documenti dei dibattiti parlamentari nella VI e VII legislatura. Milan: Rusconi Libri, 1983.

06406. Liverani, Pier Giorgio. Aborto anno uno: fatti & misfatti della Legge n. 194. Milan: Ares, [1979].

06407. Lucarini, Spartaco. Divorzio in Italia. Rome: Citta nuova, 1969.

06408. Maki, Keiji. Il ruolo del tribunale familiare nel problema del divorzio. Perugia: Accademia giuridica umbra, 1967.

06409. Mannheimer, Renato; Michelli, Giuseppe; and Zajazyk, Francesca. Mutamento sociale e comportamento elettorale: il caso del referendum sul divorzio. Milano: F. Angeli, [1978].

06410. Marinucci, Elena and Remiddi, Laura. L'aborto legale. Come applicare e gestire la legge sull'interruzione della gravidanza. Venice: Marsilio, 1978.

06411. ______________________________. Guida all'aborto legale: come applicare e gestire la legge sull'interruzione della gravidanza. Venice: Marsilio, [1978].

06412. Mattioli, Paola. Immagini del no. Milan: All'insegna del pesce d'oro, 1974.

06413. Mellini, Mauro. 1976 [i.e. Millenovecentosettantasei] brigate rosse, operazione aborto. Rome: La nuova sinistra, [1974].

06414. Menciassi, Daniele. La legge italiana sull'aborto: testo integrale e commento della Legg 22 maggio 1978, n. 194: norme per la tutela sociale della maternita e sull'interruzione volontaria della gravidanza. Poggibonsi: A. Lalli, 1979.

06415. Palagi, Umberto. _Luci e ombre della Legga 22 maggio 1978, n. 194 (Norme per ia tutela sociale delle maternita e sull'interruzione volontaria della gravidanza)_. Pisa: Pacini, 1978

06416. Palladino, Alfonso and Palladino, Vincenzo. _Il divorzio: commento teorico-pratico alla legge sulla disciplina dei casi di scioglimento del matrimonio: legge 1 dicembre 1978 n. 898_. Milan: Giuffre, 1975.

06417. Parisi, Arturo. _Questione cattolica e referendum, l'inizio di una fine_. Bologna: Il mulino, [1974].

06418. Partito della democrazia cristiana. Gruppa parlementare alla camera dei deputati. _Libro bianco sull'aborto:Cronaca di un dramma della coscienza italiana_. Milan: Rusconi, 1977.

06419. _Per una scelta di liberta_. Rome: Coines, 1974.

06420. Perico, Giacomo. _Di fronte alla legge di aborto. Diritto e morale_. Turin: Elle Di Ci, 1978.

06421. Protetti, Ettore. _Dello scioglimento del matrimonio e della separazione dei coniugi:del regime patrimoniale della famiglia_. Rome: PEM, 1979.

06422. Schooyans, Michel. _L'aborto, problema politico_. Turin: Elle Di Ci, 1975.

06423. Stella Richter, Giorgio. _L'istituto del divorzio in Italia e l'esperienza giuridica dei principali ordinamenti europei_. Milan: A. Giuffre, 1976.

06424. Studenti di sociologia dell'Universita di Napoli, ed. _Si, no: Battaglia per il referendum in due comunità del Mezzogiorno_. Naples: CLU, 1975.

06425. Teodori, Mana Adeley, ed. _Contro l'aborto di classe_. Rome: Savelli, 1975.

06426. Tettamanzi, Dionigi, ed. _Aborto e obiezione di coscienze_. Brezzo di Bedero: Edizioni Salcom, 1978.

06427. Traverso, Carlo Emilio. _La tutela costituzionale della persona umana prima della nascita_. Milan: A. Giuffre, 1977.

06428. UICEMP, ed. _L'Interruzione volontaria di gravidanza: la donna, l'uomo, il consultorio, l'ospedale, la legge_. Florence: Nuova Guaraldi, 1981.

06429. Vannini, Ottorino. _Quid iuris, vol. 5: Aborto-Omicidio preterintenzionale_. Milan: Giuffre, 1950

c) Criminal

06430. Teodori, Maria Adele. Le violentate. Milan: Sugar Company, 1977.

d) Feminism

06431. Beckwith, Karen. Feminism and Leftist Politics in Italy: The Case of the UDI-PCI Relations." Western European Politics 8 (October 1985): 19-37.

06432. Caruso, Liliana. "Tutto sottosopra--Il femminismo fuori dalle istituzioni." In Esistere comme donna, pp. 267-276. Milan: Mazzotta, 1983.

06433. Ceccolini, Laura. "L'altra meta del cielo in tempesta--Il femminismo dentro le istituzioni." In Esistere comme donna, pp. 257-266. Milan: Mazzotta, 1983.

06434. Collettivo internazionale femminista, ed. Aborto di Stato, strage delle innocenti. Venice: Marsilio, 1976.

06435. Colombo, Daniela. "The Italian Feminist Movement." In The Women's Liberation Movement, edited by Jan Bradshaw, pp. 461-469. New York: Pergamon Press, 1982.

06436. Dodds, Dinah. "Extra-Parliamentary Feminism and Social Change in Italy, 1971-1980. International Journal of Women's Studies 8 (1982): 148-160.

06437. Zaccaria, Paola. "Italy: A Mortified Thirst for Living." In Sisterhood is Global, edited by Robin Morgan pp. 370-375. Garden City, N.Y.: Anchor Books, Doubleday, 1984.

Also refer to #6439, 6442.

3. ECONOMIC

". . . To me my job is to see this land gets farmed to raise up the children, make them go to school and teach them what's right and get work, as much work as I can get while I'm still young enough to work in the fields, because that's all I know."

Teresa, quoted in
Ann Cornelisen
Woman of the Shadows

a) Women's Employment

06438. Balbo, Laura and Bianchi, Marina. Ricomposizioni: il lavoro di servizio nella societa della crisi. Milan: F. Angeli, 1982.

06439. Toronto Wages for Housework Committee and the New York Collective. Italy Now. Toronto: Wages for Housework, [1975].

06440. "Working Women in Italy." Labour Gazette 62 (September 1962): 1025.

Also refer to #5375, 6068, 6375, 6455, 6459.

b) Trade Unions

06441. Becalli, Bianca. "Italy." In Women and Trade Unions in Eleven Industrialized Countries, edited by Alice H. Cook, Val R. Lorwin, and Arlene Daniels Kaplan, pp. 182-214. Philadelphia: Temple University Press, 1984.

06442. Coordinamento nazionale femminile CISL. Questione femminile e sindacato. Rome: Nuove edizioni operaie, 1978.

4. RELIGION

"I don't believe that the faith of Italian women is the cause of their backwardness."

Togliatti

06443. L'aborto in Italia: fenomenologia dell'aborto: riflessione morale, giuridica e pastorale. Bologna: Edizioni dehoniane, 1975.

06444. Berlendis, Alfredo; Rostagno, Sergio; and Girardet, Sbaffi Maria. Protestanti e l'aborto. Perche una scelta a favore della donna. Turin: Claudiana, 1981.

06445. Bongiovanni, Pietro. L'aborto, principi, problemi, indicazioni. Turin: Elle Di Ci, 1975.

06446. Caprile, Giovanni. Non uccidere. Il magistero della Chiesa sull'aborto. Rome: La Civilta Cattolica, 1976.

06447. Ciccone, Lino. Il problema dell'aborto e la risposta cattolica. Milan: OR, 1984.

06448. La communita cristiana e l'accoglienza della vita umana nascente. Turin: Edizioni Paoline, 1979.

06449. Dichiarazione sull'aborto procurato. Turin: Elle Di Ci, 1975.

06450 Girardet, Maria. La coscienza cristiana dinanzi all'aborto. Turin: Claudiana, 1970.

06451. Marini, Emilio. Abortirei, ma. . . . Pinerolo: Alzani, 1976.

06452. Martelet, Gustave. *Chiesa e aborto*. Rome: Anonima Veritas Editrice, 1975.

06453. Tettamanzi, Dionigi. *La communità cristiana e l'aborto*. Turin: Edizioni Paoline, 1975.

Also refer to #5683, 6417, 6426.

5. SOCIAL

"A Woman in Italy is half slave to her husband."
Italian proverb

a) Generic

06454. Jalla, Daniele. "Memoria, denaro e ritulalita'domestica: ipotese di ricerca sulla famiglia operaia." *Società et Storia* 10 (1980): 863-876.

b) Demography

06455. Lenti, Libero. "Population Growth and Employment in Italy." *Review of Economic Conditions in Italy* 33 (February 1979): 7-11.

06456. Rey, Guido M. "Italy of Censuses." *Review of Economic Conditions in Italy* 37 (June 1983): 193-222.

c) Family

06457. Buonanno, Milly. "Condizioni d'origine e orientamenti iniziali della sociologia della famiglia in Italia." *Rassegna italiana di sociologia* 18 (January-March 1977): 85-109.

06458. Castellina, Luciana, ed. *Famiglia e società capitalistica*. Rome: Alfani, 1974.

06459. Saraceno, Chiara. "Shifts in Public and Private Boundaries: Women as Mothers and Service Workers in Italian Daycare." *Feminist Studies* 10 (Spring 1984): 7-29.

Also refer to #6377, 6378, 6383, 6385, 6393, 6395, 6396, 6398-6400, 6407-6409, 6412, 6416, 6419, 6421, 6423, 6424, 6438.

d) Health/Medical

(1) Birth Control/Abortion

06460. Bellino, Francesco. *Analisi delle matrici tecnocratiche dell'aborto*. Boni: Cacucci, 1976.

06461. Bonicelli, Emilio. Bambini di troppo. Il problema dell'aborto in Italia. Milan: Communione e Liberazione, 1976.

06462. Buttarelli, Armando. Noi non abbiamo abortito. Turin: Elle Di Ci, 1979.

06463. Concepito per vivere. Naples: Edizioni Dehoniane, 1978.

06464. Conoscenza dell'aborto e organizzazione sociosanitaria. Rome: Editrice Sindacale Italiana, 1979.

06465. Dalla, Vedova Arturo; Caprile, Giovanni; and Dinacci, Ugo. No all'aborto: perche? si alla vita. Rome: La Parola, 1979.

06466. Discussione sull'aborto. Rome: Libreria Ateneo Salesiano, 1975.

06467. Durand, Guy. Quale vita? Naples: Edizioni Dehoniane, 1981.

06468. Faccio, Adele. Le mie ragioni: conversazioni con 70 donne. Milan: Feltrinelli, 1975.

06469. L'interruzione volontaria di gravidanza. Florence: Guaraldi, 1981.

06470. Lichfield, Michael and Kentish, Susan. Bambini da bruciare. Turin: Edizioni Paoline, 1979.

06471. Lorenzetti, Luigi. Aborto? Cosa pensare? Cosa fare? Bologna: Edizioni Dehoniane Bologna, 1979.

06472. Manceaux, M. Aborto per non morire. Milan: Moizzi, 1983.

06473. Sardi, Paolo. L'Aborto ieri e oggi. Brescia: Paideia, 1975.

06474. Schelotto, Gianna and Arcuri, Camillo. E se soffriss: anch'io? Ansie e dolori dell'aborto maschile. Venice: Arsenale, 1981.

06475. Tocci, Arturo. Il procurato aborto. Milan: Giuffre, 1954.

Also refer to #6373, 6374, 6376, 6379-6382, 6384, 6386-6392, 6394, 6401-6406, 6410, 6411, 6413-6415, 6417, 6418, 6420, 6422, 6425-6429, 6434, 6443-6453.

(2) Women and Health

06476. Gruppo femminista per il salario al lavoro domestico di Ferrara, ed. Dietro la normalità del parto: lotta all'ospedale di Ferrara. Venice: Marsilio, 1978.

6. CULTURAL

". . . it (my revolt) has always been there, boiling inside me together with the perception that the lifeline came from education (two of my sisters had to leave school at age eleven). . . education meant knowledge--and that it would provide me with the means to escape."

Paola Zaccaria

06477. Gaboardi, Luciana; Lasagni, Ilaria; and Pedersoli, Nadia. "1945-1965: Le donne in cammino verso un nuovo progetto di società." In Esistere comme donna, pp. 237-246. Milan: Mazzotta, 1983.

06478. Macciocchi, Maria-Antonietta. "La femme au perroquet." In Les femmes et leur maîtres, pp. 95-101. Paris: C. Bourgeois, 1979.

Also refer to #5378.

G. THE LOW COUNTRIES

1. POLITICAL

"Many young girls who still have the illusion of being free and independent consider feminism 'extreme'."

Corrine Oudijk

a) Legal

06479. Avylel, G. vanden, ed. Le Divorce et la separation des époux. Brussels: Service, 1981.

06480. Bosmans, Fernand. L'avortement clandestin! ... Legal? Paris: F. Nathan, 1973.

06481. Dembour, Pierre. Le mariage et le divorce et la Cour de cassation. Brussels: E. Bruylant, 1980.

06482. de Ruiter, J. "Dutch Law." In The Reform of Family Law in Europe: The Equality of the Spouses, Divorce, Illegitimate Children, edited by A.G. Chloros, pp. 19-41. Boston: Kluwer, 1978.

06483. Marques Pereira, Bérangère. L'interruption volontaire de grossesse: un processus de politisation, 1970-1981. Brussels: Centre de recherche et d'information socio-politiques, 1981.

06484. La Séparation entre époux. Brussels: Credit communal de Belgique, 1981.

06485. Wendels, A. "The New Private International Law Legislation Regarding the Law to be Applied to International Divorce, and the Recognition of Divorces Granted Abroad." Netherlands International Law Review 29 (1982): 401-428.

Also refer to #5384, 5889, 6090.

b) Feminism

06486. Aubenas-Bastie, Jaqueline. "68-78: Dix ans de feminisme en Belgique." In Les femmes et leur maitres, edited by Maria-Antonietta Macciocchi, pp. 309-330. Paris: C. Bourgeois, 1979.

06487. Collin, Francoise. "Un autre rapport au langage: not sur l'experience des Cahiers de Grif." In Les femmes et leur maîtres, edited by Maria-Antonietta Macciocchi, pp. 331-343. Paris: C., Bourgeois, 1979.

06488. Cousineau, Parge. "The Support Function and Social Change -- A Feminist Case History." Women's Studies International Forum 8 (1985): 137-144.

06489. De Vries, Petra. "Feminism in the Netherlands." In The Women's Liberation Movement, edited by Jan Bradshaw, pp. 389-407. New York: Pergamon Press, 1982.

06490. Oudijk, Corrine. "The Netherlands: In the Unions, the Parties, the Streets, and the Bedrooms." In Sisterhood is Global, edited by Robin Morgan, pp. 469-475. Garden City, N.Y.: Anchor Press, Doubleday, 1984.

2. ECONOMIC

"On a five-hour working day more can be done and less has to be done; freedom and equality have more of a chance; the redivision of paid and unpaid labor is possible for all of us who are able to work; more people can participate in the labor-process; men and women both have a better chance to earn their own income."

Man-Vrouw-Maatschappij
1976 pamphlet

06491. Broerman, M. "Evolution de la population active féminine en Belgique: tendences de 1970 à 1977. 3 partie." Population et famille 52 (1981): 85-113.

06492. Rijk, Tineke. "Women at Work in Holland." In Working Women An International Survey, edited by Marilyn J. Davidson and Cary L. Cooper, pp. 83-102. New York: John Wiley and Sons, 1984.

3. SOCIAL

"He's sure to have his little affairs . . .
We never mention the subject . . .
Why should I
I've got everything I want
Money. A nice home. Two children."

Carta in
Herman Lutgerink
Babyfoon, 1974

a) Demography

06493. Julémont, Ghislaine. "Une enquête nationale sur la fecondité. Relations sexuelles et contraception. Evolution de leur signification sociale." *Population et famille* 53 (1981): 105-129.

06494. Morsa, Jean. "Une enquête nationale sur la fecondité. Attentes et souhaits, et descendance constituée (1966-1975)." *Population et famille* 53 (1981): 93-104.

06495. Willems, P.: Wijewickrema, S.; and Lesthaeghe, R. "L'evolution de la fecondité en Belgique de 1950 à 1980." *Population et famille* 52 (1981): 115-151.

b) Family/Marriage

06496. Tanecchio, Louis W. C.; Van Ijzendoorn, Marinus H.; Goossens, Frits A.; and Vergeer, Maria, M. "The Division of Labor in Dutch Families with Preschool Children." *Journal of Marriage and the Family* 46 (February 1984): 231-242.

06497. Van Ijzendoorn, Marinus H.; Tanecchio, Louis W. C.; Goossens, Frits A.; Vergeer, Maria M.; and Swaan, J. "How B is B4? Attachment and Security of Dutch Children in Ainsworth's Strange Situation and at Home." *Psychological Reports* 52 (June 1983): 683-691.

06498. Wiersma, Geertje Else. *Cohabitation, an Alternative to Marriage? A Cross-National Study*. The Hague: Martinus Nijhoff, 1983.

Also refer to #4912, 5384, 5889, 6479, 6481, 6482, 6484, 6485.

c) Health/Medical

(1) Birth Control/Abortion

06499. Clerck, J. ed. *Le probleme de l'avortement*. Brussels: C.R.I.S.P., 1974.

Also refer to #6090, 6480, 6483, 6493.

(2) Women and Health

06500. Goss, Simon. "The Value of a Woman's Life, and a Cost Benefit Analysis of Mass-Screening for Cancer of the Breast and Cervix." _Cahiers economiques de Bruxelles_ 98 (1983): 233-273.

06501. Pereira-d'Oliveira, E. _Women Feminists who Practiced Medicine: About Women Physicians in the Netherlands_. Amsterdam: Wetenschappel Uitgeverij, 1973.

Also refer to #5385.

4. CULTURAL

> "A very strong male dominance sets in with the early school years. Little boys are important people, and they never let little girls forget for a moment."
>
> Harry Holbert Turney-High
> _Chateau Gerard: The Life and Times in a Walloon Village_, 1953.

a) Education

06502. Jungbluth, Paul. "Covert Sex Role Socialization in Dutch Education. A Survey among Teachers." _Netherlands Journal of Sociology_ 20, no. 1 (1984): 43-57.

b) Art

06503. Musées royaux des beaux-arts de Belgique. _La Femme dans l'art: l'artiste et le modèle: Bruxelles, Musée provisoire d'art moderne, du vendredi 25 avril au dimanche 13 juillet 1975_. Brussels: Musées royaux des beaux-arts de Belgique, 1975.

SUBJECT INDEX

NAME INDEX

AUTHOR INDEX

About the Compilers

LINDA FREY, Professor of History and Chairman of the Department at the University of Montana, is co-author of *A Question of Empire, Friedrich I,* and other books. Her articles have appeared in history journals and other scholarly publications.

MARSHA FREY, Associate Professor of History at Kansas State University, is co-author of *Observations from The Hague and Utrecht* and *Les Dieux ont soif* and has published articles and book chapters on various historical subjects.

JOANNE SCHNEIDER, who is a Teaching Associate at Brown University and Visiting Assistant Professor of History at Wheaton College, collaborated with Linda and Marsha Frey on the first two volumes of *Women in Western European History.*